Footprint Patagonia

Christabelle Dilks and Janak Jani

2nd edition

To my mind there is nothing in life so delightful as that feeling of relief, of escape, and absolute freedom, which one experiences in a vast solitude, where man has perhaps never been, and has, at any rate, left no trace of his existence.

W H Hudson, *Idle Days in Patagonia (1893)*

Patagonia Highlights
See colour maps at back of book
Temuco
Villarrica
Pucón
Neuquén
Bahía Blanca
Valdivia
Parque Nacional Lanín
San Martín De Los Andes
Osorno
Parque Nacional Vicente Pérez Rosales
Parque Nacional Nahuel Huapi
Frutillar
Bariloche
Puerto Montt
Viedma
Parque Nacional Alerce Andino
Golfo San Matías
Chiloé
Chaitén
Parque Nacional Los Alerces
Esquel
Puerto Madryn
Península Valdés
Trelew
Coyhaique
Comodoro Rivadavia
Lago General Carrera
Lago Buenos Aires
Golfo San Jorge
CHILE
ARGENTINA
Villa O'Higgins
Puerto Deseado
Fitz Roy (3405m)
El Chaltén
Lago Viedma
Parque Nacional Los Glaciares
Lago Argentino
El Calafate
Parque Nacional Torres del Paine
Atlantic Ocean
Puerto Natales
Río Gallegos
To Falkland Islands
Punta Arenas
Pacific Ocean
Tierra del Fuego
Parque Nacional Tierra del Fuego
Ushuaia
SANTIAGO
BUENOS AIRES
N
0 km 100
0 miles 100
1 The lakes around Bariloche ▸▸ p92.
2 Parque Nacional Los Alerces ▸▸ p109.
3 Whale watching at Península Valdés ▸▸ p123.
4 Glaciar Perito Moreno ▸▸ p155.
5 Trekking around Cerro Fitz Roy ▸▸ p156.
6 Lago Llanquihue and Volcán Osorno ▸▸ p217 & p219.
7 A cruise to Glaciar San Rafael ▸▸ p261.
8 Trekking in Torres del Paine ▸▸ p291.
9 Isla Navarino ▸▸ p305.
10 Estancia Harberton ▸▸ p311.

Glaciar Perito Moreno
Endless silent ice fields, created millions of years ago, rupture with a roar into the lake below.

Torres del Paine
The massive granite peaks of Chile's most stunning park tower over turquoise lakes, wild-flower meadows and forests.

A foot in the door

Squeezed between two oceans and split by the tail of the Andes, Patagonia is a land of vast horizons and limitless possibilities. Unvanquished by the conquistadors, it has developed in isolation, attracting brave pioneers, hardy Welsh settlers, Wild West outlaws on the run and Che Guevara on a pre-revolutionary jaunt. It remains one of the world's last great wildernesses.

In northern Patagonia, lakes of emerald, blue and indigo nestle among snow-capped volcanoes and ancient monkey puzzle trees. East of the Andes, sheep, not cattle, roam the Argentine steppe and estancias provide a welcome haven of civilization in the emptiness. Head south on the ultimate road trip until, rising up from the flat lands, you see Fitz Roy's spires, or the granite turrets of Torres del Paine. Sculpted glaciers cleave with a roar and the raw power of nature is palpable.

Lumbering seals and migrating whales animate the deserted beaches of the Atlantic, while on the Pacific coast, the land splinters into a labyrinth of islets, fjords and looming icebergs. The oceans meet at the tip of Patagonia, where, surrounded by ice and snow, the Land of Fire is a final frontier at the end of the world.

1
2
4
5
7
8
10
11

1 *Take the 'Big Ice' hike right into the heart of Perito Moreno glacier, from El Calafate.* ▸▸ *See page 154.*

2 *Rub shoulders with Antarctic explorers at Punta Arenas, the southernmost city in the world.* ▸▸ *See page 274.*

3 *The Cueva de las Manos bears witness to one of the earliest human societies. Of the more than 800 handprints, all but 31 depict left hands.* ▸▸ *See page 149.*

4 *A cousin of the llama, the guanaco is indigenous to South America and can be seen roaming wild in Patagonia.* ▸▸ *See page 329.*

5 *The end of the world. Estancia Harberton is a haven in the vast wilderness of Tierra del Fuego.* ▸▸ *See page 311.*

6 *Laguna Amarga is a welcome sight after a steep climb in the Parque Nacional Torres del Paine.* ▸▸ *See page 293.*

7 *One of the continent's greatest journeys, the Carretera Austral stretches over 1000 km through ever-changing spectacular scenery.* ▸▸ *See page 241.*

8 *The trails at the feet of the jagged peaks of the Fitz Roy massif are one of the proverbial meccas for travellers.* ▸▸ *See page 156.*

9 *A ferry weaves its way through the icebergs in Chile's southern fjords.* ▸▸ *See page 286.*

10 *Santiago's stunning setting can best be appreciated from Cerro San Cristóbal.* ▸▸ *See page 179.*

11 *In the far south of Chile, 150,000 Magellanic penguins congregate on Isla Magdalena to breed from November to May.* ▸▸ *See page 278.*

12 *Estancias offer a great way to get to the heart of Patagonia's rural tradition and to see some spectacular scenery.* ▸▸ *See page 24.*

Parque Nacional Lanín
The grand extinct volcano Lanín watches over the Argentine Lake District, turning every snapshot into a picture postcard.

Contents

Chilean Lake District 193

Carretera Austral 241

Far South 271

Tierra del Fuego 299

Background 321

Footnotes 331

Essentials

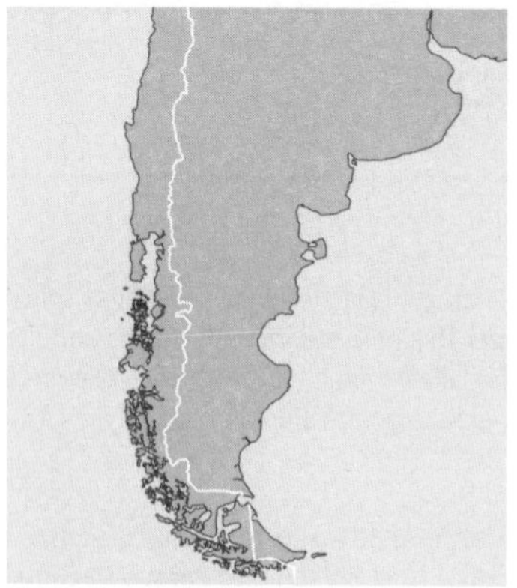

Footprint features

Planning your trip

Where to go

Possibly the most impressive characteristic of Patagonia is the sense of limitless space and freedom; it takes time to drink in the sheer size of it, the immense skies and the silence. Since it's still a wild and untamed land, allow time for spontaneity – explore a new place mentioned by a *gaucho* you meet, or take up an offer of hospitality.

One week

The **Argentine Lake District** is the most easily accessible region for a short visit. Base yourself near **Bariloche** and then either go south to **El Bolsón** and **Parque Nacional Los Alerces**, or north to **San Martín de los Andes** and **Pehuenia**, to catch a flavour of a different part of the lakes. Alternatively, fly direct from Buenos Aires to **El Calafate** for access to **Parque Nacional Los Glaciares**. From here you can either take a bus to **El Chaltén** to hike around **Cerro FitzRoy**, fly on to **Ushuaia** for the Tierra del Fuego national park and Harberton, or head across the border to Chile's **Parque Nacional Torres del Paine**. Allow time for long bus journeys between each place.

Two weeks

Two weeks in Patagonia will give you time to see the wildlife at **Península Valdés** on the **Atlantic Coast**, including whales in spring, and then fly from Trelew to either **Bariloche** for the lakes or **El Calafate** for the glaciers. Two weeks in summer is perfect for exploring the **Lake District** in detail, with time for a longer trek, or for visiting two or three different areas. Consider hiring a *cabaña* and hanging out in Butch and Sundance country, or staying at an estancia to try your hand at riding. Alternatively, cross the border by bus and ferry via Lago Todos Los Santos to explore the southern **Chilean lakes** or via Los Alerces to the **Carretera Austral**. From Puerto Chacabuco, you may just have time to cruise to the **San Rafael glacier** in the southern Chilean fjords. If you fly in to Santiago, you could catch a plane south to **Puerto Montt** or even all the way down to **Punta Arenas**, in order to hike at Torres del Paine or for access to **Tierra del Fuego**. For a complete contrast, city lovers should spend 24 hours in **Buenos Aires** at the end of their trip, to enjoy clubbing and shopping in civilisation after the wide open spaces.

One month

A month allows you to get a real feel for Patagonia's scale and extraordinary contrasts. You could get off the not very beaten track to some remote estancias in **Santa Cruz**, drive along the isolated **Ruta 40** from Los Antiguos to **El Calafate** or cycle a stretch of the wild Carretera Austral to **Futaleufú** for whitewater rafting and fishing. From Puerto Montt, head north into the lakes, visit the mystical island of **Chiloé** or take the long ferry south to **Puerto Natales**. Combine short trips to Península Valdés, the glaciers, Ushuaia and Torres del Paine, ending up in the lakes to relax.

When to go

The southern hemisphere summer lasts from December to March. The weather can be positively warm in the Lake District but the far south suffers from very strong winds at this time. **January** and **February** are when Argentine and Chilean schools have their holidays, so the main tourist centres (Bariloche, San Martín, El Calafate, Pucón, Puerto Varas, Puerto Natales and Ushuaia) can get impossibly busy and prices rise

Packing for Patagonia

You can buy hiking gear in Buenos Aires or Santiago. However, imported items can be prohibitively expensive. Prices are higher in El Calafate and El Chaltén, so unless you buy before you head south, it's best to bring the essential items with you, including a waterproof jacket, comfortable walking boots and a lightweight fleece top. If you plan to do any outdoor activities, also pack a warm hat, gloves, thermal underwear, windproof and waterproof trousers, wool or fleece jumpers, shorts, and walking socks. In El Chaltén complete hiking gear can be hired for around US$20 a day.

Wear a pouch under your clothes for your money and passport and bring a padlock if you're planning to stay in youth hostels. Carry a photocopy of your passport at all times. You'll need a universal plug adaptor if you're bringing any electrical equipment. A torch can be useful, and a folding knife is handy for camping. You'll need high-factor sun protection cream (particularly in the far south in spring), sunglasses and insect repellent.

significantly. You should book flights, buses and accommodation as far ahead as possible. However, you'll still find plenty of less popular centres offering a good range of accommodation, close to the national parks. **December** and **March** are good months for trekking, just be aware that transport services may not be running as frequently in rural areas and that the weather will be more unpredictable. **April** is a spectacular time to visit both the Lake District and Tierra del Fuego, as the leaves turn golden and scarlet, and days can be clear and windless. Rainfall tends to be higher in these months, but the tourist areas are quieter. Easter week is a major holiday in Argentina, however, so book well ahead. Much of southern Patagonia closes down entirely for winter: accommodation is often shut from May to October, transport services run a reduced schedule and many passes across the Andes are closed by snowfall. However, if you like skiing, then this is the season to visit. The best months are **July** and **August**, although many resorts have snow from late June and until September. Ski resort accommodation and transport are generally well organized but bear in mind that July is a school holiday. The rich marine life on the Atlantic Coast is most exciting in the spring, with whale-spotting possible from Península Valdés at its best in **September** and **October**. Elsewhere, there are fewer tourists and cheaper accommodation than during the summer but still enough daylight hours for trekking. Winds in the far south are less fierce at this time of year.

Summer (high season) in Patagonia is December to March. Winter is July to September.

Sport and activities

Patagonia might have been designed for adventure tourism. The spectacular geography offers a huge range of outdoor activities, from rafting and skiing to some of the finest trekking and fishing in the world. The infrastructure for 'soft' adventure tourism, such as a half-day's rafting on a Grade III river, or a day spent climbing a volcano, is particularly good in the Lake District. Patagonian estancias are appealing bases for horse riding and wildlife spotting, while further south, the terrain promises hardcore trekking and mountain biking. It is important to check the experience and qualifications of any agency offering excursions to remote areas. In Chile, **CATA** (Consejo de Autoregulación de Aventura), T02-735 8034, is an association of more reputable agencies, which regulates adventure tourism in the country. It works closely with the national park authority, **CONAF**, T02-236 1416 (see page 16).

How big is your footprint?

The Travel Foundation, www.thetravelfoundation.co.uk, provides the following tips:

→ Consider helping to compensate for the environmental impact of your flight. See www.climatecare.org.uk, www.futureforests.com and www.foc-uk.com.

→ Avoid overt displays of wealth, such as wearing expensive jewellery. Carry your camera discretely.

→ Minimize waste by re-using plastic bags, bringing your own water filter bottle, or purifier, and by taking your used batteries home with you.

→ Always carry a bag to take waste away with you, and never litter.

→ Use local taxis, and go with local guides when possible, rather than relying on big businesses, as this supports the local economy.

→ Hire a car only when you need to. Use alternatives such as public transport, bicycles and walking, which means you're more likely to meet local people, too.

→ Always, always, ask permission before taking photographs of people or their homes. Don't be offended if they decline, or expect to be paid.

→ Don't pick flowers and plants, or remove pebbles and sea shells.

→ Buy locally made products. Shop, eat and drink in locally owned outlets, rather than international chains. This brings enormous benefits to local people. At many bus stations, local people sell fruit, home-made bread and *empanadas* at a fraction of the price of the shops, and often far more delicious.

→ Always bargain with humour, and remember that a small cash saving to you could be a significant amount of money to the seller.

→ In your hotel, turn off/down air conditioning when it's not required. Switch off lights when leaving the room, and turn the TV off, rather than leaving it on standby.

→ Take quick showers instead of baths, and let staff know you're happy to reuse your towels rather than having them replaced daily.

Other useful websites for tips and inspiration: **Tourism Concern**, www.tourismconcern.org.uk, and **Responsible Tourism Awards**, www.responsibletourismawards.info.

Climbing

★ **Head for**... Volcán Lanín, Cerro Catedral, Mount Tronador, Cerro Fitz Roy, Volcán Villarrica, Volcán Osorno, Cerro Picada, Torres del Paine, ice trekking near El Chaltén.

Contact

Argentine mountain areas all have local **Club Andinos**, www.clubandino.org, which sell maps and can advise on routes, provide guides, etc. See page 103 for **Club Andino Bariloche** in the Lake District. Also see www.parquesnacionales.gov.ar.

Dirección de Fronteras y Límites, 5th fl, Ministerio de Relaciones Exteriores, Bandera 52, Santiago, T02-6714210. For permission to climb some mountains in border areas; apply 3 months in advance.

Federación de Andinismo de Chile, Almte Simpson 77A, Santiago, T02-2220888, www.feach.cl. Information on permits, expeditions and equipment hire to members. **Escuela Nacional de Montaña (ENAM)** is based at the same address (T02-2220799) for rock- and ice-climbing courses and the *Carnet de La Federación de Chile*, required to climb mountains in CONAF-controlled areas.

Cycling/mountain biking

Mountain biking is popular, particularly on descents from peaks around Bariloche. Longer routes include the Siete Lagos in the Lake District and the iconic Carretera Austral. See www.andescross.com and www.exchile.com.

★ **Head for**... Bariloche, Siete Lagos, Parque Nacional Los Alerces, Parque Nacional Villarrica, Puerto Varas, Carretera Austral.

Fishing

Patagonia has arguably the finest fly fishing in the world in incomparably beautiful surroundings. To fish anywhere in Argentina you need a permit costing US$5 per day, US$15 per week, US$50 per year. In Chile, a licence is required, whether for one day or a longer period, and is usually obtained from the local Municipalidad or some tourist offices.
★ **Head for**... Junín de los Andes, Río Baker, Río Grande (Tierra del Fuego), Lago Blanco (Chilean Tierra del Fuego).

Contact

Fly Fishing Association of Argentina, T011-4773 0821, fishing licences.
Asociación de Pesca y Caza (Sernap), San Antonio 427, 8th fl, Santiago, T02-639 1918, www.sernapesca.cl, Mon-Fri 0900-1400. Also consult the national park authorities, see box page 16, and check out www.aapm.org.ar, www.turismo.gov.ar/fishing, www.anglerstdf.com.ar, www.argentinachileflyfishing.com, www.flyfishingtravel.com, www.magallanesflyfishing.com

Horse riding

This is a great way to get to the heart of Patagonia's rural tradition and to see some varied and spectacular scenery. Expect to pay around US$10 per hour and always check the horses are tame and in good condition. Many *estancias* offer opportunities for riding. See www.estanciasdesantacruz.com, www.horseadventures.com.ar, www.horsebackridingchile.cl.
★ **Head for**... Estancias throughout Argentine Patagonia (see also page 24).

Road trips and 4WD

The sheer size and remoteness of Patagonia means that long-distance road trips are an exhilarating way of exploring the region. What's more, the terrain of endless steppes interrupted by rivers, gorges and gullies, is also ideal for off-roading. The El Calafate area has several companies dedicated to taking tourists on hair-raising trips. Hiring a 4WD vehicle, costs from US$1500 for 10 days. Buy road maps from service stations in Argentina, or in advance from **Turistel Sur**, www.turistel.cl, or the **Automóvil Club de Chile**, www.automovilclub.cl. For more on driving in Patagonia, see page 22.
★ **Head for**... Ruta de los Siete Lagos, Villa Angostura to Puyehue, Trevelín to Futaleufú, Ruta 40 from Los Antiguos to El Calafate, Carretera Austral.

Skiing

The season runs from mid-Jun to mid-Oct, but dates vary between resorts. Argentine Lake District resorts are very well run; facilities in the far south of Chile are basic. However, skiing on an active volcano looking down on 3 huge lakes (Villarrica/ Pucón) or skiing within sight of the sea at the end of the world (Cerro Castor), are memories that will truly last a lifetime.
★ **Head for**... Cerro Catedral (Bariloche), Cerro Bayo (Villa la Angostura), Cerro Chapelco (San Martín de los Andes), La Hoya (Esquel), Villarrica/Pucón, Antillanca, Cerro Castor (Ushuaia).

Contact

www.interpatagonia.com
www.andesweb.com
www.southamericaskiguide.com
www.exchile.com/ski
www.powderquest.com

Trekking

The whole of the Andes region offers superb opportunities for both short and long treks in varied landscapes. The best season for walking is Dec-Apr. National parks in the Lake District offer spectacular hikes on well-marked routes, with maps, guides and plenty of information. It's also worth exploring the lesser known lake regions, such as Pehuenia in the north, Parque Nacional Los Alerces and the Seven Lakes in Chile. The most dramatic trekking is near El Chaltén in the Parque Nacional Los Glaciares where you can walk on the Southern Ice field and climb glaciers, and in Parque Nacional Torres del Paine and Parque Nacional Tierra del Fuego. In Chile,

Patagonian national parks

Patagonia has an extensive network of reserves and protected areas, the most important of which are designated national parks (PN). Additional areas have been designated as natural monuments (MN) and natural reserves (RN).

Argentina The main office of the **Administración de Parques Nacionales** is at Santa Fe 680, near the Plaza San Martín in central Buenos Aires, T011-4311 0303, www.parquesnacionales.gov.ar. Most parks have *guardaparque* (ranger) offices at the main entrance, where you can get advice and basic maps. They are usually knowledgeable about wildlife and walks. Parks in the Lake District are particularly well set up for trekking, with signed trails, *refugios* and campsites.

Chile All reserves and national parks in Chile are managed by **CONAF** (Corporación Nacional Forestal), Avenida Bulnes 285, 1st fl, Santiago, T/F02-697-2273, www.conaf.cl. It maintains an office in each region of the country, and kiosks in some natural areas. Most of the parks have public access; details are given in the text. Camping areas are usually clearly designated, wild camping is discouraged and frequently banned.

over 1000 km of hiking opportunities have been opened up by the building of the Carretera Austral, though heavy rainfall can be a drawback outside summer. The latest plan is the *Sendero de Chile* (www.senderodechile.cl), a walking route stretching all the way from the Peruvian border to Tierra del Fuego, which is due to be completed by 2010.

You should be reasonably fit before attempting any hikes in Patagonia, especially overnight treks in the far south. Remember that conditions can be harsh at these latitudes and never overestimate your own abilities. Take account of the season, weather and terrain and make sure you are properly equipped. If trekking with a tour operator or guide, check their credentials, equipment and experience. Avoid hiking alone, even in tourist areas, and always register with *guardaparques*, or other authorities before you set out. Hikers have little to fear from the animal kingdom – in fact you are much more of a threat to the environment than vice versa; see box page 14.

★ **Head for**... Parque Nacional Lanín, Parque Nacional Nahuel Huapi, Cerro Fitz Roy (Parque Nacional Los Glaciares), Parque Nacional Los Alerces, Parque Nacional Huerquehue (Pucón), Cerro Castillo (Parque Nacional Torres del Paine), Parque Nacional Tierra del Fuego.

Contact
www.visit-chile.org, www.parquesnacionales.org.ar, www.fitzroyexpediciones.org, www.hieloyaventura.com.

Watersports

Patagonia has plenty of water and plenty to do including, canoeing, scuba diving, waterskiing, windsurfing and sailing. There's also sea kayaking around the islands off eastern Chiloé or in the fjords around Hornopirén. The tourist resorts in both lake districts offer a wide range of watersports.

★ **Head for**... Bariloche, Río Aluminé, Lago Llanquihue, Lago Villarrica, Chiloé, Hornopirén.

Whitewater rafting

Rafting is generally well organized and equipment is usually of high quality. Access to the headwaters of most rivers is easy. Choose a reputable agency who are to be found in nearby towns. Rafts should carry no more than 7 plus guide – 6 is ideal.

★ **Head for**... Río Manso, Río Aluminé, Futaleufú, Pucón, Río Petrohué (Puerto Varas), Río Manso (Bariloche).

Taking a tour

Numerous operators offer organized trips to Patagonia, ranging from a whistle-stop tour of the highlights to specialist trips that focus on a specific destination or activity. The advantage of travelling with a reputable operator is that your transport, accommodation and activities are all arranged for you in advance – particularly valuable if you only have limited time in the region or you don't speak Spanish. By travelling independently, however, you can be much more flexible and spontaneous; you will be able to explore less visited areas, practise your Spanish and you will save money, if you budget carefully. A list of specialist tour operators can be found on page 33.

Getting there and flying around

Arriving by air

It is not possible to fly directly to Patagonia from outside Argentina or Chile. Instead you must choose to fly into either Buenos Aires' **Ezeiza International Airport** (EZE; see page 40) or Santiago's **Aeropuerto Arturo Merino Benitez** (SCL; see page 172) and pick up onward transport there. There are several flights a day between Santiago and Buenos Aires, operated by **LanChile, Aerolíneas Argentinas, Air France, American, Avianca** or the new Brazilian airline, **Gol.**

Fares vary from airline to airline and according to time of year. In the low season it may be possible to get a return flight from London to Santiago or Buenos Aires for £580 (plus over £100 airport departure taxes), but in the high seasons (December/January and July/August) this may rise to £800 return. Prices are comparable for flights from the USA, but from Australia and New Zealand they may rise to £1000 return or more. Discounted fares are offered through specialist agencies (see page 18) but always check the reservation with the airline concerned to make sure the flight still exists. Note that citizens of Mexico, Australia, Canada and the USA are charged a one-off reciprocal entry tax on arrival in Chile, valid for the lifetime of the passport.

Baggage Long-haul flights generally allow one piece of luggage of up to 23 kg, or two pieces of 23 kg for flights from or via the USA. These limits may not strictly enforced if the plane is not full, so if you know you are over the limit, arrive early. However, if you're planning on catching a connecting flight, bear in mind that weight limits for internal services are usually only 20 kg for economy class.

Transport tips

→ The fastest way to get to Patagonia from the UK is to fly direct to Buenos Aires with British Airways. From there, you can fly on to Bariloche, El Calafate or Santiago in Chile. There are no direct flights from London to Santiago.

→ Internal flights are fast, but not green, so consider long-distance buses for some of your journey. Argentina and Chile have very comfortable buses that travel overnight, enabling you to sleep. However, the 24-hour bus ride along the Ruta 40 from Los Antiguos to El Chaltén has fantastic views that you'll want to stay awake for.

→ On long bus journeys, carry small packs of tissues and bottled water, as toilets on buses can be unpleasant. Also take a jumper to combat the fierce air-conditioning.

Flights from Europe

The only direct flight from the UK to **Buenos Aires** is with **British Airways,** www.ba.com, which touches down briefly in São Paulo and takes 14 hours. All other carriers stop in a European city, where you have to change planes, and the overall journey takes anything from 18 to 24 hours. Alternatively, there are daily connecting flights on one of the American carriers via New York or Miami. It is impossible to fly directly to **Santiago** from London, so connections have to be made with **British Airways** or **LanChile,** www.lan.com, via Buenos Aires; **Air France,** www.airfrance.com, via Paris; **Iberia,** www.iberia.com, or **LanChile,** via Madrid; **Lufthansa,** www.lufthansa.com, via Frankfurt; or **Swiss,** www.swiss.com.

Flights from North America

Aerolíneas Argentinas and other South American and North American airlines fly to **Buenos Aires** from Miami, New York, Washington, Los Angeles, San Francisco, Atlanta, New Orleans, Dallas and Chicago. **Air Canada** and **LanChile** fly from Toronto and Montreal. **LanChile** flies to **Santiago** from Miami (nine hours), New York (12 hours) and Los Angeles (via Mexico City and Lima) and offers connections with sister airlines from Vancouver via Los Angeles, or from Toronto via New York. Other direct flights are provided by **American Airlines,** www.aa.com, and **Delta,** www.delta.com.

Flights from Australia, New Zealand and South Africa

Aerolíneas Argentinas and **Qantas** fly to **Buenos Aires** from Sydney (via Auckland). **LanChile/Air New Zealand,** www.airnz.co.nz, or **Aerolíneas Argentinas** (via Buenos Aires) fly from Auckland to **Santiago.** **South African Airways** flies to Buenos Aires.

Discount flight agents

UK

Journey Latin America, see page 34.

Just the Ticket, Level 2, 28 Margaret St, London W1W 8RZ, T020-7291 8111, www.justtheticket.co.uk. Ticket agency, excellent deals.

STA Travel, Priory House, 6 Wrights Lane, London W8 6TA, T08701-600599, www.sta.co.uk. Specialists in low-cost student/youth flights, tours, insurance.

Trailfinders, 194 Kensington High St, London W8 7RG, T020-7938 3939. Good deals to Latin America.

North America

Air Brokers International, 685 Market St, Suite 400, San Francisco, CA 94105, T01-800-883 3273, www.airbrokers.com. Consolidator and specialist on RTW and Circle Pacific tickets.

Discount Airfares Worldwide On-Line, www.etn.nl/discount.htm. A hub of consolidator and discount agent links.

International Travel Network/Airlines of the Web, www.itn.net. Online air travel information and reservations.

STA Travel, 5900 Wilshire Blvd, Suite 2110, Los Angeles, CA 90036, T1-800-777 0112, www.sta-travel.com. Also branches in New

York, San Francisco, Boston, Miami, Chicago, Seattle and Washington DC.
Travel CUTS, 187 College St, Toronto, ON, M5T 1P7, T1-800-667 2887, www.travelcuts.com. Student discount fares, IDs and other travel services. Branches in other Canadian cities.
Travelocity, www.travelocity.com. Online consolidator.

Australia and New Zealand
Flight Centres, 82 Elizabeth St, Sydney, T13-1600; 205 Queen St, Auckland, T09-309 6171. Branches in other towns and cities.
STA Travel, T1300-360960, www.statravelaus.com.au; 702 Harris St, Ultimo, Sydney, and 256 Flinders St, Melbourne. In New Zealand: 10 High St, Auckland, T09-366 6673. Also in major towns and university campuses.

... and leaving again

Check-in two hours before departure. Some airlines allow you to check in online, after which they require you to be at the airport just 45 minutes before departure. International departure tax (US$18 in Argentina; US$30 in Chile) may be prepaid; check if it's included in your ticket when you book.

Onward flights to Patagonia

From Buenos Aires All domestic flights from Buenos Aires (as well as some flights to/ from neighbouring countries) are handled from Jorge Newbery Airport, known as **Aeroparque**, situated 4 km north of the centre of Buenos Aires (see page 40). **Manuel Tienda León**, T0800-888 5366, www.tiendaleon.com, runs efficient buses between the two airports via the city centre every 30 minutes, 0600-0100, US$8.50. They have a desk inside the arrivals hall, where you can also book a *remise* taxi, US$35. From Aeroparque, the main air routes to Patagonia are to Bariloche (US$100 one way, 2½ hours), to San Martín de los Andes (US$120, two hours), to Trelew (US$100, two hours), to El Calafate (US$120, 3¼ hours) and to Ushuaia (US$150, three hours 20 minutes).

From Santiago You will go through customs and immigration in international arrivals before transferring to the domestic section of the same terminal. **LanChile** (www.lan.com) flies between Santiago and major cities under the banner **Lan Express**. The budget airlines **Sky** (www.skyairline.cl) and **Aerolineas del Sur** (www.aerolineasdelsur.cl) also serve the main destinations but less frequently. The most important routes from Santiago are to Temuco, Puerto Montt, Valdivia (via Temuco or Concepción), Osorno (via Temuco or Concepción), Balmaceda (Coyhaique, via Puerto Montt) and Punta Arenas (via Puerto Montt).

Air services in Argentina

There are now just two operators for internal flights: **Aerolíneas Argentinas**, www.aerolineas.com, which has 178 flights to Patagonia each week, and **LanChile**, www.lan.com. This means that there are fewer airline seats than hotel beds available, and you must book well in advance. In addition, Buenos Aires' airports are currently experiencing problems with delays to internal flights; there's nothing you can do about this, but take a book and be patient. All flights to Patagonia start in Buenos Aires, though there are often connections from El Calafate to Bariloche and Ushuaia – ask your airline for details. El Chaltén does not have an airport, but is easily reached in three hours by bus from El Calafate. In addition the army airline **LADE**, T0810-810 5233 in Argentina, T+54 11-5129 9000, www.lade.com.ar, provides a weekly service connecting several towns in Patagonia, which is useful to avoid having to go back to Buenos Aires.

It's wise to leave some flexibility in your schedule to allow for bad weather, which may delay flights in the south. Most provincial airports in Argentina have a tourist information desk, banking facilities and a *confitería* (cafeteria) as well as car hire. There are usually minibus services into the nearest town and taxis are available. Don't lose your baggage ticket; you won't be able to collect your bags without it.

Air services in Chile

Departure tax for domestic flights is US$8 each way and is included in the price of the ticket. **LanChile**, www.lan.com, is the main domestic operator. It sells a **South America Airpass**, which can be used on all **LAN** routes without South America. This is only recommended if you are planning on doing several long-distance flights; visit the website in order to assess the price implications; domestic air taxes are payable in addition for each flight. The airpass must be purchased abroad at the same time as a trans-Atlantic ticket to South America. It is valid for six months, and must include at least three single flights; there is no maximum. Note that the airpass is more expensive if used in conjunction with an international flight with another carrier. Reservations should be made in advance; flight dates can be altered without penalty but route changes incur a charge of US$30 per change. A refund (minus 10%) can be obtained prior to travel.

Note that flight times may be changed without warning; always double check the time of your flight when reconfirming. The most important Patagonian routes are Puerto Montt to Balmaceda or Punta Arenas; Punta Arenas to Puerto Williams, Ushuaia or Porvenir and Puerto Natales to El Calafate (summer only). Destinations in the far south are served by **DAP** (www.dap.cl) based in Punta Arenas. **LanChile** also flies from Santiago to Port Stanley on the Falkland (Malvinas) Islands via Punta Arenas and Río Gallegos.

Choosing your bus

Argentina

→ *commún* lots of stops (*intermedios*), uncomfortable, not recommended for long journeys.
→ *semi-cama* slightly reclining seat, meals, toilet.
→ *coche-cama* fully reclining seats, meals, toilet, few stops, worth the small extra expense for a good night's sleep.

Chile

→ *classico/salón-ejecutivo* Comfortable enough for daytime travel, but not ideal for long distances.
→ *semi-cama* more leg room and fewer stops. 50% more expensive.
→ *salón cama* similar to a 'coche cama' in Argentina.
→ *cama premium* flat beds.

Getting around by land and sea

Buses in Argentina

The country is connected by a network of efficient long-distance buses, which is usually the cheapest way of getting around. They run all year, are safe and comfortable, and travel overnight, which saves time on long journeys. The main operators are **Andesmar,** www.andesmar.com, **TAC,** T011-4312-7012, **Via Bariloche,** www.viabariloche.com, and **Tecni Austral.** Book seats a day in advance in January. Regional services to tourist destinations within Patagonia tend to be limited after mid March. For general transport information, consult www.argentinatotal.com.ar. ▸▸ *Choosing your bus, above.*

Bus companies may give discounts to students with ID, and to teachers with proof of employment. Discounts aren't usually available December to March. Make sure your seat number is on your ticket. Luggage is safely stored in a large hold at the back of the bus, and you'll be given a numbered ticket to reclaim it on arrival. *Maleteros* take the bags off the bus, and may expect a small tip – 50 centavos or a peso is fine.

Buses in Chile

Bus services in Chile are frequent, and on the whole, good, although they are slightly more expensive than in Argentina. Buses tend to be punctual, arriving and leaving on time. Along the Carretera Austral, however, services are far less reliable, less frequent and usually in minibuses. Services improve again between Punta Arenas and Puerto Natales in the far south. In addition, there are long-distance international services from Santiago to Buenos Aires, from Osorno to Bariloche, from Coyhaique to Comodoro Rivadavia and from Punta Arenas to Río Gallegos.

Apart from at holiday times, there is little problem getting a seat on a long-distance bus and you only need to reserve ahead in high season. Prices are highest from December to March but competition between bus companies means you may be able to bargain for a lower fare, particularly just before departure; discounts are also often available for return journeys. Students and holders of **Hostelling International** cards may also get discounts out of season. Most bus companies will carry bicycles, but may ask for payment; on **TurBus** payment is mandatory. ▸▸ *Choosing your bus, above.*

Boat

In the Lake District, ferries on Lago Nahuel Huapi and Lago Frías in Argentina link with bus and ferry services across Lago Todos Los Santos in Chile (see page 95). There are also services across Lago Pirihueico. In the south of Chile, maritime transport is very important. The main transporter/car-ferry operators are **Naviera Austral** and **Navimag,** although there also companies offering more tourist-friendly services in summer.

Puerto Montt is the hub for boat services south, with regular sailings to Chiloé, Chaitén, Puerto Chacabuco, Puerto Natales (one a week, year round) and the San Rafael glacier. **Punta Arenas** is the departure point for ferry services to Porvenir and Puerto Williams on Tierra del Fuego. Reservations are essential for the ferries in high summer. Details of all routes are given under the relevant chapters.

Car

Hiring a car is an excellent idea if you want to travel independently and explore the more remote areas of Patagonia, although it can be complicated to take a hire car across the border between Argentina and Chile (see box, page 23). The most important routes in Argentine Patagonia are Ruta 40, which runs along the west side of the Andes and faster Ruta 3, which runs down the Atlantic coast. Most of Chile is linked by the paved toll road, the **Pan-American Highway** (or Panamericana), marked on maps as Ruta 5, which runs all the way from the Peruvian frontier south to Puerto Montt. (A coastal route running the length of Chile is under construction, and should be ready by 2010.) The **Carretera Austral**, a *ripio* (gravel) road marked on maps as Ruta 7, runs south of Puerto Montt, punctuated by three ferry crossings, with a further crossing at Villa O'Higgins for those on the overland route (summer only) from the Carretera to the far south.

Generally, main roads are in good condition but on some *ripio roads*, particularly south of Puerto Montt, a high-clearance, 4WD vehicle is required, as road surfaces can degenerate to earth *(tierra)*. Most roads in Patagonia are single lane in each direction. There's little traffic and service stations for fuel, toilets, water and food are much further apart than in Europe and the US, so always carry water and spare fuel and keep the tank full. Safety belts are supposed to be worn, if fitted. **Hitchhiking** is relatively easy and safe (although you should always exercise caution) and often involves an exhilarating ride in the back of a pick-up truck. However, traffic is sparse in the south, and roads in places like Tierra del Fuego rarely see more than a few vehicles per day.

Car hire is more expensive in Chile than in Argentina. There are few hire cars available outside the main tourist centres in either country, although small towns will have cheaper deals. Hiring a car from one place and dropping it off in another is rarely practical since very high penalties are charged. The multi-national companies (**Hertz, Avis**) are represented all over Patagonia but local companies may be cheaper and \ds usually just as reliable. You must be 25 or over in Argentina and 22 or over in Chile to hire a car; a national driver's licence should be sufficient. Vehicles may be rented by the day, the week or the month, with or without unlimited mileage. Rates quoted should include **insurance** and VAT but ALWAYS check first. Note that the insurance excess, which you'll have to pay if there's an accident, is extremely expensive. Check the vehicle carefully with the hire company for scratches and cracks in the windscreen before you set off, so that you won't be blamed for them on your return. Hire companies will take a print of your **credit card** as their guarantee instead of a deposit but are honourable about not using it for extra charges. Ensure that the hire company gives you the vehicle's ownership papers, which have to be shown at police and military checks.

Fuel facts

Petrol (known as *nafta* in Argentina, *petróleo* in Chile) becomes more expensive in Chile the further south you go, but in Argentine Patagonia, fuel prices are a third lower than in the rest of the country. Diesel (*gasoil* in Argentina, *bencina* in Chile) is available in both countries and is much cheaper than petrol. Cars in Argentina are increasingly converting to gas GNC (*gas natural comprimido*), which is about 25% the cost of petrol. However, you will not be able to hire a GNC car outside Buenos Aires and fuel stations offering GNC are very limited in Patagonia. What's more, if you're taking a gas-run vehicle from Argentina into Chile, check that it will run on Chilean gas: there is a difference.

Over the border

The main routes between Argentine and Chilean Patagonia are by boat and bus between Bariloche and Puerto Montt in the Lake District; by road from El Calafate to Puerto Natales and Torres del Paine or by road and ferry from El Calafate via Río Gallegos to Tierra del Fuego. There are many other crossings (some little more than a police post), which are detailed throughout the guide. See also http://www.difrol.cl/html/104a.htm. For some crossings, prior permission must be obtained from the authorities. Note that passes across the Andes may be blocked by snow from April onwards. See also Customs and duty free page 27; and Visas and immigration page 36.

General

→ Crossing the border is not a lengthy procedure unless you're on a bus, when each individual is checked.
→ It is your responsibility to ensure that your passport is stamped in and out when you cross borders. Do not lose your tourist card; replacing one can be inconvenient and costly.
→ Tourist card holders returning across a land border to Argentina will be given a further 90 days in the country. Visa holders should check regulations with the Chilean/Argentine embassies.
→ Fruit, vegetables, meat, flowers and milk products may not be imported into Chile; these will be confiscated at all borders. Searches are thorough.
→ Immigration and customs officials are generally friendly, helpful and efficient, however, the police at Chilean control posts a little further into the country can be extremely bureaucratic.
→ There are often no exchange facilities at the border so make sure you carry small amounts of both currencies.
→ Remember to change your watch if crossing the border between early March and September/October.

By car

Obtain an authorization form from the hire company. This is exchanged at the outgoing border control for another form, one part of which is surrendered on each side of the border. If you plan to leave more than once you will need to photocopy the authorization.
→ Make sure the number plate is etched on the car windows.
→ Ensure that the hire company gives you the vehicle's ownership papers, which have to be shown at police and military checks.
→ At some crossings, you must pay for the car's tyres to be sprayed with pesticides.

Useful contacts

Automóvil Club Argentino (**ACA**), Av Libertador Gen San Martín 1850, 1425 Buenos Aires, T011-4808 4000, www.aca.org.ar. This motoring association has fuel stations, hotels and *hosterías*, as well as a useful route service. Members of affiliated associations can use ACA facilities and get discounts.

Automóvil Club de Chile, Av Andres Bello 1863, Santiago, T02-431-1000, acchinfo@automovilclub.cl. Car-hire agency with discounts for members or affiliates. Also provides road maps.

Touring Club Argentino, Esmeralda 605 and Tucumán 781, 3rd fl, Buenos Aires T011-392-6742. Similar travel services to ACA but no service stations.

Taxis, colectivos and remises

Taxis usually have meters and can either be hailed in the street or booked in advance, although they tend to be more expensive when booked from a hotel. Surcharges are applied late at night and at weekends. Agree fares beforehand for long journeys out of city centre or for special excursions; also compare prices among several drivers.

Estancias

Estancias are the huge sheep and cattle ranches found all over Patagonia, and many of them now welcome paying guests. They offer a marvellous way to see remote landscapes and enjoy horse riding and other activities, as well as providing an authentic experience of rural Argentine life.

You'll need to stay at least two or three nights to make the most of an estancia, as they are often off the beaten track. Hire a car, or arrange with your hosts to be picked up in the nearest town. Estancias can be more expensive than hotels, but they offer a unique experience, and once you add the activities, meals and wine, are often good value. Expect to pay at least US$100 per night.

Estancias vary enormously in style and activities: **Cristina** offers total isolation and comfort; **Helsingfors** is a giant sheep farm close to glaciers; **Eolo** and **Alta Vista** are luxury estancia-style hotels on the steppe, also near glaciers; **Viamonte** and **Harberton** on Tierra del Fuego are infused with history, while on the mainland, **Monte Dinero** has a colony of Magellanic penguins on its doorstep.

For more information consult www.estanciasdesantacruz.com www.tierrabuena.com.ar; www.south trip.com and www.turismo.gov.ar.

Collective taxis (*colectivos* in Chile, *remise* in Argentina), operate on fixed routes (identified by numbers and destinations) and are a good way of getting around cities. They are usually flagged down on the street corner and advertise charges in the front windscreen. (Make sure you have small notes and coins to pay the driver.) In Chile, *colectivos* also operate on some inter-urban routes, leaving from a set point when full; they compete favourably with buses for speed but not for comfort.

Train

The main passenger service from Santiago runs to **Temuco** (see page 213); this journey is more tranquil than travelling by road along the Panamericana, and is faster than the bus. The only long-distance train within Patagonia runs from **Viedma** on the Atlantic Coast to **Bariloche** in the Lake District (see page 104). Patagonia's best known train, *La Trochita*, www.latrochita.org.ar; made famous by Paul Theroux as the *Old Patagonian Express*, is a purely tourist affair that departs from Esquel in the southern Lake District for the remote Mapuche station at Nahuel Pan (see page 108). Even more touristy is the *Tren del fin del Mundo*, www.trendelfindelmundo.com.ar, which travels from Ushuaia to the Tierra del Fuego national park (see page 311).

Sleeping

Tourist destinations in Patagonia and, especially in the Lake District, have a good range of **hotels** and **hosterías**, although on the Chilean side, there is good-value budget accommodation and some relatively high-end hotels, but not much choice in between. Hosterías have less than 20 rooms; rather than being lower quality, they are often family run and can be very good value in more remote areas. **Residenciales** and **hospedajes** tend to provide simpler accommodation but may also offer services geared specifically towards foreign backpackers, such as internet access, tours, bicycle hire, etc. **Hostales** traditionally offer dorm beds but many now also have double rooms for couples. **Cabañas** are well-equipped self-catering cottages, cabins or apartments, often in superb locations. They're very popular among Argentine holiday-makers and are a great option if you have your own transport and are travelling in a small group.

Sleeping price codes

LL +US$201 and **L US$151-200**
Top-quality hotels, mostly offering very well-equipped rooms with dataports, plus a restaurant, bar, pool, health suite, business facilities and excellent service. Also luxurious estancias (see Home on the range, page 24) and several hotels in Torres del Paine, where you're paying for location not quality.

AL US$101-150 and **A US$66-100**
Comfortable hotels with good facilities, airport transfers, tours, information and buffet breakfasts. Rooms should have TV, minibar, safe and a/c. Estancias in these categories may have simpler accommodation than an ordinary hotel, but activities are usually included.

B US$46-65 and **C US$31-45**
The quality of hotels and hosterías in these categories varies widely but most are reliable, with en suite facilities and breakfast.

D US$21-30 and **E US$12-20**
Good quality *residenciales* and *hospedajes*, especially in rural areas, where a lovely setting makes up for the lack of facilities; breakfast included. Also official Chilean youth hostels www.hostellingcl.achatj.html, which charge rates per person; IYHA or Chilean YHA card required.

F US$7-11 and **G under US$6**
Simple *residenciales* and *hospedajes*, sometimes very basic, with shared bathrooms, but usually supplying a towel and toilet paper. In Chile rates are charged per person (pp). Also beds in Argentine youth hostels (www.argentinahostels.com, www.hostels.org.ar), either in dorms (often mixed), with large communal bathrooms (US$7) or doubles (from US$10). Some have cooking facilities, internet access, lockers and laundry. At the very bottom end are Chilean *albergues*: usually just floor space in a school during the summer. They are very cheap (US$2-4 per person), very noisy and offer no privacy.

Camping is popular and there are many superbly situated sites with good facilities, although official Chilean campsites can be surprisingly expensive, with no reductions for single travellers or couples. There are also **refugios** (refuges) for walkers in national parks and reserves; standards of comfort and facilities vary hugely. Camping wild is generally safe, even in remote areas, but always consult *guardaparques* (park rangers) before pitching your tent in a national park.

Accommodation in Argentina is excellent value for visitors from Western countries. Accommodation in Chile is just under double the price of equivalent accommodation in Argentina. Prices also tend to be higher in Santiago and the further south you go from Puerto Montt. However, single travellers do not come off too badly in southern Chile, as many *hospedajes* charge per person (although you may have to share your room). The Chilean government waives the VAT charge (IVA 19%) for bills paid in dollars (cash or traveller's cheques) at designated high-end hotels, but some establishments may get round this apparent discount by offering you a low dollar exchange rate. Prices often rise in high season (*temporada alta*), especially during January and February, but off-season you can often bargain for a discount (*descuento*) if you are staying for two or more days. The ski resorts are more expensive during the winter school holidays. During public holidays or high season you should always book ahead. Few places accept credit cards. In both countries you should establish clearly in advance what is included in the price before booking. For further information on accommodation, consult the following websites: www.patagonia-chile.com, www.interpatagonia.com, www.backpackersbest.cl, www.backpackerschile.com, www.chile-hotels.com and www.i-escape.com.

Eating price codes

ΨΨΨ	over US$12
ΨΨ	US$6-12
Ψ	under US$6

Prices refer to the cost of a two-course meal for one person, excluding drinks or service charge.

Eating and drinking

Buffet-style 'American breakfasts' are served in international hotels but elsewhere, breakfast (*desayuno*) is a very simple affair. Lunch (*almuerzo*) is eaten any time from 1300 to 1530 and is followed, in Argentina, by a siesta. At around 1700, many Argentines go to a *confitería* for *merienda* (tea, sandwiches and cakes), while Chileans have a snack meal known as *las onces* (literally elevenses). Restaurants open for *cena* (dinner) at about 2000 in Chile but rarely before 2100 in Argentina, where most people don't eat until 2230 or later. Many restaurants in Chile serve a cheaper fixed-price meal at lunch time (US$2-3), called *la colación* or *el menú*. In Argentina this is known as *el menú fixo*. Those on a tight budget should also try *tenedor libre* (free fork) restaurants, where you can eat all you want for a fixed price. Some hotels, particularly in the Lake District, will offer a packed lunch to take on hikes and to see the glaciers; ask the night before.

Food and drink

Argentina may not have a particularly sophisticated cuisine, but it doesn't really need one: the meat is legendary. The classic meal is the *asado* – beef or lamb (in Patagonia) cooked over an open fire. In rural areas, a whole lamb is splayed out on a cross-shaped stick at an angle over the fire. *Parrilla* restaurants, found all over Argentina, grill cuts of meat in much the same way; they can be ordered as individual dishes or as *parrillada* (basically a mixed grill). Other meat to try includes wild boar in Bariloche and even guanaco. Italian immigration has left a legacy of pizza, *pasta casero* (homemade pasta) and *ñoquis* (gnocchi). Perhaps the most outstanding ingredient in Chilean cuisine is the seafood. Some of the best is to be had at Angelmo (Puerto Montt). The most popular fish are *merluza* (a species of hake), *congrio* (ling), *corvina* (bass – often served marinated in lemon juice as *ceviche*), *reineta* (a type of bream), *lenguado* (sole) and *albacora* (sword fish). There is an almost bewildering array of unique shellfish, particularly *erizos*, *machas*, *picorocos* and *locos*. The local *centolla* (king crab) is also exquisite.

Both Argentine and Chilean wines are excellent, and even the cheapest varieties are very drinkable. Also try the home-brewed beer around El Bolsón in Argentina. Cider (*chicha de manzana*) is popular in southern Chile. The most famous spirit in Chile is *pisco*, made with grapes and usually drunk with lemon or lime juice as *pisco sour*, or mixed with coca cola or sprite. The great Argentine drink is *mate* (pronounced mattay), an important social convention. Dried yerba leaves, similar to tea, are placed in a hollowed out gourd into which hot water (not boiling) is poured, and the resulting infusion is drunk through a metal straw with a filter at the bottom. The cup is filled with water for each person in the group, who then drinks in turn. If offered, give it a go, but be prepared for the bitter taste; you can add a little sugar to make it more palatable. The experience of sharing a *mate* is a great way to make Argentine friends and transcends social boundaries.

Essentials A-Z

Accidents

Contact the relevant emergency service and your embassy (see page 28). Make sure you obtain police/medical reports required for insurance claims.

	Argentina	Chile
Ambulance	107	131
Coastguard	101	138
Fire service	100	132
Police	101	133
Air Rescue Service	101	138

Children

Chileans and Argentines are incredibly warm and receptive to children and will go out of their way to make them welcome. More expensive hotels provide a babysitting service; children's meals are offered in many restaurants and most have high chairs. Self-catering *cabañas* may be the best sleeping option for families as they are good value and well equipped.

For most tourist attractions, there are cheaper prices for children; on sightseeing tours try to bargain for a family rate. Chilean domestic airlines charge around 66% for children under 12 but fares on long-distance buses in both Argentina and Chile are calculated for each seat, so you'll have to seat small children on your knee to save money. Bear in mind that distances are long; consider flying if possible. Trekking and adventure tourism in Patagonia are not really suitable for young children and the climate is often too cold, wet and windy for them.

Advice

→ Be very careful about sunburn in the south, due to the lack of ozone.
→ If your child has special dietary needs, learn the appropriate Spanish phrases.
→ Order mineral water rather than tap water
→ Take water, fruit, biscuits, tissues, games and books on long bus journeys; the videos shown on board are generally action movies, not suitable for under 12s.

Customs and duty free

Argentina

Visitors coming from countries not bordering Argentina are exempt from taxes on articles brought into the country, including new articles up to US$300, and an additional US$300 if goods are purchased at duty free shops within Argentina. You can claim back tax (IVA) at the airport when you leave the country, if you've bought goods over the value of US$23 and have the receipts. Ask for the necessary form when you buy goods, and take it to the IVA desk at check in.

Chile

The following may be brought into Chile duty free: 500 cigarettes or 100 cigars or 500 g of tobacco, plus 3 bottles of liquor, and all articles for personal use, including vehicles, radios, CD/MP3 players, cameras, personal computers, and similar items. Fruit, vegetables, meat, flowers, seeds and milk products may not be imported into Chile; these will be confiscated at all borders, where there are thorough searches.

Disabled travellers

Facilities for the disabled in Argentina and Chile are improving. Many buses and some metro stations are now wheelchair-friendly, however you won't find many ramps or even lowered kerbsides; pavements tend to be shoddy and broken even in big cities. Many upmarket hotels have been fully adapted for wheelchair use. Tourist sights, particularly in national parks, generally only have limited access for disabled visitors. However, the best museums have ramps or lifts and some may offer special guided tours for the visually- or hearing-impaired: the superb dinosaur museum in Trelew is setting the standard here. Boat trips to some of the glaciers should also be possible with prior arrangement. Airlines are extremely helpful, especially if you let them know your needs in advance; some long-distance buses are still unable to accommodate wheelchairs but drivers will help those with some mobility. Argentines and Chileans generally go out of their way to help you, making up for any lack of facilities with kindness and generosity. Speaking Spanish is obviously a great help, and travelling with a companion is advisable.

Useful organizations

Directions Unlimited, 123 Green Lane, Bedford Hills, NY 10507, T1-800-533-5343, T914-241 1700. A tour operator specializing in tours for disabled US travellers.
Disability Action Group, 2 Annadale Av, Belfast BT7 3JH, T01232-491011. Information about access for British disabled travellers.
Disabled Persons' Assembly, PO Box 27-524, Wellington 6035, New Zealand, T04-801-9100, www.dpa.org.nz. Has lists of tour operators and travel agencies catering for the disabled.

Drugs

Using drugs, even soft ones, without medical prescription is illegal and penalties are severe (up to 10 years' imprisonment) even for possession. The planting of drugs on travellers by traffickers or the police is not unknown. If offered drugs on the street, make no response and keep walking. People who roll their own cigarettes are often suspected of carrying drugs and may be subjected to intensive searches.

Electricity

220 volts AC. Chile has 2 or 3 round pin European-style plugs. Argentina has European-style plugs in old buildings, Australian 3-pin flat-type in the new. Bring a universal adapter, as these are not readily available.

Embassies and consulates

Argentine

Australia, 100 Miller St, Suite 6, Level 30, North Sydney, NSW 2060, T02-922 7272.
Canada, 90 Sparks St, Suite 910, Ottawa KIP 5B4, T1-613-236 2351.
Chile Miraflores 285, Casilla 9867, Santiago de Chile, T02-639 8617/638 0890/633 1076.
New Zealand, 11th fl, Harbour View Building, 52 Quay St, PO Box 2320, Auckland, T09-309757.
United Kingdom, 27 Three Kings Yard, London, W1Y 1FL, T020-7318 1340.
United States, 12 West 56th St, New York 10019, T1-212-603 0400.

Chilean

Find Chilean embassies and consulates around the world at www.minrel.cl/pages/misiones/index.html.
Argentina, Tagle 2762, Buenos Aires 1425, T011-4802 7020, F011-4804 5927, data@embajadadechile.com.ar. Also consulates up and down the country.
Australia, 10 Culgoa Circuit, O'Malley Act 2606, PO Box 69, Canberra, T02-6286 2430, chilemb@embachileaustralia.com. Also in Melbourne and Sydney.
Canada, 50 O'Connor St, Suite 1413, Ottawa, Ontario K1P 6L2, T1-613-235 4402, echileca@chile.caglobalx.net. Also in Montreal, Toronto and Vancouver.
Ireland, 44 Wellington Rd, Ballsbridge, Dublin 4, T 01-2692575, embachileirlanda@eircom.net.
New Zealand, 19 Bolton St, Wellington, T04-471 6270, echile@embchile.co.nz.
UK, 12 Devonshire St, London, W1G 7DS, T020-7580 1023, embachile@embachile.co.uk.
USA, 1732 Massachusetts Av NW, Washington DC 20036, T1-202-785 1746, F1-202-887 5579, embassy@embassyofchile.org.

Gay and lesbian travellers

In a macho culture, it is no surprise that there is quite a lot of homophobia in Chile and Argentina. Away from the capital cities, gay men and lesbian women are not encouraged to be open about their sexuality, and there are few places where you can go to meet other gay/lesbian friends.

Useful contacts

www.pride-travel.com, a helpful Argentine agency, organizing tours and trips, nights out in Buenos Aires and travel advice for the rest of the country.
www.thegayguide.com.ar, tips on the Buenos Aires gay scene
www.gaychile.com, gay-friendly hotel reservations and info on gay-friendly shops and other establishments.
Novellus, Av Vicuña Mackenna 6, 3rd fl, Providencia, Santiago, T02-6359534 novellus@tempotravel.cl, a specialist travel agency for gays and lesbians.

Health

No vaccinations are demanded by immigration officials in Chile or Argentina, but you would do well to be vaccinated against typhoid, polio, hepatitis A and tetanus. Children should, of course, also be up-to-date with any immunization programmes in their country of origin. See your GP or travel clinic at least 6 weeks before departure for general advice on travel risks and vaccinations. Try contacting a specialist travel clinic if your own doctor is unfamiliar with health in the region. Make sure you have sufficient medical travel insurance, get a dental check, know your blood group and, if you suffer a long-term condition such as diabetes or epilepsy, obtain a **Medic Alert** bracelet/ necklace (www.medicalalert.co.uk).

Health risks

Temperate regions of South America, like Patagonia, present far fewer health risks than tropical areas to the north. However, travellers should take precautions against the following: **diarrhoea/intestinal upset**; **hanta virus** (carried by rodents and causing a flu-like illness); **hepatitis A**; **hypothermia**; **marea roja** (see Fishy business, page 281); **rabies**; **sexually transmitted diseases**; **sun burn** (a real risk in the far south due to depleted ozone); and **ticks**.

Further information

www.btha.org British Travel Health Association.
www.cdc.gov US government site that gives excellent advice on travel health and details of disease outbreaks.
www.fco.gov.uk British Foreign and Commonwealth Office travel site has useful information on the country, people, climate and a list of UK embassies/consulates.
www.fitfortravel.scot.nhs.uk A-Z of vaccine/health advice for each country.
www.travelscreening.co.uk Travel Screening Services gives vaccine and travel health advice, email/SMS text vaccine reminders and screens returned travellers for tropical diseases.

Insurance

Always take out comprehensive insurance before you travel, including full medical cover and extra cover for any activities (hiking, rafting, skiing, riding etc) that you may undertake. Check exactly what's being offered, the maximum cover for each element and also the excess you will have to pay in the case of a claim. Keep details of your policy and the insurance company's telephone number with you at all times and get a police report (*constancia*) for any lost or stolen items.

Internet

The best way to keep in touch is undoubtedly by email. Broadband is widely available in Argentina and Chile, even in remote areas. Dedicated centres/internet cafés are widespread, particularly in towns and tourist centres and most *locutorios* ('phone centres, known as *centros de llamadas* in Chile) also have an internet connection. Prices are US$1-2 per hr in both countries. To access the @ symbol, you usually press the ctrl and alt keys together with q.

Language

Although English is understood in many major hotels, tour agencies and airline offices (especially in Buenos Aires and Santiago), travellers are strongly advised to learn some Spanish before setting out. Argentines and Chileans are welcoming and curious, and they're very likely to strike up conversation on a bus, shop or in a queue for the cinema. They're also incredibly hospitable (even more so away from the capital cities), and may invite you for dinner, to stay or to travel with them, and your attempts to speak Spanish will be enormously appreciated. Spanish language classes are available at low cost in a number of centres in Chile and Argentina.
Amerispan, PO Box 58129, Philadelphia, PA 19102, T215-751 1100 (worldwide) T1-800-879 6640 (USA, Canada), www.amerispan.com. Runs Spanish immersion programmes, educational tours, volunteer and internship positions throughout South America.

Spanish Abroad, 5112 N 40th St, Suite 103, Phoenix, AZ85018, T1-888 722 7623 (toll free), www.spanishabroad.com. Courses in Buenos Aires and Santiago, with tailor-made programmes, airport pickup and excursions.

Argentina

The distinctive pronunciation of Argentine Spanish is Italian-influenced – in Buenos Aires, you might even here the odd word of *lunfardo* Italian-orientated slang. It varies from standard Spanish chiefly in the replacement of the 'll' and 'y' sounds by a soft 'j' sound, as in 'beige'. The 'd' sound is usually omitted in words ending in 'd' or '-ado', and 's' sounds are often omitted altogether at the ends of words. 'S' before a consonant is usually pronounced as a Scottish or German 'ch', so that *mosca* becomes a kind of *moch-ka*. In the conjunction of verbs, the accent is on the last syllable. The big change, grammatically, is that the Spanish 'tú' is replaced by 'vos' and is used almost universally instead of 'usted'.

Chile

Chilean pronunciation is very quick and lilting, with final syllables cut off and can present difficulties to the foreigner, even those that speak good standard Spanish. Chileans also have a wide range of unique idioms that even other Latin Americans find difficult to understand, In rural areas of Region IX, travellers may encounter Mapudungún, the Mapuche language.

Media

Newspapers and magazines

The *Buenos Aires Herald* (www.buenos airesherald.com) is a daily English-language paper, with domestic news and a brief digest of world news. *News Review* (newsrevi@ mcl.cl) is a similar Chilean publication. Few foreign-language newspapers are available outside Buenos Aires and Santiago but Spanish speakers may want to check out the national dailies, especially *La Nación* (www.la nacion.com.ar) and *Clarín* (www.clarin. com.ar), both of which have good websites and excellent Sunday travel sections. Visitors should also look at *Lugares*, an informative monthly travel magazine with superb photography.

Radio and television

The *BBC World Service* broadcasts at 97.1 Mhz from 1200 to 0500 in Argentina, but no longer transmits to Chile. Many hotels have cable TV in the rooms, but rarely have any English news channels.

Money

The unit of currency in **Argentina** is the peso ($) = 100 centavos. Peso notes in circulation are 2, 5, 10, 20, 50 and 100. Coins in circulation are 1, 5, 10, 25 and 50 centavos and 1 peso. US dollar bills are also widely accepted. In **Chile**, the unit is also the peso ($). Peso notes in circulation are 1000, 2000, 5000, 10,000 and 20,000 (only in Santiago); coins come in denominations of 1, 5, 10, 50, 100 and 500. For up-to-date exchange rates see www.xe.com.

Exchange rates in Argentina (Apr 2007) £1 = Arg $6.1; €1 = Arg $4.1; US$1 = Arg $3.1; Chilean $100 = Arg $0.58.
Exchange rates in Chile (Apr 2007) £1 = Ch $1061; €1 = Ch $717; US$1 = Ch $537; Arg $1 = Ch $173.

ATMs and credit cards

In general, the easiest way to get cash while you're in Patagonia is to use an international credit or debit card at an ATM (*cajero automático*). These can be found in every town or city (with the notable exceptions of El Chaltén in Argentina and along the Carretera Austral, where the only ATM is in Coyhaique), with instructions available in English. Maestro, MasterCard, Plus/Visa and Cirrus are all widely accepted. In Chile, ATMs operate under the sign **Redbanc** and will accept daily transactions of up to US$400. A full list of Redbanc machines in Chile is listed by town at www.redbanc.cl. Commission is usually around 2-3%, but check with your card company before leaving home. You may also be charged a cash handling fee.

Credit cards are generally accepted for payment only in large hotels, city shops and restaurants and for expensive tours. In shops, ID is usually necessary. Credit card use does not usually incur a commission or higher charge in Chile, and places accepting Visa and MasterCard usually display a 'Redcompra' sticker in the window. In parts of Argentina commission of 10% is often charged.

Changing money

Most major towns in both countries have **bureaux de change** (*casas de cambio*). They are often quicker to use than banks but may not have the best rates, so shop around. US dollars (US$) and euros (€) are easier to change than other currencies but will only be accepted if in good condition. Travellers to rural areas of Chile should carry supplies of 1000-peso notes, as higher denominations are difficult to change. **Traveller's cheques** (TCs) are not very convenient for travel in Patagonia. The exchange rate for TCs is often lower than for cash and the commission can be very high (usually 10% in Argentina).

Cost of travelling

Argentina became relatively cheap for tourists after the peso was devalued in 2002, but smart hotels in tourist centres are creeping up. Comfortable en suite rooms can be found for US$50 in most places, and for US$100 you can stay somewhere very good. Dinner in a local restaurant can be found for under US$8. Touristy areas such as El Calafate and Ushuaia have inflated prices, but plenty of choice. Long-distance bus travel on major routes is very cheap (see Getting around, page 21).

Chile is more expensive than Argentina and southern Chile is even more expensive from 15 Dec to 28 Feb. A budget of US$250 per person per week will allow for basic lodgings, food, overland transport and an occasional tour. With a budget of US$500 a week, you will be able to stay in nice hotels, eat in smart restaurants and not stint on excursions.

Police and the law

The police in Chile and Argentina are usually courteous and will be helpful to tourists. However, always be wary of anyone who claims to be a plain-clothes policeman. If you get into trouble, the worst thing that you can do is offer a bribe, as this will be seen as both an insult and an admission of guilt.

Legal penalties for most offences are similar to what you might expect in a western European or North American country, although the attitude towards possession of soft drugs, such as cannabis, is very strict. If you get into trouble, your first call should be to your consulate, which should be able to put you in touch with a lawyer who speaks English.

Post

Argentina

The post service is reliable, but for assured delivery, register everything. Letters take 10-14 days to get to Europe and the USA. Post (including parcels up to 2kg) can be sent from the *correo* (post office) or through the private postal service **Oca** from any shop displaying the purple sign. Larger parcels must be sent from the town's main post office, where they are examined by customs and then taken to 'Encomiendas Internacionales' for posting. All incoming packages are also opened by customs. Poste restante (*lista de correo*) is available in every town's main post office.

Chile

The Chilean postal system is usually efficient. Letters to Europe/North America cost US$0.65 (add US$0.80 to register them). Surface mail rates for parcels to Europe cost US$16 for less than 1 kg; US$20 for 1-3 kg. The *lista de correos* (poste restante) service only holds mail for 30 days, then returns it to sender. The central post office in Santiago is good and efficiently organized, but letters are kept separately for men and women so poste restante envelopes should be marked Señor (Sr), Señora (Sra), Señorita (Srta).

Public holidays

The main holiday period are Jan and Feb, Easter and Jul, when schoolchildren are on holiday and most families go away for a few weeks. All popular tourist destinations become extremely busy at this time and you should book transport and accommodation in advance. Banks, offices and most shops close on public holidays although transport should run as normal, except on 25 and 31 Dec.

Argentina

1 Jan, Good Friday, 2 Apr (Veteran's Day), 1 May, 25 May, 10 Jun, 20 Jun, 9 Jul, 17 Aug, 12 Oct (Columbus Day), 8 Dec (Immaculate Conception Day), 25 Dec.

Chile

1 Jan, Good Friday, 1 May, 21 May, 15 Aug, 1st Mon in Sep (Day of National Unity), 18-19 Sep (Independence), 12 Oct (Columbus Day), 1 Nov, 8 Dec, 25 Dec.

Safety

Buenos Aires is much safer than most Latin American cities, but petty crime can be a problem in busy tourist areas in Buenos Aires, especially La Boca. Travelling in Patagonia itself is very safe indeed. Chile is generally a safe country to visit but, like all major cities, Santiago does have crime problems. Elsewhere, the main threats to your safety are most likely to come from natural hazards and adventure activities than from crime. Don't hike alone in remote areas and always register with *guardaparques* (rangers) before you set off.

General advice

→ Keep valuables out of sight.
→ Keep all documents and money secure.
→ Split up your main cash supply and hide it in different places.
→ Lock your luggage together with a chain/cable at bus or train stations.
→ At night, take a taxi between transport terminals and your hotel.
→ Use the hotel safe deposit box and keep an inventory of what you have deposited. Notify the police of any losses and get a written report for insurance.
→ Look out for tricks, used to distract your attention and steal your belongings.
→ Don't fight back – it is better to hand over your valuables rather than risk injury.

Student travellers

If you are in full-time education you are entitled to an **International Student Identity Card** (ISIC), www.isic.org, which is distributed by student travel offices and travel agencies in 77 countries. The **ISIC** gives you special prices on all forms of transport and access to a variety of other concessions and services, including an emergency helpline (T+44-20-8762-8110). In Chile, alternative student ID cards can be obtained from Providencia 2594, Local 421, Santiago, and cost US$8 (photo and proof of status required).

Telephone

In both countries, avoid calling from hotels, which charge very inflated prices.

Argentina

Locutorios (phone centres) are abundant in Argentina and are the easiest way to make a call. They have private booths where you can talk for as long as you like and pay afterwards, the price appearing on a small screen in your booth. They often have internet, photocopying and fax services too.

For local calls, if you can't find a *locutorio*, use a public payphone, minimum 25 centavos. For long-distance and international calls, use phone scratch cards, available from *kioskos* and *locutorios* for 5 or 10 pesos; 2 good brands are **Argentina Global** and **Hable Mas**. Dial the free 0800 number on the card, followed by the code on the card (scratch the silver panel to reveal it) and then the international number. These cards can usually be used in *locutorios* too, but the rates are more expensive.

If calling to Argentina from abroad, dial the country code (54) and then the area code of the place you want to call. Once in Argentina, dial 0 before each area code. For international calls form Argentina, dial 00, the country code and city code. Note that tariffs are reduced from 2200 to 0800.

Chile

There are 8 main phone companies (carriers) offering competing rates, which are widely advertised. The cheapest call centres (known as *centro de llamados*) tend to be run by CTC

Phone facts

	Argentina	Chile
IDD	+54	+56
International access code	00	00
Operator	19	130
International operator	000	107
Directory enquiries	110	103
International directory enquiries	110	n/a
Mobile phone prefix (within the country)	area code +15	08 or 09

Essentials Essentials A-Z

or by small independent operators. National calls cost around US$0.10 per min. A call to a mobile costs US$0.25-0.30 per min.

Telephone boxes (more widespread than call centres) are programmed to direct calls via one carrier and can be used for local, long-distance and collect calls. They accept coins or pre-paid phone cards (CTC are the most common). To make a local call, simply dial the number you require and pay the rate charged by the carrier who owns the booth. To make an inter-urban call, dial '0' plus the area code (DDD) and the number; if you wish to select a carrier, dial its code before the area code (leaving out '0'), then the number. To make an international call, you will need a phone card; dial '00' before the country code.

Mobile phones

International roaming is becoming more common, although buying a cheap local pay as you go may be a cheaper option. Major airports and hotels often have rental desks, or can advise on local outlets.

Time

Argentina is 3 hrs behind GMT. Chile is 4 hrs behind early Mar-Sep/Oct and 3 hrs behind mid Sep/Oct-early Mar.

Tourist information

Argentina

Tourism authorities in Argentina are generally better equipped than their Chilean counterparts. You might have to be patient in some parts of the country, even when requesting the most basic information, but the major centres of Bariloche, San Martín del los Andes, Villa la Angostura, Puerto Madryn, El Calafate and Ushuaia, all offer good tourist resources. Staff in these popular tourist areas usually speak at least some English and opening hours are long – typically 0800-2000 in summer although they may close at weekends or during low season. Provincial websites, with information on sights and accommodation, can be accessed via the excellent government tourist website: www.turismo.gov.ar. Also consult www.patagonia.com.ar, www.interpatagonia.com and www.revistapatagonia.com.ar. For free information within Argentina call T0800-555 0016 (daily 0800-2000).

Chile

The national secretariat of tourism, **Sernatur**, (www.sernatur.cl), has provincial offices in Temuco, Osorno, Puerto Montt, Ancud, Coyhaique, Punta Arenas and Puerto Natales (addresses are given under the relevant destination). These can provide town maps, leaflets and other useful information, otherwise contact head office in Santiago. Other towns have municipal tourist offices.

For information, contact **Tourism Promotion Corporation of Chile**, Antonio Bellet 77, oficina 602, Providencia, Santiago, T02-235 0105. Useful websites: www.visit-chile.org, www.gochile.cl, www.outdoors.cl, plus region-specific sites: www.patagoniachile.cl and www.chileaustral.com.

Tour operators

In Europe

See **Latin America Travel Association (LATA)**, www.lata.org, for a full list.

Audley Travel, 6 Willows Gate, Stratton Audley, Oxfordshire, OX27 9AU, T01869 276210, www.audleytravel.com. Tailor-made tours to Patagonia and elsewhere.

Austral Tours, 20 Upper Tachbrook St, London SW1V 1SH, T020-72335384, www.latinamerica.co.uk. Interesting and imaginative tours of Chile and Argentina.

Condor Journeys and Adventures, 2 Ferry Bank, Colintraive, Argyll, PA22 3AR, UK, T 01700 841318, www.condorjourneys-adventures.com. Adventure and ecological tour specialist including expeditions, Magellan Strait cruises and estancia visits.

Encounter Overland, 2002 Camp Green, Debenham, Stowmarket, Suffolk, IP14 6LA, UK, T0870-499 4478, www.encounteroverland.co.uk. Adventurous expeditions in groups across wild terrain. Slide shows in London to whet your appetite.

Exodus, Grange Mills, Weir Rd, London SW12 0NE, T870-240 5550, www.exodus.co.uk. Excellent, well-run tours of Patagonia, with trekking and climbing included.

Experience Chile, T07977 223 326, www.experiencechile.org. Itineraries and accommodation in Torres del Paine.

Explore, 1 Frederick St, Aldershot, GU11 1LQ, T0870 333 4002, www.explore.co.uk. Highly experienced and well respected tour operator. Small groups. Well executed.

Fidibus Tours, Postfach 178, CH-3033 Wohlen, Switzerland, T+41 79 4325904, www.fidibustours.de. All tours are organized on a private basis in off-road campers for up to 4. Tents provided.
Galapagos Classic Cruises, 6 Keyes Rd, London NW2 3XA, T020-8933 0613, www.galapagoscruises.co.uk. Good tailor-made tours.
Journey Latin America, 12-13 Heathfield Terrace, Chiswick, London, W4 4JE, T020-8747 8315, and 12 St Ann's Sq (2nd fl), Manchester, M2 7HW, T0161-832 1441, www.journeylatinamerica.co.uk. Deservedly well-regarded, this long-established company runs adventure tours, escorted groups and tailor-made tours to Patagonia and other destinations in South America. Also cheap flights and expert advice.
Last Frontiers, Fleet Marston Farm, Aylesbury, Buckinghamshire, HP18 0QT, T01296-653000, www.lastfrontiers.com. Wide range of tours in Argentina and Chile including great estancias and remote expeditions from Carretera Austral to Torres del Paine. Also fishing, skiing, birdwatching holidays.
Latin America Travel, 103 Gainsborough Rd, Richmond TW9 2ET, T0870-4424241, www.latinamericatravel.co.uk. Offers a tour taking Península Valdés and the glaciers.
Select Latin America, 79 Maltings Pl, 169 Tower Bridge Rd, London SE1 3LJ, UK, T020-7407 1478, www.selectlatin america.com. Quality tailor-made holidays and small group tours.
South American Experience, 47 Causton St, Pimlico, London SW1P 4AT, T020-7976 5511, www.southamericanexperience.co.uk. Will book flights and accommodation, also offers tailor-made trips.
Steppes Latin America, 51 Castle St, Cirencester, Glos GL7 1QD, T01285-885333, www.steppeslatinamerica.co.uk. Tailor-made escorted tours to Patagonia, including riding trips and birdwatching.
The Travel Company, 15 Turk St, Alton, Hampshire, GU34 1AG, T0870-7941009, www.adventurecompany.co.uk. For trips exploring Patagonia.
Trips Worldwide, 14 Frederick Place, Clifton, Bristol, BS8 1AS, T0117-311 4400, www.tripsworldwide.co.uk. Specialists in tailor-made holidays.

In North America

4StarSouthAmerica.com T1-800-747-4540 (US), T0871-711 5370 (UK), T+49 700 4444-7827 (rest of the world). Tour operator and flight consolidator based in Washington DC, Stuttgart, Germany and Rio de Janeiro, offering tours in Patagonia and South America. For flights, www.4starflights.com.
Argentina for Less, 7201 Wood Hollow Dr, Austin, TX 78731, USA, T1-877-269 0309, www.argentinaforless.com. Progressive tourism company with a focus solely on Latin America. US-based but with local offices and operations.
International Expeditions, 1 Environs Park, Helena, AL 35080, USA, T1-800-6334734 (toll free), T205-428 1700, www.internationalexpeditions.com. Travel company specializing in nature tours.
Ladatco Tours, 2200 S Dixie Highway, Suite 704, Coconut Grove, FL 33133, T1-800-3276162 (toll free), www.ladatco.com. Specialist operator based in Miami, runs explorer tours themed around mysticism, wine, etc.
Lost World Adventures, 337 Shadowmoor Drive, Decatur, GA 30030, T800 999 0558, F404 377 1902, www.lostworld.com. Long-time tour operator in the region. Interesting itineraries for all budgets.
Mila Tours, T1-800-3677378 (toll free), www.milatours.com. Wide range of tours from rafting to photography.
Myths and Mountains, 976 Tee Court, Incline Village, NV 89451, T1-800-670-6984 (toll free), T775-832 5454, www.mythsand mountains.com. Cultural, wildlife and environmental trips.
Wilderness Travel, 1102 Ninth St, Berkeley, CA 94710-1211, T510-5582488, T1-800-3682794 (toll free), www.wilderness travel.com. Organizes trips worldwide, including very good tours of Patagonia.

In Australia and New Zealand

Australian Andean Adventures, Suite 601, Level 6, 32 York St, Sydney, NSW 2000, T02-9299 9973, www.andean adventures.com. The specialists in trekking in South America for Australians.
South America Travel Centre, 104 Hardware St, Melbourne, T03-96425353, www.satc.com.au. Good, individual tailor-made trips to Chile.

In South America

Exploranter, Rua Joaquim Antunes 232, Jardim Paulistano, São Paulo, SP05415 000, Brazil, T+55 (11) 3085 2011, www.hotelsobrerodas.com.br. Offers a different kind of overlanding experience in Patagonia, with vehicles fully equipped with beds, hot showers, leather seats and kitchen.

Visas and immigration

Visa and immigration regulations change frequently so always check with the Argentine and Chilean embassies before you travel. Keep photocopies of essential documents and some additional passport-sized photographs, and always have a photocopy of your passport with you.

Argentina

Visitors from neighbouring countries only need to provide their ID card to enter Argentina. Citizens of the UK, western Europe, USA, Australia, New Zealand and South Africa (among other countries) require a **passport**, valid for at least 6 months, and a **tourist card**, which is given to you on the plane before you land. This allows you to stay for a period of 90 days, which can be renewed for another 90 days (US$35), either by leaving the country at a border (see page 23) and immediately re-entering, or by paying US$35 at the **National Directorate of Migration**, Antártida Argentina 1365, Buenos Aires, T011-4312 8663. No renewals are given after the expiration date.

Other foreign nationals should consult with the Argentine embassy in their home country about visa requirements.

Chile

For the latest information: www.minrel.cl.

Carry your passport at all times; it is illegal not to have ID handy and thorough searches are normal procedure. Citizens of the UK, western Europe, USA, Canada, Australia, New Zealand and South Africa require only a **passport**, valid for at least 6 months, and a **tourist card**, which is handed out at major land frontiers and at Chilean airports. This allows visitors to stay for 90 days and must be surrendered on departure from Chile.

Other foreign nationals should consult with the Chilean embassy in their home country about visa requirements. 90-day tourist card extensions (US$100) can be obtained from the **Ministerio del Interior** (*Extranjería*) in Santiago or (preferably) from any local government office (*gobernación*), where the procedure is slightly less time-consuming.

Women travellers

Argentine and Chilean men are generally respectful of a woman travelling alone, although you may hear the traditional *piropo* as you walk past: it's an inoffensive compliment that you can ignore. You can discourage unwanted attention by wearing a wedding ring and, when accepting a social invitation, ask if you can bring a friend, to check the intentions of whoever's inviting you. In other respects, women travellers should follow the safety tips given on page 32 and never go hiking alone. Women travelling in Argentina and Chile should be aware that tampons and towels must never be flushed down the pan, since the water pressure is too low to cope.

Buenos Aires

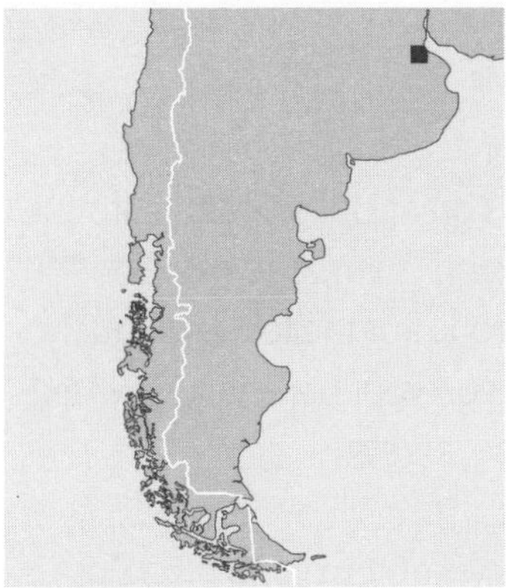

Footprint features

Introduction

Buenos Aires is one of the world's great cities. Grand baroque buildings suggest Paris, theatres and cinemas to rival London, chic shopping better than New York. But the feel is uniquely Argentine, from the steak sizzling on your plate in a crowded *parrilla* to the tango danced in the streets.

The city seethes with history. Marvel at the grand Casa Rosa where Perón addressed his people in Plaza de Mayo, then sip espresso at Borges' old haunt, Café Tortoni, and head north to Recoleta cemetery where Evita is buried in a stylish *barrio* of art galleries and buzzing cafés. Take a stroll in upmarket Palermo Viejo, with its parks and enticing cobbled streets full of chic bars and little designer shops. Or explore wonderfully seedy San Telmo, the oldest part of the city, with its antique market on Sundays, where tango dancers passionately entwine among the fading crystal and 1920's tea sets.

Buenos Aires' nightlife is legendary and requires stamina, as restaurants get don't get busy until 2300 and dancing starts at 0200. Before you fill up on piquant *empanadas*, rare steak and a glass of fine Argentina Malbec, try a tango class at a *milonga* or take in some world class opera at Teatro Colón. Then stroll around the renovated docks area of Puerto Madero, the trendy restaurants of Las Cañitas or the hip hangouts of Palermo Viejo to lap up the atmosphere in Buenos Aires' elegant eateries.

And if the city's pleasures become too intense, take a train up the coast to the pretty 1900's suburb of San Isidro or take a boat upriver in the lush jungly Tigre Delta, where you can hide away in a cabin, or retreat to a luxury lodge until you're ready for your next round of shopping, eating, and dancing.

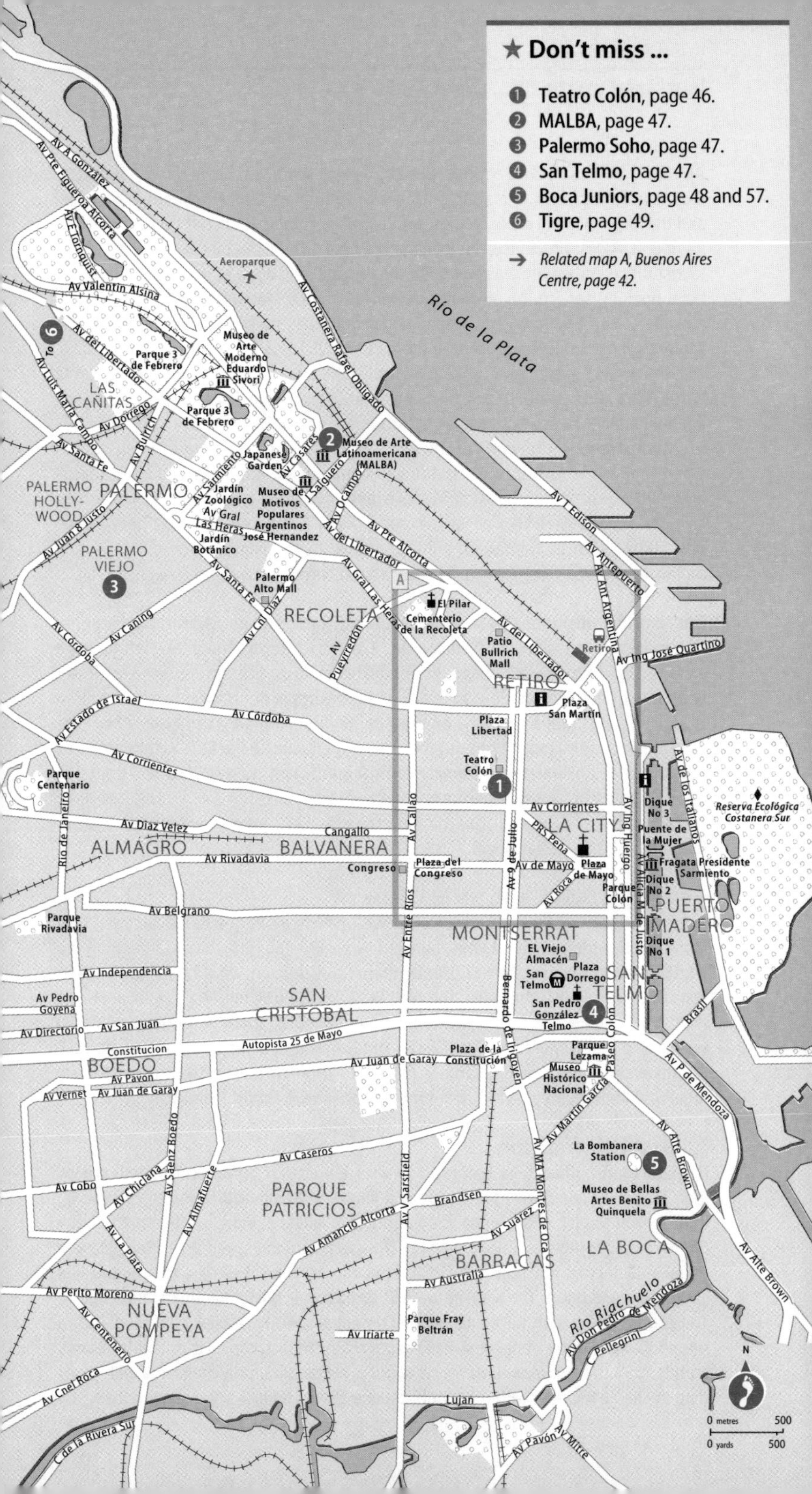
★ Don't miss ...
1 Teatro Colón, page 46.
2 MALBA, page 47.
3 Palermo Soho, page 47.
4 San Telmo, page 47.
5 Boca Juniors, page 48 and 57.
6 Tigre, page 49.
→ Related map A, Buenos Aires Centre, page 42.
Río de la Plata
Aeroparque
PALERMO
RECOLETA
RETIRO
LA CITY
MONTSERRAT
SAN TELMO
PUERTO MADERO
SAN CRISTOBAL
BOEDO
ALMAGRO
BALVANERA
PARQUE PATRICIOS
BARRACAS
LA BOCA
NUEVA POMPEYA
LAS CAÑITAS
PALERMO HOLLY-WOOD
PALERMO VIEJO
Reserva Ecológica Costanera Sur
Teatro Colón
Plaza de Mayo
Plaza San Martín
Cementerio de la Recoleta
Museo de Arte Latinoamericana (MALBA)
Río Riachuelo
0 metres 500
0 yards 500

Ins and outs » p58.

Getting there

Air Buenos Aires has two airports. **Ezeiza** ⓘ *35 km southwest of the centre, T011-5480 6111*, is the city's international airport. It has two terminals: B for **Aerolíneas Argentinas**, and the larger A for all other airlines, with *casas de cambio*, Banco de la Nación (open 24 hours), ATMs, pharmacy, left luggage (24 hours, US$1 per piece), *locutorio*, and a tourist office immediately as you enter the Arrivals hall, open 0700-2000, with a free hotel booking service. An efficient bus service, run by **Manuel Tienda León** (desk in arrivals, T0800 888 5366, www.tiendaleon.com), runs between the airports and the centre every 30 minutes 0600-0100 (from Ezeiza US$8.50 for the 40-minute journey), with free hotel transfer/pick- up. Alternatively take a reliable radio taxi (such as **Onda Verde**, T011-4867 0000), US$15; or a remise taxi, which have a fixed fare of US$18, and are booked in advance from a desk at the airport.

Aeroparque ⓘ *4 km north of Palermo, T011-4576 5111*, is the domestic airport. It is smart and modern, with bars and restaurants, shops, airport tax counter, tourist information, car rental, bank, ATMs, exchange facilities, post office, *locutorio* and luggage deposit (US$ 1.30 per piece a day). From Aeroparque **Manuel Tienda León** buses charge US$5 for the 20-minute journey to the centre, *remises* US$6 and ordinary taxis US$4. » *For flights to and from both airports, see Essentials, pages 17-20.*

Bus The long-distance bus terminal is **Retiro** at Ramos Mejía y Antártida Argentina, five blocks north of Plaza San Martín, T011-4310 0700. There are left-luggage lockers, US$2.50, but large baggage should be left at *guarda equipage* on the lower floor. City tourist information is at desk 83 on the upper floor; local bus information is at the Ramos Mejía entrance on the middle floor. Ordinary taxis leave from the official rank on the lower floor but these are unreliable. The area is insalubrious so take a *remise* taxi into town (**Remise La Terminal** T011-4312 0711, booked from one of two booths on the bus platform and paid in advance) or call a radio taxi (see Transport, page 58) and ask the company to pick you up from one of the five bridges leading from the arrivals level.

Getting around → *See metro map, page 59.*

There is a good network of **buses** (*colectivos*), which are frequent, efficient and very fast, plus five **metro** (*subte*) lines, labelled 'A' to 'E' – four link the outer parts of the city to the centre; the fifth ('C') links Plaza Constitución with Retiro station and connects with all the other lines. The central stations of 9 de Julio ('D'), Diagonal Norte ('C') and Carlos Pellegrini ('B') are linked by pedestrian tunnels. **Taxis** are painted yellow and black and carry "Taxi" flags, but for security always phone a radio taxi. Alternatively, *remise* taxis charge a fixed rate to anywhere in town and are very reliable, although they can work out more expensive for short journeys.

Tourist information

National tourist office ⓘ *Av Santa Fe 883, T011-4312 2232/5550, www.turismo.gov.ar, Mon-Fri 0900-1700*. There are also tourist kiosks at Aeroparque and Ezeiza airports, and city-run tourist kiosks open 1200-2000 on Avenida Florida, junction with Roque Sáenz Peña; at Abasto Shopping Mall (Avenida Corrientes 3200); in Recoleta (on Avenida Quintana, junction with Ortiz); in Puerto Madero, Dock 4, and at Retiro bus station (ground floor). The website www.bue.gov.ar has useful information in English. The **tourist police** can be contacted at Corrientes 436, T011-4346 5748 and T0800 9995000. **Auto Mapa**'s pocket-size *Plano guía* of the federal capital is available at news stands, US$2.70. *Buenos Aires Day & Night* is a free bimonthly magazine with a city map available together with other publications at tourist kiosks and some hotels.

Sights

The formal centre is around Plaza de Mayo, from where the broad Avenida de Mayo heads west to the congress building. Halfway, it crosses the 22 lanes of Avenida 9 de Julio, which heads north to Avenida del Libertador, the main road leading out of the city to the north and west, via the fashionable suburbs of Recoleta and Palermo. East of the centre are the city's vibrant, renovated docks at Puerto Madero, while to the south are the green spaces of Costanera Sur and the city's most atmospheric barrio, San Telmo. ▸▸ *For Sleeping, Eating and other listings, see pages 48-60.*

City centre

Plaza de Mayo

This broad open plaza is the historic heart of the city, surrounded by some of the major public buildings including the famous pink Casa de Gobierno or **Casa Rosada** ⓘ *T011-4344 3804, Mon-Fri 1000-1800, Sun 1400-1800, free, tours from Hipólito Yrigoyen 219 (passport required), changing of the guards every 2 hrs 0700-1900.* The colour derives from President Sarmiento's desire to symbolize national unity by blending the colours of the rival factions which had fought each other for much of the 19th century: the Federalists (red) and the Unitarians (white). The building has been the site of many historic events: from its balcony, Perón appeared before the masses, and when the economy crumbled in December 2001, angry crowds of *cacerolazas* (middle-class ladies banging their saucepans) rioted outside. Since 1970, the Mothers of the Plaza de Mayo (*Madres de los Desaparecidos*) have marched every Thursday at 1530 anti-clockwise around the central monument in silent remembrance of their children who disappeared during the 'dirty war'.

Opposite the Casa Rosada, on the west side of the plaza is the white-columned **Cabildo**, originally the 18th-century administrative centre. Inside is the **Museo del Cabildo y la Revolución** ⓘ *T011-4334 1782, Tue-Fri 1030-1700, Sat 1400-1800, Sun 1130-1800, US$0.35*, good for an overview of Argentine history. Of particular interest are the paintings of old Buenos Aires and the documents and maps recording the May 1810 revolution. The **Cathedral Metropolitana** ⓘ *north side of the plaza, check times for Mass at entrance*, lies on the site of the first church in Buenos Aires, built in 1580. The current structure was built in classical style between 1758 and 1807, and inside, in the right-hand aisle, is the imposing tomb of General José de San Martín (1880), Argentina's greatest hero, who liberated the country from the Spanish.

Just east of the cathedral, the **Banco de la Nación** is regarded as one of the great works of the famous architect Alejandro Bustillo (who designed **Hotel Llao Llao** in Bariloche). Built 1940-1955, its central hall is topped by a marble dome 50 m in diameter.

La City

Just north of the Plaza de Mayo lies the main banking district known as La City, with some handsome buildings to admire. The **Banco de Boston** ⓘ *Florida 99 y Av R S Pena*, dates from 1924 and boasts a lavish ceiling and marble interior. Also worth seeing is the marvellous art deco **Banco de la Provincia de Buenos Aires** at San Martín 137, built in 1940, and the **Bolsa de Comercio**, 25 de Mayo y Sarmiento, which dates from 1916 and houses the stock exchange. The **Basílica Nuesta Señora de La Merced** ⓘ *J D Perón y Reconquista 207, Mon-Fri 0800-1800*, founded in 1604 and rebuilt 1760-1769, has a highly decorated interior and an altar with an 18th-century wooden figure of Christ, the work of indigenous carvers from Misiones. Next door, the **Convento de la Merced**, originally built in 1601, has a peaceful courtyard in its cloisters.

Buenos Aires centre

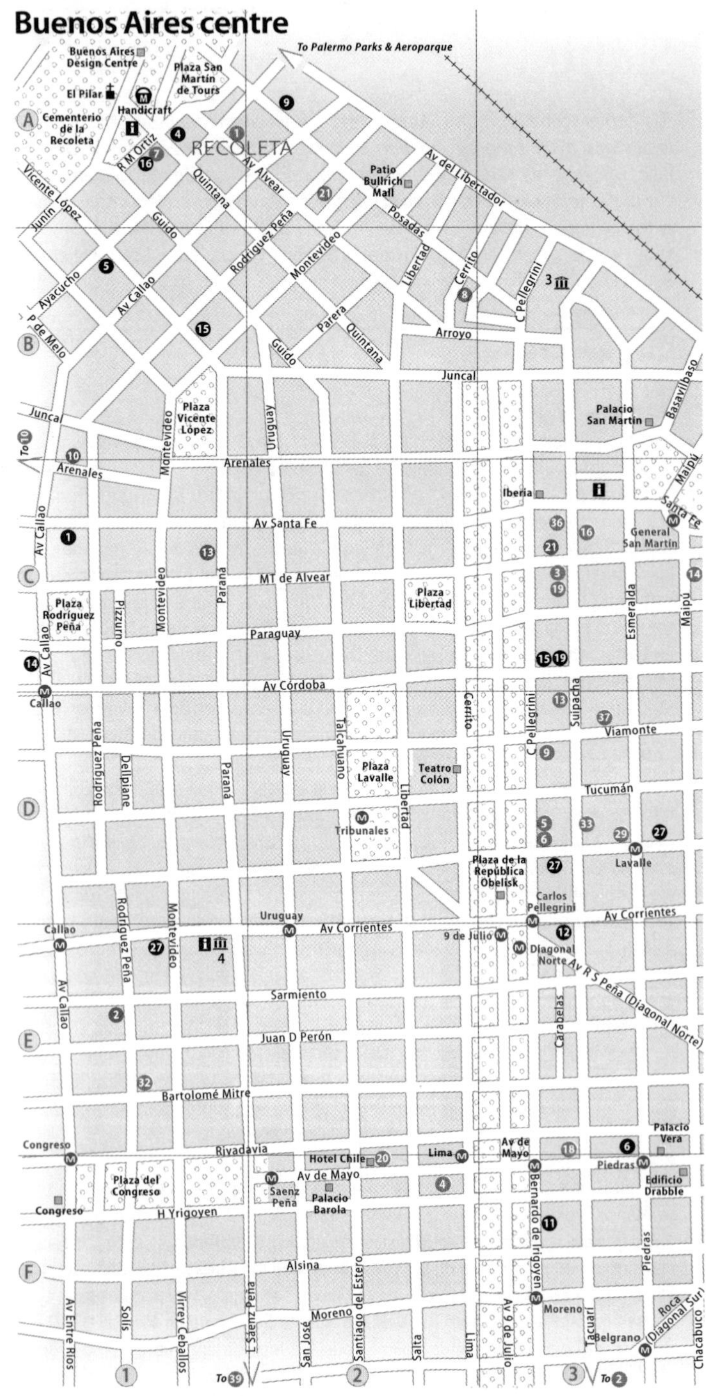

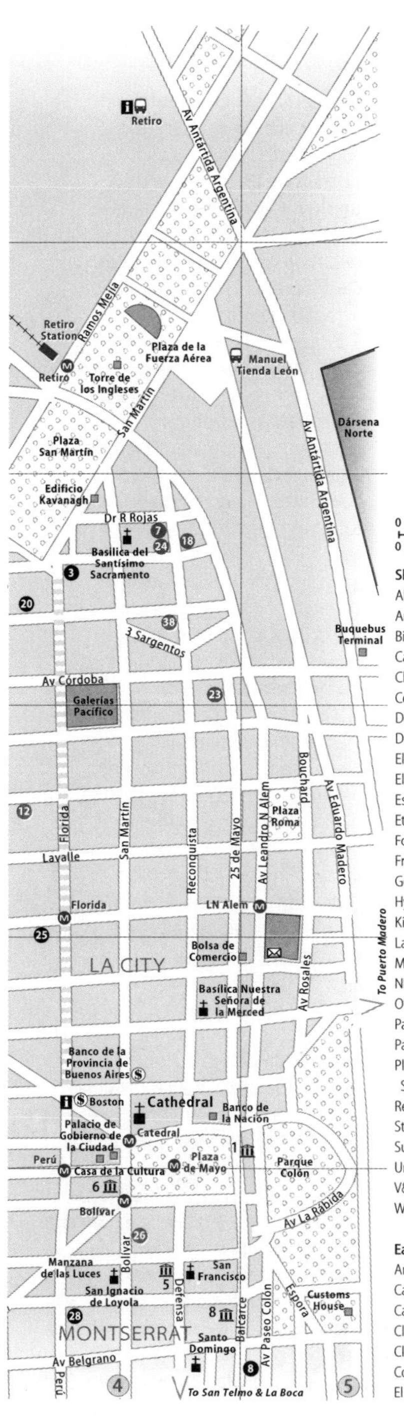

Sleeping

Alvear Palace **1** *A1*
Art **10** *B1*
Bisonte Palace **3** *C3*
Castelar **4** *F2*
Che Lagarto **2** *F3*
Colón **6** *D3*
Dolmen **16** *C3*
Dorá **14** *C3*
El Cachafaz **9** *D3*
El Conquistador **19** *C3*
España **11** *F3*
Etoile **7** *A1*
Four Seasons **8** *B2*
Frossard **12** *D4*
Goya **13** *D3*
Hyatt **21** *A2*
Kilca Hostel **39** *F1*
La Giralda **18** *E3*
Marbella **20** *F2*
NH City **26** *F4*
O'Rei **23** *D3*
Panamericano **5** *D3*
Park Hyatt **39** *F1*
Plaza San Martín Suites **36** *C3*
Regis **29** *D3*
St Nicholas **32** *E1*
Suipacha Inn **33** *D3*
Uruguay **35** *F3*
V&S **37** *D3*
Waldorf **38** *C4*

Eating

Aroma **3** *C4*
Café Tortoni **6** *E3*
Café Victoria **4** *A1*
Clásica y Moderna **14** *C1*
Club Español **11** *F3*
Confitería Ideal **12** *E3*
El Palacio de la Papa Frita **27** *D3/E1*
El Querandí **28** *F4*
El Sanjuanino **9** *A2*
Exedra **15** *C3*
La Chacra **19** *C3*
La Madeleine **1** *C1*
La Trastienda **8** *F5*
Lola **16** *A1*
Rodi Bar **5** *B1*
Sirop **15** *B1*
Sorrento **25** *D4*
Tancat **20** *C4*

Bars & clubs

Celta **2** *E1*
Druid In **7** *C4*
Kilkenny **18** *C4*
La Cigale **23** *C4*
Milion **13** *C1*
Porto Pirata **24** *C4*
Shamrock **10** *B1*
Temple **21** *C3*

Museums

Casa de Gobierno (Casa Rosada) **1** *E5*
Centro Cultural San Martín, Museo de Arte Moderno & Teatro Municipal San Martín **4** *E1*
Museo de Arte Hispanoamericano Isaac Fernández Blanco **3** *B3*
Museo de la Ciudad **5** *F4*
Museo del Cabildo y la Revolución **6** *F4*
Museo Etnográfico JB Ambrosetti **8** *F4*

24 hours in the city

Start with a traditional Buenos Aires breakfast of strong coffee and *medialunas* at **Café Tortoni**, lapping up the atmosphere of leather chairs and art nouveau loved by poets and intellectuals. Then wander down Avenida de Mayo with its splendid buildings to **Plaza de Mayo** where you can admire the bright pink **Casa Rosada**, and pop into the **Cabildo** for a taste of history. If it's a Sunday, take a short stroll along Calle Defensa to pleasingly crumbling **San Telmo**, to see live musicians, tango dancers in the fabulous antiques market. Or take a taxi to to **MALBA**, the stunning gallery of Latin American art, and have tea at its chic café before strolling through the airy galleries. From here take a taxi to **Palermo Viejo** for French, Italian, Vietnamese or Armenian food at any of the great new restaurants.

If the sun is shining, take a stroll around the **botanical gardens** in Palermo and cool off with an ice cream at **Persicco**, watching fashionable Porteños wander by. If you'd rather shop for stylish clothes instead, jump into a taxi and head to **Patio Bullrich** or **Alto Palermo**. At around 1700, it's time for *merienda* or tea, nobody does it better than the **Alvear Palace Hotel**. While you're in **Recoleta**, visit the colonial church **El Pilar**, and the cemetery next door, where Eva Perón is buried. Just outside, there's a huge **craft market**, selling cheap chic jewellery and handcarved *mate* pots, or you could pop into the **Buenos Aires Design Centre** for some quality Argentine handicrafts.

By now you'll be ready to relax in your hotel for an hour to get ready for the night out. At nine-ish, take a taxi to **Palermo Soho** and find a chic restaurant to sample some modern Argentine cuisine, such as **Dominga**, **Cabernet** or **Cluny**. Hold back from eating too much though, because your **tango** class at the *milonga* starts at 2230. Head for **Confitería Ideal** or **La Viruta**, and let the experts take you in hand. If that's too daunting, sit back and watch the city's best dancers' breathtaking display at **El Viejo Almacén**. If you've caught the infectious Porteño rhythm, have a cosy cocktail at a **Palermo Viejo** bar until the nightclubs open at 0200, perhaps at **El Living**. You'll emerge at dawn, when you can appreciate Buenos Aires' beautiful architecture in the crisp early light before staggering to **Clásica y Moderna** for a laid-back breakfast.

South of Plaza de Mayo

To the southwest of Plaza de Mayo is an entire block of buildings built by the Jesuits between 1622 and 1767, called the **Manzana de las Luces** (Enlightenment Square) – bounded by streets Moreno, Alsina, Perú and Bolívar. The former Jesuit church of **San Ignacio de Loyola** (see below for tours), begun in 1664, is the oldest colonial building in Buenos Aires and the best example of the baroque architecture introduced by the Jesuits. Its splendid golden nave dates from 1710-1734. Worth seeing are the secret **18th-century tunnels** ⓘ *T011-4342 4655, tours from Perú 272, Mon-Fri 1500, Sat and Sun 1500, 1630, 1800, (Mon 1300 free tour), in English by prior arrangement, arrive 15 mins before tour, US$1.40; weekend tours include San Ignacio*, which are thought to have been used by escaping Jesuits or for smuggling contraband from the port. For centuries the whole block was the centre of intellectual activity, and although little remains today, the history of this area is fascinating.

The **Museo de la Ciudad** ⓘ *Alsina 412, T011-4343 2123, Mon-Fri 1100-1900, Sun 1500-1900, US$1, free on Wed*, is a historical house with a permanent exhibition covering social history and popular culture, and gives an insight into 19th-century life in Buenos Aires. The **church of San Francisco** ⓘ *Alsina y Defensa, Mon-Fri 0700-1300, 1500-1900, guided visits Tue 1530 and 1630, Sat 1630 and 1730*, was built by the Franciscan Order 1730-1754 and given a new façade in 1911 in German baroque style.

The small, but beautifully designed **Museo Etnográfico J B Ambrosetti** ⓘ *a block south of the San Francisco church at Moreno 350, T011-4345 8196, www.museoetnografico.filo.uba.ar, Wed-Sun 1500-1900 (closed Jan), US$0.70, guided visits Sat and Sun 1600*, contains fascinating anthropological and ethnographic collections from all over Argentina, charting the development of various indigenous groups. One block further south at Defensa y Belgrano, the **church of Santo Domingo**, founded in 1751, where General Belgrano, a major figure in Argentine independence, is buried.

Avenida de Mayo

From the Plaza de Mayo, take a stroll down this broad leafy avenue which links the presidential palace to the congress building to the west. Constructed between 1889 and 1894 and inspired by the grand design of Paris, it's filled with elaborate French baroque and art nouveau buildings. At Perú and Avenida de Mayo is the **subte station Perú**, furnished by the Museo de la Ciudad to resemble its original state, with posters and furniture of the time. You'll need to buy a US$0.25 ticket to have a look.

Along the avenue west from here, you'll see the splendid French-style **Casa de la Cultura** at number 575, home of the newspaper *La Prensa* and topped with bronze statues. At number 702 is the fine Parisian-style **Edificio Drabble**, and at number 769, the elegant **Palacio Vera**, from 1910. Argentina's most celebrated writer, Jorge Luis Borges, was fond of the many cafés which once lined Avenida de Mayo, of which **Café Tortoni**, at number 825, is the most famous. It has been the haunt of illustrious writers, artists and poets since 1858 and its high ceilings and art nouveau stained glass plunge you straight back into another era. It's an atmospheric place for coffee, but particularly wonderful for the poetry recitals, tango and live music, which are still performed here in the evenings (see also Eating, page 53).

Continuing west over Avenida 9 de Julio, look out for the 1928 **Hotel Castelar** at number 1152 (see Sleeping, page 48), the beautiful art nouveau **Hotel Chile** at number 1297 and **Palacio Barola** at number 1370. Avenida de Mayo culminates at the Italian academic-style **congress building** ⓘ *T011-4953 3081, guided visits ext 3885, Mon, Tue, Thu, Fri 1100, 1700, 1900, free.*

Plaza San Martín and around

Ten blocks north of the Plaza de Mayo is the splendid **Plaza San Martín**, designed by Argentina's famous landscape architect Charles Thays, and filled with luxuriant mature palms and plane trees. It's popular with joggers in the early morning and office workers at lunchtimes. At the western corner is an equestrian **statue of San Martín**, 1862, and at the northern end of the plaza is the **Falklands/Malvinas memorial** with an eternal flame to those who fell in the war, 1982. The city's main shopping street, **Avenida Santa Fe**, starts from Plaza San Martín, crosses Avenida 9 de Julio and heads through Retiro and Recoleta to Palermo. Around the plaza are several elegant mansions, among them the **Palacio San Martín**. Most striking, however, is the elegant art deco **Edificio Kavanagh**, east of the plaza, once the tallest building in South America. The **Plaza de la Fuerza Aérea**, northeast of Plaza San Martín was until 1982 called the Plaza Británica; in the centre is a clock tower presented by British and Anglo-Argentine residents in 1916, known as the **Torre de los Ingleses**.

Three blocks northwest of Plaza San Martín is one of the city's most delightful museums, the **Museo de Arte Hispanoamericano Isaac Fernández Blanco** ⓘ *Suipacha 1422, Tue-Sun 1400-1900, Thu free, closed Jan, tours in English by prior arrangement T011-4327 0228, tours in Spanish Sat, Sun 1600*. Housed in a beautiful 1920s neo-colonial mansion with tiled Spanish-style gardens, it contains a fascinating collection of colonial art, with fine Cuzqueño school paintings, and dazzling ornate silverware.

Avenida 9 de Julio

This is one of the world's widest thoroughfares, with 11 lanes of traffic in each direction and the city's famous landmark at Plaza de la República: a 67-m-tall **obelisk** commemorating the 400th anniversary of the city's founding, where football fans traditionally congregate to celebrate a victory.

Just a block north of the obelisk on 9 de Julio is **Teatro Colón** ① *main entrance on Libertad between Tucumán and Viamonte, www.teatrocolon.org.ar; tour tickets from Toscanini 1168 (on C Viamonte side) or from Tucumán 1171, in Spanish and English, T011-4378 7132/33, US$4*. The theatre is characterized by exquisite opulence and an almost perfect acoustic, due to the horseshoe shape and the mix of marble and soft fabrics. Workshops and rehearsal spaces lie underneath the Avenida 9 de Julio itself, and there are stores of costumes, including 22,000 pairs of shoes. The theatre is home to three orchestras, as well as the city's ballet and opera companies (see page 56).

Four blocks west of Plaza de la República, **Centro Cultural San Martín** ① *Av Corrientes 1530, www.ccgsh.gov.ar, museum US$0.50, Wed free, tango desk daily 1400-2100, for classes see www.tangodata.com.ar*, has good photography exhibitions, a theatre and modern art museum. It's a great centre of tango, too (see page 55).

Puerto Madero

East of the city centre at Puerto Madero, the 19th-century docks have been successfully transformed into attractive modern developments of restaurants, shops, housing and even a university campus. Walk along the waterside of the old warehouses lining Avenida Alicia M de Justo from the northern end of Dique No 4, where you'll find a helpful tourist information kiosk in a glass construction under one of the cranes.

Walking south, by Dique no 3, is the **Fragata Presidente Sarmiento** ① *Av Dávila y Perón, T011-4334 9386, Mon-Fri 0900-2000, Sat and Sun 0900-2200, US$0.70*, which was the Argentine flagship from 1899 to 1938, and is now an interesting museum. Also over Dique 3 is the striking harp-like construction of the **Puente de la Mujer** (Bridge of Women), suspended by cables from a single arm.

Recoleta

Situated north of Plaza San Martín, beyond Avenida 9 de Julio, Recoleta became a fashionable residential area when wealthy families started to move here from the crowded city centre after the yellow fever outbreak of 1871. Its streets, lined with French-style mansions, cafés, art galleries and museums make for a pleasant stroll. At its heart is the **Plaza de la Recoleta**, and running down its southeastern side is Calle Ortiz. At weekends, **Plaza Alveas** has an art and craft market from 1100 until 1800, when the whole place is lively, with street artists and performers. There's a helpful **tourist information** booth at Ayacuco 1958, T011-4804 5667.

The **Cementerio de la Recoleta** ① *entrance at Junín 1790, T011-4804 7040, 0700-1800, free tours in English Tue and Thu 1100*, is a labyrinth of ornate shrines, with a vast congregation of angels on their roofs. Eva Perón is buried here in the Duarte family vault, among other illustrious figures from Argentina's history. The former Jesuit **church of El Pilar**, next to the cemetery dates from 1732 and was restored in 1930. There are stunning 18th-century gold alter pieces made in Alto Peru and an interesting, small museum of religious art downstairs.

Close to the cemetery is the **Buenos Aires Design Centre**, where you can buy stylish contemporary designs and handicrafts. There are also lots of good restaurants here, some with open terraces. To the north, the **Museo de Bellas Artes** ① *Av del Libertador 1473, T011-4803 0802, www.mnba.org.ar, Tue-Fri 1230-1930, Sat and Sun 1200-1900, closed Jan*, houses a fine collection of Argentine 19th- and 20th-century paintings and examples of European works, particularly post-Impressionist paintings and Rodin sculptures. In nearby **Plaza San Martín de Tours**, you're likely to spot one of Buenos Aires' legendary dog walkers, managing an 20 or so dogs without tangling their leads.

The wide and fast avenue **Avenida del Libertador** runs north from Recoleta towards Palermo past parks, squares and several major museums. **Museo de Motivos Populares Argentinos José Hernández** ⓘ *Av Libertador 2373, T011-4802 7294, www.mujose.org.ar, Wed-Sun 1300-1900, US$0.30, free Sun, closed in Feb, check www.malbacine.org for film screenings*, has an extensive collection of gaucho artefacts, including ornate silver *mates*, plaited leather *talebartería* and decorated silver stirrups, together with pre-Hispanic artefacts, and paintings from the Cuzco school. The museum not to be missed, however, is the **Museo de Arte Latinoamericano (MALBA)** ⓘ *Av Figueroa Alcorta 3415, T011-4808 6500, www.malba.org.ar, daily 1200-2000, Wed free till 2100, Tue closed, US$12, free for ISIC holders, cinema tickets US$7, book in advance,* which opened in 2001 to house a collection of Latin American art. It's a great building, vibrant and accessible, with stunning art and a good cinema.

North of the centre

Palermo

Northwest of Recoleta is the attractive sprawling barrio of Palermo, named after Giovanni Domenico Palermo who transformed these lands into productive orchards and vineyards in the 17th century. It has a series of great parks, designed by Charles Thays in the early 20th century. The **Parque Tres de Febrero** ⓘ *winter Mon-Fri 0800-1800, Sat and Sun 0800-2000; summer daily 0800-2000*, is the largest, with lakes, tennis courts, a rose garden and the **Museo de Arte Moderno Eduardo Sivori** ⓘ *T011-4774 9452, Tue-Fri 1200-2000, (winter 1800), US$0.70, Sat and Sun 1000-2000 (winter 1800), US$0.30, Wed free,* where you can immerse yourself in a fine collection of Argentine art. South of here is the beautifully harmonious **Japanese garden** ⓘ *T011-4804 4922, 1000-1800, US$0.70, guided visits Sat 1500, 1600,* a charming place to walk, with koi carp to feed and little bridges over ornate streams. The **Jardín Zoológico Las Heras y Sarmiento** ⓘ *1000-1900, US$2, guided visits available*, to the west, occupies impressive buildings in spacious grounds landscaped by Charles Thays, while the **Municipal Botanical Gardens** ⓘ *west of the zoo at Santa Fe 2951, daily 0800-1800, free*, designed by Thays in 1902 has areas planted with characteristic specimens representing the various regions of Argentina.

Palermo has transformed in recent years into a wonderfully chic place to shop and eat, particularly in the area known now as **Palermo Soho** (also known as **Palermo Viejo**), between avenidas Córdoba and Santa Fe, south of Juan B Justo and north of Avenida Scalabrini Ortiz. It's a very seductive area, with cobbled streets of tall bohemian houses bedecked with flowers, and leafy plazas and gardens. Many bars, cafés and chic boutiques have opened up around Calle Honduras, making it a relaxing area for an afternoon stroll. There are plenty of appealing small hotels here, too. On the northwestern edge of Palermo, and separated from the main area by a railway line, is **Las Cañitas**, a popular area of restaurants centred around Calle Báez.

South of the centre

San Telmo

The city's most atmospheric *barrio* is also its oldest. Formerly one of the wealthiest areas of the city, it was abandoned by the rich during the great outbreak of yellow fever in 1871, and it's one of the few areas where buildings remain un-modernized and crumbling. San Telmo is a delightful place to stroll, with artists' studios, cafés, antique shops and small museums hidden away in its narrow streets. On Sundays a bric-a-brac market and free tango demonstrations are held in the central **Plaza Dorrego**. This is a good place to start meandering. Behind the plaza, on Carlos Calvo, there's a wonderful indoor market, **Mercado de San Telmo** built in 1897. Walk south along Calle Defensa to the white stuccoed church of **San Pedro González Telmo** ⓘ *Humerto 1, T011-4361 1168, guided tours Sun 1500, 1600, free.* Begun by the Jesuits in 1734, but only finished in 1931, it's a wonderful confection of styles with ornate baroque columns and Spanish-style tiles.

At the end of Defensa, is the **Parque Lezama** ⓘ *Defensa y Brasil, Sat and Sun 1000-2000*, originally one of the most beautiful parks in the city, but now a little run down and not safe at night. On the west side is the **Museo Histórico Nacional** ⓘ *Defensa 1600, T011-4307 1182, Tue-Sun 1300-1800, US$0.30, tours Sat and Sun 1530*, which presents the history of the city and the country through key figures and events, with some impressive artefacts, portraits and paintings, particularly of San Martín. Among the ever-growing number of cheap and lively restaurants along Defensa, several venues offer tango shows. The best is the historical **El Viejo Almacén**, where the city's finest tango dancers demonstrate their extraordinary skills in a small atmospheric theatre, with excellent live music and singing from some the great names of tango (see page 55).

La Boca

East of the Plaza de Mayo, Paseo Colón, runs south towards the old port district of La Boca, where the Riachuelo flows into the Plata. An area of heavy Italian immigration in the early 1900s, La Boca is known for its brightly painted zinc houses, a tradition started by Genoese immigrants who used the leftover paint from ships. It's a much-touted tourist destination, but there's really only one block to see on the pedestrianized street **El Caminito**. Despite the tango demonstrations and tourist souvenirs, take extra care when visiting the area; police are on hand to stop visitors straying from El Caminito. Always take a radio taxi to and from La Boca, never the bus.

Vivid paintings of La Boca's ships, docks and workers, painted by Benito Quinquela Martín (1890-1977) can be seen in the **Museo de Bellas Artes 'Benito Quinquela'** ⓘ *Pedro de Mendoza 1835, T011-4301 1080, Tue-Fri 1000-1730, Sat and Sun 1100-1730, closed Jan, US$0.35*, along with his own collection of paintings by Argentine artists. There's a roof terrace with superb panoramic views over the whole port, revealing the marginalized poverty behind the coloured zinc façades.

La Boca is home to one of the country's great football teams, **Boca Juniors** (see page 57), and the area is especially rowdy when they're playing at home. Tour operators can arrange a ticket, and fans will be entertained by the **Museo de la Pasión Boquense** ⓘ *Brandsen 805, T011-4362 1100, www.boquense.com, daily 100-1900, US$5.*

Sleeping

The tourist offices at the airports can book rooms. Hotels and guesthouses may display a star rating, but this does not match up to international standards. Many of the upmarket hotels charge different prices for *extranjeros* (non-Argentines), in US$, and there's not much you can do to get around this as you have to prove residency. Offer to pay in pesos in cash and you may get a reduction.

Centre *p41, map p42*

LL Park Hyatt, Av Alvear 1661, T/F5171 1234, www.buenosaires.park.hyatt.com. A traditional belle-époque style palace, converted into a luxurious modern hotel with bold design, exquisite taste and superb service. Minimalist rooms, great restaurant, elegant tea rooms, spa. Recommended.

L-AL NH City Hotel, Bolivar 160, T011-4121 6464, www.nh-hoteles.com. Very chic with perfect minimalist design, this is one of 3 in the Spanish-owned chain in central Buenos Aires, with beautifully designed modern interiors in a 1930's building off Plaza de Mayo, and luxurious rooms. Small rooftop pool, good restaurant.

L-AL Panamericano, Carlos Pellegrini 551, T011-4348 5000, www.panamericano news.com. Extremely smart and modern city hotel, with luxurious and tasteful rooms, a lovely rooftop pool, superb restaurant and service.

Going further ...

If you have more than a few days to spend in the city, here are three tips for perfect escapes – all possible in a day, or overnight:

→ **Tigre Delta** Take the coastal train (*Tren de la Costa*) from Maipú station (reached by commuter train from Retiro) to the little resort of **Tigre** in the jungly overgrown river delta, 29 km north. Popular with families and the jet set in summer, it has lots of hotels and restaurants, a fruit market, excellent fishing, and you could hire a kayak if you're feeling energetic, see www.tigre.gov.ar/turismo, T011-4512 4495. Or take a river bus down the tranquil canals to stay at a luxurious riverside retreat, such as **La Pascuala**, www.lapascuala.com.ar, US$125 per person for 24 hours.

→ **Colonia de Sacramento**
East across the Río de la Plata, on the shores of Uruguay, lies **Colonia del Sacramento**, whose Portuguese colonial centre is beautifully preserved. Hire a bike (US$3 per day), or a scooter (US$4) to see the whole place at your leisure. Boats leave from Puerto Madero three times daily, three hours (US$22 return) or one hour (US$60 return) – see www.buquebus.com. Take your passport, no visa required, pesos and dollars accepted virtually everywhere.

→ **Estancias in the Pampas**
The immense flat lands stretching out from the capital are dotted with grand cattle estancias. Either visit for the day or spend the night to enjoy riding, walking, fishing, or just relaxing in complete peace and luxury. **San Antonio de Areco**, 113 km northwest, www.sanantoniodeareco.com, is a good base with a lively gaucho feel, a couple of great museums and three estancias on its doorstep. Alternatively, head 126 km south to the cowboy town of **Chascomús** where **Dos Talas** offers the most exquisite estancia stay in a historic house, www.dostalas.com.ar, from US$150 per person per night, everything included.

AL **Bisonte Palace**, MT de Alvear 910, T011-328 4751, www.hotelesbisonte.com. A rather charming place, with calm entrance foyer and courteous staff. The rooms are plain but spacious, breakfast is ample, and it's in a good location. Very good value.

AL **Colón**, Carlos Pellegrini 507, T011-4320 3500, www.colon-hotel.com.ar. With a splendid location overlooking Av 9 de Julio and Teatro Colón, extremely good value. Charming comfortable rooms, pool, gym, great breakfasts and service. Recommended.

AL **Dolmen**, Suipacha 1079, T011-4315 7117, www.hoteldolmen.com.ar. In a good location, this has a smart spacious entrance lobby, with a calm relaxing atmosphere, good professional service, comfortable modern well-designed rooms, and a little pool.

AL **El Conquistador**, Suipacha 948, T011-4328 3012, www.elconquistador.com.ar. A stylishly modernized 1970s boutique hotel, which retains the wood and chrome foyer, but has bright modern rooms, and a lovely light restaurant on the 10th floor with great views. Well situated and good value.

AL **Plaza San Martín Suites**, Suipacha 1092, T011-4328 4740, www.plazasanmartin.com.ar. Neat modern self-contained apartments, comfortable and attractively decorated, with lounge and little kitchen, so that you can relax in privacy, right in the city centre, with all the services of an hotel. Sauna, gym, room service. Good value.

A **Castelar**, Av de Mayo 1152, T011-4383 5000, www.castelarhotel.com.ar. A wonderfully elegant 1920s hotel that retains all the original features in the grand entrance and bar. Cosy bedrooms (some a bit too cosy), helpful staff, and great value. Ask if there's going to be a party as it can be noisy. Spa with Turkish baths and massage. Recommended.

A **Waldorf**, Paraguay 450, T011-312 2071, www.waldorf-hotel.com.ar. Welcoming staff and a comfortable mixture of traditional and modern. Good value, with a buffet breakfast, English spoken. Recommended.

B Dorá, Maipú 963, T011-4312 7391, www.dorahotel.com.ar. Charming old-fashioned place with comfortable rooms, good service, an attractive lounge decorated with paintings. Warmly recommended.
B Frossard, Tucumán 686, T011-4322 1811, www.hotelfrossard.com.ar. A lovely old 1940's building with high ceilings and original doors, attractively modernized, and though the rooms are small, the staff are welcoming. This is good value and near C Florida.
B Regis, Lavalle 813, T011-4327 2605, www.orho-hoteles.com.ar. Good value in this old-fashioned but modernized place, with good breakfast and friendly staff. Decent beds and spacious bathrooms. Full breakfast.
C Goya, Suipacha 748, T011-4322 9269, www.goyahotel.com.ar. Friendly and welcoming, worth paying **B** for the superior rooms, though all are comfortable and well maintained. Good breakfast, English spoken.
C Marbella, Av de Mayo 1261, T/F011-4383 3573, www.hotelmarbella.com.ar. Modernized and central, though quiet, breakfast included, English, French, Italian, Portuguese and German spoken. Highly recommended.
C Suipacha Inn, Suipacha 515, T011-4322 0099, www.hotelsuipacha.com.ar. Good value, neat small rooms with a/c, breakfast.
D La Giralda, Tacuarí 17, T011-4345 3917. Nicely maintained and good value. Popular with budget travellers, with discounts for students and for long stays.

Youth hostels

E pp **St Nicholas**, B Mitre 1691 (y Rodríguez Peña), T011-4373 5920, www.snhostel.com. Beautifully restored old house, spotless rooms, cooking facilities, large roof terrace, luggage store; also **D** double rooms. Discounts for HI members. Recommended.
E pp **V&S**, Viamonte 887, T011-4322 0994, www.hostelclub.com. **D** in attractive double rooms with bath. This is one of the city's best loved hostels, central and beautifully run by friendly English speaking staff, there's a welcoming little café and place to sit, a tiny kitchen, internet access, and lots of tours arranged, plus tango nights, etc. Good place to meet people. Highly recommended.
F pp **Che Lagarto**, Venezuela 857, T011-4343 4845, www.chelagarto.com. New location between Montserrat and San Telmo, large light dorms and **D** doubles (each with bath), attractive tango hall. The whole ground floor is a pub and restaurant open to all.
F pp **El Cachafaz**, Viamonte 982, T011-4328 1445, www.elcachafaz.com. A renovated central house, with dorms and **D** doubles, breakfast, free internet access, laundry.

Recoleta *p46*

LL Alvear Palace, Av Alvear 1891, T/F011-4808 2100, www.alvearpalace.com. The height of elegance, an impeccably preserved 1930s palace, taking you back in time to Buenos Aires' wealthy heyday. A sumptuous marble foyer, with Louis XV-style chairs, and a charming orangery where you can take tea. Antique-filled bedrooms. Recommended.
LL Four Seasons, Posadas 1086, T011-4321 1200, www.fourseasons.com/buenosaires. An entirely modern palace in traditional style, offering sumptuous luxury in an exclusive atmosphere. Spacious public areas, adorned with paintings and flowers, chic lavishly decorated rooms, and 7 suites in **La Mansión** residence, pool and health club.
AL Art Hotel, Azcuénaga 1268, T011-4821 4744, www.arthotel.com.ar. Great location on a quiet street in Recoleta and handy for the Subte and shopping in Santa Fé, this is a reliable and comfortable little hotel with small, neat, well-equipped rooms, good breakfasts. Free internet. Recommended.
AL Etoile, R Ortiz 1835 in Recoleta, T011-805 2626, www.etoile.com.ar. Outstanding location, rooftop pool, rooms with kitchenette.

Palermo *p47*

AL Krista , Bonpland 1665, T011-4771 4697, www.kristahotel.com.ar. A delightful surprise: this intimate boutique hotel is hidden behind the plain façade of an elegant townhouse, once owned by Perón's doctor, in Palermo Hollywood, well-placed for restaurants. It's a very appealing place to stay, and good value, with its comfortable, calm, individually designed rooms, all with bathrooms. The exquisite lounge was designed by the owner, Wi-Fi, wheelchair access. Recommended.

For an explanation of sleeping and eating price codes, and other relevant information, see Essentials pages 25-26.

AL Home, Honduras 5860, T 011 4778 1008, www.homebuenosaires.com. A trendy boutique hotel in Palermo Hollywood, with bold 1950's inspired textiles and minimalist concrete floors, creating a vibrant urban chic feel. A handful of minimalist rooms around a bar serving light snacks, and a small pool, a good place to hang out in the evenings.

AL Malabia House, Malabia 1555, Palermo Viejo,T011-4833 2410, www.malabiahouse.com.ar. An elegant B&B in a tastefully converted old house, with 15 light and airy individually designed bedrooms in white and pale green, and lovely calm sitting rooms. Great breakfast. This was the original Palermo boutique hotel, and while it's not the cheapest of the options available, and always booked ahead, it's recommended as a reliable and welcoming option.

AL-A Bo Bo, Guatemala 4882, Palermo Viejo, T011-4774 0505, www.bobohotel.com. Very chic, and one of the most welcoming places to stay in Palermo. Bo Bo has just 7 rooms, designed around different themes, though all are warm, elegant and minimalist, with stylish bathrooms (some with disabled access). There's also an excellent restaurant (🍴) and bar, relaxing places in the evening, with lots of dark wood and smart tables, serving very classy food. Great service from friendly staff, who all speak English. Recommended.

A Costa Petit Hotel, Costa Rica 5141, T011 4776 8296, www.costapetithotel.com. 4 spacious and exquisitely tasteful rooms in this beautifully designed B&B. Small pool, good breakfast, a peaceful haven right in the heart of Palermo. Recommended.

A-B Como en Casa, Gurruchaga 2155, T011 4831 0517, www.bandb.com.ar. Homely rustic style in this converted old house, with exposed brick walls, red stone floors, and lots of woven rugs. Rooms for 2-4, some with bathrooms, and quieter ones at the back, where there's a lovely little garden. The whole place is clean and neat, and the welcoming owner speaks English.

B Cypress In, Costa Rica 4828, Palermo Viejo, T011-4833 5834, www.cypressin.com. This cosy compact B&B offers 8 neat rooms on 2 floors, decorated in pleasing stark modern style, in a centrally located house, where the staff are very friendly. Stylish small sitting and dining area, and outside patio. Charming. Very good value. Recommended.

B Solar Soler, Soler 5676, T011-4776 3065, www.solarsoler.com.ar. Very homely and extremely welcoming B&B in a great location in an old town house in Palermo Hollywood and recommended for its excellent service. All rooms have bathrooms, ask for the quiet ones at the back, there's free internet and the breakfasts are good.

C Che Lulu, Emilio Zola 5185, T011-4772 0289, www.chelulu.com. Some double rooms and more hostel-style accommodation in this friendly, rambling, laid-back house along a quaint quiet street just a few blocks from Palermo subte. Not luxurious, but great value and very welcoming. Often recommended.

Youth hostels

F pp **Casa Esmeralda**, Honduras 5765, T011-4772 2446, www.casaesmeralda.com.ar. Laid-back, dorms and **D** doubles, neat garden with hammocks and fishpond. The owner offers basic comfort with great charm and also runs trendy bars **La Cicale** and **Zanzibar**.

F pp **Tango Backpackers Hostel**, Thames 2212, T011-4776 6871, www.tangobp.com. Well situated to enjoy Palermo's nightlife, this is a friendly hostel with shared rooms, and **D** doubles, all the usual facilities plus its own restaurant, HI discount.

San Telmo and around *p47*

A The Cocker, Av Garay 458, T011-4362 8451, www.thecocker.com. In the heart of the antiques district, this art nouveau house has been tastefully restored and offers a perfect urban retreat with stylish suites, a cosy, light living room and delightful roof terraces and gardens. Recommended.

A Dandi Royal, Piedras 922, T011-4307 7623, www.hotelmansiondandiroyal.com. Perfectly restored 1900's house with stunningly elegant entrance hall and some beautiful rooms all decorated in the original style, with luxurious bathrooms. Interesting location between San Telmo and Congreso, and the added benefit of tango classes downstairs. Charming welcome, small pool. Much better value than most of the boutique hotels. Recommended.

C La Casita de San Telmo, Cochabamba 286 T/F011-4307 5073, www.lacasitadesantelmo.com. A restored 1840's house, 7 rooms, most of which open onto a garden with a beautiful fig tree. The owners are tango fans; rooms are rented by the day, week or month.

Youth hostels
Worldwide chain **Hostel-Inn** has opened hostels in Buenos Aires, www.hostel-inn.com. **Buenos Aires Inn**, Humberto 1 No 820, T011- 4300 7992, **E** pp in double room. Also **F** pp **Tango City Hostel Inn**, Piedras 680, T011-4300 5764. Both are well organized, lively, and offer lots of activities, and the usual facilities.
D-F pp **Garden House Hostel**, San Juan 1271, T011-4305 0517, www.garden houseba.com.ar. Dorms or private rooms. Friendly, fun and relaxed hostel with a terrace, living room and kitchen. Rooms are light and have heater and fan. Breakfast included.
E pp **Buenos Ayres**, Pasaje San Lorenzo 320, San Telmo, T011-4361 0694, www.buenos ayreshostel.com. New hostel, double rooms with bath, kitchen, laundry, internet access with breakfast included.
F pp **El Hostal de Granados**, Chile 374, T011-4362 5600, www.hostaldegranados.com.ar. Small well-equipped rooms in an interesting building on a popular street with bars and restaurants. Rooms for 2 (**D**) to 4 have lots of light, bath, breakfast, kitchen, free internet, laundry service, reductions for longer stays.
F pp **Kilca Hostel & Backpacker**, Mexico 1545, Monserrat, just north of San Telmo T011- 4381 1966, www.kilcabackpacker.com. Breakfast and sheets included. Free internet access, Wi-Fi. Bar. **E** doubles.
F pp **Sandanzas**, Balcarce 1351, T011-4300 7375, www.sandanzas.com.ar. Arty hostel, run by a group of friends who've created an original and welcoming space, small but with a nice light airy feel, lounge and patio, internet, kitchen, breakfast included. Also **D** double rooms with bath.

Eating

Eating out in Buenos Aires is one of the city's great pleasures, with a huge variety of restaurants from the chic to the cheap. To try some of Argentina's excellent steak, choose from one of the many *parrillas*, where your huge slab of lean meat will be expertly cooked over a wood fire.

Argentines are very sociable and love to eat out, so if a restaurant is full, it's usually a sign that it's a good place. Remember, though, that they'll usually start eating between 2130 and 2230. If in doubt, head for Puerto Madero, where there are lots of good mid-range places. In most restaurants, a *menu fijo* is offered at around US$5-8 for 2 courses. A portion at a *comidas para llevar* (takeaway) costs US$1.50-2.50. Many cheaper restaurants are *tenedor libre*: eat as much as you like for a fixed price. The following are easily accessible for people staying in the city centre.

Retiro, and the area between Plaza de Mayo and Plaza San Martín *p45, map p42*
La Chacra, Av Córdoba 941 (just off 9 de Julio). A superb traditional *parrilla* with excellent steaks brought sizzling to your table (US$16 for complete *parrilla* and salads for 2), impeccable old-fashioned service, and a lively buzzing atmosphere.
Sorrento Corrientes 668, (just off Florida). Intimate, elegant atmosphere, with dark wood, nicely lit tables, serving traditional menu with good fish dishes and steak.
Tomo 1, Hotel Panamericano, Carlos Pellegrini 521, T011-4326 6695. Argentine regional dishes and international cuisine of a high standard in a sophisticated atmosphere.

ŸŸ **Club Español**, Bernardo de Irigoyen 180 (on Av 9 de Julio, near Av de Mayo). Faded splendour in this fine old Spanish social club serving excellent seafood.
ŸŸ **El Palacio de la Papa Frita**, Lavalle 735 and 954, Av Corrientes 1620. Great place for a filling feed, with a large menu, and quite atmospheric, despite the bright lighting.
ŸŸ **El Querandí**, Perú 302 y Moreno. Good food in an intimate atmosphere in this historical place that was opened in the 1920s. Also a popular café, good atmosphere, well known for its Gin Fizz, and a tango venue.
ŸŸ **Tancat**, Paraguay 645 . Really authentic Basque food and from other Spanish regions, delicious dishes: recommended.
Ÿ **Exedra**, Carlos Pellegrini and Córdoba. A welcoming traditional-style café right on Av 9 de Julio, serving cheap set-price menu for US$5-8, including a glass of wine.
Ÿ **Güerrín**, Av Corrientes 1368. A Buenos Aires institution, serving incredibly cheap and filling slabs of pizza and *fainá* (chick pea polenta) which you eat standing up at a zinc bar. Wonderful.

Cafés

Aroma, Florida y Marcelo T de Alvear. A great place to relax in the centre, with a huge space upstairs, comfortable chairs by big windows onto C Florida, so you can read the papers, and watch the world go by.
Café Tortoni, Av de Mayo 825-9. This most famous Buenos Aires café has been the elegant haunt of artists and writers for over 100 years: Carlos Gardel sang here, and Borges was a regular. It's self-conscious of its tourist status these days, but still atmospheric, with marble columns, stained glass ceilings and old leather chairs. Excellent coffee and cakes, and good tea, all rather pricey, but worth it.
Clásica y Moderna, Av Callao 892. One of the city's most welcoming cafés, with a bookshop at back, and lots of brick and wood, great atmosphere, good for breakfast through to drinks at night, with live music Thu to Sat. Highly recommended.
Confitería Ideal, Suipacha 384. One of the most atmospheric cafés in the city. Wonderfully old-fashioned 1930's interior, almost untouched, great coffee and cakes. Tango is taught in the afternoons and there's tango dancing at a *milonga* here afterwards, from 2200. Highly recommended.

Recoleta *p46*

ŸŸŸ **Lola**, Roberto M Ortiz 1805. Famous for its pasta dishes, lamb and fish. Recommended.
ŸŸŸ **Sirop**, Pasaje del Correo, Vte Lopez 1661, T011-4813 5900. Delightful chic design, delicious French-inspired food, superb patisserie too. Highly recommended.
ŸŸ **El Sanjuanino**, Posadas 1515. Atmospheric place offering the best of typical northwest Argentine cuisine: *humitas*, *tamale*, and *empanadas*, as well as unusual game dishes.
ŸŸ **Rodi Bar**, Vicente López 1900. Excellent *bife* and other dishes in this typical *bodegón*, a welcoming unpretentious place.
Ÿ **La Madeleine**, Av Santa Fe 1726. Great for cheap pastas in a bright cheerful place, open 24 hrs. Recommended.

Cafés

Café Victoria, Roberto M Ortiz 1865, next to the cemetery. Perfect for afternoon tea on the outdoor patio. Also popular in the evening

Palermo *p47*

There are lots of chic restaurants and bars in Palermo Viejo and the Las Cañitas district (see below). It's a sprawling district, and lovely in the evenings. Take a taxi and have a walk around before deciding where to eat.
ŸŸŸ **Cabernet**, Jorge Luis Borges 1757, T011-4831 3071. The smoked salmon and caviar blinis starter here is unmissable. Dine outside in the elegant terrace, fragrant with jasmine, and heated in winter, or in the traditional interior of *chorizo* house with a cosmopolitan twist. Sophisticated cuisine and good service.
ŸŸŸ **Dominga**, Honduras 5618, T011-4771 4443, www.domingarestaurant.com. Excellent cuisine with an Asian influence served in elegant surroundings, muted lighting with bamboo panelling, good professional service and a good wine list. Highly recommended.
ŸŸ **Bar 6**, Armenia 1676 T011-4833 6807. One of the best chic, modern bars serving food in laid back spacious surroundings in this large airy space, with bare concrete, bold colours and sofas upstairs for relaxing on. Excellent lunches, friendly atmosphere, good for a drink in the evening. Closed Sun. Recommended.
ŸŸ **Cluny**, El Salvador 4618, T011-4831 7176. A great place for lunch: the menu is as stylish as the black and cream surroundings, from the excellent home-made bread to the exquisite combinations of flavours of sauces

for fish and pasta. Friendly staff, mellow music. Very classy. Recommended.

Eterna Cadencia, Honduras 5574, T011 4774 4100. A fabulous bookshop with a good selection of English classics, and a lovely café at the back with beautiful high ceilings and comfortable sofas, great for a light lunch.

Omm, Honduras 5656, T011-4774 4224. Hip cosy wine and tapas bar with great wines and good food. Happy hour 1800-2100. Sister restaurant **Omm Carnes**, Costa Rica 5198, T011-4773 0954. For steak and meat dishes in a similarly trendy environment.

Social Paraiso, Honduras 5182. Simple delicious dishes served in a relaxed chic atmosphere in this friendly place run by art collectors. Funky paintings on the walls and a lovely patio at the back. Great for lunch with tasty fish and salads. Recommended.

Cafés

Palermo has lots of good cafés opposite the park, including the fabulous ice creams at **Persicco**, Salguero 2591, and **Volta**, Av del Libertador 3060, T011-4805 1818.

Las Cañitas *p47*

Northeast of Palermo Hollywood, separated from it by a railway track, this area has a huge number of restaurants packed into a few blocks along C Baez. Most open around 2000.

Baez, next door to Morelia. Very trendy, with lots of orange neon. Sophisticated Italian-style food, tasty goat's cheese ravioli.

Campo Bravo, Baez y Arevalo. A stylish minimalist place serving superb steaks and vegetables on the *parrilla*, in a friendly atmosphere. Popular and recommended.

De la Ostia, Baez 212. A small, and chic bistro for tapas and Spanish-style food, with a good atmosphere.

Eh! Santino, Baez 194. A trendy small restaurant for Italian style food and drinks, dark and cosy with lots of mirrors.

Morelia, Baez 260. Superb pizzas on the *parilla* or in wood ovens. Lovely roof terrace.

Novecento. Across the road from **De la Ostia** is a lively French-style bistro, stylish but unpretentious and cosy, serving good fish dishes among a broad menu.

El Primo, on the opposite corner from **Campo Bravo**. A popular and buzzing *parrilla* for slightly older crowd. Cheap set menus in a relaxed atmosphere with fairy lights.

Puerto Madero *p46*

The revamped docks area is an attractive place to eat, and to stroll along the waterfront before dinner. It's not the city's cheapest area and has long been popular with tourists, but the restaurants here are also popular with locals and there's lots of choice. Heading along Av Alicia Moreau de Justo (from north to south), the following are recommended.

El Mirasol del Puerto, No 202. Well known and loved for a broad menu.

Katrine, No 138. Delicious fish and pasta.

Las Lilas, No 516. Excellent *parrilla*, popular with Porteños, and often recommended.

La Parolaccia, 2 sister restaurants: a general bistro at No 1052, and the best seafood restaurant in Puerto Madero, at No 1160, serving fresh and deliciously cooked seafood in a lively brasserie atmosphere. Indeed both places are very stylish, and very popular with Porteños. Bargain lunches during the week, and also superb pastas. Recommended.

San Telmo *p47*

There are plenty of places along C Defensa and new places are opening all the time.

La Brigada, Estados Unidos 465, T011-4361 5557. The best choice in San Telmo, this is a really superb and atmospheric *parrilla*, serving excellent Argentine cuisine and wines in a cosy buzzing atmosphere. Very popular, and not cheap, but highly recommended. Always reserve.

Brasserie Petanque, Defensa y México, T011-4342 7930. Very good french cuisine at affordable prices, and set lunch Mon-Fri. It's an appealing little place, a tasteful combination of Paris and Buenos Aires.

Café San Juan, Av San Juan 450, T011-4300 1112. Not a café but a very small *bodegón* – looking just like a typical *restaurant de barrio* (local dive) but with an excellent cook. A short menu includes delicious *tapas de salmón*. It's very popular, book ahead.

El Desnivel, Defensa 855. Popular for cheap and basic food, jam packed at weekends, good atmosphere.

La Trastienda, Balcarce 460. Theatre café with lots of live events, also serves meals and drinks, great music. A relaxed place to hang out with an arty crowd. Recommended.

La Vieja Rotiseria, Defensa 963. Cheap café for bargain *parrilla*, packed at weekends.

Bars and clubs

There are lots of bars and restaurants in San Telmo, Palermo Viejo and Las Cañitas districts, with live music (usually beginning 2230-2400. The latest and highly recommended trend is the supper club, a fashionable restaurant serving dinner around 2200, which clears the tables at 0100 for all-night dancing. Generally it is not worth going to nightclubs before 0230 at weekends. **Pride Travel** (see Tour operators, page 57) organizes gay nights out.

City centre *p41, map p42*

La Cigale, 25 de Mayo 722, T011-4312 8275. Popular, crowded by 2400. Very good music, recommended on Tue with guest DJs.
Milion, Paraná 1048. A French-style residence with lots of space, sitting areas, cushions and tables in the sumptuous halls. It has also a garden. Recommended Fri after 2400.

Palermo *p47*

Mundo Bizarro, Guatemala 4802. This hugely popular bar gets its name from bizarre films shown on a big screen. Come for dinner first then stay all night. Electronic music on Fri and Sat; 1960s and 1980s rest of the week.
Soul Café, Báez 246, Las Cañitas. 1970's style, and a good atmosphere with soul and funk music, a 25- to 40-year-old crowd.

San Telmo *p47*

There are good bars around Plaza Dorrego.
Boquitas Pintadas, Estados Unidos 1393 (Constitución), T011-4381 6064. Hotel bar.

Entertainment

Details of events are given in the 'Espectáculos' section of newspapers, *La Nación* and *Clarín*, and the *Buenos Aires Herald* (English) on Fri, and also in www.laguia.clarin.com.

Cinemas

Films range from new Hollywood releases to Argentine and world cinema; details are listed daily in all main newspapers. Films are shown uncensored and most foreign films are subtitled in Spanish. Tickets are best booked in the early afternoon to ensure good seats (average price US$2-4; discounts on Wed). There are several good cinemas on Lavalle, also in shopping malls, in Puerto Madero (dock 1) and in Belgrano (Av Cabildo and environs). On Fri and Sat nights many central cinemas have *trasnoches*, late shows starting at 0100. Independent foreign and national films are shown during the **Festival de Cine Independiente**, every Apr.

Tango

There are 2 ways to enjoy Buenos Aires' wonderfully passionate dance: watch a show, or learn to dance at a class, and then try your new steps at a *milonga* (tango club). Tango is the key to the Argentine psyche, and you haven't experienced it unless you've tried it on the dance floor. There is tango information desk at the **Centro Cultural San Martín**, Sarmiento 1551, T011-4373 2829, and a useful website www.tangodata.com.ar. Look out for the leaflet *Passionate Buenos Aires* in tourist kiosks, which lists classes and *milongas*. **Tango Week** is in early Mar, and **National Tango Day** is 11 Dec, with free events all over the city.

Tango shows See tango at its best. Not cheap, but an unforgettable experience. A show costs around US$70, including dinner.
Café Tortoni, see Eating page 53. Daily tango shows from 2030, US$10.
El Viejo Almacén, Independencia y Balcarce, T011-4307 7388. Very impressive dancing from the city's best, excellent live band, and great singing from some of tango's great names. Highly recommended.
La Ventana, Balcarce 431, T011-4331 0217. Touristy but very good, and the only one to include traditional Argentine folklore music.
El Cabaret at Faena Hotel and Universe, Martha Salotti 445, T011-4010 9200. Fabulously choreographed and glamorous, charting tango's evolution. Recommended.
La Cumparsita, Chile 302, T011-4302 3387. Authentic, small venue, US$17 with food.
La Esquina de Carlos Gardel, Carlos Gardel 3200, T011-4867 6363, www.esquinacarlosgardel.com.ar. Recommended.

Milongas and Tango classes Tango has experienced a revival in the last few years and *milongas* are extremely popular among younger Porteños. Classes cost around US$3-4, and complete beginners are welcome. Take a class first, and then stay around to practise when the dancing starts.
La Viruta, Armenia 1366, Palermo Viejo, T011-4774 6357, www.lavirutatango.com. Most popular among a young trendy crowd.

Other recommended places include: **Confitería Ideal**, Suipacha 384, T011-5265 8069; **Central Cultural Torquato Tasso**, Defensa 1575, T011-4307 6506; **Dandi**, Piedras 936, T011-4361 3537, www.mansiondandiroyal.com; and **Porteño y Bailarín**, Riobamba 345, T011-4932 5452, www.porteybailarin.com.ar.

Theatre

Tickets for most popular shows (including rock and pop concerts) are sold through **Ticketek**, T011-5237 7200, **Entrada Plus**, T011-4324 1010 or **Ticketmaster**, T011-4321 9700, www.tm.com.ar.

Teatro Colón, see page 46. Opera and ballet tickets sold 2 days before performance. The best seats cost US$35; 'El Paraíso' tickets are available for standing room in The Gods.

Teatro San Martín, Corrientes 1530, T011-4371 0111/8, www.teatrosanmartin.com.ar. Many cultural activities, often free, including concerts. The **Sala Leopoldo Lugones** shows international classic films, daily, US$1.

Shopping

Bookshops

Foreign newspapers are available from news stands on Florida, in Recoleta and the kiosk at Corrientes y Maipú. For English language books try **Librería Rodríguez**, Sarmiento 835; and **Walrus Books**, Estados Unidos 617. The excellent **Yenny-El Ateneo** chain is found in shopping malls and also sells music. Biggest stores in Florida 340 and Av Santa Fe 1860.

Crack Up , Costa Rica 4767, T011-4831 3502. Funky open-plan bookshop and café. Open Mon-Wed till 2230, and till the early hours the rest of the week. Good place to meet people.

Eterna Cadencia, Honduras 5574, T011- 4774 4100. Excellent selection of novels in English: classics, translations of Spanish and Argentine authors. Highly recommended for its café too.

Clothes and accessories

Palermo is the best place to find chic boutiques and international designers and you will be spoilt for choice. The 2 main streets are **Honduras** and **El Salvador**.

In the city centre, head to pedestrianized **C Florida**, which stretches south from Plaza San Martín, and Santa Fe, especially west from Av 9 de Julio to Av Pueyrredon. Along Florida, **Galerias Pacificos** is a recommended mall with a good range of clothes. Designer clothes shops can be found in exclusive shopping mall **Patio Bullrich** and along Arenales and Santa Fe, between 9 de Julio and Callao. Cheaper clothes can be found in the **Abasto** shopping mall, Subte Carlos Gardel.

Camping equipment

Cacique Camping, Esteban Echeverría 3360, Munro, T011-4762 4475, caciquenet@ciudad.com.ar. Clothing and equipment.

Ecrin, Mendoza 1679, T011-4784 4799, www.ecrin.com.ar. Imported climbing gear.

Camping Center, Esmeralda 945, www.camping-center.com.ar and **Montagne**, Florida 719, Paraná 834, www.montagenoutdoors.com.ar, have a good selection of outdoor sports gear and equipment.

Handicrafts

Leather is cheap of very high quality. **All Horses**, Suipacha 1350, and **Aida**, Galería de la Flor, shop 30, Florida 670, can produce made-to-measure jackets in one day.

Arte y Esperanza, Balcarce 234, and Artesanías Argentinas, Montevideo 1386. Excellent little shop with an impressive range of indigenous crafts from all over Argentina. Chaguar bags, masks and weavings. The ethical owners give most of the profits back to the communities. Highly recommended.

El Boyero, Galería Larreta, Florida 953, T011-4312 3564. High quality silver, leather, wood work and other typical Argentine handicrafts.

Galería del Caminante, Florida 844. A variety of good shops with leather goods, arts and crafts and souvenirs.

Martín Fierro, Santa Fe 992. Good handicrafts, stonework etc. Recommended.

Plata Nativa, Galería del Sol, Florida 860, local 41, T011-4312 1398, www.platanativa .com. For Latin American folk handicrafts.

Markets

Many plazas and parks have fairs at weekends. The following are recommended:

Feria de Mataderos, 30 mins west of centre by taxi at Av de los Corrales 6436, Sun 1200-1800. Traditional gaucho crafts and games.

Plaza Dorrego, San Telmo. A wonderfully atmospheric market for souvenirs, antiques, some curious bric-a-brac. With free tango performances and live music, Sun 1000-1700.

Plaza Italia, Santa Fe y Uriarte (Palermo). Secondhand books sold daily, handicrafts market on Sat 1200-2000, Sun 1000-2000.
Recoleta, just outside the cemetery. Huge weekend crafts market, with street performers and food. Recommended.

Activities and tours

Polo

Argentina has the top polo players in the world. The high handicap season is Sep-Dec, but it is played all year round (low season: May-Aug). A visit to the national finals at Palermo in Nov and Dec is recommended. For information, **Asociación Argentina de Polo**, T011-4777 6444, www.aapolo.com. To see polo matches and visit stables, contact **Horses and Adventures** (see Tour operators)

Football

Soccer fans should go to see the **Boca Juniors** at **La Bombonera**, Brandsen 805, La Boca, www.bocajuniors.com.ar, (see page 48) but it's best to visit with **Tangol** (see Tour operators) as the area is rough. Matches on Sun 1500-1900 and sometimes Fri or Sat, cheapest entry US$5. Their arch-rivals are **River Plate**, www.carp.org.ar. The soccer season runs Mar-Jun, Aug-Dec.

Tour operators

An excellent way of seeing Buenos Aires is by a 3-hr tour, especially for those travelling alone. Longer tours might include dinner and a tango show, or a trip to an estancia.
Buenos Aires Tur (**BAT**), Lavalle 1444, of 10, T011-4371 2304, www.buenosairestur.com. City tours (US$6.50); Tigre and Delta (US$15).
Buenos Aires Vision, Esmeralda 356, 8th fl, T011-4394 4682, www.buenosaires-vision.com.ar. City tours (US$8.50), Tigre and Delta, Tango (US$60-70, cheaper without dinner) and Fiesta Gaucha (US$40).
Class Adventure Travel, Av Corrientes 2554, 2B, 1046 Buenos Aires, www.cat-travel.com. Dutch-owned and run, with 10 years of experience. Excellent for tailor-made travel solutions throughout the continent.
Eternautas, Av Roque Sáenz Peña 1124, 4th fl, T011-4384 7874, www.eternautas.com. Historical, cultural and artistic tours of the city and Pampas guided by historians and other social scientists from the University of Buenos Aires, flexible. Highly recommended.
Eves Turismo, Tucumán 702, T011-4393 6151, www.eves.com. Helpful and efficient, recommended for flights.
Flyer, Reconquista 617, 8th fl, T011-4313 8224, www.flyer.com.ar. English, Dutch, German spoken, repeatedly recommended, especially for estancias, fishing, polo, motorhome rental.
Horses and Adventures, T011 155048 2758, www.horsesadventures.com.ar. Great tours from Buenos Aires to spend a day or a night on a genuine estancia for horse riding, polo, and *asado*. Also horse riding all over Argentina arranged by friendly bilingual José Ramón Jiminez de Toro, Recommended
Lan & Kramer Bike Tours, T011-4311 5199, www.biketours.com.ar. Daily tours of the city leave at 0930 and 1400 from Plaza San Martín, also rents bikes at Florida 868.
Patagonia Chopper, www.patagonia chopper.com.ar. Helitours of Buenos Aires and its surroundings US$95-130 pp for 15-45 mins.
Pride Travel, Paraguay 523, 2nd fl, T011-5218 6556, www.pride-travel.com. The best

choice for gay and lesbian travellers in Argentina; they also rent apartments.

Say Hueque, Viamonte 749, 6th fl, T011-5199 2517/20, www.sayhueque.com. Good value tours for independent travellers.

Tangol, Florida 971, 1st fl, T011-4312 7276, www.tangol.com. Friendly, independent travel agency, specializing in football and tango. Also offers city tours, polo, paragliding, trips to ranches, plane and bus tickets and accommodation. Overland trips to Patagonia Sep-Apr. Special deals for students. A reliable and dynamic company. Recommended.

Turismo Feeling, San Martín 969, 9th fl, T011-4313 5533, www.feelingturismo.com.ar. Excellent and reliable horseback trips in the Andes and adventure tourism.

Urban biking, Moliere 2801 (Villa Devoto) T011-4568 4321, www.urbanbiking.com. 4-hr cycle tours US$24, also night city tours, US$18, and day tours to San Isidro and Tigre, US$33. Also rents bikes and runs tours in the pampas.

Transport

Air

For flight details, see pages 17-20. For transport to and from the centre, see page 40.

Airline offices Aerolíneas Argentinas, Perú y Rivadavia, Av LN Alem 1134 and Av Cabildo 2900, T0810-2228 6527. **Air Canada**, Av Córdoba 656, T011-4327 3640. **Air France-KLM**, San Martín 344, 23rd fl, T011-4317 4700 or T0800-222 2600. **Alitalia**, Av Santa Fe 887, T011-4787 7848. **American Airlines**, Av Santa Fe 881, T011-4318 1111, Av Pueyrredón 1997, branches in Belgrano and Acassuso. **Avianca**, Carlos Pellegrini 1163, 4th fl, T011-4394 5990. **British Airways**, Av del Libertador 498, 13th fl, T0800-666 0133. **Copa**, Carlos Pellegrini 989, 2nd fl, T0810-222 2672. **Delta**, Carlos Pelegrini 1141, T0800-666 0133. **Iberia**, Carlos Pellegrini 1163, 1st fl, T011-4131 1000. **LAB**, Carlos Pellegrini 131, T011-4323 1900. **Lan Chile**, Cerrito y Paraguay, T0810-999 9526. **Líneas Aéreas del Estado** (LADE), Perú 710, T011-4311 5334, Aeroparque T011-4514 1524. **Lufthansa**, M T Alvear 590, T011-4319 0600. **Malaysia Airlines**, Suipacha 1111, 14th fl, T011-4312 6971. **Mexicana**, Av Córdoba 1131. **Puna**, Florida 1, T011-4342 7000. **United**, Av Madero 900, T0810-777 8648.

Boat

Connections to the north of Argentina and Uruguay with **Buquebus**, T011-4316 6500, www.buquebus.com.ar. To **Colonia de Sacramento**, 3 daily, 3 hrs, US$18-20 one way (cars US$36-41). **Ferrylíneas Sea Cat** operates a fast service from the same terminal, 1hr, US$30-34 one-way (cars US$55-61).

Bus

Local *Colectivos* basic fare US$0.27 or US$0.45 to the suburbs, paid with coins into a machine behind the driver. Check that your destination appears on the bus stop, and in the driver's window.

Long distance Boats and buses are heavily booked Dec-Mar, especially at weekends. See also Essentials, page 21. Ticket offices are on the upper floor of **Retiro** bus terminal, Ramos Mejía y Antártida Argentina, and are organized by colour-coded regions of the country.

Car hire

AL International, San Luis 3138, T011-4312 9475. **Avis**, Cerrito 1527, T011-4326 5542. **AVL**, Alvear 1883, T011- 4805 4403. **Budget**, Santa Fe 869, T011-4311 9870. ISIC and GO 25 discount. **Hertz**, Ricardo Rojas 451, T011-4312 1317. **Localiza**, Paraguay 1122, T011-4314 3999. **Ricciard Libertador**, Av del Libertador 2337/45, T011- 4799 8514. **Unidas**, Paraguay 864, T011-4315 0777.

Metro

Trains run Mon-Sat 0500-2250, Sun 0800-2200. Free maps are available from *subte* stations and the tourist office. Single fare to anywhere US$0.25 payable in pesos only at the ticket booth.

Taxi

For security, phone for a radio taxi: **Onda Verde** T011-4867 0000; **Radio Taxi Sur**, T011- 4638 2000; **Radio Taxi 5 Minutos** T011-4523 1200; **Radio Taxi Diez** T011-4585 5007. Fares are shown in pesos, starting at US$0.35, plus US$0.04 for every 200 m or 1-min wait. A charge is sometimes made for hand luggage. *Remise* taxi **La Terminal**, T011-4312 0711, is recommended for journeys from Retiro bus station. About 10% tip is expected.

Directory

Banks and currency exchange

ATMs are widespread. Visa and MasterCard ATMs at branches of **Banco de la Nación Argentina, ABN Amro Bank, BNP, Itaú** and others. MasterCard/Cirrus also at **Argencard** offices. For lost or stolen cards, MasterCard T011-4340 5700, Visa T011-4379 3333. Casas de cambio on San Martín and Corrientes. Major credit cards usually accepted but check for surcharges. General **MasterCard** office at Perú 151, T011-4348 7000. **Visa**, Corrientes 1437, 2nd fl, T011-4379 3333.

Embassies and consulates

All open Mon-Fri unless stated otherwise. For other embassies, consult the phone book. **Australia**, Villanueva 1400 y Zabala, T011- 4779 3500, www.argentina.embassy.gov.au, 0830-1100. **Canada**, Tagle 2828, T011-4808 1000, www.dfait-maeci.gc.ca/argentina, Mon-Thu 1400-1600, tourist visa Mon-Thu 0845-1130. **Chilean Consulate**, San Martín 439, 9th fl, T011-4394 6582, www.embajadadechile.com.ar, 0900-1300. **New Zealand**, C Pellegrini 1427, 5th fl, T011-4328 0747, www.nzembassy.com/buenosaires, Mon- Thu 0900-1300, 1400-1730, Fri 0900-1300. **UK**, Luis Agote 2412 (near corner Pueyrredón y Guideo), T011-4808 2200 (call T15-5114 1036 for emergencies only out of normal office hours), www.britain.org.ar, 0900-1300 (Jan-Feb 0900-1200). **US Embassy and Consulate General**, Colombia 4300, T5777 4533/34 or T011-4514 1830, 0900-1800.

Internet

Prices range from US$0.50-1 per hr, shop around. Most *locutorios* (phone centres) have internet access.

Buenos Aires metro (Subte)

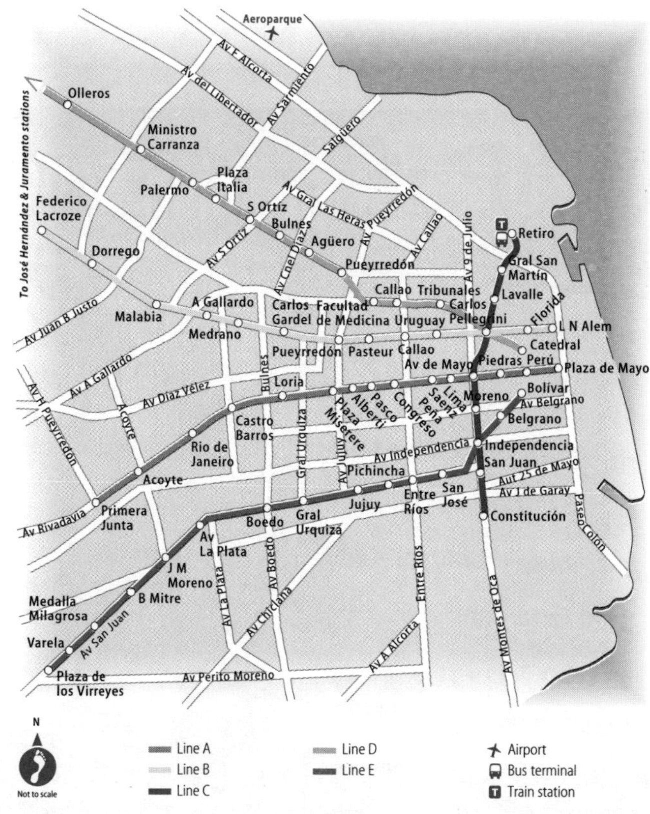

Language schools

All-Spanish, T011- 4381 3914, www.all-spanish.com.ar; **Argentina ILEE**, T011-4372 0223, www.argentinailee.com; **International Bureau of Language**, Florida 165, 3rd fl, T011-4331 4250, www.ibl.com.ar; **Instituto del Sur**, T011-4334 1487, www.delsur.com.ar; **PLS**, T011-4394 0543, www.pls.com.ar; **Universidad de Buenos Aires**, T011-4334 7512, www.idiomas.filo.uba.ar.

Medical services

For free ambulance service to an emergency department (day and night) call **Sala de guardia**, T107, or T011-4923 1051/58. **Hospital Argerich**, Almte Brown esq Pi y Margall 750, T011-4124 0700. **Hospital Juan A Fernández**, Cerviño y Bulnes, T011-4808 2600. **British Hospital**, Perdriel 74, T011-4309 6400, www.hospitalbritanico.org.ar, US$24 a visit.

Post office

Correo Central – Correos Argentinos, Sarmiento y Alem, Mon-Fri, 0800-2000, Sat 0900-1300. Poste restante on ground floor (US$0.50 per letter). **UPS**, Bernardo de Irigoyen 974, T011-4339 2877, www.ups.com.

Safety

If robbed or attacked, call the tourist police, **Comisaría del Turista**, Av Corrientes 436, T011-4346 5748 (24 hrs). English spoken. Street crime is on the rise, especially in La Boca, San Telmo and Recoleta. Be careful when boarding buses, and near train and bus stations. Don't change money on the street.

Telephone

Locutorios are available on almost every block (see Essentials, page 32). Public telephone boxes use coins (25 centavos minimum). Pre-paid cards are available at *kioskos*), don't accept cards without a wrapper or with a broken seal. International telephone calls from hotels may incur a 40-50% commission.

Useful addresses

Asatej: Argentine Youth and Student Travel Organization, Florida 835, 3rd fl, T011-4114 7600, www.asatej.com. **Asatej Travel Store**, sells travel goods. **Central Police Station**: Moreno 1550, Virrey Cevallos 362, T011-4370 5911/5800. **Migraciones**: (Immigration), Antártida Argentina 1335/55, edificios 3 y 4, T011-4317 0200. Visas extended mornings.

Argentine Lake District

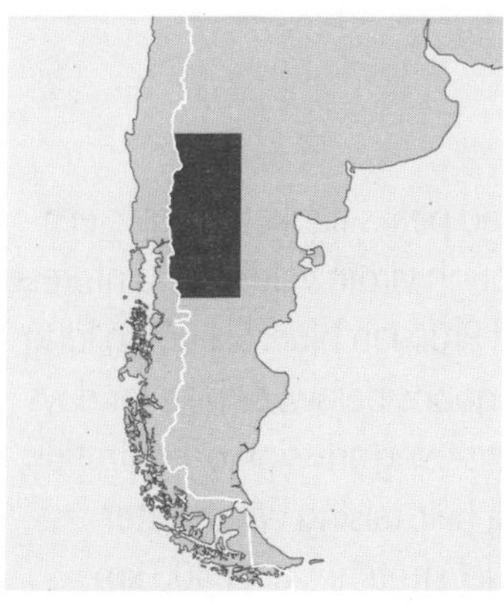

Footprint features

Introduction

Trek amongst craggy snow-capped peaks flanked by glaciers, and crystalline rivers running through virgin valdivian rainforest to lakes of peppermint green and Prussian blue. Ski down long pistes with panoramic views of lagoons below, or hike for days in a mountain-top nirvana without seeing any sign of civilization. Take a slow boat across fjords or a hair-raising whitewater rafting trip. Argentina's Lake District stretches over 400 km of spectacular forest-clad Andes mountains, and has four national parks, keeping it pristine.

With a dramatic lakeside setting, Bariloche is the central base for exploring: a friendly town with chocolate shops and chalet-style restaurants, and easy access to a towering range of peaks around Cerro Catedral. From here, a magical road winds past seven lakes to the pretty tourist town of San Martín de los Andes. Retreat to Lago Huechulafquen, where the perfectly conical Volcán Lanín is reflected in cobalt blue waters, try world-class fly fishing, or enjoy breathtaking horse riding ride at estancia Huechahue. North of here, wilder Pehuenia is a quiet haven with its forests of pre-historic monkey puzzle trees, broad lagoons, and the rich culture of the native Mapuche people.

At the southern end of the lakes, El Bolsón is a wonderfully relaxed place for a few days' hiking, where the mountains are magnificent and the local *cerveza* is excellent. Take the *Old Patagonian Express*, try a Welsh tea in quaint Trevelin, and explore the region's most unspoilt national park, Los Alerces. A jade green river flows between the cinnamon trunks of arrayanes trees and 1000-year-old alerces trees tower above you. And best of all, if you come in March or April, you'll have all this to yourself.

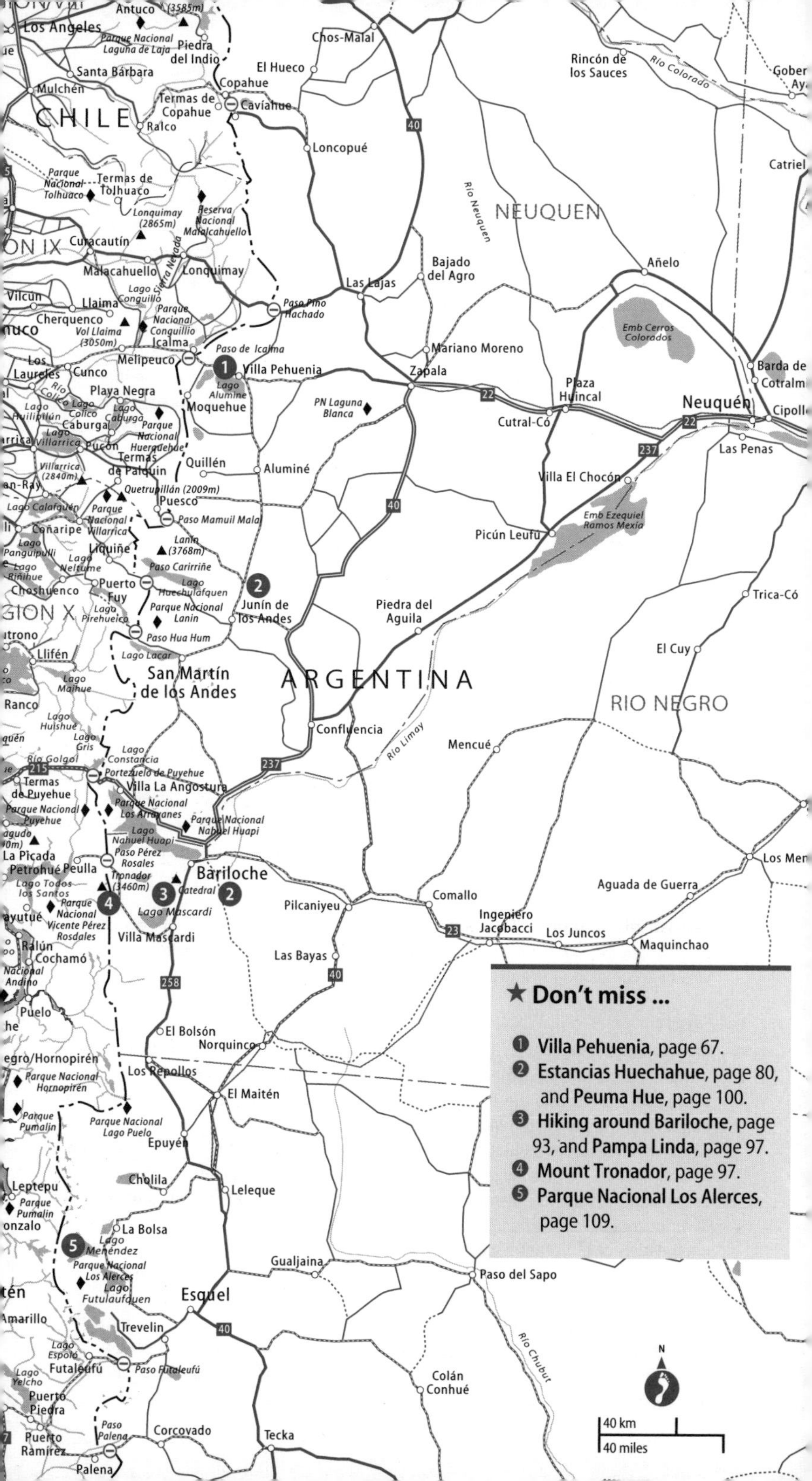

★ Don't miss ...
1 Villa Pehuenia, page 67.
2 Estancias Huechahue, page 80, and Peuma Hue, page 100.
3 Hiking around Bariloche, page 93, and Pampa Linda, page 97.
4 Mount Tronador, page 97.
5 Parque Nacional Los Alerces, page 109.
CHILE
ARGENTINA
NEUQUEN
RIO NEGRO
Los Angeles
Antuco
(3585m)
Parque Nacional Laguna de Laja
Piedra del Indio
Santa Bárbara
Mulchén
Copahue
Termas de Copahue
Caviahue
Ralco
Chos-Malal
El Hueco
Loncopué
Rincón de los Sauces
Río Colorado
Catriel
Río Neuquen
Parque Nacional Tolhuaco
Termas de Tolhuaco
Lonquimay (2865m)
Reserva Nacional Malalcahuello
Curacautín
Malacahuello
Lonquimay
Sierra Nevada
Lago Conguillo
Parque Nacional Conguillio
Vilcun
Llaima
Cherquenco
Vol Llaima (3050m)
Icalma
Paso Pino Hachado
Las Lajas
Bajado del Agro
Añelo
Emb Cerros Colorados
Mariano Moreno
Paso de Icalma
Melipeuco
Los Laureles
Cunco
Villa Pehuenia
Lago Alumine
Zapala
Barda de
Cotralm
Plaza Huincal
Neuquén
Cipoll
Playa Negra
Lago Colico
Lago Caburga
Caburga
Lago Huilipilún
Lago Villarrica
Pucón
Parque Nacional Huerquehue
Moquehue
PN Laguna Blanca
Cutral-Có
Las Penas
22
237
40
Termas de Palquin
Quillén
Aluminé
Villarrica (2840m)
Quetrupillán (2009m)
Puesco
Paso Mamuil Malal
Lago Calafquén
Parque Nacional Villarrica
Coñaripe
Villa El Chocón
Emb Ezequiel Ramos Mexia
Picún Leufú
Lago Panguipulli
Liquiñe
Lago Neltume
Lago Riñihue
Lanín (3768m)
Paso Carirriñe
Lago Huechulafquen
Choshuenco
Puerto Fuy
Lago Pirehueico
Parque Nacional Lanin
Junín de los Andes
Piedra del Aguila
Trica-Có
Paso Hua Hum
Llifén
Lago Lacar
El Cuy
Lago Maihue
San Martín de los Andes
Ranco
Lago Huishue
Lago Gris
Confluencia
Río Limay
Mencué
Río Golgol
215
Lago Constancia
Portezuelo de Puyehue
Termas de Puyehue
Villa La Angostura
Parque Nacional Puyehue
Parque Nacional Los Arrayanes
Parque Nacional Nahuel Huapi
Lago Nahuel Huapi
La Picada
Paso Pérez Rosales
Petrohué
Peulla
Lago Todos los Santos
Tronador (3460m)
Bariloche
Catedral
Los Men
Aguada de Guerra
Parque Nacional Vicente Pérez Rosales
Lago Mascardi
Pilcaniyeu
Comallo
Ingeniero Jacobacci
Los Juncos
Maquinchao
23
Villa Mascardi
Ralún
Cochamó
Las Bayas
258
Puelo
El Bolsón
Norquinco
Parque Nacional Hornopirén
Los Repollos
El Maitén
Parque Pumalin
Parque Nacional Lago Puelo
Epuyén
Cholila
Leptepu
Leleque
La Bolsa
Lago Menéndez
Parque Nacional Los Alerces
Lago Futulaufquen
Gualjaina
Paso del Sapo
Esquel
Trevelin
Río Chubut
Lago Espolo
Futaleufú
Paso Futaleufú
Lago Yelcho
Puerto Piedra
Colán Conhué
Paso Palena
Corcovado
Tecka
Puerto Ramírez
Palena
N
40 km
40 miles

Northern Neuquén

The province of Neuquén contains the northern part of the Lake District, an enormous region stretching from just north of Bariloche to the border with Mendoza province. The gateway to the area is the pleasant city of Neuquén on the province's eastern border. This is an important fruit-growing area, providing most of Argentina's apples, pears and grapes. To the southwest, enormous dinosaur footprints mark the landscape around Villa El Chocón; the skeleton in the museum there is proof that the world's largest known carnivores roamed around this area 100 million years ago.

The unspoilt wilderness in the northwest of the province has only recently started attracting visitors, although it is just as spectacular as more popular destinations to the south. The area west of Zapala, known as Pehuenia has large forests of ancient pehuén or monkey puzzle trees. Further north, Caviahue is a good base for walking and skiing in a rugged and unspoilt landscape, while bleaker Copahue is known for its high-quality thermal waters. » *For Sleeping, Eating and other listings see pages 68-72.*

Neuquén and around » *pp68-72.*

→ *Colour map 1, C5*

The provincial capital is an attractive industrial town, founded in 1904, just after the arrival of the railway. It has no major attractions but is a useful stopping point en route to the lakes and a good base for exploring the dinosaur finds in the area to the southwest.

Ins and outs

Getting there There are daily flights from Buenos Aires to the **airport** ⓘ *7 km west of town, T0299-444 0245*. Take a local bus 10 or 11 to the centre of town for US$0.40 (*tarjeta* bus card needed); taxi US$4. Long-distance buses arrive regularly at the central **bus terminal** ⓘ *Mitre 147, left luggage US$0.70 a day per item*, from Buenos Aires and towns throughout the Lake District as well as from Temuco and Puerto Montt in Chile.

Tourist information ⓘ *Félix San Martín 182, T0299-442 4089, www.neuquentur.gov.ar, daily Mon-Fri 0700-2000, Sat and Sun 0800-2000*. The office hands out helpful lists of accommodation and a good map.

Sights

At the northern end of Avenida Argentina at the Parque Centenario (not to be confused with the Centenario industrial suburb) is the **Mirador Balcon del Valle** with panoramic views over the city and the confluence of the rivers. In the university buildings at the entrance of the park is the **Museo Paleontológico de Ciencias Naturales** ⓘ *Argentina 1400*, which includes exhibitions of dinosaur fossils found in the region. The **former railway station**, at Olascaoga y Pasaje Obligado, has been converted into a cultural centre and exhibition centre. The **Museo de la Ciudad Paraje Confluencia** ⓘ *Independencia y Córdoba, T0299-442 9785*, has a small display on the colonial annihilation of indigenous groups in the Campaign of the Desert (see Background, page 324. South of the centre there is a pleasant walk along the Río Limay.

Facing Neuquén and connected by bridge is **Cipolletti**, in Río Negro province, a prosperous fruit-growing centre of the region. All the towns in the valley celebrate the **Fiesta Nacional de la Manzana** (apples are the main local crop) in the second half of March. Two lakes nearby, **Lago Pellegrini**, 36 km north, and **Embalse Cerro Colorado**, make a pleasant excursion from the city, with daily buses in summer.

Walking with dinosaurs

Few countries are as important as Argentina for palaeontologists. The relative abundance of fossils near the surface has made the country one of the most important for the study of dinosaur evolution. Patagonia was home to Jurassic dinosaurs (180-135 million years ago) and outstanding examples have been found here. Cerro Cóndor in Chubut is the only site of Middle Jurassic dinosaurs found in the Americas, and has given palaeontologists an important breakthrough in understanding the evolutionary stages of the period. At least five examples of patagosaurus have been found, indicating that these dinosaurs were social creatures, perhaps for purposes of mutual defence. In Santa Cruz traces of dinosaurs from the Upper Jurassic period have been found in rocks which indicate that the climate was arid and desert-like at the time, surprising palaeontologists with the news that dinosaurs could live and breed in such adverse conditions.

The most important discoveries of dinosaurs from the Cretacic period (135-70 million years ago) have been made in Neuquén and Chubut. Dating from the period of separation of the continents of South America and Africa, these provide evidence of the way in which dinosaurs began to evolve in different ways due to geographic isolation. For example, the *Carnotaurus sastrie* has horns and small hands, for example. The Patagonian dinosaurs are relatively huge: the *Argen tinosaurus huiculensis* is one of the largest herbivorous dinosaurs found on earth, while the carnivorous *Gigantosaurus carolinii* found near Neuquén city was larger even than the better known *Tyranosaurus rex*, discovered in North America.

The best places for dinosaur spotting in Patagonia are: **Villa El Chocón**, southwest of Neuquén city, boasts huge and perfectly preserved dinosaur footprints next to the lake. Further finds from the site can be seen in Neuquén's palaeontological museum. **Trelew** on the Atlantic Coast, has the country's finest dinosaur museum; and as part of the same foundation, there's an excellent site with 40 million years of history near the Welsh village of **Gaiman**. Many of the most interesting finds can be seen in Buenos Aires.

Villa El Chocón and around → *Colour map 1, A5*

To the southwest of Neuquén lies the huge **Embalse Ezequiel Ramos Mexía** in an area that has become famous in recent years for its wealth of dinosaur fossils. Villa El Chocón lies at the northern end of the lake, 72 km from Neuquén, on the most direct route to Bariloche. It's a neat, rather uninspiring town, but worth a stop for the amazing evidence of **dinosaurs** nearby (take Route 237 towards Piedra del Aguila, and turn left at Barrio Llanquén to the lake shore). Red sedimentary rocks have preserved bones and even footprints of the creatures that lived in this region during the Cretaceous period, about 100 million years ago. Some of these can be seen at the **Museo Paleontológico Ernesto Bachmann** ⓘ *civic centre, T0299-490 1223, www.interpatagonia.com/paseos/ernestobachmann, daily winter 0900-1900, summer 0800-2100; guided tours, website has information in English.* Exhibits include fossils of the mighty 10-ton, 15-m-long *Gigantosaurus carolinii*, a carnivorous dinosaur larger than the more famous *Tyrannosaurus rex*. There's an interesting display with information on these mind-boggling discoveries.

In the **Valle Cretacico**, 18 km south of Villa El Chocón, near the Dique with its pedestals of eroded pink rock, there are two walks beside the lake to see more dinosaur footprints, amazingly well preserved.

The monkey puzzle tree

The *Araucaria araucana*, is known in Argentina and Chile as the araucaria or pehuén and elsewhere called variously the Chilean pine, the umbrella tree, the parasol tree and the monkey puzzle tree. The species has flourished on both sides of the Andes at a latitude of 37-39° south for 200 million years, although, it is much more widespread in Chile than in Argentina. Very slow growing, it can reach up to 40 m high and live for 1200 years. The characteristic cones can weigh up to 1 kg. The araucaria was revered by the Mapuche, who ate both its cones and its sharp leathery leaves. Some isolated trees are still seen as sacred by the Mapuche who leave offerings to the tree's spirit.

Plaza Huincul → *Colour map 1, A5*

The town of Plaza Huincul, 107 km west of Neuquén, would be rather dull if it weren't for its impressive dinosaur museum. The **Museo Municipal Carmen Funes** includes the vertebrae of *Argentinossaurus huinclulensis*, believed to have weighed over 100 tons and to have been one of the largest herbivorous dinosaurs ever to have lived on earth, as well as a nest of fossilized dinosaur eggs.

Zapala and around → *Colour map 1, A4*

Zapala (1012 m) lies in a vast dry plain with views of snow-capped mountains to the west. It's a modern and unappealing town, but a useful stopover on Route 40, to cross the border into Chile at the Icalma pass (see page 67), or to explore the less-visited northern end of the Lake District. There is a **tourist office** ⓘ *San Martín y Mayor Torres, T02942-421132, summer Mon-Fri 0700-1930, Sat and Sun 0800-1300, 1600- 1900; closes earlier off-season*, for information and accommodation listings.

The **Museo Mineralógico Dr Juan Olsacher** ⓘ *Etcheluz 52 (next to the bus terminal), neumin@zapala.com.ar, Mon 0900-1500, Sat and Sun 1600-2000, free*, is one of the best museums of its type in South America; it contains over 2000 types of mineral and has the finest collection of fossils of marine reptiles and marine fauna in the country. On display is the largest turtle shell from the Jurassic period ever found and an ophthalmosaur, as well as photos of an extensive cave system being excavated nearby.

Southwest of Zapala is the **Parque Nacional Laguna Blanca** ⓘ *entrance 10 km from the junction of RN46 and RN40, www.parquesnacionales.gov.ar, US$2, no public transport*, a reserve covering large areas of high arid steppe and a vast lagoon that is one of the most important nesting areas of the black-necked swan. The landscape is very dry, and rather bleak, so take drinking water and a hat.

Pehuenia » pp68-72.

→ *Colour map 1, A3/A4*

The magical and unspoilt area of Pehuenia is named after the country's unique forests of pehuén trees, which grow here in vast numbers. Covering a marvellous open mountainous landscape, these ancient, silent trees create a mystical atmosphere, especially around the lakes of Aluminé and Moquehue. To make the most of this area, you really need to hire a car in San Martín de los Andes (see page 77), as buses from Zapala and Neuquén are slow and unreliable. Cyclists will love the view, but note that the *ripio* is rough, and there is little shade.

Villa Pehuenia and around → *Colour map 1, A3*

This picturesque sprawling village is prettily situated on the northern shores of Lago Aluminé, 107 km west of Zapala. It makes a lovely base for a few day's relaxation or gentle walks in the hills and forests around. The **Mapuche** (see box, page 197), the largest indigenous group in the south of the continent, chose this area for settlement because of its chain of eight volcanoes and its sacred pehuén trees. Villa Pehuenia is well set up for tourism: a whole cluster of upmarket *cabañas* have opened here in recent years, with one exceptionally lovely boutique hotel, **La Escondida** (see Sleeping, page 69). A **tourist kiosk** ⓘ *T02942-498027*, is signposted by the turning for the village. The peninsula stretching out into the lake offers wonderful walks along the araucaria-fringed shore and fabulous views from the **Mirador del Cipres**.

Just a few kilometres further along the main road from Villa Pehuenia, signposted to the right, is the **Batea Mahuida**, a reserve created to protect an area of pehuén trees and the majestic volcano, regarded by the Mapuche as sacred. This is a lovely area for walking in summer, with tremendous views of all seven volcanoes. There's also a winter sports centre, **Parque de Nieve**, administrated by the Mapuche people, offering snowmobiles, snowshoe walks and husky rides. Delicious home-cooked food is served.

Lago Moquehue → *Colour map 1, A3*

Another 10 km on Route 13 brings you to the sprawling village of Moquehue, on the shores of the lake. It's wilder and more remote than Villa Pehuenia with a lovely wide river that's famous for trout fishing. This is a beautiful and utterly peaceful place to relax and walk. A short stroll through araucaria forests brings you to a waterfall, while a longer hike to the top of **Cerro Bandera** (four hours return) provides wonderful views over the area as far as Volcán Llaima. You should also head along Route 13, 11 km to **Lago Norquinco**, past mighty basalt cliffs with pehuéns all around. There are fine camping spots all around and a couple of comfortable places to stay.

Aluminé and around → *Colour map 1, A3*

On Route 23 between Pehuenia and Junín lies the area's self-proclaimed rafting capital. There is indeed superb rafting (Grades II-VI) on **Río Aluminé**, but despite the grand setting, the town is a drab little place with *ripio* roads. There's a very friendly **tourist office** ⓘ *C Christian Joubert 321, T0294-496001, www.alumine.net, 0800-2100 all year*, and a service station – the first one you'll reach driving south from Villa Pehuenia. In March, the harvest of the *piñones* is celebrated in the **Fiesta del Pehuén** with horse riding and live music.

Border with Chile

Paso Pino Hachado (1864m) lies 115 km west of Zapala via Route 22. On the Chilean side the road runs northwest to Lonquimáy, 65 km west and Temuco, 145 km southwest. Buses from Zapala and Neuquén to Temuco use this crossing. **Argentine immigration and customs** ⓘ *9 km east of the border, 0700-1300, 1400-1900.* **Chilean immigration and customs** ⓘ *Liucura, 22 km west of the border, Dec- Mar 0800-2100, Apr-Nov 0800-1900.* Very thorough searches and two- to three-hour delays reported.

A more tricky route is via **Paso de Icalma** (1303 m), 132 km west of Zapala, reached by Route 13 (*ripio*). On the Chilean side this road continues to Melipeuco, but is often impassable in winter. Permission to cross must be obtained from the Policía Internacional in Temuco (Prat 19, T045-293890). **Argentine immigration and customs** ⓘ *9 km east of the border, 0800-2000 in summer, 0900-1900 in winter.* All paperwork is carried out at the customs office. **Chilean immigration and customs** ⓘ *Dec-Mar 0800-2100, Apr-Nov 0800-1900.*

From Aluminé there is access to **Lago Rucachoroi**, 23 km west, in Parque Nacional Lanín. This is the biggest Aigo Mapuche community inside the park and is set in gentle farmland surrounded by ancient pehuén forests. Access is by a rough *ripio* road, spectacular in autumn when the deciduous trees are a splash of orange against the bottle green araucarias. The *guardería* can advise about a possible trek to Lago Quillén.

▸▸ *For information on the rest of Parque Nacional Lanín, see page 73.*

Lago Quillén → *Colour map 1, A3*

At the junction by the small town of **Rahue**, 16 km south of Aluminé, a road leads west to the valley of the Río Quillén and the exquisite Lago Quillén, from where there are fine views of Volcán Lanín peeping above the mountains. The lake itself is one of the region's most lovely, jade green in colour, with beaches along its low-lying northern coast. Further west, where annual rainfall is among the heaviest in the country, the slopes are thickly covered with Andean Patagonian forest. There's no transport, and accommodation only is at the **Camping Pudu Pudu** (with food shop and hot showers) on the lake's northern shore, just west of the *guardería*.

Caviahue and Copahue ▸▸ *pp68-72.*

→ *Colour map 1, A3*

Set in an attractive lakeside setting 150 km north of Zapala, **Caviahue** is an excellent base for walking and riding in summer and for winter sports from July to September, when it is one of cheaper ski resorts in the Lake District. **Tourist information** ⓘ *8 de Abril, bungalows 5 and 6, T02948-495036, www.caviahue-copahue.com.ar.*

The arid, dramatic and other-wordly landscape of the **Reserva Provincial Copahue** is formed by a giant volcanic crater, whose walls are the surrounding mountains. The park was created to protect the araucaria trees that grow on its slopes and provides the setting for some wonderful walks through unexpectedly stunning scenery. **Copahue** (1980 m) is a thermal spa resort enclosed in a huge amphitheatre formed by mountain walls. It boasts the best thermal waters in South America, although it's decidedly bleaker than Caviahue. Information is available on Route 26, on the approach into town.

Volcán Copahue last erupted, smokily, in 2000, destroying the bright blue lake in its crater, but the views of the prehistoric landscape are still astounding. Even more highly recommended, however, is an excursion to **El Salto del Agrio**, on Route 27. This is the climax in a series of delightful waterfalls, between ancient araucaria trees poised on basalt cliffs. Other walks will take you to **Las Máquinas**, 4 km south of Copahue, where sulphurous steam puffs through air holes against a panoramic backdrop. And to **El Anfiteatro**, where thermal waters reaching 150°C, are surrounded by a semicircle of rock edged with araucaria trees. Just above Copahue, is **Cascada Escondida**, a torrent of water falling 15 m over a shelf of basalt into a pool surrounded by a forest of araucaria trees; above it is magical **Lago Escondida**

Sleeping

Neuquén *p64*

AL **Hotel del Comahue**, Av Argentina 377, T0299-443 2040, www.hoteldelcomahue.com.ar. The most comfortable by a long way is this international-style, elegant modern 4-star, with spa and pool, excellent restaurant, very good service and business facilities.

B **Amucan**, Tucumán 115, corner with Rivadavia, T0299-442 5209, www.amucanhotel.com.ar. Smart modern place with nice rooms and good breakfast.

C **Alcorta**, Alcorta 84, T0299-442 2652. Good value, breakfast, TV in rooms. Also flats for 4.

C **Royal**, Av Argentina 143, T0299-448 8902, www.royalhotel.com.ar. A smart modern hotel, but with welcoming rooms, car parking and breakfast included, good value.

Villa El Chocón and around *p65*

B **La Posada del Dinosaurio**, Costa del Lago, Barrio 1, Villa El Chocón, T0299-490 1200, www.posadadinosaurio.com.ar. Convenient for dinosaur hunting, this has very plain but comfortable rooms, with views over the lake, and a restaurant.

D **La Villa**, Club Municipal El Chocón, T0299-490 1252. Decent budget choice.

Plaza Huincul *p66*

C **Hotel Tortorici**, Cutral-Co, 3 km west, Av Olascoaga y Di Paolo, T0299-496 3730, www.hoteltortorici.com. The most comfortable option is this newly built hotel with neat rooms and a restaurant.

Zapala *p66*

A **Hostal del Caminante**, outside Neuquén 13 km south towards Zapala, T02942-444 0118. A popular place in summer, with a pool and garden.

C **Hue Melén**, Brown 929, T02942-422414. Good value 3-star hotel, with decent rooms. The restaurant serves the best food in town, including local specialities.

C **Huincul**, Av Roca 311, T02942-431422. A spacious place with a cheap restaurant, serving good home-made regional food.

D **Pehuén**, Elena de Vega y Etcheluz, T02942-423135. Comfortable, 1 block from bus terminal, with an interesting display of maps.

Camping

Hostería Primeros Pinos, RP13, T02942-422637, primerospinos@yahoo.com.ar. Municipal site.

Villa Pehuenia *p67*

There's one superb boutique hotel, and plenty of *cabañas*, many with good views over the lake and set in idyllic woodland. Email or ring first for directions, since there are no road names or numbers here.

AL **La Escondida**, western shore of the peninsula, T02942-1569 1166, www.posadalaescondida.com.ar. By far the best place to stay in the whole area, this is a really special boutique hotel, with just 9 rooms in an imaginatively designed building right on the rocky lakeside. Each room is spacious and beautifully considered, with smart bathrooms (all with jacuzzi), private decks and gorgeous views over the lake. The restaurant is superb and uses fine local produce. Non-residents can dine here with a reservation. Highly recommended.

A **Altos de Pehuén**, T02942-1566 6849, www.altosdepehuen.com.ar. Comfortable *cabañas* with lovely views. Also a *hostería*.

A **Complejo Patagonia**, T02942-1557 9434, or in Buenos Aires T011-4637 9100, www.complejopatagonia.com.ar. Very comfortable indeed, these lovely *cabañas* are traditionally designed and the service is excellent. Recommended.

A-C **Puerto Malén Club de Montaña**, T02942-498007, T011-4226 8190 (Buenos Aires), www.puertomalen.com. Well-built wooden *cabañas* with lake views from their balconies, and the highest quality interiors. Also a luxurious *hostería*. Recommended.

C **Cabañas Bahía Radal**, T02942-498057, bahiaradal@hotmail.com. Luxurious *cabañas* in an elevated position with clear lake views.

C **Las Terrazas**, T02942-498036, www.lasterrazaspehuenia.com.ar. The owner is an architect of Mapuche origin, who has retained Mapuche style in his beautiful design of these comfortable *cabañas*: tasteful, warm and with perfect views of the lake, with also D B&B. He can take you to visit Mapuche communities. Warmly recommended.

D **La Serena**, T011-547940319, www.complejolaserena.com.ar. Beautifully equipped and designed *cabañas* with great uninterrupted views, gardens going down to beach, sheltered from wind, furnished with rustic-style handmade cypress furniture, and wood stoves, all very attractive.

Camping

Camping Agreste Quechulafquen, at the end of the steep road across La Angostura. Situated among lovely steep hills and dense vegetation, run by Mapuche Puels.

Camping El Puente, La Angostura. US$2 pp, with hot showers; a simpler site, in beautiful surroundings.

Las Lagrimitas, just west of the village, T02942-498003. A lovely secluded lakeside site on the beach, US$2 pp, with food shop, hot showers and fireplaces.

Lago Moquehue *p67*

C **Hostería Moquehue**, T02946-1566 0301, www.hosteriamoquehue.netfirms.com. Set high above the lake with panoramic views, cosy, stylish, rustic rooms, nicely furnished. Excellent food: try the superb Moquehue trout and local *chivito*. Charming hosts.

D **La Bella Durmiente**, T0299-496172. In a rustic building with no heating, summer only, the welcoming owner offers good food and also offers trekking, horse riding, diving in the lake, mountain bikes. Call for directions.

Cabañas

A **Cabañas Los Maitenes**, T0299-421681, T0299-1566 5621, losmaitenes@infovia.com.ar. Right by the lake, well-equipped *cabañas*, with breakfast included, and friendly owners. Recommended.

A **La Busqueda**, T0299-4481552, www.labusquedamoquehue.com.ar. Just north of the lake. Interesting design in these well-equipped *cabañas* with TV, including breakfast. Recommended

C-D **Cabañas Melipal**, T0299-432445. Very attractive, rustic stone-built *cabañas* in secluded sites right on lake side. Lovely old-fashioned style, well equipped and warm, fabulous views from the balconies, use of boats. Highly recommended.

D **Cabañas Huerquen**, T0299-1564700, huerquen_patagoni@hotmail.com. Beyond Moquehue on the road to Ñorquinco, these lovely secluded stone *cabañas* in beautifully tranquil settings.

D **Ecocamping Ñorquinco Norquinco**, 11 km from Moquehue, towards Ñorquinco, T0299-496155, ecocamping@hotmail.com. There is one amazing rustic *cabaña* right on the lakeside, with a café. Great fishing, hot showers and a *proveduría*.

Camping

Along RN 13, 11 km to Lago Ñorquinco, past mighty basalt cliffs with pehuéns all around, there's idyllic camping. Also idyllic, reached by RN 11 are the smaller campsites of **Lagos Pilhué** and **Ñorquinco Camping**.

Camping Trenel, on the southern shore of Lago Moquehue. Beautiful shady sites in a fabulous elevated position surrounded by ñirre trees; *parrillas* overlooking lake. Hot showers, restaurant and shop Recommended.

Aluminé *p67*

A **Estancia Quillén**, RN 46 near Rahue, near the bridge crossing Río Aluminé, T02942-496196, www.interpatagonia.com/quillen/index.html. A comfortable, traditionally furnished house, with spacious rooms, and a restaurant, where you'll be welcomed by the estancia owners. Open Dec-Apr. Great for fishing and hunting.

C **Pehuenia**, just off R23, Crouzeilles 100, T02942-496340, pehuenia2000@yahoo.com.ar. A huge tin chalet-style building, not attractive, but with great views over the hills opposite. The rooms are comfortable and simple, the staff are friendly, and it's good value. Horse riding, bike hire and canoeing at the owner's campsite, **Bahía de los Sueños**, 6 km from the red bridge north of Aluminé.

Camping

La Vieja Balsa, T02942-496001, just outside Aluminé on R23 on the Río Aluminé. A well-equipped site, that offers rafting and fishing, US$1 pp per day to camp, hot showers, food shop, fireplaces, tables, open Dec to Easter.

There are 2 campsites before and after **Lago Rucachoroi**; open all year, but really ideal only Dec-Feb. The first has more facilities, with toilets, but no hot water, some food supplies, including wonderful Mapuche bread and sausages, and offers horse riding.

Caviahue *p68*

B **Lago Caviahue**, Costanera Quimey-Co, T02948-495110, www.hotellagocaviahue.com. Good value, comfortable lakeside apartments with kitchen, good restaurant, great views, 2 km from the ski centre.

B **Nevado Caviahue**, 8 de Abril s/n, T02948-495042, www.caviahue.com. Plain rooms, but modern, and there's a restaurant, and cosy lounge with wood fire. Also **A-B** for 6 *cabañas*, well-equipped but not luxurious.

C **Farallon**, Caviahue Base, T02948-495085. Neat apartments, some with kitchens.

C **La Cabaña de Tito**, Puesta del Sol s/n, T02948-495093. *Cabañas* near lake, excellent meals.

Copahue *p68*

A-C **Hotel Copahue**, Olascoaga y Bercovich, T02948-495117. Lovely old place where you'll be warmly welcomed. Recommended. Well-built wood and stone *cabañas*.

Camping

Copahue, T02948-495111; and **Hueney Municipal**, T02948-495041.

Eating

Neuquén *p64*

1900 Cuatro, at the Comahue Hotel, Av Argentina 377. Posh and a little pricey, but serves superb food.
Anonima, corner of Av Olascoaga y Félix. This supermarket has a good *patio de comidas* (food hall), and games for kids.
El Reencuentro, Alaska 6451. A popular *parrilla* recommended for delicious steaks in a warm atmosphere.
Fatto Dalla Mama, 9 de Julio 56. Fabulous filled pasta.
La Birra, Santa Fe 23. Lots of choice, and is very welcoming, with chic surroundings.
Rincón de Montaña, 9 de Julio 435. Recommended for delicious local specialities and cakes.
Tutto al Dente, Alberdi 49. Tasty home-made pasta. Recommended.

Cafés

Café El Buen Pan, Mitre y Corrientes, 0600-2300. A bright modern place for snacks and good bakery too.
El Patagonia, Bartolomé Mitre between Corrientes y Río Negro. *Lomitos* and sandwiches, with cheap(ish) deals.
Living Room, Pte Rivadaria. A lovely comfortable bar-café, with armchairs and table outside, a great place to relax.

Zapala *p66*

El Chancho Rengo, Av San Martín y Etcheluz, T02942-422795. This is where all the locals hang out.

Villa Pehuenia *p67*

La Escondida, on the western shore of the peninsula, T02942-1557 0420, www.posadalaescondida.com.ar. By far the best in town. Only open to non-residents with a reservation, this is really special cuisine, all local ingredients, imaginatively prepared and served. Highly recommended.
Anhedonia, on the lakeside, T02942-1566 9866. Fondue, beef and pasta.
Gnaien Chocolateria and tea room, on the lakeside, T02942-498082. Good for tea, with lovely views of the lake, chocolate delicacies, *picadas* and range of wines.
La Cantina del Pescador, on the lakeside, T02942-498086. Fresh trout.
Costa Azul, on the lakeside, T02942-498035. Tasty local dishes and pasta; *chivito* (kid) *al asado* is the speciality of the house.

Aluminé *p67*

La Posta del Rey, next to the service station, opposite the plaza, Cristian Joubert, T02942-496248. The best place by far, with friendly service, great trout and local kid, delicious pastas, sandwiches. Recommended.

Caviahue *p68*

Copahue Club Hotel, Valle del Volcán. Serves good *chivito al asado* and local trout.
Hotel Lago Caviahue. The most stylish place to eat with an inspired *chivo a la cerveza* (kid cooked in beer) on the menu, along with more traditional favourites and local specialities.

Activities and tours

Neuquén *p64*

Gondwana Tour, Córdoba 599, T0299-496 3355, geoda@copelnet.com.ar. Excursions to dinosaur sites nearby, and accommodation.

Zapala *p66*

Mali Viajes, Alte Brown 760, T02942-432251.
Monserrat Viajes y Turismo, Etcheluz 101, T02942-422497.

Villa Pehuenia *p67*

Los Pehuenes, T02942-498029, www.lospehuenesturismo.com. Professional helpful and friendly company offering wide range of activities including trekking, rafting (US$30, for full day, Grade IV), horse riding (US$30 full day with lunch), visits to the local Mapuche communities with fascinating local history and culture, fishing and boat trips. Ask for Fernando. Transfers to Pehuenia from San Martín and Neuquén.

Aluminé *p67*

Aluminé Rafting, Ricardo Solano, T02942-496322. US$9-15, depending on difficulty, for 3 hrs rafting, Grades II-VI. All equipment included. **Circuito Abra Ancha** 2½ hrs, Grade II, 6 km, very entertaining, suitable for everyone. **Circuito Aluminé Superior**, 12- to 15-km run, 5-6 hrs, Grade III-IV, very technical river leaving Lago Alumine, for those who like a thrill, passing little woods of araucarias and ñirres, family trips Grades I and II, costs US$20 pp for **Abra Ancha**, US$60 pp for higher level. Trekking US$80 per day, trekking in Cordon de Chachil, US$120 per day, 2 days minimum, but can be up to a week, also kayaking, and biking.

Caviahue *p68*

Caviahue Tours, San Martín 623, Buenos Aires, T02948-4314 1556. Good information.

The ski resort has 3 lifts and excellent areas for cross-country skiing; contact Caviahue Base, T02948-495079.

Transport

Neuquén *p64*

Air

To **Buenos Aires**, daily with AR, Austral, and Aerolíneas Argentinas.

Airline offices Aerolíneas Argentinas/ Austral, Santa Fe 52, T02942-442 2409, **Lapa**, Argentina 30, T02942-448 8335. **Southern Winds**, Argentina 237, T02942-442 0124.

Bus

About a dozen companies to **Buenos Aires**, daily, 12-16 hrs, US$25-35. To **Zapala** daily, 3 hrs, US$5. To **San Martín de los Andes**, 6 hrs, US$11. To **Bariloche**, many companies, 5-6 hrs, US$13, best views if you sit on left. To **Mendoza**, Andesmar, and 3 others, daily, 12 hrs, US$22. To **Junín de los Andes**, 5 hrs, US$9, many companies.

To **Aluminé**, 6 hrs, US$10, many companies. To **Zapala**, 3 hrs, US$5, Albus, Centenario. To **Plaza Huincul**, 1½ hrs, US$3, same companies. To **Caviahue** (6 hrs, US$11) and **Copahue**, 6½ hrs, US$12, Centenario.

To Chile Services to **Temuco** stop for a couple of hours at the border, 12-14 hrs, US$22. Some companies offer discount for return, departures Mon-Thu and Sat; 7 companies, some continuing to destinations en route to **Puerto Montt**.

Bus companies Andesmar, T0299-442 2216, **Via Bariloche**, T0299-442 7054, **El Valle**, T0299-443 3293.

Zapala *p66*

The bus terminal is at Etcheluz y Uriburu, T02942-423191. To **Neuquén**, 2-3 hrs, US$5, Albus, Centenario, several daily. To **San Martín de los Andes**, 3-4 hrs, US$10. To **Junín de los Andes**, 3hrs, US$9 with Albus, Centenario, several daily. To **Aluminé**, 2½ hrs, US$5, several companies, daily. To **Villa Pehuenia**, 2½ hrs, US$7, 4 a week, continue to **Moquehue** 5-6 hrs, US$8. To **Caviahue**, (3 hrs, US$8) and **Copahue** (3½-4 hrs, US$8) daily with Centenario. To **Bariloche**, Albus, TAC, Vía Bariloche via San Martín. To **Buenos Aires**, 18 hrs, US$25-35, many companies. To **Temuco** (Chile), US$16, Mon/Wed/Fri, Centenario (buy Chilean pesos in advance).

Villa Pehuenia *p67*

There are 3 buses weekly to Villa Pehuenia and **Moquehue** from **Neuquén** (less predictable in winter, when the roads are covered in snow) and **Aluminé**, 5½ hrs.

Aluminé *p67*

There are buses daily to and from **Zapala**, with either Aluminé Viajes (T02942-496231), or **Albus** (T02942-496368), 3 hrs, US$4.50. Twice a week to **Villa Pehuenia**, 1 hr, US$2.50. Twice a week to **San Martín de los Andes**, 4 hrs, US$7, with **Tilleria**, T02942-496048.

Caviahue *p68*

To/from **Neuquén**, El Petroleo and El Centenario, T02948-495024 . Daily, 6 hrs, US$13, via Zapala (US$7).

Directory

Neuquén *p64*

Banks Lots of ATMs along Av Argentina. *Casas de cambio* at: **Pullman**, Alcorta 144, Exterior, San Martin 23. **Consulates** Chile, La Rioja 241, T02942-442 2727. **Internet** Near the bus terminal at Mitre 43, T02942-443 6585, a block from bus station. **Post office** Rivadavia y Santa Fe. **Telephone** Many *locutorios* in the centre, often with internet access. Telecom, 25 de Mayo 20, daily till 0030, and Olascoaga 222, open till 2345. Cheap.

Zapala *p66*

Banks 3 banks including **Banco de la Nación Argentina**, Etcheluz 465, but difficult to change TC's, **Bansud**, Etcheluz 108. **Internet** Instituto Moreno, Moreno y López y Planes. **CPI**, Chaneton y Garayta.

Parque Nacional Lanín

Some of the most beautiful sights in the Lake District are to be found in one of the country's largest national parks, Lanín, which stretches north from Parque Nacional Nahuel Huapi along the border with Chile for 200 km. The park's centrepiece is the magnificent extinct snow-capped Volcán Lanín, a challenging three-day climb, and a dramatic backdrop to the beautiful landscapes all around the park. Lagos Huechulafquen and Paimún, west of Junín de los Andes, offer tranquillity, great hiking, fishing and camping. Southernmost parts of the park can be visited from upmarket San Martín de los Andes, on the shores of picturesque Lago Lacar, with smart hotels, boat trips and beaches. Travel south from here to Bariloche along the famous Seven Lakes Drive, or search out the remote northern areas of the park, where Mapuche communities offer horse riding and run campsites. The park is most rewarding if you hire a bike or car, as bus services are sporadic. » *For Sleeping, Eating and other listings see pages 78-84.*

Ins and outs

Access There are various points of entry to the park, with *guardaparques* at 3, 4, 7 and 8.

1 Route 18 from Aluminé to Lago Rucachoroi (see page 68).
2 Route 46 from Rahue to Quillén (see page 68).
3 Route 60 to Lago Tromen, for the ascent of Lanín and Paso Tromen.
4 Route 61 from north of Junín de los Andes to Lago Huechulafquen. The easiest entry, with regular buses in summer, fabulous walks and great camping.
5 Route 62 from Junín de los Andes to Lago Curruhué. Good walking and thermal pools.
6 Route 48 from the junction with Route 62 to Puerto Arturo and Lago Lolog.
7 Along Route 48 to Lago Lacar and Paso Hua Hum.
8 Route 234 via San Martín de los Andes.

Park information Administration ⓘ *Emilio Frey 749, San Martín de los Andes, T02972-427233, www.parquesnacionales.gov.ar, US$4 paid at point of entry.* There is a helpful **information office** in Junín de los Andes, in the same building as the tourist office, T02972-491160. You're supposed to register at the administration before setting out on major treks, but this not always practical. However, *guardaparques* at Lago Huechulafquen should always be notified before you set off. A good map is essential: pick up the excellent *Parque Nacional* map before you arrive at the park. Fires are a serious hazard: put out campfires with lots of water, not just earth.

Flora and fauna Vegetation is varied due to differences in rainfall and altitude. In the north, between lagos Norquinco and Tromen, araucaria trees dominate, interspersed with lenga and ñirre. Further south, you'll find a combination of southern beech species: roble, rauli and the majestic grey-trunked coihue. Bamboo grows in profusion along Lago Huechulafquen at the centre of the park; this prehistoric species dies en masse every 20 to 30 years, when all the plants simultaneously rot, and new life begins the following year. Wildlife includes wildcats and foxes, the elusive pudú and some red deer.

Exploring the park » *pp78-84.*

Lago Huechulafquen → *Colour map 1, A3*

In the centre of the park, Lago Huechulafquen stretches from smooth lowland hills in the east to steep, craggy mountains in the west, overlooked by Volcán Lanín on the Chilean border. The northern shore of the lake, with its grey volcanic sand, shelter beautiful, if basic, camping grounds.

Parque Nacional Lanín

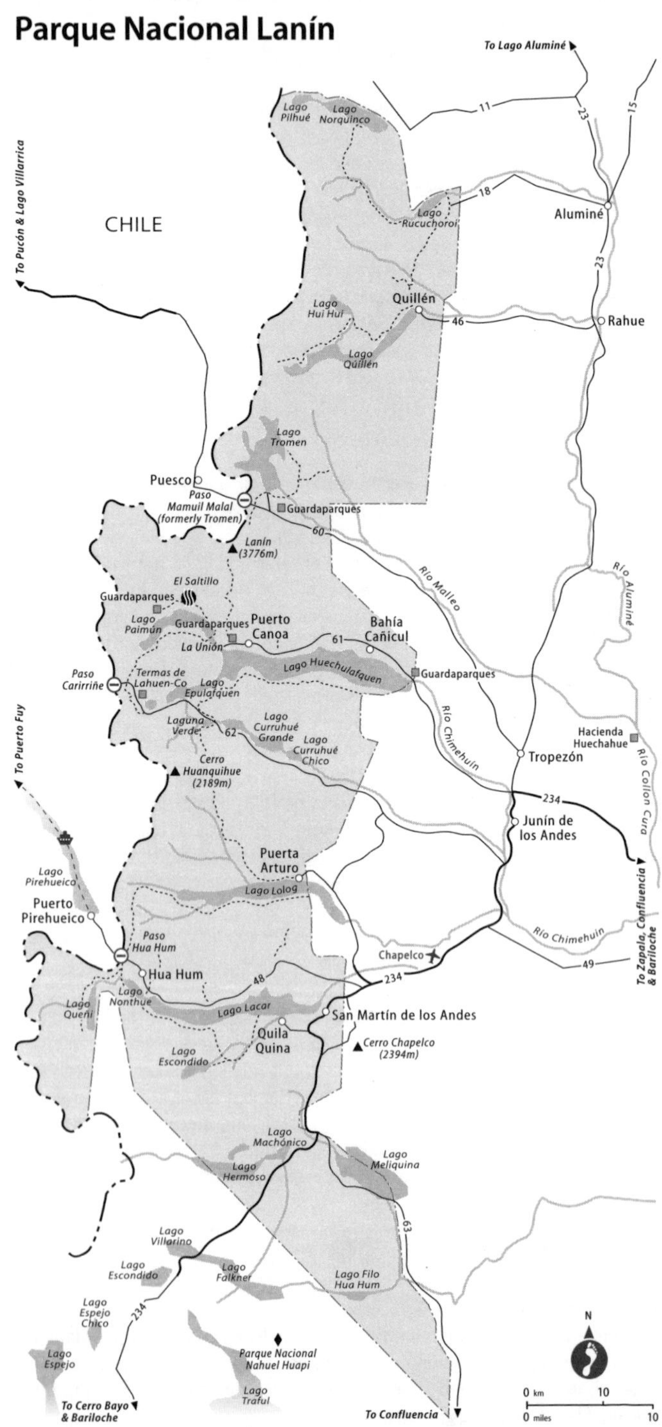

Walks around Lago Paimún

→ **El Saltillo Falls** (two hours return) fabulous views en route to the waterfall. Start from the campsite at Lago Paimún.
→ **Termas at Lahuen-Co** (12 hours) eight hours to the end of Lago Paimún, then four more to reach the Termas, best done over two days. A beautiful walk, and you'll be rewarded by a soak in the simple rustic pools.
→ **Volcán Lanín** (eight hours return) a satisfying walk to the base of the volcano and back. Start from Puerto Canoa.
→ **Cerro El Chivo** (seven hours return), a more challenging walk through forest to the summit at 2064 m. Note that heavy snow can lie till January. Set off early, and register at the campsite at Bahía Cañicul. Take a guide.

Around Lago Paimún → *Colour map 1, A3*

It's worth the trek to view the sugary peak of Lanín from the exquisitely pretty crescent-shaped Lake Paimún, further west. There is a range of excellent walks here, along paths marked with yellow arrows. Ask *guardaparques* for advice on routes before setting off and allow plenty of time for return before dark. Guides are only required for longer unmarked treks; for these, ask in the Junín park office or at San Martín de los Andes. You can also explore much of the area on horseback, including the trek to the base of Volcán Lanín. Five places along the lake hire horses: ask *guardaparques* for advice, or ask at Mapuche communities. To cross to other side of Lago Paimún there's a boat operated by the Mapuche: just ring the bell.

Lago Curruhué and Termas de Lahuen-Co → *Colour map 1, B3*

Lago Curruhué and the thermal pools at **Termas de Lahuen-Co** are a two-day hike from Lago Paimún. Alternatively, drive there along Route 62 from either Junín or San Martín de los Andes. You'll pass ancient pehuén forests along the south shore of the Lago Currhue Grande and the impressive lava field at **Escorial**. The pools are 8 km further on, with rustic camping and a *guardería*. Trips to Lago Curruhué and the termas are offered by tour companies in San Martín but there's no public transport to these places at present.

Paso Tromen and around

Paso Tromen, known in Chile as **Paso Mamuil Malal**, is 64 km northwest of Junín de los Andes and reached by *ripio* Route 60 which runs from Tropezón on Route 23, through Parque Nacional Lanín. Along this route there are several Mapuche communities that

Border with Chile

Paso Tromen (aka **Paso Mamuil Malal**) crossing is less developed than the Hua Hum and Puyehue routes further south (see page 78 and 87); although this is the route used by international buses between Junín and Temuco, it is unsuitable for cycles and definitely not usable during heavy rain or snow (June to mid-November), as parts are narrow and steep. For up-to-date information, contact the *gendarmería*, T02972-491270, or customs, T02972-492163. On the Chilean side the road continues through glorious scenery, with views of the volcanoes of Villarrica and Quetrupillán to the south, to Pucón on Lago Villarrica (see page 198). **Argentine immigration and customs** ⓘ *3 km east of the pass, 0800-2000 all year.* **Chilean immigration and customs** ⓘ *Puesco, 17 km from the border, Dec-Mar 0800-2100; Apr-Nov 0800-1900.*

 can be visited. Some 3 km east of the pass a turning leads north to **Lago Tromen**, a lovely spot where there is good camping, and south of the pass is the graceful cone of the Lanín volcano. This is the normal departure point for climbing to the summit. **Paso Tromen** is a beautiful spot, with a good campsite, and lovely walks. From the *guardería*, footpaths lead to a mirador (1½ hours round trip), or across a grassy prairie with magnificent views of Lanín and other jagged peaks, through ñirre woodland and great araucaria trees to the point where Lago Tromen drains into Río Malleo (4 km).

Climbing Lanín

One of the world's most beautiful mountains, Lanín (3768 m) is geologically one of the youngest volcanoes of the Andes; it is now extinct. It is a three-day, challenging climb to the summit; crampons and ice axe required. The ascent starts from the Argentine customs post at the Tromen pass, where you must register and where all climbers' equipment and experience are checked. A four-hour hike leads from here to two free *refugios* at 2400 m, sleeping 14 to 20 people.

It's vital to get detailed descriptions of the ascent from the *guardaparques*. To climb the north face, follow the path through lenga forest to the base of the volcano, over arroyo Turbio and up the *espina de pescado*. From here there are three paths to the *refugios*: **1** straight ahead, the *espina de pescado* is the shortest but steepest (four to five hours), **2** to the right, the *camino de mulas* is the easiest but longest (seven hours) and is marked; and **3** to the left, *canaleta* should be used only for descent. From the *refugios*, it is six to seven hours over ice fields to the summit. Because of Lanín's relative accessibility, the risks of climbing it are often underestimated. An authorized guide is absolutely necessary for anyone other than the very experienced. Crampons and ice-axe are essential, as is protection against strong, cold winds. Climbing equipment and experience is checked by the *guardaparques* at the Tromen pass.

Junín de los Andes ›› *pp78-84.*

→ *See map page 79. Colour map 1, A3/B3.*

Situated on the beautiful Río Chimehuin, the quiet town of Junín de los Andes (773 m) is justifiably known as the trout capital of Argentina. It offers some of the best fly fishing in the country in world renowned rivers, and the fishing season runs from mid-November to the end of April. Junín is also an excellent base for exploring the wonderful virgin countryside of Parque Nacional Lanín and for climbing the extinct volcano itself.

Founded in 1883, Junín is not as picturesque or tourist-orientated as its neighbour, San Martín – there are no chalet-style buildings, and few chocolate shops here – but it's a quiet neat place with friendly people.

Sights

Most of what you need can be found within a couple of blocks of the central Plaza San Martín with its fine araucaria trees among mature alerces and cedars. The small **Museo Salesiano** ⓘ *Ginés Ponte y Nogueira, Mon-Fri 0900-1230, 1430-1930, Sat 0900-1230*, has a fine collection of Mapuche weavings, instruments and arrowheads, and you can buy a whole range of excellent Mapuche handicrafts in the *galería* behind the tourist office. There's an impressive sculpture park **El Via Christi** ⓘ *just west of the town, T02972-491684, from the plaza walk up Av Ant Argentina across the main road RN 234, to the end*. Situated among pine forest on a hillside, the stations of the cross are illustrated with touching and beautifully executed sculptures of Mapuche figures, ingeniously depicting scenes from Jesus's life together with a history of the town and the Mapuche community. The sculptures are to be found along trails through the pine woods. A lovely place to walk, and highly recommended. The church, **Santuario Nuestra Senora de las Nieves y Beata Laura Vicuña**, also has fine Mapuche weavings, and is a pleasing calm space. The best fishing is at the mouth of the river Chimehuin on the road to Lago Huechulafquen, although there are many excellent spots around; see guides below. In the town itself, there are pleasant picnic sites along the river. The **tourist office** ⓘ *on the plaza, T02972-491160, www.junindelosandes.com.ar, summer 0800-2200, otherwise 0800-2100,* is friendly and hands out maps.

San Martín de los Andes and around

» *pp78-84.*

→ *Colour map 1, B3*

San Martín de los Andes is a charming tourist town nestled in a beautiful valley surround by steep mountains on the edge of Lago Lacar, with attractive chalet-style architecture and comfortable but expensive accommodation. It's a good centre for exploring southern parts of the **Parque Nacional Lanín** and lakes **Lolog** and **Lacar**, where there are beaches for relaxing and good opportunities for water sports, mountain biking and trekking. **Cerro Chapelco** (2394m), 20 km south of San Martín, offers superb views over Lanín and many Chilean peaks. In summer, this is a good place for trekking, archery, horse riding or cycling (take your bike up on the cable car, and cycle down), while in winter it transforms into a well organized ski resort (see page 83). The other most popular excursions are south along the **Seven Lakes Drive** to Lagos Traful, Meliquina, Filo Hua Hum, Hermoso, Falkner and Villarino (see below) and north to the thermal baths at **Termas de Lahuen-Co**.

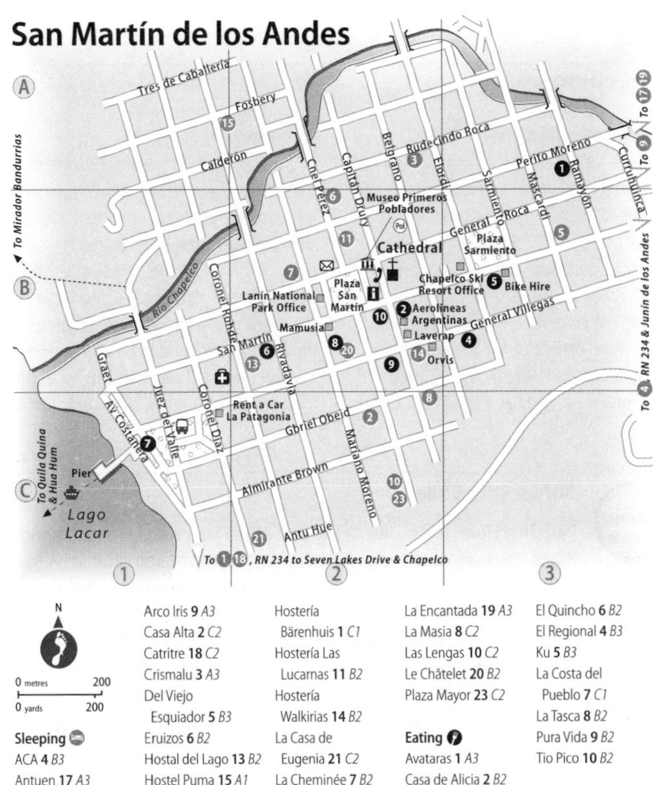

Ins and outs

Tourist information ⓘ *San Martín y Rosas 790, on the main plaza, T02972-427347, 0800-2100 all year.* The office has lists of accommodation, with prices up on a big board. Staff hand out maps and good advice and speak English and French. However, they are very busy in summer, so it's advisable to go early in the day, before they get stressed. Also check www.chapelco.com.ar and www.smandes.gov.ar.

Sights

Running perpendicular to the *costanera*, along the lake, is Calle San Martín, where you'll find most shops and plenty of places to eat. There are two plazas, of which **Plaza Sarmiento** is lovely, wooded, nicely maintained and illuminated by little lamps at night. The more functional **Plaza San Martín**, has a sporadic crafts market, and is more of a public space. It's a pleasant 1½-hour walk to **Mirador Bandurrias** with great views, and a *quincho*-like restaurant run by a Mapuche community. There's a good little museum on local history, **Museo Primeros Pobladores** ⓘ *Mon-Fri 1000-1500, 1800-2100, Sat and Sun 1300-2200.*

Lago Lacar and around → *Colour map 1, B3*

Lago Lacar can be explored by car along much of its length, as there's a *ripio* road, Route 48, leading to the Chilean border at **Paso Hua Hum**, 41 km. You can cycle or walk all the way around the lake and on to **Lago Escondido** to the south. There are beaches at **Hua Hum**, at the western end of the lake, and rafting on the nearby Río Hua Hum. On the southern shore, 18 km away, there is a quieter beach at **Quila Quina**, where you can walk either to a waterfall, along a guided nature trail, or to a tranquil Mapuche community in the hills above the lake. Both lakeshore villages can be reached by boat from the pier in San Martín. » *See also Transport, page 84.*

Sleeping

Lago Huechulafquen *p73*

There are superb campsites and 3 overpriced *hosterías* (**LL**), all rather taking advantage of their lakeside positions. **Hostería Paimún**, RN61, Km 58, T02972- 491201, is the most luxurious but not the most welcoming. **Huechulafquen**, RN61, Km 55, T02972-427598, has comfortable rooms, peaceful gardens and expert fishing advice. **Refugio del Pescador**, RN61, Km 57, T02972- 491319, is the most basic and has a small golf course.

Camping

There are lots of sites along the lake run by local Mapuche communities, often selling delicious *pan casero* or offering horse riding. **Camping Lafquen-co**, just after the sign to Bahía Coihues. Highly recommended for its friendly welcome, with a good spot on the lakeside and lots of room, US$3 pp. **Piedra Mala**, beyond Hostería Paimún, beautiful wooded site with 2 beaches, hot showers, *parrillas* and a *proveduría*, US$4.

Border with Chile

Paso Hua Hum (659 m) lies 47 km west of San Martín de los Andes along Route 48 (*ripio*), which runs along the north shore of Lago Lacar. It is usually open all year round and is an alternative to Paso Tromen (see page 75). The road (*ripio*, tough going for cyclists) continues 11 km on the Chilean side to Puerto Pirehueico (see page 203). Buses from San Martín de los Andes, connect with the boat across Lago Pirehueico to Puerto Fuy or there are buses to Panguipulli for onward connections.

Argentine immigration ⓘ *2 km east of the border, summer 0800-2100, winter 0900-2000.* **Chilean immigration** ⓘ *Puerto Pirehueico, summer 0800-2100, winter 0900-2000.*

Paso Tromen *p75*
There's a municipal campsite on the Río Curi Leuvú; a free **CONAF** site in Puesco (Chile), with no facilities, and a superb campsite, **Agreste Lanín**, at Puesto Tromen, Dec-Apr US$1 pp, with shaded areas, hot showers, toilets and *parilladas*. Take food.

Junín de los Andes *p76, map below*
L Rio Dorado Lodge and Fly Shop, Pedro Illera 448, T/F02972-491548, www.riodorado.com.ar. Expensive fishing lodge, with comfortable, spacious rooms in log-cabin style, with huge beds and private bathrooms, lovely gardens and attentive service. Big 'American' breakfast included. Good fly shop.
B San Jorge, at the very end of Antártida Argentina, Chacra 54, T/F02972-491147, www.hotelsanjorge.com.ar. Nov-Apr. A big, recently modernized 1960's hotel, beautifully located with lovely views and gardens, well furnished rooms with bath and TV. Very good value. Good restaurant and internet. English spoken. Recommended.
C Hostería Chimehuín, Suárez y 25 de Mayo, T02972-491132, hosteriachimehuin@jandes.com.ar. A long-established fishing *hostería* with beautiful gardens, and friendly owners, quaint decor, and comfortable rooms with bath and TV. Ask for the rooms with balconies next to the river. Good breakfasts, open all year. Recommended.
C Milla Piuke, off the RN234, Gral Roca y Av los Pehuenes, T/F02972-492378, millapiuke@jandes.com.ar. Delightful and welcoming *hostería*, with tastefully decorated and stylish rooms all with bath and TV, and apartments for families. Breakfast included. Highly recommended.
D Posada Pehuén, Col Suárez 560, T02972-491569, posadapehuen@fronteradigital.net.ar. A lovely quiet B&B with pretty, rather old-fashioned rooms, all rooms with TV and bathroom, charming owners, good value.

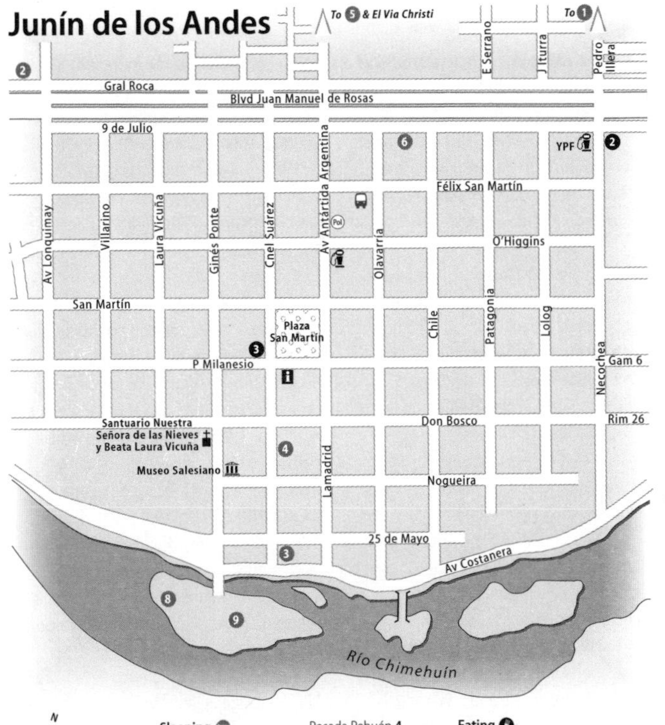

Sleeping
Hostería Chimehuín **3**
La Isla **9**
Mallin Laura Vicuña **8**
Milla Piuke **2**
Posada Pehuén **4**
Residencial Marisa **6**
Río Dorado Lodge & Fly Shop **1**
San Jorge **5**

Eating
La Aldea de Pescador **2**
Ruca Hueney **3**

E Residencial Marisa, Juan Manual de Rosas 360, T02972-491175, www.residencialmarisa.com.ar. Simple, good value, with plain clean rooms, and cheery family owners. *Confitería* downstairs. It's on the main road, so a little noisy during the day, but handy for the bus terminal and cheap eating places.

Estancias

L Estancia Huechahue, north of town, off RN 234 (reached from the Junín-Bariloche bus), T02972-491303, www.huechahue.com. A marvellous self-sufficient, traditional Patagonian estancia, where horses and cattle are bred. Guests stay in comfortable wooden cabins; evenings are spent dining together with delicious food and wine. There's fantastic riding in Parque Nacional Lanín, watching condors, cattle mustering for the adventurous, or longer pack trips over the mountains to Chile. Superb horses, great *asados* in the open air, even a jacuzzi under the stars to rest tired muscles. Highly recommended.

Camping

There are many sites in the area with 2 good ones in town: **La Isla**, T02972-492029, on the river, US$2.30 pp. **Mallin Laura Vicuña**, Ginés Ponte 861, T02972-491149, campinglv@jandes.com.ar, also on the river, with hot showers, electricity, shop, discounts for stays over 2 days, very good value *cabañas* for 4-7.

San Martín de los Andes *p77, map p77*

Single rooms and rates are scarce. Rates are much higher in Jan/Feb and Jul/Aug.

L La Casa de Eugenia, Coronel Díaz 1186, T02972-427206, www.lacasadeeugenia.com.ar. The most charming B&B in San Martín, this beautifully renovated 1900's house is more like an exclusive boutique hotel, but completely relaxing and un-snobby. Rooms are beautifully designed, incredibly cosy, and very welcoming. Breakfasts are luxurious. The friendly owners, go out of their way to make you feel at home. Highly recommended.

L Las Lengas, Col Pérez 1175, T02972-427659, www.hosterialaslengas.com.ar. A spacious hotel with plain attractive rooms, all individually designed, and a warm relaxing atmosphere, in a peaceful part of town. Recommended.

L Rio Hermoso, Ruta 63, Km 67, Paraje Rio Hermoso, T02972-410485, www.riohermoso.com. Part of the **N|A** hotel group. Rooms over US$190 per double per night.

AL La Cheminée, Gral Roca y Mariano Moreno, T02972-427617, www.hosterialacheminee.com.ar. A luxurious option, with pretty and cosy cottage-style rooms, spacious bathrooms, and a small pool. Breakfast. Overpriced in high season, but reasonable otherwise.

AL Le Châtelet, Villegas 650, T02972-428294, www.hotellechatelet.com.ar. Chic and luxurious, everything in this beautiful chalet-style hotel is designed to make you feel utterly pampered. There's a cosy wood-lined living room, gorgeous bedrooms, video library, excellent service, spa and pool with massage and facial treatments.

A Hostería Walkirias, Villegas 815, T02972-428307, www.laswalkirias.com. A lovely place, homely but smart, very spacious and well furnished, tasteful rooms with big bathrooms, breakfast and free transfer from the airport included, sauna and pool room, charming owners. Great value off season.

A Hotel Del Viejo Esquiador, San Martin 1242, T02972-427690. Very comfortable rooms with good beds, in traditional hunting lodge-style, excellent service. English spoken. Recommended.

A Plaza Mayor, Coronel Pérez 1199, T02972-421929, www.hosteriaplazamayor.com.ar. A chic and homely *hostería* in a quiet residential area, with traditional touches in the simple elegant rooms, all decorated to a high standard. Pool, *quincho*, parking. Great home-made breakfast included. English, French and Italian spoken by the helpful staff. Very welcoming. Recommended.

B La Masia, Obeid 811, T02972-427879. Spacious high-ceilinged rooms, chalet style with lots of dark wood, and nice little bathrooms, lots of cosy places to sit in the evenings in the bar and lounge.

C Casa Alta, Obeid 659, T02972-427456. Deservedly popular B&B, with charming multilingual owners. Comfy rooms, most with bathrooms, lovely gardens, delicious breakfast. Closed in low season, book in advance.

C Crismalu, Rudecindo Roca 975, T02972-427283, crismalu@smandes.com.ar. Simple rooms in attractive chalet-style place, good value, breakfast included.

C Hostería Las Lucarnas, Pérez 632, T02972-427085. Really good value, this central and pretty place with simple comfortable rooms, and friendly owner, who speaks English.

D **Hostal del Lago**, Col Rhode 854, T02972-427598, hostalago@hotmail.com. A relaxed homely place, the rooms have basic bathrooms, but a good breakfast is included.

D-E pp **Hosteria Bärenhaus**, Los Alamos 156, 5 km outside town, Barrio Chapelco, T02972-422775, www.baerenhaus.com. The owners have thought of everything to make you feel at home: very comfortable rooms with bath and heating, or great value shared dorms. Excellent breakfast. Highly recommended. Free pick-up from bus terminal and airport.

E pp **Hostel Puma**, Fosbery 535, T02972-422443, puma@smandes.com.arj. HI discounts. Excellent, lovely hostel, warm, friendly, and clean, run by an enthusiastic guide who organizes treks to Lanín. Rooms for 4 with private bathroom, also doubles **D**, kitchen, laundry, internet, cycle hire. Taxi US$0.80 from terminal. Recommended.

Cabañas

Plentiful *cabañas* are available on the hill to the north of town, and down by the lakeside. Prices increase in high season, but are good value for families or groups.

Antuen, Perito Moreno 1850, T/F02972-428340, www.interpatagonia.com/antuen. Modern well-equipped and luxurious for 2-7, jacuzzi, pool, games room, views from elevated position above valley.

Arco Iris, Los Cipreses 1850, T02972-429450, www.arcoirisar.com. Comfortable and perfectly equipped, spotless *cabañas* in a quiet area of town. Beautifully situated, with their own access to the river. Each has 2 bathrooms, cosy living rooms with TV, and spacious kitchen. The friendly owners are knowledgeable about the area and helpful. Very good value at US$35 for 4 in high season. Highly recommended.

Eruizos, Perez 428, T02972-425856, www.eruizos.com.ar. Plainer *cabañas* in rustic but comfortable style.

La Encantada, Perito Moreno y Los Enebros, T/F02972-428364, www.laencantada.com. In a spectacular position above town in wooded surroundings, large, beautifully furnished cosy *cabañas* for 2 or more families, pool, games room and fishing.

Camping

ACA, Koessler 2176 (on the access road), T02972-429430. Hot water, laundry facilities.

Catritre, R234, Km 4, southern shore of the lake, T02972-428820. Good facilities in a gorgeous position on the shore.

Quila Quina, T02972-426919. A pretty spot and a peaceful place (out of peak season) with beaches and lovely walks.

Eating

Lago Huechulafquen *p73*

There are lots of places to eat, with *proveduríasselling pan casero* at **Bahía**, **Piedra Mala** and **Rincon**, and light meals served at **La Valsa**, at Población Barriga.

Junín de los Andes *p76, map p79*

Ruca Hueney, on the plaza at Col Suárez y Milanesio, T02972-491113, www.ruca-hueney.com.ar. The best place to eat in town, with a wide menu. Try the famous (enormous) *bife de chorizo Ruca Hueney*, the local wild boar, excellent *parrilla*, and the locally caught trout: all are delicious. Also Middle Eastern dishes US$10 for 2 courses. Great atmosphere, and wonderful service. Highly recommended.

¥ **La Aldea de Pescador**, RN 234 y Necochea, on the main road by the YPF station. Good for *parrilla* and trout, very cheap.

¥ **La Posta de Junín**, Rosas 160 (RN 234), T02972-492303. Good steaks, local trout, tasty home-made pastas and good wine list.

San Martín de los Andes *p77, map p77*

¥¥¥ **Avataras**, Teniente Ramon 765, T02972-427104, Thu-Sat from 2030. The best in town, this pricey, inspired place is absolutely marvellous. The surroundings are elegant, the menu imaginative, US$13 for 3 courses and wine, an excellent treat.

¥¥ **El Quincho**, Rivadavia y San Martín. An excellent, much-recommended traditional *parrilla* for tasty steaks, also offering superb home-made pasta, with good old-fashioned service to match. Great atmosphere. Warmly recommended.

¥¥ **El Regional**, Villegas 953, T02972-425326. Hugely popular for regional specialities – smoked trout, pâtés and hams, and El Bolsón's home-made beer, all in cheerful German-style decor.

¥¥ **La Tasca**, M Moreno 866, T02972-428663. A great atmospheric family restaurant with superb food and a wonderful wine list. The wood-panelled walls are lined with fascinating paintings and bottles. The food is traditional and includes excellent smoked boar and trout-filled pasta. Recommended.

¥¥ **Pura Vida**, Villegas 745. The only vegetarian restaurant in town, small and welcoming, also fish and chicken dishes.

¥ **Ku**, San Martín 1053. An intimate *parrilla*, serving delicious home-made pastas and superb mountain specialities, with excellent service and wine list.

¥ **La Costa del Pueblo**, on the *costanera* opposite pier, T02972-429289. Decent value, overlooking the lake. A big family-orientated place with a cheerful atmosphere, offering a huge range of pastas, chicken and trout dishes. Cheap dish of the day (US$4 for 2 courses), good service, recommended.

¥ **Tio Pico**, San Martin y Capitan Drury. For a drink or lunch on the main street, this is a great bar-café, serving tasty *lomitos* in a warm atmosphere.

Teashops

Casa de Alicia, Drury 814, T02972-425830. Delicious cakes and smoked trout.

Casa de Té Arrayán, head up to Mirador Arrayán, and follow signs, T02972-425570, www.tenriverstenlakes.com. Fabulous views from this cosy rustic log cabin with delicious meals, lunch and dinner (reservations essential) and the tea room. A real treat.

Festivals and events

Junín de los Andes *p76, map p79*

Jan Agricultural show and exhibition of flowers and local crafts.

Feb Fiesta Provincial de Puestero, mid-Feb sees the election of the queen, *asados* with local foods and gaucho riding, the most important country fiesta in southern Argentina.

Jul Festival of aboriginal arts, mid-month.

Dec Inauguration of the church of **Laura Vicuña**, with a special mass on the 8th and singing to celebrate the life of Laura Vicuña.

Shopping

Junín de los Andes *p76, map p79*

Crafts stalls behind the tourist office sell good-quality local weavings and woodwork.

Patagonia Rodeo, Padre Milanesio 562, 1st fl, T01972-492839. A traditional shop selling what real gauchos wear in the field, plus quality leather belts, wallets, saddlery.

San Martín de los Andes *p77, map p77*

A great place for shopping, with chic little shops selling clothes and handmade jumpers, and a handicraft market in summer in Plaza San Martín. Lots of outdoor shops on San Martín sell clothes for walking and skiing.

Aquaterra, Villegas 795, T02972-429797. Outdoor equipment and clothing.

La Oveja Negra, San Martín 1025, T02972-428039. Wonderful handmade scarves and jumpers, esoteric crafts to a high standard.

Nomade, San Martín 881. Outdoor gear and camping equipment.

Chocolate

There are 2 recommended places for buying chocolates: **Abuela Goye**, San Martín 807, T02972-429409, also serves excellent ice creams; **Mamusia**, San Martín 601, T02972-427560, also sells homemade jams.

Activities and tours

Junín de los Andes *p76, map p79*

Fishing

The season runs from 2nd Sat in Nov to Easter. For information, consult www.turismo.gov.ar/pesca. See also **Alquimia Viajes and Turismo**, under Tour operators, below.

Estancia Quillén, Aluminé, T02942-496196, www.interpatagonia.com/quillen/index.html. Fishing on the estancia as well as trips to rivers and lakes in the surrounding area.

Jorge Trucco, based in fly shop **Patagonia Outfitters** in San Martín de los Andes, Perez 662, T02972-427561, www.jorgetrucco.com. Professional trips, good advice, and many years of experience on the lakes and rivers.

Pesca Patagonia with Alejandro Olmedo, JM Rosas 60, T02972-491632, www.pescapatagonia.com.ar. Guides, tuition, equipment.

Río Dorado Lodge, Pedro Illera 448, T02972-491548, www.riodorado.com.ar. The luxury fishing lodge at the end of town has a good fly shop, and organizes trips, run by experts and passionate fishermen.

Tour operators

Alquimia Viajes and Turismo, Padre Milanesio 840, T02972-491355, www.alquimiaturismo.com.ar. Fishing trips with expert local guides, among a range of adventure tourism expeditions, including climbing Lanín, climbing in rock and ice, rafting, and transfers.

San Martín de los Andes *p77, map p77*

Cycling

Many places rent mountain and normal bikes along San Martín, all charging similar prices.

Enduro Bikes, Elordi and Pto Moreno, T02972-427093.

HG Rodados, San Martin 1061, T02972-427345, hgrodados@smandes.com.ar. Rents mountain bikes at US$8 per day, also sells spare parts and offers expertise.

Fishing

The season runs from mid-Nov to May. For guides contact the tourist office or the park office. See www.turismo.gov.ar/pesca, www.neuquentur.gov.ar/guias2.htm or send an email to camguiasneuquen@smandes.com.ar for more information in English. The following outlets sell equipment and offer fishing excursions: **Fly Shop**, Pedro Illera 378, T02972-491548; **Jorge Cardillo Pesca Fly shop**, Villegas 1061, T02972-428372; **Los Notros**, P Milanesio y Lamadrid, T02972-492157; **Orvis Fly shop**, Gral Villegas 835, T02972-425892; **Patagonian Anglers**, M Moreno 1193, T02972-427376, patagoniananglers@smandes.com.ar. **Rosario Aventura**, Av Koessler 1827, T02972-429233.

Flying

Aeroclub de los Andes, T02972-426254, aeroclubandes@smandes.com.ar. For flights in light aircraft.

Skiing

Chapelco has 29 km of pistes, many of them challenging, with an overall drop of 730 m. Very good slopes and snow conditions make this a popular resort with foreigners and wealthy Argentines. At the foot of the mountain are a restaurant and base lodge, with 3 more restaurants on the mountain and a small café at the top. To get to the slopes, take the bus from San Martín, US$2 return, **Transportes Chapelco**, T02944-1561 8875. Details, passes, equipment hire from office at San Martín y Elordi, T02972-427845, www.sanmartindelosandes.gov.ar.

Tour operators

El Claro, Coronel Díaz 751, T02972-429363, www.interpatagonia.com/elclaro. Trips to the lakes, and also paragliding, horse riding, and other adventure trips.

El Refugio, Access from upstairs on C Pérez 830, just off San Martín, T02972-425140, www.elrefugioturismo.com.ar. Excellent company with friendly bilingual guides. Boat trips to lagos Huechulafquen and Paimún, US$18, Villa la Angustura via Seven Lakes US$18, or to Quila Quina US$12, mountain bike hire US$23 per day, rafting at Hua Hum US$33, horse riding US$20, and trekking US$20. Lots more on offer. Recommended.

Lucero Viajes, San Martín 826, 2nd fl, off B, T02972-428453, www.luceroviajes.com.ar. Rafting at Hua Hum, horse riding, 4WD trips, and tours to Hua Hum and Quila Quina. Also sells ski passes in winter.

Transport

Junín de los Andes *p76, map p79*

Bus

The terminal is at Olavarría y Félix San Martín, T02972-492038, (do not confuse with Gral San Martín). To **San Martín de los Andes**, 45 mins, US$4.50, several a day, **Centenario, Ko Ko, Airén**. To **Neuquén**, 7 hrs, US$23, several companies. To **Tromen**, Mon-Sat 1½ hrs, US$5.50. To **Caviahue** and **Copahue**, change at Zapala. 3 ½hrs, US$12. To **Bariloche**, 3 hrs US$9, Via Bariloche, Ko Ko. To **Buenos Aires**, 21 hrs, US$35, several companies.

To Chile To **Temuco** (5 hrs) US$11 via Paso Tromen/Mamuil Malal, daily with either **Empresa San Martín** or **Igi-Llaima.**

San Martín de los Andes *p77, map p77*

Air

Chapelco airport, T02972-428388, is 20 km northeast on the road to Junín de los Andes; taxi US$7. Flights to **Buenos Aires**, **Aerolíneas Argentinas**, also LADE weekly from **Bahía Blanca**, **Esquel**, and **Bariloche**. **Airline offices** Aerolíneas Argentinas, Drury 876, T02972-427003. **LADE**, in the bus terminal at Villegas 231, T02972-427672. **Southern Winds**, San Martín 866, T02972-425815.

Boat

Boats from San Martín pier, T02972-428427, depart to **Quila Quina** hourly, 30 mins each way, US$5 return, and to **Hua Hum**, US$15 return, 3 daily in season.

Bus

The bus terminal is reasonably central, at Villegas 251, information T02972-427044.

To **Buenos Aires**, 20hrs, US$55 *coche cama*, daily, 6 companies. To **Bariloche**, 3½ hrs (not via Seven Lakes Drive), US$8.30, many daily, **Via Bariloche**, T02972- 425325, **Albus**, T02972-428100, minibus along the Seven Lakes Drive via **Traful** and **La Angostura**, 4 hrs, US$7. **Ko Ko**, T02972- 427422, daily, fast route via Confluencia. To **Puerto Madryn** (via Neuquén) US$32. To **Neuquén** with **Albus** 2 daily, takes 6½ hrs, US$14.

To Chile Buses to **Puerto Pirehueico** via Paso Hua Hum leave early morning daily, 2 hrs, US$4; they connect with car and passenger ferries across Lago Pirehueico to **Puerto Fuy**. Bus to **Temuco** with **Empresa San Martín**, T02972-27294, Mon, Wed, Fri, **Igi-Llaima**, T02972-427750, Tue, Thu, Sat, US$11, 6-8 hrs (heavily booked in summer) via Paso Hua Hum.

Car hire

Hansen Rent a Car, San Martín 532, T02972-427997, www.hansenrentacar.com.ar. **Hertz**, San Martín 831, 1st floor, T02972-420820. **Nieves Rent a Car**, Villegas 668, office 2, T02972-428684, nievesrentacar@smandes.com.ar. **Rent a Car La Patagonia**, Villegas 305, T02972-421807.

Taxi

Eco Taxi, also known as **Lacar**, T02972-428817. Very helpful and efficient. If in town, find them on main street San Martín, or give Abuela Goye as useful meeting point.

Directory

Junín de los Andes *p76, map p79*

Banks TCs can be cashed at **Western Union**, Milanesio 570, 1000-1400, 1600-1930; and money changed at **Banco Provincial Neuquén**, San Martín y Lamadrid, also has ATM. **Internet** In the *galería* behind tourist office. The Parque Nacional Lanín office is in same building as tourist office, T02972- 491160, and is very helpful. **Post office** Suárez y Don Bosco. **Telephone** *Locutorío* near tourist office on plaza at Milanesio 540.

San Martín de los Andes *p77, map p77*

Banks Many ATMs along San Martín. *Casa de cambio* at **Banco de la Nación**, San Martín 687. **Internet** Lots of broadband services, **Punto.Com**, inside *galería* at San Martín 866, **Punto.Net**, Galería Azul, **Terminal**, Vilegas 150. **Laundry** Laverap, Drury 880, daily 0800-2200. **Marva**, Drury y Villegas, and Perito Moreno 980. Fast, efficient and cheap. **Medical services** Hospital **Ramón Carrillo**, San Martín y Coronel Rodhe, T02972-427211. **Post office** General Roca y Pérez, Mon-Fri 0800-1300, 1700-2000, Sat 0900-1300.

Telephones Cooperativa Telefónica, Drury 761, **Terminal**, Villegas 150.

Parque Nacional Nahuel Huapi

Nahuel Huapi is the park you're most likely to visit, as the tourist centre of Bariloche is right in the middle of it. Covering a spectacular 710,000 ha and stretching along the Andes for over 130 km, this is Argentina's oldest national park, created in 1934. It extends across some of Argentina's most dramatic mountains, with lakes, rivers, glaciers, waterfalls, bare mountains and snow-clad peaks. Among those you can climb are Tronador (3478 m) and Catedral Sur (2388 m). Base yourself either at Bariloche, where there are excellent hotels stretching for 25 km along the lakeshore, or on the northern shore, at the upmarket resort of Villa La Angostura, where the Parque Nacional Los Arrayanes, contains a rare woodland of exquisite arrayán trees with their distinctive cinnamon-coloured flaky bark.

North of here, a winding road takes you through spectacular landscapes on the famous Seven Lakes Drive to San Martín de los Andes, in Parque Nacional Lanín. Take a diversion east for to Lago Traful, with a tranquil village for fishing, camping and walking. West of Bariloche, there are glaciers and waterfalls near Pampa Linda, the base for climbing Tronador, and starting point for the trek through Paso de las Nubes to Lago Frias. Further south, lagos Mascardi, Guillelmo, and Gutiérrez have even grander scenery, with horse riding, trekking and rafting along the Río Manso. An excellent base for exploring this area is Estancia Peuma Hue on the southern shore of Lago Gutiérrez, with its beautiful, peaceful setting. » *For Sleeping, Eating and other listings see pages 88-91.*

Ins and outs

Park information Bariloche is the main centre for entering the park, where you can find information on transport, walks and maps. The **Parque Nacional Nahuel Huapi Intendencia** ⓘ *San Martín 24, T02944-423111, www.parquesnacionales.com.ar, 0900-1400*, is very helpful. Also useful for information on hiking is **Club Andino Bariloche (CAB)**, see page 103, which sells hand-drawn walking maps, showing average walking times and *refugios*. Note that these are sometimes out of date, so check the paths are open with *guardaparques*. **CAB** can also advise on transport within the park. More detailed maps are available from Buenos Aires, at the **Instituto Geográfico Militar**, www.igm.gov.ar. There are many *refugios* in the park run both privately and by **CAB**, which charge US$5 per night, plus US$2 for cooking, or US$2.50 for breakfast, US$5 for dinner. Take a good sleeping bag. Most areas of the park are free to visitors, but you must pay entry, US$4, at Puerto Pañuelo, Villa La Angostura and Pampa Linda.

Flora and fauna

Vegetation varies with altitude and climate, but includes large expanses of southern beech forest and, near the Chilean border where rainfall is highest, there are areas of virgin Valdivian rainforest. Here you will see coihues (evergreen beeches) over 450 years old and alerces over 1500 years old, with the ancient species of bamboo cane caña colihue growing everywhere. Eastern parts of the park are more steppe-like with shrubs and bushes. Wildlife includes the small pudú deer, the huemul and river otter, as well as foxes, cougars and guanacos. Among the birds, Magellan woodpeckers and austral parakeets are easily spotted as well as large flocks of swans, geese and ducks.

La Ruta de los Siete Lagos → *Colour map 1, B3*

The Seven Lakes Drive is the most famous tourist route in the Argentine Lake District. It follows Route 234 through the Lanín and Nahuel Huapi national parks from San Martín de los Andes to Villa La Angostura and passes seven magnificent lakes, all flanked by mountains clad in beech forest. It is particularly attractive in autumn (April/May) when the trees turn red and yellow. Although the road is only partially paved, the hard earth surface is usually only closed after heavy rain or snowfall. There are limited facilities for camping along the route but plenty of perfect picnic spots, especially at Pichi Traful or Lago Espejo. Five-hour round-trip excursions along the Seven Lakes Route are operated by several companies. Buses will stop at campsites on the route, but it's better to have your own transport, as you'll want to be able to explore. The route is good for cycling, although there's more traffic in January and February. The seven lakes are (from north to south) Lácar, Machónico (in Parque Nacional Lanín), Falkner, Villarino, Correntoso, Espejo and Nahuel Huapi.

Parque Nacional Nahuel Huapi

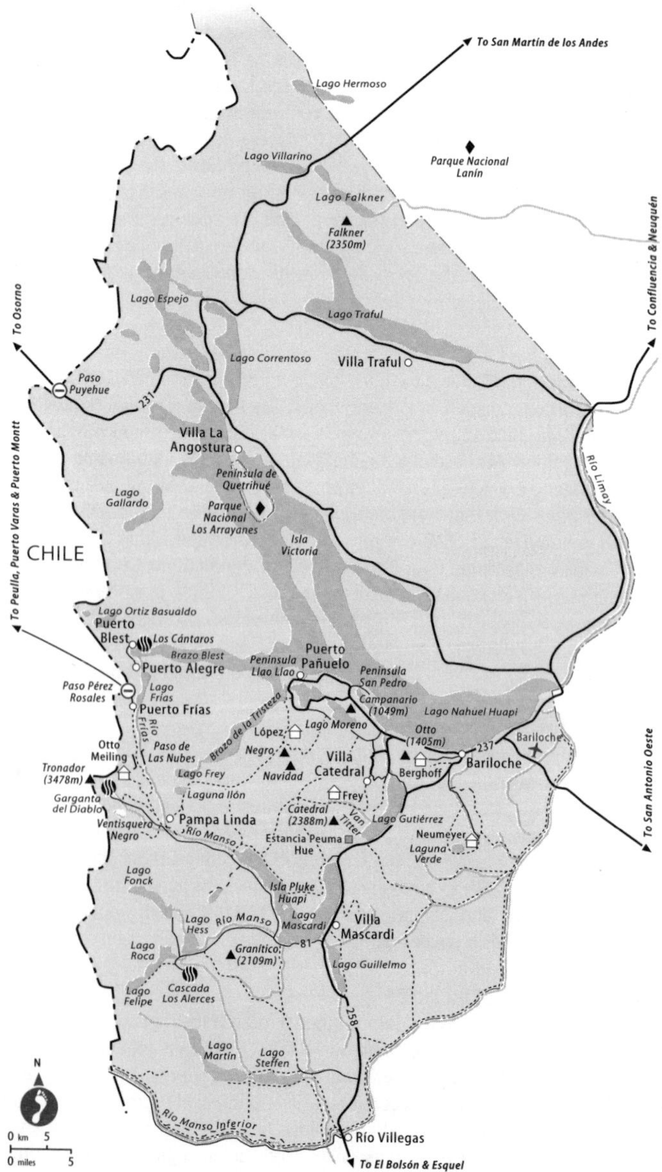

San Martín de los Andes to Bariloche

There's an alternative direct route south to Bariloche, via **Confluencia**, that's also appealing. Follow Route 234 then take Route 63, unpaved, southeast along the shore of Lago Meliquina and over the **Paso de Córdoba**, Km 77 (1300 m), where you enter Parque Nacional Nahuel Huapi. (You could turn off along an unpaved track to **Lago Filo-Hua-Hum** at Km 54, before continuing to Confluencia.) From Confluencia, take the paved Neuquén–Bariloche highway, through the astounding **Valle Encantado**, 100 km from Bariloche. Here, the road winds through mountains, whipped into jaggy peaks, alongside the milky turquoise waters of the Río Limay. The weird rock formations include *El Dedo de Dios* (The Finger of God) and *El Centinela del Valle* (The Sentinel of the Valley). The road reaches Bariloche, 157 km from San Martín de los Andes.

Villa Traful and around → *Colour map 1, B3*

If you want to get off the beaten track, Villa Traful is ideal. The quiet pretty village sprawls alongside the narrow deep-blue sliver of **Lago Traful**, enclosed on both sides by stunning sharp peaked mountains. Approaching from the west, you'll pass forests of lenga and coihue trees, their elegant tall trunks creating a woody cathedral, with idyllic spots to camp all along the shore. There are also some wonderful walks and waterfalls to see here, and little else to do but unwind. Further along the lakeshore, there's a small, but helpful **tourist office** ⓘ *past Aiken cabañas, T02944-479020, www.neuquen.gov.ar/muni/villa_traful, www.interpatagonia.com/traful*, with information on walks, riding and fishing. The *guardería* opposite the pier is open in high season for advice on walks. A 1½-hour walk from the village will bring you to the lovely **Cascadas del Arroyo Coa Có y Blanco**, which thunder down through beech forest and cañas colihues bamboo.

Villa La Angostura and around » *pp88-91.*

This pretty town with a village feel is a popular holiday resort for wealthier Argentines on the shores of Lago Nahuel Huapi and provides access to the wonderful **Parque Nacional Los Arrayanes** (see page 88) at the end of the **Quetrihué peninsula**. The town has two centres: **El Cruce**, where there are countless restaurants, hotels and *cabaña* complexes, and the picturesque port, known as **La Villa**, 3 km away at the neck of the Quetrihué Peninsula. The **tourist office** ⓘ *opposite the bus terminal, Av Siete Lagos 93, T02944-494124, www.villalaangostura.gov.ar, high season 0800-2100, low season 0800-2000*, is opposite the bus terminal north of town, and is busy and helpful.

Border with Chile

Officially known as Paso Samore, **Paso Puyehue** (1280 m) lies west of Villa La Angostura via unpaved Route 231 – a spectacular six-hour drive. Some travellers think this route is even more scenic than the ferry journey across Lago Todos Los Santos and Lago Frías (see page 95) and it's certainly far cheaper and more reliable, although it's liable to closure after snow. Heading east to west, the best views are from the southern side of the bus. From Villa La Angostura, Route 231 passes the junction with 'Ruta de Los Siete Lagos' for San Martín at Km 94. The pass itself is at Km 125. On the Chilean side the road continues via Parque Nacional Puyehue and Entre Lagos to Osorno.

Argentine customs and immigration ⓘ *Km 109, 14 km east of the border, winter 0900-2000, summer 0800-2100.* **Chilean immigration** ⓘ *Pajaritos, Km 146, 22 km west of the border, open 2nd Sat in Oct to 1 May 0800-2100, winter 0900-2000.* For vehicles entering Chile, formalities take about 30 minutes and include the spraying of tyres and the wiping of shoes on a mat, for which you pay US$2 to *Sanidad* (have Chilean pesos ready).

"" Perhaps one day, tired of circling the world, I'll return to Argentina and settle in the Andean lakes... (Ernesto 'Che' Guevara, *The Motocycle Diaries*

Bus company **15 de Mayo** runs buses between El Cruce and La Villa every two hours, but it's also a pleasant walk. About halfway between the two centres is a chapel (1936), designed by Bustillo, the architect who gave this region's buildings their distinctive chalet style. There's also the tiny **Museo Regional** ⓘ *on the raod to La Villa, Mon 0800-1400, Tue-Fri 0800-1630, Sat 1430-1700*, with interesting photos of the original indigenous inhabitants. From La Villa, a short walk leads to **Laguna Verde**, an intense emerald green lagoon surrounded by mixed coihue cypress and arrayán forests, where there's a self-guided trail.

Around Villa La Angostura

There are fine views of Lagos Correntoso and Nahuel Huapi from **Mirador Belvedere**, a 3-km drive or walk up the old road, northwest of El Cruce. From the mirador a path to your right goes to **Cascada Inacayal**, a waterfall 50 m high, situated in an area rich in native flora and forest. Another delightful walk leads to beautiful 35-m **Cascada Río Bonito**, lying 8 km east of El Cruce off Route 66. One of the country's most popular ski resorts is at **Cerro Bayo** (1782 m), see page 91, further along the same path. Alternatively, 1 km further along the road, take the ski lift to a platform at 1500 m, where there's a restaurant with great views. The ski lift functions all year; cyclists can take bikes up and cycle down.

Parque Nacional Los Arrayanes → *Colour map 1, B3*

ⓘ *Park office: C Inacayal 13, La Villa, T02944-494004, www.bosquelosarrayanes.com.ar. The park entrance is 12 km south of La Villa. See Activities and tours, page 91.*

One of the most magical spots in the Lake District, this park was created to protect a rare forest of arrayán trees. It is one of the few places where the arrayán grows to full size and some of the specimens are 300 years old. Arrayán grow in groves near water and have extraordinary cinnamon-coloured peeling trunks that are cold to the touch. They have no outer bark to protect them, but the surface layer is rich in tannins, which keep the tree free from disease. They have creamy white flowers in January and February, and produce blue-black fruit in March. The most rewarding way to see the park is to take the boat trip across the lake and to stroll along the wooden walkways through the trees, once the guided tour has left. Then walk back to the port through the mixed forest. There's a *confitería* in the park, selling drinks and confectionery.

Sleeping

La Ruta de los Siete Lagos *p85*

B pp **Hostería Los Siete Lagos**, in a secluded spot on Lake Correntoso, T02944-15497152. A lovely *hostería* with 5 small, very simple rooms, with great views. Electricity in the evenings only. Excellent restaurant. Also a campsite in summer, no facilities, free. The bus from San Martín to Villa La Angostura stops here.

C **Hostería Lago Villarino**, Lago Villarino. A lovely setting, good food, also camping.

C **Lago Espejo Resort**, Lago Espejo. A beautifully situated hotel and camping area, on the shore of the lake, surrounded by trees.

D **Hostería Lago Espejo**, Lago Espejo. Old fashioned and comfortable, with good food in the restaurant, open Jan-Mar only.

Camping

The campsite at **Lago Espejo Resort** is open all year, US$1 pp. Further along an earth track is the lovely **Lago Espejo Camping**, open all year, US$1 pp, no showers, but toilets, drinking water, fireplaces and picnic spots, busy Jan.

Villa Traful and around *p87*

B-D Ruca Lico, T02944-479004, www.interpatagonia.com/rucalico. Luxurious *cabañas* in woodland above the lake shore, lavishly furnished in rustic chic style, with jacuzzi and balcony with splendid views. Good value for 6, a treat for 2. Horse riding trips organized. Recommended.

C Marinas Puerto Traful, T02944-475284, www.marinastraful.com.ar. Gorgeous uninterrupted views of the lake from this recently modernized place, now bizarrely painted bright blue. Comfortable.

D Aiken, T02944-479048, www.aiken.com.ar. Rustic and compact, but well decorated *cabañas* in spacious gardens with open views of the lake below. All have *parrilladas* outside. Cheap for 4 or 5. Recommended.

D Cabañas del Montañes, up behind the village, T02944-479035. Accommodation in *cabañas*, offered by the company that makes *alfajores*. Lovely setting.

D Hostería Villa Traful, T02944-479005. A delightful place to stay above the lake, in pretty gardens. Cabins have comfortable furnishings and ample bathrooms. Also *cabañas* for up to 6, US$50. Charming hospitality. Offers fishing and boat trips.

F Vulcanche, T02944-494015, www.vulcanche.com. An attractive chalet-style hostel and 2 *cabañas* (**D**), very comfortable and set in lovely open gardens with good views. Also simple camping in a pleasant open site, US$4 pp with hot showers, phone, *parrilladas*.

Camping

Camping Traful Lauquen, on the shore, T02944-479030, www.interpatagonia.com/trafullauquen. With 600 m of beach, this is among the loveliest of the sites along the lake. Hot showers, fireplaces, restaurant, US$2.30 pp, Nov-Mar. Calm and beautiful.

Costa de Traful, T02944-479149. If you're under 30 and you've got a guitar, camp at this lively place, US$2.30 pp, Dec-Apr. 24-hr hot showers, restaurant, fireplaces, *proveduria*, *cabañas*, fishing, horse riding, treks to see cave paintings on the other side of the lake.

Villa La Angostura and around *p87*

L Cabañas La Ruma Andina, Blv Queitrhué 1692, La Villa, T02944-495188, www.rumaadina.com.ar. Top-quality rustic *cabañas* with lots of stone and wood, and cosily furnished, in a lovely setting with pool. Recommended.

L Correntoso, discreetly hidden off the road, RN 231, and Río Correntoso, T02944-15619728, www.correntoso.com. Really fabulous setting for this intimate and stylish hotel with a really superb restaurant. Very special. Often recommended.

L El Faro, Av 7 Lagos 2345, T02944-495485, www.hosteriaelfaro.com.ar. Swish and stylish *hosteria*. Recommended.

L Las Balsas, Bahía Las Balsas (off Av Arrayanes), T02944-494308, www.lasbalsas.com. The most famous and exclusive hotel in the area and one of the best in Argentina. Fabulous cosy rooms, impeccable service, and a wonderfully intimate atmosphere in a great lakeside location with its own secluded beach. The chef Pablo Campoy creates really fine cuisine from top local produce. There's a beautiful pool by the lake, and a fantastic spa. Excursions arranged, or transfers to the ski centre in season. Very highly recommended.

A Casa del Bosque, Los Pinos 160, T02944-475229, www.casadelbosque.com. Luxury and style in wonderfully designed *cabanas*, lots of glass, with jacuzzis and all possible comforts, in secluded in woodland at Puerto Manzana. Recommended.

A Hotel Angostura, T02944-494224, www.hotellaangostura.com.ar. Open all year, beautifully situated on the lakeside at the port, handsome stone and wood chalet was designed by Bustillo in 1938, charming old-fashioned feel, with lovely gardens, and an excellent restaurant.

A La Posada, RN 231, Km 65, west of town, T02944-494450, www.hosterialaposada.com. In a splendid elevated position with clear views over the lake, this is a welcoming, beautifully maintained hotel in lovely gardens, with pool and fine restaurant.

A Portal de Piedra, RN231, Km 56.7 y Río Bonito, T02944-494278, www.portaldepiedra.com. A welcoming *hostería* and tea room in the woods, with tastefully decorated wood-panelled rooms, and attractive gardens. Restaurant, excursions and activities.

C Verena's Haus, Los Taiques 268, T02944-494467. A quaint and welcoming wooden house for adults and non-smokers only, cosy rooms with a pretty garden, delicious breakfasts. English spoken. Recommended.

D **Hostería Del Francés**, Lolog 3057, in a great position on shore of Lago Correntoso, T02944-488055, lodelfrances@hotmail.com. Excellent value in a lovely house, chalet-style with lovely views from all the rooms,. Recommended.

F pp **Bajo Cero Hostel**, Av 7 Lagos, T02944-495454, www.bajocerohostel.com. Well situated in town, neat rooms for 2-4 with private bath, linen and breakfast included.

F **Hostel la Angostura**, Barbagelata 157, 300 m up the road behind the tourist office, T02944-494834, www.hostellaangostura.com.ar. A warm, luxurious and cheap hostel. Small dorms with bathroom, trips organized. Highly recommended.

Camping

There are many sites along the RN 231.

Osa Mayor, signposted off main road close to town, T02944-494304, osamayor@uol.com.ar. Highly recommended is this delightful leafy site on a hillside with good, shaded levelled camping spots, and all facilities and clean bathrooms US$2.30 pp. Also *cabañas*. Lovely apart from Jan, when the place is packed.

Eating

Villa Traful and around *p87*

¥ **Nancu Lahuen**, T02944, 479179. A delightful tea room and restaurant serving trout and homemade pastas, cakes and delicious chocolates. Large open fire.

¥ **Parrilla La Terraza**, T02944-479077. Delicious locally produced lamb and kid on the *asado*, with panoramic lake views. Recommended

Villa La Angostura *p87*

¥¥¥ **Cocina Waldhaus**, RN 231, Puerto Manzano, T02944-475323, www.saboresdeneuquen.com.ar. Gorgeous local delicacies created by Chef Leo Morsella, served in a charming chalet-style building. Recommended

¥¥¥ **Las Balsas**, T02944-494308, www.lasbalsas.com. Possibly the best food in all Argentina, created by chef Pablo Campoy. The wines are superb and the whole atmosphere is a real treat. Book well in advance. Highly recommended.

¥¥¥ **Tinto Bistró**, Blv Nahuel Huapi 34, T02944-494924. An interesting, eclectic menu, but it's the royal connections that make is so trendy among Argentines: the owner is the brother of the famous Maxima, married into Dutch royalty. Very chic, great wine list.

¥¥ **Correntoso**, Hotel Corentoso, Av 7 Lagos, T02944-1561 9727. A gourmet restaurant, specializing in Mediterranean cuisine, with Patagonian touches, like lamb and trout. Great wine list, gorgeous setting by the lake.

¥¥ **Los Pioneros de la Patagonia**, Av Arrayanes 263, T02944-495525. Famous for fine local dishes in a chalet style building and great Argentine steaks. Widely recommended.

¥¥ **Los Troncos**, Av Arrayanes 67. Great local dishes like trout-filled ravioli, and fabulous cakes and puddings. Warm atmosphere and live music at weekends.

¥¥ **Nativa Café**, Av Arrayanes 198. The most relaxed and welcoming eatery on the main drag with a high-ceilinged chalet feel, good music and an international menu. Excellent pizzas. Friendly efficient staff. Recommended.

¥¥ **Rincon Suizo**, Av Arrayanes 44. High season only. Delicious regional specialities with a Swiss twist, in a rather more authentic chalet-style building than most.

¥ **El Esquiador**, Las Retames 146 (behind the bus terminal). Best budget meal is the parrilla, with fixed price 3-course menu.

¥ **Gran Nevada**, opposite Nativa café. Good for cheap *parrilla* US$2, and *noquis* US$1.20 in a cheery friendly atmosphere.

¥ **Hora Cero**, Av Arrayanes 45. Hugely popular, heaving in summer, with a big range of excellent pizzas, and *pizza libre* (all you can eat US$2) on Wed and Sat.

Activities and tours

Villa Traful and around *p87*

Cycling

Del Montanes, T02944-479035, up the road behind the centre of the village, bike hire.

Fishing

The season runs mid-Nov to end Apr.

Andres Quelin, Hostería Villa Traful (see Sleeping) T02944-479005. A fishing guide who runs trips to see a submerged cypress wood.

Osvaldo A Brandeman, Bahía Mansa, T02944-479048, pescaosvaldo@mail.com. Fishing expert and guide.

Villa La Angostura *p87*

Adventure tours

Club Andino Villa La Angostura, Cerro Bayo 295. Excursions and information.
Lengas Tour, Av Arrayanes 173, T02944-494575, turismo@lengas.com. Horse riding, fishing, hunting, all with bilingual guides.
Rucan Turismo, Av 7 Lagos 90, T02944-495075, www.rucanturismo.com. Skiing, riding, mountain biking and tours.
Terpin Turismo, Los Notros 41, T02944-494551, terpinturismo@netpatagon.com. Trips to Chile and surroundings, car hire.
Turismo Cerros y Lagos, Av Arrayanes 21, T02944-495447, www.patagonianadventures.com. Skiing, adventure sports.

Fishing

For permits and a list of fishing guides, ask the tourist office. The following fly shops also arrange fishing trips: **Angler's Home Fly Shop**, Belvedere 22, T02944-495222; and **Class**, Av Arrayanes 173, T02944-494411.

Horse riding

Cabalgatas Correntoso, T02944-15552950, cabalgatascorrentoso@cybersnet.com.ar. Horseback excursions in the surrounding area and to Villa Traful, about US$5 per hr.

Skiing

Cerro Bayo, T02944-494189, www.cerrobayoweb.com, is one of Argentina's pricier resorts (adult ski pass US$20 for 1 day in high season). It has 24 pistes, many of them fabulously long, covering 20 km in total, and all with excellent views over the lakes below; it's also a great area for snowboarding.

Parque Nacional Los Arrayanes *p88*

Bus company **15 de Mayo** runs buses from El Cruce to **La Villa** every 2 hrs and takes 15 mins. A taxi to La Villa costs US$3. There's a clear path all the way from the tip of the Quetrihué peninsula where the boat arrives, through the prettiest part of the arrayán forest, and then running the length of the peninsula back to La Villa. You can walk or cycle the whole length: 3 hrs one-way walking; 2 hrs cycling.

There are 2 companies running catamarans from the pier in La Villa to the end of the peninsula, taking passengers on a guided tour through the forest before heading the boat back to La Villa. **Greenleaf Turismo** runs *Catamarán Futuleufú*, T02944- 494004, angosturaturismo@netpatagon.com; and **Catamarán Patagonia Argentina**, T02944-494463. Tickets from **Hotel Angostura**, US$12 return with the catamaran. Boats also run from Bariloche, via Isla Victoria, with **Turisur**, T02944-426109, www.barilche.com/turisur.

Transport

Villa Traful and around *p87*

Bus In summer, a daily bus between **Villa la Angostura** and **San Martín** stops here, but in low season, buses run only 3 times a week. **Kiosko El Ciervo**, by the YPF service station, sells tickets and has the timetable.

Villa La Angostura *p87*

Bus

The terminal is at Av 7 Lagos y Av Arrayanes, opposite the ACA service station.

To/from **Bariloche**, 1¼ hrs, US$4, several companies, several daily. Daily buses to **San Martín de los Andes** with **Ko Ko** and **Albus**. To **Osorno** (Chile), US$8; arrange for the bus from San Martín to pick you up in **Villa la Angostura**. For other destinations, change at San Martín de los Andes or Bariloche.

Bus companies 15 de Mayo, T02944-495104, **Albus**, T02944-1561 7578, **Andesmar**, T02944-495247, **Via Bariloche/El Valle**, T02944-495415.

Car hire

Angostura Rent a Car, T02944- 424621, info@angosturarentacar.com.ar. **Giminez Vidal**, Las Muticias 146, T02944- 494336. **Terpin Turismo**, Los Notros 41, T02944-494551, www.terpinturismo.com.

Directory

Villa La Angostura *p87*

Banks Andina, Arrayanes 256, T02944-495197. For cash and TC's. **Banco de Patagonia**, Av Arrayanes 275, and **Banco Prov de Neuquén**, Av Arrayanes 172. Both with ATMs. **Internet** Punta Arrayanes, Av Arrayanes 90, T02944-495288. **Medical services** Hospital Rural Arraiz, Copello 311 (at *barrio* Pinar), T02944-494170. **Post office** Siete Lagos 26. **Telephone** Several *locutorios* along Av Arrayanes.

Bariloche and around

Beautifully situated on the southern shore of Lago Nahuel Huapi, San Carlos de Bariloche is the best base for starting to explore the Lake District. It's right in the middle of Nahuel Huapi national park, and you could easily spend a week here, with plenty of opportunities for hiking in the mountains behind, and adventure sports. The town was founded in 1902, but took off in the 1930s once the national park was created. The chalet-style architecture was established at this time by early German and Swiss settlers. Hotel Llao Llao and the Civic Centre were designed by major Argentine architect Bustillo, which set the trend for brightly varnished wood and cute carved gable ends.

Bariloche is well set up for tourism, with lots of hotels and restaurants in the town centre, and even more appealing places along the shore of lake Nahuel Huapi, towards Llao Llao, where Argentina's most famous hotel enjoys a spectacular setting. To the immediate south of Bariloche there are tremendous hikes up giant Mount Tronador, reached from Pampa Linda, and two more gorgeous lakes, Gutiérrez, with Estancia Peuma Hue on its shores for excellent horse riding and relaxing, and Mascardi, with access to rafting on the Río Manso. Ski resort Cerro Catedral is arguably the best in South America, and makes a great base for hiking in summer. » *For Sleeping, Eating and other listings, see pages 98-104.*

Ins and outs

Getting there There are several flights daily from Buenos Aires. The airport is 15 km east of town; taxi US$5. A bus service run by **Del Lago Turismo**, T02944-430056, meets each flight, US$2.30. Bikes can be carried. Bus and train stations are both 3 km east of town; taxi US$1.50, frequent buses 10, 20, 21. If you are staying in one of the hotels on the road to Llao-Llao, west of town, expect to pay a little more for transport to your hotel.

The best walks and cycle routes around Bariloche

Consult **Club Andino Bariloche** for advice and maps (see page 103).

→ **Circuito Chico** (trek/cycle route) The classic 60-km circular route begins on Avenida Bustillo at Km 18.3, runs around Lago Moreno Oeste, past Punto Panorámico and through the Parque Munipal Llao Llao and on to Puerto Pañuelo. You could extend this circuit, by returning via Colonia Suiza and the Cerro Catedral ski resort or along the Península de San Pedro. Traffic can be a nuisance in summer, but the views are great.

→ **Around Llao Llao** (walk) Choose from an easy circuit in virgin Valdivian rainforest; an ascent of Cerrito Llao Llao, for wonderful views (three hours), or a 3-km trail to Braza Tristeza, via Lago Escondido.

→ **To Refugio López** (walk, six hours return) From the southeastern tip of Lago Moreno and climb up Arroyo López (2076 m) for fabulous views, and then along a ridge to **Refugio Lopez**.

→ **Cerro Catedral to Refugio Frey** (walk, three hours each way) via Rio Piedritas. The *refugio* at 1700 m has a beautiful lake setting.

→ **Cerro Catedral to Bariloche** (walk, six hours/cycle) descend down a rocky path to the shores of Lago Gutiérrez and follow the Route 258 back to town. Buses to Catedral will carry bikes.

→ **Bariloche to Cerro Otto** (cycle) Up a track from Avenida de los Pioneros. From the summit, the hardy could descend to Lago Gutiérrez.

→ **Around Refugio Neumayer** Cycle to **Refugio Neumayer** southeast of Bariloche then hike to Laguna Verde or through Magellanic forest to a mirador at Valle de los Perdidos.

Getting around Bariloche is an easy city to walk around and to orient yourself in: the lake lies to the north, and the mountains to the south. The main street is Calle Mitre, running east from the Centro Cívico. More accommodation and many restaurants are spread along Avenida Bustillo, which runs along the southern shore of Lago Nahuel Huapi for some 25 km, as far as **Hotel Llao-Llao**, and an area known as Colonial Suiza. Frequent local buses, run by **3 de Mayo**, shuttle along its length.

Tourist information The main **tourist office** ⓘ *Centro Cívico, T02944-429850, www.barilochepatagonia.info, daily 0900-2100*, has helpful multi-lingual staff, who can provide maps showing city buses, and arrange accommodation and campsites.

Sights

At the heart of the city is the **Centro Cívico**, designed by Bustillo in the 1930s in 'Bariloche Alpine style' and made of local wood and stone. It was inspired by the Swiss and German origins of Bariloche's early settlers. On the attractive plaza above the lake, there's the **Museo de La Patagonia** ⓘ *Tue-Fri 1000-1230, 1400-1900, Mon and Sat 1000-1300, US$1*, which, in addition to the stuffed animals, has indigenous artefacts and material from the lives of the first white settlers. Next to it is the **Biblioteca Sarmiento** ⓘ *Mon-Fri 1000-2000*, a library and cultural centre. From the plaza, the chalet style (bordering on kitsch) continues along the tourist-orientated main street, Mitre, in a proliferation of chocolate shops and restaurants serving fondue as well as delicious local trout and wild boar. The **cathedral**, built in 1946, lies six blocks east of the civic centre. Opposite the main entrance, there is a huge rock deposited here by a glacier during the last glacial period. On the lakeshore is the **Museo Paleontológico** ⓘ *12 de Octubre y Sarmiento*, which has displays of fossils mainly from Patagonia including an ichthyosaur and replicas of a giant spider and shark's jaws.

The road to Llao Llao » pp98-104.

Avenida Bustillo runs parallel to the lakeshore west of Bariloche, with **Avenida de los Pioneros** running parallel above it. From these roads, with good bus services, there's access to the mountains above. **Cerro Campanario** (1049 m) ⓘ *chairlift at Km 17.5 on Av Bustillo, T02944-427274, daily 0900-1800, extended opening in summer, 7 mins US$5*, offers a superb panorama of the lake, edged with mountains. There are more great views from **Cerro Otto** (1405 m) ⓘ *cable car at Km 5 on Av de los Pioneros*, with its revolving restaurant. To climb Cerro Otto on foot (two to three hours) turn off Avenida de los Pioneros at Km 4.6, then follow the trail past **Refugio Berghof**; don't walk this route alone, as the paths can be confusing. For a much longer trek or a good day-long cycle route, tackle **Circuito Chico**, one of the 'classic' Bariloche tours. **Cerro Catedral** ski resort (2388 m), 21 km southwest of Bariloche, is one of the major ski resorts in Argentina (see page 103), and in summer, the **cable car** ⓘ *from Villa Catedral, T02944-423776, www.catedralpatagonia.com, 0900-1700, US$8*, is a useful starting point for walks. » *See Activities and tours, page 102, and Transport, page 103.*

Llao Llao

Península Llao Llao, 25 km west of town, is a charming area for walking (see box, page 93) or for just appreciating the gorgeous views. The beautiful **Hotel Llao-Llao**, designed by Bustillo, is superbly situated on a hill with chocolate-box views. The hotel opened in 1937 as a wooden construction, but burned down within a few months and was rebuilt using local stone. It overlooks the **Capilla San Eduardo**, also designed by Bustillo, and **Puerto Pañuelo**, where boats leave for Puerto Blest. You can also take a **boat trip** ⓘ *half-day 1300-1830, full-day 0900-1830 or 1300-2000 in season, US$15*, from Puerto Pañuelo across Lago Nahuel Huapi to **Isla Victoria** and the Parque Nacional Los Arrayanes, on the Quetrihué peninsula (see page 88)

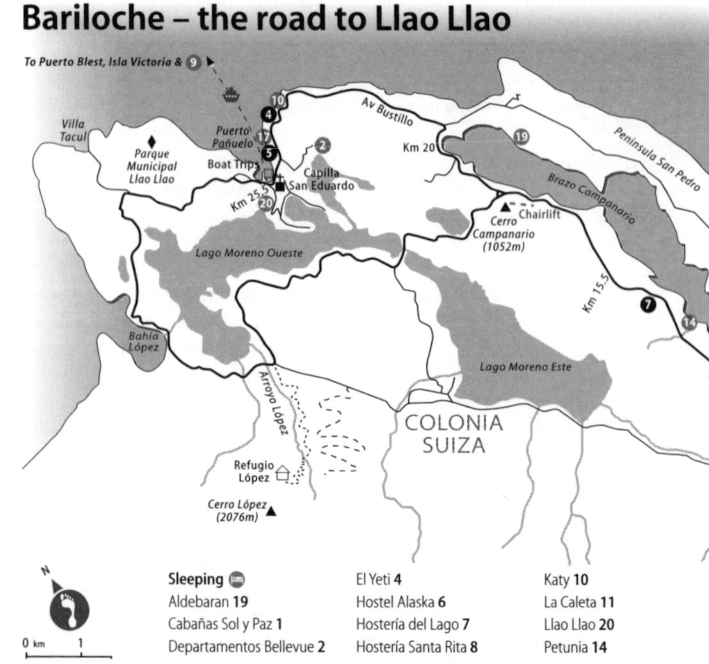

Puerto Blest

ⓘ *Tours by Catedral and Turisur (see Activities and tours, page 102). Departure time 0900. US$18, plus US$4 for bus transfer – a cheaper alternative is to take the 3 de Mayo bus at 0730 (US$0.70) to Puerto Pañuelo.*

The all-day boat trip from Puerto Pañuelo to Puerto Blest, at the western end of Lago Nahuel Huapi, is highly recommended. Boats are comfortable but fill up entirely in high season, so are much more pleasant in December and March. There's a good but expensive *cafetería* on board. The boat sails down the fjord-like Brazo Blest, with coihue-clad mountains dropping steeply into the Prussian blue water; it's usually raining, but very atmospheric. When you get to Puerto Blest, walk through beautiful forest to the **Cascada de los Cántaros** (one hour); set off while the rest of the party stops for lunch and you'll have time for your picnic by the falls before the crowd arrives by boat. The *guardaparques* can advise on other walks but the seven-hour 15-km trek to **Lago Ortiz Basualdo** is particularly recommended (summer only). From Puerto Blest, the tour continues by short bus ride to **Puerto Alegre** on Lago Frías and then crosses the peppermint-green lake by launch; for the continuation of the route into Chile, see below.

Three Lakes crossing to Chile

ⓘ *Tickets from Catedral Turismo, Palacios 263, www.crucedelagos.com. Book by 1900 the day before and further in advance during the high season. US$165 per person, plus lunch at Peulla (US$20). Credit cards accepted. Take passport when booking.*

This popular route to **Puerto Montt** in Chile, involving passenger ferries across Lago Nahuel Huapi, Lago Frías and Lago Todos Los Santos, is outstandingly beautiful whatever the season, though the mountains are often obscured by rain and heavy cloud. It's a long and tiring journey, however, and is not recommended in torrential downpours. The route is from Bariloche to Puerto Pañuelo by road, Puerto Pañuelo to Puerto Blest by boat (1½ hours), Puerto Blest to Puerto Alegre on Lago Frías by bus,

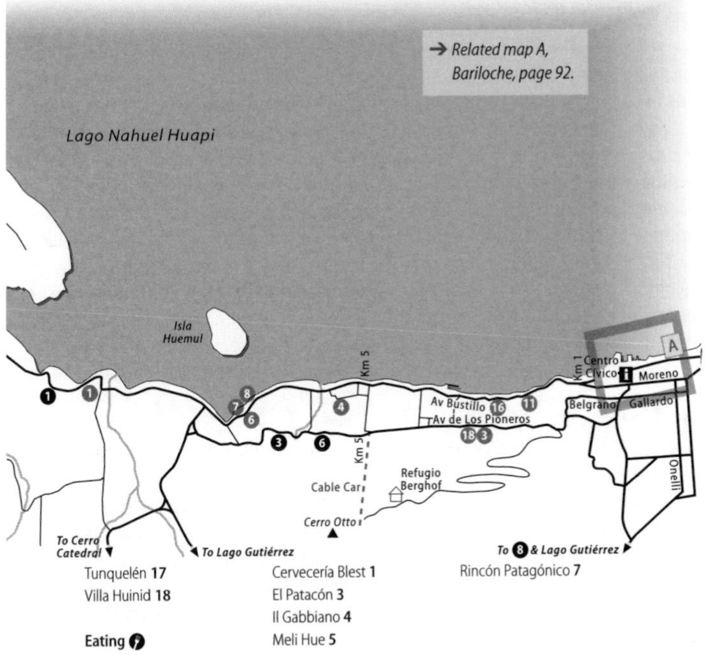

 Puerto Alegre to Puerto Frías by boat (20 minutes), then 1½ hours by road from Puerto Frías, via **Paso Pérez Rosales**, to Peulla in Chile. Cross Lago Todos Los Santos in the afternoon from Peulla to Petrohué (2½ hours), then continue by bus, via the Petrohué falls, Ensenada and Puerto Varas, to Puerto Montt.

Tickets are available from various operators, but all trips are run by **Catedral Turismo**, who own the exclusive rights, in collaboration with **Andina del Sud** on the Chilean side (see page 233). The journey can be done in one or two days: the one-day crossing (1 September to 30 April) includes a two-hour lunch stop in Peulla during the summer but does not allow you to return to Bariloche the next day. For the two-day crossing (all year round), there is an overnight stop in Peulla. Alternatively, you could do the first section from Puerto Pañuelo to Puerto Blest and Lago Frías, on a regular day trip. Note that the launches (and hence the connecting buses) on the lakes serving the direct route via Puerto Blest to Puerto Montt generally do not operate at weekends. You can't take a bike from Puerto Blest to Lago Frias, 'due to the highest level of eco protection'. » *For details of onward or return transport from Puerto Montt, see page 239.*

Towards Mount Tronador » *pp98-104.*

Lago Gutiérrez → *Colour map 1, B3*

From Bariloche, Route 258 passes the picturesque **Lago Gutiérrez**, which feels like a fjord, with mountains dropping steeply into its western side and spectacular views all around. There are many ways to access the lake, including hiking/cycling trails from Cerro Catedral or **Refugio Frey**, and it can be explored on foot or bike almost all the way round. Watersports can be practised here in summer. However, by far the best option is to stay at luxurious **Estancia Peuma Hue**, which lies right on the lakeshore and has exclusive access to hiking and riding trails, as well as offering boats and kayaks on the lake (see Sleeping, page 100).

Lago Mascardi → *Colour map 1, B3*

Route 258 continues to Lago Mascardi with its backdrop of grand jagged mountains, around which there are many places to stay and to walk, all easily reached by car (or by bus in summer). There are also boat trips across Lago Mascardi (see Activities and tours, page 102). At the southern end of the lake, **Villa Mascardi** is a small village from where a *ripio* Route 81 with a **one-way system** ⓘ *access going west 1000-1400, going east 1600-1800, 2-way 1900-0900, times may vary, so check with the tourist office, T02944-423022*, runs towards Cerro Tronador and Cascada Los Alerces. A few kilometres west of the Lago Mascardi turn-off is an entrance into the national park, US$4 for foreigners. At Km 10 is the lovely straight beach of **Playa Negro**, handy for launching boats and fishing; opposite is the peaceful **Camping La Querencia** (see Sleeping, page 100). Shortly afterwards, the road forks, with the right-hand branch following a narrow arm of Lago Mascardi towards Tronador. There's a viewpoint in pretty woodland, from where you can see **Isla Piuke Huapi** at the centre of the lake.

Lago Hess and around → *Colour map 1, B3*

The left-hand fork runs for 18 km through the beautiful valley of the **Río Manso Medio** to **Lago Hess** and on to the nearby **Cascada Los Alerces**. Lago Hess is a beautiful spot for a picnic, with good camping at **Camping Los Rapidos** (see Sleeping, page 100). It is also the starting point for trekking excursions in a remote area of small lakes and forested mountains, including lagos Fonck, Roca, Felipe and Cerros Granito and Fortaleza. Check with *guardaparques* at Lago Hess about conditions on the paths. Río Manso offers some of the best rafting in Argentina, with sections of river suitable for all levels. » *See Activities and tours, page 102.*

Pampa Linda → *Colour map 1, B3*

The quiet hamlet of Pampa Linda lies 40 km west of Villa Mascardi in the most blissfully isolated location, with spectacular views of Mount Tronador towering above. There's a ranger station with very helpful *guardaparques*, who can advise on the state of the trails and with whom you must register before trekking in the area. A good way to see the area is to take a tour with an agency from Bariloche, and then stay on at Pampa Linda for more trekking, before returning to Bariloche with the minibus service (3½ hours, US$8) run by **Transitando lo Natural** (see Activities and tours, page 103).

From Pampa Linda, a lovely track (*ripio*) leads to **Ventisquero Negro**, a rather filthy-looking glacier that hangs over a fantastically murky pool in which grey icebergs float. The colour is due to sediment and, while not exactly attractive, the whole scene is very atmospheric. The road ends at the **Garganta del Diablo**, one of the natural amphitheatres formed by the lower slopes of Mount Tronador. A beautiful walk (1½ hours there and back) from the car park through beech forest takes you to a more pristine glacier and up to the head of the gorge, where thin torrents of ice water fall in columns from the hanging glacier above.

Mount Tronador → *Colour map 1, B3*

Mighty Mount Tronador (3478 m) overshadows Pampa Linda, and can be visited in a good day's tour from Bariloche, taking in the beautiful Lagos Gutierrez and Mascardi and stopping for lunch at **Hostería Pampa Linda**. From Pampa Linda two paths head up the mountain: the first leads to a *refugio* on the south side, while the other leads to **Refugio Otto Meiling** (15 km, five hours each way), situated at 2000 m on the edge of the eastern glacier. Follow the path for another hour from the *refugio* for a view over Tronador and the lakes and mountains of the national park. Otto Meiling is a good base camp for the ascent, with lots of facilities and activities, including trekking and ice climbing; always ask the *guardaparques* in Pampa Linda if there's space (capacity 60).

Paso de los Nubes → *Colour map 1, B3*

Pampa Linda is also the starting point for a 22 km walk over Paso de los Nubes (1335 m) to **Laguna Frías** and **Puerto Frías** on the Chilean border. The spectacular glacial landscape was formed relatively recently (11,000 years ago). The pass lies on the continental divide, with water flowing north to the Atlantic and south to the Pacific. Views from the Río Frías valley are tremendous, and from Glacier Frías you enter Valdivian rainforest. Allow at least two days for the whole route: camping is available after four hours or after seven hours; then it's another five hours to Puerto Frías. You must register with *guardaparques* at Pampa Linda before setting out and check with them about conditions. The route should only be attempted if there is no snow on the pass (normally December to February only) and when the path is not excessively boggy. For further information, refer to the excellent leaflet produced by Parque Nacional Nahuel Huapi. From Puerto Frías a 30-km road leads to Peulla in Chile on the shore of Lago Todos Los Santos (see page 220), or you can take a boat back across Lago Frías and Lago Nahuel Huapi to Bariloche; three times a day in summer (check this before you leave Bariloche).

Border with Chile

Paso Pérez Rosales is west of Puerto Frías and is the crossing used by buses on the 'Three Lakes' route between Bariloche and Puerto Montt (see page 95). If you plan to make this crossing independently be prepared for some long walks, as cars are not carried on the ferries and it is impossible to buy a separate bus ticket from the border to Peulla, 26 km west.

Argentine immigration and customs ⓘ *Puerto Frías, open all year.* **Chilean immigration and customs** ⓘ *Peulla, daily summer 0800-2100, winter 0800-2000.* Chilean currency can be bought at Peulla customs at a reasonable rate.

Lago Steffen and Lago Martín → *Colour map 1, B3*

About 20 km south of Villa Mascardi, a one-way dirt road leads to Lago Steffen, where a footpath runs along both northern and southern shores of Lago Steffen to Lago Martín. Both lakes are quite outstandingly lovely, fringed with beech and alamo trees, with far-off mountains in the distance and pretty beaches where you can sit at the waters' edge. There's also great fishing here. Further south, a road leads west along the **Río Manso Inferior** towards Chile. There is excellent rafting on the river (Grade II or III), through lush vegetation, towards the Chilean border. **Extremo Sur** and **Aguas Blancas** run full-day trips and three-day expeditions from Bariloche. » *See Activities and tours, page 102.*

Sleeping

Bariloche *p92, map p92*

Prices rise in Jul-Aug for skiing, and mid-Dec to Mar for summer holidays. Prices given are lake-view high-season prices where applicable. If you arrive in the high season without a reservation, consult the listing published by the tourist office. In Jul and Oct- Dec, avoid the following hotels, which specialize in school trips: Ayelén, Bariloche Ski, Interlaken, Millaray, Montana, Piedras and Pucón.

L **Edelweiss,** San Martín 202, T02944- 445500, www.edelweiss.com.ar. A smart international 5-star with real attention to detail. Rooms are well furnished, spacious and comfortable. Good suites for families. Facilities include Wi-Fi, indoor pool, beauty salon and restaurant, **La Tavola**. Excellent service from bilingual staff. Prices are halved in low season, good value.

A-C **Hostería Tirol**, Libertad 175, T02944-426152, www.hosteriatirol.com.ar. Very neat and friendly family-run hotel just a block from the civic centre, with nice Tirolean touches in the clean welcoming rooms, and warm attention from the owners. Wi-Fi. Excellent value in low season.

B **La Pastorella**, Belgrano 127, T02944-424656, www.lapastorella.com.ar. A cosy, quaint little *hostería*, whose very welcoming owners speak English. Recommended.

B **Tres Reyes**, 12 de Octubre 135, T02944-426121, hreyes@bariloche.com.ar. Traditional lakeside hotel with spacious rooms and lounge with splendid views, all recently modernized, friendly English-speaking staff.

C **Premier**, Rolando 263, T02944-426168, www.premierhotel.com.ar. Good economical choice in centre of town, with a light spacious entrance and gallery, with neat modern rooms with bath and TV, friendly owners, internet, English spoken. Recommended.

D **Hostería Güemes**, Güemes 715, T02944-424785. A lovely quiet B&B in a residential area, with lots of space, very welcoming, all the simple rooms have bath, breakfast is included, and the owner is a fishing expert.

D **Piuké**, Beschtedt 136, T02944-423044. A delightful little B&B, with simple well-decorated rooms with bath, breakfast included. Excellent value.

D **Refugio Neumeyer**, 20 de Junio 728, 12 km south of Bariloche, T02944-428995, www.eco-family.com. Not as luxurious as an estancia, but with many of the benefits. This mountain lodge has comfortable shared accommodation and rooms for families. All kinds of activities led by expert guides. Regional cooking in the restaurant. Recommended.

E **Res No Me Olvides**, Av Los Pioneros Km 1, T02944-429140, 30 mins' walk or bus No 50/51 to corner of C Videla then follow signs. Beautiful house in quiet surroundings, use of kitchen, camping. Recommended.

Youth hostels

Bariloche has many good quality hostels, all charging around US$8 for a bed in a dorm.

E pp **La Bolsa**, Palacios 405 (y Elflein), T02944-423529, www.labolsadeldeporte.com. Recommended for its friendly relaxed atmosphere, homely rustic rooms (some with lake views), and a great deck to sit out on.

E pp **Patagonia Andina**, Morales 564, T02944-421861, www.elpatagoniaandina.com.ar. A quiet place with comfortable dorms, and double/twin rooms with shared bath. Well-equipped small kitchen, TV area, sheets included, breakfast extra, internet, advice on trekking, good atmosphere.

E pp **Periko's**, Morales 555, T02944-522326, www.perikos.com. A warm and friendly atmosphere, quiet, with an *asado* every Fri. Towels and sheets included, breakfast extra. Use of kitchen, and laundry, airy rustic rooms for 4, single sex, with bathroom. Also doubles with private bath. Garden, free internet access, can also organize horse riding, rents mountain bikes. Highly recommended.

E pp **Ruca Hueney**, Elflein 396, T02944-433986, rucahueney@bariloche.com.ar. A lovely calm and welcoming place, with comfortable beds and duvets. Spotless kitchen, quiet place to sit and eat. Fabulous double room with bathroom and great view. Also Spanish school. Highly recommended.

F pp **Albergue El Gaucho**, Belgrano 209, T02944-522464, www.hostelgaucho.com.ar. Welcoming modern place in quiet part of town, run by a very friendly German couple, offering some doubles with private bath, **E** pp. English, German and Italian spoken.

The road to Llao Llao *p94, map p94*

There are many *hosterías*, *cabañas* and campsites along Av Bustillo on the shore of Lago Nahuel Huapi. Take buses 10, 11, 20, 21.

LL Llao Llao, Av Bustillo, Km 25, T02944-448530, www.llaollao.com. Deservedly famous, one of the world's most wonderful hotels in a superb location, with panoramic views from its perfect gardens, golf course, gorgeous spa suite, pools, water sports, superb restaurants. Excellent services, but some complaints about tiny rooms. Pay the extra for more space and a view.

L Aldebaran, Península San Pedro, reached from Av Bustillo, Km 20.4, T02944- 465132, www.aldebaranpatagonia.com. A modern boutique hotel right on the rocky lake shore. Exquisite taste in warm stylish minimalist rooms and superb views across the lake. Chic food in the rustic-style restaurant, wonderful sauna and spa with outdoor pool, so you can bask under the stars. Great service from helpful bilingual staff. Highly recommended.

L Design Suites, 2.5 km from Bariloche centre, Av Bustillo, T02944-457000, www.design suites.com. Refreshingly modern, with wonderful bold design in glass and wood in the stylish bar and restaurant area. Huge spacious rooms, some with window-side jacuzzis, all very comfortable. Great spa and gym, kids' room, friendly bilingual staff, and excellent food in the bar and restaurant. Warmly recommended. Book ahead.

L Isla Victoria Resort, www.islavictoria.com. On Isla Victoria just off the coast, this is really something special with spectacular island scenery, a pool, sauna, spacious and cosy places to sit and relax, riding and trekking organized all over the beautiful island, good food. A fabulous and romantic treat.

L Tunquelén, Av Bustillo, Km 24.5, T02944-448400, www.maresur.com.ar. A comfortable 4-star hotel, on the lakeside near Llao Llao, with splendid views and a secluded feel – wilder and closer to nature than **Llao Llao**. Well-decorated cottage-style rooms, attentive service, superb food, warmly recommended. Much cheaper if you stay 4 days.

L Villa Huinid, Av Bustillo Km 2.5, T02944-523523, www.villahuninid.com.ar. Recommended luxurious *cabanas* for 2-8, beautifully furnished, and well equipped.

A Hostería del Lago, Av Bustillo, Km 7.8, T02944-525044, www.hosteriadellago. com.ar. Lovely traditional and welcoming chalet style *hostería*, on the beach, with great views of Isla Huemul, and Península San Pedro, this is particularly good value in low season, and a charming place to stay.

A-B Departamentos Bellevue, Av Bustillo, Km 24.6, T02944-448389, www.belle vue.com.ar. The famous tea room with the most beautiful view in Bariloche now has 3 extremely comfortable self-catering *cabañas* with high-quality furnishings. Access to beaches on the lake, gorgeous gardens and native forest. Delicious breakfast included. Highly recommended.

B Cabañas Sol y Paz, Av Bustillo, Km 10.63, T02944-462784, www.solypazbariloche.com.ar. Pretty *cabañas* in chalet style with lovely views of the mountains. Welcoming owner.

B La Caleta, Av Bustillo, Km 1.9, T02944-443444, bungalows@bariloche.com.ar. *Cabañas* sleep 4, open fire, excellent value.

C Hosteria Santa Rita, Av Bustillo, Km 7.2, bus 10, 20, 21 to Km 7.5. T/F02944-461028, www.santarita.com.ar. Close to the centre, but with comfortable rooms, peaceful lakeside views, lovely terrace, and great service. Warmly recommended.

C Katy, Av Bustillo, Km 24.3, T02944-448023 adikastelic@yahoo.com. A delightful peaceful place in a garden full of flowers, charming family, breakfast included. Also runs adventure tours, www.gringospatagonia.com.

E pp **Hostel Alaska**, Av Bustillo, Km 7.5, bus 10, 20, 21, T02944-461564, www.alaska-hostel.com. Well-run, cosy HI chalet-style hostel open all year, doubles and dorms. Kitchen facilities, internet, rafting and riding.

Camping

A complete list is available from the tourist office www.bariloche.org.

El Yeti, Av Bustillo, Km 5.8, T02944-442073, gerezjc@bariloche.com.ar. Pretty, also *cabañas*.

Petunia, Av Bustillo, Km 13.5, T02944-461969, www.campingpetunia.com. Well protected by trees, a lovely shady lakeside site with beach, all facilities and restaurant, and shop, recommended, also *cabañas*.

Selva Negra, Av Bustillo, Km 2.9, T02944-441013. Very attractive well-equipped site, highly recommended.

Lago Gutiérrez *p96*

AL **Estancia Peuma Hue**, on the southern shore of Lago Gutiérrez, 3 km off the road, T02944-501030, www.peuma-hue.com. One of the finest places to stay in the area, with a gorgeous rural setting on 2 km of private shoreline at the foot of Cerro Catedral Sur. Luxurious accommodation in 2 beautiful country houses and a mountain cabin. Prices include meals and activities such as trekking into virgin forest, horse riding, exploring the lake in kayaks, and rafting on the Ríos Mansos, massage, yoga. Rooms are decorated with great panache, and have wonderful views from huge windows. Jacuzzi under the stars. Delicious food. Highly recommended.

AL **El Retorno**, Villa Los Coihues, northern shore, T02944-467333, www.hosteriael retorno.com. With a stunning lakeside position, this is a traditional family-run hotel has lovely gardens running down to the beach, tennis courts and comfortable rooms. Also a restaurant. Very relaxing.

Camping

Villa los Coihues, by the lake, T02944-467479. Well-equipped and beautifully situated.

Lago Mascardi and around *p96*

A pp **Hotel Tronador**, T02944-441062, www.hoteltronador.com. A lakeside paradise, the lovely rooms have terrific lake views from their balconies, there are beautiful gardens, and a charming owner. It's a really peaceful place. Riding, fishing and excursions on the lake. Highly recommended.

B **Mascardi**, Km 36.8, towards Tronador, T02944-490518, www.mascardi.com. A few kilometres from the turning is this luxurious place with a delightful setting in lovely gardens on its own beach by the lake. Restaurant and tea room, horse riding, mountains bikes, rafting and fly fishing.

Camping

Camping La Querencia, T02944-426225, RN 258, Km 10. A pretty and peaceful spot on the side of a river, opposite the lovely straight beach of Playa Negro.

Camping Las Carpitas, Km 33, T02944-490527. Set in a great lakeside position, summer only, *cabañas* and restaurant.

Camping Los Rapidos, T/F02944-461861. Attractive site going down to the lake, with *confitería*, food store and all facilities, US$2.50pp. Also basic *albergue* US$3pp (sleeping bag needed). Trekking, kayaking, fishing and mountain bikes.

Pampa Linda *p97*

D **Hostería Pampa Linda**, T02944-442038, www.tronador.com. Comfortable retreat and a good base for trekking. Simple rooms, all with bath and stunning views. The owners are charming; Sebastian de la Cruz is one of the area's most experienced mountaineers. Horse riding, trekking and climbing courses. Full board and packed lunches available.

Camping

Pampa Linda, T02944-424531. Idyllic lakeside site, *confitería* and food shop.

Eating

Bariloche *p92, map p92*

Bariloche is famous for locally smoked trout and salmon, and for wild boar, there are other delicacies to be sampled too, like the berries in season, and the fine chocolate.

TTT **Cassis**, opposite Arelauquen golf club, just off Route 82, call first for directions, T02944-431382, www.cassis-patagonia.com.ar. Without a doubt Bariloche's finest restaurant, with a stunning setting right on Lago Gutiérrez, in secluded gardens. Amazing food including exquisite local delicacies. Highly recommended. Open evenings only except in high season. Book ahead.

TTT **Chez Philippe**, Primera Junta 1080, T02944-427291. Delicious local delicacies, really fine French-influenced cuisine, and delicious fondue, in this cosy place with a living room feel. Book ahead.

Dias de Zapata, Morales 362, T02944-423128. Great atmosphere. The Mexican food is tasty but not remotely spicy. The staff are welcoming. Recommended.

Familia Weiss, also Palacios y VA O'Connor. Excellent local specialities in chalet-style splendour, with live music. The wild boar is particularly recommended. US$6, menu US$4.

Hasta Que Llegue el Tren, next to the train station 3km from centre, 12 de Octubre 2,400, T02944-457200. Tasty food such as Patagonian ostrich, lamb and quail, with great wine list. Frequently recommended.

Jauja, Quaglia 366, T02944-422952. Specializes in local delicacies such as local trout and wild boar. Friendly and good value. Recommended.

Kandahar, 20 de Febrero 698, T02944-424702. Highly recommended for its excellent food and intimate warm atmosphere. Reserve in high season. Dinner only. Argentine dishes, and other imaginative cuisine served in style, in a cosy place, run by ski champion Marta Peirono de Barber, superb wines. The pisco sour are recommended. US$7 for 2 courses.

La Marmite, Mitre 329. A cosy place with good service, perfect for a huge range of fondues, good wild boar and delicious cakes for tea too. Recommended, US$5.

Vegetariano, 20 de Febrero 730, T02944-421820. Also serves fish in its excellent set menu, beautifully served in a warm friendly atmosphere. Highly recommended.

Friends, Mitre 302. A good lively café on the main street, convenient for lunch, open 24 hrs, US$3 for dinner.

La Jirafa, Palacios 288. A cheery family-run place for good food, good value, US$3.

Rock Chicken, Quaglia y Moreno. Small, busy, good value fast food (also takeaway).

Simoca, Palacios 264. Recommended for delicious and cheap Tucumán specialities, such as *humitas* and huge *empanadas*, US$3.

The road to Llao Llao *p94, map p94*

Il Gabbiano, Av Bustillo, Km 24.3, T02944-448346. Excellent Italian food in this intimate restaurant on the lakeside. Delicious trout and sea food and extensive wine list. Booking essential. Closed Tue. Highly recommended.

Bellevue, Av Bustillo Km 24.6, same location as **Departamentos Bellevue** (see Sleeping) T02944-448389, Wed-Sun 1600-2000. The best tearoom, perched high up among lovely gardens with incredible views. It's worth a special trip on the bus to taste the raspberry cheesecake and chocolate cake. A real treat.

Punta Bustillo, Av Bustillo, Km 5.8, T02944-442782, www.puntabustillo.com.ar. Very cutesy chalet-style exterior, but the food is great. Lots of steak, Patagonian lamb, wild boar, smoked delicacies, and locally brewed beer. Cosy, welcoming and a great wine list.

Rincón Patagónico, Av Bustillo, Km 14, T02944-463063. Traditional *parrilla*, with tasty Patagonian lamb cooked *al palo* speared over an open fire. Come out of season when there aren't huge coach loads.

Cerveceria Blest, Av Bustillo, Km 11.6, T02944- 461026, 1200-2400. Wonderful brewery with delicious beers (try La Trochita stout), imaginative local and German dishes in a rustic atmosphere. Recommended.

El Patacón, Av Bustillo Km 7, T02944-442898. Good *parrilla* and game.

El Boliche de Alberto, Villegas 347. Very good steak and live folklore music.

Meli Hue, Av Bustillo, Km 24.7, T02944-448029. Tearoom and B&B, in a lavender garden, selling fragrant produce. Lovely views.

Bars and clubs

Bariloche *p92, map p92*

Cerebro, JM de Rosas 406, T02944-424948, www.cerebro.com.ar. This is where everybody who doesn't go to **Roxy** goes.

La Esquina, Moreno 10. A traditional pub with good food and a relaxed atmosphere.

Pilgrim, Palacios 167, between O Connor and Mitre. Lively Irish pub with a good range of beers and decent regional dishes.

Roxy, San Martín 490, T02944-400451. Food, and then dancing from 0130. It's where everybody goes.

Wilkenny, San Martín 435, T02944-424444. Another Irish pub, also lively.

Shopping

Bariloche *p92, map p92*

The main commercial centre is on Mitre between the Centro Civíco and Beschtedt. The local chocolate is excellent; try **Abuela Goye**, Mitre 258; **Mamushka**, Mitre 216; and **Fenoglio**, Mitre 301 y Rolando.

Arbol, Mitre in the 400 block. Good quality outdoor gear, clothes and gifts.

La Barca Libros, Quaglia 247, T02944-423170, www.patagonialibros.com. Bookshop with a wonderful range on Patagonia, good selection in English.
Martin Pescador, Rolando 257, T02944-422 2275, Also at Cerro Catedral in winter. Fishing, camping and skiing gear.
Patagonia Outdoors, Elflein 27, T02944-426768, www.patagonia-outdoors.com.ar Maps and loads of equipment, plus adventure tours, trekking and rafting.

Activities and tours

Bariloche *p92, map p92*

Most agencies in Bariloche charge the same. They get very booked up in season, and many trips only run in Jan and Feb.

Tours include: San Martín de los Andes, (360 km) US$25, via the Seven Lakes Drive and returning via Paso de Córdoba and the Valle Encantado, 12-hr minibus excursions. There are also tours around the Circuito Chico (60 km), US$8, half-day. 'Cerro Tronador' (they mean a view of Tronador, not climbing it) and Cascada los Alerces full day (255 km) U$20, El Bolsón full day (300 km, including Lago Puelo) US$22. Whole-day excursions to Lagos Gutiérrez, Mascardi, Hess, the Cascada Los Alerces and Cerro Tronador and the Ventisquero Negro, leaving at 0800, US$32, lots of time spent on the bus. Useful as a way to get to walks at Pampa Linda if the bus from **CAB** isn't running.

Boat trips

Catedral Turismo, Palacios 263, T02944-425444. Tickets for the crossing to Puerto Montt in Chile, www.crucedelagos.com, see page 95 and Transport, page 103. US$178 for one day; US$220 for 2 days.
Turisur, Mitre 219, T02944-426109, www.bariloche.com/turisur, offers trips from Puerto Pañuelo to Isla Victoria and Bosque de Arrayanes full or half-day US$11/US$16; to Puerto Blest and Lago Frías full day, including buses, US$20. Also offers conventional tours.

Cycling

This is a great area for mountain biking, with some challenging descents. **CAB** (see under Trekking) has detailed maps and advice on where to go. Also contact Diego Rodriguez, www.adventure-tours-south.com.
Dirty Bikes, V O'Connor 681, T02944- 425616, www.dirtybikes.com.ar. Very helpful for repairs, if pricey. Also guided excursions on bikes, with bikes for hire. Recommended.
Diversidad, 20 de Junio 728, T02944-428995, www.eco-family.com. Excellent mountain biking around **Refugio Neumeyer**.
Huala, San Martín 66, T02944-522438, www.huala.com.ar. More unusual rides onto the steppe with trips to *chacras* (farms). Also amazing 12 day bike expedition to Traful via Villa la Angostura. Book well ahead as this is very popular. Also crossing by bike to Chile.

Fishing

Excellent trout fishing Nov-Mar (permits required); arrange boat hire with tackle shops. For guides, consult **AGPP**, T02944-421515, www.guiaspatagonicos.com/guias.
Baruzzi Deportes, Urquiza 250, T02944-424922, www.baruzzi.com. Guided fishing excursions (flycast, trolling, spinning) for experts and newcomers; US$150-300.
Martin Pescador, Rolando 257, T02944-422275, martinpescador@bariloche.com.ar. Great for fishing supplies (also camping and skiing) and excursions with experts.

Horse riding

Estancia Fortín Chacabuco, T02944-441766, www.estanciaspatagonicas.com. Superb riding for all levels, bilingual guides, lovely landscape east of Bariloche.
Tom Wesley, Bustillo km 15.5, T02944-448193, tomwesley@bariloche.com.ar. Relaxed ranch. Tuition and day rides.

Paragliding

Parapente Bariloche, T02944-462234, para pente@bariloche.com.ar. At Cerro Otto.

Rafting

Río Manso, south of Bariloche, offers some of the best rafting in Argentina, with sections of river suitable for all levels.
Aguas Blancas, Mitre 515, T02944-429940, www.aguasblancas.com.ar. Rafting on the Manso river with expert guides, equipment and lunch. Also bikes and horse riding.
Extremo Sur, Morales 765, T02944-427301, www.extremosur.com. Rafting and kayaking, all levels, full day all-inclusive packages offered, US$30 to US$50, or a 3-day trip for US$180 including accommodation.

Skiing

Cerro Catedral, T02944-460125, open mid-Jun to end Aug, ski lifts open 0900-1700, lift pass adults US$15 per day, see also page 94. One of South America's most important ski resorts, with 70 km of slopes of all grades, a total drop of 1010 m and 52 km of cross-country skiing routes. There are also snowboarding areas and a well-equipped base with hotels, restaurants, equipment hire, ski schools and nursery care. The resort is busiest from mid-Jul to mid-Aug.
Xtreme Snow Solutions, at the resort, T02944-460309, www.skipacks.com, has a ski school and equipment hire.

Tour operators

Active Patagonia, ask in Club Andino Bariloche, T02944-527966, www.activepatagonia.com.ar. Excellent company with very knowledgeable and well-trained guides. Produce good walking books. Recommended.
Diversidad, 20 de Junio 728, T02944-428995, www.eco-family.com. All kinds of adventures offered by this friendly company with a base in **Refugio Neumeyer**, 12 km south of Bariloche. Treks can be tailormade for you. Highly recommended.
Extremo Sur, Morales 765, T02944-427301, www.extremosur.com. Professional company offering rafting and kayaking, all levels, full day all-inclusive packages, and longer trips including accommodation.
Huala, San Martín 66, T02944-522438, www.huala.com.ar. Excellent company with all kinds of adventure tourism on offer: rafting, riding, climbing, biking, and more. English speaking guides. Highly recommended.
Sebastian de la Cruz, in Bariloche T02944-442038, pampalindaa@bariloche.com.ar. Renowned mountaineer, who owns the **Pampa Linda Hostería** (see Sleeping). Enormously knowledgeable. Recommended.
Transitando lo Natural 20 de Febrero 25, T02944-527926, transitando1@hotmail.com. Buses to Pampa Linda daily at 0900 in season, US$8, rafting, paragliding and horse riding.

Trekking and climbing

There's a good range of peaks around Bariloche, offering walks ranging from 3 hrs to several days (see box, page 93). The season runs Dec-Apr; winter storms can begin as early as Apr making climbing dangerous.
Club Andino Bariloche (**CAB**), 20 de Febrero 30, T02944-422266, www.clubandino.com.ar, Mon-Fri 0900-1300, and 1600-2100 high season only. The club arranges guides; ask for a list. Its booklet *Guía de Sendas y Picadas* gives details of climbs and provides maps (1:150,000) and details of *refugios* and paths. There's also a book *Excursiones, Andinismo y Refugios de Montaña en Bariloche*, by Tonchek Arko, available in local shops, US$2.

Recommended trekking guides include: **Andescross.com**, T02944-467502, www.andescross.com; **Angel Fernandez**, T02944-524609, T156 09799; **Daniel Feinstein**, T/F02944-442259; and **Sebastian de la Cruz**, (see Tour operators).

Transport

Bariloche *p92, map p92*

Air

Aerolíneas Argentinas runs several flights a day to **Buenos Aires**, and to **El Calafate** (2 hrs) and **Ushuaia** (2 hrs) in summer. **LAN** also run flights to **Buenos Aires** and Chilean cities. **LADE** flies weekly to many destinations in Patagonia, including **Bahía Blanca, Comodoro Rivadavia, Mar del Plata, Puerto Madryn**; book well in advance in peak seasons. There are **LanChile** flights to/from **Santiago** (2 hrs) and **Puerto Montt** (45 mins).

Airline offices Aerolíneas Argentinas, Mitre y Villegas, T02944-423682, free phone T0810-222 86527, www.aerolineas.com. **LADE**, Mitre 531, 1st fl, T02944-423562. **LAN**, Moreno 234, 2nd fl, T02944-431043, www.lan.com.

Bus

The bus terminal, T02944-432860, has toilets, a *confiteria*, *kiosko* and phones. Left luggage US$1 per day. Frequent buses 10, 20, 21 to centre, US$1, and Av Bustillo, with **3 de Mayo**.

Local **3 de Mayo** buses leave from the big bus stop on Moreno y Rolando. Useful routes include: bus 20 to **Llao Llao**, for lakeside hotels and restaurants, every 20 mins, journey 45 mins, US$0.70; bus 10 to **Colonia Suiza** and **Bahia Lopez** for trekking; bus 50 to **Lago Gutiérrez**.

Bus marked 'Catedral' for **Cerro Catedral**, leaves from terminal or from Moreno y Palacios, every 90 mins, journey 35 mins, US$1. Bus to **Cerro Otto**, T02944-441031, leaves from hut at the Civic Centre, hourly 1030-1730 to connect with cable car, returning hourly 1115-1915, combined ticket for bus and cable car US$8 pp.

Long distance To **Buenos Aires**, several daily, 22½ hrs, US$60 *coche cama*, **Andesmar**. To **Bahía Blanca**, 3 companies, US$38. To **Mendoza**, US$38, **TAC** and **Andesmar**, 19 hrs, via Piedra de Aguila, Neuquén, Cipolleti and San Rafael. To **Esquel**, via El Bolsón, several companies, 4 hrs, US$8. To **Puerto Madryn**, 14 hrs, US$35 with **Mar y Vale** and **Don Otto**. To **San Martín de los Andes**, **Ko Ko**, 4 hrs, US$10. No direct bus to **Río Gallegos**; you have to spend a night in **Comodoro Rivadavia** en route: **Don Otto** daily, US$55, 14½ hrs. To **El Calafate**, ask at youth hostel **Alaska**, or **Periko's** about the *Safari Route 40*, a 4-day trip down Ruta 40 to **El Calafate** via the Perito Moreno national park, Cueva de Las Manos and Fitz Roy, staying at Estancia Melike and Río Mayo en route, US$128 plus accommodation at US$10 per day, www.visitbariloche.com/alaska.

To Chile To **Osorno** (4-6 hrs) and **Puerto Montt**, 7-8 hrs US$30, daily, **Bus Norte**, **Río de la Plata**, **TAS Choapa**, **Cruz del Sur**, **Andesmar** (sit on left side for best views). For **Santiago** or **Valdivia** change at Osorno.

Bus companies **3 de Mayo**, for local services, Moreno 480, T02944-425648; **Andesmar/Albus**, Mitre 385, T02944-430211, bus station T02944-430211; **Chevallier/La Estrella/Ko Ko**, Moreno 105, T02944-425914; **Cruz del Sur**, T02944-437699; **Don Otto/Río de La Plata**, 12 de Octubre T02944-437699; **Flechabus**, Moreno 107, T02944-423090, www.flechabus.com; **TAC**, Moreno 138, T02944-434727; **Vía Bariloche/El Valle**, Mitre 321, T02944-429012, www.viabariloche.com.

Car hire

Let your hire company know if you're planning to drive over the border into Chile, as you need a vehicle which has its registration number engraved on the windows, by law. Give 24 hrs. Rates are around US$40 a day. You can arrange to drop the car at San Martín de los Andes, or Esquel for an extra charge, from US$35. **Budget**, Mitre 106, 1st fl, T02944-426700, www.budgetbariloche.com.ar. **Localiza**, O' Connor 602, T02944-435374. **Rent a Car Bariloche**, Rolando 258, T02944-426420, www.rentacarbariloche.com.

Taxi

Puerto Remises, T0800-9990885 (freephone), **Radio Taxi Bariloche**, T02944-422103; **Remises Bariloche**, T02944- 430222.

Train

Booking office T02944-423172. Closed 1200-1500 weekdays, Sat afternoon and all Sun. Information from the tourist office. Tourist service to **Viedma** (16 hrs, US$35), also with sleeper section, and carries cars, T02944-423172, www.trenpatagonico.com.ar.

Lago Mascardi *p96*

Buses from Bariloche to **El Bolsón** pass through **Villa Mascardi**. Buses to **Los Rapidos** from the terminal in Bariloche, 0900, 1300, 1800 daily in summer.

Pampa Linda/Mount Tronador *p97*

Bus marked 'Tronador' departs from outside **CAB**, 20 de Febrero 28, daily Jan-Apr, and according to demand in Dec. Run by **Transitando lo Natural**, T02944-1560 8581, T02944-423918, 3½ hrs, US$8. From Pampa Linda you can often get a lift with an excursion trip returning to **Bariloche**, US$8.

Directory

Bariloche *p92, map p92*

Banks ATMs at many banks along Mitre. Exchange and TCs, best rates at *casas de cambio*: **Sudamérica**, Mitre 63, T02944-434555. **Consulates** **Chile**, Rosas 180, T02944-422842. **France**, T02944-441960. **Germany**, Ruiz Moreno 65, T02944-425695. **Italy**, Beschtedt 141, T02944-422247. **Switzerland**, Quaglia 342, T02944-426111. **Customs** Bariloche centre T02944-425216, Rincon (Argentina) T02944-425734, Pajarito (Chile) T002944- 236284. **Internet** Many along Mitre, and in the first block of Quaglia. **Immigration office** Libertad 191, T02944-423043, Mon-Fri 0900-1300. **Language schools** **La Montana**, Elflein 251, 1st fl, T02944-156 11872, www.lamontana.com. **Medical services** Dial 107 for emergencies, or San Carlos Emergencias, T02944-430000, Clinic: **Hospital Zonal**, Moreno 601, T02944-426100. **Post office** Moreno 175, Mon-Fri 0800-2000, Sat 0830- 1300. **Telephone** Many *locutorios* along Mitre, **Telecom** at Mitre y Rolando is helpful.

Southern Lake District

The southern end of the Lake District offers quite different scenery from that further north, with dense forests hugging the Andean foothills and contrasting with the Patagonian steppe further east. At the pretty and easy-going town of El Bolsón, there are beautiful rivers, waterfalls and mountains to explore, and a small national park, Lago Puelo, for fishing and walking. The pioneer town of Esquel is the southernmost centre in the lakes and can be reached via Cholila, a wild small settlement where Butch Cassidy hid out. From Esquel, you can explore the magnificent Parque Nacional Los Alerces, go skiing in winter, take a ride on La Trochita or visit the appealing Welsh pioneer village of Trevelin. » *For Sleeping, Eating and other listings see pages 111-116.*

El Bolsón and around » *pp111-116.*

El Bolsón is situated in a broad fertile valley 130 km south of Bariloche, surrounded by the mountains of the *cordillera* on either side, (hence its name: the big bowl), and dominated by the dramatic peak of **Cerro Piltriquitrón** (2284 m). With a river running close by and a warm sunny microclimate, it's a magical setting that inspired thousands of hippies to create an ideological community here in the 1970s. The result is a laid-back town with a welcoming, rather nonchalant atmosphere that still produces the handicrafts, home-brewed beers, fruit and jams for which the town is famous. There are many beautiful mountain walks and waterfalls nearby and swimming and rafting on Río Azul. The small national park of Lago Puelo is within easy reach, with fishing and walking, but if you'd rather just sit and relax, this is a wonderful place to spend a few days. The helpful and friendly **tourist office** ⓘ *San Martin y Roca, opposite the post office, T02944-492604, www.elbolson.gov.ar, daily 0900-2100 all year, till 2400 in summer*, is on the side of the semi-circular plaza and has plenty of English-speaking staff. They provide an excellent map of the town and the area and can suggest places to stay. **Club Andino Piltriquitrón** ⓘ *Sarmiento y Roca, T02944-492600, summer daily 0800-2200, otherwise closed*, can advise on hikes; all walkers must register here before setting off.

Around El Bolsón

There's an impressive long sweep of waterfalls at **Cascada Escondida**, 10 km northwest of town, a good place for a picnic, with a botanical garden and *casa de té* (tea room) nearby, serving delicious homemade beer, cakes and waffles. All along **Río Azul** are lovely places to bathe, camp and picnic. For a pleasant hour-long walk, with views over the town, climb **Cerro Amigo**. There are also good views from **Cabeza del Indio**, so called because the rock's profile resembles a face. It's a good 6-km drive or bike ride from the centre; take Azcuénaga west to cross the bridge over Río Quemquemtreu and follow signs. See also box, page 106.

Parque Nacional Lago Puelo → *Colour map 1, B3*

This lovely green and wooded national park is centred around the deep turquoise-coloured Lago Puelo, 18 km south of El Bolsón on the Chilean border, surrounded by southern beech forest. With relatively low altitude (200 m) and high rainfall, the forest is rich in tree species, particularly the arrayán and the pitra, coihues (evergreen beech) and cypresses. The lake is glorious in April, when the trees turn a vivid yellow. There's lots of wildlife, including the huemul, pudú and foxes, and the lake is known for its good fishing for trout and salmon. There are gentle walks on marked paths around the northern shore area, boat trips across the lake and canoes for rent.

The best walks around El Bolsón

For maps, guides and advice contact the tourist office or **Club Andino Pilquitrón**, see page 105.

→ **Cerro Piltriquitrón** (six to seven hours round trip if you walk all the way) Walk or drive 10 km east up winding roads towards the jagged peak that looms over the town. Then it's an hour's walk through the sculpture park of the Bosque Tallado to the mirador with fabulous views over the valley. Food and shelter are available at the refugio (1400 m).

→ **Cerros Lindo and Hielo Azul** (two days) Hike up Río Motoco, with **Refugio Motoco** at the top of the path, up Arroyo Lali to Cerro Lindo (2135 m), with **Refugio Cerro** Lindo at the top, and up to Cerro Hielo Azul (2270 m), also with a *refugio*. Club Andino Piltriquitrón has details of routes and transport.

→ **Cajón de Azul** (four hours one way) Walk up Río Azul, which flows from a deep canyon to the *refugio* along a well marked path. It's a bit hairy crossing the two wood and wire bridges, but worth it for a dip in the turquoise water on the way down. Set off early to allow for a leisurely lunch at the top, or spend the night in the *refugio*, with its lovely gardens. To start the walk, take a Nehuén minibus from Belgrano y Perito Moreno to Wharton, leaving El Bolsón at 0900. You'll be collected at 2000.

The main entrance is along a pretty road south from El Bolsón, through *chacras* (small farms) growing walnuts, hops and fruit, to **Villa Lago Puelo**, 3 km north of the park, where there are shops, plenty of accommodation and fuel. From here the road is unpaved. The **intendencia** ① *500 m north of the lake, T02944-499232, lagopuelo@apn.gov.ar, year round Mon-Fri 0800-1500*, has a booth at the pier in summer. Staff provide a helpful leaflet and can advise on walks. To the left of the entrance, **Bosque de las Sombras** (Forest of the Shadows), is a delightful overgrown forest, which you wander through on wooden walkways, on the way to the shingle beach at 'La Playita'. **Senda a los Hitos** (10-km, three hours each way) is a walk through marvellous woods to the rapids at Río Puelo on the Chilean border (passport required).

Entrance is also possible at **El Desemboque**, on the eastern side of the park: take the bus from El Bolsón to Esquel, alight at El Hoyo, then walk 14 km to El Desemboque. From El Desemboque, you can hike (seven hours) to **El Turbio**, where there's a *guardaparque*, and on to **Cerro Plataforma** (12 hours); allow three days for the whole trip. There's also a three-day trek through magnificent scenery to **Glaciar y Cerro Aguaja Sur**: get advice and directions from the *guardaparques* ▸▸ *For boat trips and fishing, see page 115.*

South towards Esquel ▸▸ *pp 111-116.*

Cholila → *Colour map 1, C3*

The peaceful scrappy village is sprawled out in a broad open landscape, surrounded by far off mountains. There is good fishing for those with a 4WD and a dedicated guide. Otherwise, your only reason for stopping in Cholila would be to see the wooden cabins where **Butch Cassidy** and the **Sundance Kid** hung out for six years (see box, page 108). The cabins were once rather evocative, falling to pieces, patched up with bits of wood and with a lichen-stained slatted roof. However, they are now being 'renovated' and have lost all their charm. It's not worth the long detour to get there (from Route 258 heading south from El Bolsón, towards Los Alerces national park's northern entrance; 13 km north of Cholila along Route 71, look out for a sign on the right, park by the little kiosk; US$1); head straight for Parque Nacional Los Alerces instead.

Leleque → *Colour map 1, C3*

Route 40 (paved) is a faster way to get from El Bolsón to Esquel and is the route that the bus takes. Stop off at Leleque to see the **Museum of Patagonia**ⓘ *off RN 40, Km 1440, Mar-Dec 1100-1700, Jan and Feb 1100-1900, closed Wed and May, Jun and Sep, US$1*, located in the vast estate owned by Benetton, the Italian knitwear company. There's a beautifully designed exhibition on the lives of indigenous peoples, with dwellings reconstructed of animal skins, using the original construction techniques, a huge collection of delicate arrowheads and the original *boleadoras* for catching cattle. Another moving exhibit highlights the first pioneers in Patagonia, especially the Welsh. And there's an attractive café in a reconstructed *boliche* (provisions shop and bar).

Esquel » *pp111-116.*

Esquel is a pleasant breezy town in a fertile valley with a dramatic backdrop of mountains. It was originally an offshoot of the Welsh colony at Chubut, 650 km to the east and still has a pioneer feel to it, thanks to the old-fashioned general stores and architecture from the early 1900s. It's a busy country town, not at all touristy and with few sights, but all the more appealing for that. It's the best base for visiting Parque Nacional Los Alerces and for skiing at La Hoya in winter. Esquel is also famous for the steam train *La Trochita*, immortalized by Paul Theroux as the *Old Patagonian Express*.

Ins and outs → *See map page 112. Colour map 1, C3.*

Getting there and around There's an airport 20 km east, reached by bus or taxi, and a smart modern bus terminal on Avenida Elver, six blocks from the main commercial centre around Avenida Fontana. Buses arrive here from Comodoro Rivadavia and Bariloche, with connections from those places to other destinations in Patagonia and to the north. Buses also run daily to Los Alerces national park. » *See also Transport, page 115.*

Tourist information The basic **tourist office**ⓘ *Alvear y Sarmiento, T02945-451927, www.esquel.gov.ar, www.esquelonline.com.ar, daily 0800-2000, summer 0730-2200, closed weekends off-season*, is friendly but has little information. It has a useful town map, however, with a plan of Los Alerces national park.

Sights

The town has two mildly interesting museums: the **Museo Indigenista y de Ciencias Naturales**ⓘ *Belgrano 330 y Chacabuco, Wed-Mon 1600-2000*, which has indigenous

Border with Chile

There are two border crossings south of Esquel. On the Chilean side, these crossings both link with route 7 north to Chaitén.

Paso Futaleufú lies 70 km southwest of Esquel via Route 259 (ripio from Trevelin) towards Futaleufú (see page 250). The border is a bridge over the Río Futaleufú. When entering Chile, change money in Futaleufú and then continue towards Puerto Ramírez; outside Ramírez, take the right turn to Chaitén, or you'll end up at Paso Palena. **Argentine immigration and customs**ⓘ on the Argentine side of the bridge; **Chilean immigration and customs**ⓘ at the border 9 km east of Futaleufú. Formalities should take no longer than an hour

Paso Palena lies 120 km southeast of Esquel and is reached by ripio Route 17, 26 km west of Corcovado. On the Chilean side, the road continues to Palena. **Argentine immigration and customs**ⓘ *at the border, daily 0900- 1800.* **Chilean immigration and customs** ⓘ *Palena, 8 km west of the border.*

Butch and Sundance

Butch Cassidy (real name Robert LeRoy Parker) and the Sundance Kid (Harry Longabaugh) pursued careers in which periods of legal employment was mixed with distinctly illegal activity. In the late 1890s they were part of a gang known variously as the Train Robbers' Syndicate, the Hole in the Wall Gang and the Wild Bunch, which operated out of a high valley on the borders of Utah, Colorado and Wyoming. Gang members specialized in hold-ups on railway payrolls and banks. In 1900 they celebrated the wedding of one of their colleagues by having their photo taken: a big mistake. The photo was recognized and, with their faces on 'Wanted' posters across the land, Cassidy, Sundance and his girlfriend Etta left for Argentina in February 1901.

Using the names Santiago Ryan and Harry Place, the outlaws settled on government land near Cholila but they were soon tracked down. They lay low, in the house which you can now visit (see page 106); but by 1905 it was time to move on. The gang raided banks in Villa Mercedes and Río Gallegos, posing as ranching company agents. They opened a bank account with US$7000, spent two weeks at the best hotels and socialized with the city's high society, and then entered the bank to close their accounts and empty the safe before escaping to Chile. At this point, Etta returned to the States.

No longer welcome in Argentina, Butch and Sundance moved to Bolivia, finding work at the Concordia tin mine. In 1908 they seized an Aramayo mining company payroll; with military patrols in pursuit and the Argentine and Chilean forces alerted, they rode into the village of San Vicente where they were besieged. The 1969 movie showed Butch and Sundance gunned down by the Bolivian army, but rumours have persisted that, having faked their deaths, they returned to the USA. Butch was said to have become a businessman, a rancher, a trapper and a Hollywood movie extra, while Sundance had run guns in the Mexican Revolution, migrated to Europe, fought for the Arabs against the Turks in the First World War, sold mineral water, founded a religious cult, and still found time to marry Etta. (Adapted from *Digging up Butch and Sundance* by Ann Meadows, London, 1996).

artefacts, and the **Museo de Arte Naíf** ⓘ *Av Fontana y Av Alvear,* which displays Argentine 'modern primitive' paintings. It's also the departure point for the famous narrow-gauge steam train, **La Trochita** ⓘ *Estación Viejo Expreso Patagonico, T02945-451403, www.latrochita.org.ar, Jan-Feb daily 0900, 1000, otherwise Sat 1000, 2½ hrs, US$30, tickets from tour operators, or station office*. Although it's a touristy experience, this is a thoroughly enjoyable trip, taking in the lovely valley and mountains of the *precordillera* framed through the windows of the quaint old train, with its wood stoves and little tea room. There's Spanish commentary along the way, and homemade cakes and handicrafts for sale at the Mapuche hamlet **Nahuel Pan**, where the train stops en route to El Maitén at the northern end of the line.

Trevelin » *pp111-116.*

The pretty village of Trevelin, 22 km southwest of Esquel, was once an offshoot of the Welsh colony in the Chubut valley (see box page 126). With a backdrop of snow-capped mountains, it's an appealing place to stay, with fishing and rafting on **Río Futuleufú**, and beautiful waterfalls at **Nant-y-fall**. The enthusiastic **tourist office** ⓘ *central plaza, T02945-480120, www.trevelin.org*, offers maps, accommodation and fishing advice.

Sights

The Welsh chapel of 1910, **La Capilla Bethel**, is now closed but the building can be seen from the outside. There is also a fine old flour mill dating from 1918, which houses the **Museo Histórico Regional** ⓘ *daily 1100-1800, US$1.30*, with fascinating artefacts from the Welsh colony. **El Tumbo del Caballo Malacara** ⓘ *200 m from plaza, tours US$2*, is a private house and garden that belonged to John Evans, one of the first settlers. The house contains his belongings and outside is the grave of his horse, Malacara, who once saved his life. Eisteddfods are still held in Trevelin every year and *té galés* (Welsh tea), including an excess of delicious cakes, is served at **Nain Maggie** tea rooms.

Around Trevelin

Molino Nant Fach ⓘ *RN 259, 22 km southwest towards the Chilean border, US$2.50*, is a beautiful flour mill built by Merfyn Evans, descendant of the town's founder Thomas Dalar Evans. It's an exact replica of the first mill built in 1899. Merfyn's fascinating tour (English booklets available) recounts a now familiar tale of the government's mismanagement of natural resources and industry, through the suppression of the Welsh prize-winning wheat industry. It's a beautiful spot and Merfyn tells the rather tragic story in a wonderfully entertaining way. The **Nant-y-fall Falls** ⓘ *US$4 including guide, 1½-hr walk*, lie 17 km southwest on the road to the border and are reached via an easy trail through the forest. The series of waterfalls is spectacular and the area is great for picnics. Both Molino Nant Fach and Nant-y-fall Falls are only accessible by car or on a tour.

Parque Nacional Los Alerces » pp111-116.

ⓘ *33 km west of Esquel, via ripio RN17, between Cholila and Trevelin, T02945-471020, www.parquesnacionales.gov.ar, US$4, daily bus along RN 71 stops at campsites and hosterías*. One of the most magnificent and untouched expanses of the whole Andes, this park was established to protect the tall and stately alerce trees (*Fitzroya cupressoides*) that grow deep in the Valdivian rainforest. Access is possible only at the eastern side of the park, via *ripio* Route 71, which runs along Lagos Futalaufquen, Verde and Rivadavia. The western side of the park, where rainfall is highest can only be accessed by boat or by hiking to Lago Krügger. The park offers several good treks, rafting and fishing, plus idyllic lakeside campsites and *hosterías*.

The park contains four major lakes: **Lago Rivadavia** at the northern entrance; vivid blue **Lago Futalaufquen**, with some of the best fishing in the area; **Lago Menéndez**, which can be crossed by boat to visit the ancient *alerce* trees, and the emerald-green **Lago Verde**. At the southern tip of Lago Futalaufquen is **Villa Futalaufquen**, a village with a visitor centre with useful information on the park. Helpful *guardaparques* at the *Intendencia* here give out maps and advise on walks. There is a service station, *locutorio*, two food shops and a restaurant.

Exploring the park → See map page 110.

From Puerto Limonao, there are boat trips across Lago Futalaufquen and along the pea-green **Río Arrayanes**, which is lined with extraordinary cinnamon-barked arrayán trees. Even more spectacular, is the trip from **Puerto Chucao** across **Lago Menéndez** (1½ hours) to see the majestic 2600-year-old alerce tree, known as *El Abuelo* at the lake's northwestern tip. From *El Abuelo*, walk to the hidden and silent, jade-green **Lago Cisne** and then back past the rushing white waters of Río Cisne. If walking, register with *guardaparques* before you set off; bear in mind that it takes 10 hours to reach the *refugio* at Lago Krügger. Camping is possible (one night only) at Playa Blanca, but fires are not permitted. Boat trips run frequently in high season (1 December to 31 March) and all can be booked through **Safari Lacustre**, www.brazosur.com, through **Patagonia Verde** (see page 115), or when you get to the piers, though tickets sell out in high season.

Walks

For all walks, get the *Sendas y Bosques* (walks and forests) map and book for El Bolsón, Lago Puelo and Los Alerces. Maps are 1:200,000, laminated and easy to read, and the book is full of great walks, with English summaries, and detailed directions in Spanish. www.guiasendasybosques.com.ar.

Cave paintings There are *pinturas rupestres* to be found just 40 minutes stroll from the park *Intendencia* (Km 1). Also a waterfall, and a mirador with panoramic views over Lago Futalaufquen.

Lago Verde The most beautiful walk in the park, and unmissable, is across the suspension bridge over Río Arrayanes (Km 34.3) to heavenly Lago Verde. A self-guided trail leads around a peninsula and to Lago Menéndez, to the pier where boat trips begin, Puerto Chucao. Go in the early evening, to see all kinds of bird life from the beach by Lago Verde, swifts and swallows darting all around you. Signposted off Route 71, Pasarella (walkway) Lago Verde. While you're in the area, take a quick 20-minute stroll up to **Mirador Lago Verde** where you'll be rewarded with gorgeous views up and down the whole valley and can appreciate the string of lakes, running from Lago Futalaufquen in the south, Lago Verde, and Lago Rivadavia in the north.

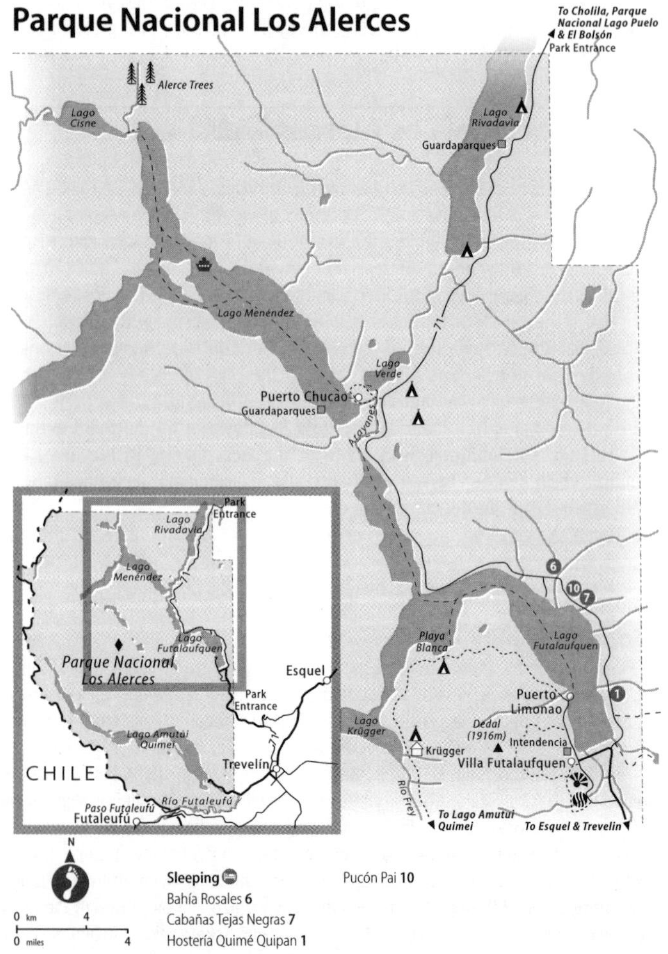

Cerro Dedal For a great day hike, there is a longer trek up Cerro Dedal (1916 m), a circular walk, at least eight hours return, with a steep climb from the *Intendencia*, and wonderful views over the lake and mountains further west. Register with *guardaparques* and get detailed instructions. You're required to start before 1000. Carry plenty of water.

Lago Krügger This is a rewarding two- to three-day (12- to 14-hour) hike though coihue forest to the southernmost tip of Lago Krügger, where there is a *refugio* (open only January and February), and campsite, as well as a *guardaparque's* office. Here you can take a boat back to Puerto Limonao; check it's running before you set off, and always register with the *Intendencia*. For information on the boat service, and the *refugio* contact **Hostería Lago Krügger**, www.lagokruger.com, a little rustic fishing lodge. US$60 for two, full board.

Sleeping

El Bolsón *p105*

There are *cabañas* and *hosterías* in beautiful settings in the Villa Turismo, 3 km southeast of the centre. Buses run by **Comarca Andina**, opposite Via Bariloche, T02944-455400.

C **Hostería Casa Blanca**, José Hernández y Onelli, T02944-493784, losalerces@elbolson.com. Charming chalet-style *hostería* with comfortable rooms with bath/TV. Good service.

C **La Casona de Odile**, Barrio Lujan, T02944-492753, odile@elbolson.com. A really special place to stay, in rustic wooden cabins in this idyllic lavender farm by a stream, with delicious French cooking. Recommended.

C **Sukal**, Villa Turismo, T02944-492438, www.sukal/elbolson.com. Gorgeous B&B, a haven of peace in a flower-filled garden, with glorious views. Also a *cabana*. Delightful.

D **La Posada de Hamelin**, Int Granollers 2179, T02944-492030, www.posadadehamelin.com.ar. Exceptionally welcoming with an outstanding breakfast, including homemade jams and cakes. Lovely chalet-style house with quaint and comfortable rooms all with bathroom, very central. Highly recommended.

D **Hostería Steiner**, San Martín 670, T02944-492224. Worth going out of the centre to this peaceful place with huge lovely gardens, simple rooms, wood fires. Recommended.

D **Valle Nuevo**, 25 de Mayo y Belgrano, T02944-1560 2325. Small and basic rooms in this quiet place, good value but no breakfast.

E pp **Refugio Patagónico**, Islas Malvinas y Pastorino, T02944-1563 5463, diegogfe@hotmail.com. High-quality hostel, with small dorms with bathrooms, in a spacious house with great views of Piltriquitrón, 5 blocks from the plaza. Recommended. Camping possible.

E pp **Sol del Valle**, 25 de Mayo 2329, T02944-492087. A bright hostel with basic rooms, shared bathrooms, big kitchen and a garden with views of Piltriquitrón.

F **Altos del Sur**, Villa Turismo, T02944-498730, www.altosdelsur.bolsonweb.com. In a lovely setting with beautiful views, this peaceful hostel has shared rooms, and an en suite double, **D**. Breakfast included, dinner available. Highly recommended.

Cabañas

These cost around US$40 per night for 5 people in the Villa Turismo.

Cabañas Paraíso, T02944-492766, www.cabanasparaiso.com.ar. Lovely wooden cabins in a gorgeous setting. Pool, good service.

La Montana, T02944-492776, www.montana.com.ar. Well equipped smart *cabañas* with pool and play area.

Los Teros, off the road leading up via Los Tres Cipreses, T02944-455 5569, www.cabañaslosteros.com.ar. Lovely cabins, well spaced in park land with good views. Recommended.

Camping

Arco Iris, T02944-15558330. Blissful wooded site near Rio Azul, helpful owners.

La Chacra, Belgrano 1128, T02944-492111. 15 mins walk from town, well shaded, good facilities, lively in season.

Quem Quem, Rio Quemquemtreu, T02944-493550, quemquem@elbolson.com. Well-kept with hot showers, pick-up from town.

Parque Nacional Lago Puelo *p105*

There are lots of *cabañas*, shops and fuel. Apart from wild camping, there's no accommodation in the park itself, but plenty in Villa Lago Puelo, just outside, with *cabañas*, restaurants and campsites spread out along RN 16 through the little village.

Cabañas

A Lodge Casa Puelo, RN 16, T02944-499539, www.casapuelo.com.ar. *Cabañas* for up to 6. Beautifully designed rooms and self-catering cabins in forested mountains. The owner knows the local area intimately. Free internet. Very comfortable. Recommended.

B Río Azul, RN 16, T02944-499345, www.complejoazul.com. Beautifully designed rooms in pretty area next to Río Azul, with gardens, Swimming pools, volley ball,

B-C Frontera, off the main road to Esquel, T02944-473092, www.frontera-patagonia.com.ar. *Cabañas* for 4 and a *hostería*, furnished to a very high standard, in a lovely building in isolated woodland. Delicious meals.

C La Yoica, just off RN 16, Km 5, T02944-499200, www.layoica.com.ar. Charming Scottish owners make you feel at home in these lovely traditional cabañas set in lovely countryside with great views.

C San Jorge, a block from the main street, on Plaza Ilia, T02944-491313, www.elbolson.com/sanjorge. Excellent value, these neat little self-catering apartments in a pretty garden, with friendly helpful owners.

Cholila *p106*

A-B pp **Hostería La Rinconada**, T02945-498091, larinconada@interlink.com.ar. Meals and excursions available.

C pp **El Trébol**, Lago Los Mosquistos, T02945-498055, eltrebol@teletel.com.ar Comfortable rooms with stoves, meals available, popular with fishing expeditions, reservations advised.

D Cabanas Cerro La Momia, RN71 in Villa Rivadavia, T0297-446 1796, www.cabanascerrolamomia.com.ar. Peaceful setting, basic *cabañas*, but breakfast is included.

Esquel *p107, map below*

A-B Cumbres Blancas, Ameghino 1683, T/F02945-455100, www.cpatagonia.com/esq/cblancas. A little out of town, with great views, comfortable traditional rooms and an airy restaurant serving dinner US$7.

B Angelina, Alvear 758, T02945-452763. A warm welcoming place, open high season only, serving good food.

B Canela, C Los Notros, Villa Ayelén, T02945-453890, www.canela-patagonia.com. Helpful, comfortable B&B and tearoom.

C La Tour D'Argent, San Martín 1063, T02945-454612, www.cpatagonia.com/esq/latour. The bright modern rooms are very good value in this friendly family-run hotel. Breakfast.

D La Chacra, Km 4 on Ruta 259 towards Trevelin, T02945-452471. Tranquil place with spacious modern rooms and huge breakfast, Welsh/English spoken.

D La Posada, Chacabuco 905, T02945-454095 laposada@art.inter.ar. A real gem. Welcoming tasteful *hostería* in a quiet part of town, with a lovely lounge and good, spacious rooms, breakfast included. Excellent value.

E pp **Casa de Pueblo**, San Martin 661, T02945-450581, www.epaadventure.com.ar. A friendly welcoming hostel with smallish rooms, kitchen, laundry. Also rafting, trekking, climbing and mountain biking.

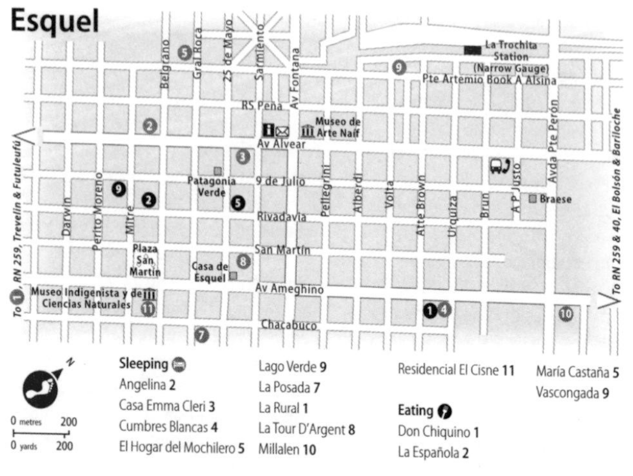

E Lago Verde, Volta 1081, T02945-452251, patagverde@teletel.com.ar. Modern and comfortable, kitchen, laundry. Handy for the bus terminal. Excursions. Recommended.
E Res El Cisne, Chacabuco 778, T02945-452256. With cooking facilities, this quiet and well-kept family guesthouse is good value.
F El Hogar del Mochilero, Roca 1028, T02945-452166. Jan-Mar only. Hostel and campsite with laundry, 24-hr hot water, friendly owner, internet, free firewood.
G pp **Mrs Elvey Rowlands' guesthouse**, behind Rivadavia 330, T02945-452578. Welcoming, though the rooms are simple with shared bath. Breakfast. Recommended.

Camping

El Hogar del Mochilero, Roca 1028, T02945-452166. Jan-Mar only, laundry, 24-hr hot water, friendly, internet, free firewood.
La Rural, 1 km on road to Trevelin, T02945-1568 1429. Well organized and shady site.
Millalen, Ameghino 2063, T02945-456164. Good services.

Trevelin *p108*

A Challhuaquen, Los Cipreses, T02945-1550 4072, www.challhuaquen.com. Charming place set high up with beautiful views over the river, and high quality accommodation and food, aimed at the fly fishing market with expert resident fishing guide.
B Patagonia Lodge, RN 71, Km 1, T02945-480752, tom@lapatagnialodge.com. Has been recommended.
D Pezzi, Sarmiento 353, T02945-480146, hpezzi@intramed.com.ar. Jan-Mar only. Attractive small hotel with a garden.
D-E Casa Verde Hostal, Los Alerces s/n, T/F02945- 480091, www.casaverdehostel.com.ar. 'The best hostel in Argentina' is a cosy log cabin, with gardens, and views over Trevelin. Comfortable dorms for 4-6 with bathrooms. Kitchen, laundry, lounge, meals available. Trekking and rafting trips in Los Alerces national park. Also a very comfortable *cabaña*. Highly recommended. HI affiliated.

Cabañas

Ask for a full list at the tourist office.
A-B Casa de Piedra, Brown 244, T02945-480357, casadepiedratrevelin@yahoo.com.ar.
A-B El Tropezón, San Martín y Saavedra, T02945-480016, eltropezon@ciudad.com.ar.

Camping

Many sites on the road to Futuleufú and Chile.
Aikén Leufú, on the road to Futaleufú dam, T02945-1568 1398. Full facilities and *cabañas*.
Puerto Ciprés, on the banks of Río Futuleufú, T02945-450913. Peaceful place, right on river bank, simple facilities.

Parque Nacional Los Alerces

p109, map p110
The following are on the east side of Lago Futalaufquen. **Hostería Futalaufquen** on the west side of the lake is not nearly as good.
L El Aura: Lago Verde Wilderness Resort, www.tenriverstenlakes.com/elaura-i.htm. Exquisite taste in these 3 stone cabins and guesthouse by the lake. Luxury, attention to detail, ecologically friendly. Impressive.
A Hostería Quimé Quipan, T02945-471021. Delightful, comfortable rooms, impeccably clean, with lake views, dinner included. Very peaceful. Paths lead to a small rocky beach.
C Bahía Rosales, T02945- 471044. Welcoming and family-run. Spacious *cabañas* in an elevated position above the lake, also *refugio*-style *cabañas* and camping , fireplaces, hot showers; restaurant and *quincho*.
D Cabañas Tejas Negras, T02945-471046. Comfortable. Good camping. Tea room.
D Pucón Pai, T02945- 471010, puconpai@ciudad.com.ar. Spartan rooms, but a good restaurant with lovely views, great for fishing. Camping US$2 pp.

Camping

Several campsites at **Lagos Rivadavia, Verde** and **Río Arrayanes**, ranging from free to US$3. All have marvellous views, lake access and fireplaces; can be busy in high season. **Krügger Lodge** has a *refugio* and campsite, with hot showers, food shop, meals provided, fishing guides, boat trips.

Eating

El Bolsón *p105*

¶¶ Cerro Lindo, San Martín y Hube. An elegant place for dinner, delicious pastas.
¶¶ Jauja, San Martín 2867. A great meeting place, welcoming atmosphere, good music and tasty food. Try the trout-filled pasta and the hand-made ice cream.
¶¶ Martin Sheffield, Av San Martín 2760, T02944-491920. Conveniently central

and serving good food, Patagonian specialities, menu of the day.

🍴🍴 **Parrilla El Quincho**, 10 mins north of town, signposted from RN 258, near Cataratas del Mallín, T02944-492870. Excellent *asado*, and delicious lamb are the specialities at this rustic *parrilla* with garden going down to the river, and tables in the open air. Recommended.

🍴🍴 **Parrilla Patagonia**, on the RN 258, 2 km out of town. Superb *parrilla* for steak, and Patagonian lamb and kid on the *asado* at weekends. Cheap set menu and *parrilla libre*.

🍴 **Acrimbaldo**, San Martin 2790. Good value *tenedor libre*, smoked fish and beer.

🍴 **Dulcinea**, on the road to El Hoyo. This delightful tea room is not to be missed. Famous for cakes and rose hip tea, and fondu at nights in season.

🍴 **La Tosca**, San Martín y Roca. Café, restaurant in summer, warm atmosphere.

Parque Nacional Lago Puelo *p105*

🍴🍴 **Familia von Fürstenberg**, RN 16 on the way to the national park, T02944-499392, www.vonfuerstenberg.com.ar. In a delightful perfectly decorated Swiss-style chalet, try the beautifully presented traditional waffles and homemade cakes. Also *cabañas* to rent.

🍴🍴 **Sabores de Patagonia**, RN 16 on the way to the national park, T02944-499532. Good for lunch or tea, locally caught trout, and smoked s. Service is slow, but the food is worth waiting for.

Cholila *p106*

🍴 **La Casa de Piedra**, RN 71 outside village, T02945-498056. Welsh tea room, chocolate cake recommended.

Esquel *p107, map p112*

🍴🍴 **Vascongada**, 9 de Julio y Mitre. Good trout and local specialities.

🍴 **Don Chiquino**, behind Av Ameghino 1649. A fun atmosphere: the walls are lined with number plates, and there are games while you wait for your pasta and pizzas.

🍴 **La Española**, Rivadavia 740. Excellent beef, salad bar, and tasty pastas. Recommended.

🍴 **La Tour D'Argent**, San Martin 1063. Delicious local specialities, good value set meals, and a warm atmosphere.

🍴 **Maria Castaña**, Rivadavia y 25 de Mayo. Popular for excellent coffee, reading the papers and watching street life.

Trevelin *p108*

🍴🍴 **Patagonia Celta**, 25 de Mayo s/n. The best place to eat by a long way. Delicious local specialities, superb fresh trout, steaks and vegetarian dishes, in elegant stylish surrounds. Very welcoming, and reasonably priced.

🍴 **Parrilla Mirador del Valle**, RN 259, Km 46, Excellent *parrilla* and other delicious dishes.

🍴 **Parrilla Oregon**, Av San Martín y Murray Thomas. Large meals (particularly breakfast).

🍴 **Nain Maggie**, P Moreno 179, T02945-480232, www.patagoniaexpress.com/nainmaggie.htm. The best tea room with a huge *té galés* and excellent *torta negra*. Recommended.

Festivals

El Bolsón *p105*

Jan Fiesta de la Fruta Fina (Berry Festival) at the nearby El Hoyo.

Feb Fiesta del Lúpulo (Hops Festival).

Oct The homebrewed beer festival, Fiesta de la Cerveza Artesanal, much more civilized than an Oktoberfest

Dec The **jazz festival** attracts many famous musicians, for 10 days.

Shopping

El Bolsón *p105*

The handicraft and food market is on Tue, Thu, and Sat in season 1000-1600 around the main plaza, for leather and jewellery, carved wood and organic produce.

Centro Artesanal, Av San Martín 1059, daily 1100-1900. For handicrafts.

Granja Larix, RN 258, Km 118.5, T02944-498018, alejandra@bariloche.com.ar. For fabulous smoked trout, homemade jams.

Mercado Artesanal, Av San Martín 1920. Wonderful Mapuche weavings can be bought here in this co-operative of local weavers, and you can watch women spin and weave beautiful rugs, scarves and bags, in the traditional way. Recommended.

Esquel *p107, map p112*

Casa de Esquel, 25 de Mayo 415. Rare books on Patagonia, also souvenirs.

Librería Patagonica, 25 de Mayo 415, T02945-452544. Rare books on Patagonia and recent editions, with friendly service.

Braese, at 9 de Julio 1959. Home-made chocolates and regional specialities.

Activities and tours

El Bolsón *p105*

Ask at the tourist office for their *Agroturismo* leaflet, with information on the *chacras* (fruit farms) you can visit in summer, for delicious freshly picked soft fruits and berries, jams and other delights. Throughout El Bolsón and El Hoyo further south.

Grado 42, Av Belgrano 406 y Av San Martín, T02944-493124, www.grado42.com. Excellent company offering wide range of tours, including *La Trochita*'s lesser-known trip from El Maitén, where there is a superb steam railway workshop and you can learn all about the trains. Also rafting on the Río Manso, horse riding in glorious countryside at Cajón de Azul, fishing in Lago Puelo, paragliding from Plitriquitron, information on buses. Recommended.

Kayak Lago Puelo, T02944-499197, www.kayaklagopuelo.com.ar. Kayaking on the lake with instructor Alberto Boyer.

Patagonia Adventures, Pablo Hube 418, T02944-492513, patagoniaadventures@elbolson.com. Horse riding, fly fishing, rafting and boat trips, crossing to Chile.

Puelo Extremo, T02944-499588, www.pueloextremo.com.ar. Trekking and canoeing.

Puelo Trout, T02944-499430. Boat trips, and all-inclusive fishing trips with equipment.

Parque Nacional Lago Puelo *p105*

Juana de Arco, T02945-493415, T02945-15-602290, juanadearco@red42.com.ar. Boat trips across Lago Puelo, US$2 for 45 mins, US$6 to the Chilean border, including walk through woodland. Recommended.

Zona Sur, T02945-15- 615989, alemaca@yahoo.com.ar. All-inclusive fishing trips Nov-Apr, US$100 for 3, with equipment.

Esquel *p107, map p112*

Fishing

Lots of guides and equipment for hire. See also **Frontera Sur**, under Tour operators.

Jorge Trucco and Patagonia Outfitters, Tte Cnel Pérez 662 (San Martín de los Andes) T/F02972-427561, www.jorgetrucco.com.

Skiing

La Hoya, 15 km north, 22 km of pistes for beginners and experienced skiers, 7 ski-lifts. Popular and cheap. Ski pass US$7 per day in high season, equipment hire US$4 a day. Contact **Club Andino Esquel**, Volta 649, T02945- 453248, www.esquelonline.com.ar.

Tour operators

Frontera Sur, Av Alvear y Sarmiento, T02945-450505, www.fronterasur.net. Good company offering adventure tourism and traditional excursions, ski equipment and trekking.

Patagonia Verde, 9 de Julio 926, T/F02945-454396, patagoniaverde@ciudad.com.ar. Excellent tour to Los Alerces, including the boat across Lago Menéndez. Helpful.

Trevelin *p108*

Adventure tours

Gales al Sur, Patagonia s/n, T/F02945-480427, correo@galesalsur.com.ar. Tours to the border, Los Alerces national park and Futaleufú dam; also *La Trochita*. Recommended for rafting, trekking, bike, 4WD and horse riding. Friendly.

Fishing

Fishing is popular in many local rivers and lakes, most commonly in ríos Futuleufú and Corintos and lagos Rosario and Greda. The season runs from mid-Nov to mid-Apr, and the tourist office can advise on guides.

Parque Nacional Los Alerces *p109, map p110*

Boat trips

Boat trips, US$16-27 run frequently in high season, and can be booked through **Safari Lacustre**, T02945-471008, www.brazosur.com, **Patagonia Verde** in Esquel, or **Gales al Sur** in Trevelin. US$5 extra for transport from Esquel.

Fishing

Lago Futalaufquen has some of the best fishing in the area; local guides offer trips and boat transport. Ask in the *intendencia* or at **Hostería Cume Hue**, T02945-453639 (am) or T02945-450503 (pm). Fishing licences can be obtained either from the food shops, the *kiosko* or **Hosteria Cume Hue**.

Transport

El Bolsón *p105*

Bus

Several buses daily from **Bariloche** and **Esquel**, with **Don Otto, Via Bariloche, Vía Bariloche/El Valle**, Mitre 321, T02944-429012, www.viabariloche.com . Heavily booked in high season. US$7.50, 2 hrs. **La Golondrina** runs 3 buses daily Mon-Sat from the plaza to **Mallin Ahogado**, from where you'll have to walk to reach the falls. Buses to **Lago Puelo** with **Via Bariloche** every 2 hrs, 4 on Sun, 45mins, US$1.30. To **Parque Nacional Los Alerces** (highly recommended route), with **Transportes Esquel** (from ACA service station), once a day, US$5, 4-5 hrs, via Cholila and Epuyén.

Parque Nacional Lago Puelo *p105*

Buses from **El Bolsón** with **Via Bariloche** every 2 hrs Mon-Sat, 4 on Sun, 45mins, US$2. **Transportes Esquel** daily connecting Lago Puelo with **Cholila**, **Parque Nacional Los Alerces** (4-5 hrs) and **Esquel**.

Esquel *p107, map p112*

Air

Airport, 20 km east of town, U$9 by taxi, US$3 by bus. To **Buenos Aires**, 3 per week, **Aerolíneas Argentinas** (agent) Av Fontana 408, T02945-453614. **LADE**, Alvear 1085, T02945-452124, to **Bariloche** and elsewhere.

Bus

The modern terminal at Alvear 1871, T02945-451566, has toilets, kiosko, *locutorio*, left luggage and taxis. 3 daily buses to **La Hoya**, US$5 return.

Long distance To **Bariloche**, 4-5 hrs, US$6, **Don Otto**, **Andesmar**, **Mar y Valle**, T02945-453712, **Vía Bariloche**, T02945-453528. To **El Bolsón**, 2 hrs, US$4, on bus to Bariloche, or via Los Alerces national park, see below. To **Trelew**, 9 hrs, US$16. **Mar y Valle**, **Emp Chubut**, **Don Otto**, daily. To **Trevelin**, **Jacobsen** , T02945-453528, Mon-Fri, hourly 0700-2100, every 2 hrs at weekends, US$2. To **Parque Nacional Los Alerces**, **Jacobsen** , T02945-453528, runs a daily bus through the park from Esquel bus terminal at 0930, arriving at **Futalaufquen** (the entrance and *guardería*) 1100, and on to **Lago Verde** 1215. You can get on or off at any of the campsites or *hosterías* in park. US$4 each way. Returns to Esquel from **Futalaufquen** at 2000, arriving **Esquel** 2115. Ring to check times as they vary from season to season.

To **Buenos Aires** travel via Bariloche: **Andesmar**, T02945-450143, including change in Bariloche, 24 hrs, *semi cama US$50*. *To* **Comodoro Rivadavia**, 9 hrs US$13, **Don Otto**, T02945-453012, 4 times a week (but usually arrives full in season).

To Chile From Esquel to **Paso Futaleufú**, 0800 daily in Jan/Feb, otherwise Mon, Fri, sometimes Wed, with **Jacobsen** US$3.50. From the border, **Transportes Cordillera** T02945-258633, and **Ebenezer**, to **Futuleufú** and **Chaitén**, 4 times a week (daily Jan/ Feb). From Chaitén there are services to **Coyhaique**.

Trevelin *p108*

Bus

To **Esquel**, with **Via Trevelin**, T02945-455222, Mon-Fri, hourly 0700-2100, every 2 hrs weekends, US$2. To the **Chilean border**, **Jacobsen** bus from Esquel runs through Trevelin, 0830 daily in Jan/Feb, otherwise Mon, Fri, sometimes Wed, US$3, connecting bus at border to **Futuleufú** and on to **Chaitén**.

Parque Nacional Los Alerces *p109, map p110*

From Esquel there are 2 services running at the time of writing: **Jacobsen**, as described above, and **Transportes Esquel**, T02945-453529, runs daily buses at 0800 from Esquel (returning at 2115) along the east side of **Lago Futalaufquen**, passing **Villa Futalaufquen** 0915 (return 2000), **Lago Verde** 1030 (return 1845), **Lago Rivadavia** 1120 (return 1830), and continuing on to **Cholila**, **El Bolsón** and **Lago Puelo** (return 1500). The driver will drop you at your accommodation, and you can stop the bus at any point on the road. US$4 each way.

Directory

El Bolsón *p105*

Banks Exchange cash and TCs at **Banco Patagonia**, San Martín y Roca, with ATM outside. **Internet** Ciber Café La Nuez, Av San Martín 2175, T02944-455182. **Post office** San Martín 1940.

Esquel *p107, map p112*

Banks ATMs at **Banco de la Nación**, Alvear y Roca; **Banco Patagonia**, 25 de Mayo 739; **Bansud**, 25 de Mayo 752. **Internet** lots in the centre. **Post office**, Alvear 1192 y Fontana, Mon-Fri 0830-1300, 1600-1930, Sat 0900-1300. **Telephone** many *locutorios* in centre and at bus terminal.

Atlantic Coast

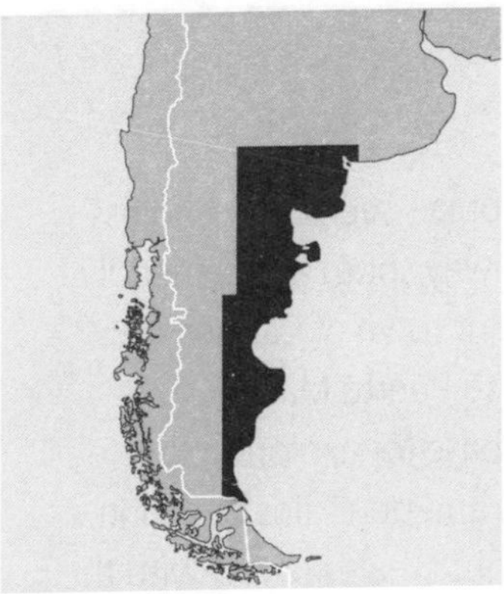

Footprint features

Introduction

Marine life abounds along Patagonia's seemingly endless virgin coastline. Stop off on your way south at the friendly city of Bahía Blanca or at the quaint town of Carmen de Patagones and then head down to Puerto Madryn. This pleasant seaside town is a great base for exploring the Península Valdés, where sealions and penguins gather in their thousands, and southern right whales cavort with their young in the spring. Take a walk on the shore and then try the excellent seafood. Nearby, Trelew has a superb dinosaur museum, while Gaiman keeps the Welsh pioneer heritage alive with a fascinating museum, *eisteddfods* and delicious Welsh teas.

Further south, you'll find colonies of cormorants in Ría Deseado and dolphins frolicking in the beautiful bay at Puerto San Julián. Leaving the sublime shorelines behind, venture inland to explore the weird lunar landscapes of the *bosques petrificados* – an unforgettably eerie sight. There are quiet towns for rest at Piedrabuena and Río Gallegos, and the new national park Monte León offers superb accommodation in a wild and splendidly isolated setting.

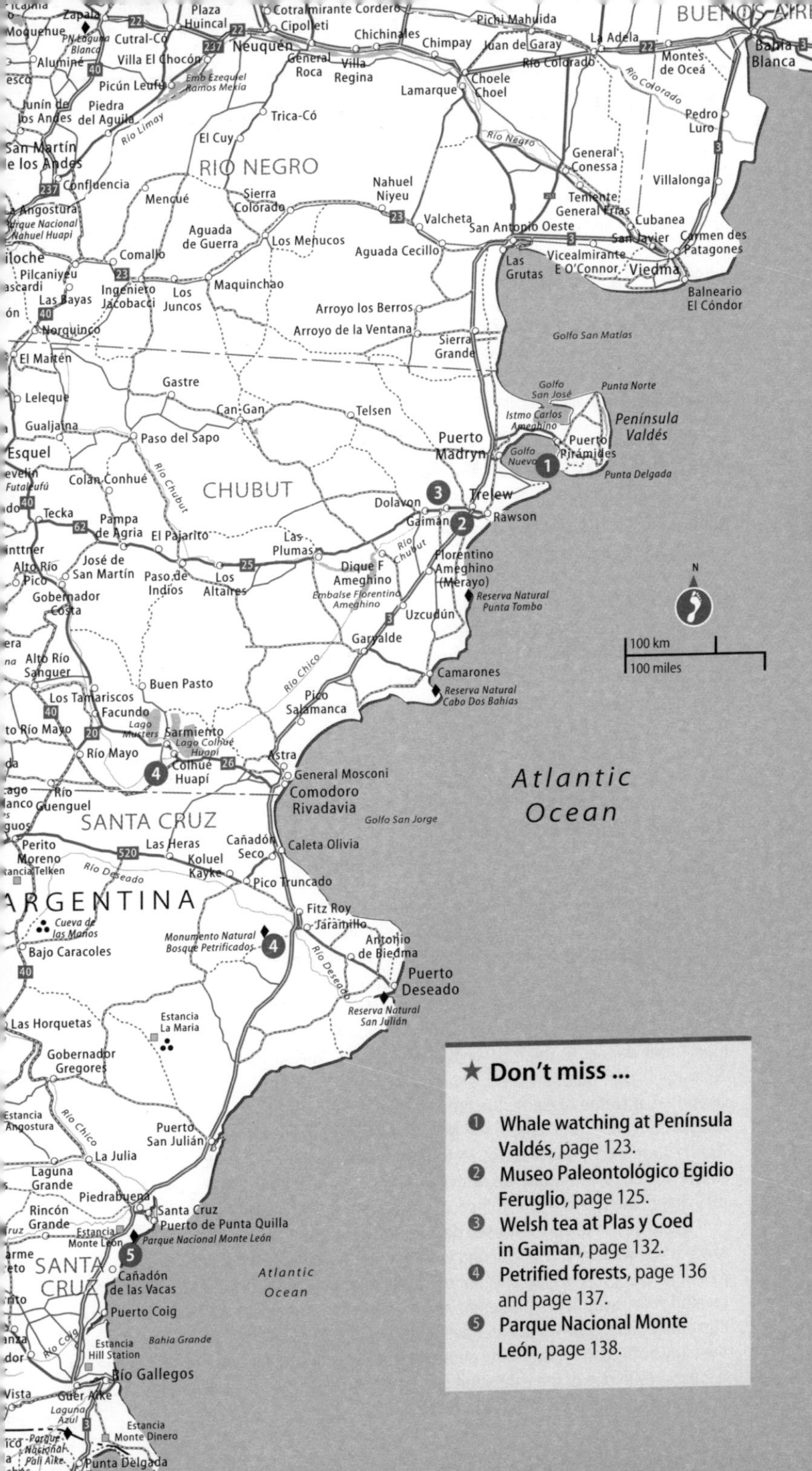
BUENOS AIRES
Zapala
Moquehue
PN Laguna Blanca
Plaza Huincal
Cutral-Có
Cotralmirante Cordero
Cipolleti
Neuquén
Aluminé
Villa El Chocón
Emb Ezequiel Ramos Mexía
Picún Leufú
Junín de los Andes
Piedra del Aguila
Río Limay
San Martín de los Andes
Confluencia
General Roca
Villa Regina
Chichinales
Chimpay
Pichi Mahuida
Juan de Garay
La Adela
Río Colorado
Montes de Oceá
Bahía Blanca
Choele Choel
Lamarque
Trica-Có
El Cuy
RIO NEGRO
Río Negro
General Conessa
Pedro Luro
Villalonga
Teniente General Frías
Cubanea
San Javier
Carmen des Patagones
Viedma
Balneario El Cóndor
Vicealmirante E O'Connor
Las Grutas
San Antonio Oeste
Valcheta
Nahuel Niyeu
Sierra Colorado
Mencué
La Angostura
Parque Nacional Nahuel Huapi
Bariloche
Aguada de Guerra
Los Menucos
Aguada Cecillo
Comallo
Pilcaniyeu
Ingeniero Jacobacci
Los Juncos
Maquinchao
Las Bayas
Norquinco
Arroyo los Berros
Arroyo de la Ventana
Sierra Grande
Golfo San Matías
El Maitén
Gastre
Leleque
Gualjaina
Can Gan
Telsen
Golfo San José
Punta Norte
Istmo Carlos Ameghino
Península Valdés
Puerto Pirámides
Golfo Nuevo
Punta Delgada
Puerto Madryn
Esquel
Paso del Sapo
Río Chubut
Futaleufú
Colán Conhué
CHUBUT
Trelew
Rawson
Dolavon
Gaiman
Tecka
Pampa de Agria
El Pajarito
Las Plumas
Alto Río Pico
José de San Martín
Paso de Indios
Los Altares
Dique F Ameghino
Embalse Florentino Ameghino
Florentino Ameghino (Merayo)
Reserva Natural Punta Tombo
Gobernador Costa
Uzcudún
Garyalde
N
100 km
100 miles
Alto Río Senguer
Río Chico
Camarones
Reserva Natural Cabo Dos Bahías
Buen Pasto
Los Tamariscos
Facundo
Pico Salamanca
Lago Musters
Sarmiento
Lago Colhué Huapí
Río Mayo
Colhué Huapí
Astra
General Mosconi
Comodoro Rivadavia
Atlantic Ocean
Río Guenguel
SANTA CRUZ
Golfo San Jorge
Perito Moreno
Las Heras
Cañadón Seco
Caleta Olivia
Koluel Kayke
Río Deseado
Pico Truncado
ARGENTINA
Fitz Roy
Jaramillo
Cueva de las Manos
Monumento Natural Bosque Petrificados
Antonio de Biedma
Bajo Caracoles
Puerto Deseado
Reserva Natural San Julián
Estancia La Maria
Las Horquetas
Gobernador Gregores
Estancia Angostura
Río Chico
Puerto San Julián
La Julia
Laguna Grande
Piedrabuena
Santa Cruz
Puerto de Punta Quilla
Rincón Grande
Estancia Monte León
Parque Nacional Monte León
SANTA CRUZ
Cañadón de las Vacas
Atlantic Ocean
Puerto Coig
Río Coig
Estancia Hill Station
Bahía Grande
Río Gallegos
Guer Aike
Laguna Azul
Estancia Monte Dinero
Parque Nacional Pali Aike
Punta Delgada
★ Don't miss ...
1 Whale watching at Península Valdés, page 123.
2 Museo Paleontológico Egidio Feruglio, page 125.
3 Welsh tea at Plas y Coed in Gaiman, page 132.
4 Petrified forests, page 136 and page 137.
5 Parque Nacional Monte León, page 138.

Bahía Blanca to Camarones

Many visitors to Patagonia head for Península Valdés, a splay of land stretching into the Atlantic which hosts an array of wildlife, most famously the southern right whales that come here to breed in spring. The seaside town of Puerto Madryn makes a good base for exploring the area. Just south, Trelew is worth a visit for its superb palaeontological museum, and for access to the old Welsh pioneer villages of Gaiman and Dolavon in the Chubut Valley to the west. Halfway from Buenos Aires you could break your journey at the friendly town of Bahía Blanca, spend a night at historic Carmen de Patagones on the Río Negro, or go shark fishing at Bahía San Blas. Viedma has a direct train to Bariloche and Bahía Blanca has excellent transport links all parts of the country. » *For Sleeping, Eating and other listings see pages 128-135.*

Bahía Blanca » *pp 128-135.*

Bahía Blanca is the best stopping point on the route south. It's a busy city, yet relaxed and attractive, with superb early 20th-century architecture around its large plaza.

Ins and outs → *Colour map 4, A3*

Getting there and around There are several flights daily from Buenos Aires to **Comandante Espora airport** ⓘ *T0291-486 1456, 11 km northeast of centre*, taxi US$3. Also weekly flights with **LADE** to many places in Patagonia. Bahía Blanca is a transport hub, with buses from all over the country to the **terminal** ⓘ *2 km east of the centre, Estados Unidos y Brown, T0291-481 9615*, from where local buses 512, 514 run to the centre; taxi US$2. Trains from Buenos Aires arrive at the **station** ⓘ *6 blocks east of the plaza at Av Gral Cerri 750, T0291-452 9196*. There is a good network of local buses, taking *tarjebus* cards (available from shops and kiosks) rather than cash. Taxis are cheap. » *See also Transport, page 134.*

Sights

At the city's heart is the large **Plaza Rivadavia**, a broad, well-kept leafy space, planted with a wide variety of trees, with a striking sculpture at its centre. On the west side is the Italianate **Municipalidad** (1904), which houses the **tourist office** ⓘ *Alsina 65, T0291-459 4007, www.bahiablanca.gov.ar, Mon-Fri 0730-1900, Sat 1000-1300*. To the south is the impressive French-style **Banco de la Nación** (1927). Three blocks north there's the classical **Teatro Colón** (1922) ⓘ *T0291-456 3973*, which hosts regular theatre, live music and dance. At the side of the theatre, the **Museo Histórico** ⓘ *Dorrego 116, T0291-456 3117, Tue-Sun 1500-2000*, has interesting displays on the city's history. Outside is a statue of Garibaldi, erected by the Italian community in 1928. There are lively, changing exhibitions at the **Museo de Arte Contemporánea** ⓘ *Sarmiento 450, Tue-Fri 1000-1300, 1600-2000*. To the northwest of the centre, along the attractive Avenida Além, the **Parque de Mayo**, is filled with eucalyptus trees, with children's play areas, bars, and a fine golf course and sports centre nearby.

Not to be missed is the **Museo del Puerto** ⓘ *Torres y Carrega, weekends in summer 1700-2030, winter 1500-2000, and weekdays for schools, and public by arrangement, free, take bus 500A or 504 from the plaza, running hourly at weekends, or a taxi, US$3*, located 7 km away at the port area, which is known as *Ingeniero White*. Set in a former customs building, this has entertaining and imaginative displays on immigrant life in the early 20th century, with witty photographs, evocative music and sound. And there's a great café in one of the exhibition spaces on Sundays. The port also has a couple of fine fish restaurants in its red light district.

Carmen de Patagones and Viedma

» pp128-135.

These two pleasant towns straddle the broad sweep of the Río Negro, 250 km south of Bahía Blanca. Viedma, on the south bank, was founded in 1779, but destroyed almost immediately by floods, after which Carmen de Patagones was founded on higher ground to the north. The **Fiesta de 7 de Marzo** (for a week around 7th March) is worth a visit, although accommodation is heavily booked. » *See Festivals and events, page 132.*

Ins and outs

Aeropeuerto Gobernador Castelo ⓘ *5 km south of Viedma*, receives flights from Buenos Aires and other Patagonian destinations. There are comfortable buses direct from Buenos Aires several times a day to the **terminal** ⓘ *Av Pte Peron y Guido, 15 blocks from plaza in Viedma, taxi US$1*, and a train three times a week between Viedma and Bariloche in the Lake District. Patagones (as it's known) and Viedma are linked by two bridges and a very small ferry, which takes four minutes and leaves every 15 minutes, US$0.20. Patagones has a very helpful **tourist office** ⓘ *Bynon 186, T02920-462054, www.vivalaspampas.com*. Viedma has a rather impoverished **tourist office** ⓘ *on the costanera, 3 blocks east of Plaza Alsina, T02920-427171, www.rionegrotur.com.ar, 0900-2100*.

Carmen de Patagones → *Colour map 4, A3/B3*

Carmen de Patagones is by far the most picturesque of the two towns. Its town centre, just east of the river, lies around the Plaza 7 de Mayo, and just west is the **Iglesia del Carmen**, built by the Salesians in 1880. Take a stroll down the pretty adobe streets winding down to the river, to find many early pioneer buildings, including the **Casa de la Tahona**, a disused 18th-century flour mill, that now houses the **Casa de la Cultura**. Nearby is the fascinating **Museo Historico** ⓘ *Viedma 4, T02920-462729, daily 0930-1230, 1900-2100, Sun pm only*, which gives a great insight into early pioneer life.

Viedma → *Colour map 4, B3*

Viedma is the provincial administrative centre and a duller place than Carmen de Patagones. However, it does have better accommodation and a pretty bathing area on the river, with large grassy banks shaded by willow trees, where everyone hangs out to swim and drink *mate* on warm summer afternoons. The river water is pleasantly warm in summer and completely uncontaminated.

There are two plazas, with the cathedral, built by the Salesians in 1912, on the west of Plaza Alsina. Two blocks east, on the Plaza San Martín, are the French-style **Casa de Gobierno** (1926) and, opposite, the **Museo Gobernador Tello** ⓘ *summer 0900-1230, 1700-1930*, with fossils, rocks and indigenous *boleadoras*. Along the attractive *costanera*, the **Centro Cultural**, opposite Calle 7 de Marzo, houses a small **Mercado Artesenal** selling beautifully made Mapuche weavings and woodwork.

South and west of Viedma

This whole stretch of coast is great for shore fishing, with pejerrey, variada and even shark among many other species. At **El Cóndor** ⓘ *30 km south of Viedma, 3 buses a day in summer*, there is a beautiful beach, with the oldest *faro* (lighthouse) in the country, dating from 1887. **Playa Bonita**, 12 km further south is known as a good fishing spot, with pleasant beaches. The sealion colony at **Lobería Punta Bermeja**, 60 km south, is visited by some 2500 sealions in summer. You can see the animals at close range and get further information at the impressive visitor centre. There's another stretch of lovely coastline at **Bahia San Blas**, www.bahiasanblas.com, a well-established shark fishing resort 100 km from Patagones.

Puerto Madryn and around » pp128-135.

→ See map page 129. Colour map 4, B2.

Puerto Madryn is a pleasant breezy seaside town with a grand setting on the wide bay of Golfo Nuevo, the perfect base for seeing the extraordinary array of wildlife on Península Valdés, just 70 km east. During the breeding season you can see whales, penguins and seals at close range or go diving to explore life underwater. If you want to stay on the peninsula itself, there's the small popular resort of Puerto Pirámides as well as several estancias to choose from, but Puerto Madryn makes a good place to enjoy the sea for a couple of days. The town was the site of the first Welsh landing in 1865 and is named after the Welsh home of the colonist, Jones Parry. It is a modern, relaxed and friendly place and hasn't been ruined by its popularity as a tourist resort.

Ins and outs

Getting there The **airport**ⓘ *10 km west of centre, taxi US$5*, has regular flights from Buenos Aires and El Calafate plus weekly flights with **LADE** to other towns in Patagonia (see Essentials, page 20). There are more frequent services to/from Trelew airport. **Mar y Valle** runs an hourly bus that links Trelew airport with Puerto Madryn's bus terminal; a taxi will cost US$20. Puerto Madryn is connected to all the main tourist destinations by long-distance buses from Buenos Aires, Bahía Blanca and south to Río Gallegos. The **bus terminal**ⓘ *Irigoyen y San Martín, T02965- 451789*, is behind the old railway station. Walk three blocks down R S Pena to get into town. » See also Transport, page 134.

Tourist information ⓘ *Av Roca 223, off 28 de Julio, T02965-453504, www.madryn.gov.ar, Mon-Fri 0700-2100, Sat and Sun 0830-2300*. This is one of the country's best tourist information centres, located on the seafront next to the shopping complex. Its staff are friendly, extremely well organized and speak English and French. They have leaflets on Península Valdés, accommodation lists and can advise on tours.

Around Puerto Madryn

You're most likely to be visiting the town to take an excursion to Península Valdés but there are other worthwhile destinations along the coast nearby. You can stroll along the long stretch of town beach to **El Indio**, a statue marking the gratitude of the Welsh to the native Tehuelche people, whose shared expertise ensured their survival. As the road curves up the cliff here, there's the splendid **EcoCentro** ⓘ *Julio Verne 784, T02965-457470, www.ecocentro.org.ar, daily 1000- 1800 (Tue closed in winter, check with tourist office), US$6, bus linea 2 from 25 de Mayo y Belgrano, then 5-min walk from the university*, an inspired interactive sea-life information centre that combines an art gallery, café and fabulous reading room with comfy sofas at the top of a turret. The whole place has fantastic views of the bay; great for an afternoon's relaxation or for finding out about whales.

Less exciting is the **Museo de Ciencias Naturales y Oceanográfico** ⓘ *Domecq García y J Menéndez, T02965-451139, Mon-Fri 0900-1200, 1430-1900, Sat 1430-1900 entry US$1*. It's an old-fashioned museum but its displays on local flora and wildlife are informative and worth a look.

You can spot whales from the *ripio* road at the long **Playa El Doradillo**, 16 km northeast of Puerto Madryn, and sea lions 15 km southeast at the **Punta Loma Reserve** ⓘ *open during daylight hours, US$3.50, but free with ticket to Península Valdés*. Access is via the coastal road from town and, like the road to the north, makes a great bike ride – allow 1½ hours to get there. The reserve is best visited at low tide in December and January.

Península Valdés » pp128-135.

→ Colour map 4, B2

Whatever time of year you visit Península Valdés, you'll find a wonderful array of marine life, birds and a profusion of Patagonian mammals such as guanacos, rheas, Patagonian hares and armadillos. But in spring, this treeless splay of land is host to a quite spectacular numbers of whales, penguins and seals, who come to breed in the sheltered waters of the gulf and on beaches at the foot of the peninsula's chalky cliffs. The land is almost flat, though greener than much of Patagonia, and at the heart of the peninsula are large saltflats, one of which, **Salina Grande**, is 42 m below sea level. The peninsula is privately owned – many of its estancias offer grand places to stay in the middle of the wild beauty – but it is also a nature reserve and was declared a World Heritage Site by UNESCO in 1999. The beach along the entire coast is out of bounds and this is strictly enforced. The main centre for accommodation and whale trips is **Puerto Pirámides**, on the southern side of the isthmus.

Ins and outs

Getting there Península Valdés is best visited by taking one of the well-organized full-day excursions from Puerto Madryn but you could also hire a car relatively inexpensively for a group of four, and then take just the boat trip to see the whales (September to November) from Puerto Pirámides. Note that distances are long on the peninsula, and roads beyond Puerto Pirámides are *ripio*, so take your time. A cheaper option is the daily bus to Puerto Pirámides. » *See also Transport, page 134.*

Tourist information The **entrance** ⓘ *US$12, tickets are also valid for Punta Loma*, is 45 km northeast of Puerto Madryn. About 20 km beyond, on the isthmus, there's an interesting **interpretation centre** with stuffed examples of the local fauna, many fossils and a wonderful whale skeleton. Ask for the informative bilingual leaflet on southern right whales. Contact the tourist office in Puerto Madryn or the small office on the edge of Puerto Pirámides, T02965-495084, which has useful information on hikes and driving tours.

Whale watching

Puerto Pirámides, 107 km east of Puerto Madryn, is the main centre for visits to the peninsula and whale-watching boat trips leave from its broad sandy beach. Every year between June and December 400-500 **southern right whales** migrate to the Gulfo Nuevo to mate and give birth. It is without doubt one of the best places in the world to watch these beautiful animals, as the whales often come within just a few metres of the coast. Take a boat trip and, with luck, you'll be very close to a mother and baby. Sailings are controlled by the Prefectura, according to weather and sea conditions (if you're very prone to sea sickness think twice before setting off on a windy day).

Wildlife colonies

Isla de los Pájaros In the Golfo San José, 5 km from the entrance. Bird Island's seabirds can only be viewed through fixed telescopes (at 400 m distance). Only recognized ornithologists can get permission to visit. Between September and April you can spot wading birds, herons, cormorants and terns.

Punta Norte At the northern end of the peninsula, 97 km from the entrance. Punta Norte is not often visited by tour companies, but it has colonies of Magellanic penguins and sea lions. Killer whales (orca) have also been seen here, feeding on sea lion pups at low tide in March and April. **Estancia San Lorenzo** is nearby (see Sleeping, page 130).

Península Valdés – top tips

→ Take an organized tour rather than hiring a car. The excess charged for turning them over is huge and you'll be too tired after driving on the *ripio* roads to enjoy the wildlife to the full.
→ Whale-watching trips in boats from Puerto Pirámides are not for those who get sea sick. If it's a rough day and you're prone to sickness, bring good binoculars and head for the Playa El Doradillo, 16 km north of Puerto Madryn where you can often spot whales close to the shore in season.
→ To spend more time on the peninsula and see more wildlife, stay at one of several estancias there: **Rincón Chico** and **Faro Punta Delgada** are right in the middle of the land.

Caleta Valdés About 45 km south of Punta Norte in the middle of the eastern shore, has huge colonies of **elephant seals**, which can be seen at close quarters. During the first half of August the bull-seals arrive to claim their territory, and can be seen at low tide engaging in bloody battles for the females. From September to October, you'll see them hauling their blubbery mass up the beach to breed. Just south of here, at Punta Cantor, you'll find a good café and clean toilets. There are also three marked walks, from 45 minutes to two hours. A short distance inland is **Estancia La Elvira** (see Sleeping, page 130).

Punta Delgada At the southeastern end of the peninsula, 91 km from the entrance, is where **elephant seals** and **sea lions** can be seen from the high cliffs in such large numbers that they seem to stretch out like a velvety bronze tide line on the beautiful beach below. It's mesmerizing to watch as the young frolic in the shallow water, and the bulls lever themselves around the females. There's an estancia nearby, **Faro Punta Delgada** (see Sleeping, page 129), a good base for exploring this beautiful area further.

Trelew and the Chubut Valley » *pp128-135.*

The Río Chubut flows a massive 820 km from the foothills of the Andes to enter the Atlantic at Rawson. Welsh pioneers came to this part of the world in 1865 and their irrigation of the arid land around the river enabled them to survive and prosper. You can trace their history west along the valley from the pleasant airy town of Trelew, past little brick chapels sitting amidst lush green fields, to the villages of Gaiman and Dolavon (see box, page 126). If you're keen to investigate further into the past, there's a marvellous museum full of dinosaurs at Trelew and some ancient fossils in the Parque Palaeontológico Bryn-Gwyn near Gaiman.

Ins and outs

Getting there There are daily flights from Buenos Aires, El Calafate, Ushuaia and Bariloche in high season to Trelew's airport, 5 km north of the town. A taxi to the centre costs US$3 and local buses to Puerto Madryn will stop at the airport entrance if asked. The bus terminal is north of the centre on the east side of Plaza Centenario, T02965-420121.

Tourist information A 10-minute walk south is the main plaza, where you'll find the very helpful **tourist office** ⓘ *Mitre 387, T02965-420139, www.trelew.gov.ar, Mon-Fri 0800-1400, 1500-2100, Sat and Sun 0900-1300, 1500-2000.* It has an excellent map, directing you to the town's older buildings. Visit in mid-October for the *eisteddfod*.

Trelew → *Colour map 4, C1*

Located some 70 km south of Puerto Madryn, Trelew (pronounced *'Trel-Yeah-Oo'*) is the largest town in the Chubut Valley. Founded in 1884, it was named in honour of Lewis Jones, an early settler, and the Welsh colonization is still evident in the remaining chapels in the town's modern centre and in the Welsh language still spoken by some residents.

The lovely, shady Plaza Independencia in the town centre is packed with mature trees and hosts a small handicraft market at weekends. Nearby is the **Capilla Tabernacle** ⓘ *Belgrano between San Martín and 25 de Mayo*, a red-brick Welsh chapel dating from 1889. Heading east, rather more impressive is the **Salon San David**, a Welsh meeting hall first used for the Eisteddfod of 1913 and now, sadly, used for bingo. The most wonderful building in the town, however, is the 1920s **Hotel Touring Club** ⓘ *Fontana 240*. This was the town's grandest hotel in its heyday; politicians and travellers met in its glorious high-ceilinged mirrored bar, which is now full of old photographs and relics. You can eat lunch here and there's simple accommodation; ask the friendly owner to see the elegant meeting room at the back.

The town's best museum – and indeed one of the finest in Argentina – is the **Museo Paleontológico Egidio Feruglio** ⓘ *Fontana 140, T02965-432100, www.mef.org.ar, spring and summer daily 0900-2000, otherwise Mon-Fri 1000-1800, Sat and Sun 1000-2000, US$5, full disabled access and guides for the blind.* Imaginatively designed and beautifully presented, the museum traces the origins of life through the geological ages, displaying dynamically poised dinosaur skeletons, with plentiful information in Spanish. Tours are free and are available in English, German and Italian. There is also a reasonably cheap café and shop. Ask for information about the Parque Paleontológico Bryn Gwyn near Gaiman.

The **Museo Regional Pueblo de Luis** ⓘ *Fontana y 9 de Julio, T02965-424062, Mon-Fri 0800-2000, Sat and Sun 1400-2000, US$2*, is appropriately housed in the old railway station, built in 1889. It was Lewis Jones that founded the town and started the railways that exported Welsh produce so successfully. The museum has displays on indigenous societies, failed Spanish attempts at settlement and on Welsh colonization.

A little Wales beyond Wales

Among the stories of early pioneers to Argentina, the story of the Welsh emigration, in search of religious freedom, is courageous. The first 165 settlers arrived in Patagonia in July 1865. Landing on the bay where Puerto Madryn now stands, they were forced, by lack of water, to walk south across the parched land to the valley of the Chubut river, where they found cultivatable land and settled. The first 10 years were harsh indeed, and they were saved by trade with local Tehuelche indigenous peoples, who taught them essential survival skills. The British navy also delivered supplies, and there was support from the Argentine government, eager to populate its territory.

The settlement was partly inspired by Michael D Jones, a non-conformist minister who provided much of the early finance and recruited settlers through the Welsh language press and through the chapels. Jones, whose aim was to create a 'little Wales beyond Wales', far from the intruding influence of the English, took particular care to recruit people with useful skills such as farmers and craftsmen. Between 1865 and 1915, the colony was reinforced by another 3000 settlers from Wales and the United States. The early years brought persistent drought, and finding that the land was barren unless irrigated, the pioneers created a network of irrigation channels. Early settlers were allocated 100 ha of land, and when, by 1885, all irrigable land had been allocated, settlement expanded westwards along the valley. The charming town of Trevelin (near Esquel, see page 108), where Welsh is still spoken, was the result of this westward migration.

The success of the Welsh colony was partly due to the creation of their own successful Cooperative Society, which sold their produce and bought necessities in Buenos Aires. Early settlers were organized into chapel based communities of 200-300 people, which were largely self-governing and organized social and cultural activities. The colony thrived after 1880, growing prize-winning wheat in the valley, and exporting successfully to Buenos Aires and Europe, but was badly weakened by the great depression in the 1930s, and the poor management of the Argentine government. Many of the Welsh survived, however, and most of the owners of Gaiman's extra-ordinary Welsh tea rooms are indeed descendants of the original settlers. The Welsh language is kept alive in both Gaiman and Trevelin, and musical *eisteddfods* are held every October. So, as you tuck into your seventh slice of Welsh cake, spare a thought for the harsh conditions endured by those brave early pioneers.

Just outside town, on the road to Rawson, you'll find one of the oldest standing Welsh chapels, **Capilla Moriah**. Built in 1880, it has a simple interior and a cemetery with the graves of many original settlers, including the first woman born in the Welsh colony.

Gaiman → *Colour map 4, C1*

West of Trelew, Route 25 heads through the beautifully green and fertile floodplain of the Río Chubut to Gaiman and Dolavon before continuing through attractive scenery all the way to Esquel (see page 107) and the Welsh colony of Trevelin (see page 108).

Gaiman is a small pretty place with old brick houses, retaining the Welsh pioneer feel, and hosts an annual **eisteddfod** (Welsh festival of arts) in October. The **tourist office** ⓘ *near the old railway on Belgramo between 28 de Julio and Rivadavia, T02965-491571, www.gaiman.gov.ar, Oct-Mar, Mon-Sat 0900-2100, Sun 1400-2000, Apr-Sep, Mon-Sat 0900-1700, Sun 1100-1700,* is housed in the Casa de Cultura.

Around the town plaza are several **tearooms**, many of them run by descendants of the original settlers, serving delicious and 'traditional' Welsh teas (see Eating, page 132). It's hard to imagine their abstemious ancestors tucking into the vast plates filled with seven kinds of cake and scones, so for a reminder of the spartan lives of those idealistic pioneers, visit the wonderful, tiny **Museo Histórico Regional Galés** ⓘ *Sarmiento y 28 de Julio, T02965-491007, Tue-Sun 1500-1900, US$1*. Its impressive collection of Welsh artefacts, objects and photographs is an evocative and moving testimony to extraordinary lives lived in harsh conditions. The curator is helpful and hugely knowledgeable.

Many older buildings remain: the low, stone 'first house' **Primera Casa** (1874) ⓘ *on the corner of the main street, Av Tello y Evans, daily 1400-1900*; the old **railway station** (1909), which now houses the regional museum; the **old hotel** (1899) ⓘ *Tello y 9 de Julio*, and the **Ty Nain tea room** ⓘ *Plaza at Yrigoyen 283*, (1890). On the south side of the river there are two old chapels: **Capilla Bethel** (1913) and the **Capilla Vieja** (1888). A far more recent monument to human energy and inspiration is the extraordinary **El Desafío** ⓘ *2 blocks west of plaza, daily until 1800, US$1.70*, an imaginative sculptural world, made entirely from rubbish by the eccentric Joaquín Alonso – painted plastic bottles, cans and wire form pergolas and dinosaurs, sprinkled liberally with plaques bearing words of wisdom and witty comments. It's beginning to fade now, but still good fun.

Some 8 km south of town, there are fossil beds dating back 40 million years at the **Parque Paleontológico Bryn Gwyn** ⓘ *T02965-432100, www.mef.org.ar, Oct-Feb daily 1000-1900, Mar-Sep daily 1100-1700, US$2.70, taxi from Gaiman US$2*. A mind-boggling expanse of time is brought to life by the guided tour. It takes 1½ hours to do the circuit and see the fossils. There's also a visitor centre where you can experience some fieldwork in palaeontology.

Dolavon and around → *Colour map 4, C1*

Founded in 1919, the most westerly Welsh settlement in the valley is quiet and not as inviting as Gaiman, although if you stroll around its two intersecting streets, you'll find a few buildings reminiscent of the Welsh past.

If you have your own transport, it's worth driving from Dolavon back towards Gaiman through the neat squared fields of the beautiful irrigated valley, where you'll see Welsh chapels tucked away among poplar trees and silver birches. The **San David chapel** (1917) is a beautifully preserved brick construction, with an elegant bell tower and sturdy oak-studded door, in a quiet spot surrounded by birches, an impressive testimony to Welsh pioneer spirit.

South of Trelew » pp128-135.

Reserva Natural Punta Tombo → *Colour map 4, C1*

ⓘ *107 km south of Trelew, access from ripio RN 1 towards Camarones. Sep-Mar, US$7. Tours from Trelew and Puerto Madryn, US$20, including 45 mins at the site, where there's a café and toilets.*

There is a lovely rock and sand beach with birds and other wildlife at **Playa Isla Escondida**, 70 km south of Trelew, with secluded camping but no facilities. Head south from here to see the penguin colony at the **Reserva Natural Punta Tombo**. This reserve is the largest breeding ground for Magallenic penguins in Patagonia. The birds come here in September, chicks hatch from mid-November and first waddle to the water in January or February. It's fascinating to see these creatures up close, but noisy colonies of tourists dominate the place in the morning; it's quieter in the afternoon. You'll see guanacos, hares and rheas on the way.

Camarones and the Reserva Natural Cabo dos Bahías

Camarones is a quiet fishing port on Bahía Camarones, 275 km south of Trelew, whose main industry is harvesting seaweed. This is prime sheep-rearing land, and Camarones wool is world-renowned for its quality. Aside from the salmon festival that takes place in early February, the only real attraction is the penguin colony at the **Reserva Natural Cabo Dos Bahías** ⓘ *28 km southeast of Camarones at the southern end of the bay via a dirt road, US$5*. It protects around 12,000 pairs of penguins, which you can see close up, but also lots of other marine life. You can see seals and sea lions any time, plus whales from March to November and even killer whales from October to April.

Sleeping

Bahía Blanca *p120*

B Argos, España 149, 3 blocks from the plaza, T0291-455 0404, www.hotelargos.com.ar. The city's finest is a 4-star business hotel with comfortable rooms, and good breakfast. Also a restaurant.

B Austral, Colón 159, T0291-456 1700, www.hoteles-austral.com.ar. A friendlier 4-star with plain spacious rooms, good bathrooms, and good views over the city, attentive service, and decent restaurant.

C Bahía Hotel, Chiclana 251, T0291-455 0601, www.bahia-hotel.com.ar. A modern business hotel, good value, with well- equipped rooms, a bright airy bar and *confitería* on street level.

C Italia, Brown 181, T0291-456 2700. Set in a lovely 1920s Italianate building, this is one of the town's oldest, full of character, but some rooms are badly in need of a face lift.

D Barne, H Yrigoyen 270, T0291-453 0294. Friendly, low-key and family-run. Good value.

Viedma *p121*

C Austral, 25 de Mayo y Villarino, T02920-422615, paradoresviedma@infovia.com.ar. Along the *costanera*, this modern hotel has well-equipped, if slightly old-fashioned, rooms.

C Nijar, Mitre 490, T02920-422833. Very comfortable, smart modern rooms, a quiet relaxed atmosphere, and good attentive service. Recommended.

D Peumayen, on the plaza, Buenos Aires 334, T02920-425222. Old-fashioned and friendly.

E Hotel Spa, 25 de Mayo 174, T02920-430459. A real find, this is a great-value hotel in a quiet complex with steam baths, a very relaxing atmosphere and welcoming staff.

Puerto Madryn *p122, map p129*

Accommodation often gets full in spring and summer, when prices rise; book in advance. Watch out for the 'international tourist' price in more expensive hotels.

A Tolosa, Roque Sáenz Peña 253, T02965-471850, www.hoteltolosa.com.ar. An extremely comfortable modern place with faultless service and great breakfasts. The superior rooms are much more spacious and have full wheelchair access. Free use of bicycles and internet. Highly recommended.

B Bahía Nueva, Av Roca 67, T/F02965-451677, www.bahianueva.com.ar. One of the best seafront hotels, with a welcoming reception area and high standards in all details. Rooms are on the small side, but comfortable. Breakfasts are generous, and staff are helpful and professional. Cheaper in low season. Recommended.

B-C Villa Pirén, Av Roca 439, T/F02965-456272, www.piren.com.ar. Excellent modern rooms and apartments in smart seafront building with great facilities. Ask for the junior suite, or rooms with a view.

C Muelle Viejo, H Yrigoyen 38, T02965-471284, www.muelleviejo.com. Ask for the stylish, comfortable modernized rooms in this funny old place. Excellent value large rooms sleep 4 and there are *parrilla* and kitchen facilities if you want to cook.

D Gran Palace Hotel, 28 de Julio 400, T 02965-471009. Attractive entrance to this central and economical place, but rooms are a bit squashed and rather dark, thanks to the mahogany effect wallpaper. But they're clean and have bathroom and TV, making this good value.

D Hostería Torremolinos, Marcos A Zar 64, T02965-453215. Nice modern place with simple, well decorated rooms.

D Santa Rita, Gob Maiz 370, T02965-471050, www.hostelsantarita.com.ar. Welcoming place and comfy rooms with wash basin – this is good value with dinner included or you can use the kitchen facilities. Helpful hosts. Often recommended by travellers.

E-F pp **El Gualicho**, Marcos A Zar 480, T02965-454163, www.elgualichohostel.com.ar. By far the best budget place in Puerto Madryn, this hostel is beautifully designed and run by a friendly and enthusiastic owner. Free pick up from bus terminal, *parrilla*, breakfast included, garden, attractive double rooms, and bikes for hire. Book ahead. Discounts to HI members. Highly recommended.

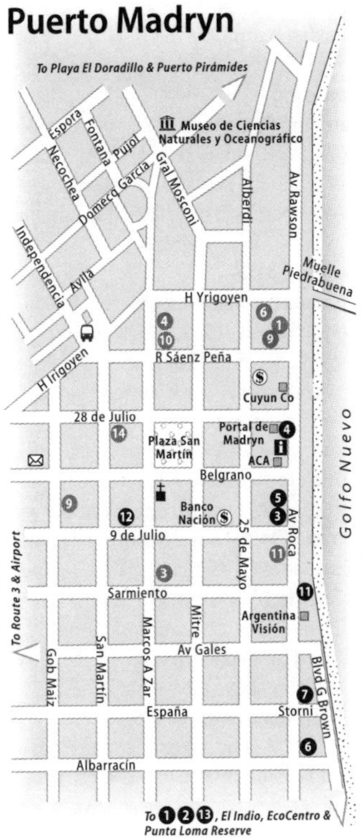

Sleeping
Bahía Nueva **1**
El Gualicho **3**
Gran Palace **14**
Hostería Torremolinos **4**
Muelle Viejo **6**
Santa Rita **9**
Tolosa **10**
Villa Pirén **11**

Eating
Caccaros **3**
Cantina El Náutico **6**
Centro de Difusión de la Pescada Artesanal **2**
Havanna **4**
La Casona de Golfo **5**
La Vaca y el Pollito **7**
Nativo Sur **1**
Plácido **11**
Taska Beltza **12**
Yoaquina **13**

Bars & clubs
Margarita **9**

Península Valdés *p123*

Accommodation is good quality, but can be pricey. The following are all in Puerto Pirámides unless otherwise stated.

L Las Restingas, T02965-495101, www.lasrestingas.com. The top hotel in town has an exclusive location on the beach, and 8 of its 12 suites have their own balcony for splendid sea views. All very comfortable, with minimalist decoration and there's a small restaurant serving a sophisticated selection of regional food.

A Cabañas del Mar, Av Roca s/n, T02965-495049, cabanas@piramides.net. Comfortable *cabañas*, well equipped, but no heating.

A The Paradise, far end of the main street, T02965-495030, www.hosteriaparadise.com. Huge very comfortable light rooms, smart bathrooms, and splendid suites with jacuzzis. Also a fine restaurant, serving delicious squid, among other seafood.

C Motel ACA, on beach front, at Av Roca s/n, T02965-495004, 02965-156 61629, curti@satlink.com.ar. Slightly old fashioned, this has welcoming rooms, handy for the beach. Also a good seafood restaurant, from whose terrace you might even spot whales.

Estancias

To really appreciate the space and natural beauty of the peninsula, staying at an estancia is an appealing (if slightly expensive) option. Ask the tourist office for advice. Day trips to estancias can also be arranged, with access to some of the most beautiful places.

LL Estancia La Ernestina, T156-61079, www.laernestina.com.ar. Near Punta Norte, the welcoming owners offer comfortable accommodation in simple rooms, all meals and excursions included. Open mid-Sep to mid-Apr. No credit cards.

L Faro Punta Delgada, T02965-15406304, www.puntadelagada.com. Comfortable accommodation right on the cliffs, offering half and full board, excellent food, and horse riding, guided walks, English-speaking guides. Recommended.

L Rincón Chico, south of Puerto Pirámides, T02965-471733, www.rinconchico.com.ar. A working sheep farm, still owned by the original pioneer family who built it. Luxurious, beautifully situated, great for walking. Recommended.

AL Estancia La Elvira, T156-69153 (office in Puerto Madryn: Av Yrigoyen 257, T02965-474248), www.laelvira.com.ar. Traditional Patagonian dishes, and comfortable accommodation in an outstanding location on Caleta Valdés, near Punta Cantor.

AL Estancia San Lorenzo, on RP3, 20 km southwest of Punta Norte (contact through **Argentina Visión** in Puerto Madryn, see Tour operators). For day excursions to a beautiful stretch of coast to see penguins close up in one of the peninsula colonies.

Trelew *p125, map p125*

Trelew is not touristy, but there are a few decent places to stay and a good campsite.

B Rayentray, San Martín y Belgrano, T/F02965-434702, www.cadena rayentray.com.ar. Huge modernized 1960s place with comfortable rooms and professional staff – the spacious 'superior' rooms are worth the extra, with sitting area and good bathrooms, and splendid 1970s leather panelling. Swimming pool on top floor is free for guests, but gym, sunbed and sauna are extra.

C Centenario, San Martín 150, T02965-420542, www.hotelcentenario.com.ar. This vast 1970s relic is worth seeing for the untouched decor, though it's more amusing than comfortable, and service is poor. Popular with Argentines, but you can always get a room here; not great value.

C Libertador, Rivadavia 31, T/F02965-420220, www.hotellibertadortw.com.ar. Breakfast is included in this large modern place, highly recommended for its friendly service and comfortable rooms – the newer more spacious rooms are slightly pricier but worth it. Book ahead.

D Galicia, 9 de Julio 214, T02965-433802, www.hotel-galicia.com.ar. Breakfast included in this recently refurbished and central hotel, whose smallish rooms don't quite live up to the grand entrance, but are extremely comfortable and well decorated, and the staff are friendly. Excellent value and recommended.

D pp Rivadavia, Rivadavia 55, T02965-434472, www.cpatagonia.com/rivadavia. Simple, comfortable rooms with TV and bath, and some even cheaper rather spartan rooms without, in this well-located place. This is the best value in town, if you can ignore the grumpy owner. Breakfast extra.

D Touring Club, Fontana 240, T02965-433997, htouring@ar.inter.net. The best budget option. Gorgeous, faded bar, vast staircase and light corridors. The rooms are on the plain side, but they're quiet and spacious, with big bathrooms, and well kept. Breakfast is extra, but this is still good value.

Camping

Camping Patagonia, 11 km south on RN 7 towards Rawson, T02965-428968. US$2. Pretty site with *parrillas*, hot showers, football pitch and *proveduría* (food shop).

Gaiman *p126*

C Posada Los Mimbres, Chacra 211, 6 km west of Gaiman, T02965-491299, www.posada losmimbres.com.ar. A farmstead in idyllic surroundings with just a few rooms in the charming old house or in a modern one. Gorgeous meals. A wonderful place to unwind.

C Unelem, Av Tello y 9 de Julio, T02965-491663, www.unelem.com. Pricey, but very comfortable, this is a restored hotel from 1867. The restaurant serves Welsh cuisine.

D Casa de Té Ty Gwyn, 9 de Julio 147, T02965-491009, tygwyn@cpsarg.com. The next best option in town are the smart new rooms above the tea house.

D Plas Y Coed, Yrigoyen 320, T02965-15585219. A good place run by the charming Marta Rees, descended from a Welsh tea pioneer family, with double and twin rooms with bath and TV including breakfast.

E Gwesty Tywi, Jones 342, T02965-491292, gwestywi@infovia.com.ar. A pretty and very well-kept B&B.

Camping

Los Doce Nogales is an attractive site south of the river at Chacra 202, close to **Ty Te Caerdydd** tea room, T155-18030, with showers.

Camarones *p128*

B Kau I Keu Kenk, Sarmiento y Roca. Good food, recommended, owner runs trips to penguin colony.

Eating

Bahía Blanca *p120*

Lola Mora, Av Alem and Sarmiento. The city's most sophisticated restaurant serves delicious Mediterranean-style food, in an elegant colonial-style house. US$8 for 3 courses and wine. Excellent.

El Mundo de la Pizza, Dorrego 53. Fabulous pizzas, thin bases loaded with toppings, lots of choice in this big atmospheric place, the city's favourite.

Micho, Guillermo Torres 3875, Ingeniero White, T0291-457 0346. There are several good fish restaurants in the port area, but this elegant restaurant is the best. Be sure to take a taxi at night.

Santino, Dorrego 38. Italian-influenced, with a relaxed but sophisticated atmosphere and a welcoming glass of champagne, very good value. US$6 for 2 courses and wine.

Viedma *p121*

Camilla's Café, Saavedra and Buenos Aires. A smart and relaxing place for coffee, to watch Viedma trundle by on its errands.

La Balsa, on the river at Colon y Villarino. By far the best restaurant, inexpensive with a pleasant atmosphere. Delicious seafood, and a bottle of superb Río Negro wine, Humberto Canale Merlot, is highly recommended.

Parrilla Libre, Buenos Aires and Colón. Cheap *tenedor libre* steaks in a cheerful atmosphere, US$2.50 for dinner.

Puerto Madryn *p122, map p129*

One of the unmissable pleasures of Puerto Madryn is the great seafood served in its beachfront restaurants. While you're here, try at least one plate of *arroz con mariscos* (rice with a whole selection of squid, prawns, mussels and clams). Most restaurants are mid-range and charge similar prices, but quality varies widely. Without doubt, the best place to eat in town is the wonderful **Taska Beltza**, though there's plenty of choice along the coast road.

Plácido, Av Roca 508, T02965-455991. Overlooking the sea and beautifully designed, with stylish tables and intimate lighting, this is perfect for a romantic dinner. Excellent service and a good range of seafood, with cheaper pasta dishes too, lots of options for vegetarians.

Caccaros, Av Roca 385, T02965-453767. Stylish simple place on sea front with relaxing atmosphere, good value seafood menu, and cheap lunch menu.

Cantina El Náutico, Av Roca 790, T02965-471404. Long-established and now resting on its laurels, this is still popular for its seafood, and family atmosphere. The individual dishes are better than the set menu.

Centro de Difusión de la Pescada Artesanal, Blv Brown, 7th roundabout, T02965-15-538085. Grandly named, but with no sign outside, this is a basic *cantina* on the coast road east, opposite the municipal campsite, where the fishermen's families cook delicious meals with their catch. Hugely popular with locals, so come early.

La Vaca y el Pollito, Av Roca y A Storni, T02965-458486. You can't miss this place as it's partly built into the wooden hull of a boat. A big place but with a cosy atmosphere, the speciality is *parrilla*, very reasonably priced, but there's seafood and pastas too. Great for families, with a big soft play area for kids.

Nativo Sur, Blv Brown 2000, T02965-457403. Smarter than its more popular sister restaurant **Yoaquina**, this is a good place for a quiet dinner on the beachfront, with an imaginative menu of local Patagonian produce and seafood.

Taska Beltza, 9 de Julio 345, T02965-1566 8085, closed Mon. Chef and owner 'El Negro' cooks superb seafood with great passion and a Basque influence. The *arroz con mariscos* is cheap and superb. Highly recommended. Book ahead.

Yoaquina, Blv Brown between 1st and 2nd roundabouts, T02965-456058. Great in the summer when you can eat outside, this is a relaxed spacious beachfront place, serving good seafood, if slightly pricey, and open from breakfast to after dinner. Cheap lunch menu, play area for kids, good service. Recommended.

Havanna, Av Roca y 28 de Julio. Smart, buzzing café selling the famous *alfajores* you see all over Argentina, coffees and sandwiches *de miga*. Very central, and open from breakfast to the early hours.

La Casona de Golfo, Av Roca 349, T02965-15511089. Good value *tenedor libre* with lots of choices including good *parrilla* and seafood, and '*helados libre*' – as much ice cream as you can eat. Great for families. Kids pay half price.

Península Valdés *p123*

The following are all on the beach in Puerto Pirámides. There are also reasonably priced restaurants at Punta Norte, at Punta Cantor and at **Faro Punta Delgada**.

ΨΨΨ **Las Restingas**. Perfect for a romantic dinner for the sea views and tranquillity. An imaginative menu combines quality local produce with a touch of sophistication.

ΨΨ **Paradise**. Just off the beach, good atmosphere and seafood.

ΨΨ **Patagonia Franca**, T02965-495006. Good seafood restaurant in the new hotel on the beach front, with perfect sea views.

ΨΨ **Quimey Quipan**, T02965-156 93100. By the beach, and next to **Tito Bottazzi**, this family-run place specializes in delicious seafood and has a cheap set menu. Recommended. Open for lunch, ring to reserve for dinner.

Ψ **Mi Sueno**. Close to the beach, good cheap pizzas to share.

Trelew *p125, map p125*

ΨΨ **El Quijote**, Rivadavia 463, T02965-402937. Traditional *parrilla*, popular with locals.

ΨΨ **El Viejo Molino**, Gales 250, T02965-428019, 1130-0030, closed Mon. The best in town, and well worth a visit to see the first flour mill that was built here in 1886. It is now beautifully restored as a fine restaurant and café in relaxed and stylish surroundings. There's an imaginative menu with Patagonian lamb and home-made pastas, good value set menu, and Welsh teas. Recommended.

ΨΨ **La Bodequita**, opposite the cinema on Belgrano. Serves superb homemade pastas, in a warm and lively atmosphere. Recommended.

ΨΨ **Norte**, Soberanía y Belgrano. Cheap takeaway food is available at this supermarket.

Ψ **Café Mi Ciudad**, Belgrano y San Martín. A smart café serving great coffee; read the papers watching street life.

Ψ **Hotel Touring Club**, Fontana 240. Open from breakfast to the small hours for sandwiches and drinks, worth a visit to see the splendid 1920s bar.

Gaiman *p126*

There's a stylish small restaurant **El Angel**, Rivadavia 241, serving delicious food in an old-fashioned intimate atmosphere. Also a high-quality *panadería*, **La Colonia**, on the main street. **Siop Bara**, Tello and 9 de Julio, sells cakes and ice creams.

Welsh teas

You're unlikely to be able to resist the scrumptious Welsh teas for which Gaiman has become famous. Tea is served from 1500, all the tea rooms charge about the same (US$4) and include the most well known of the Welsh cakes *torta negra* – a delicious dense fruit cake.

Plas Y Coed, Jones 123. The first house to start serving tea, has lovely gardens, and the owner Marta Rees is a wonderful raconteur and fabulous cook who can tell you all about her Welsh forebears, married in this very house in 1886. Highly recommended.

Ty Cymraeg, down by the river. In a lovely spot, selling good cakes.

Ty Gwyn, 9 de Julio 111. This large tea house serves a very generous tea in a more modern place with traditional features; the owners are welcoming. Recommended.

Ty Nain, Yrigoyen 283. Quite the prettiest house and full of history. The charming owner's grandmother was the first woman to be born in Gaiman.

Ty Te Caerdydd, Finca 202, 2 km from the centre, but well sign posted. A staggering theme park of its own, with manicured lawns and dressed-up waitresses; its main claim to fame is that Princess Di took her tea here. The atmosphere is entirely manufactured.

Bars and clubs

Bahía Blanca *p120*

Lots of discos on Fuerte Argentino (along the stream leading to the park) mainly catering for under 25s: **Chocolate**, **Bonito** and **Toovaks**. The best place for anyone over 25 is **La Barraca**.

Puerto Madryn *p122, map p129*

Margarita, RS Pena, next to Ambigu on RS Pena and Av Roca. Late night bar for drinks and live music.

Festivals and events

Carmen de Patagones *p121*

Mar Fiesta de 7 de Marzo, celebrates the victory at the Battle of Patagones with a week of music and handicrafts, fine food, a huge procession, horse riding displays, and lots of meat on the *asados*. Great fun. Book accommodation ahead.

Shopping

Bahía Blanca and around *p120*

There's a smart modern shopping mall **Bahía Blanca Plaza Shopping**, 2 km north of town on Sarmiento. Cheap food hall, cinema (0291-T453 5844) and supermarket. Also supermarket **Cooperativa** on Donado. Plenty of clothes and shoe shops on Alsina and San Martín within a couple of blocks of the plaza.

Puerto Madryn *p122, map p129*

The sleek new indoor shopping centre **Portal de Madryn**, 28 de Julio y Av Roca, has all the smart clothes shops, **Café Havanna** on the ground floor, and a kids games area with a fast, but not cheap, food place **Mostaza** on the top floor. **Cardon**, is recommended for regional goods and leather bags.

You'll find lots more clothes, T-shirts, high quality Patagonian crafts, leather goods, and artesanal *alfajores* on 28 de Julio and Av Roca.

Trelew *p125, map p125*

The main shopping area is around San Martín, and from the plaza to Belgrano, though Trelew can't compare with Puerto Madryn for souvenirs, it has a good little handicrafts market on the plaza.

There's a supermarket, **Norte**, Rivadavia y 9 de Julio, opposite Banco Río.

Activities and tours

Viedma *p121*

Fishing

Fishing equipment is available in Viedma at **Patagonia Out Doors Life**, 25 de Mayo 340, and **Tiburón**, Zatti 250, among others. Ask the tourist office for a leaflet, T02920-427171.

Puerto Madryn *p122, map p129*

Diving

Madryn Buceo, Blv Brown, 3rd roundabout in Balneario Nativo Sur, T02965-1551 3997, www.madrynbuceo.com. All levels from beginners' dives to the week-long PADI course, US$160, US$30 for a day excursion. **Ocean Divers**, Blv Brown (between 1st and 2nd roundabout), T02965-472569. Advanced courses (PADI) and courses on video, photography and underwater communication. **Scuba Duba**, Blv Brown 893, T02965-452699. Courses, excursions, night dives.

Fishing

Contact **Raul Diaz**, T02965-450812; or **Juan Dominguez**, T02965-1566 4772.

Horse riding

Huellas y Costas, Blv Brown 860, T02965-1568 0515. Also has kayaks and windsurfs for hire.

Mountain bike hire

El Gualicho, Marcos A Zar 480, T02965-454163. **Vernardino Club Mar**, on beach at Blv Brown 860, T02965-455633. **XT Mountain Bike**, Av Roca 742, T02965-472232.

Tour operators

Lots of agencies in Puerto Madryn do tours to Península Valdés, taking in the same places: the interpretation centre and viewing point for the Isla de los Pájaros, (both on the narrow isthmus at the entrance to the peninsula), and then Puerto Pirámides, where the boat trip to see the whales costs US$25 extra. They go on to Punta Delgada and Caleta Valdés, with time to look at wildlife. Trips take 12 hrs. All charge around US$40, plus US$12 entrance to the peninsula. Shop around to find out how long you'll spend at each place, how big the group is, and if your guide speaks English.

On all excursions take drink, food (if you don't want to eat in the expensive restaurants), and binoculars. Tours are also offered to see the penguins at Punta Tombo, or the Welsh village of Gaiman with Ameghino Dam thrown in, but these are both 400 km round trips and better from Trelew.

Alora Viaggio, Av Roca 27, T/F02965-455106. A helpful company which also has an office at the bus terminal.

Argentina Visión, Av Roca 536, T02965-451427, www.argentinavision.com. 4WD adventure trips and can arrange estancias at Punta Delgada. English and French spoken.

Cuyun Co, Av Roca 165, T02965-451845, www.cuyunco.com.ar. Friendly personal service and a huge range of tours: guided walks with biologists, 4WD expeditions, and estancia accommodation. Recommended.

Flamenco Tour, Av Roca 331, T02965-455505, www.flamencotour.com.ar. For slightly more sedate trips and charming staff.

Golfo Azul, Mitre y H Yrigoyen, T02965-451181. For windsurf boards, kayaks, jet ski, sailing boats for hire.

Hydrosport, near the ACA, T02965-495065, hysport@infovia.com.ar. Rents boats and scuba equipment, and organizes land and sea wildlife tours to see whales and dolphins.
Jorge Schmidt, Puerto Pirámides, T02965-495012. Recommended for whale watching.
Juan Benegas, Puerto Pirámides, T02965-495100. Diving expeditions with equipment.
Tito Botazzi, Blvd Brown y Martín Fierro , T/F02965-474110, and at Puerto Pirámides. Recommended for small groups, popular for whale watching. Bilingual guides.

Trelew *p125, map p125*

Tour operators

Agencies run tours to Punta Tombo, US$22, Chubut Valley (half-day), US$30, both together as a full day US$40. Tours to Península Valdés are best done from Puerto Madryn.
Nieve Mar, Italia 98, T02965-434114, www.nievemartours.com.ar. Punta Tombo and Península Valdés, bilingual guides (reserve ahead). Organized and efficient.
Patagonia Grandes Espacios, Belgrano 338, T02965-435161, infopge@speedy.com.ar. Good excursions to Punta Tombo and Gaiman, and palaeontological trips, staying in *chacras*; also whale watching. Recommended.

Transport

Bahía Blanca *p120*

Air

Several daily flights to **Buenos Aires** with AR/Austral. LADE has weekly flights to various Patagonian destinations (see Air services in Argentina, page 19). Book ahead in summer.

Airline offices Aerolíneas Argentinas, San Martín 198, T0291- 426934. AR/Austral, T0291-456 0561/0810-2228 6527. LADE, Darregueira 21, T0291-437697.

Bus

Local Buy *tarjetas* (Tarjebus cards) from kiosks for 1 (US$0.50), 2, 4 or 10 journeys.

Long distance To **Buenos Aires** frequent, 8½ hrs, several companies, shop around, US$15-18; most comfortable by far is Plusmar suite bus US$25, with completely flat beds. To **Neuquén**, 6 a day, 8 hrs, US$12. To **Viedma**, Ceferino, Plusmar and Río Paraná (to **Carmen de Patagones**), 4 hrs, US$6-8. To **Trelew**, Don Otto and others, US$30, 10½ hrs. To **Río Gallegos**, Don Otto US$36.

Bus companies Andesmar T0291-4815462; **Ceferino** T0291-481 9566; **Don Otto** T0291-481 8585; **Plusmar** T0291-456 0616; **Rápido del Sur** T0291-481 3118.

Train

To **Buenos Aires**, 3 weekly, 12½ hrs, Pullman US$30, first class US$15, tourist class US$12.

Carmen de Patagones and Viedma *p121*

Air

LADE (Saavedra 403, T/F02920- 424420) flies to **Buenos Aires** and places in Patagonia.

Bus

To **Buenos Aires**, 3 daily, 14 hrs, US$20, Don Otto/La Estrella/Cóndor. To **Bahia Blanca**, 4 daily, 4 hrs, US$5, Rio Parana.

Train

A comfortable sleeper train, T02944-431777, www.trenpatagonico.com.ar, which also carries cars, goes from Viedma to **Bariloche** overnight once a week, Fri 1800, arriving in the morning. Restaurant and a cinema car showing videos. US$30 for a bed, US$18 for a *semi-cama* seat. Book ahead.

Puerto Madryn *p122, map p129*

Air

Only LADE operate from here. Flights, once a week to and from **Buenos Aires**. Also weekly services by LADE to other destinations (see Essentials page 21). More frequent flights serve Trelew airport.

Airline offices LADE, Roca 117, T02920-451256. **Aerolíneas Argentinas**, Roca 303, T02920-421257/0800-2228 6527.

Bus

To **Buenos Aires**, 19-20 hrs; US$36-67, several companies daily, **Andesmar** recommended. To **Comodoro Rivadavia**, 5 hrs, US$12, many companies. To **Río Gallegos**, 17 hrs; US$40, (from here to **El Calafate, Puerto Natales, Punta Arenas**), many companies. To **Trelew**, 1 hr, every hr, US$4 with **28 de Julio**, **Mar y Valle**. To **Puerto Pirámides**, 1 hr, US$2, daily, 28 de Julio. To **Bariloche**, 15 hrs, US$46, daily, except Wed, Mar y Valle. To **Esquel**, 9-10 hrs; US$ 23-30, many companies.

Bus companies 28 de Julio/Mar y Valle, T02965-432429; **Andesmar**, T02965-433535; **El Cóndor**, T02965-431675; **El Ñandú**, T02965-

427499; **El Pingüino**, T02965-427400; **Que Bus**, T02965-422760; **Transportadora Patagónica/Don Otto**, T02965-429496; **TUS**, T02965-421343.

Car hire
More expensive than other parts of Argentina, and a large insurance excess. Drive slowly on unpaved *ripio* roads. **Localiza**, Roca 15 , T02965-458000. Efficient and helpful. **Madryn Rent a Car**, Roca 624, T02965-452355.

Península Valdés *p123*
Join a full day excursion from Puerto Madryn, hire a car or catch the daily bus from Puerto Madryn to **Puerto Pirámides**, departs 1000 daily, **28 de Julio**, 1 hr, returns 1800, US$2 each way. Then take the boat trip to see the whales (Sep-Nov) from Puerto Pirámides with **Jorge Schmidt**, T02965-451511/495012.

Trelew *p125, map p125*
Air
Aerolíneas Argentinas flies to/from **Buenos Aires**, **Río Gallegos**, **Ushuaia** and Río Grande; **Lapa** (and TAN) fly to **Comodoro Rivadavia**. **LADE** also flies to several Patagonian airports. Local buses to/from **Puerto Madryn** stop at the airport entrance, turning is 10 mins walk.

Airline offices Aerolíneas Argentinas, 25 de Mayo 33, T02965- 420170. **LADE**, Terminal de Omnibus, T02965-435925.

Bus
Local Mar y Valle and **28 de Julio** both go frequently to **Rawson**, 30 mins; US$0.70, to **Gaiman**, 30 mins; US$1, and **Dolavon** 1 hr, US$1.50, to **Puerto Madryn**, 1hr, US$2.50, to **Puerto Pirámides**, 2½ hrs, US$5, daily.

Long distance To **Buenos Aires**, 20 hrs; US$36-67, several companies daily. To **Comodoro Rivadavia**, 5 hrs, US$12, many companies. To **Río Gallegos**, 17 hrs; US$40, (from here to El Calafate, Puerto Natales and Punta Arenas), many companies. To **Esquel**, 9-10 hrs; US$23-30, many companies.

Bus companies 28 de Julio/Mar y Valle, T02965-432429; **Andesmar**, T02965-433535; **El Cóndor**, T02965-431675; **El Pingüino**, T02965-427400; **El Ñandú**, T02965-427499; **Que Bus**, T02965-422760; **Transportadora Patagónica/Don Otto**, T02965-429496; **TUS**, T02965-421343.

Car hire
Car hire desks at the airport desks are staffed only at flight arrival times. All have offices in town. **AVIS**, Italia 98, T02965-436060; **Hertz**, airport, T02965-1540 5495; **Localiza**, H Yrigoyen 1416, T02965-430070.

South of Trelew *p127*
Bus
Don Otto from Trelew to **Camarones**, Mon and Fri, 2½ hrs, return 1600. Also **El Nañdu**, Mon, Wed, Fri 0800 to **Reserva Natural Cabo Dos Bahías**, 2½ hrs, return 1600, US$4.20.

Directory

Bahía Blanca *p120*
Banks Many ATMs on plaza. **Citibank**, Chiclana 232. **Lloyds TSB Bank**, Chiclana 299, T0291-455 3263. **Pullman**, San Martín 171, changes TCs. **Consulates** Chile, Güemes 102, T0291-455 0110; **Italy**, Colón 446, T0291-454 5140; **Spain**, Drago 70, T0291-422549. **Migraciones**, Brown 963. **Laundry** Laverap, Av Colón 197; **Las Heras**, Las Heras 86. **Post office** Moreno 34. **Telephone** *Locutorio* at Alsina 108, also internet.

Carmen de Patagones and Viedma *p121*
Banks ATMs at Colon and San Martín in Viedma, and Carmen de Patagones at Bynon and Alsina or Bynon and Paraguay. **Travel agencies** Mona Tour, San Martín 225, Viedma. Sells flights and tickets for the train to Bariloche, www.trenpatagonico.com

Puerto Madryn *p122, map p129*
Banks ATMs at: **Banco Nación**, 9 de Julio 117. **Banco del Chubut**, 25 de Mayo 154 and Río, 28 de Julio 56. **Medical services** Chemist on 28 de Julio, late night pharmacy on Belgrano y 25 de Mayo. **Post office**, Belgrano y Maiz, 0900- 1200, 1500-1900. **Telephone** Many *locutorios* in centre.

Trelew *p125, map p125*
Banks Banco de la Nación, 25 de Mayo y Fontana. **Banco del Sud**, 9 de Julio 320, cash advance on Visa. **Post office** 25 de Mayo and Mitre. **Telephone** Telefónica, Roca y Pje Tucumán, and several *locutorios* in the centre. **Travel agencies** Turismo Sur (aka Patagonia Grandes Espacios), Belgrano 338, also currency exchange.

South to Río Gallegos

Lovers of marine life will want to head south towards Río Gallegos and beyond, where the Atlantic coastline is extraordinarily rich in sea birds, penguins, whales and sealions. The southernmost town, Río Gallegos, is a quiet but pleasant place, with accommodation and tours offered. Beyond, on the last spit of land before Tierra del Fuego, is Cabo Vírgines. Inland, Route 26, known as the Bioceanic Corridor, runs west across the steppe amid oil wells, towards Río Mayo, the border and the Chilean towns of Coyhaique and Puerto Aisén and provides access to two petrified forests of ancient araucaria trees. Comodoro Rivadavia is a rather dull base for exploring these forests, but the little town of Sarmiento is far more pleasant. » *For Sleeping, Eating and other listings see pages 140-144.*

Comodoro Rivadavia and inland

» *pp140-144.*

This is a useful transport hub for all areas of Patagonia – if you have the time to travel by bus. Comodoro Rivadavia is the largest city in the province of Chubut and was established primarily as a sheep-exporting port but flourished when oil was discovered here in 1907. However, since the petrol industry was privatized in the 1990s, there's been increasing unemployment and now the town has a slightly sad, unkempt feel. There's little to make you want to stay, although there's a popular beach at **Rada Tilly**, 12 km south, where you can see sea lions at low tide.

If you're fascinated by oil, you could visit the **Museo del Petroleo** ⓘ *T02967-455 9558, Tue-Fri 0900-1800, Sat and Sun 1500-1800, taxi US$4, 3 km north of the centre at San Lorenzo 250*, for a history of local oil exploitation, or the **Museo Paleontológico** ⓘ *20 km north, Sat and Sun 1400-1800*, to look at fossils and reconstructions of dinosaurs. There's a good view of the city from **Cerro Chenque** (212 m), a dun-coloured hill, unattractively adorned with radar masts, whose cliffs give the town its drab backdrop. The **tourist office** ⓘ *Rivadavia 430, T02967-446 2376, www.comodoro.gov.ar, Mon-Fri 0900-1400, or in the bus terminal, daily 0800-2100*, is very helpful and staff speak good English.

Sarmiento and around → *Colour map 2, A4*

Sarmiento lies on the Río Senguer, 150 km west of Comodoro and just south of two great lakes, **Lago Musters** and **Lago Colhué Huapi**, both of which offer good fishing in summer. Founded in 1897, it's a quiet and relaxed place, sitting in fertile, well-irrigated land, and little visited by tourists, despite being close to two areas of petrified forest.

Most accessible is the huge park, **Bosque Petrificado de Sarmiento (José Ormachea)** ⓘ *32 km south along a ripio road, entry US$2.50*. Less easy to reach is the rather bleaker **Bosque Petrificado Víctor Szlapelis** ⓘ *40 km further southwest along the same road; minibus from Sarmiento twice daily Dec-Mar, taxi US$16*. These 60-million-year-old forests of fallen araucaria trees, nearly 3 m in circumference and 15-20 m long, are a remarkable sight, best visited in summer as the winters here are very cold. **Señor Juan José Valero** ⓘ *Uruguay 43, T0297-4898407*, the *guardaparque*, can give guided tours and provide information on camping. Otherwise contact Sarmiento's helpful **tourist office** ⓘ *Av San Martín, near Alberdi, T0297-489 8220, www.interpatagonia.com/sarmiento*. There is also a small museum – ask the tourist office for directions.

Puerto Deseado and around » pp140-144.

Puerto Deseado is a pleasant fishing port on the estuary of the Río Deseado, which drains, curiously, into the Lago Buenos Aires in the west. The estuary encompasses a wonderful nature reserve, and provides easy access to more reserves, protecting sea lions and penguins. Outside the former railway station is the **Vagón Histórico** ⓘ *San Martín 1525, T0297-487 0220, T0297-15-623 4351, www.scruz.gov.ar*, an 1898 carriage, now used as the **tourist office**.

Reserva Natural Ría Deseado → *Colour map 2, B6*

The submerged estuary (*ría*) of the Río Deseado is an important nature reserve and a stunning area to visit. Among many varieties of seabird, there's a colony of Magellanic penguins, and the crumbling chalky cliffs, mauve and ochre, splattered with guano, are home to four species of cormorants including the unique red-legged cormorant, most appealing with their smart dinner-jacketed appearance. These birds nest from October to April on four offshore islands. The reserve is also the breeding ground for Commerson's dolphins: beautiful creatures, which frolic playfully around the tour boats that run from the town's pier. » *See Activities and tours, page 143.*

Around Puerto Deseado

North of Puerto Deseado, on the shore of the peninsula, is **Cabo Blanco**, the site of the largest fur seal colony in Patagonia. It's another magnificent area, a rocky peninsula bursting out from flat lands, with one of the oldest lighthouses on the coast perched on top, and thousands of seals resting on the rocks below. The breeding season is December to January. A little further west, you should also visit **Reserva Cañadón de Duraznillo** within **Estancia La Madrugada** (see Sleeping, page 141). Here you'll see lots of guanacos, ñandues, foxes and birds, as well as the largest seal colony in the province on spectacular unspoilt beaches.

South of Puerto Deseado are two more reserves: **Isla Pingüino**, an offshore island, with a colony of Magellanic penguins, as well as cormorants and steamer ducks, and the **Reserva Natural Bahía Laura**, an uninhabited bay 155 km south along *ripio* and dirt roads, where black-necked cormorants, ducks and other seabirds can be found in abundance. **Darwin Expediciones** and **Los Vikingos** run tours. » *See Activities and tours, page 143.*

Monumento Natural Bosques Petrificados → *Colour map 2, B5*

ⓘ *RN 49, 86 km south of Fitz Roy, T0297-4851000, www.parquesnacionales.gov.ar, Oct-Mar 0900-1900, Apr-Sep 1000-1700. Entry by donation. No services or water anywhere close by, and no accommodation.*

Extending over 10,000 ha in a bizarre, wind-wracked landscape surrounding the **Laguna Grande**, this park contains much older petrified trees than the forests further north around Sarmiento. The trunks, mainly of giant araucaria trees, are up to 35 m long and 150 cm in diameter and were petrified in the Jurassic period 140 million years ago by intense volcanic activity in the Andes *cordillera* which covered the area in ash. The place is more eerie than beautiful, but it does exert a strange fascination, especially when you consider that the fossils of marine animals that you see on the site are a mere 40 million years old, belonging to a sea that covered the land long after the trees had turned to stone. There is a small visitor centre and a well signposted 2-km nature walk. Don't be tempted to take any souvenirs.

Puerto San Julián and around » pp140-144.

The quiet port town of Puerto San Julián, on the Bahía San Julian, is the best place for breaking the 834 km run from Comodoro Rivadavia to Río Gallegos. The first Mass in Argentina was held here in 1520 after the Portuguese explorer Magellan had executed a member of his mutinous crew. Then in 1578, Francis Drake also stopped by in order to behead Thomas Doughty. In 1780, Antonio Viedma founded the colony of Florida Blanca here but it failed due to scurvy; you can visit the ruins 10 km west of the present town. Puerto San Julián was finally founded in 1901 to serve as a port for the sheep estancias in this part of Santa Cruz. A small regional museum, **Museo Regional** ⓘ *Rivadavia y Vieytes*, houses the amazingly well-preserved dinosaur footprint found in the town. Enquire at the **tourist office** ⓘ *Av Costanera y 9 de Julio, or San Martín 1126, T02962-454396, www.scruz.gov.ar/turismo*, about tours to see the wildlife in Reserva San Julian. It's also worth visiting **Estancia La María** (see Sleeping, page 141), 150 km west, which incorporates one of the main archaeological sites in Patagonia: a huge canyon with 87 caves of paintings including human hands and guanacos, 4000-12,000 years old.

Reserva San Julián → *Colour map 2, C5*

The **Reserva San Julián**, on the shores of Bahía San Julián, includes the islands **Banco Cormorán** and **Banco Justicia** (thought to be the site of the 16th-century executions), where there is a colony of Magellanic penguins and nesting areas for several species of cormorants and other birds. You're also very likely to spot Commerson's dolphins in the bay, particularly if you visit in December. However, there's plenty to see right through until April. It's a lovely location and the concentration of marine life is stunning. **Cabo Curiosa**, 15 km to the north, has 30 km of spectacular coastline and fine beaches.

Piedrabuena → *Colour map 2, C4*

Known officially as Comandante Luís Piedrabuena, this quiet town is named after the famous Argentine explorer and sailor, Piedra Buena, who built his home on an island in the Río Santa Cruz here, in 1859. On the island is **Casa Histórica Luis Piedra Buena**, a reconstruction of the original building where he carried on a peaceful trade with local indigenous groups. In recent years, **Isla Pavón**, T02966-1562 3453, has become most popular as a weekend resort for those fishing steelhead trout. Accommodation includes a smart four-star *hostería* as well as an attractive campsite. In March there's a national trout festival. Piedrabuena is a good base for exploring the **Parque Nacional Monte León**. The **tourist office** ⓘ *Av Gregorio Ibáñez 388, T02962-497498*, is helpful and informative.

Parque Nacional Monte León → *Colour map 2, C4*

ⓘ *Access along 23 km of poor ripio road that branches off RN 3, 36 km south of Piedrabuena, 210 km north of Río Gallegos, www.parquesnacionales.gov.ar. Contact Vida Silvestre in Buenos Aires, T011-4311 6633, www.vidasilvestre.org.ar.*

Monte León incorporates 40 km of coastline, where there are many species of seabirds and an enormous penguin colony. Sea lions occupy the many caves and bays, and the tiny island Monte León is an important breeding area for cormorants and terns. The park is owned by US millionaire Douglas Tompkins and looked after by the organization **Vida Silvestre**, but so far access is difficult. However, the effort of getting here is rewarded by wonderful walks along wide isolated beaches, with extraordinary rock formations and cliffs riven with vast caverns – fabulous at low tide. The old house at the heart of the park has been converted to a *hostería*, which is the best way to enjoy the park in comfort. There are plans to turn the old shearing shed into a visitor centre.

Río Gallegos and around » pp140-144.

→ *Colour map 3, A4*

The capital of Santa Cruz province lies on the estuary of the Río Gallegos, the river famous for its excellent brown trout fishing. It's a pleasant airy town, founded in 1885 as a centre for the trade in wool and sheepskins, and is by far the most appealing of the main centres on southern Patagonia's east coast. It was once the main access point for trips to the Parque Nacional Los Glaciares (see page 152) but receives fewer visitors since the airport opened at El Calafate. However, you may well come here to change buses, and could visit the penguin reserve at Cabo Vírgenes some 130 km south, or Monte León 210 km north. The town itself has a couple of museums, and boasts a few smart shops and restaurants.

Ins and outs → *Río Gallegos is pronounced 'rio ga-shay-gos'*

Getting there Flights arrive at the airport, 10 km from centre, from Buenos Aires, El Calafate and Ushuaia. There are also **LADE** flights connecting all major Patagonian towns, see Essentials, page 20. A taxi into town costs US$4. The crowded **bus terminal** ⓘ *corner of RN 3 y Av Eva Perón*, is inconveniently located 3 km from the centre. Buses 1 and 12 will take you into town, or take a taxi for US$1.30.

Tourist information ⓘ *Av Roca 863, T02966-438725, www.scruz.gov.com.ar/turismo, Mon-Fri 0900-2100, Sat 1000-2000, Sun 1000-1500, 1600-2000.* An excellent and well-organized office with information for the whole province. The staff are extremely helpful, speak English and have a list of estancias in Santa Cruz. There's also an office at the airport and a small desk at the bus terminal, T02966-442159.

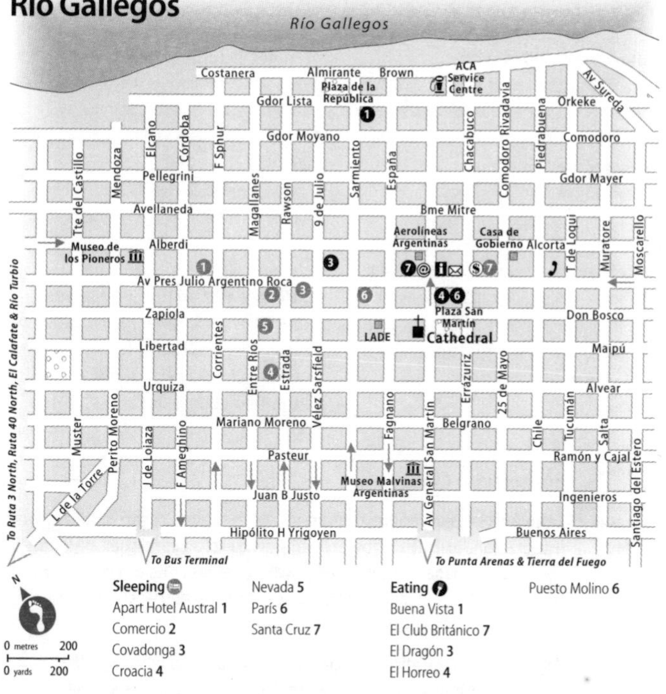

Sights

The tidy, leafy Plaza San Martín, two blocks south of the main street, Avenida Roca, has an interesting collection of trees (many planted by the early pioneers) and a diminutive corrugated iron cathedral, with a wood-panelled ceiling in the chancel and stained-glass windows. The best of the town's museums is the small **Museo de los Pioneros** ⓘ *Elcano y Alberdi, T02966-437763, daily 1000-2000, free*, housed in a building that was shipped here from Britain in 1890. The museum has interesting photographs and artefacts telling the story of the first Scottish settlers, who came here in 1884 from the Falkland Islands/Las Malvinas to take up government grants of land. Also stimulating is the **Museo Malvinas Argentinas** ⓘ *Pasteur 74, T02966-420128, Mon and Thu 0800-1200, Tue and Fri 1300-1730, 3rd Sun in the month 1530-1800*, which aims to inform visitors about Argentine claims to Las Malvinas.

Reserva Provincial Cabo Vírgenes

ⓘ *Branch off RN 3, 15 km south of Río Gallegos, onto RN 1 for 119 km, 3½ hrs, US$3.* This nature reserve protects the second largest colony of Magellanic penguins in Patagonia. There's an informative self-guided walk to see their nests among the calafate and fragrant mata verde bushes. It's good to visit around November, when the chicks are born and there are nests under every bush. You can climb the Cabo Vírgenes **lighthouse** (owned by the Argentine Navy) for wonderful views and there's a *confitería* close by for snacks. **Estancia Monte Dinero** (see Sleeping, page 142), 13 km north of Cabo Vírgenes, is a wonderful base for visiting the reserve.

South of Cabo Vírgenes are the ruins of **Nombre de Jesús**, one of two doomed settlements founded by Pedro Sarmiento de Gamboa in 1584. **Laguna Azul**, near the Monte Aymond border crossing, is a perfect, royal blue lagoon in the crater of an extinct volcano. It's set in an atmospheric and arid lunar landscape and is a good place for a walk. Take a tour, or get off the bus along Route 3, which stops on the main road.

Sleeping

Comodoro Rivadavia *p136*

B Lucania Palazzo Hotel, Moreno 676, T02967-449 9338, www.lucania-palazzo.com. A stylish and luxurious business hotel, with a lovely airy spacious reception, and superb rooms, many with sea views, good value. A huge American breakfast, and use of sauna and gym included. Recommended.

D Hotel Azul, Sarmiento 724, T02967-447 4628. This is a nice quiet old place, with lovely bright rooms, friendly owners, and great panoramic views from the *confiteria*, though breakfast is extra.

D Hotel Victoria, Belgrano 585, T02967-446 0725. An old fashioned city *hostería*, mostly used by workers in the oil industry, but it's friendly, and clean and comfortable enough. Breakfast US$1.20.

D Rua Marina, Belgrano 738, T02967-446877. All rooms have TV and bath and breakfast; newer rooms are particularly comfortable. Friendly welcome.

E Hospedaje Cari Hue, Belgrano 563, T02967-472946. Sweet rooms, with separate bathrooms off a central hallway. Very nice owners who like backpackers. Breakfast extra. Best budget choice.

Border with Chile

From Río Gallegos, Route 3 continues south to the Chilean border at **Paso Integración Austral**. On the Chilean side, the road continues as Route 255 via Punta Delgada to Punta Arenas, where ferries cross to Tierra del Fuego (see pages 274 and 302). For bus passengers the border crossing is easy, but hire cars will need special documentation.

Argentine immigration and customs ⓘ *24hrs in summer, Apr-Nov 0800-2200.* **Chilean immigration and customs** ⓘ *daily 0800-2200.*

Camping

Municipal site, Rada Tilly, reached by **Expreso Rada Tilly** bus from town. Hot showers.
San Carlos, 37 km north on RN3, T02967-4560425.

Sarmiento *p136*

C Chacra El Labrador, 10 km from Sarmiento, T0297-489 3329, agna@coopsar.com.ar. This is an excellent place to stay on a small estancia, breakfast included, other meals available, also for non-residents. Tours to petrified forests at good prices, will collect guests from Sarmiento (same price as taxi).

Puerto Deseado *p137*

C Isla Chaffers, San Martín y Mariano Moreno, T0297-487 2246, www.islachaffers.wm.com.ar. The town's best hotel, modern and central.
C Los Acantilados, Pueyrredón y España, T0297-487 2167, www.pdeseado.com.ar/acantour. Beautifully located hotel, popular with anglers, comfortable rooms with bathrooms, good breakfast.

Camping

There is a **municipal campsite** on the seafront, T0297-1562 52890, or **Camping Cañadon Jiminez**, 4 km away on RN 281.

Estancias

A Estancia La Madrugada, on the Atlantic Coast, 120 km from Puerto Deseado, reached from the RN281 to Km 79, then RN 68, T0297-1559 4123, walker@caminosturismo.com.ar. Splendid views, and plenty of places to spot wildlife, good Patagonian home cooking, and comfortable accommodation. The owners also arrange excursions to sea lion colony and cormorant nesting area. Recommended.

Puerto San Julián *p138*

B Bahía, San Martín 1075, T02962-453144, nico@sanjulian.com.ar. Modern and comfortable rooms, good value.
C Municipal, 25 de Mayo 917, T02962-452300. Attractive rooms, well-run, good value, no restaurant.

Camping

Municipal campsite, Magellanes 650 y M Moreno, T02962-452806. US$2 per site plus US$1 pp, recommended, all facilities.

Estancia

B Estancia La María, 150 km west, contact Fernando Behm, Saavedra 1163, T02962-452328. Simple accommodation in a modern house, with amazing cave paintings. Trips to see marine and birdlife organized.

Piedrabuena *p138*

A-B ACA Motel, T02962-47145. Simple, functional but good, warm and nice food.
A-B Hostería El Alamo, Lavalle 08, T02962-47249. Quiet, breakfast extra. Recommended.
A-B Hostería Municipal Isla Pavon, Isla Pavón, T02962-1563 8380. Luxurious 4-star catering to fishermen of steelhead trout.
C Res Internacional, Ibáñez 99, T02962-47197. Recommended.

Camping

There are a couple of sites south of town on RN 3; also on Isla Pavón.

Parque Nacional Monte León *p138*

A-B Estancia Monte León, on RN3, www.monteleon-patagonia.com, Nov-Apr. Beautifully modernized but traditional *estancia* with 4 impeccably tasteful rooms, decorated with Tompkins' considerable style. See also www.vidasilvestre.org.ar.

Río Gallegos *p139, map p139*

Most hotels are within a few blocks of the main street, Av Roca, running northwest–southeast. Do not confuse the street Comodoro Rivadavia with (nearby) Bernardino Rivadavia.
C Apart Hotel Austral, Roca 1505, T02966-434314, apartaustral@infovia.com.ar. A smart newly built apart hotel, with bright rooms, and attractive sunny decor. Very good value, particularly the superior duplexes. Kitchen facilities are basic, but certainly adequate for a couple of nights. Breakfast US$1.50 extra.
C Comercio, Roca 1302, T02966-422458, hotelcomercio@informacionrgl.com.ar. Good

For an explanation of sleeping and eating price codes, and other relevant information, see Essentials pages 25-26.

value, well-designed comfortable en suite rooms, breakfast included. There is an attractive cheap *confitería* on the street.

C **Croacia**, Urquiza 431, T02966-421218. Cheaper, and one of the most reasonably priced places, with comfortable beds, bright spotless rooms with bath, huge breakfasts, and helpful owners. Recommended.

C **Santa Cruz**, Roca 701, T02966-420601, www.advance.com.ar/usuarios/htlscruz. This modern city-style hotel is excellent value. Go for the slightly pricier, spacious new rooms with excellent bathrooms and full buffet breakfast included. Highly recommended.

D **Covadonga**, Roca 1244, T02966-420190. Attractive old 1930s building. Rooms are basic but clean and well maintained, with bath and TV. Courtyard. Breakfast included, .

D **Nevada**, Zapiola 480, T02966-435790. A good budget option, with clean, simple spacious rooms, nice beds and good bathrooms, and welcoming owners.

D **París**, Roca 1040, T02966-420111. Simple rooms with bath, set back from the street, a good value choice, though breakfast is extra.

Estancias

A **Hill Station**, 63 km north of Río Gallegos on RN 58. An estancia with 120 years of history, run by descendants of the founder, William Halliday. A sheep farm, also breeding criollo horses, this offers wonderful horse riding to see flora and fauna of the coast.

A **Monte Dinero**, near Cabo Vírgines, T02966-428922, www.montedinero.com.ar. On this working sheep farm accommodation is comfortable. The house is lined with wood rescued from ships wrecked off the coast, and the food is delicious and home grown. They'll take you on a tour of the reserve, and give you an impressive demonstration of the incredible prowess of their sheep dogs. Highly recommended.

Camping

Camping ATSA, RN 3, towards bus terminal, T02966-420301. US$2.50 pp, US$0.50 for tent.

Chacra Daniel, Paraje Río Chico, 3.5 km from town, T02966-423970. US$4 pp per day, with *parrilla* and full facilities. Recommended.

Club Pescazaike, Paraje Güer Aike, T02966-421803, some 30 km west of town on RN 3. Well equipped, and an attractive place US$2 pp per day, also *quincho* and restaurant.

Eating

Comodoro Rivadavia *p136*

🍴🍴 **Cayo Coco**, Rivadavia 102. A welcoming little bistro, with very cheery staff, and excellent pizzas. Recommended.

🍴🍴 **Dionisius**, 9 de Julio y Rivadavia. A smart and elegant *parrilla*, popular with a more sedate clientele. Excellent set menus US$5.

🍴🍴 **La Barra**, San Martín 686. A pleasant bright café for breakfast, very good coffee or a light lunch.

🍴🍴 **La Tradición**, Mitre 675. Another popular and recommended *parrilla*.

🍴🍴 **Peperoni**, Rivadavia 348. A cheerful modern place with good range of home made pastas, filled with exciting things like king crab, as well as serving seafood and *parrilla*. US$4-7, for main dish.

🍴 **La Barca**, Belgrano 935. Welcoming and cheap *tenedor libre*.

Puerto Deseado *p137*

🍴 **El Pingüino**, Piedrabuena 958. Established *parrilla* which serves fabulous rice pudding.

🍴 **Puerto Cristal**, Espana 1698. Panoramic views of the port, a great place for Patagonian lamb and *parrilla*.

Puerto San Julián *p138*

🍴🍴 **El Muelle Viejo**, Mitre 1. Good seafood on this seafront restaurant. The *pejerrey* is recommended. Also bars and tearooms.

🍴🍴 **Rural**, Ameghino y Vieytes. Best after 2100.

🍴🍴 **Sportsman**, Mitre y 25 de Mayo. Excellent value.

Río Gallegos *p139, map p139*

There are lots of good places to eat here, many serving excellent seafood, and some smart new inexpensive restaurants.

🍴 **Buena Vista**, Sarmiento y Gob Lista, T02966-444114. Most chic, and not expensive. Near the river, with open views across the Plaza de la República, this has an imaginative menu.

🍴 **El Club Británico**, Roca 935. Doing its best to look like a London gentleman's club, though lacking in atmosphere, set lunches.

🍴 **El Dragón**, 9 de Julio 29. Cheap and varied *tenedor libre*.

🍴 **El Horreo**, Roca 863. Next to **Puesto Molino**. A more sophisticated option, rather like a bistro in feel, serving delicious lamb dishes and good salads. Recommended.

Puesto Molino, Roca 862, opposite the tourist office. A relaxed airy place, its design inspired by life on estancias, with bold paintings, wooden tables and excellent pizzas (US$5 for 2) and *parrilla* (US$10 for 2). Recommended.

Activities and tours

Comodoro Rivadavia *p136*

Aonikenk Viajes, Rawson 1190, T02967-446 6768, aonikenk@satlink.com. Tours to the petrified forests, with 2 hrs at the site.
Marco Sur, San Martín 263 Local 9, Galería San Martín, T/F02967-4477490, www.marcosur.com.

Puerto Deseado *p137*

Darwin Expediciones, España 2601, T0297-15-624 7554, www.darwin-expeditions.com, and **Los Vikingos**, Estrada 1275, T0297-487 0020, both offer excursions by boat to Rio Deseado reserve, and Reserva Provincial Isla Pinguino, as well as trips to see the Monumento Natural Bosques Petrificados.

Monumento Natural Bosques Petrificados *p137*

The site can be visited in a day trip with a tour from San Julián, or from Puerto Deseado with **Los Vikingos**, Estrada 1275, T0297-4870020, www.losvikingos.com.ar.

Puerto San Julián *p138*

Tur Aike Turismo, Av San Martín 446, T02962-452086. Excellent 1½-hr zodiac boat trips.

Río Gallegos *p139, map p139*

Fishing

The southern fishing zone includes the rivers Gallegos, Grande, Fuego, Ewan and San Pablo plus Lago Fagnano, near Ushuaia. It is famous for runs of sea trout. Ask the tourist office for fishing guides and information on permits, www.scruz.gov.ar/pesca.

Tours

Macatobiano Turismo, Roca 908, T/F02966-434201, macatobiano@macatobiano.com. Tours to Pingüinero Cabo Vírgenes, also to Laguna Azul, a beautiful lake in a volcanic crater, and to Estancia Monte León. Air tickets to El Calafate and Ushuaia. Recommended.

Transport

Comodoro Rivadavia *p136*

Air

Airport 9 km north. Bus No 6 to airport from bus terminal, hourly (45 mins), US$0.40. Taxi to airport US$3. To **Buenos Aires**, with **Aerolíneas Argentinas/Austral**, 9 de Julio 870, T0297-444 0050. Also **LADE**, Rivadavia 360, T0297-447 6565, once a week to **Puerto Madryn**, **Esquel**, **Bariloche**, and **El Calafate**, among other towns in Patagonia.

Bus

The terminal, Pellegrini 730, T02967-3367305, has an excellent tourist office 0800-2100. To **Buenos Aires**, 2 daily, 28 hrs, US$45. To **Bariloche**, 14 hrs, US$19 (**Don Otto**, T02967-447 0450). To **Esquel** (paved road) 8 hrs direct with **ETAP** and **Don Otto**, US$18; in summer buses usually arrive full, so book ahead. To **Río Gallegos**, **Don Otto**, **Pingüino** and **TAC**, T02967-444 3376, daily, 11 hrs, US$9. To **Puerto Madryn**, US$8. To **Trelew**, **Don Otto** 3 daily 4 hrs US$6. To **Caleta Olivia**, **La Unión** hourly, US$1.50. To **Sarmiento**, US$4, 2½ hrs, 3 daily.

To Chile To **Coyhaique**, US$15, 12 hrs, and **Santiago**, 35 hrs $155, **Etap Angel Giobbi**, twice a week.

Car rental

Avis, 9 de Julio 687, T/F02967-496382. **Patagonia Sur Car**, Rawson 1190, T02967-4466768.

Sarmiento *p136*

There are 3 buses daily to **Comodoro** with **Etap**, T0297-447 4841, and overnight services to **Esquel**, T0297-454756, daily except Sat. To **Chile** via Río Mayo, **Giobbi**, 0200, 3 weekly; seats are scarce.

Puerto Deseado *p137*

Bus terminal, T0297-155 928598. **Sportman** and **La Unión**, daily to **Caleta Olivia**, US$5, for connections to Comodoro Rivadavia.

Puerto San Julián *p138*

Air

LADE, San Martín 1552, T02962-452137, flies each Mon to various Patagonian destinations (see Essentials, page 19).

Bus

To **Buenos Aires**, **Transportadora Patagónica**, T02962-452072, **Pingüino**, T02962-452425. To **Río Gallegos**, **Pingüino**, 6 hrs, US$7.

Río Gallegos *p139, map p139*

Air

Río Gallegos used to be the nearest airport to **El Calafate**, but there are fewer flights now that Lago Viedma airport has opened. Both **Pingüino** and **Interlagos** arrange packages to El Calafate including accommodation and trip to Moreno glacier from offices at the airport.

Regular flights to/from **Buenos Aires**, **Ushuaia** and **Río Grande** direct with Aerolíneas Argentinas. Also LADE to **Río Turbio**, **El Calafate**, **Ushuaia** and **Comodoro Rivadavia** once a week (book as far in advance as possible). The **Ladeco** service from **Punta Arenas** to **Port Stanley** on the **Falkland Islands/Islas Malvinas** stops here once a month in either direction.

Airline offices Aerolíneas Argentinas, San Martín 545, T02966-422020/0810-222 86527, also at airport T02966-442059. LADE, Fagnano 53, T02966-422316. **Southern Winds**, San Martín 661, T02966-437171.

Bus

To **El Calafate**, 4-5 hrs, US$9, **Taqsa** and **Interlagos**. To **Los Antiguos**, **Sportman** daily at 2100, US$20. To **Comodoro Rivadavia**, **Pingüino**, **Don Otto** and **TAC**, 10 hrs, US$10. To **Bariloche**, **Transportadora Patagonica**, daily at 2130. To **Buenos Aires**, 33 hrs, several daily, **Pingüino**, **Don Otto**, **TAC**, US$35. To **Río Grande** and **Ushuaia**, **Tecni Austral**, Tue, Thu, Sat, 1000, US$18-23, 8-10 hrs.

To Chile To **Puerto Natales**, **Pingüino**, Sat, 7 hrs, US$7 or **Bus-Sur** Tue and Thu 1700. To **Punta Arenas**, **Pingüino** and others, US$11, daily.

Car

Book car rental in advance in high season. Hire companies include: **Cristina**, Libertad 123, T02966-425709; **Localiza**, Sarmiento 237, T02966-424417; **Taxi Centenario**, Maipú 285, T02966-422320.

Taking a car to Chile Make sure your car papers are in order (go first to tourist office for necessary documents, then to the customs office at the port, at the end of San Martín, very uncomplicated). Let the hire company know, and allow 24 hrs to get the appropriate papers. The car's windows should be etched with the licence plate number.

Directory

Comodoro Rivadavia *p136*

Consulates **Belgium**, Rivadavia 283. **Chile**, Sarmiento 936. Italy, Belgrano 1053. **Internet**, Rivadavia 201 and along San Martín. **Post office** San Martín y Moreno.

Puerto San Julián *p138*

Banks **Banco de la Nación**, Mitre y Belgrano, and **Banco de la Provincia de Santa Cruz**, San Martín y Moreno. **Post office** Belgrano y San Martín.

Río Gallegos *p139, map p139*

Banks Change TCs here if going to El Calafate. 24-hr ATMs are plentiful. **Thaler**, San Martín 484, will change Chilean pesos and US$. **Consulates** **Chile**, Mariano Moreno 136, Mon-Fri, 0900-1300; tourist cards issued at the border. **Internet/telephone** **J@va cybercafe** (next to British Club on Roca); also various *locutorios* with internet, US$0.60 per hr. **Post office** Roca 893 y San Martín.

Ruta 40 to the glaciers

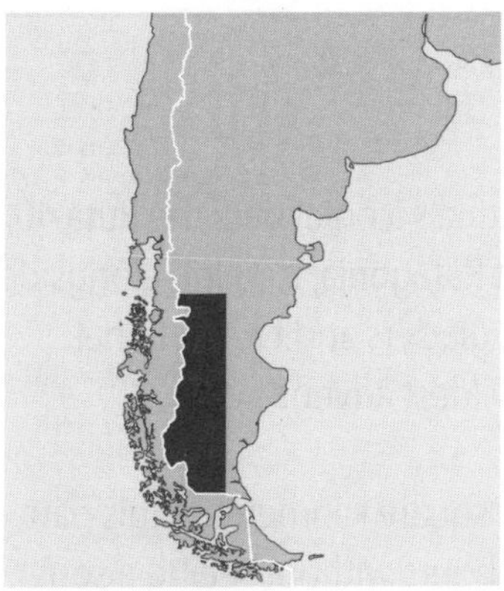

Footprint features

Introduction

The southernmost part of Argentina's iconic road, the Ruta 40, penetrates the remotest heart of Patagonia, running alongside the Andes, with access to peaks, glaciers and two national parks – perfect terrain for your wildest adventure.

There's less than one person per square kilometre in this part of Patagonia and you'll drive for hours without seeing a soul. Head south to the mysterious Cueva de las Manos, where thousands of handprints were painted by pre-historic people or west to the Perito Moreno national park, a virgin wilderness, where jagged peaks are reflected in limpid lakes and condors wheel overhead. For a little civilization in your wilderness, stay at an estancia, where you can experience the timeless life on the land and feast on Patagonian lamb.

At the northern end of Parque Nacional Los Glaciares, El Chaltén is the base for trekking around the magnificent peaks of Mount Fitz Roy, where you can hike for days, and even climb glaciers, or get access to expeditions on the Southern Ice Field. Further south, El Calafate is the gateway to the spectacular Perito Moreno glacier. Walk with crampons on the sculpted surface, or watch with wonder as great walls of ice cleave with a mighty roar into the milky lake below. Best of all, take a boat to Estancia Cristina and see Upsala glacier from above: just you and millions of years of time and space.

★ Don't miss ...
❶ Driving the Ruta 40, page 148.
❷ Cueva de las Manos, page 149.
❸ Trekking on the glaciers, pages 154 and 155.
❹ Cerro Fitz Roy, page 158.
❺ Estancia Cristina, page 167.
40 km
40 miles
N
Hudson
Río Ibáñez
Reserva Nacional Cerro Castillo
Cerro Castillo
Balmaceda
Lago Blanco
Paso Huemules
Lago Blanco
Río Guenguel
Villa Cerro Castillo
Puerto Ibáñez
Río Murta
Puerto Grosse
Levicán
Bahía Murta
Lago General Carrera
Lago Buenos Aires
SANTA CRUZ
Fachinal
Chile Chico
Los Antiguos
Perito Moreno
Río Tranquilo
Reserva Nacional General Carrera
Pico del Sur (2190m)
Estancia La Serena
520
Las H
Río Tranquilo
Mallín Grande
Reserva Nacional Lago Jeinemeni
Lago Bertrand
Puerto Guadal
Lago Bertrand
El Maitén
Jeinemeni (2600m)
Cevallos (2743m)
Estancia Telken
Río Pinturas
Río Deseado
Puerto Bertrand
Río Chacabuco
Paso Roballos
ARGENTINA
Reserva Nacional Tamango
40
Cochrane
Lago Cochrane
Lago Pueyrredón
Cueva de las Manos
Campo de Hielo Norte
Río Baker
Lago Posadas
Lago Salitroso
Bajo Caracoles
Tortel
Estancia La Oriental
Puerto Yungay
Parque Nacional Perito Moreno
Herros (2770m)
San Lorenzo (3706m)
Las Horquetas
Villa O'Higgins
L Strobel
Lago O'Higgins
Gobernador Gregores
Lago San Martín
L Cardiel
Estancia La Angostura
Estancia La Maípu
Río Chico
Fitz Roy (3405m)
El Chaltén
40
La Julia
Glaciar Viedma
Lago Viedma
Laguna Grande
Estancia Helsingfors
Tres Lagos
Cerro Norte
Estancia La Leona
Parque Nacional Los Glaciares
Glaciar Upsala
Estancia Cristina
Leona
Santa Cruz
Puerto de Punta Quilla
Rincón Grande
Lago Argentino
El Galpón del Glacier
Río Santa Cruz
Puerto Bandera
Río Bote
Gendarme Barreto
SANTA CRUZ
Glaciar Perito Moreno
El Calafate
40
Cañadón de las Vacas
Estancia Alta Vista
Estancia Nibepo Aike
El Cerrito
Atlantic Ocean
Fuentes del Coyle
Puerto Coig
Lago Sarmiento
Parque Nacional Torres del Paine
La Esperanza
Paso Cancha Carrera
Cerro Castillo
Gobernador Mayer
REGION XII
Monumento Nacional Cueva Milodón
Río Coig
Estancia Hill Station
Balmaceda (2035m)
Paso Dorotea
Río Turbio
Güer Aike
Río Gallegos
Seno Ultima Esperanza
Paso Casas Viejas
El Turbio
Río Gallegos
3
Puerto Natales
Cordillera Sarmiento
El Zurdo
Bella Vista
Laguna Azul
Morro Chico
Parque Nacional Pali Aike
9

South on the Ruta 40

Route 40 (paved) heads south from Esquel across a deserted landscape that provides a taste for the full experience of Patagonia. The main reason for travelling along this route is to visit the extraordinary Cueva de las Manos, south of Perito Moreno, but the journey itself will also leave a lasting impression: you might not see a soul all day, and passing a car is a major event. However, there are estancias hidden in the emptiness, where a night or two can give you a wonderful flavour of Patagonian life. When at last you arrive at Mount Fitz Roy, you may think you've imagined it. The sight of the great turrets of granite is made all the more spectacular by days spent crossing endless flatlands, with only condors and clouds for company. ⏩ *For Sleeping, Eating and other listings, see pages 150-152.*

Ins and outs

Getting there and around **Chalten Travel** and **Itinerarios y Travesías** run a daily bus service between Los Antiguos and El Chaltén; you're unlikely to stop in between, except to see the Cueva de las Manos from Perito Moreno. Various companies organize tours, with estancia stays included (for example www.tierrabuena.com.ar or www.estanciasdesantacruz.com). For drivers travelling south, the road is paved as far as Perito Moreno, and then good *ripio*, improving greatly after Las Horquetas. Fuel is available in most places but carry extra to avoid a 72 km detour to Gobernador Gregores. If cycling, note that food and water stops are scarce, the wind is fierce and there is no shade.

Perito Moreno and around → *Colour map 2, B3*

Your most likely stop on the long road south is the spruce little town of Perito Moreno, 25 km west of Lago Buenos Aires and accessible by bus from Esquel or Comodoro Rivadavia. It's the nearest base for exploring the mysterious cave paintings at the **Cueva de las Manos** to the south (see page 149). The town has no sights as such, but southwest of the town is **Parque Laguna**, where you can see varied bird life, including flamingos and black-necked swans, and go fishing. You could also walk to the crater of **Cerro Volcán**, from a path 12 km outside Perito Moreno: ask at the friendly **tourist office** ⓘ *San Martín 1222, T02963-432222, www.epatagonia.gov.ar, 0700-2300*, for directions. Staff can also advise on tours and estancia stays.

Los Antiguos → *Colour map 2, B3*

From this part of Argentina, the easiest and most commonly used route to Chile is via the pretty little village of Los Antiguos, which lies just 2 km east of the border, on the southern shore of **Lago Buenos Aires**. This is the second largest lake in South America and extends into Chile as Lago General Carrera (see page 263). The landscape is beautiful and unspoilt and the Río Baker, which flows from the lake, is world-renowned for excellent trout fishing. The main reason to enter Chile here is to take the ferry over the lake to Puerto Ibáñez with bus connections to Coyhaique on the Carretera Austral. (You can also drive to Puerto Ibáñez from Perito Moreno, via the paved road around the north-east side of Lago Buenos Aires.)

Los Antiguos is a sleepy little place, but has a rather pleasant quiet atmosphere, thanks largely to its warm microclimate. It's a rich fruit-growing area with a popular cherry festival in early January that attracts national *folclore* stars. There's a small but willing **tourist office** ⓘ *Av 11 de Julio 446, www.losantiguos-sc.com.ar, summer 0800-2200, at other times 0800-1200 only*. While you're here, visit two local *chacras* (small farms). You can walk to **Chacra Don Neno**, where strawberries are grown and good jam is sold, or (if you have transport) head further afield to idyllic **Chacra el Paraiso**, which grows and sells perfect cherries.

Cueva de las Manos → *Colour map 2, B4*

ⓘ *Access is via an unpaved road east off RN 40, 3 km north of Bajo Caracoles, US$1.50, 6 hrs return journey by car from Perito Moreno. Estancia Los Toldos (60 km from Perito Moreno, 18 km from the caves) organizes trips, page 150.*

Situated 163 km south of Perito Moreno and 47 km northeast of Bajo Caracoles, the canyon of the **Río Pinturas** contains outstanding examples of handprints and cave paintings, estimated to be between 3000 and 9300 years old. In the cave's four galleries are over 800 paintings of human hands (all but 31 of which depict left hands), as well as images of guanacos and rheas, and various geometrical designs painted by the Toldense peoples. The red, orange, black, white and ochre pigments were derived from earth and calafate berries and fixed with a varnish of guanaco fat and urine. The canyon itself is also worth seeing: 270 m deep and 480 m wide, with strata of vivid red and green rock; it's especially beautiful in the early morning or evening light. A *guardaparque* living at the site provides helpful information.

Bajo Caracoles and beyond → *Colour map 2, B3*

After hours of spectacular emptiness, even tiny Bajo Caracoles is a relief. It's nothing more than a few houses, facing into the wind, with an expensive grocery store and very expensive fuel. From here, Route 41 (unpaved) heads 99 km northwest, past Lago Ghio and Lago Columna, to the **Paso Roballos** border and on to **Cochrane** (see page 266). Although it's passable in summer, the route is often flooded in spring and there's no public transport. **Chilean immigration** ⓘ *11 km from border, winter 0800-2000, summer 0800-2200.* Route 39, meanwhile, heads west for 72 km to **Lago Posadas** and **Lago Pueyrredón**, two beautiful lakes with contrasting blue and turquoise waters, separated by a narrow isthmus, where guanacos and rheas can be seen.

South of Bajo Caracoles, Route 40 crosses the Pampa del Asador and then, near Las Horquetas, swings southeast to follow the Río Chico. There is a turning off west to Lago Belgrano and **Parque Nacional Perito Moreno** (see 150). South of this junction, Route 40 improves considerably. At Km 464, Route 25 branches off towards **San Julian** on the Atlantic Coast, via **Gobernador Gregores** (72 km, fuel), while Route 40 continues southwest towards Tres Lagos. There is no food between Bajo Caracoles and Tres Lagos, although there are estancias roughly every 25 km.

Border with Chile

Two roads cross the border into Chile west of Río Mayo to take you to Coyhaique (see page 252). Further south, the road from Perito Moreno to Los Antiguos leads to a border on the shores of Lago Buenos Aires.

Coyhaique Alto is reached by a 133 km road (87 km *ripio*, then dirt) that branches off Route 40 about 7 km north of Río Mayo, continuing on the Chilean side 50 km west to Coyhaique. **Chilean immigration** ⓘ *Coyhaique Alto, 6 km west of the border, May-Aug 0800-2100, Sep-Apr 0700-2300.*

Paso Huemules is reached by a road that branches off Route 40, some 31 km south of Río Mayo and runs west 105 km via Lago Blanco (fuel), 30 km from the border. This crossing has better roads than Coyhaique Alto. On the Chilean side, this road continues via Balmaceda airport, 61 km to Coyhaique. **Chilean immigration** ⓘ *3 km from the border, winter 0800-2000, summer 0800-2200.*

From **Los Antiguos** a bridge crosses the border heading towards Chile Chico, (see page 265). **Chilean immigration** ⓘ *20 km from the border, winter 0800-2000, summer 0800-2200.*

Parque Nacional Perito Moreno → *Colour map 2, B3*

ⓘ Southwest of Bajo Caracoles on the Chilean border. Entrance 90 km west of Las Horquetas via RN 37, Nov-Mar, free, no public transport. Information from Av San Martín 409, Gobernador Gregores (220 km away), T02962-491477, peritomoreno@apn.gov.ar. This is one of the wildest and most remote parks in Argentina. The large, interconnected system of lakes and glaciated peaks offers good trekking and abundant wildlife but much of the park is dedicated to scientific study and inaccessible.

About 10 km beyond the park entrance, the *guardaparque*'s office has maps and leaflets on walks and wildlife. The most accessible section of the park is a little further on, around turquoise **Lago Belgrano**. Several good hikes are possible from here around the peninsula, with fine views of Cerro Herros; to **Cerro Léon**, starting from **Estancia La Oriental**, good for spotting condors; and the one- or two-day hike to **Lago Burmeister**, via Cerro Casa de Piedra, 16 km. At the foot of **Cerro Casa de Piedra** is a network of caves containing paintings, accessible only with a guide.

The **Sierra Colorada** dominates the northeast of the park and the erosion of its multicoloured rocks is responsible for the lakes' vibrant colours. Between the lakes are snow-covered peaks, the highest of which is **Cerro Herros** (2770 m), while outside the park itself, but towering over it to the north, is **Cerro San Lorenzo** (3706 m), the highest peak in southern Patagonia. Vegetation changes with altitude: dense coiron grasses and shrubs cling to the windswept steppe, while beech forest, lenga and coihue occupy the higher slopes. Wildlife includes guanacos, foxes and the rare huemul, plus flamingos, ñandus, steamer ducks, grebes, black-necked swans, Patagonian woodpeckers, eagles and condors. The lakes and rivers are unusual for Argentina in that they contain only native species of fish.

Sleeping

Perito Moreno *p148*

D **Austral**, San Martín 1327, T02963-42042. Bath and breakfast, and a decent restaurant. The slightly better of the 2 hotels in town.

D **Belgrano**, San Martín 1001, T02963-42019. Also pleasant, with simple rooms.

Estancia

L pp **Telken**, 28 km south on RN40, T02963-432079, Buenos Aires T011-4797 7216, jarinauta@santacruz.com.ar. Formerly a sheep station, with comfortable wood-lined rooms in the farmhouse, and charming simple bedrooms. All meals shared with the welcoming owners, who also offer horse riding. Highly recommended.

Los Antiguos *p148*

A **Hostería La Serena**, 29 km east of Los Antiguos, T02963-432340. Comfortable accommodation, excellent home-grown food, fishing and trips to the Chilean and Argentine lake districts, open Oct-Jun.

B **Antigua Patagonia**, on the lakeside, signposted from RN43, T02963-491038, www.antiguapatagonia.com.ar. An excellent hotel and worth a detour. Luxurious rooms with beautiful views on the shore of the lake. There's also a great restaurant. Tours to the Cueva de los Manos and nearby Monte Cevallos can be arranged. Recommended.

D **Argentino**, 11 de Julio 850, T02963-491132. Comfortable rooms, and a decent restaurant.

F pp **Albergue Padilla**, San Martín 44 (just off main street) T02963-491140. Big shared rooms for 4-8 with bathrooms, *quincho* and garden, where you can also camp. Very friendly. El Chaltén travel tickets sold.

Camping

Municipal, T02963-491308, T02963-15-621 1855. Outstanding site with every facility, lovely grounds 2 km from centre, US$1.25 pp.

Cueva de las Manos *p149*

L **Estancia Los Toldos**, 7 km off the RN 40, 60 km south of Perito Moreno, T02963-432856, T011-4901 0436, www.estanciasdesanta cruz.com/lostoldos. The closest estancia to the caves. A modest building in a wonderful landscape. The owners run trips by horse or 4WD, as well as to the lakes and PN Perito Moreno. They also have an albergue, the **Hostería Cueva de Las Manos** (**B**), Nov-Easter.

Bajo Caracoles and beyond *p149*
There are some superb estancias around Gobernador Gregores, tricky to get to without your own transport, but offering an unforgettable slice of Patagonian life.

L Hostería Lagos del Furioso, Lago Posadas, on the peninsula between the lakes, reached along RN 39, T02963-490253, www.lagosdelfurioso.com. Open Mid Oct-Easter. Extremely comfortable accommodation in cabins in a really incredible setting by the lake shore, offering superb Patagonian cooking with home produced food, and good wines. Also offers horse riding, trekking and excursions in 4WD vehicles. 2 nights minimum – you'll want to stay longer.

D Hotel Bajo Caracoles, Bajo Caracoles, T0297-434963. Very old-fashioned 1920s building, with plain spacious rooms and meals, but a rather institutional feel. Given the wilderness, you'll probably be glad of a bed.

Camping

G At the campsite, rooms **E** pp, are also available. A simple and welcoming place, also running excursions to Cueva de las Manos, 10 km by vehicle then 1½- to 2-hrs' walk, and to nearby volcanoes by car or horse. Ask for **Señor Sabella**, Av Perón 941, Perito Moreno, T02963-432199.

Estancias

There are some superb estancias in this region: tricky to get to without your own transport, but offering an unforgettable experience of Patagonian life.

A pp **La Angostura**, 55 km from Gobernador Gregores isT02962-452010. Horse riding, trekking and fishing. Recommended.

Parque Nacional Perito Moreno *p150*
B Estancia La Oriental, T02962-452196, elada@uvc.com.ar. Open Nov-Mar, full board. In a really splendid setting, rooms are comfortable, and there's superb horse riding.

Camping

Camping is possible and there are 4 free sites inside the park: **Lago Burmeister, Mirador Lago Belgrano, Cerro de Vasco** and **Alberto de Agostini**. No facilities, no fires.

Eating

Perito Moreno *p148*
There's good food at **Pipach**, next to Hotel Austral, **Parador Bajo Caracoles**, or pizzas at **Nono's**, on 9 de Julio y Saavedra. **Rotiseria Chee's I** is a cheap and cheery place to eat and does takeaways.

Los Antiguos *p148*
I La Perla del Lago, Fitzroy y Perito Moreno. The best *parrilla*.

Activities and tours

Perito Moreno *p148*
Tour operators
Señor Sabella, Av Perón 941, T02963-432199. Tours to Cueva de las Manos, including a spectacular 2-hr trip along the river valley.

Transporte Terrestre Guanacondór, Juan José Nauto 432079 and **Transporte Lago Posados**, T02963-432431, both offer the 'Circuito Grande Comarca Noroeste', which includes Perito Moreno to Bajo Caracoles, Cueva de los Manos, Lago Posada, Paso Roballos, Monte Cevallos and Los Antiguos. Also day tours to Cueva de los Manos, with option of collecting from Bajo Caracoles, US$30-40.

Transport

Perito Moreno *p148*
Air
The airport is 7 km east out of town, and the only way to get there is by taxi. **LADE**, Av San Martín 1207, T02963-432055, has flights to/from **Río Gallegos**, **Río Grande**, **Ushuaia**, **El Calafate** and **Gobernador Gregores**.

Bus
The terminal is on the edge of town, T02963- 432072. **La Union**, T02963-432133, to **Comodoro Rivadavia**, 6 hrs US$12, and to **Chile** via Los Antiguos, 2 buses daily in summer, 1hr, US$2. **Co-op Sportman** also daily to **Comodoro Rivadavia**. To **El Chaltén**, **Chaltén Travel**, www.chaltentravel.com, depart 1000 on even dates (ie 2nd, 4th, 6th); **Itinerarios y Travesias**,

For an explanation of sleeping and eating price codes, and other relevant information, see Essentials pages 25-26.

www.elchalten.com/ruta40, 1800 on odd dates (ie 1st, 3rd, 5th), US$30. It's a bleak 14-hr, 582-km journey; see also page 168.

Los Antiguos *p148*

Bus

Co-op Sportman to **Comodoro Rivadavia**, via Perito Moreno and Caleta Olivia, daily, 7½ hrs, US$9. Chaltén Travel and Itinerarios y Travesias to **El Chaltén** and **El Calafate**, US$40, see above for details. Tickets from Albergue Padilla, San Martín 44 Sur, T02963-491140. La Union across the border to **Chile Chico** (Chile), 45 mins, US$1; also Transportes VH, US$2.

Cueva de las Manos *p149*

Bus

Northbound buses run by Itinerarios y Travesias stop here at dawn for a couple of hours en route between **El Chaltén** and **Los Antiguos**, see page 148. It's a great way to see the caves. Tickets are available from Albergue Patagonia in El Chaltén, Av San Martín 495, T02962-493088, alpatagonia@infovia.com.ar. The Perito Moreno tourist office can advise on tours, see page 148.

Parque Nacional Perito Moreno *p150*

There is no transport into the park but it may be possible to get a lift with estancia workers. Also consult www.parquesnacionales.com.

Directory

Perito Moreno *p148*

Banks There are 2 ATMs in the main street, at Banco de la Provincia de Santa Cruz and Banco de la Nación, but nowhere to change TCs.

Parque Nacional Los Glaciares

Of all Argentina's impressive landscapes, the sight of the immense glaciers stretching out infinitely and silently before you, may stay with you longest. This is the second-largest national park in Argentina, extending along the Chilean border for over 170 km. Almost half of it is covered by the Southern Ice Cap; at 370 km long, it's the third largest in the world. From it, 13 major glaciers descend into two great lakes: Lago Argentino in the southeast and Lago Viedma to the northeast.

There are two main areas to explore: the glaciers can be visited by bus and boat trips from El Calafate, while from El Chaltén, 230 km northwest, there is superb trekking around the dramatic Fitz Roy massif and ice climbing near its summit. The central section, between Lago Argentino and Lago Viedma, is the Ice Cap National Reserve, inaccessible to visitors apart from a couple of estancias.

East of the ice fields, there's southern beech forest before the land flattens to the wind-blasted Patagonian steppe. Birdlife is prolific; often spotted are black-necked swans, Magallenic woodpeckers, and, perhaps, even a torrent duck, diving in the rivers. Guanacos, grey foxes, skunks and rheas can be seen on the steppe, and the rare huemul inhabits the forest. » For Sleeping, Eating and other listings, see pages 160-168.

Ins and outs

Getting there Access to the park is via **El Calafate**, 50 km from the park's eastern boundary, for the glaciers, or via **El Chaltén**, 230 km northwest, for trekking, near Fitz Roy on the northeastern edge of the park. There are regular flights to El Calafate airport, 20 km east of town, as well as buses from Río Gallegos and Puerto Natales. El Chaltén is three hours' drive north then west, with several buses daily from El Calafate and Río Gallegos. » *See also Transport, page 167.*

Best time to visit Although this part of Patagonia is generally cold, there is a milder microclimate around Lago Viedma and Lago Argentino, which means that summers can be reasonably pleasant, with average summer temperatures between 5°C and 22°C, though strong winds blow constantly at the foot of the *cordillera*. In the forested area, around 1500 mm of rain falls annually, mainly between March and late May. In winter, the whole area is inhospitably cold and most tourist facilities are closed. The best time to visit, therefore, is between November and April, avoiding January and early February, when Argentines take their holidays, campsites are crowded and accommodation is hard to find. Park entry US$10. For further information contact T02962 491477, peritomoreno@apn.gov.ar.

Parque Nacional Los Glaciares

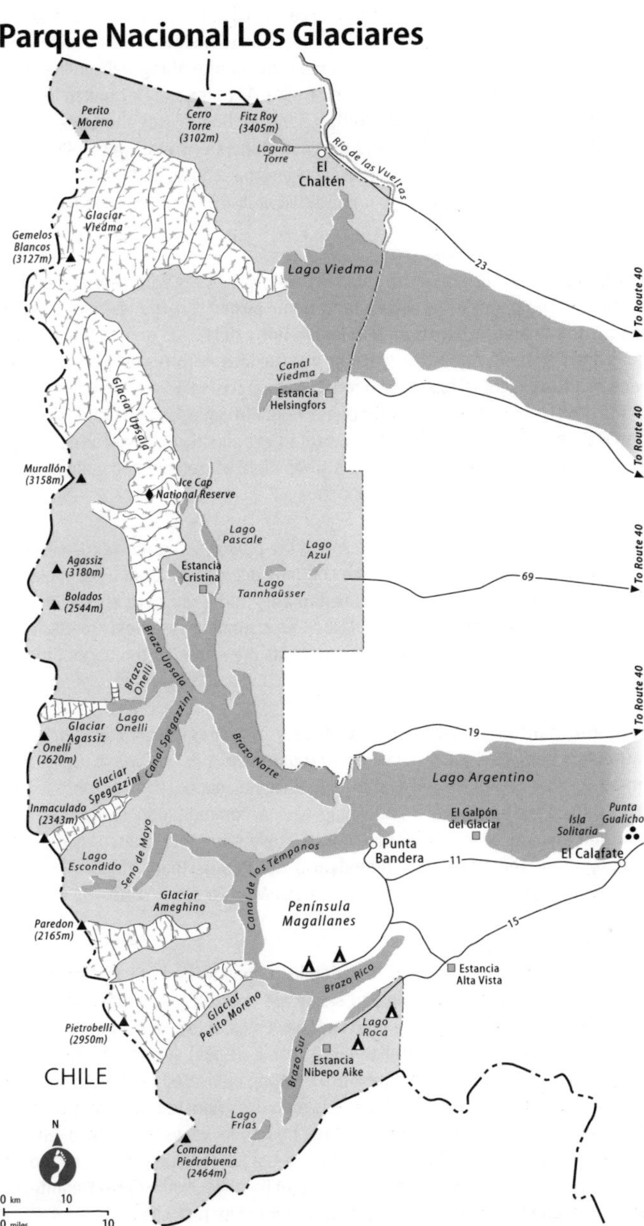

El Calafate » p160-168.

El Calafate sits on the southern shore of Lago Argentino, and as it's the only base for exploring the magnificent glaciers to the west. The town has expanded rapidly in the last few years, with hotels mushrooming everywhere to exploit tourism. There is accommodation to cater for all budgets, including some excellent hostels, but if you can afford it, stay at an estancia-style hotel out of town such as **Eolo, Alta Vista** or **Los Notros,** where you will feel close to nature and can avoid the unattractive town altogether.

From El Calafate, tours take you on boat trips and to walkways right beside the wall of Perito Moreno glacier. Highly recommended is the **Minitrekking** walk on the glacier's surface, or the more intrepid six-hour **Big Ice** hike. All these can be booked in town, or by your hotel. You could also head further north by boat to see the Spegazzini and Upsala glaciers, or stay a night at the remote **Estancia Cristina**, which offers superb hiking and horse riding to see the Upsala glacier from above, and down a fossil-filled canyon. Whatever you do, this is an unmissable part of any trip to Patagonia.

Ins and outs → *See map page 161. Colour map 3, A3.*

Getting there The easiest way to get to El Calafate is by air, with several daily flights in summer from Buenos Aires to its international **airport** ⓘ *Lago Viedma, 22 km east of town*. You can also fly here from Ushuaia in Tierra del Fuego or from Puerto Natales in Chile and combine a trip to the glaciers with trekking in Torres del Paine. A minibus service meets all flights, US$6 (open return), a taxi costs US$9.

Bus travel is convenient too, with buses from Río Gallegos and Ushuaia and from Puerto Natales, via Cerro Castillo, if you want to get directly to/from Torres del Paine. The bus terminal is centrally located up a steep flight of steps off the main street, and has a small tourist office. » *See Transport, page 167.*

Getting around From El Calafate, access to the park is straightforward, with regular bus services and organized tours, which combine access with boat trips, walking and even ice trekking. El Calafate's shops, restaurants and tour operators can mostly be found along its main street, Avenida del Libertador, running east-west. Hotels lie within two blocks north and south and smaller *hosterías* are scattered throughout the newly built residential area sprawling up the hill.

Tourist information El Calafate **tourist office** ⓘ *in the bus terminal, T02902-491090, www.turismo.elcalafate.gov.ar or www.interpatagonia.com in English, daily Oct-Apr 0700-2200, May-Sep 0800-2100*, may look disorganized, but the efficient staff speak several languages and have a good map with accommodation shown, as well as helpful information on estancias and tours. There's another branch at the airport, T02902-491230. There's also an **Intendencia del Parque** (park office) ⓘ *Libertador 1302, T02901-491005, losglaciares@apn.gov.ar, Mon-Fri 0800-1600.*

Around El Calafate

Just west of the town centre is **Bahía Redonda**, a shallow part of Lago Argentino that freezes in winter, when ice-skating and skiing are possible. From the **Intendencia del Parque**, an hour's stroll will take you to **Laguna Nimez** at the eastern edge of the bay, where there's a bird reserve with flamingos, black-necked swans and ducks. To get there, follow Calle Bustillo up the new road among cultivated fields and orchards to cross the bridge. Keep heading north: the laguna is signposted. Hike to the top of the **Cerro Calafate**, behind the town (2½ to three hours), for views of the silhouette of the southern end of the Andes, Bahía Redonda and Isla Solitaria on Lago Argentino. There is also scope for good hill-walking to the south of the town, while **Cerro Elefante**, to the west, on the road to the Perito Moreno glacier, is good for rock climbing.

Francisco Moreno, El Perito

You can't miss the name of Argentina's favourite son as you travel around Patagonia. Francisco Pascasio Moreno (1852-1919) is commemorated by a national park, a town and a world- famous glacier. Moreno, a naturalist and geographer, explored areas previously unknown to the authorities. At the age of 20, he travelled up the Río Negro to Lago Nahuel Huapi, along the Río Chubut, and then up the Río Santa Cruz to reach the giant lake which he named Lago Argentino. Expeditions such as these were dangerous: apart from physical hardships, relations with the indigenous populations were poor. On one expedition, Moreno was seized as a hostage, but escaped on a raft which carried him for eight days down the Río Limay to safety.

His fame established, Moreno was elected to congress and became an expert (*perito*) adviser to the Argentine side in the negotiations to draw the border with Chile. His reward was a grant of land near Bariloche, which he handed over to the state to manage, the initial act in creating the national parks system in Argentina, and an inspiring gesture at a time when anyone who could was buying up land as fast as possible. Moreno's remains are buried in a mausoleum on Isla Centinela in Lago Nahuel Huapi.

In addition to the glaciers, El Calafate provides access to some other good places for trekking, horse riding and exploring by 4WD, if you're here for a few days. There are several estancias within reach of the town, which offer a day on a working farm, a lunch of superb Patagonian lamb, cooked *asado al palo*, and outdoor activities. **El Galpón del Glaciar** (formerly **Estancia Alice**, see page 162) offers displays of sheep shearing, walking and horse-riding trips to the Perito Moreno glacier and Cerro Frias. Overnight accommodation is available in the lovely house with views of Lago Argentino.

Lago Roca, 40 km southwest of El Calafate, is set in beautiful open landscape, with hills above offering panoramic views. The lake is perfect for lots of activities, including trout and salmon fishing, climbing and walking, and there are several estancias, where you can see farm activities, such as the branding of cattle in summer. There is also good camping in a wooded area and a restaurant.

Lago Argentino and the glaciers » p160-168.

Perito Moreno glacier → Colour map 3, A2

Perito Moreno is one of the few glaciers in the world that is still advancing. Some 30 km long, it reaches the water at a narrow point on one of the fjords, **Brazo Rico**, opposite **Peninsula Magallanes**. Every few years, the glacier blocks the fjord and, as water pressure builds up behind the ice wall, the ice suddenly breaks, reopening the channel and sending huge icebergs (*témpanos*) rushing down the Canal de los Témpanos. This happened most recently in March 2006. Naturally, there are concerns about the effects of climate change on the glacier, but these are not straightforward, and the glacier's calving has no relationship with increased temperature.

Viewing the glacier There are various ways to approach the glacier. All excursions (and the regular bus service) will take you 85 km from El Calafate direct to the car park on Peninsula Magallanes, where you begin the descent along a series of wooden walkways (*pasarelas*) to see the glacier slightly from above, and then, as you get lower, directly head-on. There are several wide viewing areas, where, in summer, crowds wait expectantly, cameras poised, for another hunk of ice to fall from the vertical blue walls at the glacier's front. Never walk down to the rocks overlooking the channel; there is a real danger of being washed away if a large chunk of ice breaks off the glacier. However, you can also approach the glacier by walking around the tranquil lake shore. From the restaurant at the car park, a path leads over big bald rocks, carved smooth by ancient glaciers, until the Perito Moreno appears through rich lenga forest. *Guardaparques* (park rangers) guide an hour-long walk along the lakeshore, leaving from the park ranger's office in the car park (check for times T02902-491005).

Boat trips leave constantly during the day from the tourist pier (well signposted from the car park), to survey the glacier from the water below, giving you a chance to appreciate its magnitude and its varied sculptural forms. To get closer still, there are guided treks on the ice itself, known as *minitrekking*, which allow you to walk along the crevices and frozen crests in crampons. This is possible for anyone with a reasonable level of fitness and is not technically demanding. Highly recommended for the fitter and more intrepid are the longer six-hour hikes on the ice (known as Big Ice); the sight of the glacier from within, with its cobalt blue ice caves in female forms and turquoise rivers, is utterly magical. **Hielo y Aventura** offers both and can be booked through any hotel or tour operator. » *See Activities and tours, page 165.*

Upsala glacier → *Colour map 3, A2*

The fiords at the northwestern end of Lago Argentino are fed by four other glaciers. The largest is the Upsala glacier, named after the Swedish university that commissioned the first survey of this area in 1908. It's a stunning expanse of untouched beauty, covering three times the area of the Perito Moreno glacier, and is the longest glacier flowing off the Southern Patagonian icefields. Unusually it ends in two separate frontages, each about 4 km wide and 60 m high, although only the western frontage can be seen from the lake excursion. The best way to see the glacier is to stay at **Estancia Cristina** (see box, page 167) and take the trip up to the viewpoint, where vermillion rocks have been polished smooth by the glacier's approach. The estancia can be reached only by boat from Punta Bandera, 50 km west of El Calafate. Further south, the **Spegazzini** glacier has a frontage 1½ km wide and 130 m high. In between are **Agassiz** and **Onelli**, both of which feed into **Lago Onelli**, a quiet and very beautiful lake, full of icebergs of every shape and size, surrounded by beech forests on one side and ice-covered mountains on the other.

Around Cerro Fitz Roy » *p160-168.*

At the northern end of Parque Nacional Los Glaciares, the soaring granite of **Cerro Fitz Roy** (3405 m) rises up from the smooth baize of the steppe, more like a ziggurat than a mountain, surrounded by a consort of jagged snow-clad spires, with a stack of spun cotton cloud hanging constantly above them. It is one of the most magnificent mountains in the world and towers above the nearby peaks: **Torre** (3128 m), **Poincenot** (3076 m) and **Saint-Exupery** (2600 m). Its Tehuelche name was El Chaltén, ('smoking mountain' or 'volcano'), perhaps because at sunrise the pink towers are occasionally lit up bright red for a few seconds in a phenomenon known as the *amanecer de fuego* ('sunrise of fire'). Perito Moreno named the peak after the captain of the *Beagle*, who saw it from afar in 1833, and it was first climbed by a French expedition in 1952. It stands in the northern end of Parque Nacional Los Glaciares at the western end of Lago Viedma, 230 km north of El Calafate, in an area of lakes and glaciers that makes marvellous trekking country. The base for walking and climbing around Fitz Roy is the modern town of El Chaltén, which has been built right next to the mountains.

Ins and outs

Getting there and around The quickest way to reach El Chaltén is to fly to El Calafate and then catch one of the frequent buses for the 230-km journey north. There are also daily buses to El Chaltén from Los Antiguos along Route 40, useful if you've come from the Lake District. Access to the park is free and it is not necessary to register before you set out. Most paths are very clear and well worn but a map is essential, even on short walks: the park information centre has photocopied maps of treks but the best is one published by *Zagier and Urruty*, US$6, and is available in shops in El Calafate and El Chaltén.

Best time to visit Walking here is only really viable mid-October to April, with the best months usually March to April when the weather is generally stable and not very cold, and the autumn colours of the beech forest are stunning. Mid-summer (December and January), and spring (September to October), are generally very windy. And in December and January the campsites can be full to bursting, with many walkers on the paths.

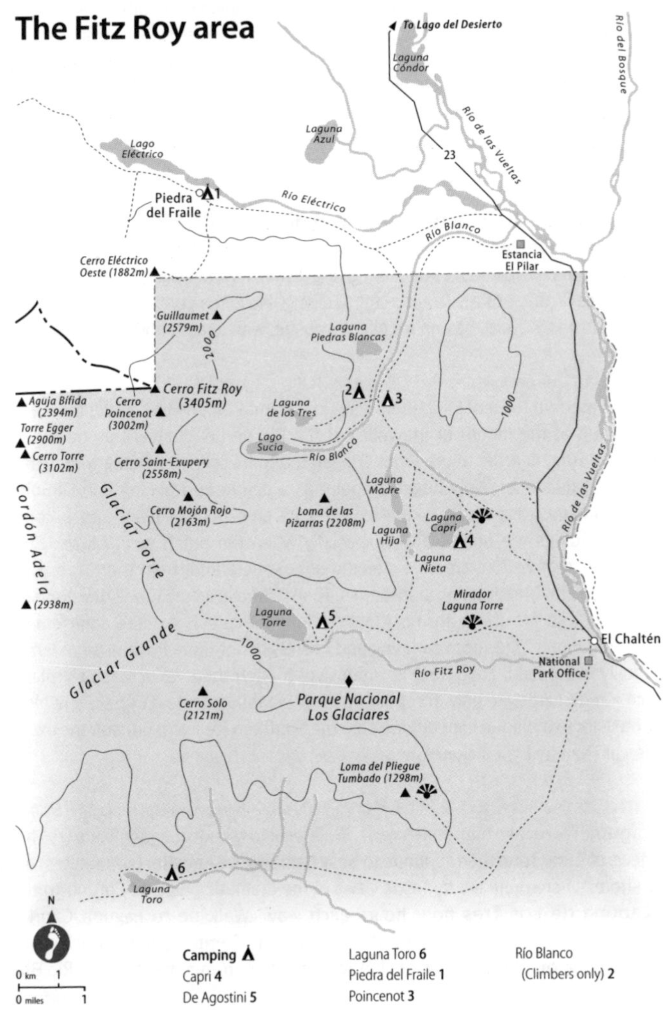

Hiking around El Chaltén and Cerro Fitz Roy

→ **Equipment** A map is essential, even on short walks. Also take plenty of warm clothes and a four-season sleeping bag, if you're camping. A gas or alcohol stove is essential, as fires are prohibited in the park. It is possible to rent equipment in El Chaltén; ask at the park office or Rancho Grande.

→ **Information** The park's *Intendencia* provides a good map, showing walks and campsites. *Guardaparques* can advise on walks and, although you're not required to register, it's a good idea to check with them about the state of the paths. Some speak English.

→ **Paths** Paths are well marked. Stick to the centre of the path so as not to make it any bigger and walk in single file (this means at times that you're walking in a rut).

→ **Rubbish** Take all rubbish back down the mountain with you.

→ **Water** All river water in the national park is drinkable. Don't bathe in rivers and lakes; do not wash or bury waste within 70 m of a water source. Never go to the toilet near water sources.

→ **Weather** The weather changes hourly, so don't wait for a sunny day to go hiking and be prepared for a sudden deterioration in conditions. Always wear sun screen (factor 30 at least).

→ **Wildlife** As you leave El Chaltén, don't let the dogs follow you, as they frighten the huemules (a rare and endangered species of deer).

Tourist information The **Intendencia del Parque** is in El Chaltén, across the bridge at the entrance to the town, T02962-493004. It hands out helpful trekking maps of the area, with paths and campsites marked, giving distances and walking times. El Chalten's **tourist office** ⓘ *Güemes 21, T02962-493011, www.elchalten.com, Mon-Fri 0900-2000, Sat and Sun 1300-2000*, has an excellent website, with accommodation lists.

El Chaltén → *See map page 163. Colour map 2, C2.*

The small modern town of El Chaltén is set in a wonderful position at the foot of Cerro Fitz Roy and at the mouth of the valley of the Río de las Vueltas but, having been founded in 1985 in order to pre-empt Chilean territorial claims, it has grown with little thought for aesthetics. Now hugely popular as a centre for trekking and climbing in summer, and for cross-country skiing in winter, it's an expensive place and its concrete and tin buildings are unattractive, especially when the harsh wind blows. But the steady stream of visitors create a cheerful atmosphere and, from the town, you can walk directly into breathtaking landscapes. Tourist infrastructure is still developing in El Chaltén and, so far, there are no ATMs (or internet cafés), so take sufficient cash. Accommodation ranges from camping and hostels to not-quite-luxurious *hosterías*, all hideously overpriced. Food, too, is expensive, though there is increasingly plenty of choice. Credit cards are only accepted in larger establishments. El Chaltén is also the only base for two unique expeditions onto the Southern Ice Field. Consult the excellent guides at **Fitz Roy Expediciones.** » *See Activities and tours, page 167.*

Hiking around Cerro Fitz Roy → *These are the most popular walks from El Chaltén.*

▲ **Laguna Torre** (two hours each way) Walk west to Mirador Laguna Torre (1½ hours) for views of Cerro Torre then continue to busy **Camping De Agostini** (30 minutes) on the lake shore, where there are fantastic views of the dramatic peaks of Cordon Torre.

▲ **Laguna de Los Tres** (four hours each way) Walk up to Laguna Capri (two hours), with great views of Fitz Roy, then continue to **Camping Poincenot** (one hour) and **Camping Río Blanco** (only for climbers, by prior arrangement). From Río Blanco you can head southwest to Laguna de los Tres, where you'll get a spectacular view on a fine day (one hour) but in bad weather, you're better off walking to Piedras Blancas.

▲ **Laguna Torre** (seven hours each way) A marvellous walk with views of both mountain groups. Climb past Laguna Capri and take the signed path to your left, passing two lakes (Madre and then Hija), to reach the path that leads to Laguna Torre.

▲ **Loma del Pliegue Tumbado** (four hours each way) A marked path from the *guardería* (park ranger's office) leads southwest to this viewpoint where you can see both cordons and Lago Viedma. This is a good day walk, best in clear weather. More experienced trekkers can continue to the glacial Laguna Toro (six hours from El Chaltén).

▲ **Río Blanco to Piedra del Fraile** (seven hours each way) This beautiful walk starts at **Camping Río Blanco** and runs north along the Río Blanco and then west along the Río Eléctrico to **Camping Piedra del Fraile** (four hours), just outside the national park. From here a path leads south, up Cerro Eléctrico Oeste (1882 m) towards the north face of Fitz Roy (two hours); it's tough going but with spectacular views. You should take a guide for the last bit. Ask at **Estancia El Pilar** and outdoor centre, www.elpilar.com.ar.

Climbing Cerro Fitz Roy → *Colour map 2, C2*

Base camp for ascents of Fitz Roy (3375 m) is **Camping Río Blanco**. Other peaks include Cerro Torre (3102 m), Torre Egger (2900 m), Cerro Solo (2121 m), Poincenot (3002 m), Guillaumet (2579 m), Saint-Exupery (2558 m), Aguja Bífida (2394 m) and Cordón Adela (2938 m): all of these are for very experienced climbers only. However, most climbers can try ice climbing at the foot of Cerro Torre; contact **Fitz Roy Expediciones**, page 167. The best time to climb is mid-February to the end of March; November and December are very windy and the winter months are extremely cold. Permits for climbing are available at the national park information office and guides are available in El Chaltén.

Border with Chile

Three crossings provide access to Puerto Natales and Torres del Paine. They are open, subject to weather conditions, 24 hours a day from September to May and 0700-2300 at other times. Most buses use the Río Turbio crossing but Cancha Carrera is quicker if you're driving to the national park from El Calafate. Note that Argentine pesos cannot be exchanged in Torres del Paine.

Paso Cancha Carrera 129 km west of La Esperanza and 42 km north of Río Turbio. The most northerly of the crossings is the most convenient (though desolate) crossing between Argentina and Torres del Paine but it is often closed in winter. On the Chilean side the road continues to Cerro Castillo, where it meets the good ripio road that runs between Puerto Natales (65 km south) and the national park. **Argentine customs and immigration** ⓘ *Cancha Carrera, 2 km east of the border*, is fast and friendly. **Chilean customs and immigration** ⓘ *Cerro Castillo, 7 km west of the border, 0800-2200.*

Paso Dorotea 14 km south of Río Turbio, 27 km from Puerto Natales. On the Chilean side the road runs south for 11km to join Route 9 between Puerto Natales and Punta Arenas. **Chilean customs and immigration** ⓘ *2 km from the border, winter 0800-2400, for summer times, check in Puerto Natales.*

Paso Casas Viejas 33 km south of Río Turbio via 28 de Noviembre. On the Chilean side, the road continues west to join Route 9 east of Puerto Natales at Km 14. **Argentine customs and immigration** ⓘ *winter 0800-2200, summer 0800-2400.* **Chilean customs and immigration** ⓘ *1 km from the border, winter 0800-2200, summer 0800-2400.*

Around El Chaltén

The main attraction here is the trekking around Fitz Roy, but there is also stunning virgin landscape to explore outside the park, around **Lago del Desierto**, 37 km north. The long skinny lake is fiord-like and surrounded by forests. It's reached by unpaved Route 23, which leads along the Río de las Vueltas via **Laguna Condor**, where flamingos can be seen. A mirador at the end of the road gives fine views over the lake and a path runs along the east side of the lake to its northern tip, from where a trail leads west along the valley of the Río Diablo to **Laguna Diablo**, and north to Lago O'Higgins in Chile, see page 267.

En route to the lake is **Estancia El Pilar**, www.elpilar.com.ar, in a stunning position with views of Fitz Roy. Accommodation is available here but you can also visit for tea or use it as an excellent base for trekking up **Río Blanco** or **Río Eléctrico.**

Lago Viedma to the south of El Chaltén can also be explored by boat. The trips usually pass Glaciar Viedma, with the possibility of ice trekking on some excursions. » *See Activities and tours, page 166.*

Towards Torres del Paine » *p160-168.*

From El Calafate

From El Calafate you can take the paved combination of Routes 11, 40 and 5 to **La Esperanza** (165 km), where there's fuel, a campsite and a large but expensive *confitería.* From La Esperanza, *ripio* Route 7 heads west along the valley of the Río Coyle towards the border crossing at Cancha Carrera. A shorter route (closed in winter) misses Esperanza and goes via El Cerrito direct to **Estancia Tapi Aike**, T02966 420092, bvdesing@fibertel.com.ar. » *See Transport, page 167.*

Río Turbio → *Colour map 3, A3*

A charmless place you're most likely to visit en route to or from Torres del Paine in Chile. The site of Argentina's largest coalfield hasn't recovered from the recent depression hitting the industry. It has a cargo railway connecting it with Punta Loyola, and visitors can see Mina 1, where the first mine was opened. There's a small ski centre nearby, **Valdelén**, which has six pistes and is ideal for beginners; there's also scope for cross-country skiing between early June and late September. The **tourist office** is in the municipal building on San Martín.

Sleeping

El Calafate *p154, map p161*

LL Esplendor, Presidente Perón 1143, T492488, T011-52175700 in Buenos Aires, www.esplendorcalafate.com. Exceptionally stylish, large and pricey, this is a top hotel.

LL Kau-Yatún, Estancia 25 de Mayo (10 blocks from town centre, east of arroyo Calafate), T02902-491059, www.kauyatun.com. A very comfortable former estancia, surrounded by 4 ha of gardens, where vegetables are grown for the meals served in its 2 excellent restaurants. The building is homely and rustic.

L Kosten Aike, Gob Moyano 1243, T02902-492424, www.kostenaike.com.ar. A special place with large elegant rooms, king-sized beds, jacuzzi and gym. The restaurant has an excellent chef, there's a cosy bar with a wood fire, and a garden. Staff are attentive and speak English. Recommended.

AL El Quijote, Gobernador Gregores 1155, T02902-491017, www.quijotehotel.com.ar. This spacious, modern hotel is Italian-owned and designed. Tasteful and comfortable rooms with excellent bathrooms and TV. Great restaurant **Sancho**. Recommended.

AL Los Alamos, Gobernador Moyano y Bustillo, T02902-491144, www.posada losalamos.com. An extremely comfortable hotel in 2 separate chalet-style buildings, with charming rooms, good service, lovely gardens and without doubt the best restaurant in town, **La Posta**. Recommended.

A Cabañas Nevis, Av del Libertador 1696, T02902-493180, www.canasnevis.com.ar.

Complex of spacious, A-shaped *cabañas* for 5 and 8, some with lake views. Great value.
A Vientos del Sur, up the hill at Río Santa Cruz 2317, T02902-493563, www.vientosdelsur.com. This tranquil retreat is worth the short taxi ride for the views over the lake, comfortable rooms with bath and TV in a large wooden cabin. Recommended.
B Michelangelo, Espora y Gobernador Moyano, T02902-491045, www.michelangelohotel.com.ar. A modern, stylish and welcoming place with an innovative restaurant. All rooms en suite, breakfast included. Recommended.
C Casa de Grillos, Pasaje Las Bandurrias, T02902-491160, www.casadegrillos.com.ar. A warm welcome awaits at this B&B situated next to Nímez nature reserve. All the comfort and charm of a family house.
C Sir Thomas, Comandante Espora 257, T02902-492220, www.sirthomas.com.ar. A chalet-type house with comfortable, spacious en suite rooms.
F pp **Lago Azul**, Perito Moreno 83, T2902-491419. This pioneer house with a couple of simple and spotless rooms to shire is the most welcoming budget choice, offering traditional Patagonian hospitality. Recommended.

Camping

AMSA, Olavarría 65 (50 m off the main road, turn south at the fire station), T02902-492247, US$3.50 pp, hot water, security, summer only.

There are 2 campsites in the park en route to Lago Roca: **El Huala**, 42 km from El Calafate, free, basic facilities, open year round; and **Lago Roca** (see Lago Argentino, page 162).

Youth hostels

E-F pp **Albergue Buenos Aires**, Buenos Aires 296, 200 m from terminal, T02902- 491147, www.glaciarescalafate.com. Homely, with kitchen facilities, bikes for hire, simple and comfortable rooms to share and doubles with or without own bath. Breakfast extra.

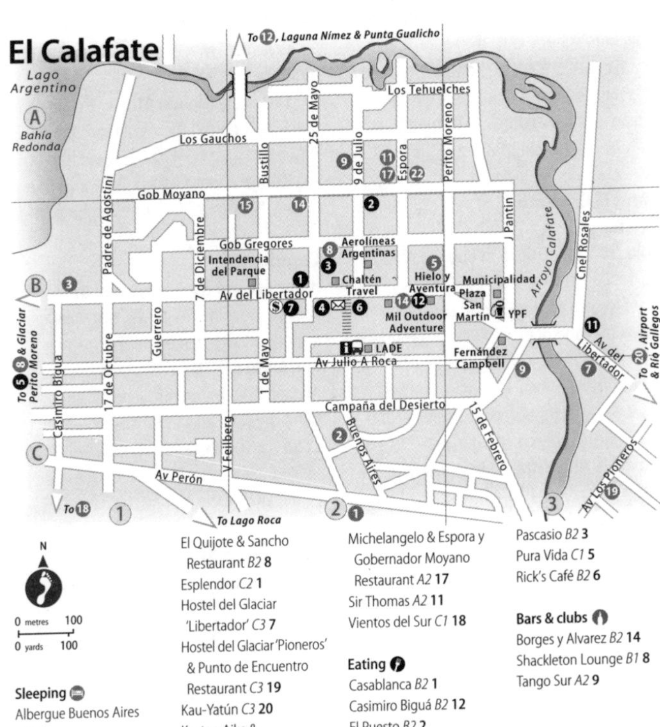

Sleeping
Albergue Buenos Aires *C2* **2**
AMSA *C3* **9**
Cabañas Nevis *B1* **3**
Calafate Hostel *A2* **22**
Casa de Grillos *A2* **12**
El Quijote & Sancho Restaurant *B2* **8**
Esplendor *C2* **1**
Hostel del Glaciar 'Libertador' *C3* **7**
Hostel del Glaciar 'Pioneros' & Punto de Encuentro Restaurant *C3* **19**
Kau-Yatún *C3* **20**
Kosten Aike & Restaurant *B2* **14**
Lago Azul *B2* **5**
Los Alamos & La Posta Restaurant *B2* **15**
Michelangelo & Espora y Gobernador Moyano Restaurant *A2* **17**
Sir Thomas *A2* **11**
Vientos del Sur *C1* **18**

Eating
Casablanca *B2* **1**
Casimiro Biguá *B2* **12**
El Puesto *B2* **2**
Heladería Aquarela *B2* **4**
La Cocina *B2* **7**
La Tablita *B3* **11**
Mi Viejo *B2* **6**
Pascasio *B2* **3**
Pura Vida *C1* **5**
Rick's Café *B2* **6**

Bars & clubs
Borges y Alvarez *B2* **14**
Shackleton Lounge *B1* **8**
Tango Sur *A2* **9**

E-F pp **Hostel del Glaciar 'Libertador'**, Av del Libertador 587 (next to the bridge on the access to town), T02902-491792, www.glaciar.com. Closed Jun. The modern and 'exclusive' sister of the **Del Glaciar** hostel, with good, well-heated doubles or dorms for 4, all with private bath. Quiet relaxed atmosphere. Free transfer from bus station. Discounts to HI members. Recommended.
F pp **Calafate Hostel**, Gobernador Moyano 1226, 400 m from bus terminal, T02902-492450, www.calafatehostels.com. Huge with well-built dorms for 4, **B-C** doubles or superior rooms with private bath and breakfast. Kitchen, internet and a lively sitting area. Book a month ahead for Jan and Feb. They also run the helpful travel agency **Chaltén Travel**.
F pp **Hostel del Glaciar 'Pioneros'**, Los Pioneros 251, T/F02902-491243, www.glaciar.com. Oct-Mar. A long-established and lively hostel with dorms for 4, doubles (**C**), and superior rooms with bath (**B**). Internet, kitchen facilities. The cosy restaurant has a good value fixed menu. They run **Patagonia Backpackers** agency with the much loved *Alternative Glaciar Tour* (see page 166). Free shuttle service from the bus terminal. Book well in advance. Discounts to HI members. Beautifully run, and highly recommended.

Around El Calafate *p154*

Estancias

LL Eolo, T011-4700 0075 in Buenos Aires, on RP 11, 23 km west of El Calafate, www.eolo.com.ar. With a wild setting on the windswept slope of Cerro Frías, this modern fabulously stylish hotel is the perfect base for exploring the glaciers, with grand views over the steppe, excellent food and service, and horse riding. Highly recommended.
LL Hostería Alta Vista, 33 km west of El Calafate, T02902-491247, www.hosteriaaltavista.com.ar. The area's most expensive estancia, set within a staggering 74,000 ha. Absurdly exclusive with all the facilities you could need, with lovely gardens, excellent cuisine and wines, and good service.
L El Galpón del Glaciar, formerly **Estancia Alice**, 22 km west of El Calafate, T/F02902-491793, www.estanciaalice.com.ar. Lovely house with views of Lago Argentino. 16 very comfortable rooms. Sheep shearing, birdwatching and horse riding. Trips to the Perito Moreno glacier and Cerro Frias.
E pp **La Leona**, 106 km north of Calafate near east end of Lago Viedma, T02902-491418, carlosk@polarstar.com.ar. A historic estancia with fishing. The perfect stopping point between El Calafate and El Chaltén, with a delightful café and restaurant and a lovely welcome.

Lago Argentino *p155*

LL Estancia Helsingfors, T/F02966-420719, T/F011-4315 1222, www.helsingfors.com. A fabulous place in a splendid position on Lago Viedma, 150 km from El Calafate, with stylish rooms, a welcoming lounge, delicious food, and excursions directly from there to glaciers and to Laguna Azul, by horse or trek, plus boat trips. Recommended.
LL Los Notros, www.losnotros.com. Comfortable accommodation in simple rooms with staggering views over the Perito Moreno glacier. This is one of Patagonia's most famous hotels, and earns its reputation with excellent service, fine food and wine. Excursions run by **Fitz Roy Expediciones**. For all-inclusive packages see www.experiencepatagonia.com. Highly recommended.
B pp **Estancia Nibepo Aike**, in the far south of the park on the shores of Brazo Sur of Lago Argentino, T02966-436010, www.nibepoaike.com.ar. Open Oct-Apr for horse riding, fishing, boat tours to glacier. Recommended.

Camping

Bahía Escondida, 7 km east of the glacier. Facilities include fireplaces, hot showers and a shop. Crowded in summer, US$3 pp.
Correntoso, 10 km east of the glacier. An unmarked site with no facilities but a great location. No fires. US$2 pp.
Lago Roca, 50 km from El Calafate, T02902-499500. Beautifully set, with hot water, public phone, restaurant, bike hire, US$4 pp.

Cerro Fitz Roy *p156*

There are campsites in the park at **Poincenot**, **Capri** and **Laguna Toro**. **Río Blanco** is for climbers with prior permission. Campsites have no services but all have latrines, apart from Toro. A gas/alcohol stove is essential as fires are prohibited. See box, page 158.
Camping Piedra del Fraile, on Rio Electrico, just north of the park boundary. Privately owned with *cabañas* and hot showers (**E** pp) as well as camping (US$5 pp).

El Chaltén *p158, map opposite*
See www.elchalten.com for a full list.
LL Los Cerros, T02962-493182, www.loscerrosdelchalten.com. On a hill above the town, this large hotel is by far the most sophisticated choice. Stylish, yet informal, all rooms are very comfortable with impressive attention to detail. Half-board and all-inclusive packages with excursions run by **Fitz Roy Expediciones**. Superb restaurant and wine list.
AL Hostería El Puma, Lionel Terray 212, T02962-493095, www.hosteriaelpuma.com.ar. The most desirable place in town, set a little apart, and with splendid views up the valley, a welcoming lounge with log fire and tasteful furnishings, spacious rooms and plush bathrooms. Transfers and breakfast included. Good restaurant. Tours arranged through their agency **Fitz Roy Expediciones**, see Activities and tours, page 167. Recommended.
AL Hostería Posada Lunajuim, Trevisán s/n, T/F02962-493047, www.elchalten.com/lunajuim. Stylish, relaxed and welcoming with comfortable rooms (thick duvets on the beds) with bathrooms and a lovely big lounge with wood fire. Full breakfast included. Charming hosts. Recommended.
C Hospedaje La Base, Lago de Desierto 97, T02962-493031. A friendly little place with basic en suite doubles or dorms for 3-4 (**E**). Tiny kitchen for guests to use, self service breakfast included, and a great video lounge.
B-C Northofagus, Hensen s/n T02962-493087, www.elchalten.com/northofagus. A small cosy B&B, with simple double rooms with shared bath, including breakfast. Welcoming and good value.

Youth hostels
F pp **Albergue Patagonia**, San Martín 493, T/F02962-493019, www.elchalten.com/patagonia. HI-affiliated. The most appealing hostel. Cosy and friendly with rooms for 4-6, kitchen, video room, bike hire and laundry. Information and excursions available. Next door is their restaurant **Fuegia**.
F pp **Albergue Rancho Grande**, San Martín s/n, T02962-493005, chaltenrancho@yahoo.com.ar. HI-affiliated, in a great position at the end of town with good views, and an attractive restaurant and lounge. Rooms for 4, with shared bathrooms, doubles (**C**) and a family room. Well run and friendly. Breakfast and sheets extra. Recommended.

El Chaltén

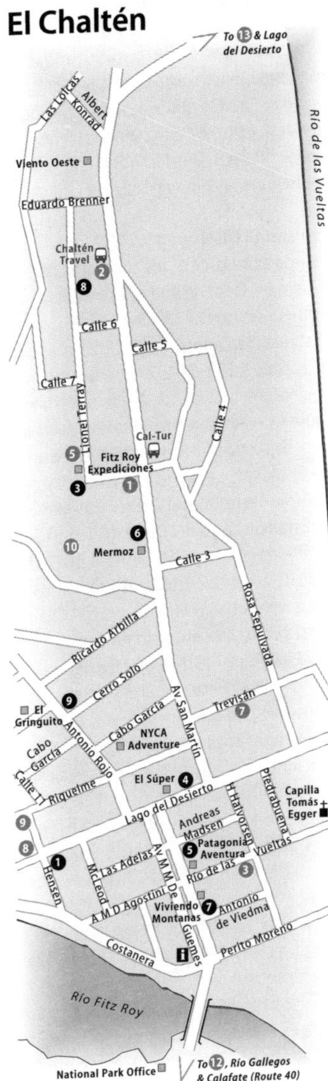

Not to scale

Sleeping
Albergue Patagonia **1**
Albergue Rancho Grande **2**
Cóndor de los Andes **3**
El Pilar **13**
Estancia La Quinta **12**
Hospedaje La Base **8**
Hostería El Puma & Restaurant Terray **5**
Hostería Posada Lunajuim **7**
Los Cerros & Restaurant **10**
Northofagus **9**

Eating
Estepa **9**
Fuegia **6**
Josh Aike **1**
Las Lengas **7**
Pangea **4**
Patagonicus **5**
Ruca Mahuida **3**
Zafarrancho **8**

F pp **Cóndor de los Andes**, Av Río de las Vueltas y Halvorsen, T02962-493101, www.condordelosandes.com. Friendly, small and modern, with nice little rooms for 4-6 or en suite doubles, sheets included, breakfast extra. Washing service, library, kitchen facilities. Quiet atmosphere. HI-discount. Recommended.

Around El Chaltén *p160*

There is a campsite at the southern end of Lago del Desierto and *refugios* at its northern end and at Laguna Diablo.

L **Estancia La Quinta**, on RP 23, 2 km south of El Chaltén, T02962-493012, www.estancialaquinta.com.ar. Oct-Apr. A spacious pioneer house with renovated rooms and beautiful gardens. A superb breakfast is included and the restaurant is open for lunch and dinner. Free transfer to/from El Chaltén bus terminal.

AL **Estancia Lago del Desierto**, Punto Sur, southern tip of Lago del Desierto, T02962-493010, www.lagodeldesierto.com. Basic place with *cabañas* for 5, camping US$6 pp, hot showers, kitchen. Recommended.

A **El Pilar**, on RP 23, Km 17, T/F02962-493002, www.hosteriaelpilar.com.ar. A special place to stay a little way out of town on the road to Lago del Desierto. This simple country house, in a spectacular setting with views of Fitz Roy, offers the chance to access less visited parts of the park. Spacious rooms and great food. Tailor-made trekking tours. Recommended.

Towards Torres del Paine *p160*

In La Esperanza, **Restaurant La Esperanza** has bunk beds, with bath. There are also 6-person *cabañas* at the YPF service station.

C **De La Frontera**, 4 km from Rio Turbio, Paraje Mina 1, T02962-421979. The most frequently recommended option.

D **Hostería Capipe**, Dufour, 9 km from town, T02902-482930, www.hosteriacapipe.com.ar. Simple rooms with bath, friendly. Restaurant.

Eating

El Calafate *p154, map p161*

For cheap meals, there are 2 lively, packed places on the main street, Libertador, with good atmosphere and cheapish food: **Rick's Café**, No 1105, serving *tenedor libre* for US$5, and **Casablanca**, Libertador and 25 de Mayo. A welcoming place, serving omelettes, hamburgers, US$4 for steak and chips.

TTT **Casimiro Biguá**, Av del Libertador 963, T02902-492590. A popular upmarket place with quality food, including the excellent stew *cazuela de cordero.*

TTT **El Puesto**, Gobernador Moyano y 9 de Julio. Tasty thin-crust pizzas in a cosy old house. Also pricier regional meals and take-away service. Recommended

TTT **Espora y Gobernador Moyano**, Hotel **Michelangelo**. Excellent regional meals and some other more eclectic, but all very good such as hare, steak and ink squid ravioli.

TTT **La Posta**, **Los Alamos Hotel**, Gobernador Moyano y Bustillo. Undoubtedly the best in town. With elegant decor, slightly reminiscent of a traditional mountain lodge and a really superb menu. Patagonian lamb and rose hip sauce, king crab-stuffed raviolis, with a refined, but definitely not stuffy, atmosphere, and very friendly staff. Pricey but worth it.

TTT **Pascasio**, 25 de Mayo 52. Cosy, exclusive and a very good spot for romantic dinners. Try the risotto with mushrooms.

TTT **Sancho**, restaurant at Hotel El Quijote, 25 de Mayo and Gobernador Gregores is one of the best for its varied and top quality menu, in a relaxed atmosphere.

TT **La Cocina**, Av del Libertador 1245. Pizzería, a large variety of pancakes, pasta, salads, in cosy warm atmosphere.

TT **La Tablita**, Coronel Rosales 28 (near the bridge). The best place for a typical *parrilla* with generous portions and quality beef.

TT **Mi Viejo**, Av del Libertador 1111. Popular *parrilla*, try the grilled lamb for US$7.

TT **Pura Vida**, Av del Libertador 1876. Recommended for a relaxed place to eat, with comfortable sofas, homemade food, lots of veggie options, and a lovely lake view.

El Chaltén *p158, map p163*

TTT **Los Cerros**, **Hotel Los Cerros**. Top cuisine in a sophisticated atmosphere, where regional meals such as *puchero patagónico* and *carbonada de liebre* sit well among other more international standards. The wine list includes produce from the best *bodegas*.

TT **Bahía Túnel**, 16 km south of town, access from RP 23. Its setting right on the shores of Lago Viedma is a spectacular and peaceful. Delicious trout, lamb and rich stews. Home-made cakes and pastries at tea time.

Estepa, Cerro Solo y Antonio Rojo. Small, intimate place with a varied menu that includes excellent lamb, selected wines and imaginative vegetarian options.
Fuegia, San Martín. The usual international menu in a warm atmosphere, plus some Patagonian dishes and more imaginative options, such as curries and veggie food.
Pangea, Lago del Desierto y San Martín. Open for lunch and dinner, drinks and coffee, in calm comfortable surroundings with good music, a varied menu, from pastas to steak, trout and pizzas. Recommended.
Patagonicus, Güemes y Madsen. A lovely warm cosy stylish place with salads, home made pastas and the best pizzas. Great family photos of mountain climbers on the walls. Open from 1200-2400. Recommended.
Ruca Mahuida, Lionel Terray s/n. Widely regarded as the best restaurant in El Chaltén, for imaginative and carefully prepared food.
Terray, Lionel Terray 212, **Hostería El Puma**. Climbers, trekkers and other visitors chat about their expeditions, over excellent food in a homely atmosphere.
Zafarrancho, behind Rancho Grande. A great lively bar-restaurant, serving a good range of reasonably priced dishes.
Josh Aike, Lago del Desierto 105. Excellent *confitería*, delicious homemade food, in a beautiful building. Recommended.
Las Lengas, Viedma y Güemes. Opposite the tourist office, this place is a little cheaper than most. Big meals, basic pastas and meat dishes. US$4 for the meal of the day.

Bars and nightclubs

El Calafate *p154, map p161*
Borges y Alvarez, Av del Libertador 1015, 1st floor, Galería de los Gnomos. Lively café and bookshop open late. Good for hanging out.
Shackleton Lounge, Av del Libertador 3287, on the outskirts of town (US$1.70 in taxi). A great place to relax, lovely views of the lake, old photos of Shackleton, great atmosphere, good music. Highly recommended for a late drink or some good regional dishes.
Tango Sur, 9 de Julio 265, T02902-491550. Live music and, amazingly, a long way from Buenos Aires, a tango show. US$5, Tue-Sun from 2000 (Oct-Apr), in charming old-style house that became the informal refuge of Alejandro, a nostalgic Porteño.

Festivals

El Calafate *p154, map p161*
15 Feb People flock to the rural show **Lago Argentino Day**, and camp out with live music, dancing and *asados*.
10 Nov Displays of horsemanship and *asados* on **Día de la Tradición**.

Shopping

El Calafate *p154, map p161*
All along Libertador there are souvenir shops selling hats and gloves for those chilly boat rides to the glacier. There are lots of fine quality handicrafts; look out for Mapuche weavings and woollen items. Handicraft stalls are on Libertador at around 1200.
Ferretería Chuar, a block away from bus terminal. The only place selling white gas for camping and camping supplies.
La Anónima, Av del Libertador and Perito Moreno. Supermarket.

El Chaltén *p158, map p163*
Camping Center, San Martín, T02962-493264. Buy or rent equipment for climbing, trekking and camping.
El Gringuito, Av San Martín. The best of many supermarkets. All are expensive and have little fresh food. Fuel is available.
El Súper, Lago del Desierto y Av Güemes, T02902-493039. A supermarket that also rents and sells camping and climbing equipment, maps, postcards, books and handicrafts.
Viento Oeste, Av San Martín s/n, (northern end of town), T02962-493021. Equipment hire such as tents and sleeping bags. Also arranges mountain guides and sells handicrafts.

Activities and tours

El Calafate *p154, map p161*
Ballooning
Hotel Kau Yatun, (see Sleeping, page 160). Organizes balloon trips over El Calafate and Lago Argentino, weather permitting, US$150 per hr for a group of up to 7 people.

Birdwatching
Cecilia Scarafoni, T02902-493196, ecowalks@cotecal.com.ar. Expert-led birdwatching walks to Laguna Nimenez, lasting 2 hrs, US$4, Mon-Sat.

Boat trips

Boat trips are also run by **Hielo y Aventura**, see Ice trekking, below.

Fernández Campbell, Av del Libertador 867, T02902-491298, www.solopatagonia.com.ar. The main operator for trips on Lago Argentino to the Perito Moreno and Upsala glaciers.

Mar Patag, www.crucerosmarpatag.com or call T011-50310756 in Buenos Aires. Run the *'Spirit of the Glaciers'* luxurious boat trip, a recommendable 2-day exclusive experience for viewing Moreno, Upsala and Spegazzini glaciers (US$350 pp, full board).

Fishing

Calafate Fishing, 9 de Julio 29, T02902-493311, www.calafatefishing.com. From half-day excursions to 3-day expeditions.

Ice trekking

Hielo y Aventura, Av del Libertador 935, T02902-492205, www.hieloyaventura.com. *Safari Náutico* 1-hr boat trip for viewing Moreno glacier from the south side, leaves from Bajo de las Sombras pier, US$8.50 (tickets also sold at the pier); *Brazo Sur* boat trip, the same as Safari plus a landing to give you the chance to see more glaciers, US$30; the famous *minitrekking*, with 90 mins on the glacier with crampons, US$85, and *Big Ice*, a much longer walk on ice in the same area of the minitrekking, US$115. Recommended.

Horse riding

Cabalgata en Patagonia, Av del Libertador 3600, T02902-493203, www.cabalgaten patagonia.com. For 2-hr rides (US$20 pp) or 6-hr excursions (US$40 pp, lunch included) to see the Gualicho cave paintings by the lake.

Mountain bikes

On Rent a Car, Av del Libertador 1831, T02902-493788. US$20 per day.

Offroading

Mil Outdoor Adventure, Av del Libertador 1029, T02902-491437, www.miloutdoor.com. Exciting excursions in 4WD to see wild places with wonderful views, 3-6 hrs, US$42-70.

Rafting

Nonthue Aventura, Libertador 1177, T02902-491179. Rafting on the Río Santa Cruz, 4-5 hrs, US$40 with transport.

Tour operators

Most agencies charge the same rates for excursions: to the Perito Moreno Glacier US$20; to Lago Roca, a full-day including lunch at Estancia Anita, US$30; horse riding to Gualichó caves, 2 hrs, US$20.

Chaltén Travel, Av del Libertador 1174, T2902-492212, www.chaltentravel.com. The most helpful, with a huge range of tours: glaciers, estancias, trekking, and trips to El Chaltén with a visit to Torres del Paine, US$67; also sells tickets along Ruta 40 to Los Antiguos. English spoken. Highly recommended.

Lago San Martín, Av del Libertador 1215, 1st fl, T02902-492858, www.lagosanmartin.com. Specializes in reservations to *estancias* in Santa Cruz province, very helpful.

Leutz Turismo, Av del Libertador 1341, T02902-492316, www.leutzturismo.com.ar. Daily excursion to Lago Roca 1000-1800, US$ 35 pp, plus US$ 17 for optional lunch at Estancia Nibepo Aike, and an interesting tour of the sheep and fruit. **Estancia Quien Sabe** with a traditional *cordero asado* for dinner.

Mundo Austral, Av del Libertador 1114, T02902-492365. All kinds of tours to the park and cheaper trips to the glaciers with helpful bilingual guides. Also books bus travel.

Patagonia Backpackers, at Hostels del Glaciar: Los Pioneros 251 or Av del Libertador 587, T/F2902-491243, www.glaciar.com. Offers the 'Alternative Tour to Moreno Glacier'. Highly recommended, it includes lots of information on the landscape and wildlife with some light walking to approach the glacier along the lake shore, followed by the boat trip, to see it up close. US$30. Other trips include 'Supertrekking en Chaltén', a 2-day hiking trip, featuring the best treks in the Fitz Roy massif, including camping and ice trekking; and a 2-day visit to Torres del Paine including camping and trekking (US$180). They also sell tickets for the Navimag ferries in the Chilean fjords. Highly recommended.

El Chaltén *p158, map p163*

Boat trips

Patagonia Aventura, Av Güemes s/n, T02962-493110, www.elchalten.com/viedmadiscovery. Boat trips along Lago Viedma to see the Glaciar Viedma, informative; transfers US$10 extra. Also a good full day's trip along Lago Viedma, with ice trekking on Glaciar Viedma. They also operate Lago del Desierto crossings, US$15 pp.

Estancia Cristina

For many visitors, a visit to historical **Estancia Cristina** is the highlight of their trip. A boat leaves Puerto Bandera early in the morning and travels for two hours to the northernmost reaches of Lago Argentina, strewn with mighty icebergs, to see the Upsala glacier from the water. Then, having taken in the sheer size of and unspoilt beauty, the boat continues to the remote estancia situated in isolation on the shores of the lake under a crown of mountains. Visit for the day to enjoy a real Patagonian *asado*, or better still, stay overnight in comfortable rooms with superb views. An overnight stay allows for a wonderful horse-riding trip, or an excursion by 4WD to a viewpoint high above the Upsala glacier, with the still milky Prussian blue lake below, and fire coloured rocks all around. From here hike down the staggering Canyon de los Fosiles, with your own private guide: mind blowingly beautiful. Day trips cost from US$110, all included. See www.experiencepatagonia.com for packages including their other hotels **Los Notros** and **Los Cerros** in El Chaltén.

Tour operators and trekking guides

Fitz Roy Expediciones, Lionel Terray 212 (next to **Hosteria El Puma**), T02962-493017, www.fitzroyexpediciones.com.ar. The best and most experienced company with excellent guides. Trekking, rock climbing and ice-climbing courses, adventure expeditions, including 2-day ascents of Cerro Solo (2121 m), 3-day trekking crossing from Lago Viedma to Lago San Martín, and 8-day trekking expeditions on the Campo de Hielo. Also organizes superb kayaking down the Río de las Vueltas from its wonderful adventure camp, the FRAC, on the way to Lago del Desierto. Great *asados*, hiking, biking, and guides on hand too. Highly recommended.

Transport

El Calafate *p154, map p161*

Air

Aerolíneas Argentinas, 9 de Julio 57, T02902- 492814, flies daily to/from **Buenos Aires**, with many more flights in summer. **LADE**, Julio Roca 1004, at the bus station, T02902- 491262) flies twice a week to **Río Gallegos**, **Comodoro Rivadavia**, **Esquel** and **Bariloche**. To **Puerto Natales**, **Aerovias Dap**, www.aeroviasdap.cl, daily, Nov-Mar only. Airport charge for departing passengers US$6.

Bus

The terminal is on Roca, 1 block up steep stairs from Libertador.

Long-distance To **Ushuaia** take a bus to Río Gallegos; (the **Taqsa** 0300 is the best connection). To **Río Gallegos**, daily with **Interlagos**, T02902-491179, **Sportman**, T02902-492680, and **Taqsa**, 4 hrs, US$7-10. To **El Chaltén**, daily with **Cal-Tur**, **Chaltén Travel**, T02902-491833, and **Taqsa**, 4-4½ hrs, US$15-17. To **Perito Moreno glacier**, daily with **Cal-Tur**, T02902-491842, 1½ hrs, US$10. **Taqsa**, T02902-491843, goes only in summer. To **Perito Moreno** and **Los Antiguos**, contact **Chaltén Travel**. To **Bariloche** along Ruta 40 with **Overland Patagonia**, www.overlandpatagonia.com, 4 days via the Perito Moreno national park, Cueva de las Manos, Estancia Melike, Río Mayo and Fitz Roy, US$95 plus accommodation at US$5 per day; bookings in El Calafate from **Patagonia Backpackers** (Hostels del Glaciar), T02902-491243, www.glaciar.com.

To Chile To **Puerto Natales**, daily with either **Cootra** T02902-491444, or **Bus Sur** T02902-491631, US$16, advance booking recommended. **Bus Sur** (Tue, Sat 0800) and **Zaahj** (Wed, Fri, Sun 0800) also run to Puerto Natales via **Cerro Castillo**, where you can pick up a bus to **Torres del Paine** in summer. Take your passport when booking tickets to Chile.

Car hire
Adventure Rent a Car, Av del Libertador 290, T02902-492595, adventurerentacar@cotecal.com.ar. **On Rent a Car**, Av del Libertador 1831, T02902-493788, onrentacar@cotecal.com.ar. Average US$50 per day for a small car including insurance.

Taxi
To **Río Gallegos**, 4 hrs, US$100 irrespective of number of passengers, up to 5 people.

Perito Moreno glacier *p155*
The cheapest way to get to the glacier is on the regular daily **bus** services run by **Taqsa** T02902-491843, and **Cal-Tur** T02902-491842, to the car park above the walkways. Many agencies in El Calafate (see Activities and tours) also run minibus **tours** (park entry not included) leaving 0800 and returning 1800, giving you 3 hrs at the glacier; the return ticket is also valid if you come back next day (student discount available). **Patagonia Backpackers** run an extended alternative itinerary. **Boat** trips for up to 60 passengers are run by **Fernandez Campbell** (see Activities and tours). 'Safari Náutico' offers the best views, US$10 pp, 1 hr. Boats leave from the tourist pier signposted from the car park in Parque Nacional Los Glaciares, bus travel is included. Out of season, trips to the glacier are difficult to arrange, but you can gather a party and hire a **taxi** (*remise* T02902-491745/ 492005). These will charge US$45 for 4 passengers, round trip.

Upsala glacier *p156*
Tour boats usually run daily. The main operator is **Fernández Campbell** (see Activities and tours) who charges US$25, including transfer bus and park entry fees. The bus departs at 0730 from El Calafate for Punta Bandera, with time allowed for lunch at the restaurant (not included, so take your own food) near the Lago Onelli track. The return bus to El Calafate is at 1930. A more expensive but also more spectacular trip is offered by **Estancia Cristina**, see box page 167.

El Chaltén *p158, map p163*
Bus
In summer, buses fill quickly, so book ahead. The following are high-season services; they are less frequent in winter. Daily buses to **El Calafate**, 4-4½ hrs, US$15-17 one way: run by **Chaltén Travel**, San Martín 635 (at Albergue Rancho Grande), T02902-493005, www.chaltentravel.com, **Cal-Tur**, San Martín 520 (at Fitz Roy Inn), T02902-493062, and **Taqsa**, Av Güemes 68, T02902-493068. To **Los Antiguos** along the RN 40, **Itinerarios y Travesías**, T002902-493088 overnight, even dates (ie 2nd, 4th, 6th), includes trip to Cueva de las Manos in the early morning. **Chaltén Travel** runs a service Nov-Mar, leaving on odd days to go along RN 40 up to Bariloche, with a stopover at the small town of Perito Moreno, US$113 transport only.

Overland Patagonia does trips to **Bariloche** in 4 days, staying at *estancias* and visiting Cueva de las Manos.

Río Turbio *p160*
Bus
Bus To **Puerto Natales**, 1hr, US$ 3, several daily with: **Cootra**, Tte del Castillo 01, T02902- 421448. **Bus Sur**, Baquedano 534, Pto Natales, T+56(0)61-411859, www.turismo zaahj.co.cl. **Lagoper**, Av de Los Mineros 262, T02902- 411831, **El Pingüino. To El Calafate, Cootra**, **Taqsa**, daily, US$13, 4½ hrs. To **Río Gallegos**, **Taqsa**, www.taqsa.com.ar, daily, 4 hrs, US$10.

❻ Directory

El Calafate *p154, map p161*
Banks Best to take cash as high commission is charged on exchange. Plenty of ATMs. Change money at **Thaler**, 9 de Julio 57, www.cambio-thaler.com. **Post office** Av del Libertador 1133. **Telephone** Open **Calafate**, Libertador 996, huge *locutorio* for phones and internet. **Centro Integral de Comunicaciones**, Av del Libertador 1486, is cheaper.

Santiago

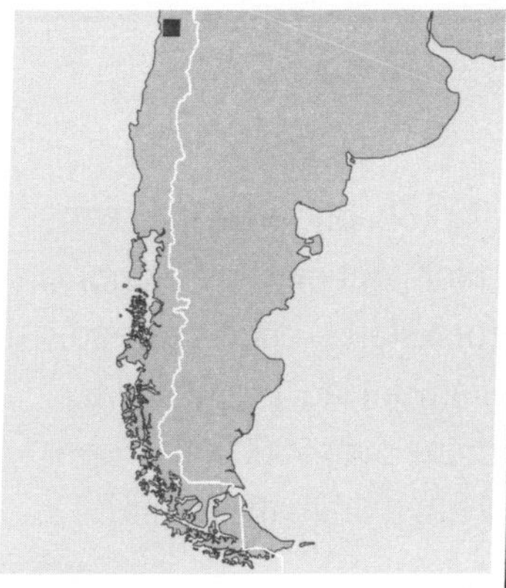

Footprint features

Introduction

If you are flying into Chile, you will probably arrive in Santiago. It is unlikely to prove a highlight of your Patagonian adventures – it's 1000 km away for a start – but it's a good place to acclimatize and get over any jet lag. In a hollow surrounded by mountains with peaks over 5000 m, no one can deny that the Chilean capital has a dramatic setting.

Santiago is a vibrant, progressive city. Its many parks, excellent museums, glittering high-rises and boutiques, not to mention ebullient nightlife, burst with possibilities. Santiago has grown to become the sixth largest city in South America, as well as the political, economic and cultural capital of Chile. But life isn't easy for everyone here. Many people, particularly those originally from rural areas, live in appalling *villas misérias* on the city's outskirts.

The region near the capital can be seen as a microcosm of the country as a whole. Coastal resorts are less than two hours away, and the city is within easy reach of the best ski resorts in South America, which are great spots for weekend hikes in summer. Meanwhile, the area south of Santiago is perhaps the best wine-producing area in Chile. Autumn is a particularly good time to visit the vineyards.

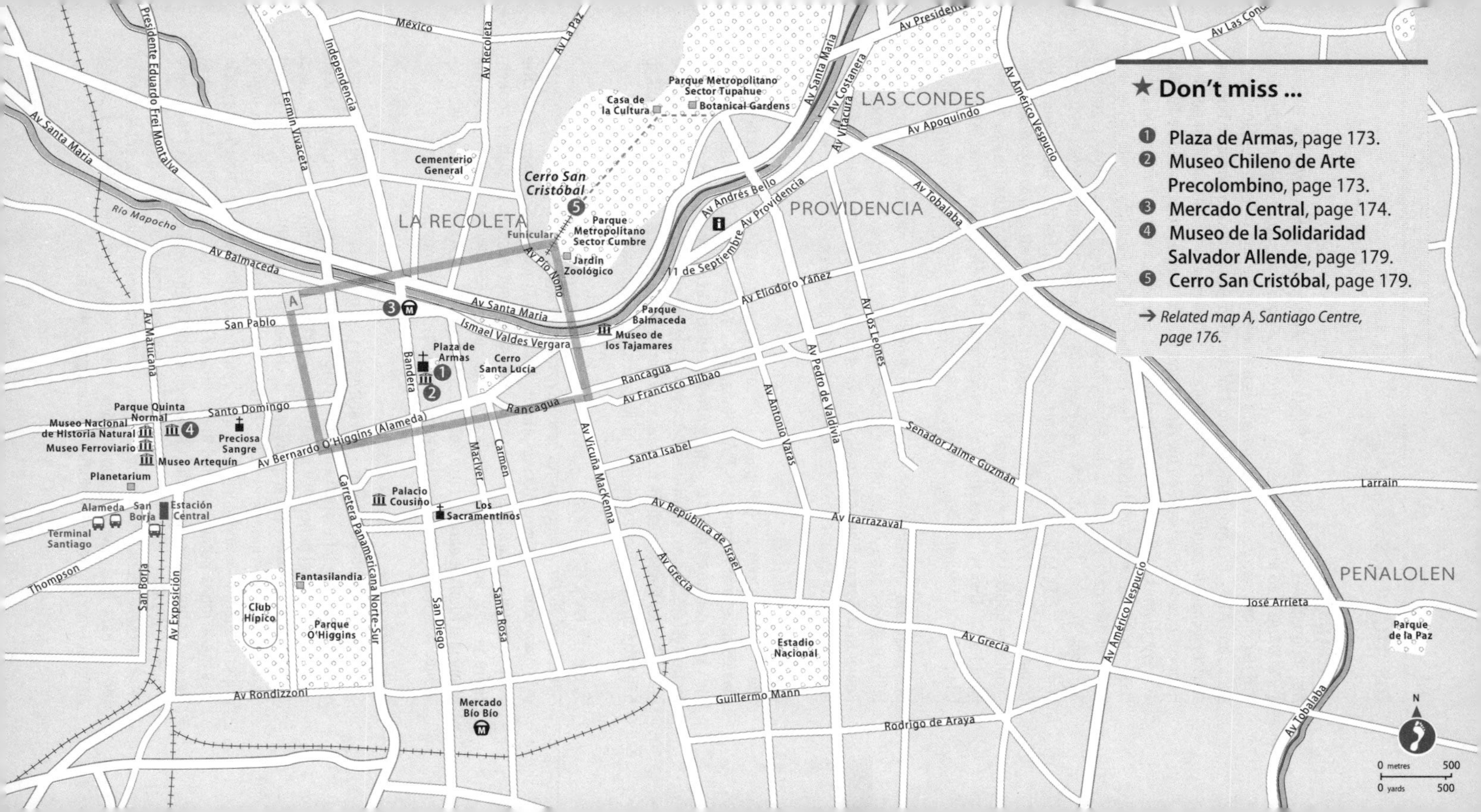
★ Don't miss ...
1 Plaza de Armas, page 173.
2 Museo Chileno de Arte Precolombino, page 173.
3 Mercado Central, page 174.
4 Museo de la Solidaridad Salvador Allende, page 179.
5 Cerro San Cristóbal, page 179.
→ Related map A, Santiago Centre, page 176.
LAS CONDES
PROVIDENCIA
LA RECOLETA
PEÑALOLEN
Parque Metropolitano Sector Tupahue
Casa de la Cultura
Botanical Gardens
Cementerio General
Cerro San Cristóbal
Parque Metropolitano Sector Cumbre
Funicular
Jardín Zoológico
Parque Balmaceda
Museo de los Tajamares
Plaza de Armas
Cerro Santa Lucía
Parque Quinta Normal
Museo Nacional de Historia Natural
Museo Ferroviario
Museo Artequín
Preciosa Sangre
Planetarium
Alameda
San Borja
Estación Central
Terminal Santiago
Palacio Cousiño
Los Sacramentinos
Fantasilandia
Club Hípico
Parque O'Higgins
Estadio Nacional
Mercado Bío Bío
Parque de la Paz
México
Av Recoleta
Av La Paz
Independencia
Fermín Vivaceta
Presidente Eduardo Frei Montalva
Av Santa María
Río Mapocho
Av Balmaceda
Av Santa Maria
San Pablo
Av Matucana
Santo Domingo
Av Bernardo O'Higgins (Alameda)
Bandera
Ismael Valdes Vergara
Av Pío Nono
Rancagua
Av Francisco Bilbao
Av Vicuña MacKenna
MacIver
Carmen
Carretera Panamericana Norte-Sur
San Diego
Santa Rosa
Santa Isabel
Av República de Israel
Av Grecia
Av Irarrazaval
Av Rondizzoni
Guillermo Mann
Rodrigo de Araya
Av Exposición
San Borja
Thompson
Av Andrés Bello
Av Providencia
11 de Septiembre
Av Eliodoro Yáñez
Av Antonio Varas
Av Pedro de Valdivia
Av Los Leones
Senador Jaime Guzmán
Av Costanera
Av Vitacura
Av Apoquindo
Av Tobalaba
Av Américo Vespucio
Av Presidente
Av Las Condes
Larrain
José Arrieta
N
0 metres 500
0 yards 500

Ins and outs » p190.

Getting there

Air International and domestic flights use **Aeropuerto Arturo Merino Benitez** ⓘ *Pudahuel, 26 km northwest of centre, T02-6901900, flight information T02-6763149, www.aeropeurtosantiago.cl.* It is a modern, safe and efficient terminal, with banks and ATMs, fast food outlets, tourist information with an accommodation booking service, a *casa de cambio* and car hire offices. Left luggage is US$8 per item per day. Frequent bus services between the airport and the city centre are operated by **Tur Bus** ⓘ *every 30 mins, US$3*, and **Centropuerto** ⓘ *T02-6019883, every 15 mins, 0600-2230, US$2.50*. All airport buses stop at the new terminal at Metro Pajaritos, where buses also leave for the coast. En route to the airport, buses also pick up at Estación Central and Terminal Santiago. Minibus services between the airport and hotels or other addresses in the city (US$5 to/from the city centre, US$7 to/from Las Condes) are operated by **Transfer** ⓘ *T02-7777707*, **Delfos** ⓘ *T02-6011111*, and **Navett** ⓘ *T02-6956868*, and should be booked the previous day. Taxis to/from centre cost around US$20, to/from Providencia US$25; agree the fare beforehand. There is a taxi office inside the international terminal. » *For flights, see Essentials, page 17 and page 20.*

Bus and train Intercity buses arrive at one of four terminals, all located close to each other, just west of the centre and not far from the train station, along Avenida Libertador Bernardo O'Higgins. This is the main east-west avenue through the city and within easy reach of line 1 of the metro. » *For information on long-distance services, see Essentials, page 21.*

Getting around

The city's main avenue, O'Higgins, is almost always referred to as the Alameda, and Plaza Baquedano is known as Plaza Italia (this book follows suit). Although parts of the centre can be explored on foot, you will need to master the city's fast but crowded metro system. Buses, known as micros also ply the city's streets but these can be confusing for foreign visitors and are slow during peak periods. It is not advisable to hail taxis on the street for night-time journeys. » *See metro map, page 190.*

Tourist information

Sernatur ⓘ *Av Providencia 1550, next to Providencia Municipal Library, T02-7318336, info@sernatur.cl, Metro Manuel Montt, Mon-Fri 0845-1830, Sat 0900-1400*. The national tourist board has maps, many brochures and posters. English is spoken. There is also an information office at the airport. For city information, visit the **Municipal tourist board** ⓘ *Casa Colorada, Merced 860, T02-336700, Metro Plaza de Armas,* which also offers walking tours of the city, on Wednesdays at 1500.

Background

Santiago was founded by Pedro de Valdivia in 1541 on the site of a small indigenous settlement between the southern bank of the Río Mapocho and the Cerro Santa Lucía. During the colonial period, it was one of several Spanish administrative and cultural centres. Much of the fledgling city was destroyed by two earthquakes in 1647 and 1730 but following Independence, Santiago became more significant. In the 1870s, under Benjamín Vicuña MacKenna, an urban plan was drafted, the Cerro Santa Lucía was made into a public park and the first trams were introduced. As the city grew at the end of the 19th century, the Chilean elite built their mansions west of the centre around Calle Dieciocho. The spread of the city east towards Providencia began in 1895. In the latter part of the 20th century, Santiago grew rapidly as affluent residents moved east into new neighbourhoods in the foothills of the Andes and poorer neighbourhoods were established to the west of the centre.

Playing it safe

Like all large cities, Santiago has problems of theft. Pickpockets and bagsnatchers operate in the central area, mostly on the metro, around the Plaza de Armas, in Barrio Brasil, near Cerro Santa Lucía and around the restaurants in Bellavista, and can easily be avoided with common sense. The biggest risk is in unwittingly entering a dangerous *barrio* away from the centre; avoid Pudahuel in the west, Conchalí in the north and Macul and La Pintana in the south. At night, take a public bus (*micro*) for safety in numbers or call for a radio taxi.

Sights

The centre of the old city lies between the Río Mapocho and the city's main avenue, Alameda. From Plaza Italia, in the east of the city's central area, the river flows to the northwest and the Alameda runs to the southwest. From Plaza Italia, Calle Merced runs due west to the Plaza de Armas, the heart of the city, which lies five blocks south of the Río Mapocho. ▸▸ For Sleeping, Eating and other listings see pages 181-192.

Plaza de Armas

On the eastern and southern sides of the Plaza de Armas, there are arcades with shops; on the northern side is the post office and the Municipalidad; and on the western side the cathedral and the archbishop's palace. The **cathedral**, much rebuilt, contains a recumbent statue in wood of San Francisco Javier and the chandelier that lit the first meetings of Congress after Independence; it also houses a museum of religious art and historical pieces. In the Palacio de la Real Audiencia is the **Museo Histórico Nacional** ⓘ *Plaza de Armas 951, T02-4117000, www.museohistoriconacional.cl, Tue-Sun 1000-1730, US$1, free on Sun*, which covers the period from the Conquest until 1925 and contains a model of colonial Santiago.

Around the plaza

Southwest of the cathedral are the courts and **Museo Chileno de Arte Precolombino** ⓘ *Bandera 361, www.precolombino.cl, Tue-Sun 1000-1800, US$4*. Housed in the former Real Aduana, this is one of the best museums in Chile with an excellent representative exhibition of objects from the pre-Columbian cultures of Central America and the Andean region. Displays are well labelled in English. Two blocks west is **Palacio de la Alhambra** ⓘ *Compañía 1340, T02-6890875, www.snba.cl, Mon-Fri 1100-1300, 1700-1930*, a national monument, with art exhibitions and a permanent display.

Just east of the Plaza de Armas is the Casa Colorada. Built in 1769, it was the home of the governor in colonial days and then of Mateo de Toro, first president of Chile. It now holds the **Museo de Santiago** ⓘ *Merced 860, www.munistgo.cl/colorada, Tue-Sat 1000-1800, Sun and holidays 1100-1400, US$3, students free*, which covers the history of Santiago from the Conquest to modern times with excellent displays, models and guided tours.

From the Plaza de Armas, Paseo Ahumada runs south to the Alameda, four blocks away. **Ahumada** is a pedestrianized street and the commercial heart of the centre. Ahumada and nearby **Calle Huérfanos** are always interesting places to come for a stroll, especially at night, when those selling pirated CDs or playing the three-card trick mix with evangelist preachers and satanists.

Four blocks north of the Plaza de Armas is the interesting **Mercado Central** ⓘ *Av 21 de Mayo y San Pablo*. This is the best place to come for seafood in Santiago and is so prominent in the Chilean psyche that it was the setting for a recent national soap opera, *Amores del Mercado*. The building faces the **Parque Venezuela**, on which is the Cal y Canto metro station on Line 2; at its western end, the former Mapocho railway station is now a cultural centre and concert venue. If you head east from Mapocho station, along the river, you arrive at the **Parque Forestal**. The **Museo Nacional de Bellas Artes** ⓘ *www.mnba.cl, Tue-Sun 1000-1900,* US$1.20, is located in the wooded grounds and is an extraordinary example of neo- classical architecture. Inside is a large display of Chilean and foreign painting and sculpture; contemporary art exhibitions are held several times a year. In the west wing is the **Museo de Arte Contemporáneo** ⓘ *www.mac.uchile.cl, US$1.20, Bellas Artes metro*.

Along and around the Alameda

The Alameda runs through the heart of the city for over 3 km. It is 100 m wide, choked full of *micros*, taxis and cars day and night and ornamented with gardens and statuary.

At the eastern end of the Alameda is **Plaza Italia**, where there is a statue of General Baquedano and the Tomb of the Unknown Soldier. Four blocks south is the **Museo Nacional Benjamín Vicuña MacKenna** ⓘ *Av V MacKenna 94, www.dibam.cl/subdirec_museos/mbm_mackenna, Mon-Sat 0930-1300, 1400-1750, US$1.20*, which records the life and works of the 19th-century Chilean historian and biographer who became one of Santiago's most important mayors. It also has occasional exhibitions.

Between the Parque Forestal, Plaza Italia and the Alameda is the **Lastarria** neighbourhood (Universidad Católica metro). For those interested in antique furniture, pieces of art and old books, the area is worth a visit, especially the **Plaza Mulato Gil de Castro** (Calle Lastarria 305). Occasional shows are put on in the plaza, and surrounding it are restaurants, bookshops, handicraft and antique shops, an art gallery, the **Instituto de Arte Contemporáneo** and the **Museo Arqueológico de Santiago** ⓘ *Lastarria 307, Tue-Sun 1030-1830, US$2, free,* with temporary exhibitions of Chilean archaeology, anthropology and pre-Columbian art. The museum also houses the **Museo de Artes Visuales** ⓘ *Tue-Sun 1030-1830, free*.

From here, the Alameda skirts **Cerro Santa Lucía**, a cone of rock rising steeply to a height of 70 m. It can be scaled from the Caupolicán esplanade, but the ascent from the northern side of the hill – wit h its statue of Diego de Almagro – is easier. On clear days you can see across to the Andes from the top and even when it is smoggy the sunset is good. There is a fortress, the **Batería Hidalgo** (closed to visitors) on the summit. The hill closes at 2100; visitors must sign a register at the entrance, giving their ID card number. It is best to descend the eastern side, to see the small **Plaza Pedro Valdivia** with its waterfalls and **statue of Valdivia**. The area is known to be dangerous after dark and you should beware of thieves.

Past the hill, on the right, the Alameda goes past the **Biblioteca Nacional** ⓘ *Av Libertador Bernardo O'Higgins 651, Santa Lucía metro, www.dibam.cl, Mon-Fri 0900-1900, Sat 0910-1400, free*. Beyond, on the left, between Calle San Francisco and Calle Londres, is the oldest church in Santiago: the red-walled church and monastery of **San Francisco** (1618). Inside is the small statue of the Virgin that Valdivia carried on his saddlebow when he rode from Peru to Chile. Free classical concerts are sometimes given in the church in summer; arrive early for a seat. Annexed to the church, near the cloisters, is the **Museo Colonial** ⓘ *Londres 4, T02-6398737, www.museosanfransisco.cl, Tue-Sat 1000-1300, 1500-1800, Sun1000-1400, US$1.50*, containing displays of religious art and Gabriela Mistral's Nobel Prize medal.

Two blocks north of the Alameda is the **Teatro Municipal** ⓘ *C Agustinas, www.municipal.cl, guided tours Tue 1300-1500 and Sun 1100-1400, US$4*. A little

24 hours in the city

First, try to make sure you are here on a Saturday. If you're staying in the centre, get up early and walk down to Calle San Diego for breakfast. Afterwards, walk down San Diego to the **Iglesia de los Sacramentinos** – Santiago's answer to Sacré Coeur – and then west through gardens until you reach the **Palacio Cousiño** in time for the first tour at 0930. This extraordinary building gives a real insight into the Chilean aristocracy and the opulence to which the upper classes became accustomed. After the tour, stroll to Toesca metro and head south to Franklin. Here you will find swarms of people all making their way to the **Mercado Bío Bío**. This market will show you how most of Santiago lives and it provides a striking contrast to Palacio Cousiño.

When you start feeling hungry, head back to Franklin metro and take the train north to Cal y Canto, where you will find the **Mercado Central**, with some of the best seafood restaurants in Santiago – don't be put off by all the choice.

After lunch, it's time to remind yourself that Santiago has one of the most dramatic settings of any of the world's major cities. Cross back over the Río Mapocho and stroll east towards the conical hill of **Cerro San Cristóbal**. If it's summer, the heat may be making you feel a little tired by now. If so, you could go up the hill on the **funicular railway**. If you are lucky and it is a clear day, you will have an unforgettable view of the Andes. Stroll through tree-lined lanes and discover a world away from the clutter of the city. There are even swimming pools to cool off in and the chance to do some wine tasting. Towards dusk, have a drink in the café near the funicular railway station and watch the sun go down over the coastal mountain range, lighting up the snows of the Andes.

After dark, go back down the hill by funicular railway (it's not advisable to walk here in the evening) in time to sample Santiago's nightlife. At the foot of Cerro San Cristóbal is **Barrio Bellavista**. Here you can take your pick of any one of dozens of excellent (and expensive) restaurants, before going out to one of the area's buzzing *salsotecas*. These don't really get going until midnight and you'll usually find that you don't leave much before five, so perhaps head back to your hotel room for some sleep after dinner and then go out dancing later on.

further west along the Alameda is the **Universidad de Chile** and the **Club de la Unión**, an exclusive social club founded in 1864. The current building dates from 1925 and houses a restaurant where wonderful meals are served at exorbitant prices. Nearby, on Calle Nueva York, is the **Bolsa de Comercio** (stock exchange). The public are allowed access to view the trading, but you must have your passport checked in order to get inside.

One block further west there are three plazas: **Plaza de la Libertad** to the north of the Alameda, **Plaza Bulnes** in the centre and **Plaza del Libertador O'Higgins** to the south. To the north of Plaza de la Libertad, hemmed in by the skyscrapers of the Centro Cívico, is **Palacio de la Moneda** ⓘ *Mon-Fri 1000-1800, guided tours of the palace 0900-1300 last Sun of every month*, (1805), the presidential palace containing historic relics, paintings, sculptures and the elaborate Salón Rojo used for official receptions. Although the Moneda was damaged by air attacks during the military coup of 11 September 1973 it has been fully restored. Only the courtyards are open to the public. In front of the palace is the statue of former President Arturo Alessandri Palma. Ceremonial changing of the guard every other day at 1000.

South of the Alameda

Four blocks south of Plaza del Libertador O'Higgins is **Parque Almagro**, notable for the **Iglesia de los Sacramentinos**, a Gothic church loosely designed in imitation of Sacré Coeur in Paris, which is best viewed from the nearby Palacio Cousiño against the backdrop of the *cordillera*. **Palacio Cousiño** ⓘ *C Dieciocho 438, www.palaciocousino.co.cl, Metro Toesca, admission by guided tour only (Spanish or English), Tue-Fri 0930-1330, 1430-1700 (last tour 1600), Sat, Sun and holidays 0930-1330, US$3*, on the west side of the Parque Almagro and five blocks south of the Alameda, is a large mansion in French rococo style. It was built by Luis and Isadora Cousiño, part of a wealthy Chilean dynasty that made its money in the mining and wine industries.

Furnished with tapestries, antiques and pictures imported from France, the palace startled Santiago society with its opulence and its advanced technology, including its own electricity generators and the first lift in the country. Even today, the word 'luxurious' falls short when describing the palace: one of the chandeliers is made with 13,000 pieces of crystal and the superb Italian staircase was built using 20 different types of marble. Look out also for the '*indiscretos*', three-seater armchairs designed for courting couples and a chaperone. Now owned by the Municipalidad, the palace is used for official receptions but is also open as a museum. Unfortunately part of the upper floor was recently damaged by fire. It has been restored to some extent but not to its original state, however, a visit is still highly recommended.

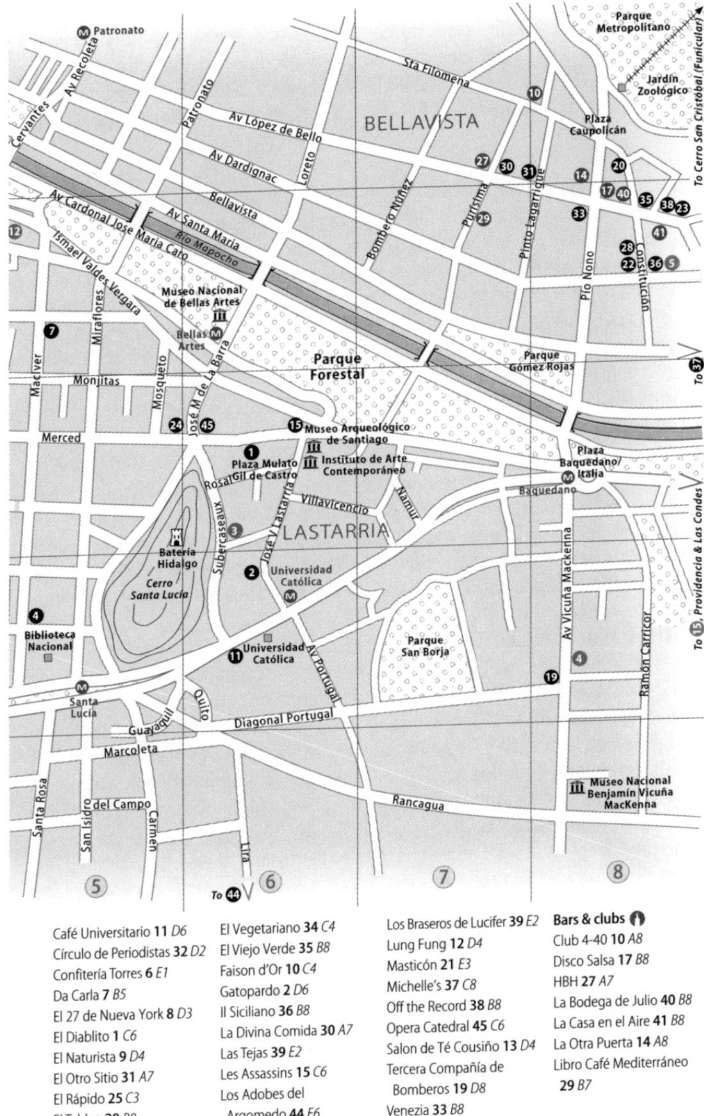

Café Universitario **11** *D6*
Círculo de Periodistas **32** *D2*
Confitería Torres **6** *E1*
Da Carla **7** *B5*
El 27 de Nueva York **8** *D3*
El Diablito **1** *C6*
El Naturista **9** *D4*
El Otro Sitio **31** *A7*
El Rápido **25** *C3*
El Tablao **28** *B8*
El Vegetariano **34** *C4*
El Viejo Verde **35** *B8*
Faison d'Or **10** *C4*
Gatopardo **2** *D6*
Il Siciliano **36** *B8*
La Divina Comida **30** *A7*
Las Tejas **39** *E2*
Les Assassins **15** *C6*
Los Adobes del Argomedo **44** *E6*
Los Braseros de Lucifer **39** *E2*
Lung Fung **12** *D4*
Masticón **21** *E3*
Michelle's **37** *C8*
Off the Record **38** *B8*
Opera Catedral **45** *C6*
Salon de Té Cousiño **13** *D4*
Tercera Compañía de Bomberos **19** *D8*
Venezia **33** *B8*

Bars & clubs

Club 4-40 **10** *A8*
Disco Salsa **17** *B8*
HBH **27** *A7*
La Bodega de Julio **40** *B8*
La Casa en el Aire **41** *B8*
La Otra Puerta **14** *A8*
Libro Café Mediterráneo **29** *B7*

In 1981, a thief made off with the statue of the Virgen del Carmen, but hastily returned it the next day after an earthquake rocked the city.

Parque O'Higgins lies about 10 blocks south of the Alameda. It has a small lake and various entertainment including the **Club Hípico** racecourse, and an amusement park, **Fantasilandia** ⓘ *daily in summer, Sat and Sun only in winter, US$10, children US$7.50*. There are kite-flying contests on Sundays and, during the Independence celebrations around 18 September, there are many good *peñas*. There are also three small museums. The park can be reached by Metro Line 2 to Parque O'Higgins station or by bus from Parque Baquedano via Avenida MacKenna and Avenida Matta.

Barrio Brasil

On the northern side of the Alameda, immediately to the west of the Panamericana, is the Barrio Brasil, a tranquil area in which many of the houses are brightly painted. This historic part of the city was the first area to be colonized by Santiaguinos away from the centre, at the end of the 18th century. It is now a more bohemian, studenty neighbourhood than the surrounding areas and has rich colonial architecture, inexpensive hotels and good restaurants. It is also a centre for nightlife with underground bars, clubs and Santiago's most radical shop, **La Lunita**, stocking feminist books and Santiago's only gay monthly, *Lambda News*.

The heart of the *barrio* is **Plaza Brasil**, easily reached by walking straight up Calle Concha y Toro from the República metro stop. This is a narrow, winding cobblestone street that passes elegant old stone homes in rococo and German Gothic styles, before reaching the plaza, which is shaded by palms, lime trees and silk cottons. Just west of the plaza, on Compañía, is the **Basilica del Salvador**, a striking yellow- and rose-coloured church built between 1870 and 1872, with stained glass and a statue of the Virgen del Carmen. A little further along Compañía is the **Iglesia Preciosa Sangre**, a bright red church of neoclassical design, with impressive reliefs and twin towers.

Around Estación Central

The Alameda continues westwards across the Pan-American Highway towards the impressive railway station, **Estación Central**, which is surrounded by several blocks of market stalls. Opposite Estacíon Central is the **Planetarium** ⓘ *US$6*, while to the north on Avenida Matucana y Diego Portales is **Parque Quinta Normal**. The park was founded as a botanical garden in 1830, and is a pleasant, popular spot, which gets very crowded on Sundays with families and the street entertainers who vie with one another to get their pesos.

The park contains several museums. **Museo Ferroviario** ⓘ *www.corpdicyt.cl, Tue-Fri 1000-1800, Sat and Sun 1100-1900, US$2*, contains the former presidential stagecoach and 13 steam engines built between 1884 and 1953, including a rare surviving Kitson-Meyer. The **Museo Nacional de Historia Natural** ⓘ *www.mnhn.cl, Tue-Sat 1000-1730, Sun and holidays 1100-1830,US$1.20, Sun free, students free*, was founded in 1830 and is one of Latin America's oldest museums. Housed in a neoclassical building, it has exhibitions on zoology, botany, mineralogy, anthropology, ethnography and archaeology. **Museo Artequín** ⓘ *Av Portales 3530, T02-6825367, www.artequin.cl, Tue-Fri 0900-1700, Sat, Sun and holidays 1100-1800, US$1.60*, is housed in the Chilean pavilion built for the 1889 Paris International Exhibition. It contains prints of famous paintings and explanations of the techniques of the great masters.

Moving mountains

While Santiago's smog is not too bad in spring, summer and autumn, those who arrive here during winter could be in for an unpleasant shock. It might not take more than half an hour for your throat to begin to itch and your eyes to water due to one of Santiago's biggest problems – pollution. In 2001, it was rated the eighth most polluted city in the world. When Pedro de Valdivia founded the city in 1541, between the coastal mountains and the Andes, it must have seemed like a perfect site; he could never have imagined that the city would one day engulf the whole valley, and that the mountains would become a serious problem.

The principal reason for Santiago's high levels of pollution is that it lies in a bowl, encircled by mountains, which means that the smog is trapped. This, combined with the centralization of Chilean industry in Santiago, the fact that many buses are not equipped with catalytic converters and the sheer volume of cars that choke the city's highways, conspires to create a problem that cannot easily be resolved. It is a serious issue: asthma rates are high and older people sometimes die during the winter *emergencias*, when the pollution gets particularly bad.

Over the years, all sorts of solutions have been proposed. A team of Japanese scientists once even suggested blowing up the part of the Andes nearest the city, so that the pollution could disperse more easily. Each weekday, cars that have number plates ending in one of two digits are prohibited from circulating. But, until the government finds a means of dispersing the population more widely throughout the country, the problem is likely to remain.

Recommended. Two blocks east of the park is the **Museo de la Solidaridad Salvador Allende** ⓘ *Herrera 360, T02-6817542, www.mssa.cl, Tue-Sun 1000-1900, US$1.20*. Located in a beautiful listed building with a cobbled patio and palm trees with nesting birds, it houses a collection of over 400 art works produced by Chilean and foreign artists in support of the Unidad Popular government and in opposition to the Pinochet dictatorship. Artists include Alexander Calder, Joan Miró, Oswaldo Guayasamin and Roberto Matta. There are also videos of interviews (in Spanish) with survivors of the 1973 coup and an information sheet in English. You need to give four days' notice for guided tours, but they are recommended. The good café serves a cheap set lunch.

Bellavista and Cerro San Cristóbal

Santiago's bohemian face is most obvious in the **Bellavista** district, on the north bank of the Río Mapocho at the foot of **Cerro San Cristóbal**. This is the main focus of nightlife in the old city; the area around Pío Nono and López de Bello buzzes, especially at weekends. In the bars you can see everything from live Cuban music to local imitations of Georges Brassens, while eating options range from classic Italian to sushi and West African palm-nut stew. There are also theatres, art galleries and craft shops specializing in lapis lazuli.

La Chascona ⓘ *Márquez de la Plata 192, T02-7778741, www.uchile.cl/neruda/chascona.html, Tue-Sun 1000-1300, 1500-1800, US$4 guided visits only*, is the house of the poet Pablo Neruda. There are really three houses, built on a steep hillside and separated by gardens. It was completed in 1955 and Neruda lived here whenever he was in the capital. The house was fully restored after being damaged in the 1973 coup and is now the headquarters of the **Fundación Pablo Neruda**.

Parque Metropolitano

Bellavista lies at the foot of the **Cerro San Cristóbal**, which forms the **Parque Metropolitano** ⓘ *daily 0900-2100, cars US$4*, the largest and most interesting of the city's parks. On a clear day it provides excellent views over the city and across to the Andes. More usually, however, the views provide a graphic demonstration of Santiago's continuing smog problem. From the top, the **Cemeterio General** can also be seen, situated in the *barrio* of La Recoleta to the north. This cemetery contains the mausoleums of most of the great figures in Chilean history, including Violeta Parra, Victor Jara and Salvador Allende. There is also an impressive monument to the victims of the 1973-1990 military government. There are two sectors, **sector Cumbre** on Cerro San Cristóbal and, further east, **sector Tupahue**. There are two entrances: west from Pío Nono in Bellavista and east from Pedro de Valdivia Norte. When the weather is good, the walk up the access road from Bellavista is very pleasant, providing unexpected views of distant and little-visited northern parts of the city. Near the Bellavista entrance is the **Jardín Zoológico** ⓘ *www.zoologico.cl, Tue-Sun 1000-1800, US$4*, which has a well cared-for collection of animals. On **Cerro Cumbre** (300 m), there is a colossal statue of the Virgin, which is floodlit at night; beside it is an astronomical observatory.

The Tupahue sector is reached by taxi either from the Bellavista entrance or on foot from the Pedro de Valdivia metro. This section of the park contains terraces, gardens and paths. One building houses the **Camino Real** ⓘ *T02-2321758, www.eventos caminoreal.cl*, a good restaurant with a splendid view from the terrace, especially at night, and an **Enoteca** of Chilean wines from a range of vineyards, which you can taste (US$2 per glass), or buy, although prices are higher than in shops. Nearby is the **Casa de la Cultura**, which has art exhibitions and free concerts at midday on Sunday. There are also two good **swimming pools** in the park. East of Tupahue are the **botanical gardens** ⓘ *daily 0900-1800, tours available*, with a collection of native plants.

If you don't want to walk to the top of Cerro San Cristóbal, take the **funicular** ⓘ *from Plaza Caupolicán at the northern end of C Pío Nono, daily 1000-2000, US$2 return*, or the **teleférico** ⓘ *from Estación Oasis, Av Pedro de Valdivia Norte via Tupahue, summer only, Mon 1430-1830, Tue-Fri 1030-1830, Sat and Sun 1030-1900, US$4 combination ticket including funicular*. An open-top bus runs to San Cristóbal and Tupahue from the Bellavista entrance to the same schedule as the *teleférico*.

East to Providencia and Las Condes

East of Plaza Italia, the main east-west axis of the city is known as **Avenida Providencia**, as it heads towards the affluent areas of Providencia and Las Condes. On the south bank of the Mapocho is **Parque Balmaceda**, also known as Parque Gran Bretaña. It is one of the more attractive parks in Santiago and houses the **Museo de los Tajamares** ⓘ *Av Providencia 222, T02-340 7329, Mon-Fri 0900-1400 and 1500-2100*, an exhibition of the 17th- and 18th-century walls built to protect the city from flooding by the river. There is also an exhibition of photographs.

South of Las Condes

Parque de la Paz, the new peace park in the southwestern suburb of Peñalolén, stands on the site of **Villa Grimaldi**, the most notorious torture centre during the Pinochet regime. The Irish missionary, Sheila Cassidy, has documented the abuses that she underwent when imprisoned without trial in this place. The walls are daubed with human rights' graffiti and the park makes a moving and unusual introduction to the conflict that has eaten away at the heart of Chilean society for the past 30 years. To reach the park, take a metro to Tobalaba and then any bus marked Peñalolén heading south down Tobalaba. Get off at the junction of Tobalaba y José Arrieta and then walk five minutes up Arrieta towards the mountains.

Sleeping

Expensive hotels in the city centre, Providencia and Las Condes tend to be slightly characterless but with good service. Most budget accommodation is located in the city centre or further west around the bus terminals. Decent *hostales* are also starting to appear in Barrio Brasil and around Providencia. Accommodation in Santiago tends to be more expensive than the rest of the country (see Essentials, page 24).

Around Plaza de Armas *p173, map p176*

A **Majestic**, Santo Domingo 1526, T02-695 8366, www.hotelmajestic.cl. With breakfast, pool, US-chain standard. The rooms, while spacious, retain their 1970s decor. Internet ports in the rooms. Excellent Indian restaurant. English spoken.
E **Indiana** (no sign), Rosas 1339, T02-688 0008, hostal_indiana@hotmail.com. **F** singles. Very basic but friendly. Facilities include a kitchen and internet.
E **Olicar**, San Pablo 1265, T02-673 0837, hotel_olicar@chile.com. **F** singles. Basic, cooking facilities.
E **Residencial San Antonio**, San Antonio 811, T02-638 4607, ressnant@ctcinternet.cl. **F** singles. Good place, decent value.
E **San Felipe**, Gral MacKenna 1248, T02-6714598. **F** singles. Cheap laundry service, kitchen, noisy (2nd floor quieter), luggage stored.

Along and around the Alameda *p174, map p176*

L **Fundador**, Paseo Serrano 34, T02-387 1200, www.hotelfundador.cl. In a nice area with helpful staff. Pool, bar, restaurant, internet. Some rooms on the small side. Universidad de Chile metro, south exit.
AL **Galerías**, San Antonio 65, T02-470 7400, www.hotelgalerias.cl. Large rooms, good location, generous breakfast. Excellent value if booked over the internet.
B **El Marqués del Forestal**, Ismael Valdés Vergara 740, T02-633 3462, www.apart-hotel-elmarques.cl. Good value, apartments.
B-C **Montecarlo**, Victoria Subercaseaux 209, T02-639 2945, www.hotelmontecarlo.cl. At the foot of Cerro Santa Lucía in quiet street, modern but with nice art-deco touches, restaurant, helpful. Recommended.
C-D **Hostal Che Lagarto**, Tucapel Jiménez 24, T02-699 1493, www.chelagarto.com. **F** pp in dorms. Some rooms with bath. Branch of the South American chain hostel. Comfortable common areas, kitchen facilities, internet.
C-D **París**, París 813, T02-6640921, www.hotelparis.cl. Clean no-frills rooms with bath. Quiet, good value, breakfast extra, luggage store. Book in advance in summer. Recommended.
D **Residencial Londres**, Londres 54, T02-638 2215, unico54@ctcinternet.cl. **F** singles. Near San Francisco Church, in a former mansion with large old-fashioned rooms and furniture, some rooms with bath, few singles, no heating so cold in winter, some English spoken, book exchange, great value, very popular, highly recommended, usually full, no advance bookings high season, arrive early.

Barrio Brasil *p178*

B **Happy House Hostel**, Catedral 2207, metro Cumming or República, T02-688 4849, www.happyhousehostel.cl. **E** pp in dorms. In a completely refurbished mansion, this is one of the best hostels in the country. High-ceilinged spacious rooms, excellent fully equipped kitchen, internet, bar, pool room. One room even has an en suite sauna. Friendly and informative staff who speak English. The only downside is that some rooms facing the main street can be a little noisy. Expensive, but still highly recommended.
C **Ducado**, Agustinas 1990, T02-696 9384, hotelducado@entelchile.net. With breakfast. Reasonable value, clean, quiet at back. Secure parking. Also self-contained apartments.
C **Hostal Río Amazonas**, Rosas 2234, T02-698 4092, www.hostalrioamazonas.cl. With breakfast and bath, internet, good value if paying in US$ or euros. Recommended.
D **Hostal Americano**, Compañia 1906, T02-698 1025, www.hostalamericano.cl. Non-descript brick and concrete building. Clean, comfortable rooms, some with private bathroom. Friendly atmosphere. There is a pleasant garden at the back. Better value if paying in US$. Recommended.
D **La Casa Roja**, Agustinas 2113, T02-696 4241, www.lacasaroja.cl. **F** pp in dorms. Huge old house slowly being restored. Without breakfast, kitchen facilities, internet,

Spanish lessons. Large garden with table tennis and pool. Also runs trips to ski resorts. Can be noisy. Recommended if you want to party, not if you want to sleep. Camping available.

E Residencial Turístico, Catedral 2235, T02-695 4800. **G** singles. Basic, clean, hot showers, quiet location, good value.

Around Estación Central *p178*

Staying in this area is convenient for those on a quick visit or arriving late.

B Conde de Anzúrez, Av República 25, T02-696 0807, www.ansurez.cl. República metro. Convenient for airport, central station and bus terminals, clean, helpful, safe, luggage stored, good car hire deals and occasional special offers.

B Tur Hotel Express, Av Libertador Bernardo O'Higgins 3750, 3rd fl, in the Turbus Terminal, T02-685 0100, www.turbus.com/html/turhotel_stgo.html . Comfortable business standard with breakfast, cable TV, a/c, free internet. Useful if you have an early flight as buses leave for the airport from here.

C-D Residencial Mery, Pasaje República 36, off 0-100 block of República, T02-696 8883, www.residencialmery.virtuabyte.cl. Art deco building down an alley, some rooms with bath, breakfast extra, friendly owners, quiet. Recommended.

D Residential Alemana, República 220 (no sign), T02-6712388, ralemana@entelchile.net. República metro. **F** singles. Without bath, clean, with breakfast, pleasant patio, central, heating on request, good cheap meals available. Recommended.

E SCS Habitat, San Vicente 1798, T02-6833732, scshabitat@yahoo.com. **G** pp in dorms. English spoken, lots of information, hot showers, laundry facilities, bicycle rental, internet, maps, guidebooks and camping equipment sold/rented, safe parking for bikes and motorbikes. Often recommended but some mixed reports. Camping available.

Bellavista and Plaza Italia *p179, map p176*

A Presidente, Eliodoro Yáñez 867, almost at Providencia, T02-2358015, www.Presidente.cl. Salvador metro. Slightly soulless, medium-sized chain hotel. Good value and good location.

C Bellavista Hostel, Dardignac 0184, T02-7328737, www.bellavistahostel.com. **F** pp in dorms. Fun hostel in the heart of this lively area. European-style hostel. With breakfast. Kitchen facilities, free internet, satelite TV in common area, bicycles lent to guests. Good meeting place.

D Hostal Casa Grande, Vicuña MacKenna 90, T02-222 7347, www.hostalcasagrande.cl. Baquedano metro. **F** singles. On the 2nd floor of an old high-ceilinged building. Some rooms with bath and TV, quiet, good value.

Providencia *p180*

A Orly, Pedro de Valdivia 027, T02-231 8947, www.orlyhotel.com, Pedro de Valdivia metro. Small, comfortable, convenient location. Small café attached. Recommended.

B El Patio Suizo, Condell 847, T02-494 1214, www.patiosuizo.com, Metro Parque Bustamante. Comfortable Swiss-run B&B in a quiet residential area. Rooms with bath, TV. Patio, internet. English spoken

B-C Marilú's Bed and Breakfast, Rafael Cañas 246 C, T02-2355302, www.bedandbreakfast.cl. Comfortable, no credit cards, very friendly, good beds. Highly recommended.

C-D Casa Condell, Condell 114, T02-209 2343, Salvador metro, www.casacondell.cl. 4-bed dorms, **F** pp. Pleasant old house, central but quiet roof terrace. Shared baths, no breakfast, kitchen facilities, free local phone calls, friendly. Recommended.

F pp **Santiago Hostel**, Dr Barros Borgoño 199, T02-226 49894, hostelsantiago@yahoo.com. European-style hostel, with dorms, breakfast, kitchen, garden, internet. Skiing information.

Las Condes *p180*

LL Grand Hyatt Santiago, Av Kennedy 4601, T02-950 1234, www.santiago.grand.hyatt.com. Beautifully decorated, large outdoor pool, gym. Thai restaurant. Recommended.

A Manquehue, Esteban Dell'Orto 6615, T02-430 1100, www.hotelmanquehue.com. Very good with new wing, new pool, 4 star.

A Montebianco, Isidora Goyenechea 2911, T02-233 1808, www.hotelmontebianco.cl. Small, smart hotel. Good value. Can arrange tours to vineyards and trips to the ski centres.

C Urania's Bed and Breakfast, Boccaccio 60, T02-201 2922, uraniae@hotmail.com. Comfortable, friendly, good beds, English and French spoken. Good value. Recommended, though not particularly convenient for public transport.

Eating

El Mercurio's website has an excellent restaurant guide: www.emol.com. For cheap meals in the evening try the *fuentes de soda* and *schoperias* scattered around the centre.

Around Plaza de Armas *p173, map p176*
For excellent cheap seafood make for the Mercado Central (Cal y Canto metro).
¥¥¥-¥¥ **Da Carla**, MacIver 577, T02-633 3739. Intimate old-time Italian trattoria, good service and has maintained its quality over the years.
¥¥¥-¥¥ **Les Assassins**, Merced 297, T02-638 4280. Small family-run French bistro. Excellent food with friendly service and a decent wine list. Good value set lunches. Recommended.
¥¥¥-¥¥ **Los Adobes del Argomedo**, Argomedo 411 y Lira, T02-2222104. Good Chilean food, floor show (Mon-Sat) includes *cueca* dancing, salsa and folk.
¥¥¥-¥¥ **Majestic**, Santo Domingo 1526. This hotel has an excellent Indian restaurant, good range of vegetarian dishes.
¥¥ **El Naturista**, Moneda 846. Excellent vegetarian, serving quiches, tortillas, a wide range of soups and sandwiches. Also serves organic coffee, fruit and vegetable juice as well as beer and wine. Closes 2100.
¥¥ **Faisan d'Or**, Plaza de Armas. Good *pastel de choclo*, pleasant place to have a drink and watch the world go by.
¥¥ **Lung Fung**, Agustinas 715. The oldest Chinese restaurant in Santiago. Pricey but serves decent food. There is a large cage in the centre with noisy parrots.
¥ **Bar Nacional**, Bandera 317. Good restaurants, popular, local specialities. There is another branch at Huérfanos 1151.
¥ **El Rápido**, C Bandera, next door to **Bar Nacional**. Famed for its *empanadas* and *completos*, cheap, quick service, popular.
¥ **El Vegetariano**, Huérfanos 827, Local 18. Popular vegetarian fast food, good juices. There are other branches in the centre.

Cafés
Café Caribe and **Café Haití**, Paseo Ahumada, are institutions among Santiago's business community and good places to see the people who make Chile tick; also branches throughout the centre and in Providencia.
Bombón Oriental, Merced 345, T02-639 1069, www.bombonoriental.cl. Superb Turkish coffee, arabic snacks and sweets.
Café Colonia, MacIver 133. Splendid variety of cakes, pastries and pies, efficient if somewhat brusque service by staff who haven't changed for decades. Recommended.
Salón de Té Cousiño, Matías Cousiño 107. Good coffee, snacks and *onces*, very popular, not cheap.

Along and around the Alameda *p174, map p176*
¥¥¥-¥¥ **Opera Catedral** , José Miguel de la Barra 407, Bellas Artes metro, line 5, T02-664 5491, www.operacatedral.cl. Very good, if expensive, French restaurant on the ground floor. Upstairs there is a minimalist pub-restaurant, usually packed at night, serving fusion food at reasonable prices.
¥¥ **El 27 de Nueva York**, Nueva York 27, a stone's throw from the Alameda. T02-699 1555. Large and slightly soulless restaurant serving international cuisine, good and varied menu. Tends to fill up with the lunchtime executive crowd.
¥¥ **Gatopardo**, Lastarria 192, T02-633 6420. A mix of Bolivian and Mediterranean cuisine. Good value lunch buffet. Recommended.
¥¥-¥ **El Diablito**, 336, Local 2, Bellas Artes metro, line 5. Fashionable Bohemian bar-restaurant wide range of beer.
¥ **Círculo de Periodistas**, Amunátegui 31, piso 2. Unwelcoming entrance, good value lunches. Recommended.
¥ **Confitería Torres**, Av Libertador Bernardo O'Higgins 1570. Chile's oldest bar/restaurant dating from 1570, good atmosphere, live tango music at weekends. Cheap lunches are served in a large underground *comedor*.

Cafés
Café Universitario, Alameda 395 y Subercaseaux (near Santa Lucía), Lastarria. Good, cheap *almuerzos*, lively at night, separate room for rock videos, very pleasant.

South of the Alameda *p176, map p176*
Those on a very tight budget should make straight for C San Diego to the following:
¥¥-¥ **Los Braseros de Lucifer**, No 397. Excellent *parrilladas*, also seafood, popular, recommended. A little more expensive than the ones listed below.

¶ Las Tejas, No 234. Lively, rowdy crowd, very cheap cocktails and drinks such as *pisco sour* and *pipeño*, excellent *cazuelas*.
¶ Masticón, No 152. Good service, excellent value, popular, wide range.
¶ Tercera Compañía de Bomberos, Vicuña Mackenna 097, near the junction with Diagonal Paraguay. Good food, very cheap, recommended.

Barrio Brasil *p178*
¶¶¶-¶¶ Las Vacas Gordas, Cienfuegos 280, T02-697 1066. Excellent *parrillada*. Very popular, so book in advance.
¶¶ Los Buenos Muchachos, Cumming 1031, T02-698 0112, www.losbuenosmuchachos.cl. Cavernous hall seating over 400 and serving traditional Chilean food in abundant portions. Very popular, especially at night when shows of traditional Chilean dances are held.
¶¶ Los Chinos Ricos, Brasil 373, T02-6963778, www.chinosricos.cl, on the plaza. Famed Chinese. The restaurant used to be called Los Chinos Pobres, but was so popular it had to change its name. Fills up with noisy families on Sun lunchtimes.
¶¶ Ostras Azócar, Bulnes 37. Specializes in oysters. Several reasonable seafood restaurants on the same street.

Bellavista *p179, map p176*
Most restaurants in Bellavista close on Sun and public holidays, but this is one of the liveliest places to come out and eat at night, with many excellent and costly restaurants. There are dozens more restaurants than those listed below, with a new place seeming to open every few weeks.
¶¶¶ Azul Profundo, Constitución 111. Fish and seafood with a touch of invention. Good range of cocktails.
¶¶¶ El Otro Sitio, Antonia López de Bello 053. Upmarket Peruvian. Good service, excellent range of starters. If you are feeling brave try the *Rocoto relleno*. Recommended.
¶¶¶ El Viejo Verde, Antonia López de Bello 94. Excellent vegetarian food.
¶¶¶ Il Siciliano, Dardignac y Constitución. Elegant trattoria serving excellent pasta and seafood. Extensive wine list.
¶¶¶ La Divina Comida, Purísima 093. Italian with 3 rooms: Heaven, Hell and Purgatory. Recommended.
¶¶¶ Off the Record, Antonia López de Bello 0155, T02-777 7710, www.offtherecord.cl. Bar-restaurant. Period design, nice atmosphere with live music on Fri-Sat nights, cheaper set lunch.
¶¶ Ají Verde, Constitución 284, T02- 735 3329. Specializes in Chilean food, open for lunch.
¶¶ El Tablao, Constitución 110, T02-737 8648. Traditional Spanish restaurant. The food is reasonable, but the main attraction is the live flamenco show on Fri-Sat nights.
¶¶ Michelle's, C del Arzobispo 0615, T02-777 9919. Mediterranean bistro, excellent seafood and fish dishes. Recommended.
¶¶ Venezia, Pío Nono y Antonia López de Bello, Bellavista. Traditional Chilean home-cooked fare. Large servings, good value. One of Neruda's favourite haunts.
¶ Café de la Dulcería Las Palmas, Antonia López de Bello 190. Good pastries and lunches.
¶ Cafetería La Nona, Pío Nono 099. Real coffee, good *empanadas* and cakes, fresh fruit juices. Recommended.
¶ Empanatodos, Pío Nono 153. Serves 25 different types of *empanada*.

Providencia *p180*
¶¶¶ El Giratorio, 11 de Septiembre 2250, 16th fl, T02-232 1827. Good French food eaten while the whole city rotates outside your window. Recommended for the view.
¶¶¶ El Huerto, Orrego Luco 054, T02-233 2690. Open daily, live music Fri and Sat evenings, varied menu, very good, popular. Recommended.
¶¶¶ Salvaje, Av Providencia 1177. Excellent international menu, open-air seating, good-value lunches. Recommended.
¶¶¶-¶¶ A Pinch of Pancho, Gral del Canto 45, T02-235 1700. Seafood and fish specialities, very good.
¶¶¶-¶¶ Oriental, M Montt 584, T02-352 389. One of the best Chinese restaurants in Santiago. Excellent service.
¶¶ Café El Patio, Providencia 1652, next to Phone Box Pub. Tofu and pasta as well as

For an explanation of sleeping and eating price codes, and other relevant information, see Essentials pages 25-26.

fish dishes, nice sandwiches, popular. Good drinks. Internet. Very pleasant.

ΨΨ **Gatsby**, Providencia 1984, T02-2330732. Nationwide chain serving American food, all-you-can-eat buffet and lunch/dinner, also coffees and snacks, open till 2400, tables outside in warm weather, good.

ΨΨ **La Pez Era**, Providencia 1421. Seafood, smart but reasonably priced.

Ψ **Kimomo**, Av Providencia 1480. Vegetarian. Tofu, miso soup, good snacks.

Cafés

Cafetto, Pedro de Valdivia 030, next to **Hotel Orly**. Upmarket café with tasty sandwiches.

There are several good places for snacks and ice cream on Av Providencia including: **Copelia**, No 2211; **Bravissimo**, No 1406; **El Toldo Azul**, No 1936. Also, **Salón de Té Tavelli**, Drugstore precinct, No 2124.

Las Condes *p180*

This area has many first-class restaurants, including grills, serving Chilean (often with music), French and Chinese cuisine. They tend to be more expensive than central restaurants. Lots of expensive eateries are located on El Bosque Norte, near the Tobalaba metro stop.

ΨΨΨ **Cuerovaca**, El Mañío 1659, Vitacura, T02-2468936. The place to head for a fantastic steak, both Argentine and Chilean cuts. Recommended.

ΨΨΨ **El Madroñal**, Vitacura 2911, T02-2336312. Excellent, Spanish cuisine, one of the best restaurants in town, booking essential.

ΨΨΨ **El Mesón del Calvo**, El Bosque Norte y Roger de Flor. Seafood specials.

ΨΨΨ **Isla Negra**, next door to **Coco Loco**, El Bosque Norte. Seafood a speciality.

ΨΨΨ **Pinpilinpausha**, Isidora Goyenechea 2900, T02-2325800. Basque specialities, good.

ΨΨΨ **Sakura**, Vitacura 4111. Renowned sushi restaurant. Recommended.

ΨΨΨ-ΨΨ **Diego Pizza**, El Bosque Norte y Don Carlos. Friendly, good cocktails, popular. Recommended.

ΨΨΨ-ΨΨ **Puerto Marisko**, Isidora Goyenechea 2918, T02-2332096. Good seafood.

ΨΨ **Le Fournil**, Vitacura 3841, opposite Cuerovaca, T02-2280219. Excellent French bakery and restaurant. Particularly popular at lunchtime. Good soups.

Bars and clubs

As in most of South America, a night out in Santiago begins late. Arrive in a restaurant before 2100 and you may be eating alone, while bars and clubs are often empty before 2400. There is a good selection of bars, discos and *salsotecas* from the reasonably priced in **Bellavista** (Baquedano metro) to the smarter along Av Suecia and G Holley in **Providencia** (Los Leones metro). El Bosque Norte in **Las Condes** (Tobalaba metro) is lined with chic bars and expensive restaurants for the Chilean jetset, while **Barrio Brasil (República metro)** is popular with Chilean students. Most clubs and bars playing live music charge around US$2 (for student- orientated places), usually with a drink included, although some clubs in Las Condes and Providencia may charge US$20 or more.

Bellavista *p179, map p176*

Club 4-40, Santa Filomena 081. Named after popular singer Juan Luis Guerra's backing group from the Dominican Republic, live Cuban music, packed at weekends.

Disco Salsa, Pío Nono 223. Good atmosphere, salsa dance classes downstairs.

HBH Bar, Purísima y Antonia López de Bello. Good beer, good atmosphere.

La Bodega de Julio, Constitución 256. Cuban staff and Cuban cocktails, excellent live music and dancing, very popular, free entry before 2300, good value. Highly recommended.

La Casa en el Aire, Antonia López de Bello 125. Pleasant atmosphere, live music. Recommended.

La Otra Puerta, Pío Nono 348. Lively *salsoteca* with live music. Recommended.

Libro Café Mediterráneo. Popular with students, lively, expensive. US$4.50 charge on Mon nights, when a local man does good Georges Brassens impressions.

Providencia *p180*

Brannigan's Pub, Suecia 35, T02-232 7869. Good beer, live jazz, lively.

Golden Bell Inn, Hernando de Aguirre 27. Popular with expats.

Ilé Habana, Bucaré just off Suecia. Bar with salsa music, often live, and a good dance floor.

Louisiana River Pub, Suecia y General Holley. Live music.

Phone Box Pub, Providencia 1670, T02-2350303. Very popular with expats, serves numerous European beers including Pilsener Urquell, and canned British beers including Newcastle Brown Ale, Beamish Stout and Old Speckled Hen. A good place to go if you are missing home.

Las Condes *p180*

Country Village, Av Las Condes 10680. Mon-Sat from 2000, Sun from lunch onwards, live music Fri and Sat.
Flannery's Irish Geo Pub, Encomenderos 83, T02-2336675, www.flannerys.cl. Irish pub, serving Guinness on draft, good lunches including vegetarian options, popular among gringos and Chileans alike.
Las Urracas, Vitacura 9254. US$20 but free before 2300 if you eat there. Huge variety of cocktails.
Morena Pizza and Dance Bar, Av Las Condes 10120. Good sound system, live music at weekends, happy hour before 2200.
Tequila, Av Las Condes at Paseo San Damián. One of a few popular bar-restaurants nearby.

Entertainment

For all entertainment, clubs, cinemas, restaurants, concerts, *El Mercurio Online* website has listings and a good search feature. Look under the *tiempo libre* section: www.emol.com. There are also listings in weekend newspapers, including *Santiago What's On* (in English).

Cinemas

A good guide to daily cinema listings can be found in the 2 free newspapers, *La Hora* and *tmg*, handed out at metro stations early on weekday mornings. Tickets cost US$4-7 with reductions on Mon, Tue and Wed.

There are many mainstream cinemas showing international films, usually in original English with Spanish subtitles. 'CineArte' (art-house cinemas that show quality foreign films) are also very popular and include the following:
Casa de Extensión Universidad Católica, Av B O'Higgins 390, T02-6351994. Universidad Católica metro, south exit, line 1.
Centro Arte Alameda, Av Bernado O'Higgins 139, Baquedano metro, line 1, T02-6648821, www.centroartealameda.cl.
Cine Arte Normandie, Tarapacá 1181, T02-6972979. Varied programme, altered frequently, films at 1530, 1830 and 2130 daily, students half price. Moneda metro, south exit.
El Biógrafo, Lastarria 181, T02-6334435. Universidad Católica metro, north exit.
Tobalaba, Av Providencia 2563, T02-2316630. Tobalaba metro.

Performing arts

Teatro Municipal, Agustinas y San Antonio, www.municipal.cl. Stages international opera, concerts by the Orquesta Filarmónica de Santiago and performances by the Ballet de Santiago, throughout the year. On Tue at 2100 there are free operatic concerts in the Salón Claudio Arrau. Tickets range from US$10 for a very large choral group with a symphony orchestra, and US$12 for the cheapest seats at the ballet, to US$100 for the most expensive opera seats. Some cheap seats are often sold on the day of concerts.
Teatro Municipal de Ñuñoa, Av Irarrázaval 1564, www.ccn.cl, T02-2777903. Dance, art exhibitions, cinema, children's theatre.
Teatro Universidad de Chile, Plaza Baquedano, www.teatro.uchile.cl, T02-978 2203. Home of the Orquesta y Coro Sinfónica de Chile and the Ballet Nacional de Chile.

A great number of more minor theatres around the city stage plays, including **Abril**, Huérfanos 786; **Camilo Henríquez**, Amunátegui 31; **Centro Arrayán**, Las Condes 14891; **El Galpón de los Leones**, Av Los Leones 238; **El Conventillo**, Bellavista 173 and **La Comedia**, Merced 349. Events are listed in *El Mercurio* and *La Tercera*.

Festivals and events

Mar/Apr Religious festivals and ceremonies continue throughout **Holy Week**, when a priest ritually washes the feet of 12 men.
End of May A food festival called **Expo gourmand**. Its location changes every year.
16 Jul The image of the **Virgen del Carmen** (patron saint of the armed forces) is carried through the streets by cadets.
18 Sep Chile's **Independence Day** when many families get together or celebrate in *fondas* (small temporary constructions made of wood and straw where people eat traditional dishes, drink *chicha* and dance *cueca*).

19 Sep Armed Forces Day is celebrated with an enormous military procession through the Parque O'Higgins. It takes 4 hrs.
Nov A free **art fair** lasting a fortnight is held in the Parque Forestal on the banks of the Río Mapocho.

Shopping

The shops in the centre and to the north of the Plaza de Armas are cheaper and more downmarket than the countless arcades and boutiques strung along Providencia, especially near Av Ricardo Lyon. Specialist shops tend to be grouped together, eg bikes and second-hand books on San Diego, new bookshops on Providencia, opticians on Mac Iver, lapis lazuli in Bellavista. Many stalls on Paseo Ahumada/ Huérfanos sell overseas newspapers.

Bookshops

Book prices are very high compared with Europe, even for second-hand books. There are many bookshops in the Pedro de Valdivia area on Av Providencia. Much better value but with a smaller selection are the bookshops in the shopping mall at Av Providencia 1114-1120. For cheap English-language books try the second-hand book kiosks on San Diego, 4 blocks south of Plaza Bulnes, next to Iglesia de los Sacramentinos.
Books, Providencia 1652, Local 5, in a court-yard beside the **Phone Box Pub** and **Café El Patio**. Wide selection of English-language books for sale or exchange, English spoken. On the expensive side.
Feria Chilena del Libro, Huérfanos 623. Largest bookstore in Santiago, good for travel books and maps; also at Nueva York 3, Agustinas 859, Mall Parque Arauco and Providencia 2124.
Librería Inglesa, Huérfanos 669, local 11, Pedro de Valdivia 47, Vitacura 5950, Providencia 2653, T02-2319970, www.libreriainglesa.cl. Sells only books in English, good selection.
LOM Ediciones, Estación Mapocho, Mon-Fri 1000-2000, Sat 1000-1400. Sells a stock of literature, history, sociology, art and politics from its own publishing house. Also a bar and a reading room with recent Chilean newspapers and magazines.
South American Way, Av Apoquindo 6856, Las Condes, T02-2118078. Books in English.

Camping and outdoors equipment

Club Andino and **Federación de Andinismo** (see page 188) sell expensive products as the stocked articles are imported.
Fabri Gas, Bandera y Santo Domingo. Camping gas cartridges.
Industria Yarur, Rosas 1289 y Teatinos, T02-6723696. Good value for money, discounts available.
Luz Emperatriz Sanhuela Quiroz, Portal de León, Loc 14, Providencia 2198. Los Leones metro. Second-hand equipment.
Outdoors & Travel, Encomenderos 206, Las Condes, T02-3357104. For wide range of imported and locally made camping goods.
Patagonia, Helvecia 210, Providencia, T02-3351796. Good range of clothing and equipment, comparatively expensive.

Handicrafts

The gemstone, lapis lazuli, can be found in a few expensive shops in Bellavista but is cheaper in the arcades on the south side of the Plaza de Armas. Antique stores can be found in Plaza Mulato Gil de Castro and elsewhere on Lastarria (Merced end). Other craft stalls can be found: in an alleyway, 1 block south of Av O'Higgins between A Prat and San Diego; on the 600-800 blocks of Santo Domingo; and at Pío Nono y Av Santa Maria in Bellavista.
Amitié, Av Ricardo Lyon y Av Providencia. Los Leones metro. Recommended.
Dauvin Artesanía Fina, Providencia 2169, local 69. Los Leones metro. Recommended.
El Almacén Campesino, Purísima 303, Bellavista. Cooperative association in a colonial building. Sells handicrafts from all over Chile, including Mapuche weavings, woodcarvings, pottery and beautiful wrought copper and bronze. Prices similar to those in Temuco. Ask about shipping.
Plaza Artesanos de Manquehue, Av Manquehue Sur, block 300-600, just off Apoquindo in Las Condes. The biggest craft market in Chile. A good range of modern crafts from ceramics to textiles, and places where the artisans can be seen working on wood, silver, glass and so on. Although more expensive than, for instance, the market in Santa Lucía. This is a good and attractive place to come; take any bus east from Providencia or Escuela Militar which goes via Apoquindo.

Maps

Automóvil Club de Chile, Av Andrés Bello 1863, Pedro de Valdivia metro, T02-431 1000, www.automovilclub.cl). Mon-Thu 0900-1815, Fri 0900-1700. Route maps of Chile, US$6 each, free to members of affiliated motoring organizations; very helpful.
CONAF, see page 16. Maps of national parks.
Instituto Geográfico Militar, Dieciocho 369, near Toesca metro, T02-4109463. Detailed geophysical and topographical maps of the whole of Chile, very useful for climbing. Expensive (about US$15 each), but **Biblioteca Nacional**, Av Libertador Bernardo O'Higgins 651, T02-360 5200, stocks them and will allow you to photocopy parts of each map.
Librería Australis, Av Providencia 1670, local 5. All sorts of local, regional and trekking maps.

Markets

For craft markets, see Handicrafts, above.
Bío Bío flea market, C Bío Bío. Every Sat and Sun morning. This is the largest and cheapest flea market in the city and sells everything from spare parts for cars and motorbikes to second-hand furniture. Those trying to do up a new flat on the cheap, a car on the hoof, or who are simply interested in sharing a street with tens of thousands of others, should find their way here; just go to Franklin metro, line 2 and follow the crowds. Beware of rip-offs.
Mercado Central, Puente y 21 de Mayo by the Río Mapocho. Cal y Canto metro. Brilliant for seafood, with many places to eat cheaply, **Donde Augusto** is recommended. Otherwise an excellent range of goods, but quite expensive.
Vega Central, on the opposite bank of the river, is cheaper than Mercado Central.

Wine

There's a good selection of wines at **Jumbo**, **Líder** and **Santa Isabel** supermarkets.
El Mundo del Vino, Isidora Goyenechea 2929. Also in the Alto Las Condes and Plaza Vespucio malls.
Vinopolis, Pedro de Valdivia 036, Pedro de Valdivia metro, line 1. Mon-Fri 0900-2300, Sat 1000-2300, Sun 1000-2200. Exclusively Chilean wines. Good selection.
The Wine House, Portada de Vitacura 2904.

Activities and tours

Boat operators

Cruceros Australis, El Bosque Norte 0440, T02-442 3110, www.australis.com. Punta Arenas to Puerto Williams, Cape Horn and Ushuaia.
M/N Skorpios, Augusto Leguía Norte 118, Las Condes, T02-231 1030, www.skorpios.cl, for Puerto Montt-Laguna San Rafael.
Naviera Austral, Agustinas 715, of 403, T02-633 5959, www.navieraustral.cl. For Chiloé and the Carretera Austral.
Navimag, Av El Bosque Norte 0440, 11th fl, Las Condes, T02-442 3120, www.navimag.com. For Puerto Montt-Puerto Natales.
Patagonia Connection SA, Fidel Oteíza 1921, oficina 1006, Providencia, T02-225 6489, www.patagonia-connection.com. For Puerto Montt–Coyhaique/Puerto Chacabuco–Laguna San Rafael.

Climbing

Federación de Andinismo de Chile, Almte Simpson 77A, T02-222 0888, www.feach.cl. It has the addresses of all the mountaineering clubs in chile. Runs a mountaineering school.
La Cumbre Ltda, Av Apoquindo 5258, T02-220 9907, www.lacumbreonline.cl. Mon-Fri 1100-2000, Sat 1100-1600. Dutch proprietors very helpful, good climbing and trekking equipment.
Mountain Service, Santa Magdalena 75, T02-234 3439, Providencia, www.mountain service.cl. English spoken, tents, stoves, clothing, equipment rental. Recommended.

Football

If you decide to visit the **Estadio Nacional**, where international matches are played, find a space high up on the terraces and you will be able to watch the sun set over the mountains behind Santiago. See box, page 189.
Colo Colo, play at the Estadio Monumental, reached by any bus to Puente Alto or Pedrero metro, line 5; tickets from Av Marathon 5300, Macul, T02-294 7300.
Universidad Católica, play at San Carlos de Apoquindo, reached by bus from Escuela Militar metro; tickets from Andrés Bello 2782, Providencia, T02-231 2777.
Universidad de Chile, play at Estadio Nacional, Av Grecia 2001 Ñuñoa, Ñuble metro, line 5. Tickets from Av General Miranda 2094, Ñuñoa.

Soccer nation

Football arrived in Chile towards the end of the 19th century, courtesy of the British. The role of British workers – most of whom were employed in the construction of the railway system – is reflected in the names of several of the leading teams, notably Santiago Wanderers (based in Valparaíso), Everton (based in Viña) and Rangers (based in Talca). The game's popularity grew rapidly and by the 1940s most large towns boasted their own team and stadium. In 1962, Chile's importance as a soccer nation was recognized internationally when it hosted the World Cup and the national side finished third.

The season is split into two tournaments, the *apertura* running from March to June and the *clausura* from August to December. Most of the support (and money) goes to the big three clubs, all based in Santiago: **Universidad de Chile** (known as 'La U'), **Colo-Colo** (known as Los Indios, as their strip carries an image of the great Mapuche leader) and **Universidad Católica**.

A visit to a match is an unforgettable experience as the supporters dance, sing and wave their team colours beneath a rain of confetti, fireworks and coloured smoke. Cheap tickets cost around US$5.

Skiing

Farellones, 1½ hours from the city, has good accommodation and facilities but can get very busy at weekends. Expect to pay US$40-50 for a combined ticket for the four resorts in the area. Buses organized by **Ski Travel**, T02-246 6881, www.skitotal.cl, also rents equipment

Portillo, www.skiportillo.cl. Widely regarded as one of the best resorts in Chile. Only one hotel but extra activities are available, such as a visit to the Laguna del Inca. All buses from Santiago to Mendoza pass through Portillo.

Ski clubs **Club Andino de Chile**, Av Libertador Bernardo O'Higgins 108, local 215, T02-274 9252, www.skilagunillas.cl. **Skitotal**, Av Apoquindo 4900, of 40-42, T02-246 0156. Rents equipment, organizes accommodation and lessons. Also provides transport.

Tour operators

Altue Expediciones, Encomenderos 83, piso 2, Las Condes, T02-232 1103, www.altue.com. For wilderness trips including tour of Patagonia and sea-kayaking in Chiloé.

Andina del Sud, Av El Golf 99, Las Condes, T02-388 0101, www.andinadelsud.com. Climbing and trekking in the Lake District.

Azimut 360, General Salvo 159, Providencia, T02-235 1519, www.azimut.cl. Salvador metro. Reasonable prices. Adventure and eco-tourism throughout Chile, including tours to the Atacama Desert. Aconcagua base camp services and mountaineering expeditions to Parinacota and Sajama. Highly recommended.

Cascada Expediciones, Camino al Volcán 17710, T02-861 1777, www.cascada-expediciones.cl. Activity tours in remote areas.

Mountain Service, Paseo Las Palmas 2209, T02-233 0913, info@mountainservice.cl, Los Leones metro. Recommended climbing trips.

Patagonia Connection SA, Fidel Oteíza 1921, of 1006, Providencia, T02-225 6489, www.patagonia-connection.com, Pedro de Valdivia metro. For cruises to Patagonia.

Rapa-Nui, Huérfanos 1160, oficina 912, piso 9, T02-672 1050. www.rapanuiturismo.cl. Specializes in trips to Easter Island.

Southern Cross Adventure, Victor Rae 5994, Las Condes. T02-639 6591, www.scadventure.com. Offers biking, mountaineering, horse riding, trekking, high-altitude archaeology, visits to volcanoes, fishing in the Andes. Multi-lingual guides, camping gear provided.

Sportstours, Moneda 970, piso 18 T02-549 5200, www.sportstour.cl. Helpful, 5-day trips to Antarctica. Another branch at **San Cristóbal Tower**, Av Santa María 1742.

Turismo Cabo de Hornos, www.turismocabodehornos.cl. Agustinas 814, oficina 706, T02-664 3458. For **DAP** flights and Tierra del Fuego/Antarctica tours.

Transport

Air

For details of the Aeropuerto Arturo Merino Benitez, see page 172. For flights see Essentials, pages 17-20.

Airline offices Aerolíneas Argentinas, oficina Generales Roger de Flor 2921 y 2907, Las Condes, T02-210 9000; **Aeroméxico**, Isidora Goyenechea 2939, oficina 602, Las Condes, T02-390 1000; **Air France**, Av Américo Vespucio Sur 100, oficina 202, Las Condes, T02-290 9330; **Alitalia**, El Bosque Norte 107, oficina 21, T02-3788230; **American**, Huérfanos 1199, T02-6790000; **British Airways**, Ebro 2743, 1st fl, oficina 1 T02-232 9563 or Don Carlos 2939, Las Condes, airport T02-690 1845; **Continental** (Chilean agents are Copa Airlines) Fidel Oteíza 1921, oficina 703, T02-200 2100; **Delta**, Isidora Goyenechea 2939, oficina 601, Las Condes, T02-280 1600; **Iberia**, Bandera 206, 8th fl, T02-870 1000, reservations T02-870 1070; **KLM**, San Sebastián 2839, oficina 202, Las Condes, T02-233 0011 (sales), T02-233 0991 (reservations); **LACSA**, Dr Barros Borgoño 105, 2nd fl, Providencia, T02-235 5189 ; **LanChile**, Huérfanos 926, also at Av Providencia 2006, Providencia, and Isidora Goyenechea 2888, T02-600-526 2000; **Lufthansa**, Av El Bosque Norte 500, 16th fl, Las Condes, T02-630 1655, airport 6901112; **South African Airways** (Chilean agents, Space, Adriana Frugone), 11 de Septiembre 1881, oficina 713, Providencia, T02-376 9042; **Sky Airline**, Andrés de Fuenzalida 55, Providencia, T02-600-6002828; **United**, Av Andrés Bello 2687, 16th fl, Las Condes, T02-337 0000.

Bus

Local

Micros display their route in the windows. Routes are all numbered and buses will only halt at stops on main roads. Destinations are clearly marked at the stops. When you get on the bus, you should put exact change into the machine to get a ticket, but as the machines

are unpredictable, you may have to pay the driver instead. Single fare US$0.75, but price rises are frequent. Green and white trunk buses serve the main routes of the capital while local feeder buses serve different neighbourhoods depending on their colour.

Long distance There are frequent, good inter-urban buses to all parts of Chile (see Essentials page 21). Fares from/to the capital are given in the text. Bear in mind that on Fri in summer, when the night buses depart, the terminals are nightmarishly chaotic and busy.

Terminal Alameda, O'Higgins 3712, T02-2707 1500, has the best left luggage facilities in the city, and 2 of the best companies, **Tur Bus**, www.turbus.com, and **Pullman Bus**, www.pullman.cl, leave from here.

Terminal Santiago, O'Higgins 3878, T02-376 1755, 1 block west of Terminal Alameda. Sometimes referred to as 'Terminal Sur', this terminal is used by services to and from the south, as well as buses to **Valparaíso** and **Viña del Mar**. It is the only terminal with services to **Punta Arenas** (48 hrs), and is also the centre for most international services.

Terminal Los Héroes, Tucapel Jiménez, just north of the Alameda, T02-420 0099. Los Héroes metro. A smaller terminal for 8 companies to some useful destinations.

International Almost all international buses leave from the Terminal Santiago. There are frequent services via **Mendoza** to **Buenos Aires** and **Bahía Blanca**, but if you're going to destinations such as **Bariloche** or **Neuquén** in Argentine Patagonia, it is better to travel south to Temuco or Osorno and connect there. There are also services to destinations throughout the rest of South America; consult bus companies at the terminal.

Car

Driving in the city is restricted according to licence plate numbers; each day, certain plates are prohibited from circulating (numbers are given in the press).

Hertz, Avis, Budget and others are available from the airport; **Alameda**, Av Bernado O'Higgins 4332, T02-779 0609, www.alamedarentacar.cl, San Alberto Hurtado metro (ex Pila del Ganso), line 1, also in the airport, very good value; **ANSA**, Av Eleodoro Yáñez 1198, Providencia , T02-251 0256; **Automóvil Club de Chile**, Av Vitacura 9511, Providencia, T02-431 1106, 25% discount for members of associated motoring organizations; **Avis**, San Pablo 9900, T02-331 0121, poor service reported; **Hertz**, Costanera Andrés Bello 1469, T02- 6010477, and at Hotel Hyatt T02-245 5936, has a good network in Chile and cars are in good condition; **Rosselot**, Francisco Bilbao 2032, Providencia, T02-3813690, www.rosselot.cl, and airport, T02-690 1374, reputable Chilean firm with national coverage; **Seelmann**, www.seelmann.cl, Monseñor Edwards 1279, La Reina , T02-277 9259; **Trekker Ltd**, www.trekkerchile.com, has camper vans, trucks and 4WD vehicles available; **Verschae**, Manquehue Sur 660, T02-202 7266, www.verschae.cl, good value, branches throughout the country.

Colectivo/taxi

Collective taxis operate on fixed routes between the centre and the suburbs. They display destinations and route numbers. Fares vary, depending on the length of the journey, but are usually US$1-2. Higher fares at night.

Regular taxis (black with yellow roofs) are abundant, minimum charge US$0.40, plus US$0.15 per 200 m, more at night. Avoid taxis with more than 1 person in them, especially at night. For journeys outside the city arrange the charge beforehand. **Radio Taxis Andes Pacífico**, T02-2253064/2888, www.andespacifico.cl.

Metro

The metro, www.metrosantiago.cl, is fast, quiet and very full. First train 0630 Mon-Sat, 0800 Sun and holidays; last train 2245. Fares US$0.80, 0715-0900 and 1800-1930, US$0.60 at all other times. Buy a *tarjeta Bip*, US$3 from any metro station, from which the appropriate fare is deducted from each journey. The card can also be used on buses and if you use a bus-metro combination to make a single journey you will be charged a reduced rate. **Metrobus** (blue buses, US$0.70) connects Lo Ovalle, San Pablo, Las Rejas, Salvador, Cal y Canto, Escuela Militar, Pedrero and Bellavista de la Florida with outlying areas.

Train

For the **Temuco** service, see page 213. Booking office at Estación Central, T02-689 5718/689 1682, www.efe.cl.till 2230.

Directory

Banks and currency exchange

Redbanc ATMs (for Cirrus) are everywhere. Official exchange rates are published in *El Mercurio*, *La Nación*, and on www.xe.com. The best rates are offered by *casas de cambio* around Paso Ahumada and Huérfanos (Metro Universidad de Chile or Plaza de Armas). Most charge 3% commission to change TCs into dollars. Avoid street money changers (common on Ahumada and Agustinas).

American Express, Av Isidora Goyenchea 3621, 10th fl, Las Condes, T02-350 6700, no commission but poor rates; **Turismo Tajamar**, Orrego Luco 023, T02-366 8165, Thomas Cook/MasterCard agent.

Embassies and consulates

Argentina, Miraflores 285, T02-582 2500. Also Argentine consulate, Vicuña MacKenna 41, T02-582 2608, open 0900-1400 (visa US$25, free for US citizens), if you need a visa for Argentina, get it here or in the consulates in Puerto Montt or Punta Arenas; Australians will need a letter from their embassy to get a visa here. **Australia**, Isidora Goyenechea 3261, Torre B, Las Condes, T02-550 3500; **Canada**, Nueva Tajamar 481, Torre Norte, 12th fl, T02-362 9660; **New Zealand**, El Golf 99, of 703, Las Condes, T02-290 9802; **South Africa**, Av 11 de Septiembre 2353, Torre San Román, 17th fl, T02-231 2862; **UK**, El Bosque Norte 0125, Casilla 72-D, 6th fl, T02-370 4100, will hold letters; **USA**, Av Andrés Bello 2800, T02-232 2600, www.embajadaeeuu.cl, consulate at Merced 230, T02-710 133, for visas.

Medical services

If you need to get to a hospital, take a taxi rather than waiting for an ambulance. **Clínica Central**, San Isidro 231, T02-4631400, open 24 hrs; **Emergency hospital**, Marcoleta 377, US$60, for vaccinations (not cholera); **Hospital de Urgencia**, Portugal 125, from US$125, cheapest public hospital; **Vaccinatoria Internacional**, Hospital Luis Calvo, MacKenna, Antonio Varas 360. **Emergency pharmacy**, Portugal 155, T02-382 439.

Internet

Internet cafés are ubiquitous. Prices vary from US$0.60-1 per hr.

Language schools

Escuela de Idiomas Violeta Parra, Ernesto Pinto Lagarrigue 362A, Recoleta-Barrio Bellavista, T02-735 8240, www.tandemsantiago.cl; **Instituto Chilena de la Lengua**, Ernesto Requelme 226, 2nd fl, T02-697 2728, www.ichil.cl; **Instituto Chileno Suizo de Cultura**, José Victorino Lastarria 93, T02-638 5414, www.chilenosuizo.cl; **Natalislang Language Centre**, Vicuña Mackenna 06, piso 7, of 4, T02- 222 8721, info@natalislang.com; **Pacifica**, Guillermo Acuña 2884, Providencia, T02-205 5129, pacifica@netline.cl; **Top Language Services**, Huérfanos 886, of 1107, T/F02-639 0321.

Post office

The main post office is at Plaza de Armas (0800-1900), poste restante (30 days max) is well organized with a list of post received on display (one list for men, another for women, indicate Sr or Sra/Srita on envelope), passport essential for collection. Sub offices in Providencia, Av 11 de Septiembre 2092, Manuel Montt 1517, Pedro de Valdivia 1781, Providencia 1466, and in **Estación Central** shopping mall, Mon-Fri 0900-1800, Sat 0900-1230. Paper, tape etc on sale, Mon-Fri 0800-1900, Sat 0800-1400.

Telephone

The cheapest call centres are on Bandera, Catedral and Santo Domingo, all near Plaza de Armas. International calls from here are half the price of the main company offices: to the US and Europe, US$0.20 per min, eg at Catedral 1033 and Santo Domingo 1091. The main company offices are **Telefónica CTC**, Moneda 1151, closed Sun, and **ENTEL**, Huérfanos 1133, Mon-Fri 0830-2200, Sat 0900-2030, Sun 0900-1400, calls cheaper 1400-2200.

Useful addresses

Asatej Student Flight Centre, Hernando de Aguirre 201, of 401, T02-335 0395, chile@asatej.com.ar. Cheap flights, tours, car rental, ISIC cards, insurance, hotels. **Ministerio del Interior**, Departamento de Extranjería, Teatinos 950 (near Estación Mapocho), T02-674 4000, www.extranjeria.gob.cl, Mon-Fri 0900-1200. For extension of tourist visa or any enquiries regarding legal status.

Chilean Lake District

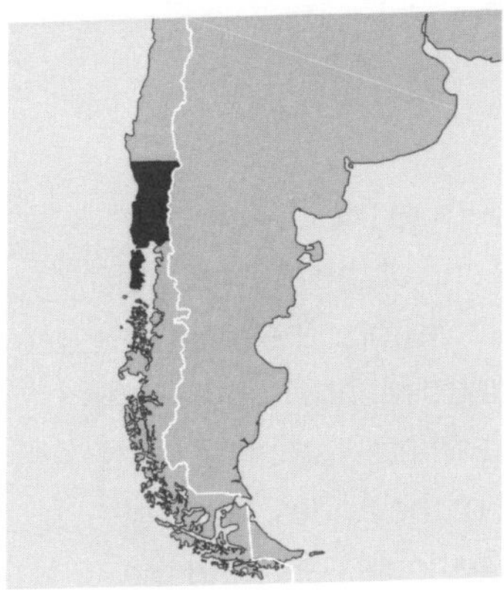

Footprint features

Introduction

Extending from the Río Biobío south to the city of Puerto Montt, the Lake District is one of the most popular destinations for both Chileans and visitors. The main cities are Temuco, Valdivia, Osorno and Puerto Montt, but the most attractive scenery lies further east where a string of lakes stretches down the western side of the Andes. Much of this region has been turned into national parks and the combination of forests, lakes and snow-capped volcanoes is unforgettable.

In the north, the major resort is Pucón on Lago Villarrica, while, in the south, Volcán Osorno keeps watch over Lago Llanquihue and the Argentine border. Puerto Varas or the nearby city of Puerto Montt can both be used as a base for sea voyages south to Puerto Natales, Puerto Chacabuco and the San Rafael glacier, as well as east across the lakes and mountains to the Argentine resort of Bariloche.

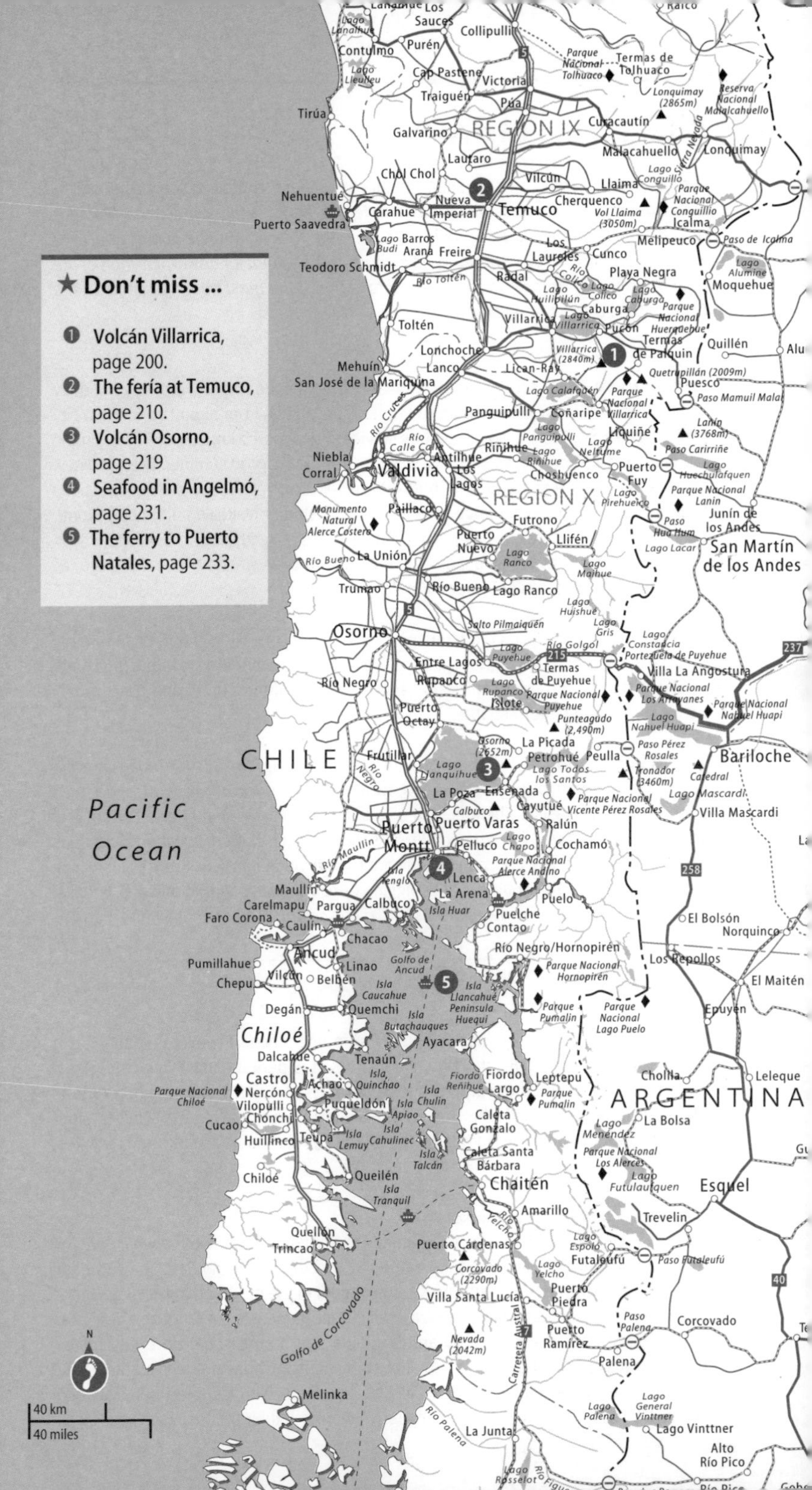
★ Don't miss ...
❶ Volcán Villarrica, page 200.
❷ The fería at Temuco, page 210.
❸ Volcán Osorno, page 219
❹ Seafood in Angelmó, page 231.
❺ The ferry to Puerto Natales, page 233.
Pacific Ocean
CHILE
ARGENTINA
REGION IX
REGION X
Chiloé
Los Sauces
Collipulli
Lago Lanalhue
Contulmo
Purén
Lago Lleulleu
Cap Pastene
Victoria
Traiguén
Púa
Tirúa
Galvarino
Lautaro
Chol Chol
Nehuentué
Carahue
Nueva Imperial
Temuco
Puerto Saavedra
Lago Budi
Barros Arana
Freire
Teodoro Schmidt
Río Toltén
Toltén
Parque Nacional Tolhuaco
Termas de Tolhuaco
Lonquimay (2865m)
Reserva Nacional Malalcahuello
Curacautín
Malacahuello
Sierra Nevada
Lonquimay
Vilcún
Llaima
Cherquenco
Vol Llaima (3050m)
Lago Conguillío
Parque Nacional Conguillío
Icalma
Melipeuco
Paso de Icalma
Los Laureles
Cunco
Lago Alumine
Moquehue
Radal
Río Colico
Playa Negra
Lago Huilipilún
Lago Colico
Lago Caburga
Caburga
Parque Nacional Huerquehue
Villarrica
Lago Villarrica
Pucón
Termas de Palquín
Quillén
Lonchoche
Lanco
Villarrica (2840m)
Licán-Ray
Quetrupillán (2009m)
Puesco
Paso Mamuil Malal
Mehuín
San José de la Mariquina
Lago Calafquén
Parque Nacional Villarrica
Río Cruces
Panguipulli
Coñaripe
Lago Panguipulli
Liquiñe
Lanín (3768m)
Río Calle Calle
Antilhue
Riñihue
Lago Riñihue
Lago Neltume
Paso Carirriñe
Niebla
Corral
Valdivia
Los Lagos
Choshuenco
Puerto Fuy
Lago Huechulafquen
Parque Nacional Lanín
Lago Pirehueico
Monumento Natural Alerce Costero
Paillaco
Futrono
Paso Hua Hum
Junín de los Andes
Puerto Nuevo
Lago Ranco
Llifén
Lago Lacar
San Martín de los Andes
Río Bueno
La Unión
Lago Maihue
Trumao
Río Bueno
Lago Ranco
Lago Huishue
Salto Pilmaiquén
Lago Gris
Osorno
Río Golgol
Lago Constancia
Portezuela de Puyehue
Lago Puyehue
Entre Lagos
Termas de Puyehue
Villa La Angostura
Río Negro
Rupanco
Lago Rupanco
Parque Nacional Puyehue
Parque Nacional Los Arrayanes
Parque Nacional Nahuel Huapi
Islote
Puerto Octay
Punteagudo (2,490m)
Lago Nahuel Huapi
Osorno (2652m)
La Picada
Paso Pérez Rosales
Frutillar
Petrohué
Peulla
Bariloche
Lago Llanquihue
Lago Todos los Santos
Tronador (3460m)
Catedral
Río Negro
La Poza
Ensenada
Parque Nacional Vicente Pérez Rosales
Lago Mascardi
Calbuco
Cayutué
Villa Mascardi
Puerto Varas
Ralún
Puerto Montt
Pelluco
Lago Chapo
Cochamó
Río Maullín
Parque Nacional Alerce Andino
Isla Tenglo
Lenca
La Arena
Maullín
Carelmapu
Pargua
Calbuco
Puelo
Isla Huar
Puelche
Faro Corona
Caulín
Contao
El Bolsón
Norquinco
Chacao
Ancud
Río Negro/Hornopirén
Los Repollos
Pumillahue
Golfo de Ancud
Linao
Parque Nacional Hornopirén
Chepu
Vilcún
Belbén
Isla Llancahue
El Maitén
Isla Caucahue
Peninsula Huequi
Degán
Quemchi
Parque Pumalín
Parque Nacional Lago Puelo
Isla Butachauques
Epuyén
Ayacara
Dalcahue
Tenaún
Isla Quinchao
Fiordo Reñihue
Fiordo Largo
Leptepu
Cholila
Leleque
Parque Nacional Chiloé
Castro
Nercón
Achao
Isla Chulín
Parque Pumalín
Vilopulli
Puqueldón
Isla Apiao
Caleta Gonzalo
Lago Menéndez
La Bolsa
Cucao
Chonchi
Isla Cahuilinec
Huillinco
Teupa
Isla Lemuy
Isla Talcán
Caleta Santa Bárbara
Parque Nacional Los Alerces
Chiloé
Queilén
Lago Futulaufquen
Isla Tranquil
Chaitén
Esquel
Amarillo
Río Yelcho
Trevelin
Quellón
Trincao
Puerto Cárdenas
Lago Espolo
Futaleufú
Paso Futaleufú
Corcovado (2290m)
Lago Yelcho
Villa Santa Lucía
Puerto Piedra
Golfo de Corcovado
Carretera Austral
Paso Palena
Corcovado
Nevada (2042m)
Puerto Ramírez
Palena
Melinka
Lago Palena
Lago General Vinttner
Lago Vinttner
Río Palena
La Junta
Alto Río Pico
Lago Rosselot
N
40 km
40 miles

Northern lakes

Patagonia really starts with the southern lakes but there's plenty to see further north, including Volcán Villarrica, which has erupted 10 times in the last century. Popular resorts around Lago Villarrica provide access to the volcano and the opportunity for a wealth of outdoor activities. Temuco is a good starting point for any exploration of the region, providing an accessible gateway to some of the most beautiful spots in the Chilean Lake District. » *For Sleeping, Eating and other listings, see pages 204-214.*

Ins and outs

Getting there 6 km southwest of Temuco is **Manquehue Airport**, with several daily flights north to Santiago and south to Puerto Montt. Taxis from airport to Temuco city centre cost US$6; there is no airport bus service. The airport 2 km east of Pucón on the Caburga road also has several flights a week to/from Santiago in summer. There is a new long-distance bus terminal on the outskirts of Temuco, with many daily connections to/from Santiago and other large Chilean towns, including Valdivia and Puerto Montt, plus Neuquén and Bariloche in Argentina. There is also a nightly train to Santiago. Pucón is served by one or two daily buses from Puerto Montt, several daily from Santiago, as well as regular services from Temuco and Villarrica. » *For further details, see Transport page 212.*

Getting around Temuco is the transport hub for the Lake District and its municipal bus station serves much of the region, as well as the communities towards the coast. Pucón is the main tourist centre on Lago Villarrica, offering tours and transport to nearby lakes and national parks.

Tourist information In Temuco, **Sernatur** ⓘ *Bulnes 586, T045-211969, infoaraucania @sernatur.cl, summer daily 0830-2030, winter Mon-Fri 0900-1200, 1500- 1700,* has good leaflets in English. There is also a tourist kiosk in the market and an office of **CONAF** ⓘ *Bilbao 931, T045-234420.* Pucón's **tourist office** ⓘ *Municipalidad, O'Higgins 483, T045-293002, www.pucon.com,* provides information and sells licences for fishing on the lake. The **CONAF** office is at O'Higgins 669. Villarrica's **tourist office** ⓘ *Valdivia 1070, T045-411162, daily in summer, Mon-Fri off season,* has information and maps.

Temuco » *pp204-214.*

At first sight, Temuco may appear a grey, forbidding place. However in reality it is a lively industrial and university town. For visitors, it is perhaps most interesting as a contrast to the more European cities in other parts of Chile. Temuco is proud of its Mapuche heritage, and it is this that gives it a distinctive character, especially around the *feria* (outdoor market). North and east of the city are national parks and reserves, and several hot springs.

Sights → *See map page 205. Colour map 1, A2.*

The city is centred on the newly redesigned **Plaza Aníbal Pinto**, around which are the main public buildings including the cathedral and the municipalidad. The cathedral was destroyed by the 1960 earthquake, when most of the old wooden buildings in the city were also burnt down. On the plaza itself is a monument to 'La Araucanía' featuring figures from local history. Nearby are fountains and a small *Sala de Exposiciones*, which stages exhibitions. More compelling, though, is the huge produce **market** *(feria)* at Lautaro y Aníbal Pinto, which is always crammed with people (many of them Mapuche), who have come from the countryside to sell their produce (see page 212).

The Mapuche

The largest indigenous group in southern South America take their name from the words for 'land' (*mapu*) and 'people' (*che*). They were known as Araucanians by the Spanish.

Never subdued by the Incas, the Mapuche successfully resisted Spanish attempts at conquest. At the time of the great Mapuche uprising of 1598 they numbered 500,000, concentrated in the area between the Río Biobío and the Reloncaví estuary. The 1641 Treaty of Quilín recognized Mapuche autonomy south of the Biobío.

Although tools and equipment were privately owned, the Mapuche held land in common, abandoning it when it became exhausted. This relatively nomadic lifestyle helped them to resist the Spanish. They became formidable guerrilla fighters and pioneered the use of horses by two men. Horses also enabled the Mapuche to extend their territory to the eastern side of the Andes and the Argentine pampas.

The conquest of the Mapuche was made possible by the building of railways and the invention of new weapons. The settlement of border disputes between Chile and Argentina allowed Argentine troops to occupy border crossings, while the Chileans subjugated the Mapuche.

Under the 1881 treaty, the Mapuche received 500,000 ha from the government. They were confined to reservations, most of which were situated near large estates for which they provided a labour force. By the 1930s, the surviving Mapuche, living in more than 3000 separate reservations, had become steadily more impoverished and dependent on government money. Today Mapuche communities remain among the poorest in Chile and occupy only 1.5 % of the lands they inhabited at the time of the conquest.

Between Temuco and the Pacific coast is the indigenous heartland of Chile, home to the largest Mapuche communities. Here you will find traditional thatched houses (*rucas*) and villages still fiercely proud of their traditions, hinting at the sort of country that the first *conquistadors* might have found. It is well worth making a trip to the dusty, friendly town of **Chol Chol**. Buses (Huincabus, 4 daily 1100-1800, one hour, US$1), laden with people and produce, make the 30 km journey from Temuco across rolling countryside. You will see people travelling by ox cart on the tracks nearby, and a few traditional round *rucas*. The town has a small museum dedicated to Mapuche culture.

West of the centre, the **Museo de la Araucanía** ⓘ *Alemania 084, Mon-Fri 0900-1700, Sat 1100-1700, Sun 1100-1300, US$1.50, bus 1 from centre*, houses a well arranged collection devoted to the history and traditions of the Mapuche nation; there's also a section on German settlement.

On the northern edge of the city is the **Monumento Natural Cerro Ñielol** offering views of the city and surrounding countryside. The final peace treaty between the Chilean army and the Mapuche was signed on Cerro Nielol in 1881, under 'La Patagua', a tree that can still be seen. It is a good spot for a picnic. There is an excellent **visitor centre** ⓘ *0830-2030, US$1.50*, run by **CONAF** and a fine collection of native plants, including the copihue rojo, the national flower. Note that the hill has a one-way system for drivers (entry by Prat, exit by Lynch) and that bicycles are only allowed in before 1100.

Southeast of the centre is the predominantly Mapuche suburb of **Padre las Casas**. Here you will find the **Casa de la Mujer Mapuche** ⓘ *Corvalín y Almte Barroso, T09-1694682, Mon-Fri 0930-1300, 1500-1830, bus 8a/10, colectivo 13a*, which sells crafts and textiles made by a co-operative of 135 Mapuche weavers. The items are very good quality, but expensive.

Lago Villarrica

» pp204-214.

Backed to the southeast by the active and snow-capped Villarrica volcano (2840 m), wooded Lago Villarrica, 21 km long and about 7 km wide, is one of the most beautiful lakes in the region. Its resorts – Villarrica and Pucón – are among the priciest in Chile and are busy with tourists in summer but those with the money will find them well worth the expense. Within easy reach is some of the most dramatic scenery in the Chilean Lake District, encompassing two lakes, two national parks and several hot spring resorts, perfect for relaxation after a hard day's trekking.

Villarrica

→ *Colour map 1, A3*

Pleasantly set at the extreme southwest corner of the lake, Villarrica can be reached by a paved road southeast from **Freire**, 24 km south of Temuco on the Pan-American Highway, or from **Loncoche**, 54 km south of Freire, also paved. Less significant as a tourist resort than nearby Pucón, it is also cheaper. Founded in 1552, the town was besieged by the Mapuche in the uprising of 1599: after three years the surviving Spanish settlers, 11 men and 13 women, surrendered. The town was refounded in 1882.

There is a small museum, the **Museo Histórico** ⓘ *Pedro de Valdivia 1050 y Zegers, Mon-Sat 0900-1730, 1800-2200, Sun 1800-2200, reduced hrs in winter, US$0.50*, containing a collection of Mapuche artefacts. Next to it is the **Muestra Cultural Mapuche**, featuring a Mapuche *ruca* and stalls selling good-quality handicrafts in summer. There are good views of the volcano from the *costanera*; for a different perspective over the lake, head south along Aviador Acevedo and then take Poniente Ríos towards the **Hostería de la Colina**.

Pucón

→ *See map page 207. Colour map 1, A3.*

On the southeastern comer of the lake, 26 km east of Villarrica, Pucón is one of the most popular destinations in the Lake District, famous above all as a centre for visiting Volcán Villarrica (2840 m), which lies to the south. Built across the neck of a peninsula, it has two black sand beaches, which are popular for swimming and watersports. Whitewater rafting is also offered on the nearby rivers and excursions

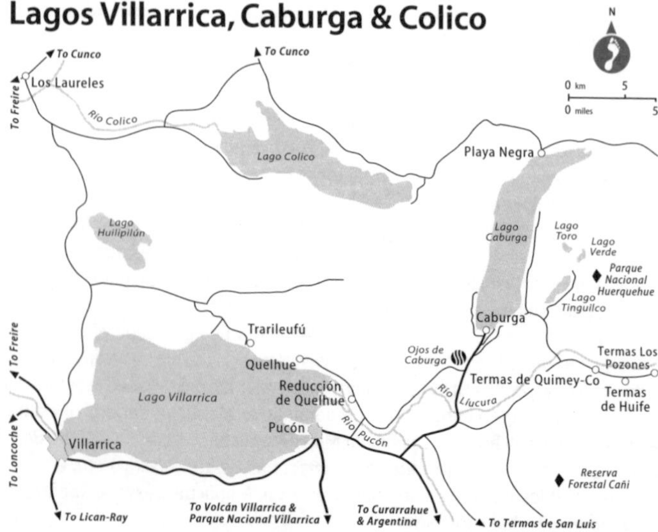

Going further ... Parque Nacional Conguillio

One of the most popular national parks in Chile lies 80 km east of Temuco and is a good stopping point en route to the Argentine border at Paso Pino Hachado (see page 67). At the centre of the park is the still-active Volcán Llaima. It is possible to climb the volcano, hike throughout the park and also ski. The best means of visiting is with a hired 4WD or as part of a tour. The three park entrances are accessible from Curacautín, Melipeuco and Cherquenco, respectively. There is a visitor centre at the entrance by Lago Conguillio. Open December to March, US$6.

can be made into the Parque Nacional Huerquehue and Parque Nacional Villarrica, which both lie east of the town.

The Pucón of today is very different from the town of 30 years ago, when it was a small, pleasant, quiet village with seasonal Chilean tourism, but no foreign backpackers. It is now a thriving tourist centre, full of Chileans in summer and gringos in the autumn. Neon signs are forbidden and road signs and telephone kiosks are made of wood, but the streets are full of bars, restaurants and *artesanía*. The commercial centre lies between **Avenida O'Higgins**, the main thoroughfare, and the **Gran Hotel Pucón**. Private land (ask for permission at the entrance) leads west from the centre to **La Peninsula**, where there are views of the lake and volcano, as well as pony rides and golf. There is also a nice walk, along the **Costanera Otto Gudenschwager**, starting at the northern end of Calle Ansorena and following the lakeside to the north.

Boat trips ⓘ *daily 1500 and 1900, summer only, 2 hrs, US$6*, on the lake leave from the landing stage at La Poza at the western end of O'Higgins. Walk a couple of kilometres north along the beach from here to the mouth of the Río Pucón for views of volcanoes. Or take a boat ⓘ *summer only, US$12*, to the mouth of the river from near the Gran Hotel.

From the road to the Villarrica volcano, a *ripio* road branches off for 5 km to some privately managed *cuevas volcanicas* (**volcanic caves**) ⓘ *US$12*, surrounded by a small attractive park with tunnels and a museum, as well as paths through the forest. Entry to the site is expensive, but it's recommended as a bad-weather option.

Lago Caburga and around » *pp204-214.*

→ *Colour map 1, A3*

Lago Caburga (spelt locally Caburgua) is a very pretty lake in a wild setting 25 km northeast of Pucón. It is unusual for its beautiful white sand beach (other beaches in the area have black volcanic sand), and is supposedly the warmest lake in the Lake District. The western and much of the eastern shores are inaccessible to vehicles, but the village of **Caburga**, at the southern end of the lake, is reached by a turning off the main road to Argentina, 8 km east of Pucón.

If walking or cycling, there is a very pleasant alternative route: turn left 3 km east of Pucón, cross the Río Pucón via Puente Quelhue, then turn right and follow the track for 18 km through beautiful scenery. (From the bridge, there are also pleasant walks along the north shore of Lago Villarrica to the Mapuche settlement of **Quelhue** and the village of **Trarilelfú**.) Just off the main road from Pucón, Km 15, are the **Ojos de Caburga** ⓘ *US$0.60*, beautiful pools fed from underground, particularly attractive after rainl.

The northern tip of Lago Caburga can be reached by a road from Cunco, which runs east along the northern shore of **Lago Colico**. This is one of the less accessible lakes, and lies north of Lago Villarrica in a remote setting.

Parque Nacional Huerquehue → *Colour map 1, A3*

ⓘ *Open officially Jan-Mar, US$4, parking 500 m along the track, US$1.*

Located a short distance east of Lago Caburga, Parque Nacional Huerquehue covers 12,500 ha at altitudes rising to 1952 m at the **Picos del Caburgua**. It also encompasses about 20 lakes, some of them very small, and many araucaria (monkey puzzle) trees. The entrance and administration is on the western edge, near **Lago Tinguilco**, the largest lake in the park. From the entrance there is a well-signed track north up a steep hill to **Lago Chico**, where the track divides left to **Lago Verde** and right to **Laguna Toro**. The lakes are surrounded by trees and are very beautiful. The tracks rejoin at **Lago Huerquehue**, where a further 20 km of trails begin. None of the routes is particularly taxing, making the park a good warm-up for the volcán Villarrica hike. An adequate map is available at the entrance and the warden is very helpful. People in the park rent horses and boats, and there is a restaurant.

Reserva Forestal Cañi

ⓘ *Information from Fundación Lahuén, Urrutia 477, Pucón, T045-441660, lahuen@interaccess.cl. Park entrance is US$ 5 per person; tours run by Outdoor Experience, Urrutia, Pucón, T045-442809, www.outdoorexperience.org.*

Situated south of Parque Nacional Huerquehue and covering 500 ha, this is a private nature reserve owned by the **Fundación Lahuén**, and only accessible on a guided tour – it is definitely worth a visit. The reserve contains 17 small lakes and is covered by ancient native forests of coigue and lenga; it also has some of the oldest araucaria trees in Chile. From its highest peak, **El Mirador**, (1550 m) there are panoramic views over neighbouring parts of Argentina and Chile, including four volcanoes: Lanín, Villarrica, Quetrupillán and Llaima. As the reserve is above the snowline, tours are normally restricted to summer, though visits in winter are sometimes possible.

Parque Nacional Villarrica » pp204-214.

This park, which covers 61,000 ha, stretches from Pucón to the Argentine border near Puesco. There are three sectors: around Volcán Villarrica; around Volcán Quetrupillán and the Puesco sector, which includes the slopes of the Lanín volcano on the Argentine frontier. Each sector has its own entrance and ranger station. Between July and November it is possible to ski at the **Pucón resort**, which is situated on the eastern slopes of Villarrica and reached by a badly maintained track (see page 211).

Climbing Villarrica → *Colour map 1, A3*

The Villarrica volcano, 2840 m high and still active, lies 8 km south of Pucón. Due to accidents, access to the volcano, US$5, is restricted only to groups with a guide – several agencies offer excursions (see Activities and tours, page 212) – and to individuals who can show proof of membership of a mountaineering club in their own country. Tours from Pucón cost US$70, including park entry, guide, transport to park entrance and hire of equipment (no reduction for those with their own equipment). Bargain for group rates. Entry is refused if the weather is poor. Good boots, crampons and ice picks are essential; these can be rented for US$8 per day from tour operators. You should also take sunglasses, sun block, plenty of water and chocolate or some other snack; equipment is checked at the park entrance.

It is a three- to four-hour trek to the summit, but you can skip the first 400 m by taking the ski lift (US$9). At the summit look down into the crater and you may see bubbling molten lava, but beware of the sulphur fumes; the better tour agencies provide gas masks, otherwise take a cloth mask moistened with lemon juice. On clear days you can see six other volcanoes. Conditions permitting, groups may carry ski or snowboard equipment for the descent; otherwise just slide down toboggan style – great fun.

The legend of Lican-Ray

At the height of the wars between the Spanish and the Mapuche a young Spanish soldier was lost and strayed into the forests near Lago Calafquén. He came across a beautiful young Mapuche woman drying her hair in the sun and singing. He began to sing along and as they exchanged glances, they fell in love. She called him Allumanche, which means white man in Mapuche, and, indicated that her name was Lican Rayan, meaning the flower of magic stone. They began to live together near the lake.

Lican Rayan's father, Curtilef, a powerful and fearsome chief, feared she might be dead. One day a boy came to him and said: "Lican Rayan is alive. I have seen her near the lake with a white man but she is not a prisoner: it is clear they are in love".

Lican Rayan saw the warriors coming to look for her. They escaped by riding on logs to one of the islands where they hid for several days. The north wind blew and it rained heavily. Unable to bear the cold and thinking that the warriors would have given up the search, they lit a fire. The smoke was spotted by Curtilef's men, so Lican Rayan and the solider fled to another island further away but again they were discovered and had to escape. This happened so many times that, although they were never caught, they were never seen again.

In the town of Lican-Ray, it is said that on spring afternoons it is sometimes possible to see a distant column of smoke from one of the islands, where Lican Rayan and the soldier are still enjoying their love after over 400 years.

Abridged and translated from *Lengua Y Costumbres Mapuches* by Orietta Appelt Martin, Imprenta Austral, Temuco, 1995.

Towards Paso Mamuil Malal

From Pucón a road runs southeast along the southern bank of the valley of the Río Trancura to the Argentine border at Paso Mumuil Malal/Tromen (see page 75) and on through Parque Nacional Lanín to Junín de los Andes. Unless the pass is closed by snow, this is the route used by international buses from Temuco. The road provides access en route to thermal springs and a number of hikeable waterfalls (*saltos*) in the Quetrupillán and Puesco sectors of the Villarrica national park.

At Km 18, a *ripio* road heads south 10 km to the Quetrupillán section of the park. On the edge of the park are the **Termas de Palguín** ⓘ *www.termasdepalguin.cl, US$10*, and the spectacular **Saltos del Puma** and **del León** ⓘ *also accessible at Km 27 on the Pucón-Curarrehue road, US$2 for both*. From the springs a very rough dirt road, great for horse riding, runs south across the national park to Coñaripe. Palguín is also the starting point for a four- to five-day hike to Puesco, with vistas over the Villarrica and Lanín volcanoes.

Back on the Curarrehue road, at Km 23, a turning leads north to the indoor and outdoor pools at **Termas de San Luis** ⓘ *www.sanluis.pucon.com, US$9*, from where it is 30 minutes' walk to **Lago del León**. At Km 24, the **Salto Palguín** can be seen (but not reached), and beyond that is the impressive **Salto China** ⓘ *Km 26, US$1.50*, where there's a restaurant and camping. At Km 35 another turning leads north for 15 km to the **Termas de Pangui** ⓘ *US$10*, where there are three pools beautifully situated in the mountains. » *See also box, page 208.*

Beyond the small town of **Curarrehue**, 36 km east of Pucón, the road deteriorates as it turns south to the customs post in the Puesco sector of the park. The road then climbs via **Lago Quellelhue**, to reach the border at **Paso Mamuil Malal** (Paso Tromen). To the south of the pass rises the graceful cone of **Volcán Lanín** (3747 m), one of the world's most beautiful mountains (see page 76).

Seven Lakes » pp204-214.

Heading south from Villarrica, you can rejoin the Pan-American highway towards Valdivia and Osorno or take a more leisurely route southeast to Lican Ray and the 'Siete Lagos'. These lakes tend to be less developed than the resorts to the north and south. They form a picture-postcard necklace of water, with a backdrop of thick woods and distant snows. Six of the lakes lie in Chile, with the seventh, Lago Lacár, in Argentina. After the final peace settlement of 1882 the area around these lakes was reserved for Mapuche settlements. Most of the lakes have black-sand beaches, although as the water level rises in spring, these all but disappear.

Lago Calafquén and around → *Colour map 1, A3*

The most northerly of the seven lakes, **Lago Calafquén** is a popular tourist destination, readily accessible by a paved road from Villarrica, along which there are fine views of the Villarrica volcano. Wooded and dotted with small islands, the lake is reputedly one of the warmest in the region and is good for swimming. A partly paved road runs around the lake.

The major resort on the lake is **Lican-Ray**, named after a legendary Mapuche woman (see box, page 201). It is 30 km south of Villarrica on the north shore, and although crowded in summer, most facilities close by April. There are two beaches, one on each side of the peninsula. Boats can be hired (US$3 an hour) and there are catamaran trips (US$5 per hour or US$18 to the islands). Some 6 km to the east is the river of lava formed when the Villarrica volcano erupted in 1971. There is a **tourist office** on the plaza ⓘ *daily in summer, Mon-Fri in winter.*

Coñaripe, lies 21 km southeast of Lican-Ray with a black sand beach surrounded by mountains. The **tourist office** ⓘ *on the plaza, mid Nov-mid Apr daily; late Apr-early*

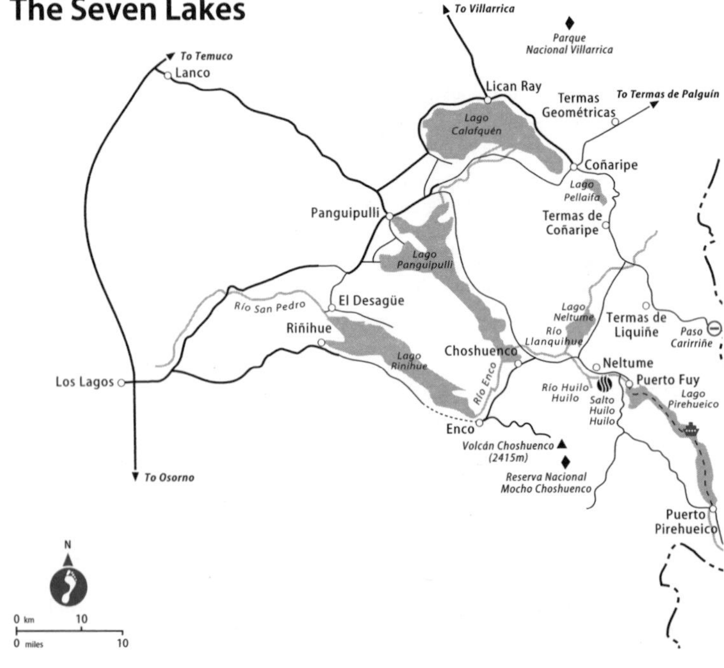

Nov Sat and Sun only, can arrange excursions to local thermal springs. From Coñaripe a road (mostly *ripio*) around the lake's southern shore leads to **Lago Panguipulli**, 38 km west, with views over Volcán Villarrica.

Another route heads southeast towards the Argentine border at **Paso Carirriñe** (see page 204). As it crosses the steep Cuesta Los Añiques, there are views of **Lago Pellaifa**, a tiny lake with rocky surroundings and a small beach. The **Termas de Coñaripe** ⓘ *Km 16, 2km from the lakeshore, T063-411407, www.termasdeconaripe.cl*, has four pools, accommodation, restaurant, cycles and horses for hire. Further south are the **Termas de Liquiñe** ⓘ *Km 32, T/F063-317377, US$6-10 per person*, with eight thermal springs and accommodation (but little other infrastructure), surrounded by a small native forest. About 8 km north of Liquiñe is a road going southwest (20 km) along the southeast shore of **Lago Neltume** to meet the Choshuenco-Puerto Fuy road.

Lagos Panguipulli and Pirehueico → *Colour map 1, A3*

Covering 116 sq km, Lago Panguipulli, the largest of the seven lakes, is reached by paved road from Lanco or Los Lagos on the Pan-American Highway or by *ripio* roads from Lago Calafquén. A road leads along the beautiful northern shore, which is wooded with sandy beaches and cliffs.

The site of a Mapuche settlement, **Panguipulli**, meaning 'hill of pumas', is situated on a hillside at the northwest corner of the lake and is the largest town in the area. On Plaza Prat is the Iglesia San Sebastián, built in Swiss style, with three bells from Germany. The plaza also has a tourist office (open December to February only). In summer, catamaran trips are offered on the lake and excursions can be made to Lagos Calafquén, Neltume, Pirehueico and Riñihue.

Choshuenco lies 45 km east of Panguipulli on the Río Llanquihue, at the eastern tip of the lake and can only be reached by road from Panguipulli or Puerto Fuy. To the south is the **Reserva Nacional Mocho Choshuenco** (7536 ha), which has two volcanoes: Choshuenco (2415 m) and Mocha (2422 m). On the slopes of Choshuenco the **Club Andino de Valdivia** runs a small ski resort and three *refugios*. From Choshuenco a road leads east towards Neltume and Lago Pirehueico, via the impressive waterfalls of **Huilo Huilo**. The falls are three hours' walk from Choshuenco, or take the Puerto Fuy bus and get off at **Alojamiento Huilo Huilo**.

Lago Pirehueico is a 36-km-long, narrow and deep glacial lake surrounded by virgin lingue forest. It is beautiful and largely unspoilt, although there are plans to build a huge tourist complex in Puerto Pirehueico. There are two ports on the lake: **Puerto Fuy** at the northern end and **Puerto Pirehueico** at the southern end. The ports are linked by a ferry service (the crossing is beautiful) and can also be reached by the road that runs east from Neltume to the Argentine border crossing at **Paso Hua Hum** (see page 78). The road south from Puerto Fuy, however, is privately owned and closed to traffic.

Sleeping

Temuco *p196, map p205*
Many cheaper *residenciales* and *pensiones* can be found in the market area.
AL Terraverde, Prat 0220, T045-239999, www.panamericanahoteles.cl. This 5-star is the best in town.
B Hotel Don Eduardo, Bello 755, T045-214133, www.hoteldoneduardo.cl. Parking, suites with kitchen, recommended.
B-C Bayern, Prat 146, T045-276000, www.hotelbayern.cl. Standard 3-star. Small rooms, clean, helpful, buffet breakfast, parking. Cheaper if paying in US dollars.
C Continental, Varas 708, T045-238973, www.turismochile.cl/continental. Charming old-fashioned building with large rooms and antique furniture. Breakfast, decent restaurant, a popular bar, cheaper rooms without bath. Neruda stayed here once. Recommended.
C-D La Casa de Juanita, Carrera 735, T045-213203. Quiet B&B. Hot water, laundry, heating, parking. Cheaper without bath. Similar places on Bello, west of the plaza.
C-D Oriente, M Rodríguez 1146, T045-233232, h-oriente@123mail.cl. Old, but clean and friendly. Good value rooms with bath, cheaper without (these rooms do have sinks). Heating, TV, parking, laundry. Some rooms with no windows. Recommended.
D Chapelco, Cruz 401, T045-749393 www.hotelchapelco.cl. Rooms with bath and cable TV. Breakfast, internet in lobby, comfortable, good service, recommended.
D Hospedaje Aldunate, Aldunate 187, T045-270057, cristorresvalenzuela@hotmail.com. **F** singles. Friendly, cooking facilities. Some rooms with TV and bath.
D Hospedaje Maggi Alvarado, Recreo 209, off Av Alemania, T045-409804, cppacl@gmail.com. **G** singles. Small rooms, but very clean, friendly, helpful, in a pleasant part of town. Also has a good value *cabaña* sleeping 4.

Villarrica *p198*
Off-season is 30-40% cheaper. Upmarket hotels tend to be on the lakefront.
A El Ciervo, Koerner 241, T045-411215, www.hotelelciervo.cl. 4-star. Comfortable rooms with heating, in pleasant grounds. German-style breakfasts, pool, terrace, Wi-Fi. Recommended.
A Parque Natural Dos Ríos, 13 km west of Villarrica, T09-94198064, www.dosrios.de. With full board. Tranquil 40-ha nature park with *cabañas* on the banks of the Río Toltén (there is a white sand beach), horse riding, birdwatching, children-friendly.
A-B Hostería de la Colina, Las Colinas 115, overlooking town, T045-411503, www.hosteriadelacolina.com. Large gardens, breakfast and restaurant,Wi-Fi, views. Recommended.
A-B Hotel y Cabañas El Parque, 3 km east on Pucón road, T045-411120, www.hotelelparque.cl. Lakeside with beach, tennis courts, breakfast, good restaurant with set meals. Highly recommended.
B Hostería Bilbao, Henríquez 43, T045-411186, www.interpatagonia.com/bilbao. Clean rooms, pretty patio, good restaurant.
C Hotel-Yachting Kiel, Koerner 153, T045-411631, www.yachtingkiel.cl. All rooms with lake views, clean, friendly, rooms with bath, cable TV and heating. Restaurant. Good value.
C-D La Torre Suiza, Bilbao 969, T045-411213, www.torresuiza.com. **F** pp in dorms. Some rooms with bath. Excellent breakfast, kitchen and laundry facilities, camping, bike rental, book exchange. Recommended.
D Villa Linda, Pedro de Valdivia 678, T045-411392. **F** singles. Hot water, clean, basic, cheap, good restaurant.
D-E Chilepeppers, Vicente Reyes 546, T045-414694, www.chilepeppers.cl. **F** pp in dorms. Lively backpackers' hostel with basic cramped dorms. Kitchen, internet, BBQ.

Border with Argentina

Paso Carirriñe across the Argentine border is open between 15 October and 31 August, and is reached by unpaved road about 15 km from the Termas de Liquiñe. On the Argentine side the road continues through the Parque Nacional Lanín to Junín de los Andes (see page 76). This route is only used by international buses, when Paso Tromen is closed with snow. **Chilean immigration and customs** ⓘ *daily 0800-2000*. **Argentine immigration and customs** ⓘ *daily 0800-2000*.

D-E Hospedaje Nicolás, Anfion Muñoz 477, T045-410232. **F** singles. Basic rooms with cable TV and bath. With breakfast. Good value, although the walls are thin.
D-E Señora Nelly, Aviador Acevedo 725, T045-412299. **F** singles. Hot water all day, good value, camping, recommended.
G pp **Residencial San Francisco**, Julio Zegers 646. Dorms and rooms in private homes usually **D**, or **G** singles; several on Koerner 300 block and O'Higgins 700.

Camping

Many sites east of town on Pucón road, but these are expensive and open in season only. It may be cheaper to stay in a *hospedaje*; those nearest to town are **El Edén**, 1 km southeast of centre, T045-412772, US$6 pp, recommended, and **Los Castaños**, T045-412330, US$15 per site.

Pucón *p198, map p207*

Rooms may be hard to find in high season (Dec-Feb). Look for signs for rooms in private houses – or ask in bars/ restaurants. Price codes are based on high season rates; off season prices are 20-40% lower and it's often possible to negotiate.
LL-L Hotel Antumalal, Km 2 Pucón-Villarrica Hwy, T045-441011, www.antumalal.com. Very small, picturesque Bauhaus chalet-style, set in 5 ha of parkland, magnificent views of the lake, tennis court, lovely gardens, open year round, pool.
AL Interlaken, Caupolicán 720, T045-441276, www.hotelinterlaken.cl. Chalets, pool, water-skiing, tours arranged, no restaurant. Recommended.
A-B Gudenschwager, Pedro de Valdivia 12, T045-442025, www.hogu.cl. Refurbished 1920s hotel. 20 simple centrally heated

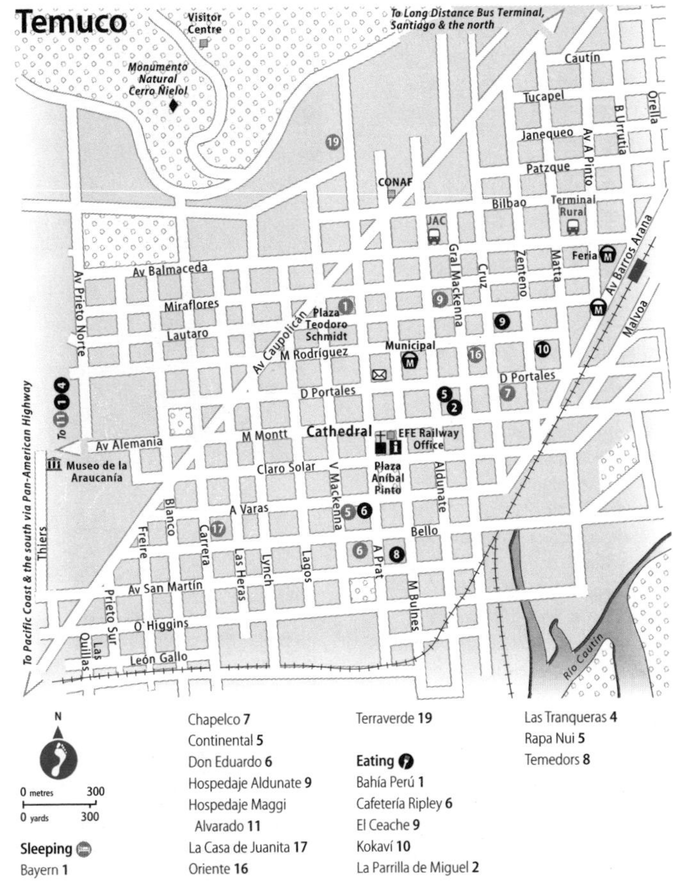

Sleeping
Bayern 1
Chapelco 7
Continental 5
Don Eduardo 6
Hospedaje Aldunate 9
Hospedaje Maggi Alvarado 11
La Casa de Juanita 17
Oriente 16
Terraverde 19

Eating
Bahía Perú 1
Cafetería Ripley 6
El Ceache 9
Kokaví 10
La Parrilla de Miguel 2
Las Tranqueras 4
Rapa Nui 5
Temedors 8

rooms some with lake and volcano view. Much cheaper rooms with exterior bathroom. Also good rates off season. Living room with big screen TV and Wi-Fi area. Large breakfast included. Meals served (special needs catered for). English spoken.

A-B La Posada Plaza-Pucón, Valdivia 191, T045-441088, www.hotelplazapucon.cl. Pleasant rooms with bath, restaurant, also spacious cabins, gardens and a pool. Cheaper when paying in dollars.

B-C Hostal Gerónimo, Alderete 665, T045-443762, www.geronimo.cl. Recently refurbished. Rooms with bath and cable TV. Comfortable, friendly, quiet, with restaurant, bar and terrace. Recommended.

C La Tetera, Urrutia 580, T045-441462, www.tetera.cl. Rooms with and without bath. Good breakfast with real coffee, good Spanish classes, book swap, lots of information. Recommended, book in advance.

C-D Hostal Willy, Arauco 565, T045-444578, www.hostalyturismowilly.com. **F** singles. Pleasant carpeted and heated rooms with cable TV and spacious bathrooms. Breakfast available, internet, use of kitchen. Friendly, good value, recommended. The annex across the street is not nearly as good.

C-D Hostería Ecole, Urrutia 592, T045-441675, www.ecole.cl. **F** pp in dorms without breakfast, some rooms with bath, good vegetarian and fish restaurant, ecological shop, forest treks, rafting, biking, information, language classes, massage, recommended.

D Hospedaje M@yra, Colo Colo 485, T045-442745, www.myhostelpucon.com. **F** singles. Good backpackers' hostel. Some rooms with bath and cable TV. Kitchen, internet, laundry, parking, tours offered. Recommended.

D Hospedaje Victor, Palguín 705, T045-443525, www.pucon.com/victor. **F** singles. Some rooms with bath. Kitchen facilities, TV, laundry. Friendly. A decent choice.

D Tr@vel Pucón, Blanco Encalada 190, T045-444093, www.interpatagonia.com/travelpucon. **F** singles. Near Turbus terminal, garden, kitchen facilities, Spanish classes.

D-E Hospedaje Graciela, Pasaje Rolando Matus 521 (off Av Brasil). **F** singles. Comfortable rooms, good food.

D-E Hospedaje Lucía, Lincoyán 565, T045-441721. **F** singles. Friendly, quiet, garden, recommended, cooking facilities.

D-E Hospedaje Sonia, Lincoyán 485, T045-441269, www.myhostelpucon.com/sonia. **F** singles. Basic but clean rooms, some with bath. Use of kitchen, noisy and somewhat crowded, friendly. Basic English spoken.

Camping

Buy supplies in Villarrica where it is cheaper.
La Poza, Costanera Geis 769, T045-441435. Hot showers, clean, quiet, good kitchen facilities, open all year. Recommended.
L'etoile, Km 2 towards Volcán Villarrica, T045-442188. Attractive forest site.
Millaray, Km 7 west of Pucón, T045-212336. Lakeside campsite.
Saint John, Km 7 west of Pucón, T045-441165, Casilla 154. Beside the lake.

Lago Caburga and around *p199*

AL-A Trailanqui, 20 km west of Lago Colico (35 km north of Villarrica), T045-578218, www.trailanqui.com. Luxurious hotel on the riverbank, with suites, *cabañas*, a campsite, restaurant, horse riding and golf course.
B Hostería Los Robles, 3 km from Caburga village, T045-236989. Lovely views, good restaurant; also campsite, expensive in season, but cheap out of season.
C Landhaus San Sebastián, east of Lago Caburga, T045-1972360, www.landhaus-chile.com. With bath and breakfast, tasty meals, laundry facilities, good walking base, English and German spoken, Spanish classes.

Pucón

Sleeping
Antumalal 2 *C1*
Gran Pucón 8 *A2*
Gudenschwager 4 *A1*
Hospedaje Graciela 13 *C2*
Hospedaje Lucía 17 *C2*
Hospedaje M@yra 10 *B3*
Hospedaje Sonia 18 *B2*
Hospedaje Victor 11 *C2*
Hostal Gerónimo 26 *B3*
Hostal Willy 5 *C3*
Hostería Ecole 21 *B3*
Interlaken 24 *C1*
La Posada Plaza-Pucón 28 *B1*
La Poza 9 *C1*
La Tetera 29 *B2*

Eating
Arabian 1 *B2*
El Refugio 2 *B1*
En Alta Mar 4 *B2*
Il Baretto 5 *B2*
La Buonatesta 8 *B2*
La Maga 7 *B2*
Puerto Pucón 10 *B2*
Rap Hamburguesa 9 *B3*
Senzo 11 *B2*

... and relax

More than a third of all the thermal spas in Chile are in the Lake District, thanks to the high level of volcanic activity in this area. There are several east of Pucón, ranging from luxurious hotel complexes with extensive spa treatments to rustic bathtubs in the forest and natural pools or rivers. Easing your aching muscles in thermal water is the perfect way to recover after an arduous volcano trek.

The most upmarket are the **Termas de Huife**, Km 33, T045-1975666, www.termashuife.cl, US$12, reached via a turning off the Pucón-Caburga road. The complex has three modern pools on the banks of the river Liucura. Overnight guests at Hostería Termas de Huife (AL) stay in cabins on site and can indulge in various treatments.

Closer to Pucón and more low-key are the **Termas de Quimey-Co**, Km 29, T045-441903, US$9, with a hotel (B), campsite and two cabins.

Further on are the **Termas los Pozones**, Km 35, US$7 per day, US$9 at night, which have six natural rock pools but little infrastructure and are popular with backpackers.

Termas de Palguín, T045-441968, www.termasdepalguin.cl, US$9, are in a beautiful spot in the Quetrupillán section of the Villarrica national park, close to the spectacular Saltos del Puma and del León. There's a swimming pool, private baths and cabins.

Termas de San Luis, T045-443965, www.sanluis.pucon.com, US$11, are reached north off the Curarrehue road at Km 23. There's an indoor and outdoor pool, a sauna and *cabañas* (A), plus a pick-up service for overnight guests from Pucón.

At Km 35, another turning leads north for 15 km to the **Termas de Pangui**, US$12, where there are three pools beautifully situated in the mountains. Accommodation is in a lodge (D-E) or in 3-person teepees right next to the hot pools. There are also camping facilities, good vegetarian meals, trekking and aromatherapy; contact O'Higgins 555, of 2, Pucón, T045-442039, ingeluz@yahoo.com.

Camping

The southern end of Lago Caburga is lined with campsites, but there are no shops, so take your own food. There are 2 campsites at the entrance to Parque Nacional Huerquehue, US$8, but no camping is allowed in the park. There are also 2 sites about half-way along north shore of Lago Colico: **Quichelmalleu**, Km 22 from Cunco, T045-573187. **Ensenada**, Km 26, T045-221441.

Parque Nacional Villarrica *p200*

Avoid the *refugio* 4 km inside the park towards Volcán Villarrica, which is insecure and in desperate need of renovation. There is a **CONAF** campsite at Puesco and another, near Lago Tromen, free, but no facilities.

Towards Paso Mamuil Malal *p201*

See box, above, for Hotel **Termas de Pangui**.

B-G Cabañas La Tranquera, Puesco. Cabins for 6, also dorms, restaurant, campsite.

C Rancho de Caballos, 36 km southeast of Pucón on the dirt road to Coñaripe, T045-441575. Restaurant with vegetarian dishes, laundry and kitchen facilities; also *cabañas* and camping, self-guided trails, horse riding excursions US$70 per day, English and German spoken, recommended.

D Kila Leufu, Km 20, Pucón-Curarrehue road, T09-97118064, www.kilaleufu.cl. **E** pp in shared rooms. Rooms on the Martínez family farm, contact daughter Margot in advance, friendly, English spoken, full board available including spit-roast lamb in the *ruca* and other home-grown food, also offers trekking information, horse riding and mountain bike hire, camping possible. Recommended.

Camping

There is a **CONAF** campsite at Puesco and another, 5 km from the frontier near Lago Tromen, free, no facilities.

Lago Calafquén and around *p202*
There are plenty of options along the north shore of Lago Calafquén towards Coñaripe.
A pp **Termas de Liquiñe**, Km 32 , T/F063-317377. Full board, cabins, restaurant, tours. Also accommodation in private houses.
C **Hospedaje Los Nietos**, Manquel 125, Lican Ray, T045-431078. Without breakfast.
C **Hostería Inaltulafquen**, Casilla 681, Playa Grande, Lican Ray, T045-431115. With breakfast and bath, English spoken.
D **Cabañas Cacique Vitacura**, Urrutia 825, Playa Grande, Lican Ray, T02-2355302, tradesic@intermedia.cl. For 2, also larger cabins with kitchen.
D-E **Residencial Temuco**, G Mistral 515, Playa Grande, Lican Ray, T045-431130. F singles, with breakfast. Clean, good.

Camping
There are also 6 sites just west of Lican Ray.
Forestal, ½ km east of town, T045-211954. Sites for up to 6 people.
Isla Llancahue, 5 km east, T063-317360. Campsite with *cabañas* on an island in Río Llancahue. More campsites on the north and south sides of the lake, US$15 per site.
Prado Verde,1 km east of town, T045-431161.

Lagos Panguipulli and Pirehueico *p203*
Beds are available in private houses around Lago Pirehueico, and free camping is possible on the beach.
C **Hostal España**, O'Higgins 790, Panguipulli, T063-311166, hostal_espana@elsitio.com. Rooms with breakfast.
C **Hostería Quetropillán**, Etchegaray 381, Panguipulli, T063-311348. Comfortable.
D **Hospedaje Familiar**, Los Ulmos 62, Panguipulli, T063-311483. **F** singles. Kitchen facilities, helpful, good breakfast.
D **Hostería Rayen Trai**, María Alvarado y O'Higgins, Choshuenco. **F** singles. Former yacht club serving good food, open all year.
D pp **Hotel Central**, Valdivia 115, Panguipulli, T063-311331. Clean rooms, with breakfast.

Eating

Temuco *p196, map p205*
Those on a very strict budget should make for the **Mercado Municipal**, Aldunate y Portales, where there are several restaurants and fierce touting for business, or the rural bus terminal, where countless restaurants serve very cheap set meals at lunch. *Humitas* are on sale in the street in summer/autumn.
♈♈ **Bahía Perú**, Alemania y Recreo, near the Mall Mirage, about 10 blocks west of centre. One of several good mid-priced restaurants on Av Alemania (take bus 1), reasonable Peruvian food, good *pisco sours*.
♈♈ **Caletas Restaurante**, Mercado Municipal, Aldunate y Portales. One of several in the covered market serving fish and seafood.
♈♈ **La Cumbre del Cerro Ñielol**, Cerro Ñielol. Food and dancing on top of the hill, not always open.
♈♈ **La Parrilla de Miguel**, Montt 1095, T045-275182. Good for large servings of meat and wine. One of the best in the town centre.
♈♈ **Las Tranqueras**, Alemania 0888, T045-385044. Meat specialists, great grills, but vegetarian options also available.
♈ **El Ceache**, Cruz 231. Typical Chilean food. Good value set lunch.
♈ **Kokaví**, Rodríguez y Zenteno, T045-951625. Popular restaurant serving traditional Mapuche food. Gets busy at lunchtime.
♈ **Rapa Nui**, Aldunate 415. For take-away lunches and snacks, recommended.
♈ **Restaurante Temedors**, San Martín 827. Good-value lunch.

Cafés
Good coffee can be found at **Café Marriet**, Prat 451; **Cafetería Ripley**, Prat y Varas; **Dino's**, Bulnes 360. For ice cream try **Il Gelato**, Bulnes 420.

Villarrica *p198*
♈♈♈ **El Tabor**, Epulef 1187, T045-411901. Excellent but pricey.
♈♈♈ **La Cava del Roble**, Valentin Letelier 658, 2nd fl, T045-416446. Excellent grill. Specializes in exotic meat and game. Extensive wine list. Recommended.
♈♈ **El Rey de Mariscos**, Letelier 1030. Good seafood.
♈♈ **Rapa Nui**, Vicente Reyes 678. Good and cheap end of the range, closed Sun.
♈♈ **The Travellers**, Letelier 753, T045-413617. Varied menu including vegetarian and Asian food, bar, English spoken.
♈ **Café 2001**, Henríquez 379. Good ice cream.
♈ **Casa Vieja**, Letelier y Muñoz. Good value set lunch. Family run, friendly.
♈ **Chito Fuentes**, Reyes 665. Chilean fast food.

Pucón *p198, map p207*
Vegetarians should check out the deli at O'Higgins y Fresia. Boutique restaurants can be found on Fresia; there are several cheap restaurants around Urrutia y Ansorena.
YYY Ana María, O'Higgins 865, T045-444288. Chilean food including game and seafood.
YYY En Alta Mar, Urrutia y Fresia. Fish and other seafood, very good.
YYY Puerto Pucón, Fresia 251. One of Pucón's older restaurants. Spanish, stylish.
YYY-YY La Buonatesta, Fresia 243, T045-441434. Pucón's original pizzeria. Good, but a little on the expensive side.
YYY-YY La Maga, Fresia 125, T045-444277. Uruguayan Parillada serving possibly the best steak in Chile. So good that imitations have opened up beside it to take the overspill.
YYY-YY Senzo, Fresia 284, T045-449005. Fresh pasta and risotto prepared by a swiss chef.
YY Arabian, Fresia 354-B, T045-443469. Arab specialities – stuffed vine leaves, falafel etc.
YY El Refugio, Lincoyán 348. Some vegetarian dishes, expensive wine.
YY Il Baretto, Fresia 124, T045-443515. Stone-baked pizzas. Relatively good value.
Y Rap Hamburguesa, O'Higgins 625. Freshly made hamburgers and Chilean fast food.

Cafés

Café de la P, O'Higgins y Lincoyán. Real coffee.
Holzapfel Backerei, Holzapfel 524. German café. Recommended.
Patagonia Express, Fresia 223. Chocolates, ice creams, pancakes and snacks.

Lago Calafquén and around *p202*
YY-Y Café Ñaños, Urrutia 105, Lican-Ray. Very good, reasonable prices, helpful owner.
YY-Y Restaurant-Bar Guido's, Urrutia 405, Lican-Ray. Good value.

Lago Panguipulli *p203*
There are cheap restaurants in Panguipulli on O'Higgins 700 block.
YY Didáctico El Gourmet, Ramón Freire s/n. Restaurant linked to a professional hotel school. Excellent food and wine, mid price but high quality, open in school terms only.
YY-Y Café Central, M de Rozas 750. Good cheap lunches, expensive evening meals.
YY-Y El Chapulín, M de Rozas 639. Good food, good value, friendly.

Bars and clubs

Pucón *p198, map p207*
El Bosque, O'Higgins 524. Lively bar with occasional live jazz music. Wide range of wines and cocktails. Also serves good food. At weekends in summer, there are discos 2-3 km east of town, near the airport: **Kamikaze** and **La Playa**. There are several more discotheques in the same area.
Mamas and Tapas, O'Higgins y Arauco. Drink and snacks. Several others also on O'Higgins.

Festivals and events

Villarrica *p198*
Jan-Feb Many events are organized, including music, regattas, rodeo and the Festival Cultural Mapuche, with a market, based around the Muestra Cultural Mapuche, usually in 2nd week of Feb.

Pucón *p198, map p207*
Feb Pucón is home to an international triathlon competition every year.

Shopping

Temuco *p196, map p205*
Crafts
Mapuche crafts and textiles are sold inside and around the Mercado Municipal, Aldunate y Portales, and also in the Casa de la Mujer Mapuche (see Sights above).

Food
Temuco feria, Lautaro y Aníbal Pinto. This is one of the most fascinating markets in Chile, where people from the surrounding countryside come to sell their wares. You will find excellent cheap fruit and vegetables, local spices like *merquén* (made from smoked chillies), fish, grains, cheese and honey; there are many inexpensive bars and restaurants nearby.

Pucón *p198, map p207*
There is a large handicraft market just south of O'Higgins on Ansorena. The local specialities are painted wooden flowers. Camping equipment is available at Eltit Supermarket, O'Higgins y Fresia, and from Outdoors and Travel, Lincoyán 361. Pucon Express, O'Higgins y Colo Colo, is a 24-hr supermarket.

Activities and tours

Tours to **Volcán Villarrica** will not run if the weather is bad; some travellers have had difficulties getting a refund. Establish in advance what terms apply in the event of cancellation and be prepared to wait a few days. For information on individual guides, all with equipment, ask at the tourist offices; prices, schedules and operators can change very quickly in this popular tourist area.

There are plenty of tour operators in Temuco, but it is far better to book with a company in Villarrica or Pucón.

Villarrica *p198*

Tour operators

Prices are fairly standard: to Parque Nacional Villarrica, US$18; to climb Volcán Villarrica, US$70; to Valdivia US$45; to Termas de Coñaripe US$30. With **Karina Tour**, Letelier 825, T045-412048. **Politur**, Henríquez 475, T045-414547. Recommended. **Turismo Coñaripe**, P Montt 525, T045-411111. **Vuelatour**, Camilo Henríquez 430 local 1, T045-415766. General tour agency. Trips to thermal springs etc, Navimag, Lan Chile agent, airport transfer, car hire.

Pucón *p198, map p207*

Canopy

Several agencies offer canopy tours – ziplining from treetop to treetop in native forests. **Bosque Aventura**, O'Higgins 615, T09-93254795, www.canopypucon.cl. Has one of the longest runs as well as being the most responsible safety-wise.

Fishing

Pucón and Villarrica are celebrated as bases for fishing on Lago Villarrica and on the beautiful Lincura, Trancura and Toltén rivers. The local tourist office will supply details on licences and open seasons etc. Prices are much more reasonable than further south. **Mario's Fishing Zone**, O'Higgins 580, T045-444259, www.pucon.com/fishing. Expensive, but good fishing guide. **Off Limits**, O'Higgins 560, T045-442681, www.offlimits.cl. Fishing specialists, English and Italian spoken, offer fly-fishing excursions and courses between half and three days. Recommended. Birdwatching trips also offered as well as cycle hire.

Horse riding

Horse hire is about US$40 half day, US$70 full day; enquire at **La Tetera** in Pucón, or try **Rancho de Callabos** at the Termas de Palguín; for both see Sleeping above. **Centro de Turismo Ecuestre Huepil-Malal**, T09-96432673, www.huepil-malal.cl. Small groups, excursions ranging from half-day to 11-day trips to Argentina.

Mountaineering

Outdoor Experience, Urrutia, next to **Hostal école**, T045-442809, www.outdoorexperience.org. Runs mountaineering trips for people of all levels. Experienced guides. It also organizes excursions to the Cañi nature reserve.

Skiing

Pucón resort, 35 mins from Pucón on the slopes of the Villarrica Volcano, T045-441901, www.skipucon.cl. The resort is owned by **Gran Hotel Pucón**, which can provide information on snow, ski lifts and, perhaps, transport; otherwise consult the tourist office in Pucón. There are 8 lifts (day ticket US$23-33, depending on the season, US$7 to the restaurant only), though rarely do more than 2 or 3 work and piste preparation is mediocre. The snow is generally soft and good for beginners, though more advanced skiers can try the steeper areas. The season runs from mid-July to mid-Sep (longer during exceptionally good years). The ski centre offers equipment rental (US$20 per day, US$110 per week), ski instruction, first aid, and has a restaurant and bar with wonderful views from the terrace.

Tour operator

Travel Aid, Ansorena 425, local 4, T045-444040, www.travelaid.cl. Helpful general travel agency selling trekking maps, guidebooks, lots of other information, agents for **Navimag** and other boat trips. English and German spoken.

Whitewater rafting and Volcán Villarrica trek

Most operators can arrange a variety of trips, including climbing Villarrica, 12 hrs, US$70 including park entry, equipment provided; ski hire and transport to slopes US$25 per person; tours to Termas de Huife, US$25 including entry. Whitewater rafting, Trancura bajo (basic, Grade II-III) US$25, Trancura alto (advanced, Grade III-IV) US$40. Shop around, prices vary, as well as the quality of guides and equipment. Unfortunately, while several agencies offer acceptable levels of service, none is exceptional. To reach the falls, lakes and *termas* it is cheaper for groups to flag down a taxi and negotiate a price. Also try **Hostería école**, see Sleeping above.

Aguaventura, Palguín 336, T045-444246, www.aguaventura.com. French-run kayaking and rafting specialists.

Anden Sport, O'Higgins 535, T045-441475, www.andensport.cl. Skiing specialist, but also does volcano trips. Slightly disorganized.

Enjoy Tour, Ansorena 123, T045-442303, www.enjoytour.cl. Owned by the upmarket **Hotel del Lago**. Prices are slightly above average, but equipment is generally first rate.

Politur, O'Higgins635, T045-441373, www.politur.com. Good for volcano trek and rafting. A little more expensive than most, but generally responsible.

Ronco Track, O'Higgins 615, esq Arauco, T045-449597, roncotrack@hotmail.com. Small group quadbike excursions from 1½ hrs to 1½ days. Good fun. Rents good-quality bicycles.

Sol y Nieve O'Higgins, esq Lincoyán, T/F045-441070, www.solynieve.cl. Previously held in high esteem, with guides and equipment, but now some mixed reports about organization. Most guides speak English.

Spirit Palguín 323, T/F045-442481, www.spiritexplora.com. Offers the usual tours as well as diving and canyoning.

Sur Expediciones, O'Higgins 615. One of the better agencies for the volcano trip.

Trancura, O'Higgins 211, T045-443436, www.trancura.com. The biggest agency in Pucón with several branches. Very competitive prices but lax safety record. Recommended for trips to thermal springs but not for any sort of adventure tourism.

Watersports

Equipment for water-skiing (US$13 for 15 mins), dinghy sailing (lasers US$16 per hr) and windsurfing (sailboards US$13 per hr) can be hired in summer at Playa Grande, the beach by the **Gran Hotel**. Rowing boats can also be hired for US$6 per hr. The outlets on La Poza beach are more expensive and not recommended.

Parque Nacional Villarrica *p200*

Tours from Pucón cost US$70, including park entry, guide, transport to park entrance and hire of equipment (no reduction for those with their own equipment). Bargain for group rates. Travel agencies will not start out if the weather is bad and some travellers have experienced difficulties in obtaining a refund: establish in advance what terms apply in the event of cancellation and be prepared to wait a few days. For information on individual guides, all with equipment, ask for recommendations at the tourist office.

Lagos Panguipulli and Pirehueico *p203*

Fishing

The following fishing trips on Lago Panguipulli are recommended: **Puntilla Los Cipreses** at the mouth of the Río Huanehue, 11 km east of Panguipulli, 30 mins by boat; the mouth of the **Río Niltre**, on east side of lake. Boat hire US$3, licences available from the Municipalidad, Librería Colón, O'Higgins 528, or from **Club de Pesca**.

Whitewater rafting

Good rafting opportunities on the **Río Fuy**, Grade IV-V; **Río San Pedro**, varying grades, and on the **Río Llanquihue** near Choshuenco.

Transport

Temuco *p196, map p205*

Air

LanChile and **Sky** fly to Manquehue airport from **Santiago**, 1¼ hrs, **Osorno**, 40 mins, and **Puerto Montt**, 45 mins.

Airline offices LanChile, Bulnes 687, on Plaza, T600-5262000; **Sky Airline**, T600-600 2828 for information.

Bus

Local Services to neighbouring towns leave from **Terminal Rural**, Pinto y Balmaceda or from bus company offices nearby: **Erbuc**, Miraflores y Bulnes; **JAC**, **NarBus** and **Igi Llaima**, Balmaceda y Aldunate; **Tur Bus**, Lagos 549.

JAC runs buses to **Villarrica** and **Pucón**, many daily 0705-2045, 1½ hrs, US$4, and to **Coñaripe**, 3 hrs, and **Lican Ray**, 2 hrs. To **Panguipulli**, Power and Pangui Sur, 3 hrs, US$4. **Pangui Sur** also has services to **Loncoche**, US$2 and **Los Lagos**, US$3.

Long distance The terminal is north of city at Pérez Rosales y Caupolicán; to get there, take buses 2, 7 or 10 from the centre. To **Santiago**, several companies, 9 hrs, most overnight, US$11 (*salón cama* US$22); to **Valdivia** 2½hrs, US$5; to **Osorno** 4hrs, US$5; to **Puerto Montt**, **Cruz del Sur**, 10 daily, 5½ hrs, US$10; to **Castro** (Chiloé), **Cruz del Sur**, 3 daily; also buses to cities further north.

To Argentina To **Neuquén** via Pucón, Paso Tromen and Junín de los Andes, **Buses San Martín**, 3 a week, US$15. To **Neuquén** via Curacautín, Lonquimay and the Paso Pino Hachado, **Igi Llaima**, **Buses Caraza** and **Buses El Valle**, daily between them, US$25; see page 72 for onward services from Neuquén. To **Bariloche** via Osorno, **Tas Choapa**, daily, US$23; see page 103 for onward services.

Car hire

Automóvil Club de Chile, Varas 687, T045-248903 and at airport; **Budget**, Lynch 471, T045-214911; **Euro**, MacKenna 426, T045-210311, helpful, good value; **Full Famas**, at airport and in centre T045-215420, recommended. Several others.

Train

The **station** is at Barros Arana y Lautaro Navarro, T045-233416, www.efe.cl. There is also another ticket office at Bulnes 582, T045-233522, Mon-Fri 0900-1300, 1430- 1800, Sun 0900-1300. To **Santiago**, overnight service on a modern train, daily 2200, 10 hrs, *Preferente* US$22-35, *salón* US$19-26. There is a connecting bus service from Pucón at 1900. There is a somewhat unreliable service south of Temuco as far as **Puerto Montt**.

Villarrica *p198*

Bus

The main terminal is at Pedro de Valdivia y Muñoz; **JAC** has 2 terminals, at Muñoz y Bilbao (long-distance) and opposite for Pucón and Lican-Ray (local). Other services leave from the **Terminal Rural**, Matta y Vicente Reyes.

Buses to **Santiago**, 10 hrs, US$15, *salón cama* US30, several companies; to **Pucón**, both **Vipu-Ray** (main terminal) and **JAC**, every 15 mins in summer, 40-min journey, US$1; to **Puerto Montt**, US$8; to **Valdivia**, **JAC**, 5 a day, 2½ hrs, US$5; to **Lican-Ray** services in summer, **JAC** and **Vipu-Ray**, US$1.50; to **Coñaripe**, US$2, and **Liquiñe** at 1600 Mon-Sat, 1000 Sun; to **Temuco**, **JAC**, every 30 mins in summer, US$4; to **Loncoche** (Route 5 junction for hitching), US$2. There are also occasional direct buses to **Panguipulli**, via Lican Ray.

To Argentina Buses from Temuco to Junín de los Andes stop in Villarrica en route to Paso Tromen; fares are the same as from Temuco, see page 212. There are no services from Villarrica when the Tromen pass is blocked by snow; buses go via Paso Carirriñe.

Car and bicycle hire

Car hire: **Christopher Car**, Pedro de Valdivia 1061, T/045-F413980; **Castillo Propiedades**, Anfion Muñoz 417, good value. Bike hire: **Mora Bicicletas**, Körner 760, helpful.

Pucón *p198, map p207*

Air

Lan Express flies to **Santiago**, 4 times weekly in summer. **LanChile**, Urrutia 103 y Caupolican, T045-443516, Mon-Sat 1000-1400, 1800-2200.

Bus

There is no municipal terminal; each company has its own: **JAC**, Uruguay y Palguín; **Tur Bus**, O'Higgins 910, east of town; **Igi Llaima** and **Condor**, Colo Colo south of O'Higgins.

To **Villarrica**, **JAC**, every 15 mins, US$1; to **Valdivia**, **JAC**, 5 daily, US$6; to **Temuco** hourly, 2 hrs, US$4, or *rápido*, 1½ hrs, US$5; to **Puerto Montt**, 6 hrs, US$9, daily with **Tur Bus**, or change at Valdivia. To **Santiago**, morning and evening, 10 hrs, US$15; *salón cama* service by **Tur Bus** and **JAC**, US$33.

To Argentina Buses from Temuco to **Junín de los Andes** arrive in Pucón at 1000; for fares see Temuco, page 212. There are no services from Pucón, when the Tromen pass is blocked by snow.

Car and bicycle hire

Christopher Car, O'Higgins 335, T/F045-449013; **Hertz**, Fresia 220, T045-441664, more expensive; **Pucón Rent A Car**, Camino Internacional 1395, T045- 441922, kernayel@cepri.cl; **Sierra Nevada**, Palguín y O'Higgins, also 4WDs.

Bicycles cost US$2 per hr or US$7 for 5 hrs from several travel agencies, many on O'Higgins; shop around as quality varies

Taxi
Taxis are useful for out-of-town trips: Cooperative, T045-441009.

Lago Caburga and around *p199*
JAC runs buses from Pucón to **Caburga**, several daily, US$1.50; there are also minibuses every 30 mins from Ansorena y Uruguay in Pucón. Tour agencies arrange transport for groups to **Parque Nacional Huerquehue**, US$8. Taxis cost US$35 return to Caburga. Minibuses from Ansorena y Brasil.

Towards Paso Mamuil Malal *p201*
Several minibuses daily to **Curarrehue** from Pucón. Daily bus from Pucón to the **border**, 1800, 2 hrs, US$3, returns to Pucón 0700.

Lago Calafquén and around *p202*
From Lican-Ray, buses leave from offices around the plaza to **Villarrica**, JAC, frequent, 1 hr, US$1.50; to **Santiago**, Tur Bus and JAC, 10 hrs, US$14, *salón cama* US$40; to **Temuco**, JAC 2½ hrs, US$6; to **Coñaripe**, 4-7 daily.

From Coñaripe, buses run to **Panguipulli**, 7 daily (4 off season), US$2; to **Villarrica**, 16 daily, US$2; to **Lican-Ray**, 45 mins, US$1. Also a nightly bus direct to **Santiago** run by Tur Bus and JAC, 11½ hrs, US$15, *salón cama* in summer US$40.

Lagos Panguipulli & Pirehueico *p203*
Bus
The bus terminal in Panguipulli is at Gabriela Mistral y Portales. To **Santiago** daily, US$15; to **Valdivia**, Mon-Sat, 4 only on Sun, several companies, 2 hrs, US$5; to **Temuco**, frequent, Power and Pangui Sur, US$5; to **Puerto Montt**, US$8; to **Calafquén**, 3 daily at 1200, 1545 and 1600; to **Choshuenco**, **Neltume** and **Puerto Fuy** (3 hrs), 3 daily, US$4.5; to **Coñaripe**, for Lican-Ray and Villarrica, 4-7 daily.

Ferry
The *Hua Hum* ferry sails across Lago Pirehueico from **Puerto Fuy** to **Puerto Pirehueico**, twice daily in summer, twice a week, other times, 2-3 hrs, foot passengers US$2, cars US$20. For reservations and information see www.panguipulli.cl/pasohuahum/index.html. This is a recommended journey and compares with the famous lakes crossing from Puerto Montt to Bariloche but at a fraction of the price. The ferry connects with buses to **San Martín de los Andes** (Argentina), via Paso Hua Hum, daily in summer, weekly in winter (out Sat 0930, return Sun 1330).

Directory

Temuco *p196, map p205*
Banks and currency exchange ATMs at several banks on or around Plaza A Pinto also at the new JAC bus terminal. There are many *cambios* around the Plaza; all deal in dollars and Argentine pesos. **Honorary consulate** Netherlands, España 494, honorary consul, Germán Nicklas, is friendly and helpful. **Internet** Gral MacKenna 445; several others, generally US$0.75 per hr. **Laundry** Alba, Zeneto 480, opposite the church, and at Aldunate 324 and Aldunate 842; Marva, M Montt 415 and 1099, Mon-Sat 0900-2030. **Post office** Portales 839. **Telephone** CTC, A Prat just off Claro Solar and plaza, Mon-Sat 0800-2400, Sun and holidays 1030-2400; Entel, Bulnes 303, daily 0830-2200; also call centres at Lautaro 1311 and Montt 631.

Villarrica *p198*
Banks and currency exchange There are ATMs at the major banks. Rates at *casas de cambio* are generally poor. Exceptions are: Central de Repuestos, Muñoz 415, and Cristopher, Valdivia 1061, for TCs. **Internet** Cybercafé Salmon, Letelier y Henríquez. **Laundry** Lavacenter, Alderete 770; Lavandería y Lavaseco Villarrica, Andrés Bello 348. **Post office** Muñoz y Urrutia, Mon-Fri 0900-1300, 1430-1800, Sat 0900-1300. **Telephone** CTC, Henríquez 544; Chilesat, Henriquez 473; Entel, Henríquez 440 and 575.

Pucón *p198, map p207*
Banks and currency exchange
There are 3 or 4 banks with ATMs on o'Higgins. Several casas de cambio on O'Higgins, although rates are universally poor. Much better to change money in Temuco. **Internet** Several on O´Higgins. **Laundry** Urrutia 520; Palguín 460; Fresia 224; Colo-Colo 475 and 478, several others. **Post office** Fresia 183. **Telephone** CTC, Gen Urrutia 472; Entel, Ansorena 299.

Southern lakes

The southern lakes are the real gateway to Patagonia. The virgin forest becomes thicker, the volcanoes more remarkable, the settlements fewer. In spite of the fact that tourism is booming on Llanquihue and Todos Los Santos, there are numerous spots where you can still escape to the old heart of Patagonia. And with activities from windsurfing and horse trekking to ice climbing, this region will keep even the most active traveller happily occupied. ▸▸ *For Sleeping, Eating and other listings, see pages 221-230.*

Ins and outs

Getting there Osorno is a key crossroads for bus routes in southern Chile and to the Argentine Lake District. Passengers heading for Bariloche, Neuquén, Coyhaique or Punta Arenas will pass through here before making for the Puyehue Pass into Argentina. There are hourly local services to Puerto Montt and frequent services north to Temuco and Valdivia. Puerto Varas is the main centre on Lago Llanquihue and is served by shuttle buses from Puerto Montt every few minutes; there are connections north to Osorno, Valdivia, Temuco and Santiago and east across Lago Todos Los Santos to Bariloche. A taxi to Puerto Varas from Puerto Montt airport costs US$22.

Getting around There are local bus services around Lago Llanquihue but the eastern shore is difficult to visit without your own transport. Beyond Las Cascadas, the road is narrow with lots of blind corners, necessitating speeds of 20-30 kph at best in places. There is almost no public transport on this section and hitching is very difficult. Minibuses run along the southern shore of the lake to Ensenada for access to the Parque Nacional Vicente Pérez Rosales. ▸▸ *For further details, see Transport, page 229.*

Tourist information Information is available form the regional government office of **Sernatur** ⓘ *Gobernación Provincial building, Plaza de Armas, Puerto Montt, T065-256999,* and from **CONAF** ⓘ *Rosas 430, Osorno, T064-234393*. Puerto Varas has a **tourist office** ⓘ *in the Municipalidad, San Francisco 413, T065-321330*. Other places in town also claim to offer information, but may only give information about their paying members' services. There is no general information centre for Lago Llanquihue, but each town has its own municipal tourist office.

Osorno and around ▸▸ *pp221-230.*

Situated at the confluence of the Ríos Rahue and Damas, Osorno is grey and nondescript and has little to attract tourists, but if you're travelling by bus, you're likely to just pass through it. Founded in 1553, the city was abandoned in 1604 and was refounded by Ambrosio O'Higgins and Juan MacKenna O'Reilly in 1796. It later became one of the centres of German immigration to Chile. The **municipal tourist office** is based in the bus terminal and in a kiosk on the Plaza de Armas, both open December to February, and offer free **city tours** ⓘ *Mon-Fri 1500 and 1700, Jan-Feb only, book in advance.*

Sights → *See map page 222. Colour map 1, B2.*

On the large **Plaza de Armas** stands the modern, concrete and glass cathedral, with many arches and a tower that is itself an open, latticed arch with a cross superimposed. West of the centre on a bend overlooking the river is the **Fuerte María Luisa,** built in 1793 and restored in 1977; only the river front walls and end turrets are still standing. East of the main plaza along Calle MacKenna are a number of late 19th-century wooden mansions built by German immigrants, now preserved as national monuments. Two blocks south of the Plaza is the **Museo Histórico Municipal** ⓘ *Matta 809, summer daily 1100-1900; winter Mon-Fri 0930-1730, Sat 1500-1800, US$1.50*, which has displays on natural history, Mapuche culture, the refounding of the city and German colonization. Three blocks southwest of the plaza, in the former train station, is the **Museo Interactivo de Osorno (MIO)** ⓘ *T064-212996, www.municipalidadosorno.cl, Mon-Thu 0815-1300, 1445-1815, Fri 0815-1300, 1445-1745, Sat 1415-1745*, an interaactive science museum designed for both children and adults.

East of Los Lagos

The southernmost of the Seven Lakes, **Lago Riñihue**, is most easily reached from Los Lagos on the Pan American Highway. **Riñihue**, a beautiful but small and isolated village at its western end, is worth visiting but the road around the southern edge of the lake from Riñihue to Enco is closed and there is no road around the northern edge of the lake.

South of Lago Riñihue is **Lago Ranco**, one of the largest lakes in the region, covering 41,000 ha. It has a rough road round its edge, characterized by lots of mud and animals, including oxcarts. However it is worth taking the opportunity to witness an older lifestyle and to see the beautiful lake, starred with islands, and the sun setting on the distant volcanoes. There is excellent fishing on the southern shore around the ugly town of Lago Ranco and to the west around **Puerto Nuevo**; several hotels organize fishing expeditions. The main town on the northern shore is **Futrono**, which has a daily boat service to **Huapi**, the island in the middle of the lake. On the eastern shore is **Llifén**, Km 22, a picturesque place, from where it is possible visit **Lago Maihue**, 33 km further east. From Llifén the road around Lago Ranco continues via the Salto de Nilahue (Km 14) to **Riñinahue**, Km 23, with access to beaches.

Lago Puyehue and around → *Colour map 1, B3*

Surrounded by relatively flat countryside, 47 km east of Osorno, **Lago Puyehue** extends over 15,700 ha. The southern shore is much more developed than the northern shore, which is accessible only by unpaved road from **Entre Lagos** at the western end. On the opposite side of the lake are the **Termas de Puyehue** ⓘ *daily 0900-2000, US$5 outdoor, US$18 indoor*, an upmarket spa resort with extensive facilities (see page 226). Two thermal pools are open to day visitors. From the

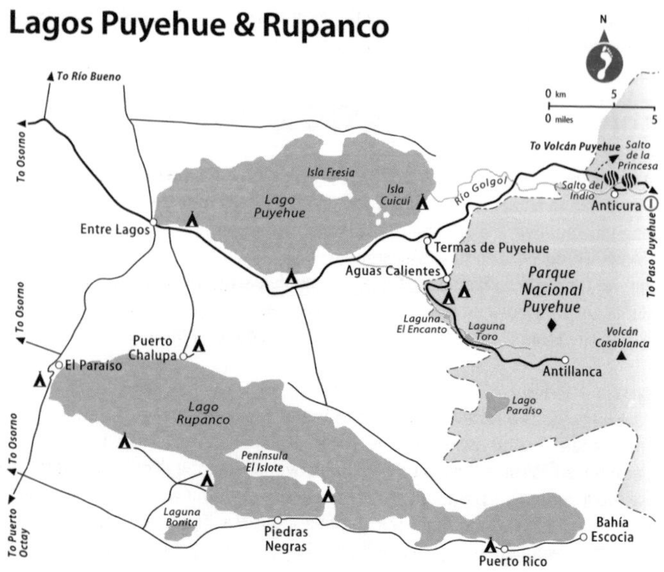

termas, Route 215 heads northeast to the Anticura sector of Parque Nacional Puyehue and on towards the border, while another road leads southeast to the Aguas Calientes and Antillanca sectors of the park.

Parque Nacional Puyehue → *Colour map 1, B3*

Stretching east from Lago Puyehue to the Argentine frontier, **Parque Nacional Puyehue** covers 107,000 ha, much of it in the valley of the Río Golgol. On the eastern side are several lakes, including Lago Constancia and Lago Gris. There are two volcanic peaks: **Volcán Puyehue** (2240 m) in the north (access via a private track US$10) and **Volcán Casablanca** (also called Antillanca, 1900 m). Leaflets on walks are available from the park administration at Aguas Calientes and from the ranger station at Anticura.

Four kilometres southeast of the Termas de Puyehue, in a thickly forested valley beside the Río Chanleufú, is **Aguas Calientes** ⓘ *Mon-Fri 0830-1230, 1400-1800 in summer only; Sat, Sun and holidays 0830-2030 all year; outdoor pool US$3; indoor pool US$8*, where you'll find the park administration and a dirty, open-air pool with very hot thermal water. From Aguas Calientes the road continues 18 km past three small lakes and through forests to the ski resort at **Antillanca** on the slopes of Volcán Casablanca. In winter (and sometimes summer, depending on the weather) a one-way traffic system operates on the last 8 km of the narrow and icy road: ascending traffic 0800-1200 and 1400-1730; descending traffic from 1200-1400 and after 1730. This is a particularly beautiful area of the park, especially at sunrise, with views over Lago Puyehue to the north and Lagos Rupanco and Llanquihue to the south, as well as the snow-clad peaks of Calbuco, Osorno, Puntiagudo, Puyehue and Tronador forming a semicircle. From Antillanca it is possible to climb Casablanca for even better views; there's no path and the hike takes about seven hours there and back; information from **Club Andino** in Osorno.

The paved Route 215, meanwhile, heads northeast from the Termas de Puyehue to **Anticura**. In this section of the park are three waterfalls, including the spectacular 40-m wide **Salto del Indio**. Legend has it that an Indian, enslaved by the Spanish, was able to escape by hiding behind the falls. Situated just off the road, the falls are on a marked path through dense forest that includes a 800-year-old Coihue tree known as 'El Abuelo'. The **Argentine border** at Paso Puyehue is reached 26 km east of Anticura (see page 87).

Lago Rupanco → *Colour map 1, B2/B3*

Lying south of Lago Puyehue and considerably larger, this lake covers 23,000 ha and is far less accessible and less developed for tourism than most of the other larger lakes. Access from the northern shore is via two unpaved roads that branch off Route 215. **El Paraíso** (aka Marina Rupanco), at the western tip of the lake, can be reached by an unpaved road south from Entre Lagos. A 40-km dirt road runs along the southern shore, via **Laguna Bonita**, a small lake surrounded by forest, and **Piedras Negras** to **Bahía Escocia** at the eastern end. From the south, access is from two turnings off the road between Osorno and Las Cascadas.

Puerto Varas and Lago Llanquihue

» pp221-230.

→ *See map page 224. Colour map 1, B2.*

The second largest lake in Chile and the third largest natural lake in South America, Lago Llanquihue is one of the highlights of the Lake District. Three snow-capped volcanoes can be seen across the vast expanse of water: the perfect cone of Osorno (2680 m), the shattered cone of Calbuco (2015 m) and the spike of Puntiagudo (2,480 m), as well as, when the air is clear, the distant Tronador (3460 m). On a cloudless night with a full moon, the snows reflect eerily in the lake and the peace and stillness are hard to match.

Situated on the southwestern corner of the lake, Puerto Varas is the commercial and tourist centre of Lago Llanquihue. In the 19th century Puerto Chico (on the southern outskirts) was the southern port for shipping on the lake. With the arrival of the railway the settlement moved to its current location and is now a resort, popular with South American tourists. Despite the numbers of visitors, it has a friendly, compact feel and its location near centres for trekking, rafting, canyoning and fly fishing make it one of the best bases for exploring the southern Lake District. It can also be used as an alternative to Puerto Montt for catching the Navimag ferry.

Around town

Parque Philippi, on top of a hill, is a pleasant place to visit, although the views are a bit restricted by trees and the metal cross at the top is unattractive. To reach the summit walk up to **Hotel Cabañas del Lago** on Klenner, cross the railway and the gate is on the right. The centre lies at the foot of the hill, but the town stretches east along the lake to **Puerto Chico**, where there are hotels and restaurants. The imposing **Catholic church** was built by German Jesuits in 1918 in Baroque style as a copy of a church in the Black Forest. North and east of the **Gran Hotel Puerto Varas** (1934) are a number of German-style mansions.

The southern shore

Puerto Varas is a good base for trips around the lake. A paved road runs along the south shore to Ensenada on the southwestern corner of the lake. Two of the best beaches are **Playa Hermosa**, Km 7 and **Playa Niklitschek**, Km 8, where an entry fee is charged. At Km 16 narrow channels overhung with vegetation lead south from Lago Llanquihue to the little lake of **La Poza**. There are boat trips (US$2.50) to the beautiful **Isla Loreley**, on the lake, and a channel leads from La Poza to yet another lake, the **Laguna Encantada**. At Km 21 there is a watermill and a restaurant run by the Club Alemán.

Frutillar and the western shore → *See map page 225. Colour map 1, B2.*

Lying about half-way along the western side of the lake, Frutillar is in fact two towns: **Frutillar Alto**, just off the main highway, and **Frutillar Bajo**, beautifully situated on the lakeside, 4 km away. The latter is possibly the most attractive and expensive town on the lake, with superb views from the *costanera* over the water with volcanoes Osorno and Tronador in the background. The town's atmosphere is very German and somewhat snobbish, but the **tourist office** ⓘ *on the lakeside, T065-420198, summer only*, is helpful. In the square opposite is an open-air chess board and the **Club Alemán** restaurant. A new concert hall has recently been built on the lakeside to host the town's prestigious music festival in late January (see Festivals and events, page 227).

Away from the waterfront, the appealing **Museo Colonial Alemán** ⓘ *off Prat, summer daily 1000-1930; winter Tue-Sun 1000-1330, 1500-1800, US$3*, is set in spacious gardens, with a watermill, replicas of two German colonial houses with furnishings and utensils of the period and a blacksmith's shop selling personally engraved horseshoes for US$8. It also has a *campanario*, a circular barn with agricultural machinery and carriages inside, as well as a handicraft shop. At the northern end of the town is the **Reserva Forestal Edmundo Winckler**, run by the Universidad de Chile and extending over 33 ha, with a guided trail through native woods. Named after one of the early German settlers, it includes a very good collection of native flora as well as plants introduced from Europe.

Some 20 km south of Frutillar, **Llanquihue** lies at the source of the Río Maullín, which drains the lake. The site of a large dairy processing factory, this is the least touristy town on the lake, and makes a cheaper alternative to Puerto Varas and Frutillar. It has uncrowded beaches and hosts a German-style beer festival at the end of January.

Puerto Octay → *Colour map 1, B2*

Puerto Octay is a small town at the north tip of the lake. It's 56 km southeast of Osorno, set amid rolling hills, hedgerows and German-style farmhouses with views over the Osorno volcano. Founded by German settlers in 1852, the town enjoyed a boom period in the late 19th century when it was the northern port for steamships on the lake: a few buildings survive from that period, notably the church and the enormous German-style former convent. Since the arrival of railways and the building of roads, the town has declined. Much less busy than Frutillar or Puerto Varas, Puerto Octay offers an escape for those seeking peace and quiet.

Museo el Colono ⓘ *Independencia 591, Tue-Sun 1000-1300, 1500-1900, Dec-Feb only*, has displays on German colonization. Another part of the museum, housing agricultural implements and machinery for making *chicha*, is just outside town on the road towards **Centinela**. This peninsula, about 3 km south (taxi US$2 one way) along an unpaved road has accommodation, camping, a launch dock, bathing beaches and watersports. It is a very popular spot in good weather, especially for picnics, with fine views of the Osorno, Calbuco and Puntiagudo volcanoes.

Eastern shore

The eastern lakeside, with the Osorno volcano on your left is very beautiful. From Puerto Octay two roads run towards Ensenada, one *ripio* along the shore, and one paved. (They join up after 20 km.) At Km 10 along the lakeside route is **Playa Maitén**, a lovely beach, often deserted, with a great view of Volcán Osorno. Continue for another 24 km past **Puerto Fonck**, which has fine 19th century mansions, and you'll reach **Las Cascadas**, surrounded by picturesque agricultural land, old houses and German cemeteries. To reach the waterfalls that give the village its name follow signs along a *ripio* road east to a car park, continue along a footpath over two or three log bridges over a stream, and after a final wade across you will arrive at a 40-m high natural cauldron, with the falls in the middle. The round trip takes about one-and-a-half hours.

Volcán Osorno → *Colour map 1, B3*

The most lasting image of Lago Llanquihue is the near perfect cone of Volcán Osorno, situated north of Ensenada on the eastern edge of the lake. Although the peak is on the edge of the Parque Nacional Pérez Rosales (see page 220), it is climbed from the western side, which lies outside the park. Access is via two roads that branch off the Ensenada-Puerto Octay road along the eastern edge of Lago Llanquihue: the northern one at Puerto Klocker, 20 km south of Puerto Octay; the other 2 km north of Ensenada (turning unmarked, high clearance vehicle necessary).

Guided ascents of the volcano – with transport from Puerto Montt or Puerto Varas, food and equipment – are organized by agencies in Puerto Varas (see page 233), weather permitting. Weather conditions are checked the day before and a 50% refund is available if the climb is abandoned due to weather. Guided ascents start from the *refugio* at **La Burbuja**, from where it is six hours to the summit. Those climbing from La Burbuja must register with **CONAF** and show they have suitable equipment. The volcano can also be climbed from the north (La Picada); this route is easier and may be attempted without a guide, although only experienced climbers should attempt the summit as ice climbing equipment is essential. ⏩ *See Activities and tours, page 228.*

Ensenada → *Colour map 1, B3*

Despite its lack of a recognizable centre, Ensenada is beautifully situated at the southeast corner of Lago Llanquihue, almost beneath the snows of Volcán Osorno. A good half-day trip from Ensenada is to **Laguna Verde**, about 30 minutes from **Hotel Ensenada**, along a beautiful circular trail behind the lake (take first fork to the right behind the information board), and down the road to a secluded campsite at Puerto Oscuro on Lago Llanquihue.

Parque Nacional Vicente Pérez Rosales

▸▸ *pp221-230.*

ⓘ *CONAF administration, Petrohué. Also a guardaparque office in Peulla. Hourly minibuses in summer from Puerto Montt, Puerto Varas and Ensenada to Petrohué; it is impossible to reach the national park independently out of season.*

Established in 1926, this is the oldest national park in Chile, stretching east from Lago Llanquihue to the Argentine frontier. The park is covered in woodland and contains a large lake, Lago Todos Los Santos, plus three major volcanic peaks: Osorno, Puntiagudo and Tronador. Several other peaks are visible, notably Casablanca to the north and Calbuco to the south. Near the lake are the Saltos de Petrohué, waterfalls on the Río Petrohué. A memorable journey by road and water takes you through the park from Puerto Montt to Bariloche in Argentina (see pages 95 and 239). A combination of walking and hitching rides in locals' boats is the best way to explore the park. No maps are available in the park; buy them from a tour agency in Puerto Varas (see page 228). In wet weather many treks are impossible.

Lago Todos Los Santos → *Colour map 1, B3*

The most beautiful of all the lakes in southern Chile, Lago Todos Los Santos is a long, irregularly shaped sheet of emerald-green water, surrounded by a deeply wooded shoreline and punctuated by several small islands that rise from its surface. Beyond the hilly shores to the east are several graceful snow-capped mountains, with the mighty Tronador in the distance. To the north is the sharp point of **Cerro Puntiagudo**,

Parque Nacional Pérez Rosales & the lakes route to Argentina

and at the northeastern end **Cerro Techado** rises cliff-like out of the water. The lake is fed by several rivers, including the Río Peulla to the east, the ríos Techado and Negro to the north, and the Río Blanco to the south. At its western end the lake is drained by the Río Petrohué. The lake is warm and sheltered from the winds, and is a popular location for watersports, swimming and for trout and salmon fishing. The only scheduled vessel on the lake is the **Andina del Sud** service between Petrohué and Peulla, with connections to Puerto Montt and Bariloche. There are no roads round Lagos Todos Los Santos and only those with houses on the lakeshore are allowed access by boat, but private launches can be hired for trips.

Petrohué and around → *Colour map 1, B3*

At the western end of the lake, 16 km northwest of Ensenada, **Petrohué** is a good base for walking tours with several trails around the foot of Volcán Osorno, or to the *miradors* that look over it, such as **Cerro Picada**. The Petrohué office of **CONAF** incorporates a visitor centre, small museum and three dimensional model of the national park.

Near the Ensenada-Petrohué road, 6 km west of Petrohué, is the **Salto de Petrohué** ⓘ *US$2*, which was formed by a relatively recent lava flow of hard volcanic rock. Near the falls are a snack bar and two short trails, the Sendero de los Enamorados and the Sendero Carileufú. Boat trips from Petrohué visit **Isla Margarita**, the largest island on the lake, with a lagoon in the middle of it, in summer only, and boats can also be hired to visit the **Termas de Callao** – actually two large Alerce tubs in a cabin – north of the lake. The boat will drop you at the uninhabited El Rincón (arrange for it to wait or collect you later), from where it's a 3½-hour walk to the baths through forest beside the Río Sin Nombre. The path twice crosses the river by rickety hanging bridges. Just before the baths is a house, doubling as a comfortable *refugio*, where you collect the keys and pay.

Peulla and around → *Colour map 1, B3*

Peulla, at the eastern end of the lake, is a good starting point for hikes in the mountains. The **Cascadas Los Novios**, signposted above the **Hotel Peulla**, are a steep walk away, but are stunning once you reach them. There is also a good walk to **Laguna Margarita**, which takes four hours. Peulla is also the location of Chilean immigration and customs for those crossing into Argentina via the **Paso Pérez Rosales**, see page 97.

Cayutué and around → *Colour map 1, B3*

On the south shore of Lago Todos Los Santos is the little village of **Cayutué**, reached by hiring a boat from Petrohué, US$30. From Cayutué (no camping on the beach but there are private sites) it is a three-hour walk to **Laguna Cayutué**, a jewel set between mountains and surrounded by forest, where you can camp and swim. From the laguna it is a five-hour hike south to **Ralún** on the Reloncaví estuary (see page 232): the last half of this route is along a *ripio* road built for extracting timber and is part of the old route used by missionaries in the colonial period to travel between Nahuel Huapi in Argentina and the island of Chiloé.

Sleeping

Osorno *p215, map p222*

A Inter-Lagos, Cochrane 515, T064-234695, www.hotelinterlagos.cl. Small 3-star with decent sized rooms, parking, restaurant.

B Gran Hotel Osorno, O'Higgins 615, T064-232171, granhotelosorno@entelchile.net. Cable TV, well furnished. Comfortable 3-star.

C Eduviges, Eduviges 856, T064-235023, www.hoteleduviges.cl. Cheaper rooms without bath. Spacious, clean, quiet, attractive, gardens, also *cabañas* and restaurant. Laundry and internet facilities. Recommended.

C-D Residencial Riga, Amthauer 1058, T064-232945, resriga@telsur.cl. Clean, pleasant. Internet. Recommended but booked ahead.

D Hostal Bilbao Express, Bilbao 1019, T064-262200, pazla@telsur.cl. With bath and breakfast, parking, restaurant. Also **Residencial Bilbao II**, MacKenna 1205, T064-264444.

D-E Residencial Hein's, Errázuriz 1757, T064-234116. **F** singles. Some rooms with bath. Old- fashioned, spacious, family atmosphere.

There are lots of cheap options (**E** or **F** singles) near the bus terminal, including the following: **Hospedaje de la Fuente**, Los Carrera 1587; **Residencial Ortega**, Colón y Errázuriz; **Residencial San Diego**, Los Carrera 1551; **Residencial Carillo**, Angulo 454.

Camping

Municipal site off Pan-American Highway near southern entrance to city, open Jan-Feb only, poor facilities, US$9 per site.

East of Los Lagos *p216*

A Hostería Huinca Quinay, 3 km east of Riñihue, Lago Riñihue, T063-1971811, gcristi@hotmail.com. 4-star *cabañas* with restaurant and lots of facilities.

A-B Hostería Chollinco, 3 km out of Llifén, on the road towards Lago Maihue in the Lago Ranco area, T063-1971979, www.hosteriachollinco.cl. Remote country lodge with swimming pool, trekking, horse riding, fishing, hunting and other activities.

A-B Riñimapu, northwest edge of Lago Riñihue, T063-311388, www.rinimapu.cl. Comfortable rooms and suites with views over the lake, excellent food.

B Huequecura, Llifén, T09-96535450. Includes meals and fishing, good restaurant.

D-E Hospedaje Futronhue, Balmaceda 90, Futrono, T063-481265. Good breakfast.

Camping

There are campsites all around Lago Ranco and several on Lago Maihue, though many are open in summer only and prices are high.

Lago Puyehue and around *p216*

A private house close to the *termas* provides cheap lodging, with full board available.

LL-AL Hotel Termas de Puyehue, Termas de Puyehue, T600-2936000, www.puyehue.cl. Large resort containing 2 thermal swimming pools (one indoors, very clean), theatre, conference centre, well maintained, meals expensive, beautiful scenery, heavily booked Jan-Feb (cheaper May to mid-Dec).

B Cabañas Ñilque, on the southern lake-shore, T064-371218, www.turismonilque.cl. Cabins (half-price May-Oct), fishing trips, watersports, car hire.

C Hospedaje Millaray, Ramírez 333, Entre Lagos, T064-371251. **F** singles. With breakfast, excellent, clean, friendly.

C Hostal y Cabañas Miraflores, Ramírez 480, Entre Lagos, T064-371275, olivia.hostalmiraflores@gmail.com. Pleasant rooms and cabins.

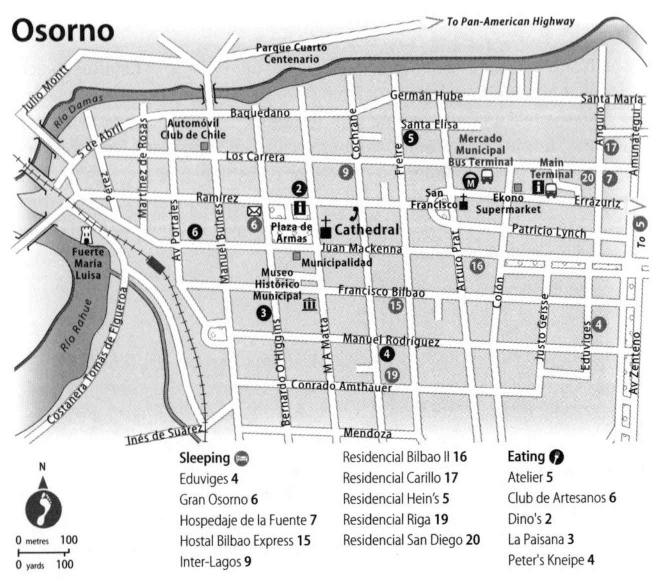

C Hostería Entre Lagos, Ramírez 65, Entre Lagos, T064-371225. Rooms with lake view.
E Ruta 215 Gasthaus, Osvaldo Muñoz 148, Entre Lagos, T064-371357. **F** singles with bath and good breakfast. Clean, friendly, German spoken. Good value.

Parque Nacional Puyehue *p217*
A Hotel Antillanca, at foot of Volcán Casablanca, T064-235114, www.skiantillanca.com. Attached to the antillanca ski resort, decent restaurant/café, pool, sauna, friendly atmosphere, also a *refugio*.

Camping
Camping No Me Olvides, Km 56, on southern lakeshore. US$15, also *cabañas*.
Chanleufu, Aguas Calientes, T064-236988. US$305 per site with hot water, also *cabañas*, an expensive café and a small shop.
Los Derrumbes, 1 km from Aguas Calientes. No electricity, US$25 per site.
Playa Los Copihues, Km 56.5, on the southern lakeshore. Hot showers, good.

There is also a CONAF *refugio* on Volcán Puyehue (check with CONAF in Anticura whether it is open) and a campsite beside the Río Chanleufú (US$5 pp).

Lago Rupanco *p217*
There is no accommodation on the northern shore of the lake.
AL-A Puntiagudo Lodge, Bahía Escocia, T064-1974731, www.puntiagudolodge.cl. With breakfast, very comfortable, good restaurant, fly-fishing, horse riding, boat excursions. Advance bookings only.
B-C Refugio Club de Pesca y Caza, Sector Islote, 7 km east of Piedras Negras, T064-232056. Basic *refugio* with breakfast and bath.

Camping
There are several campsites on the southern shore, including at Puerto Rico.
Desague del Rupanco, just south of El Paraíso. No facilities.
Puerto Chalupa, on northern shore, T064-232680. US$32 per site.

Puerto Varas *p217, map 224*
There are many hotels all along the lake front, but in high season can be tourist traps.
AL-A Cabañas del Lago, Klenner 195, T065-232291, www.cabanasdellago.cl. Recently rebuilt 4-star hotel on Philippi hill with superb views of the lake. Also self-catering *cabañas* sleeping 5, cheaper rates in low season, heating, sauna, swimming pool, games room, bar and restaurant.
AL Bellavista, Pérez Rosales 060, T065-232011, www.hotelbellavista.cl. 4 star with good views over the lake, king size beds, restaurant and bar, sauna, parking..
AL Colonos del Sur, Estación 505, T065-235555, www.colonosdelsur.cl. Overlooking the town, decent rooms, good restaurant and tea room. The sister hotel at Del Salvador 24, on the lakeside, is being refurbished.
AL-A Licarayén, San José 114, T065-232305, www.hotelicarayen.cl. Overlooking the lake, comfortable, clean, gym and sauna, 'the perfect place for bad weather'. Book in season.
A-B Gran Reserva, Mirador 134, T065-346876, www.granreserva.cl. New boutique hotel overlooking the town and lake. Conference centre and pleasant living room.
B El Greco, Mirador 104, T065-233388, www.hotelelgreco.cl. Recently refurbished German-style mansion with wooden interior and full of artworks. Simple rooms with bath and cable TV. A good choice.
B Terrazas del Lago, Pérez Rosales 1571, T/F065-232622. Good breakfast, views over Volcán Osorno, restaurant.
B-C Hostería Outsider, San Bernardo 318, T065-232910, www.turout.com. With bath, breakfast with real coffee, meals, friendly, comfortable. German and English spoken, book in advance.
C Amancay, Walker Martínez 564, T065-232201, cabamancay@chile.com. With bath and breakfast. Friendly, German spoken, also *cabañas*, sleep 4. Recommended.
C Canales del Sur, Pasage Ricke 224, T065-346620, www.canalesdelsur.com. Very friendly and helpful, tours arranged. Laundry, internet and car hire service.
C-D Casa Azul, Manzanal 66 y Rosario, T065-232904, www.casaazul.net. **F** pp in shared rooms. Some rooms with bath. German/Chilean owners, good buffet breakfast with homemade muesli (US$5 extra), large kitchen, good beds with duvets, central heating, internet, book exchange, comfortable common area, tours organized, friendly, helpful. Highly recommended.
C-D Compass del Sur, Klenner 467, T065-232044, compassdelsur.cl. **F** pp in

shared rooms. Kitchen facilities, internet, cable TV in comfortable lounge, good breakfast, friendly, helpful, lots of information, tours, highly recommended. Also camping, car hire.

C-D **Ellenhaus**, Walker Martínez 239, T065-233577, www.ellenhaus.cl. Some rooms with bath. **F** pp in dorms. Kitchen and laundry facilities, luggage stored, lounge, tours offered. German and English spoken, recommended.

D **Casa Margouya**, Santa Rosa 318, T065-511648, www.margouya.com. **F** pp in shared rooms. Bright and colourful hostel in the town centre with breakfast and kitchen facilities. Friendly, lots of info.

D **Hospedaje Carla Minte**, Maipo 1010, T065-232880. **F** singles. Rooms with bath and breakfast in a family home. Cable TV, very comfortable.

D **Las Dalias**, Santa Rosa 707, T065-233277, las_dalias@hotmail.com. **F** singles. Some rooms with bath. In a family home, peaceful , clean, good breakfast with real coffee, parking, German spoken.

D **Villa Germania**, Nuestra Sra del Carmen 873, T065-233162. **F-G** singles. Old wooden mansion north of the centre. Also *cabañas*.

E **Hospedaje Don Raúl**, Salvador 928, T065-310897, hospedajedonraul@ hotmail.com. **G** singles. Laundry and cooking facilities, very friendly, garden with hammock, clean. Recommended. Camping by main road.

Camping

Campo Aventura, San Bernardo 318, T065-232910, www.campo-aventura.com. 2 lodges with camping facilities, excellent horse riding, fishing, birdwatching, Spanish classes and vegetarian food.

Los Troncos, 10 km east of Puerto Varas, T09-9206869. US$15 per site, no beach access.

Playa Hermosa, 7 km east of Puerto Varas. Fancy ground, US$22 per site, bargain off season. Recommended. Take own supplies.

Playa Niklitschek, 8 km east of Puerto Varas, T065-338352. Full facilities.

Trauco, Imperial 433, T065-236262. Expensive but central (in Puerto Varas).

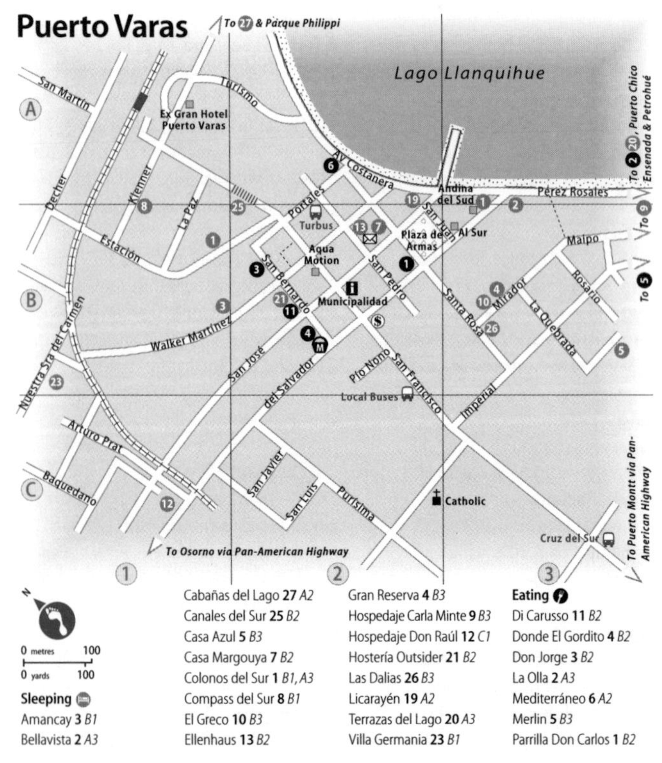

Frutillar and around *p218, map p225*
During the music festival (see page 227) rooms should be booked well in advance; alternatively stay in Frutillar Alto or Puerto Varas. There are several cheap options along Carlos Richter (main street) in Frutillar Alto.
A **Casona del 32**, Caupolicán 28, Frutillar Bajo, T065-421369. Comfortable old house, central heating, With breakfast. Groups-only off season. Recommended.
A **Salzburg**, Playa Maqui, 7 km north of Frutillar Bajo, T065-421589, www.salzburg.cl. Excellent restaurant, plus sauna, swimming pool, mountain bikes, tours and fishing.
B **Hostal Cinco Robles**, 1 km north of Frutillar Bajo, T065-421351, www.cinco-robles.com. In pleasant large grounds with

Sleeping
Apart Hotel Frutillar **2**
Casona del 32 **1**
Hospedaje Tía Clara **4**
Hospedaje Vivaldi **6**
Hostal Cinco Robles **5**
Hostería El Arroyo **3**
Hostería Los Maitenes Rincón Alemán **8**
Pérez Rosales 590 **12**
Philippi 451 **10**
Residenz am See **13**
Salzburg **11**

Eating
Andes **1**
Casino de Bomberos **2**
Club Alemán **3**
Selva Negra **4**

views. Rooms with wooden interiors. With breakfast, restaurant, parking.
B **Hostería Los Maitenes Rincón Alemán**, 3 km north of Frutillar Bajo, T065-330033, www.interpatagonia.com/losmaitenes. An old country house in 16 ha of land by the lake (private beach), fishing trips, free pickup from terminal. Disabled-friendly. Also *cabañas*.
B **Residenz am See**, Philippi 539, Frutillar Bajo, T065-421539, www.hotelamsee.cl. Good breakfast and views. Café downstairs serving German specialities.
C **Apart Hotel Frutillar**, Philippi 1175, Frutillar Bajo, T065-421388, mwikler@vtr.net. Also cabins, good breakfasts, meals available.
C **Hospedaje Vivaldi**, Philippi 851, Frutillar Bajo, T065-421382. **E** singles. Quiet, comfortable, excellent breakfast and lodging, also family accommodation. Recommended.
C **Hostería El Arroyo**, Philippi 989, Frutillar Bajo, T065-421560, alarroyo@surnet.cl. With breakfast. Highly recommended.
D **Hospedaje Tía Clara**, Pérez Rosales 743, Frutillar Bajo, T065-421806. **G** singles, kitchen facilities, very friendly, good value.
D **Pérez Rosales 590**, Frutillar Bajo. *Cabañas* and excellent breakfast.
D **Philippi 451**, Frutillar Bajo, T065-421204. Clean accommodation and good breakfast.
D-E **Hospedaje Juana Paredes**, Aníbal Pinto y Winkler, Frutillar Alto, T065-421407. **G** singles. Recommended, also *cabañas* for up to 5 and parking.

Camping

Los Ciruelillos, 2 km south of Frutillar Bajo, T065-339123. Most services.
Playa Maqui, 7 km north of Frutillar, T065-339139. Fancy, expensive site.
Sr Guido González, Casa 3, Población Vermont, T065-421385. Recommended site.

Puerto Octay *p219*
Several farms on the road around the north and east side of the lake offer rooms. Camping is also possible.
AL **Hotel Centinela**, T064-391326, www.hotelcentinela.cl. Built in 1914 as a summer mansion, this hotel has been recently restored. It is idyllically situated and has superb views, 12 rooms, also *cabañas*, restaurant with grand minstrels' gallery and bar, open all year. Edward VIII once stayed here.

D Hospedaje Raquel Mardorf, Germán Wulf 712. **F** singles with enormous breakfast, clean, comfortable.
D Hostería Irma, on lake, 2 km south of Las Cascadas, T064-396227, julietatrivino @yahoo.es. **G** singles. Attractive former residence, good food, very pleasant.
D Zapato Amarillo, 35 mins' walk north of town, T064-210787, www.zapatoamarillo.8k.com. **G** pp in shared rooms. Excellent for backpackers, spotless kitchen, great breakfasts with homemade bread, very friendly, German and English spoken. Lots of information, mountain bike rental, tours, canoes and sailing boat, luggage storage, phone for free pickup from town. Main house has a grass roof or there's the roundhouse next door with restaurant. Highly recommended.
E Hostería La Baja, Centinela, T064-391269, irisbravo1@hotmail.com. **G** singles, with breakfast and bath. Beautifully situated at the neck of the peninsula. Good value.

Camping

Camping Municipal, on lakeside, T064-391326. US$18 per site.
El Molino, beside lake. US$5 pp, clean, friendly, recommended.

Volcán Osorno *p219*

F There are 2 *refugios*, both of them south of the summit and reached from the southern access road: **La Burbuja**, the former ski-club centre, 14 km north of Ensenada at 1250 m) and **Refugio Teski Ski Club**, just below the snow line. Price per person, meals served. **Refugio La Picada** marked on the northern slopes on many trekking maps burned down several years ago.

Ensenada *p219*

LL Yan Kee Way Lodge, T065-212030, www.southernchilexp.com. Plush resort specializing in fly-fishing expeditions. Excellent restaurant.
AL-A Ensenada, Casilla 659, Puerto Montt, T065-212028, www.hotelensenada.cl. With bath, old-world style, good food, good view of lake and Volcán Osorno, runs tours, hires mountain bikes (guests only). Closed in winter. Also much cheaper *hostal* in the grounds with cooking facilities.
A-C Cabañas Brisas del Lago, Km 42, T065-212012, www.brisasdellago.cl. On beach, rooms and cabins sleeping 2-6, good restaurant nearby. Recommended.
C Hospedaje Ensenada, Km 43, T065-212050, www.hospedajensenada.blogspot.com. **F** singles. Most rooms with bath. Very clean, excellent breakfast.
C-D Hospedaje Arena, Km 43, T065-212037. Some rooms with bath. Breakfast. Recommended.

Camping

Montaña, centre of town. Charges per site, good beach space.
Playa Larga, 1 km east of **Hotel Ensenada**, US$15 per site.
Puerto Oscuro, 2 km north of Ensenada, US$12 per site.
Trauco, 4 km west of Ensenada, T065-212033. Large site with shops, fully equipped, US$5-10 pp.

Petrohué *p221*

The CONAF office in Petrohué can help find cheaper family accommodation. Camping wild and picknicking forbidden.
LL Fundo El Salto, near Salto de Petrohué, www.fly-fish-chile.com. Very expensive fishing lodge.
AL Hotel Petrohué, T065-212025, www.petrohue.com. Half board available. Magnificent views, log fires, cosy. Sauna and heated swimming pool. Hiking, fishing and other activities arranged.

Camping

In Petrohué, there's a campsite beside the lake, US$6 per site, no services (local fishermen will ferry you across for US$2). Camping wild and picnicking is forbidden at Petrohué; car parking US$4 per day.

Peulla *p221*

AL Hotel Peulla, Peulla, T02-1964182, hpeullareservas@terra.cl. Price includes dinner and breakfast, direct personal reservations, cheaper out of season. Beautiful setting by the lake and mountains, restaurant and bar, poor meals, cold in winter, often full of tour groups (tiny shop at back of hotel).
E Residencial Palomita, 50 m west of **Hotel Peulla**. Price pp for half board, lunches available. Family-run, simple, comfortable but not spacious, separate shower, book ahead in season.

Camping

The campsite in **Peulla** is opposite the CONAF office, US$4 per site. There's also a good campsite 1¾ hrs' walk east of the village, or ask at the *carabineros* station if you can camp on the beach; no facilities.

Eating

Osorno *p215, map p222*
The bakery at Ramírez 977 sells good wholemeal bread.
ΨΨ **Atelier**, Freire 468, T064-213735. Fresh pasta and other Italian delights.
ΨΨ **Dino's**, Ramírez 898, on the plaza. Good restaurant upstairs, bar/cafeteria downstairs.
ΨΨ **La Paisana**, O'Higgins 827, piso 2. Arab specialities including vegetarian options.
ΨΨ **Peter's Kneipe**, M Rodríguez 1039. Excellent German restaurant.
ΨΨ-Ψ **Club de Artesanos**, MacKenna 634. Hearty traditional Chilean fare.
Ψ **Waldis**, on Plaza de Armas. Real coffee.

Puerto Varas *p217, map p224*
ΨΨΨ **Merlin**, Imperial 0605, on the road east out of town, T065-233105, www.merlinrestaurant.com. Reputed to be one of the best restaurants in the Lake District, but occasional adverse reports.
ΨΨΨ-ΨΨ **Mediterráneo**, Santa Rosa 068, T065-237268. On the lakefront, varied and interesting menu with a Mediterranean influence, recommended.
ΨΨ **Di Carusso**, San Bernardo 318, T065-233478. Italian tratoria. Good fresh pasta dishes on Fri. Recommended.
ΨΨ **La Olla**, Pérez Rosales 1071, T065-233540. 1 km east of centre along the lakefront. Seafood Chilean cuisine. Recommended.
ΨΨ-Ψ **Donde El Gordito**, downstairs in market. Large portions, good range of meat dishes.
ΨΨ-Ψ **Parrilla Don Carlos**, Del Salvador 450. Typical Chilean grill.
Ψ **Don Jorge**, San Bernardo 240. Sandwiches and good value lunches.

Cafés
Café Danés, Del Salvador 441. Good coffee and cakes.
El Molino, on road to Ensenada, 22 km east. Café next to an old water mill.
Punto Café, Del Salvador 348. Café with internet and art gallery.

Frutillar and around *p218, map p225*
ΨΨ **Andes**, Philippi 1057, Frutillar Bajo. Good set menus and à la carte.
ΨΨ **Club Alemán**, Av Philippi 747. Good but not cheap, hostile to backpackers.
ΨΨ **Selva Negra**, Varas 24 y Philippi, Frutillar Bajo. Located in a traditional German mill, with scores of toy witches hanging from the ceiling, open 1100-2300.
Ψ **Casino de Bomberos**, Philippi 1060, Frutillar Bajo. Upstairs bar/restaurant, open all year, memorable painting caricaturing firemen in action. Great value but service can be poor.

Cafés
There are several German-style cafés on C Philippi, including **Salón de Te Frutillar** at No 775 and **Guten Apetit** at No 1285.

Puerto Octay *p219*
ΨΨ **El Rancho del Espanta-Pajaros**, 6 km south on the road to Frutillar, T065-330049. In a converted barn with wonderful views over the lake, serves all kind of spit roasted meat. All you can eat, with salad bar and drinks included, for US$12. Also arranges horse riding trips. Recommended.
ΨΨ **Fogón de Anita**, 1 km out of town, T064-391455. Mid-priced grill. Also German cakes and pastries.
Ψ **Restaurante Baviera**, Germán Wulf 582. Cheap and good. Salmon and *cazuelas*.

Ensenada *p224*
ΨΨΨ **Latitude 42**, Yan Kee Way resort, T065-212030. Expensive, excellent and varied cuisine, very good quality wine list. Views over the lake.
Ψ **Canta Rana**. Recommended for bread and *küchen*.
Ψ **Donde Juanito**, west of Ensenada. Excellent value cheap set lunch.

Festivals and events

Frutillar *p218, map p225*
Jan/early Feb A highly regarded classical **music festival** is held in the town; tickets must be booked well in advance from the Municipalidad, T065-421290.

Llanquihue *p218*
End Jan A German-style **beer festival** with oom-pah music is held here.

Shopping

Osorno *p215, map p222*
There is a mall on C Freire 542 with 3 internet cafés and a bookshop, **CM Books**, which sells some English titles.
Alta Artesanía, MacKenna 1069. Excellent handicrafts, not cheap.
Climet, Angulo 603. Fishing tackle.
Ekono, Colón y Errázuriz. Supermarket.
The Lodge, Los Carrera 1291, local 5. Fishing tackle.

Puerto Varas *p217, map p224*
El Libro del Capitán, Martiínez 417. Book shop with a large selection in German and English. Also book swap.
Las Brisas, Salvador 451. Supermarket.
Mamusia, San José 316. Chocolates.
VYH Meistur, Walker Martínez. Supermarket with a good selection, reasonably priced.

Frutillar *p218, map p225*
Services and shops are generally much better in Frutillar Alto, although in Frutillar Bajo, seek out **Der Volkladen**, O'Higgins y Philippi, for natural products, including chocolates, cakes and cosmetics.

Ensenada *p224*
There are several shop selling basic supplies. Most places are closed off season, other than a few pricey shops, so take your own provisions.

Activities and tours

Most tours operate in season only (Sep-May).

Osorno *p215, map p222*
Skiing
Club Andino, O'Higgins 1073, T064-235114. Information and advice on skiing in the area.
Hotel Antillanca, see Sleeping above, is attached to one of Chile's smaller ski resorts; 17 pistes are served by 3 lifts, ski instruction and first aid available. Piste preparation is unreliable. Skiing is not difficult but quality depends on the weather: though rain is common it often does not turn to snow. See www.skiantillanca.cl for information on the state of the pistes.

Trekking up Volcán Osorno
Weather permitting, agencies in Puerto Varas organize climbing expeditions with a local guide, transport from Puerto Montt or Puerto Varas, food and equipment, US$150 per person, payment in advance (minimum group 2, maximum 6 with 3 guides). Weather conditions are checked the day before and a 50% refund is available if the climb is abandoned due to weather. Those climbing from La Burbuja must register with **CONAF** at La Burbuja, and show they have suitable equipment. Those climbing from the north (La Picada) are not subject to any checks.

Lago Rupanco *p217*
Fishing
Lago Rupanco is very popular for fishing. **Bahía Escocia Fly Fishing**, offers excursions from the Puntiagudo Lodge (see Sleeping, above); advance booking required. In Osorno, fishing tackle is available from **Climet**, Angulo 603, and **The Lodge**, Los Carrera 1291, local 5.

Puerto Varas *p217, map p224*
Fishing
The area around Puerto Varas is popular for fishing. A licence (obligatory) is obtainable from the Municipalidad. Fishing expeditions are organized by many operators (see below). The Río Pescado (25 km east of Puerto Varas) is a good easy alternative for those who do not want to hire a guide.

Horse riding
Cabañas Puerto Decher, Fundo Molino Viejo, 2 km north of Puerto Varas, T065-338033. Guided tours, horse riding, minimum 2 people, mixed reports.
Campo Aventura, San Bernardo 318, T065-232910, www.campo-aventura.com. English and German spoken, offers 1- to 10-day trips on horseback.

Mountain biking
Bikes available from many tour operators, see below, for around $US14 per day; check equipment carefully

Tour operators
Al Sur, Del Salvador 100, T065-232300, www.alsurexpeditions.com. Rafting on Rió Petrohué. Official tour operator to the Parque Pumalín. Sells trekking maps.

Andina del Sud, Del Salvador 72, T065-232811, www.andinadelsud.cl. Operates 'lakes' trip to Bariloche, Argentina via Lago Todos Los Santos, Peulla, Cerro Tronador, plus other types of excursions.
Aqua Motion, San Francisco 328, T065-232747, www.aquamotion.cl. Rafting, trekking, mountain biking, fishing, birdwatching.
Kokayak, San José 320, T065-346433, www.paddlechile.com, French/Chilean-run, offers bike hire, whitewater rafting and sea kayaking.
Tranco Expeditions, San Pedro 422, T065-311311, www.trancoexpediciones.cl Trekking, rafting and climbing, Norwegian and English spoken, good equipment.
Travel Art, Imperial 0661, T065-232198, www.travelart.coml. General all-inclusive multi-day tours.
Turismo Biker, Café Terranova, on the plaza, turismobiker@yahoo.es. Specialists in downhill mountain bike trips. Not for the fainthearted.

Transport

Osorno *p215, map p222*

Air

LanChile, E Ramírez 802, T600-5262000, flies daily to **Santiago** via Temuco.

Bus

Main terminal 4 blocks from Plaza de Armas at Errázuriz 1400, bus from centre, US$0.50. Left luggage open 0730-2030.

Local Some local services leave from the Mercado Municipal terminal, 1 block west of the main terminal. To **Entre Lagos**, frequent in summer, reduced service off-season, Expreso Lago Puyehue, T064-234919, and Buses Puyehue, 45 mins, US$1.50; buses by both companies also continue to **Aguas Calientes**, off-season according to demand, 2 hrs, US$3. To **Puyehue**, 4-5 daily, 1½ hrs, US$3.50, but the buses don't stop by the lakeside (unless you want to get off at Hotel Termas de Puyehue and clamber down).

Bus from Osorno to **Piedras Negras** from the main terminal, leaves 1230 Mon-Fri, 1630 on Sat, returns from Piedras Negras early morning.

Long distance To **Santiago**, frequent, 11½ hrs, US$15, *salón cama* US$35; to **Temuco**, US$8; to **Panguipulli**, Buses Pirehueico, 4 a day; to **Pucón** and **Villarrica**, Tur Bus, frequent, US$10; to **Valdivia**, frequent, 2 hrs, several companies, US$4, but Igi Llaima only US$3; to **Frutillar**, US$2, **Llanquihue**, **Puerto Varas** and **Puerto Montt**, every 30 mins, US$4; to **Puerto Octay**, Vía Octay, hourly 0815-1930 (return 0800-1930) Mon-Sat, 5 daily 0800-2000 Sun, (4 return buses), US$3; to **Lago Ranco** (town), 6 a day, Empresa Ruta 5, 2 hrs, US$3; to **Punta Arenas**, several each week, US$65; to **Anticura**, daily at 1620, 3 hrs .

To Argentina Several buses run daily services from Puerto Montt via Osorno to **Bariloche** via Paso Puyehue (see page 239).

Lago Ranco *p217*

Buses from Valdivia to **Llifén** via Futrono, Cordillera Sur, 4 daily, US$3; to **Riñihue** via Paillaco and Los Lagos, frequent. To **Osorno**, Empresa Ruta 5, 6 daily.

Parque Nacional Puyehue *p217*

Expreso Lago Puyehue, T064-23499, and Buses Puyehue, run from Osorno to **Aguas Calientes**, according to demand, 2 hrs, US$2. Note that buses from Osorno to Entre Lagos and Aguas Calientes do not stop at the lakeside (unless you want to get off at Hotel Termas de Puyehue and clamber down). There is no public transport from Aguas Calientes to **Antillanca**; hitching is always difficult, but it is not a hard walk. Buses run from Osorno to **Anticura**, daily at 1620, 3 hrs.

Puerto Varas *p217, map p224*

Minibuses to **Ensenada** and **Petrohué** leave from San Bernardo y Martínez; regional buses stop on San Francisco 500 block; long distance buses leave from their own terminals.

To **Santiago**, Turbus, Igi Llaima, Cruz del Sur and several others, US$20, semi cama US$30, salón cama US$40. Thaebus, Full Express and others have services to **Puerto Montt**, every 15 mins, 30 mins, US$1; same companies, same frequency to **Frutillar**, 30 mins, US$1, and **Osorno**, 1 hr, US$3. Same companies hourly to **Petrohué**, US$3. To **Valdivia**, 3 hrs, US$6; to **Temuco**, US$9; to **Cochamó** via Ensenada, 5 a day, US$3. Services from Puerto Montt to **Bariloche**

(Argentina) also stop here. For the **Andina del Sud** lakes route via Lago Todos Los Santos, see page 239.

Car and bicycle hire

Adriazola Expediciones, Santa Rosa 340, T065-233477; **Turismo Nieve**, Gramado 560, T065-346115. Bicycle hire is available from many tour operators, see above, for around $US18 per day; check equipment carefully.

Train

There are 2 daily trains north to **Temuco**, US$6 and south to **Puerto Montt**, US$1. Trains leave from the station at Klenner 350.

Frutillar and around *p218, map p225*

Colectivos run between the 2 towns, 5 mins, US$0.60. Most buses to other destinations leave from opposite the Copec station in Frutillar Alto. **Thaebus** and others have frequent services to **Puerto Varas**, US$1, and **Puerto Montt**, US$1.25. To **Osorno**, Turismosur, 1¼ hrs, US$2.50; to **Puerto Octay**, Thaebus, 5 a day.

Train

There are 2 daily train services north to **Temuco**, US$5 and south to **Puerto Varas** and **Puerto Montt**, US$1.80. Trains leave from the staion at Alessandri s/n.

Puerto Octay *p219*

Buses to **Osorno**, 9 a day, US$2; to **Las Cascadas** Mon-Fri 1730, return next day 0700. **Thaebus** runs 5 daily services to **Frutillar**,1 hr, US$0.90, **Puerto Varas**, 2 hrs, and **Puerto Montt**, 2¼ hrs, US$2.

Lago Todos Los Santos *p220*

Boat

The **Andina del Sud** catamaran sails between **Petrohué** and **Peulla**, departing Petrohué 1030 Mon-Sat, departing Peulla 1500 Mon-Sat, 2 hrs, US$22 per person one way, bicycles free (book in advance); most seating indoors, no cars carried, commentaries in Spanish and English, expensive refreshments. This is the only public service across the lake and it connects with the **Andina del Sud** tour bus between Puerto Montt and Bariloche (see page 239). Local fishermen also make the trip across the lake and for a group this can be cheaper than the public service, allow 3½ hrs.

Bus

Minibuses from **Puerto Varas** to **Ensenada** continue to **Petrohué** in summer; last return bus from Petrohué to Puerto Varas, 1800. Note that apart from the **Andina del Sur** service from Puerto Montt, there is no transport from Peulla to the border at Paso Pérez Rosales.

Ensenada *p224*

Frequent minibuses run from **Puerto Varas** in summer. Buses from Puerto Montt via Puerto Varas to **Cochamó** also stop here. Hitching from Puerto Varas is difficult.

Directory

Osorno *p215, map p222*

Banks and currency exchange Several banks and *casas de cambio* in the centre. **Internet** Chat-Mail MP3, Patricio Lynch 1334; **Dream House**, Matta 510, opposite Chung Hwa Restaurant; **Pub Sa Tanca**, Patio Freire 542. **Laundry** Prat 678, allow at least a day. **Post office** O'Higgins 645. **Telephone** Ramírez at central plaza, Juan MacKenna y Cochrane.

Puerto Varas *p217, map p224*

Banks Good exchange rates at **Banco Osorno**, Del Salvador 399. Also numerous *casas de cambio*. **Internet** Several in the centre, although if you want coffee while you browse try **Punt Café**, Del Salvador 348. **Laundry** Gramado 1090; **Lavanderia Delfin**, Martínez 323, expensive. **Medical emergencies** Clinica Alemana, Otto Bader 810, T065-232336, emergencies T065-232274, usually has English-speaking doctors. **Post office** San José y San Pedro; Del Salvador y Santa Rosa. **Telephone Bellsouth**, San Bernardo 555; **CTC**, Salvador 320; **Telefónica del Sur**, Del Salvador 314; **Entel**, San José 314.

Puerto Montt and around

The capital of Región X (Los Lagos), Puerto Montt lies on the northern shore of the Seno de Reloncaví 1016 km south of Santiago. The jumping-off point for journeys south to Chiloé and southern Patagonia, it is a busy modern city, the fastest growing in Chile, flourishing with the salmon-farming boom. It was founded in 1853, as part of the German colonization of the area, on the site of a Mapuche community known as Melipulli, meaning four hills. There are good views over the city and bay from outside the Intendencia Regional on Avenida X Region. There is a wide range of accommodation here, but you might prefer to stay in Puerto Varas, which is more picturesque and only 20 minutes' away by bus. » *For Sleeping, Eating and other listings, see pages 235-240.*

Ins and outs → *See map page 236. Colour map 1, B2.*

Getting there **El Tepual airport** ⓘ *13 km northwest of town*, served by **ETM** buses from the **bus terminal** ⓘ *T065-294292, 1½ hrs before departure, US$3*; there's also a minibus service to/from hotels, US$6 per person. There are several daily flights north to Santiago and Temuco, and south to Coyhaique and Punta Arenas. Ferries serve Chaitén (four times weekly) and Puerto Chacabuco (four times weekly); there's also a weekly service south to Puerto Natales. Puerto Montt is the departure point for bus services south to Coyhaique and Punta Arenas, and for buses north to Santiago and all the intermediate cities. » *See also Transport, page 239.*

Tourist information **Sernatur** ⓘ *Gobernación Provincial, Plaza de Armas, summer daily 0900-1300, 1500-1900; winter Mon-Fri 0830-1300, 1400-1800*. Ask for information on Chiloé here as this is often difficult to obtain on the island. **Regional tourist office** ⓘ *Intendencia Regional, Av Décima Región 480, Casilla 297, T065-254580, infloslagos@sernatur.cl*. There's also an information kiosk on the Plaza de Armas, which has town maps, but little information on other destinations. **CONAF** is at Ochogavia 458. Information on **Parque Pumalín** (see page 246) is available from Buin 356, T065-250079, www.pumalinpark.org.

Sights

The **Plaza de Armas** lies at the foot of steep hills, one block north of Av Diego Portales, which runs east-west parallel to the shore. The **Palacio del Arte Diego Rivera** ⓘ *Quillota 116, off the Plaza de Armas, T065-261817*, hosts temporary exhibitions, concerts and plays. Two blocks west of the square is the **Iglesia de los Jesuitas** on Calle Gallardo, dating from 1872, which has a fine blue-domed ceiling; behind it on a hill is the **campanario** (clock tower). Further west, near the bus terminal, is the **Museo Regional Juan Pablo II** ⓘ *Diego Portales 997, 1030-1800 daily, US$1*, documenting local history. It has a fine collection of historic photos of the city and memorabilia of the Pope's visit in 1988. » *For Parque Nacional Alerce Andino, see page 245.*

Angelmó

The little fishing port of Angelmó, 2 km west along Avenida Diego Portales (a pleasant 30-minute walk) has become a tourist centre thanks to its dozens of seafood restaurants and handicraft shops. Launches depart from Angelmó for the wooded **Isla Tenglo**, a favourite place for picnics, with views from the summit. The island is famous for its *curanto*, served by restaurants in summer. Boat trips round the island from Angelmó last for 30 minutes, US$8. A longer boat trip (two hours) will take you to **Isla Huar**.

Towards Chiloé

The road west from Puerto Montt is very beautiful. **Chinquihue** (the name means 'place of skunks'), beyond Angelmó, has many seafood restaurants, oysters being a speciality. Further south is **Calbuco**, scenic centre of the fishing industry. It is on an island linked to the mainland by a causeway and can be visited direct by boat or road. West of here is the Río Maullin, which drains Lago Llanquihue, and has some waterfalls and good salmon fishing. At its mouth is the fishing village of **Maullín**, founded in 1602. On the coast to the southeast is **Carelmapu**, with an excellent beach and *cabañas* at Playa Brava, about 3 km away. At the southern tip of the mainland, **Pargua** is the departure point for car ferries to Chiloé (see box, page 233).

Seno de Reloncaví » *pp235-240.*

The Seno de Reloncaví situated east of Puerto Montt and south of the Parque Nacional Pérez Rosales, is the northernmost of Chile's glacial inlets. It is a quiet and beautiful estuary, often shrouded in mist, but stunning nonetheless, and recommended for its wildlife, including sea lions and dolphins, and for its peaceful atmosphere. It is relatively easily reached by a road that runs along the wooded lower Petrohué valley south from Ensenada and then follows the eastern shore of the estuary for almost 100 km to join the Carretera Austral.

Ralún and around → *Colour map 1, B3*

A small village situated at the northern end of the estuary, Ralún is 31 km southeast from Ensenada by a poorly paved road. There is a village shop and post office, and on the outskirts are **thermal baths** ⓘ *US$2, reached by boat, US$2.50 across the Río Petrohué*. Ralún is the departure point for a five-hour walk north to **Laguna Cayutué** in the Parque Nacional Vicente Pérez Rosales. From Ralún you can either travel along the eastern shore of the estuary to Cochamó or take the road that branches off and follows the western side of the estuary south, 36 km to Lago Chapo and the Parque Nacional Alerce Andino (see page 245).

Cochamó and further south → *Colour map 1, B3*

Some 17 km south of Ralún along a poor *ripio* road is the pretty village of Cochamó. It's situated in a striking setting, on the east shore of the estuary with the volcano behind, and has a small, frequently deserted waterfront, where benches allow you to sit and admire the view. Cochamó's fine wooden church dates from 1900 and is similar to those on Chiloé. It has a clock with wooden hands and an unusual black statue of Christ.

Further south, on the south bank of the Río Puelo (crossed by a new bridge) is **Puelo**, a most peaceful place. From here the road continues 36 km further southwest to Puelche on the Carretera Austral (see page 246). The Gaucho Trail east from Cochamó to **Paso León** on the Argentine frontier was used in the colonial period by the indigenous population, Jesuit priests and later by *gauchos*. It runs along Río Cochamó to La Junta, then along the north side of Lago Vidal, passing waterfalls and the oldest surviving Alerce trees in Chile at El Arco. The route takes three to four days by horse, five to six days on foot.

Sea routes south of Puerto Montt » *p239.*

Puerto Montt is the departure point for several popular voyages along the coast of southern Chile. All sailings are from Angelmó; timetables should be checked carefully in advance as schedules change frequently.

Going further ... Chiloé

The mysterious archipelago of Chiloé is one of the most fascinating areas of Chile. Isolated from mainstream Spanish development for 200 years, Chiloé is different to the mainland and retains many unique traditions, including the belief in witchcraft and local mythical figures such as 'El Trauco', an ugly, smelly creature who is said to seduce virgins and the 'La Fiura', who attracts men with her colourful clothes before putting them to sleep with her foul breath.

Chiloé consists of one main island, La Isla Grande de Chiloé (180 km long), and numerous islets. There are two main towns, Ancud and Castro, in which most of the island's 116,000 people live, and a number of small villages. The Parque Nacional de Chiloe covers extensive areas of uninhabited temperate rainforest on the wild western and southern sides of the island. At Cucao, an immense 20 km long beach a is battered by thundering Pacific surf. The more sheltered east coast and offshore islands are covered with wheat fields and dark green plots of potatoes and the roads are lined with wild flowers in summer. There are often dolphins playing in the bay, and, on a clear day, views across to Corcovado volcano on the mainland. The Humboldt Current ensure a wide variety of fresh shellfish are available all year; try *curanto* (a stew, traditionally cooked in a hole in the earth). Chiloé is famous for its painted churches, now designated UNESCO World Heritage sites. The earliest example from 1730 is in Achao on the island of Quinchao.

Ferry and catamaran services connect the island with Chaitén and the Carretera Austral (see page 249), but the main sea link is the frequent vehicle ferry service between Pargua on the mainland (55 km southwest of Puerto Montt) across the Chacao straits to Chacao (30 minutes, cars US$11.40 one way, foot passengers US$1). Frequent bus services meet the ferriesa, linking Ancud and Castro with Puerto Montt and beyond. Local services, however, can be crowded and slow. Mountain bikes and horses are ideal for travelling through the more remote parts of Chiloe; there are also limited opportunities for hiking.

The agrotourism network (T065-628333) enables visitors to stay with a local family and share their way of life. Prices per person are all D-E with breakfast. Further information can be obtained from the tourist office in Ancud, Libertad 665, T065-622665, Mon-Fri 0900-1300, 1430-1730.

To Puerto Natales

One of the highlights of many journeys to Chile is the 1460-km voyage between Puerto Montt and the southern port of **Puerto Natales**, made by the *M/V Magallanes*; it is quicker to fly and cheaper to go by bus via Argentina but the voyage by boat is spectacular. The route south from Puerto Montt crosses the Seno de Reloncaví and the Golfo de Ancud, then continues south through the Canal Moraleda and the Canal Errázuriz, which separate the mainland from the outlying islands. It then heads west through the Canal Chacabuco to Bahía Anna Pink and across the open sea and the infamous Golfo de Penas (Gulf of Sorrows) to reach a series of channels, which provide one of the narrowest routes for large shipping in the world. There are spectacular views of the wooded fjords, weather permitting, particularly at sunrise and sunset, and a sense of desolate peace pervades everything except the ship, which is filled with cows in transport containers mooing day and night, and people having a good time.

The only regular stop on this route is at the fishing village of **Puerto Edén** on Isla Wellington, one hour south of the Angostura Inglesa. It has three shops, one off-licence,

Going further ... Valdivia

For a complete contrast to the rural communities around the lakes, visit the lively student city of Valdivia to the west. It's a good place to rest after arduous treks in the mountains.

Founded in 1552 by Pedro de Valdivia, the city was abandoned as a result of the Mapuche insurrection of 1599 and was not refounded until 1645 when it became the only Spanish mainland settlement south of the Río Biobío. The Spanish fortified the area throughout the 1600s but the defences proved of little avail during the Wars of Independence, when the Chilean naval squadron under Lord Cochrane seized control of Valdivia's forts in two days. Until the 1880s Valdivia remained an outpost of Chilean rule, reached only by sea or by a coastal route. In 1960, a devastating earthquake and tidal wave caused the land around Valdivia to drop by 3 m, creating new lagunas to the north of the city.

Ins and outs There are daily flights to the airport, 29 km north of the city from Santiago, as well as numerous buses from Santiago, Puerto Montt and Temuco. Access from the Panamericana is via Loncoche (toll US$2.50), Paillaco or by *ripio* road from Los Lagos. Tourist information is available from Prat 555, T063-342300.

Don't miss...

→ **Cervecería Kunstmann**, T063-292969, www.cerveza-kunstmann.cl. Tour the working brewery and museum before tucking into German food and five types of beer.

→ **Plaza de la República** The heart of the city and the site of the cathedral museum, for four centuries of Christian history.

→ **Isla Teja** This island is home to the university, the botanical gardens and two good museums.

→ **Santuario de la Naturaleza Río Cruces** Boat trips from the city dock run north to this flooded nature reserve, which now attracts many bird species.

→ **Niebla and Corral** Take a boat downstream to visit two of the most important 17th-century Spanish forts. The boat also stops midstream at Isla Mancera, a small island dominated by the Castillo de San Pedro de Alcántara, the earliest of the Spanish forts.

→ **Semana Valdiviana** This festival in mid February, culminates in Noche Valdiviana, when a procession of elaborately decorated boats sail past the Muelle Fluvial.

Sleeping and eating

E-G pp **Aires Buenos**, Gral Lagos 1036, T063-206304. Some rooms with bath. Kitchen facilities, bar, internet, tours, Spanish and tango lessons, Argentinian run, English spoken, recommended.

Restaurante Camino de Luna, Prat s/n. A floating restaurant next to the costanera, unique in Chile.

one café, and a *hospedaje* (open intermittently) for up to 20 people. The population of 185, includes a few remaining native Alacaluf people. **Isla Wellington** is largely untouched, with stunning mountains. If you do stop here, take all food; maps (not very accurate) are available in Santiago. The onward fare to Puerto Natales is US$50.

This is a cargo ferry rather than a cruise liner; standards of service and comfort vary, depending on the number of passengers and weather conditions. Economy class is basic, cramped and near the engine room, in 24-berth dormitories; book a cabin instead. The food is variable, and, apart from videos, entertainment on board is limited. However, wine is available and you are welcome to bring your own.

To Puerto Chacabuco and Laguna San Rafael

A weekly catamaran service sails between Puerto Montt and **Puerto Chacabuco,** 80 km west of Coyhaique. This beautiful voyage passes forested cliffs, seemingly within touching distance, and offers glimpses of distant snows. However, taking this route south means that travellers miss out on the attractions of the Carretera Austral. The **Navimag** ferry *M/N Edén* also sails this route, continuing (September to April only) from Puerto Chacabuco to visit **Laguna San Rafael** (see page 261). However, the cabins are on the expensive side and be sure to double check departure times. A better option is to take a catamaran service direct to the Laguna from Puerto Chacabuco (see page 261) or to charter a small plane from Coyhaique (see page 260). A luxury alternative is to board *Skorpios II* for a cruise to Chiloé and Laguna San Raphael. Generally service is excellent, the food superb and, at the laguna, you chip ice off the face of the glacier for your whisky. After San Rafael the ship visits **Quitralco fjord,** where there are thermal pools and boat trips. There are also four- to six-day tours from Puerto Montt with **Patagonia Connection,** which visit Puerto Chacabuco, Laguna San Rafael and the Termas de Puyuhuapi (see page 252).

To Chaitén

The sea route to Chaitén through the Golfo de Ancud is quicker and more reliable than the Carretera Austral but you'll miss much of the spectacular scenery encountered along the way. However, if you are pushed for time, **Navimag** and **Naviera Austral** both offer ferry services on a weekly basis. The journey normally takes 10 hours. **Catamaranes del Sur** and **Aysen Express** also run a much faster cataraman service six times weekly.

Sleeping

Puerto Montt *p231, map p236*
Accommodation is expensive in season, much cheaper off season. There are lots of *cabañas* on the outskirts of the city and in Pelluco.

L-AL **Gran Hotel Don Vicente**, Varas 447, T065-432900, www.granhoteldonvicente.cl. Business class hotel. Some rooms noisy, restaurant serving seafood, fine views.

AL **Club Presidente**, Portales 664, T065-251666, www.presidente.cl. Comfortable 4-star with breakfast. Large rooms or suites. English spoken.

AL-A **Gran Hotel Don Luis**, Quillota 146, T065-259001, www.hoteldonluis.cl. Another comfortable 4-star hotel and very good restaurant as well as a gym and sauna. Recommended.

A **Apart Hotel Colón**, Pedro Montt 65, T065-264290, www.aparthotelcolon.cl. Fully furbished studio apartments, good value, especially when paying in dollars.

A **O'Grimm**, Gallardo 211, T065-252845, www.ogrimm.com. Pleasant rooms with lounge area, cosy restaurant with occasional live music, central.

B-C **Le Mirage**, Rancagua 350, T065-255125. A basic business class hotel with breakfast, small rooms, clean.

C **Hostal Pacífico**, J J Mira 1088, T065-256229. With bath, some rooms a little cramped, breakfast, cable TV, parking, comfortable.

C **Millahue**, Copiapó 64, T065-253829, www.hotelmillahue.cl. With breakfast and bath, slightly run down, restaurant, also apartments at Benavente 959, T/F065-254592.

C-D **Colina**, Talca 81, T065-253502, hotcolina@surnet.cl. With bath. Spacious, restaurant, bar, car hire, can be noisy, good value. Recommended.

C-D **Hospedaje Suizo**, Independencia 231, T/F065-252640, rossyoelckers@yahoo.es. **G** singles, with breakfast. Some rooms with bath. Attractive house near the bus terminal, clean, German and Italian spoken, painting and Spanish classes. Convenient for Navimag. Recommended.

D **Alda González**, Gallardo 552, T065-253334. **G** singles. Some rooms with bath, breakfast included, cooking facilities, English and German spoken, good value, near the Plaza de Armas.

D Hospedaje Emita, Miraflores 1281, T065-250725, hospedaje_emita@hotmail.com. persons singles with breakfast, including home-made bread. Some rooms with bath. Clean, friendly, safe, near the bus terminal.
D-E Casa Perla, Trigal 312, T065-262104, www.casaperla.com. **G** per person in shared rooms. With breakfast. Near the bus terminal, helpful, friendly, meals, laundry, internet, pleasant garden, English spoken, Spanish classes offered, good meeting place. Recommended.
D-E Hospedaje Rocco, Pudeto 233, T/065-272897, www.hospedajerocco.cl. **G** singles. With breakfast, but without bath, real coffee, English and Italian spoken, friendly atmosphere, laundry. Quiet residential area, convenient for Navimag. Recommended.
D-E Vista al Mar, Vivar 1337, T065-255625, www.hospedajevistaalmar.unlugar.com . **F** singles. Friendly, helpful, welcoming, good breakfast. Phone for lift from bus terminal.
E Casa Gladis, Ancud y Mira. Some double rooms. **G** pp for dormitory beds, kitchen and laundry facilities, near bus terminal.
E Vista Hermosa, Miramar 1486, T/F065-268001, vistahermosa@mixmail.com. **G** singles without bath, 10 mins' walk from bus terminal. The room at the front has the best views.

Camping

Wild camping is possible along the sea front. There are also several official sites west of Puerto Montt.
Anderson, 11 km west. American run, hot showers, private beach, home-grown fruit, vegetables and milk products.
El Ciervo, 3 km west. Good site.
Municipal, Chinquihue, 10 km west. Open Oct-Apr, fully equipped with tables, seats, barbecue, toilets and showers, small shop, no kerosene, bus service from town.

Towards Chiloé *p232*

C Cabañas El Pangal, 5 km from Maullin, T065-451244, m_essedin@hotmail.com. Campsite and cabins on the beach.
C Hotel Colonial, Calbuco, T065-461546, www.hotelcolonial@hotmail.com. One of several decent hotels.

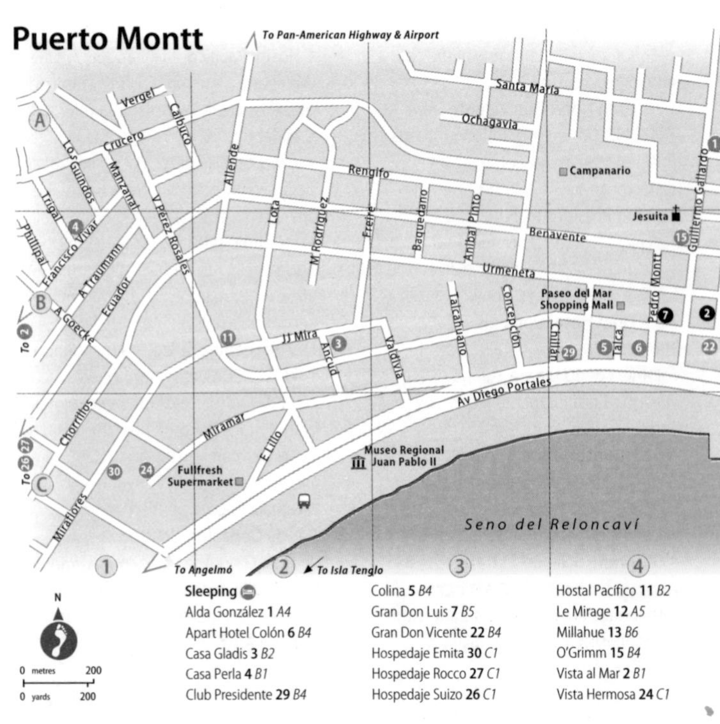

Seno de Reloncloví *p232*
Accommodation in Puelo is also available with local families.

LL Río Puelo Lodge, Puelo, T02-2298533, www.rio-puelo-lodge.cl. Plush lodge offering all-in fly-fishing packages from US$500.

B Campo Aventura, 4 km south of Cochamó, T065-232910, www.campo-aventura.com. For details of riding and trekking expeditions, see below. Accommodation is offered at the base camp (signpost on road) with great breakfast, kitchen, sauna. Camping is also possible. Very fresh milk from Campo Aventura's cow, herb garden, expensive but good food using local produce, vegetarian also available, book exchange. There's another base in a renovated mountain house in the valley of La Junta. Write to **Campo Aventura**, Casilla 5, Correo Cochamó for information.

D-E Cochamó, T065-216212. **G** singles. Basic but clean, friendly, often full with salmon farm workers, good meals, recommended.

D-E Mercado Particular Sabin, Catedral 20, Cochamó. One of several *pensiones*, next to **Hotel Cochamó**.

D-E Navarrito, Ralún. **G** singles in basic accommodation. Also restaurant.

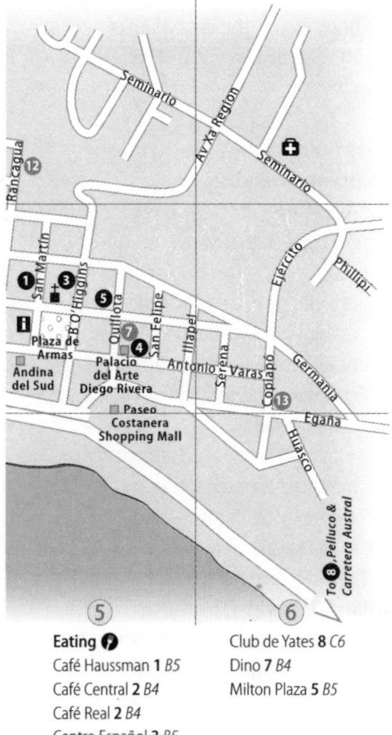

Eating
Café Haussman **1** *B5*
Café Central **2** *B4*
Café Real **2** *B4*
Centro Español **3** *B5*
Club Alemán **4** *B5*
Club de Yates **8** *C6*
Dino **7** *B4*
Milton Plaza **5** *B5*

E Hospedaje Edicar, Cochamó. **G** singles. Breakfast available. Without bath, spacious, recommended.

E Hospedaje Maura, JJ Molina 12, Cochamó. **G** singles. Some rooms with bath. Beautifully situated, good food.

E Posada Campesino, Ralún. **G** singles. Without breakfast, very friendly, simple, clean.

Camping

Camping Los Castaños, Cochamó, T065-216212.

Eating

Puerto Montt *p231, map p236*
For seafood enthusiasts, the only place to go is **Angelmó**, where there are many small, very popular seafood restaurants in the old fishing port past the fish market, serving excellent lunches only. There is fierce touting for business. Look out for local specialities such as *curanto* and *picoroco al vapor*, a giant barnacle whose flesh looks and tastes like a crab, and ask for *té blanco* (white wine; the stalls are not legally allowed to serve wine). There are more good seafood restaurants on the other side of the city in Pelluco (see page 245). Cheap food is available at the bus terminal. In Puerto Montt itself, try the following eateries:

TTT Club de Yates, Juan Soler s/n. Excellent, expensive seafood.

TTT-TT Club Alemán, Varas 264, T065-252551. Old fashioned, good food and wine.

TT Café Haussman, San Martín y Urmeneta. German-style cakes, beer and *crudos* (raw meat).

TT Centro Español, O'Higgins 233, T065-343753. Decent traditional Chilean and Spanish food. Vegetarian options.

TT Dino, Varas 550, T065-252785. Restaurant upstairs, snacks downstairs (try the lemon juice). Often has an all you can eat buffet.

T Café Central, Rancagua 117, T065-482888. Spartan decor, generous portions (sandwiches and *pichangas*). Giant TV screen for football enthusiasts.

T Café Real, Rancagua 137, T065-253750. For *empanadas*, *pichangas*, *congrío frito* and cheap lunches.

T Milton Plaza, Urmeneta 326 y O'Higgins, T065-295790. Good seafood and snacks. Doubles as a pool hall. Recommended.

Restaurant de las Antiqüedades, Av Angelmó. Attractive and unusual decor, real coffee, interesting menu.

Cafés

Asturias, Angelmó 2448. Limited menu but often recommended.
Café Alemana, Rancagua 117. Real coffee, good.

Towards Chiloé *p232*

Kiel, Chinquihué, T065-255010. Good meat and seafood dishes.

Seno de Reloncaví *p232*

Eateries in Cochamó include **Donde Payi**, opposite the church and **Reloncaví**, on the road down to the waterfront. On the seafront there is a cheap fish/seafood restaurant, which also hires out canoes, US$1.50 for 30 mins.

Bars and clubs

Puerto Montt *p231, map p236*

Watch out: several of the 'bars' near the port and along Pérez Rosales have more to them than meets the eye.
Star, RN 5 north of the city. Disco. Several more in Pelluco, east of Puerto Montt.

Shopping

Puerto Montt *p231, map p236*

Woollen goods and Mapuche-designed rugs can be bought at roadside stalls in Angelmó and on Diego Portales opposite the bus terminal. Prices are much the same as on Chiloé, but quality is often lower.
Fullfresh, opposite bus terminal. Supermarket open 0900-2200 daily.
Libros, Diego Portales 580. Bookshop with a small selection of English novels, also maps.
Paseo del Mar, Talca y Antonio Varas. Large modern shopping mall. There is also a new mall, the **Paseo Costanera** on the seafront.

Activities and tours

Puerto Montt *p231, map p236*

There are many agencies. Most offer 1-day excursions to **Chiloé** (US$30) and to **Puerto Varas**, **Isla Loreley**, **Laguna Verde**, and the **Petrohué Falls**: these tours are cheaper from bus company kiosks inside the bus terminal. Some companies offer 2-day excursions along the Carretera Austral to **Hornopirén**, US$100, with food and accommodation.
Alsur, Antonio Varas 445, T/F065-287628, www.alsurexpeditions.com. Rafting and watersports as well as trips to Pumalín Park.
Andina del Sud, Varas 437, close to central tourist kiosk, T065-257797. Sells a variety of tours, and offers the lakes trip to Bariloche in collaboration with **Catedral Turismo**, www.crucedealgos.com, in Argentina (see page 102).
Eureka Turismo, Gallardo 65, T065-250412, www.chile-travel.com/eureka.htm. Helpful, German and English spoken.
Kayaking Austral, T09-6980951, or book through **Casa Perla**. Guided sea kayaking.
Petrel Tours, Benavente 327, T065-251780, petrel@telsur.net. Recommended.
Travellers, General Bulnes 1009, 22 de Mayo, T065-262099, www.travellers.cl. Booking office for **Navimag** ferry to Puerto Natales, bespoke excursions, also sells imported camping equipment and runs computerized tourist information service, book swap ("the best south of Santiago"), map display, TV, real coffee, English-run.

Seno de Reloncaví *p232*

Horse riding/trekking

Campo Aventura, Casilla 5, Correo Cochamó, T065-232910, www.campo-aventura.com. Specializes in all-inclusive riding and trekking expeditions with packhorses along the Gaucho trail between the Reloncaví Estuary and the Argentine border, 2-10 days, roughly US$100 per person, per day; good guides, spectacular scenery, English, French and German spoken, highly recommended. It also organizes other activities including combined sea kayaking-horse riding trips with **Kokayak** in Puerto Varas.
Sebastián Contreras, C Morales, Cochamó, T065-216220. An independent guide who offers tours on horseback and hires out horses, recommended.

Transport

Puerto Montt *p231, map p236*

Air

LanChile, **Sky** and **Aerolíneas del Sur** have several flights daily to **Santiago**, from US$150 return (best one way prices with **Aerolíneas del Sur**); to **Balmaceda** for Coyhaique, from US$120 return; to **Punta Arenas**, from US$170 return. In Jan, Feb and Mar you may be told that flights are booked up, however, cancellations are sometimes available from the airport. To **Chaitén**, **Cielomar Austral** and **Aerotaxis del Sur**, daily, US$70. To **Bariloche** and **Neuquén** (Argentina), **TAN**, 2 weekly, 40 mins; to **Port Stanley** (Falkland Islands/Islas Malvinas), from Santiago via Punta Arenas, **LanChile**, Sat, US$700 return.

Airline offices Aerotaxis del Sur, A Varas 70 , T065-731315, www.aerotaxisdelsur.cl; **Cielomar Austral**, Quillota 245, loc 1, T065- 264010; **LanChile**, O'Higgins 167, T600-5262000; **Sky**, T600-600 2828 for information.

Bus

The very crowded terminal on the seafront at Diego Portales y Lota has telephones, restaurants, a casa de cambio and left luggage (US$1.80 per item for 24 hrs).

Expreso Puerto Varas, **Thaebus** and **Full Express** run minibuses every few mins to **Puerto Varas**, US$1, **Llanquihue** and **Frutillar**, US$1.50, and to **Osorno**, US$2.50. Buses and *colectivos* nos 2, 3 and 20 ply the route to **Anglemó**, US$0.50 each way.

To **Ensenada** and **Petrohué**, several companies, hourly; to **Ralún**, **Cochamó** and **Puelo**, **Buses Fierro** and **Buses Bohle**, 5 daily via Puerto Varas and Ensenada; to **Pucón**, several daily, 6 hrs, US$10; to **Santiago**, several companies, 13 hrs, US$20, semi cama US$30, salón cama US$40; to **Temuco**, US$9; to **Valdivia**, US$6; to **Concepción**, US$11. For services to Chiloé, see box page 233.

To **Punta Arenas**, **Pacheco** and **Queilen Bus**, 1-3 weekly, 32-38 hrs, approximately US$55 (bus goes through Argentina via Bariloche; take US$ cash to pay for meals etc in Argentina); book well in advance in Jan-Feb and check if you need a multiple-entry Chilean visa; also book any return journey before setting out. To **Coyhaique** via Bariloche, 2 weekly, **Turibus**, US$60.

International Buy tickets for international buses from the bus terminal, not through an agency. **Andes Mar** has through-services to Buenos Aires, Neuquén and Bahía Blanca; less in winter.

To **Bariloche** via Osorno and the Puyehue pass, daily, 7hrs, **Andes Mar**, **Rio de la Plata** and **Tas Choapa**, US$17. **Andina del Sud** (see page 238) in partnership with **Catedral Turismo** in Bariloche, runs services to **Bariloche** via Lago Todos Los Santos and Paso Pérez Rosales, depart company offices in Puerto Montt daily at 0800, US$160 one way (plus US$150 May- Aug for overnight stay in the **Hotel Peulla**; for a cheaper alternative see page 226). The trip may be cancelled if the weather is poor; there are reports of difficulty in obtaining a refund. If you have time but are short of money, you can buy tickets for the boat in Puerto Montt or Puerto Varas and do the rest of the trip independently, but bear in mind that there is no transport from Peulla to the border, 26 km.

Car hire

Automotric Angelmó, Talca 79, cheap and helpful; **Automóvil Club de Chile**, Ensenada 70, T065-254776, and at airport; **Autovald**, Diego Portales 1330, T065-256355, cheap rates; **Avis**, Urmeneta, 1037, T065-253307, and at airport; **Budget**, Gallardo 450, T065-254888 and at airport; **Dollar**, Hotel Vicente Pérez Rosales, Antonio Varas 447; **Egartur**, Benavente 575, loc. 3, T065-257336, egartur@telsur.cl, will deliver to your hotel; **First**, Antonio Varas 447, T065-252036; **Full Famas**, Diego Portales 506, T065-258060, F065-259840, and airport, T065-263750, helpful, good value, has vehicles that can be taken to Argentina; **Hertz**, Antonio Varas 126, T065-259585, helpful, English spoken; **Travicargo**, Urmeneta 856, T065-257137.

Ferry

Shipping offices **Bohemia**, Antonio Varas 947, T065-254675; **Catamaranes del Sur**, Diego Portales 510, T065-267533, www.catamaranesdelsur.cl; **Navimag**, Terminal Transbordadores, Av Angelmó 2187, T065-253318, www.navimag.com; **Skorpios**, Angelmó 1660 y Miraflores (Castilla 588), T065-252619, www.skorpios.cl; **Naviera Austral**, Terminal Transbordadores, Angelmó 2187, T065-270400, www.navieraustral.cl.

Train

The station is 2 km north of the city centre at Cuarta Terraza s/n, La Paloma, T600-5855000, www.efe.cl. Two daily services north to **Temuco**, US$6 via **Puerto Varas**, US$1, **Frutillar**, US$1.80 and **Osorno**, US$2.75.

Seno de Reloncaví *p232*

Bus

Buses Fierro and **Bohle** from Puerto Montt via Puerto Varas and Ensenada, to **Ralún**, **Cochamó** and **Puelo**, 5 daily all year.

Boat

In summer boats sail up the estuary from **Angelmó**. Get a group of people together and convince one of the fishermen to take you. For information on (irregular) scheduled trips, contact the Regional Sernatur office in Puerto Montt.

Sea routes south of Puerto Montt *p232*

To Puerto Natales

Navimag ferries the *Eden* or the *Magellanes* sail once a week, Nov-Apr, departing Puerto Montt Mon 1600, returning Fri 0400 (although departures are frequently delayed so double check depature times), 3½ days, economy from US$355 pp (take sleeping bag), private cabin with view US$1720 (double US$1750), all prices include meals, 10% discount for ISIC holders in cabin class only, fares 10-20% lower Apr-Oct. Book well in advance for cabin class departures Dec-Mar (more than 2 weeks in advance in Feb), especially for the voyage south; Puerto Natales to Puerto Montt is less heavily booked; it is worth putting your name on the waiting list for cancellations at busy periods. Tickets can be bought in advance through **Travellers** in Puerto Montt (see Activities and tours above), from **Navimag** offices in Puerto Montt, Puerto Natales and Punta Arenas, from travel agencies throughout the country, or online at www.navimag.com.

To Puerto Chacabuco and Laguna San Rafael

Navimag ferry *M/V Magallanes* sails this route throughout the year, once or twice a week, 24 hrs, bunks from US$60 to US$200, cars US$180, motorcycles US$40, cycles US$28. In the summer (Sep-Apr) the Magallanes continues once a week (usually at the weekend) from Puerto Chacabuco to **Laguna San Rafael**, 21-24 hrs, return fare Puerto Montt-Laguna San Rafael US$400-800; better offers are available from Puerto Chacabuco to Laguna San Rafael (see page 261).

Skorpios Cruises luxury ship *Skorpios 2* leaves Puerto Montt Sat 1100 for a 6-day cruise to **Laguna San Rafael**, returning to Puerto Montt Fri, double cabin from US$1100 pp. For further details (and information about routes sailed by Skorpios II , consult www.skorpios.cl).

Raymond Weber, Av Chipana 3435 Pasaje 4, T02-8858250, www.chilecharter.com, charters 2 luxury sailing catamarans to visit Golfo de Ancud and Laguna San Rafael.

Other sea routes

To **Chaitén**, **Naviera Austral**, 4 ferries weekly, 10 hrs, passengers US$25, reclining seat US$33, cars US$120, bicycles US$11; **Catamaranes del Sur** 2 weekly in summer, less frequently off season, catamaran service, 4 hrs, US$35 including transfer to port from company offices.

To **Río Negro**, Isla Llancahué, Baños Cahuelmó and Fiordo Leptepu/Coman, m/n Bohemia, 6 days/5 nights, US$745-920 per person depending on season.

Directory

Puerto Montt *p231, map p236*

Banks ATMs at several banks and supermarkets in the centre and in both malls; commission charges for TCs vary widely. **Consulates** Argentina, Cauquenes 94, piso 2, T065-253996, quick visa service; **Germany**, Antonio Varas y Gallardo, piso 3, Oficina 306, Tue-Wed 0930-1200; **Netherlands**, Chorillos 1582, T065-253003; **Spain**, Rancagua 113, T065-252557. **Internet** Several in the centre and on Av Angelmó. **Laundry Center**, Antonio Varas 700; **Lavatodo**, O'Higgins 231; **Narly**, San Martín 187, Local 6, high prices, US$7 for 3 kg; **Nautilus**, Av Angelmó 1564, cheaper, good; **Unic**, Chillán 149; **Yessil't**, Edif Caracol, Urmeneta 300, service washes. **Medical services** Seminario s/n, T065-261134. **Post office** Rancagua 126, open 0830-1830 Mon-Fri, 0830-1200 Sat. **Telephone** Several in the centre and along Av Angelmó.

Carretera Austral

Footprint features

Introduction

Travelling along the Carretera Austral (also known as the Camino Austral) is one of the greatest journeys South America has to offer. The Carretera is a largely unpaved *ripio* road stretching over 1000 km through ever-changing spectacular scenery. Before the opening of the Carretera, this part of Chile was largely inaccessible; it remains breathtaking. Deep tree-lined fiords penetrate into the heart of a land of spiralling volcanoes and sparkling glaciers, rushing rivers, crystal blue lakes and temperate rainforest, rich with southern Chile's unique flora.

The only town of any size, Coyhaique, lies in the valley of the Río Simpson. South of Coyhaique are Lago General Carrera, the largest lake in Chile, and the Río Baker, one of the country's longest rivers. Further south still is Villa O' Higgins and the icefields of the Campo de Hielo Sur, which feed several magnificent glaciers and prevent further road building, although a route (by boat and on foot or mountain bike) exists to El Chaltén in Argentina. Coyhaique enjoys good air connections with Puerto Montt and Santiago, while nearby Puerto Chacabuco can be reached by ferry or catamaran from Puerto Montt, Chaitén and Chiloé. The most appealing parts of this region, however, can only be visited by travelling along the Carretera Austral.

★ Don't miss ...
❶ Cycling along the Carretera Austral, page 244.
❷ Parque Pumalín, page 246.
❸ Whitewater rafting at Futaleufú, page 250.
❹ Cruising to the San Rafael glacier, page 261.
❺ Trekking around Chile Chico, page 265.
N
50 km
50 miles
Pacific Ocean
CHILE
ARGENTINA
SANTA CRUZ
REGION XI
Puerto Montt
Puerto Varas
Frutillar
Ensenada
La Poza
Lago Llanquihue
La Picada
Peulla
Petrohué
Cayutué
Ralún
Cochamó
Pelluco
Lenca
Puelo
Paso Pérez Rosales
Tronador (3460m)
Bariloche
Catedral
Lago Mascardi
Villa Mascardi
Las Bayas
El Bolsón
Norquinco
Los Repollos
El Maitén
Epuyén
Cholila
Leleque
La Bolsa
Gualjaina
Esquel
Trevelin
Paso Futaleufú
Futaleufú
Lago Futalaufquen
Parque Nacional Los Alerces
Lago Menéndez
Maullín
Faro Corona
Caulín
Pargua
Calbuco
Isla Tenglo
Isla Huar
La Arena
Contao
Río Negro/ Hornopirén
Parque Nacional Hornopirén
Parque Pumalín
Parque Nacional Lago Puelo
Pumillahue
Ancud
Chacao
Linao
Chepu
Vilcún
Golfo de Ancud
Isla Llancahué
Peninsula Huequi
Degán
Quemchi
Isla Butachauques
Ayacara
Fiordo Largo
Leptepu
Dalcahue
Tenaún
Castro
Achao
Vilopulli
Puqueldón
Isla Chulin
Cucao
Chonchi
Teupa
Caleta Gonzalo
Caleta Santa Bárbara
Chiloé
Queilén
Isla Talcán
Isla Tranquil
Chaitén
Amarillo
Trincao
Quellón
Puerto Cárdenas
Corcovado (2290m)
Lago Yelcho
Lago Espoló
Puerto Piedra
Villa Santa Lucía
Nevada (2042m)
Puerto Ramírez
Palena
Paso Palena
Corcovado
Tecka
Carretera Austral
Golfo de Corcovado
Melinka
Lago Palena
Lago General Vinttner
Lago Vinttner
Alto Río Pico
La Junta
Lago Rosselot
Lago Risopatrón
Paso Las Pampas-Lago Verde
Lago Verde
Río Pico
Gobernador Costa
Termas de Puyuhuapi
Puyuhuapi
Parque Nacional Queulat
Parque Nacional Isla Magdalena
La Tapera
Paso Río Frias-Appeleg
Puerto Cisnes
Villa Amengual
Lago La Plata
Lago Fontana
Reserva Nacional Lago Las Torres
Alto Río Sanguer
Parque Nacional Isla Guamblin
Archipiélago de las Chonos
Puerto Aguirre
Mañihuales
Paso Pampa Alta
Puerto Aisén
Santa Maria del Mar
Coyhaique
Puerto Chacabuco
Paso Coyhaique Alto
Paso Triana
Reserva Nacional Río Simpson
Lago Elizalde
Alto Río Mayo
Hudson
Lago Atravesado
El Blanco
Balmaceda
Lago Blanco
Reserva Nacional Cerro Castillo
Cerro Castillo
Paso Huemules
Río Guenguel
Villa Cerro Castillo
Reserva Nacional Las Guaitecas
Puerto Grosse
Puerto Ibáñez
Levicán
Lago Buenos Aires
Bahía Murta
Lago General Carrera
Los Antiguos
Parque Nacional Laguna San Rafael
Fachinal
Chile Chico
Perito Moreno
Laguna San Rafael
Río Tranquilo
Estancia La Serena
Mallín Grande
Puerto Guadal
Cevallos (2743m)
Estancia Telken
Lago Bertrand
El Maitén
Puerto Bertrand
Campo de Hielo San Valentín
Reserva Nacional Tamango
Paso Roballos
Golfo de Peñas
Cochrane
Campo de Hielo Norte
Lago Cochrane
Lago Pueyrredón
Río Baker
Lago Posadas
Lago Salitroso
Cueva de los Manos
Canal Messier
Bajo Caracoles
Río Pinturas
Tortel
Estancia La Oriental
Puerto Yungay
Parque Nacional Perito Moreno
Herros (2770m)
San Lorenzo (3706m)
Reserva Nacional Katalalixar
Villa O'Higgins
Las Horquetas
L Strobel
Lago O'Higgins
Gobernador Gregores
Lago San Martín
L Cardiel
Estancia La Maipu
Estancia La Angostura
Puerto Edén
Isla Wellington
258
40
7

Ins and outs

Travelling the length of the Carretera Austral can be quite a challenge. The first and most important piece of advice is to take enough cash. While there are Cirrus and MasterCard ATMs in Chaitén and Cochrane, Coyhaique is the only place between Puerto Montt and Villa O'Higgins with Visa ATMs. After heavy rain, parts of the Carretera are liable to flood, so check the weather carefully and be prepared to be stuck in one place for a few days while conditions improve. Off season much of the northern section of the Carretera is inaccessible when the Arena–Puelche and Hornopirén–Caleta Gonzalo ferries are suspended. You will have to go to Chaitén directly from Puerto Montt or Chiloé instead.

Getting around

The road can be divided into three sections: **Puerto Montt to Chaitén** (242 km), including two or three ferry crossings; **Chaitén to Coyhaique** (435 km); and **Coyhaique to Villa O'Higgins** (582 km), including one ferry crossing. There is also a branch that runs along the southern shore of **Lago General Carrera** from Puerto Guadal to Chile Chico. The Puerto Montt–Chaitén section can only be travelled in summer, when the ferries are operating, but an alternative route, through Chiloé to Chaitén, exists year round (see page 233). The road is paved around Coyhaique from Mañihuales and Puerto Chacabuco to Villa Cerro Castillo and Puerto Ibañez.

Bus Most of the buses that ply the Carretera Austral are minibuses (and in more than one case converted transit vans) operated by small companies and often driven by their owners. Services are less reliable than elsewhere in Chile and timetables change frequently. Booking your ticket in advance means that if your bus does not leave for whatever reason, the company is liable to pay for your accommodation until the bus is ready to depart. Complaints should be directed to **SERNAC**, the government consumer rights department, in Coyhaique.

Driving Some sections of the road can be difficult or even impossible after heavy rain or snowfall, so check the weather carefully and be prepared to be stuck in one place for a few days while conditions improve. Take a 4WD and fill up your tank whenever possible. Although tourist infrastructure is growing rapidly and unleaded fuel is available all the way to Villa O'Higgins, you should protect windscreens and headlamps and carry adequate spare fuel and parts, especially if you are intending to detour from the main route.

Hitching is popular in summer, but extremely difficult out of season, particularly south of Cochrane. Watching the cloak of dust thrown up by the wheels from the back of a pick-up, while taking in the lakes, forests, mountains and waterfalls, is an unforgettable experience, but be prepared for long delays and allow at least three days from Chaitén to Coyhaique.

Cycling The Carretera Austral is highly recommended for cycling as long as you have enough time and are reasonably fit. A good mountain bike is essential and a tent is an advantage. Most buses will take bicycles for a small charge. An excellent online guide to cycling the Carretera, can be found at www.salamandras.cl

Best time to visit

January and February are probably the best months for a trip to this area. From April to September it is bitterly cold inland; roads are subject to snowfall or flooding, and some ferry services are suspended.

Puerto Montt to Chaitén

This 242-km section of the Carretera Austral is the most inaccessible and secluded stretch along the entire route, passing through two national parks and the private Parque Pumalin. Beautiful old trees close in on all sides, the rivers and streams sparkle and, on (admittedly rare) clear days, there are beautiful views across the Golfo de Ancud to Chiloé. » For Sleeping, Eating and other listings, see pages 248-249.

Parque Nacional Alerce Andino → *Colour map 1, B3*

ⓘ Entrances 2½ km from Correntoso (35 km west of Puerto Montt) and 7 km west of Lenca (40 km south of Puerto Montt), US$8.

This national park covers 39,255 ha of steep forested valleys between the beautiful Seno de Reloncaví (see page 232) and Lago Chapo, and contains ancient alerce trees, some over 1000 years old (the oldest are estimated to be 4200 years old). There are also some 50 small lakes and many waterfalls in the park. Wildlife includes pudú, pumas, vizcachas, condors and black woodpeckers. There are ranger posts at Río Chaicas, Lago Chapo, Laguna Sargazo and at the north entrance and a map is available from **CONAF** in Puerto Montt.

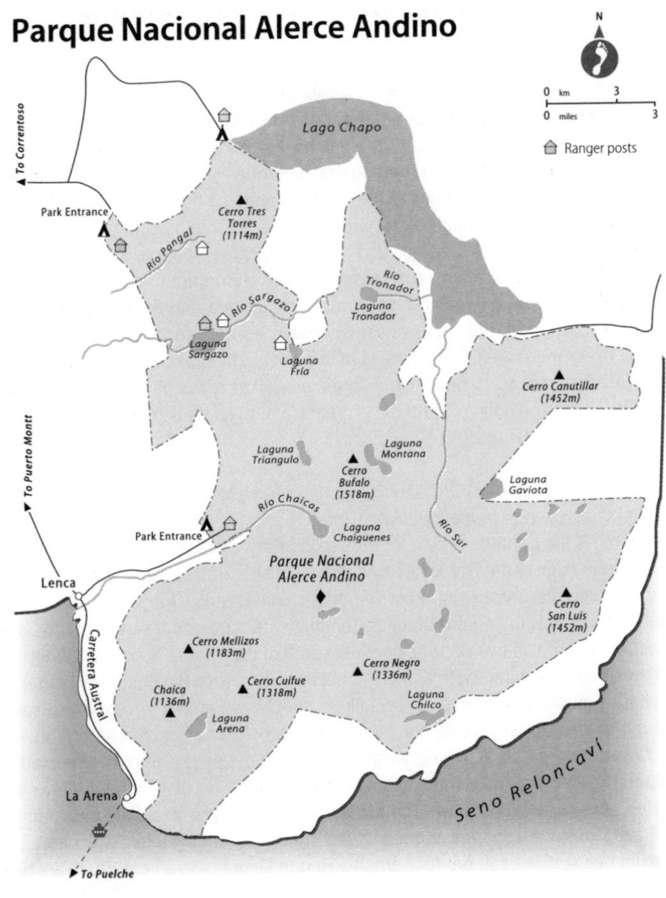

The long road south

Although the first town in this area, Balmaceda, was founded in 1917, followed by Puerto Aisén in 1924, the first road, between Puerto Aisén and Coyhaique, was not built until 1936. It was not until the 1960s, when new roads were built and airstrips were opened, that this region began to be integrated with the rest of the country.

The Carretera Austral has helped transform the lives of many people in this part of Chile, but the motivation behind its construction was mainly geopolitical. Ever since Independence, Chilean military and political leaders have stressed the importance of occupying the southern regions of the Pacific coast and preventing any incursion by Argentina. Building the Carretera Austral was seen by General Pinochet as a means of achieving this task: a way of occupying and securing territory, just as colonization had been in the early years of the 20th century.

Begun in 1976, the central section of the Carretera Austral, from Chaitén to Coyhaique, was opened in 1983. Five years later, the northern section, linking Chaitén with Puerto Montt, and the southern section, between Coyhaique and Cochrane, were officially inaugurated. Since then, the Carretera has been extended south of Cochrane to Puerto Yungay and Villa O'Higgins. Work is continuing, building branch roads and paving the most important sections.

Hornopirén and around → *Colour map 1, B3*

Some 46 km south of Puerto Montt (allow one hour), **La Arena** is the site of the first ferry, across the Reloncaví estuary to **Puelche**. From Puelche there is an unpaved road north to Puelo but the Carretera Austral continues 58 km south to **Hornopirén**, also called Río Negro, which lies at the northern end of a fjord. At the mouth of the fjord is **Isla Llancahué**, a small island with a hotel and thermal springs. The island is reached by **boat** ⓘ *T09-96424857, US$50 one way shared between group*, look out for dolphins and fur seals on the crossing. From Hornopirén, excursions can be made to the Hornopirén volcano (1572 m), Lago Cabrera and the **Parque Nacional Hornopirén**. The park lies 16 km east by *ripio* road and encompasses the Yates volcano (2187 m) as well as the basins of two rivers, the Blanco and the Negro. The park protects some 9000 ha of alerce forest as well as areas of mixed native forest including lenga and coigue. From the entrance a path leads 8 km east up along the Río Blanco to a basic *refugio*.

Parque Pumalin and around → *Colour map 1, B3*

ⓘ *T065-250079, www.pumalinpark.org, free.*

Hornopirén is the departure point for the second ferry, to Caleta Gonzalo, situated on the southern edge of the Fiordo Reñihue. This is the base for visiting Parque Pumalin, seen by many as one of the most important conservation projects in the world. Created by the US billionaire Douglas Tompkins, this private reserve extends over 700,000 ha and is in two sectors, one just south of the Parque Nacional Hornopirén and the other stretching south and east of Caleta Gonzalo to the Argentine border. Its purchase aroused controversy, especially in the Chilean armed forces, which saw it as a threat to national sovereignty, but now the park has nature sanctuary status.

Covering large areas of the western Andes, most of the park is occupied by temperate rainforest and is intended to protect the lifestyles of its inhabitants as well as the physical environment. Tompkins has established a native tree nursery, producing 100,000 saplings of endangered species, and developed apiculture; the Pumalin bee stations can produce around 30,000 kg of honey a year. There are treks ranging from short trails into the temperate rainforest to arduous hikes lasting for several days. Three marked trails lead to Cascadas Escondidas; to an area of very old alerce trees; and to Laguna Tronador.

The road through these forests was only built in the 1980s, meaning that, unlike areas to the north and south, endangered trees have been protected from logging (laws protecting alerces, araucaria and other native species were passed in the 1970s). As a result, Parque Pumalín is home to perhaps the most diverse temperate rainforest in the world, and is the only place where alerce forests remain intact just a few metres from the main road. It is a truly humbling experience looking up from the base of a 3000-year-old, 3-m-wide alerce, and this, in itself, is a reason to visit the park. There are only three buses a week, but hitching is not difficult in season.

The Carretera Austral runs through the park, climbing steeply before reaching two lakes, Lago Río Negro and Lago Río Blanco. The coast is reached at Santa Bárbara, 48 km south, where there is a black sand beach. Camping, although not officially allowed, is tolerated. Towards sunset dolphins often swim right up to the beach. You can join them, although the water is very cold.

Chaitén → *Colour map 1, C2*

The capital of Palena province, Chaitén lies in a beautiful spot, with a forest-covered hill rising behind it, and a quiet inlet leading out into the Patagonian channels. The town is important as a port for catamarans and ferries to Puerto Montt and to Chiloé (see page 249), and is a growing centre for adventure tourism. There is excellent fishing nearby, especially to the south in the ríos Yelcho and Futaleufú and in lagos Espolón and Yelcho. Fishing licences are sold at the Municipalidad. Visits are also possible to an offshore sea-lion colony on **Isla Puduguapi**.

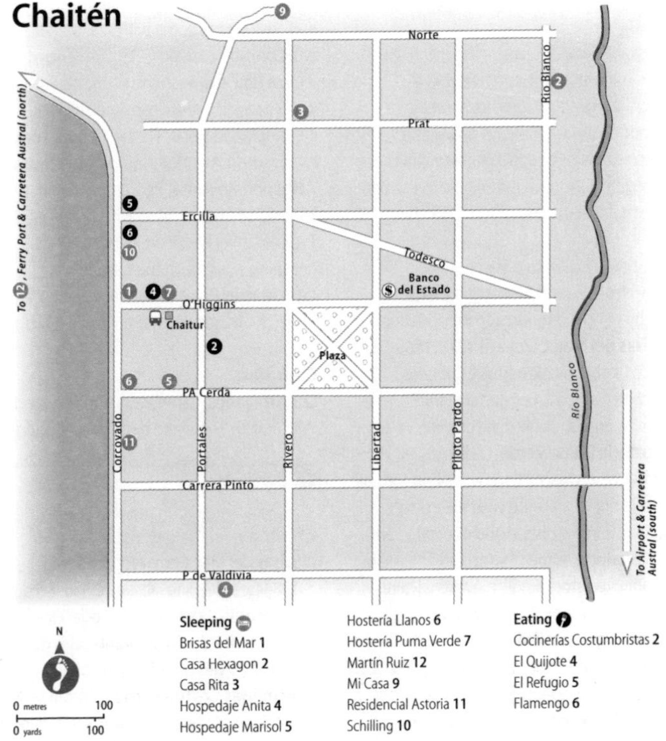

Sleeping

Parque Nacional Alerce Andino *p245*
There are basic *refugios* at Río Pangal, Laguna Sargazo and Laguna Fría, and campsites at Río Chaicas and at the northern entrance; no camping is permitted within the park.

Hornopirén and around *p246*
Lots of *cabañas* and *residenciales* here.
B **Termas de Llancahue**, Llancahue Island, T099-6424857. Full board, good food, access to thermal springs.
C-D **Holiday Country**, O'Higgins 637, T065-217220. Restaurant, also *cabañas*.
C-D **Hostería Catalina**, Ingenieros Militares s/n, T065-217359, www.hosteriacatalina.cl. Comfortable rooms with breakfast and bath. Recommended.
D **Hornopirén**, Carrera Pinto 388, T065-217256. Rooms with shared bathrooms. Recommended, also *cabañas*.

Camping
There's a good site on Ingenieros Militares, US$14 per site, and 4 more sites south of Hornopirén on the road to Pichanco.

Parque Pumalin and around *p246*
There is a restaurant, *cabañas* and a campsite in Caleta Gonzalo, as well as a visitors' centre (not always open) and demonstrations of agricultural techniques in the region. Camping is available in the park at several well-run sites from US$8 per tent.

Chaitén *p247, map p247*
Ferries from Puerto Montt and Chiloé are met by people offering accommodation.
B **Brisas del Mar**, Corcovado 278, T065-731284, cababrisas@telsur.cl. *Cabañas* opposite the coast, comfortable for 3. Friendly, English spoken in summer, Wi-Fi.
B **Hostería Puma Verde**, O'Higgins 54, T065-731184, reservasalsur@surnet.cl. Comfortable upscale hostel affiliated with the Pumalín organization. Furnished and decorated with local products, some of which are for sale in the annexed store. English spoken. There is also an apartment, AL, sleeping up to 5.
B **Schilling**, Corcovado 320, T065-731295. With breakfast, heating, restaurant. No views from rooms despite the location, overpriced, unfriendly. No advance reservations.
C **Mi Casa**, Av Norte, T065-731285, hmicasa@telsur.cl. On a hill offering fine views. Sauna, gymnasium and restaurant with good value set meal. Recommended.
D **Casa Hexagon**, Blanco 36, T09-82862950. F singles. Extraordinary hexagonal hostel with a tree trunk at its centre. Very comfortable and with excellent kitchen facilities. Pleasant walks along the river. Owned by an eccentric German, who built the house himself, and has furnished it with contemporary art and oriental carpets. Highly recommended.
D **Residencial Astoria**, Corcovado 442, T065- 731263. With bath, G pp without. A couple of the rooms have a sea view. There is a nice living room upstairs over-looking the sea, where breakfast is served.
D-E **Hospedaje Marisol**, Pedro Aguirre Cerda 66, T065-731188, rumer@surnet.cl. G singles. With breakfast. Friendly and clean family home. Kitchen facilities, internet, cable TV in living room. There is a nice cabin in the garden, B-C for up to 5 people. Recommended.
D-D **Hostería Llanos**, Corcovado 378, T065-731332. G Singles. Slightly cramped but clean and cosy rooms, some with sea view. No bath, basic breakfast, friendly. Recommended.
E **Casa Rita**, Rivero y Prat. G singles. Friendly, good beds, kitchen, clean, open all year, heating. Good value. The best budget option, highly recommended. Camping also available.
E **Hospedaje Anita**, Pedro de Valdivia 129, T065-731413. G singles. With breakfast. Typical family home. Very low ceilings. Camping possible in the garden.
G pp **Martín Ruiz**, Carretera Austral, 1 km north of Chaitén. With breakfast. Friendly.

Camping
Los Arrayanes, Carretera Austral, 4 km north. With hot showers and close to sea, good.

Eating

Chaitén *p247, map p247*
TT **Brisas del Mar**, Corcovado 278. T065-731284 (see Sleeping, above). Good fish dishes.
TT **El Refugio**, Corcovado y Ercilla. One of the better seafood restaurants with rustic furniture carved out of tree trunks.
T **Cocinerías Costumbristas**, Portales 300 block. Several tiny restaurants serving local

fare such as *curanto* at reasonable prices and in large portions. Recommended.

¥ **El Quijote**, O'Higgins 42, T065-731293. Basic food and bar snacks.

¥ **Flamengo**, Corcovado 218. Popular seafood restaurant.

Activities and tours

Chaitén *p247, map p247*

Chaitur, O'Higgins 67, T/F065-731429, nchaitur@hotmail.com. Travel agent selling bus and boat tickets. Also trekking, horse riding, fishing and trips to Parque Pumalín, Termas de Amarillo and Yelcho Glacier. Highly recommended. Another branch at Diego Portales 350.

Transport

Before setting out, check when the ferries are running and, if driving, make a reservation for your vehicle: do this at **Naviera Austral**, in Puerto Montt (see page 239).

Parque Nacional Alerce Andino *p245*

To reach the northern entrance, take **Fierro** or **Río Pato** bus from Puerto Montt to **Correntoso** (or **Lago Chapo** bus which passes through Correntoso), several daily except Sun, then walk. To reach the southern entrance, take any **Fierro** bus to Chaicas, La Arena, Contau and Hornopirén, US$1.50, get off at **Lenca** sawmill, then walk (signposted).

A ferry makes the 30-min crossing, from La Arena to **Puelche**, 10 daily Dec-Mar, reduced service off season. Arrive 30 mins early for a place; buses have priority, cars US$15.

Hornopirén and around *p246*

Bus

Fierro 2 buses daily from Puerto Montt. No buses south from Hornopirén.

Ferry

In Jan and Feb only, the **Naviera Austral** ferry *Mailen* sails from Hornopirén to **Caleta Gonzalo**, 1600 daily, 6 hrs, return departures 0900 daily, cars US$110 one way, foot passengers US$18, bicycles US$11. Advance booking required: there can be a 2-day wait. **Chaitur** organizes connecting transport between the ferry port in Caleta Gonzalo and Chaitén (see Activities and tours).

Chaitén *p247, map p247*

Air

Flights to **Puerto Montt** by Aerosur, **Aeropuelche** and **Aeromet**, daily 1200, 35 mins, US$50. Bookings through **Chaitur** (see Activities and tours). Note that flying in bad weather in a small aircraft is not necessarily safe and there have been a number of accidents in recent years.

Bus

Terminal at O'Higgins 67. Several companies run minibuses along the Carretera Austral to **Coyhaique**, most days direct in summer, 2 a week with overnight stop in La Junta or Puyuhuapi in winter, departures usually 0800-0900. Minibuses usually travel full, so can't pick up passengers en route. Chaitur acts as an agent for all these services (see Activities and tours). **Buses Norte**, Libertad 432, T065-731390, has buses to **Coyhaique**, US$30, and intermediate points such as La Junta (US$10) and Puyuhuapi. To **Futaleufú**, 4 hrs, with **Chaitur**, 1530 Mon-Sat, US$12; with **B y V**, 0900 daily, US$9; with **Buses Ebenezer**, Mon-Sat 1530, Sun 1700.

Sea

The ferry port is about 1 km north of town. Schedules change frequently and are infrequent off season. To **Chiloé**, **Naviera Austral**, Corcovado 266, T065-731272, www.navieraustral.cl, operates ferry services to **Castro** or **Quellón**, 4 per week Dec-Mar, reduced service off season, 5 hrs, US$30 one way, US$130 cars, US$13 bikes. **Catamaranes del Sur**, Todesco 180, T065-731199, www.catamaranesdelsur.cl, operates catamaran services on the same route for foot passengers only, 2-3 weekly in summer, less regularly off season, 2 hrs, US$25.

To **Puerto Montt**, **Naviera Austral**, 4 weekly, 10 hrs, US$25, car US$120, bike US$11; **Catamaranes del Sur** 2 weekly weather permitting, 3 hrs, US$35.

Directory

Chaitén *p247, map p247*

Banks **Banco del Estado**, O'Higgins y Libertad, charges US$10 for changing TCs, ATM accepts MasterCard and Cirrus but not Visa. Rates are poor along the Carretera Austral; change money in Puerto Montt.

Chaitén to Coyhaique

This section of the Carretera Austral, 422 km long, runs through long stretches of virgin rainforest, passing small villages, the still white waters of Lago Yelcho and the Parque Nacional Queulat, with its glaciers and waterfalls. Roads branch off east to the Argentine frontier and west to Puerto Cisnes and Puerto Aisén. Near Coyhaique, the road passes huge tracts of land destroyed by logging, where only tree-stumps remain as testament to the depredations of the early colonists. Founded in 1929, Coyhaique is the administrative and commercial centre of Region XI and is the only settlement of any real size on the Carretera Austral. A lively city, it provides a good base for excursions in the area. » *For Sleeping, Eating and other listings see pages 253-262.*

Ins and outs » *For further details, see Transport, page 260.*

Getting there Coyhaique is the transport hub for Region XI. There are two airports in the area: **Tte Vidal** ⓘ *5 km southwest of Coyhaique, taxi US$7*, which handles only smaller aircraft, and **Balmaceda** ⓘ *56 km southeast of Coyhaique, taxi 1 hr US$11*, near the Argentine frontier at Paso Huemules. Flying to Balmaceda is the most direct way to reach Coyhaique, with three or four flights daily from Santiago and Puerto Montt and a weekly flight to/from Punta Arenas. Minibuses, known as 'transfers', run between Balmaceda and Coyhaique, collecting/delivering to hotels; contact **Travell** ⓘ *Parra y Moraleda, T067-230010, US$5* and **Transfer** ⓘ *Lautaro 828, T067-233030, US$5*.

There are long-distance buses (several weekly) from Puerto Montt to Coyhaique but they do not travel along the Carretera Austral, using instead the long and expensive route via Argentina. Another enjoyable way to reach this part of the country is to take the boat from Puerto Montt to Puerto Chacabuco (see page 240).

Lago Yelcho and the border → *Colour map 1, C3*

Surrounded by forest, 45 km south of Chaitén, **Puerto Cárdenas** lies on the northern tip of **Lago Yelcho**, a beautiful glacial lake on the Río Futaleufú surrounded by hills and the beautiful Yelcho glacier. The lake is frequented by anglers. At Puerto Cárdenas, there is a police post where you may have to register your passport. Further south at Km 60, a path leads to the **Yelcho glacier**, a two-hour walk. The Argentine frontier is reached at Futaleufú and Palena, along a road that branches off the Carretera Austral at **Villa Santa Lucía** (Km 81). The road to the border is single track, *ripio*, best with a 4WD. At **Puerto Ramírez**, at the southern end of **Lago Yelcho**, the road divides: the north branch runs along the valley of the Río Futaleufú to Futaleufú, while the southern one continues to Palena. The border is 8 km east of both Futaleufú and Palena. Both crossings lead to the Welsh settlement of Trevelin (45 km east of Futaleufú, 95 km east of Palena; see page 108) and Esquel (23 km northeast; see page 107). » *For full details, see page 107.*

Futaleufú → *See map pag 253. Colour map 1, C3.*

Futaleufú (big river in the Mapuche language) has now established itself as the centre for the finest whitewater rafting in the southern hemisphere. Every year, hundreds of fanatics travel to spend the southern summer here and there is no shortage of operators offering trips. The river is an incredible deep blue colour and offers everything from easy Grade II-III sections downstream to the extremely challenging Grade V Cañon del Infierno (Hell Canyon), surrounded by spectacular mountain scenery.

The village, hemmed in by mountains and the Río Espolón, is peaceful, with wide streets and Chilote-style houses. There is a **tourist office** ⓘ *on the plaza, T065-721241, daily in summer 0900-2100*. **Lago Espolón**, west of Futaleufú, is reached by a turning 41 km northeast of Puerto Ramírez. The beautiful lake enjoys a warm microclimate: 30°C in the day in summer, 5°C at night. If you take a quick dip, beware of the currents.

“” Ciudad de los Césares was a fabulously wealthy mythological city built between hills made of gold and diamonds and inhabited by immortal beings.

La Junta and around → *Colour map 1, C3*

From Villa Santa Lucía, the Carretera Austral follows the Río Frío and then the Río Palena to **La Junta**, a tranquil, nondescript village at the confluence of Río Rosselot and Río Palena, 151 km south of Chaitén. Fuel is available here. From La Junta roads head northwest to **Puerto Raúl Marín Balmaceda** on the coast and east for 9 km to **Lago Rosselot**, surrounded by forest and situated at the heart of a *reserva nacional* (12,725 ha). From Lago Rosselot the road continues for 74 km to a **border crossing** ① *summer 0730-2200; winter 0800-2000*, at **Lago Verde** towards Las Pampas and Gobernador Costa in Argentina.

Puyuhuapi and around → *Colour map 2, A2*

The Carretera Austral continues south from La Junta, along the western side of Lago Risopatrón, past several waterfalls, to **Puyuhuapi** (also spelt Puyuguapi). Located in a beautiful spot at the northern end of a fjord, the village is a tranquil stopping place between Chaitén and Coyhaique. It was founded by four Sudeten German families in 1935 and its economy is based around fishing, tourism and the factory where Puyuhuapi's famous handmade carpets are produced. From Puyuhuapi, the road follows the eastern edge of the fjord along one of the most beautiful sections of the Carretera Austral, with views of the **Termas de Puyuhuapi** on the other side (see page 252).

Covering 154,093 ha of attractive forest around Puyuhuapi, the **Parque Nacional Queulat** ① *administration at the CONAF office in La Junta, T067-314128*, is, supposedly, the former location of the legendary Ciudad de los Césares. According to myth, the city was protected by a shroud of fog and hence was impossible for strangers to discover. The Carretera Austral passes through the park, close to **Lago Risopatrón**, where boat trips are available. Some 24 km south, a two-hour trek leads to the **Ventisquero Colgante** hanging glacier. From here the Carretera Austral climbs out of the Queulat valley through a series of hairpin bends offering fine views of several glaciers.

Río Cisnes → *Colour map 2, A2*

Stretching 160 km from the Argentine border to the coast at Puerto Cisnes, the Río Cisnes is recommended for rafting or canoeing, with grand scenery and modest rapids – except for the horrendous drop at Piedra del Gato, about 60 km east of Puerto Cisnes. Good camping is available in the forest. Possibly the wettest town in Chile, **Puerto Cisnes** is reached by a 33-km winding road that branches west off the Carretera Austral about 59 km south of Puyuhuapi. The **Argentine border** is reached via a road that follows the Río Cisnes east for 104 km, via La Tapera. In Argentina, the road continues via Río Frías to meet up with Route 40, the north-south road at the foot of the Andes (see page 148). **Chilean immigration** ① *12 km west of the border, daylight hours only.*

Towards Coyhaique

The **Reserva Nacional Lago Las Torres** is 98 km south of Puyuhuapi and covers 16,516. It includes the wonderful Lago Las Torres, which offers good fishing and a small **CONAF** campsite. Further south, at Km 125, a road branches east to El Toqui where zinc is mined. From here the Carretera Austral is paved.

Termas de Puyuhuapi

Situated on the western edge of the fjord, 18 km southwest of Puyuhuapi, are the Termas de Puyuhuapi, T067-325103, US$15 per person, under-12s US$10. This resort, accessible only by boat (US$3 each way, 10-minute crossing) has several 40°C springs filling three pools near the beach. Accommodation at the resort (L-AL) includes use of the pools and the boat transfer. Price depends on the season and type of room. The hotel restaurant is good; full board US$40 extra. The resort can be visited on a four- or six-day tour with **Patagonia Connection** (see page 254). Transport to the hotel can also be arranged independently via hydroplane from Puerto Montt.

Coyhaique and around » pp253-262.

→ *See map page 255. Colour map 2, A2.*

Located 420 km south of Chaitén, Coyhaique (also spelt Coihaique) lies in the broad green valley of the Río Simpson. The city is encircled by a crown of snow-capped mountains and, for a few hours after it has rained, the mountainsides are covered in a fine layer of frost – a spectacular sight. Although there are many more attractions outside Coyhaique, it is a pleasant, friendly place, perfect for relaxing for a couple of days or as a base for day trips. The town is centred around an unusual pentagonal plaza, built in 1945, on which stand the cathedral, the Intendencia and a handicraft market. Further north on Baquedano is a display of old military machinery outside the local regimental headquarters. In the Casa de Cultura the **Museo Regional de la Patagonia Central** ⓘ *Lillo23, Tue-Sun 0900-2000 (summer), 0830-1730 (winter), US$1*, has sections on history, mineralogy, zoology and archaeology, as well as photos of the construction of the Carretera Austral. The very helpful **Sernatur** office ⓘ *Bulnes 35, T067-231752, infoaisen@sernatur.cl, Mon-Fri 0830-1700*, has bus timetables. **CONAF** is at ⓘ *Ogana 1060, T067-212125, Mon-Fri 0830-1730*. Maps (photocopies of 1:50,000 IGM maps) are available from **Dirección de Vialidad** on the plaza.

From Coyhaique there are two routes into Argentina: via Coyhaique Alto and Paso Huemules (see page 149). The former route takes you past the **Monumento Natural Dos Lagunas** ⓘ *25 km east of Coyhaique, US$2, camping US$15 per site*, a small park that encompasses Lagos El Toro and Escondido. The latter route passes Balmaceda airport.

Around Coyhaique

There are two national reserves close to Coyhaique: 5 km northwest off the Carretera Austral is **Reserva Nacional Coyhaique**, which covers 2150 ha of forest (mainly introduced species), while west of Coyhaique (take any bus to Puerto Aisén) is the **Reserva Nacional Río Simpson**, covering 40,827 ha of steep forested valleys and curiously rounded hills rising to 1878 m. One of these, near the western edge of the park, is known as '*El Cake Inglés*'. There are beautiful waterfalls, lovely views of the river and very good fly fishing here. The southeastern sector of the reserve is designated as the **Reserva Nacional Río Clara** and is one of the best places to see the native huemul (see page 264), although visitors must be accompanied by a warden. Other wildlife includes pudú and pumas, and a variety of birds ranging from condors to several species of ducks. Administration is 32 km west of Coyhaique, just off the road.

Puerto Aisén and Puerto Chacabuco → *Colour map 2, A2*

Puerto Aisén lies at the confluence of the rivers Aisén and Palos. First developed in the 1920s, the town grew as the major port of the region until the silting up of the Río Aisén forced the port to move 15 km further downriver to Puerto Chacabuco. Today boats lie

Puerto Aisén is much wetter than Coyhaique – local wags say that it rains for 370 days a year.

high and dry on the bank when the tide is out and the foundations of buildings by the river are overgrown with fuchsias and buttercups. To see any maritime activity you have to walk to **Puerto Aguas Muertas** where the fishing boats come in. There is a helpful **tourist office** ⓘ *Prat y Sgto Aldea, Dec-Feb only*, in the Municipalidad.

The town is linked to the south bank of the Río Aisén by the Puente Presidente Ibáñez, once the longest suspension bridge in Chile. From the far bank a paved road leads to **Puerto Chacabuco**, from where ferry services depart for Puerto Montt and **Laguna San Rafael** (see page 261).

A good 10 km walk north along a minor road from Puerto Aisén leads to **Laguna Los Palos**, calm, deserted and surrounded by forested hills. **Lago Riesco**, 30 km south of Puerto Aisén, can be reached by an unpaved road that follows the Río Blanco. In season, the *Apulcheu* sails regularly to **Termas de Chiconal** ⓘ *US$50*, about one hour west of Puerto Chacabuco on the northern shore of the Seno Aisén, offering a good way to see the fjord.

Sleeping

Lago Yelcho and the border *p250*

AL **Cabañas CAVI**, Lago Yelcho, near Puerto Cárdenas. Sauna, restaurant, video room, laundry. 6 *cabañas* with bathrooms, hot water, kitchen facilities. Also campsite with electricity, hot showers, laundry, barbecue area and fishing boats for hire. Book via **Turismo Austral Ltda**, Santa Magdalena 75, of 902, Providencia, Santiago, T02-3341309.

AL-A **Cabañas Yelcho en La Patagonia**, Lago Yelcho, 7 km south of Puerto Cárdenas, T065- 731337, www.yelcho.cl. Cabins and rooms on the lake shore. Also camping and café.

B **Termas de Amarillo**, Termas de Amarillo, T065-731326. Also camping and *cabañas*.

D **Residencial Yelcho**, Puerto Cárdenas, T065-264429. Clean, full board available.

E **Residencial Marcela**, Amarillo, T065-264442. Also *cabañas* and camping.

Futaleufú *p250, map p253*

L-AL **El Barranco**, O'Higgins 172, Futaleufú, T065-721314, www.elbarrancochile.cl. Probably the best rooms in town, but still overpriced. There is a bar, restaurant, outdoor swimming pool and free bicycles for the guests. Fishing trips organized.

AL-A **Hostería Río Grande**, O'Higgins 397, Futaleufú, T065-721320, www.pacchile.com. Overpriced though comfortable, en suite bathrooms, friendly, bar, good restaurant.

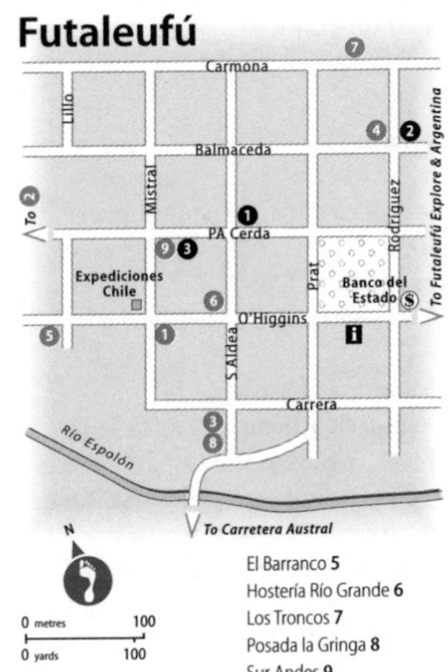

A **Posada la Gringa**, Sargento Aldea 498, Futaleufú, T065-721260. Elegant and charming guesthouse set in large gardens and with the best view in town. Price includes a large brunch. Recommended.

B-C **Cabañas Veranada**, Sargento Aldea 480, Futaleufú, T065-721266. Well-equipped cabins with excellent beds and good kitchens. Most have slow-burning wood stoves. Friendly owners. Recommended.

C **Cabañas Río Espolón**, PA Cerda s/n, 5 mins' walk west of centre, Futaleufú, T065-721216, rioespolon@yahoo.es. Secluded cabins with bar and restaurant overlooking the river, the sound of which is a constant in the background. Book ahead as it often fills up with rafting groups.

C **Sur Andes**, Cerda 308, Futaleufú, T065-721405, www.surandes.tk. Rustic but tasteful apartment, fully equipped but with no kitchen.

D **Adolfo B&B**, O'Higgins 302, Futaleufú, T065- 721256. F-G singles. Well-kept and friendly family home. With breakfast and kitchen facilities.

D **Los Troncos**, Carmona 541, Futaleufú, T065-721269. G singles. Basic clean *hospedaje* on the northern edge of town. With breakfast and kitchen facilities.

F **Continental**, Balmaceda 595, Futaleufú, T065-721222. G singles. Pokey rooms, creaky floors, squeaky beds and no toilet paper provided, but clean and you can't ask for more at this price.

Camping

There is a decent, if basic, campsite on the west edge of town next to Laguna Espejo, US$5 per person with hot water.

Los Copihues, T065-721413, is on the river, 500 m from Futaleufú. Horse-riding trips.

La Junta and around *p251*

A-B **Espacio y Tiempo**, La Junta, T067-314141, www.espacioytiempo.cl. Attractive garden, English spoken, good restaurant, fishing expeditions and other tours.

D **Hostería Patagonia**, Lynch 331, La Junta, T067-314120. Good meals, small rooms.

D **Residencial Copihue**, Varas 611, T067-314184. F singles. With breakfast, without bath, good meals, changes money, poor rates.

D **Residencial Valdera**, Varas s/n, T067-314105. F singles. Breakfast and bath, excellent value.

Puyuhuapi and around *p251*

There's a CONAF campsite at Lago Risopatrón.

LL-L **Fiordo Queulat Ecolodge**, Seno Queulat, Parque Nacional Queulat, T067-233302, www.aisen.cl. Half board. Has a good reputation, offers hikes and fishing trips. Campsite nearby, US$5.

L-AL **Cabañas El Pangue**, north end of Lago Risopatrón, Carretera Austral Norte, Km 240, Parque Nacional Queulat, T067-325128, www.elpangue.com. Cabins sleep 4, private bathrooms, hot water, heating, telephone, parking, swimming pool, fishing trips, horse riding, mountain bikes. Recommended.

L-AL **Puyuhuapi Lodge and Spa**, T067-325103, www.patagonia-connection.com. For reservations contact **Patagonia Connection**, Fidel Oteiza 1921, oficina 1006, Santiago. Rooms from US$118 including in/out boat transfer, breakfast and use of outside hot-spring pools (low season). Good restaurant. Recommended. Boat schedule from jetty, 2 hrs' walk from town, frequent in season, US$5 each way, 10-min crossing. Transport to the hotel may be arranged independently via hydroplane from Puerto Montt. See also Activities and tours, page 258.

C **Hostería Alemana**, Av Otto Uebel 450, T067-325118. A large, comfortable, wooden house on the main road, owned by Señora Ursula Flack Kroschewski. Highly recommended, closed in winter.

C-D pp **Casa Ludwig**, Av Otto Uebel s/n, on the southern edge of town, T067-325220, www.contactchile.cl/casaludwig. English and German spoken. Highly recommended.

E **Sra Leontina Fuentes**, Llantureo y Circunvalación. G singles. Clean, hot water, good breakfast for US$2.

Camping

CONAF, reservations T067-212125, runs a basic campsite (cold water) 12 km north of Puyuhuapi on the shores of Lago Risopatrón, and another near the Ventisquero Colgante. There is also a dirty campsite by the fjord behind the general store in Puyuhuapi.

Río Cisnes *p251*

A-C **Cabañas Río Cisnes**, Costanera 101, Puerto Cisnes, T067-346404. Cabins sleep 4-8. Owner, Juan Suazo, has a boat and offers good sea trout/salmon fishing.

B Manzur, Dunn 75, Puerto Cisnes, T067-346453. *Cabañas.*
D Pensión, Carlos Condell y Dr Steffen, Puerto Cisnes. With breakfast, hot shower, friendly.
F Hostería El Gaucho, Holmberg 140, Puerto Cisnes, T067-346514. With breakfast, dinner available, hot water.
F Residencia Bienvenido, Ibar 248, Villa Mañihuales. Clean, friendly, with a restaurant.
F Villa Mañihuales, E Ibar 200, Villa Mañihuales, T067-234803. Friendly, with breakfast.

Coyhaique *p252, map p255*
The tourist office has a list of all accommodation, but look out for notices in windows since any place with fewer than 6 beds does not have to register with the authorities.
AL-A Hostería Coyhaique, Magallanes 131, T067-231137. Coyhaique's premier hotel. 4-star, though showing its age a little. Set in spacious gardens, decent rooms, doubles have full bathtub.
A El Reloj, Baquedano 828, T067-231108, www.elrelojhotel.cl. In a former saw mill. With good restaurant, nice lounge, conference room, some rooms have wonderful views. English spoken. Highly recommended.
A-B Cabañas Mirador, Baquedano 848, T067-233191. Fully equipped cabins sleeping 2-4. The last cabin has tremendous views.

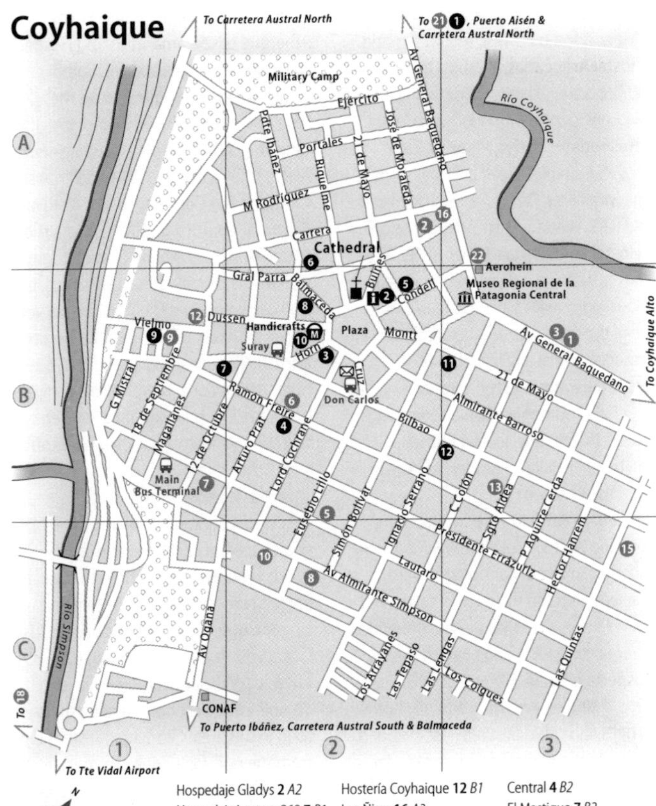

Sleeping
Albergue Las Salamandras **18** *C1*
Cabañas Mirador **1** *B3*
El Reloj **3** *B3*
Hospedaje Gladys **2** *A2*
Hospedaje Lautaro 269 **7** *B1*
Hospedaje María Ester **5** *B2*
Hospedaje Mondaca **8** *C2*
Hospedaje Natti **10** *C2*
Hospedaje Patricio y Gedra Guzmán **21** *A3*
Hospedaje Pochi **6** *B2*
Hostal Araucarias **9** *B1*
Hostal Español **13** *B3*
Hostal Las Quintas **15** *C3*
Hostería Coyhaique **12** *B1*
Los Ñires **16** *A3*
San Sebastián **22** *A3*

Eating
Café Alemana **5** *B2*
Café Oriente **2** *B2*
Café Ricer **3** *B2*
Calor y Comida **1** *A3*
Casino de Bomberos **6** *A2*
Central **4** *B2*
El Mastique **7** *B2*
Histórico Ricer **3** *B2*
La Casona **9** *B1*
La Fiorentina **10** *B2*
La Olla **8** *B2*
Las Piedras **11** **B3**
Yangtse **12** *B3*

Advance booking essential in season (deposit required). Long-term lets off season.

A-B **Cabañas Río Simpson**, 3 km north of town, T067-232183, www.cabanas-rio-simpson.cl. Fully equipped cabins for 4-9 people. Horse riding, fishing and tours. Several tame alpacas in the grounds.

A-B **Los Ñires**, Baquedano 315, T067-232261, www.doncarlos.cl/hotel.htm. With breakfast, small rooms, comfortable, parking.

B **Hostal Español**, Sargento Aldea 343, T067-242580, www.hostalcoyhaique.cl. New, small family-run hotel. 7 rooms all with views, carpets, bathrooms and cable TV. Spacious living room downstairs. Recommended.

B **San Sebastián**, Baquedano 496, T067-233427. Small hotel with spacious rooms, all with view, good breakfast, recommended.

B-C **Hostal Araucarias**, Vielmo 71, T067-232707. Spacious, creaky rooms with bath and TV, pleasant lounge with good view, quiet.

C-D **Hospedaje Gladys**, Parra 65, T067-251076. **E-F** singles. Clean and well-kept rooms with cable TV. Some with bathrooms. A little dark. Breakfast extra. Beauty salon.

C-D **Hostal Las Quintas**, Bilbao 1208, T067-231173. Spartan, but clean and extremely spacious rooms with bath and breakfast. Some of the rooms are architecturally among the most bizarre of any hostel in Chile.

D **Hospedaje María Ester**, Lautaro 544, T067-233023. **G** singles. Some rooms with bath and TV. Friendly, local information given, breakfast extra, laundry facilities, kitchen use charged for.

D **Hospedaje Patricio y Gedra Guzmán**, Baquedano 20, T067-232520, www.balasch.cl/cabanas. Small but comfortable self-contained cabins on the edge of town with extensive views. Good value. Recommended. Preference to those taking Spanish classes.

D **Hospedaje Pochi**, Freire 342, T067-256968. **F** singles. Rooms in a family home with bath and cable TV. Breakfast included. Very pleasant owners. English spoken by the daughter. Good value. Recommended.

D-E **Hospedaje Lautaro 269**, T067-237184. **G** singles. Large old wooden house with creaky floors. With parking, internet access and kitchen facilities.

D-E **Hospedaje Mondaca**, Av Simpson 571, T067-254676. **G** singles. Small (only 3 rooms) but spotless family home. Friendly, breakfast extra, will heat up pre-prepared food.

D-G **Albergue Las Salamandras**, 2 km south of town, T067-211865, www.salamandras.cl. Double rooms, dorm beds, *cabañas* and camping in attractive forest location. Kitchen facilities, winter sports, trekking and tours. Maps, including good trekking maps, and cycling information provided. English spoken. Excellent website. Highly recommended.

E **Hospedaje Natti**, Av Simpson 417, T067-231047. **G** singles. Clean, very friendly, kitchen facilities, breakfast US$2 extra. Also good-value camping including access to hot showers. Recommended.

Campsites

Sernatur in Coyhaique (see page 252) has a full list of all sites in Region XI. Also see **Albergue Las Salamandras** and **Hospedaje Natti** above. There are several other campsites in Coyhaique and on the road to Puerto Aisén, including:

Camping Alborada, Km 1 towards Puerto Aisén, T067-238868. US$14, with hot shower.

Camping Río Correntoso, Km 42 towards Puerto Aisén, T067-232005. US$20, showers and fishing. Automobile Club discount.

In the Reserva Nacional Coyhaique, there are basic campsites, US$7, at Laguna Verde and at Casa Bruja, 4 km and 2 km respectively from the entrance, and a *refugio*, US$2, 3 km from the entrance. There's also a campsite near the turning to Santuario San Sebastián, US$7, in the Reserva Nacional Río Simpson.

Puerto Aisén and around *p252*

Accommodation can be hard to find, most is geared towards workers in the fishing industry in both Puerto Aisén and Puerto Chacabuco. There's no campsite but free camping is easy.

LL-L **Parque Turístico Loberías de Aisén**, Carrera 50, Puerto Chacabuco, T067-351112, www.loberiasdelsur.cl. Recently rebuilt 5-star complex, the best hotel serving the best food in this area. Climb up the steps direct from the port for a drink or a meal overlooking boats and mountains before boarding your ferry. Car hire available.

C **Hotel Caicahues**, Michimalonco 660, Puerto Aisén, T067-336633. With bath, heating, telephone and internet; book in advance.

D **Hotel Plaza**, O'Higgins 613, Puerto Aisén, T067-332784. **G** singles. Basic, without breakfast, some rooms with no windows.

D **Mar Clara**, Carrera 970, Puerto Aisén, T067-330945. **G** singles. More expensive with bath. Basic, clean, thin walls, looks nicer from outside than within.
D **Roxy**, Aldea 972, Puerto Aisén, T067-332704. **F-G** singles. Friendly, clean, large rooms, restaurant. Rooms at the back are quieter and have a view. Recommended.
D-E **Moraleda**, O'Higgins 82, Puerto Chacabuco, T067-351155. **G** singles, also food.

Eating

Futaleufú *p250, map p253*

ŸŸ **Martín Pescador**, Balmaceda y Rodríguez, Futaleufú, T065-721279. Decent meat and fish.
ŸŸ **Futaleufú**, Cerda 407, Futaleufú, T065-721295. All the normal Chilean fare plus, of course, trout.
ŸŸ-Ÿ **Sur Andes**, Cerda 308, Futaleufú, T065-721405, www.surandes.tk. Pleasant little café serving real coffee as well as a variety of cakes, sweets, snacks and light meals. Local handicrafts also sold.

Puyuhuapi and around *p251*

ŸŸ **Café Rossbach**, Costanera, Puyuhuapi. Limited menu, including excellent salmon; also good for tea and *küchen*; building is in the style of a German Black Forest inn.
Ÿ **Restaurante Marili**, Otto Ubel s/n, Puyuhuapi. Cheaper option.
Ÿ **K-Cos Café Restaurante**, Prat 270, Puerto Cisnes. Good snacks.

Coyhaique *p252, map p255*

ŸŸŸ **Restaurant Histórico Ricer**, Horn 48 y 40, 2nd fl, T067-232920. Regional specialities, historical exhibits, recommended, though slightly over-priced.
ŸŸŸ-ŸŸ **Calor y Comida**, Baquedano 022, T067-25183, yelisa@patagoniachile.cl. Bizarre entrance through someone's house leading to a restaurant with as breathtaking a view as any in Coyhaique. Aims for rustic elegance, occasionally at odds with the music they play. Patagonian-Mediterranean cuisine. Abundant portions. Decent food. Wine sold by the glass.
ŸŸ **El Reloj**, Baquedano 444, T067-231108 (see Sleeping, above). Unusual dishes using all local ingredients. Good service, recommended.
ŸŸ **La Casona**, Obispo Vielmo 77, T067-238894. Good lamb and fish dishes, recommended.
ŸŸ **La Olla**, Gral Prat 176, T067-242588. Spanish, excellent cuisine, not cheap but there are good-value lunches. Recommended.
ŸŸ **Las Piedras**, 21 de Mayo 655, T067-233243. Slightly upmarket but with good-value set lunches. Dishes include venison and emu. Fills up at weekends. Recommended.
ŸŸ **Yangtse**, Bilbao 715, T067-242173. Better than average (in Chilean terms) Chinese. You can hear your food being stir-fried fresh to order. Reasonable prices but the quantity of MSG leaves you almost happy to fork out for the exorbitantly expensive drinks.
ŸŸ-Ÿ **Casino de Bomberos**, Gral Parra 365, T067-231437. Wide range, large portions, very good value. Slow service, especially if the overdressed tip-hungry waiters are doting on a table of cruise ship tourists.
ŸŸ-Ÿ **Restaurant Central**, Freire 319, T067-256885. Decent basic set lunches. Big screen TV. A good place to watch football matches.
Ÿ **El Mastique**, Bilbao 141. Cheap but good pasta and Chilean food. Recommended.
Ÿ **La Fiorentina**, Prat 230, T067-238899. Good value pizza and pasta.

Cafés

Café Alemana, Condell 119. Excellent cakes, coffee, vegetarian dishes. Recommended.
Café Oriente, Condell 201 y 21 de Mayo. Good bakery, serves tea.
Café Ricer, Horn 48. Also serves light food.

Puerto Aisén *p252*

ŸŸ **Café Restaurante Ensenada**, O'Higgins 302, Puerto Chacabuco. Basic grub.
ŸŸ **Restaurante La Cascada**, Km 32 between Coyhaique and Puerto Aisén. Waterfalls nearby. Recommended for meat and fish.
ŸŸ **Restaurante Martina**, Av Municipal, near bridge, Puerto Aisén. Good Chilean fare. Probably the best place to eat in town.

There are many cheap places on Aldea in Puerto Aisén, between Municipal and Dougnac.

Bars and clubs

Coyhaique *p252, map p255*
Bar West, Bilbao y 12 de Octubre. Western-style bar.
Kamikaze, Moraleda 428. Disco.
Piel Roja, Moraleda y Condell. Friendly, laid-back atmosphere, meals served, not cheap.
Pub El Cuervo, Parra 72. Good cocktails and snacks, relaxed ambience, live music at weekends.

Puerto Aisén and around *p252*
The following are all in Puerto Aisén. There are a couple of smaller bars on Sargento Aldea; one has a wildly sloping pool table.
Crazzy Pub, Aldea 1170. Make up your own mind how 'crazzy' it is.
Dina's, Carrera 1270. Disco.
Eko Pub, Tte Merino 998.

Festivals and events

Puerto Aisén and around *p252*
2nd week of Nov Local **festival of folklore** is held in Puerto Aisén.

Shopping

Coyhaique *p252, map p255*
Food, especially fruit and vegetables, is more expensive here than in Santiago. For *artesanía* try the **Feria de Artesanía** on the plaza or **Manos Azules**, Riquelme 435. **The Wool House**, Horn 40, loc 101, T067-255107, sells good-quality woollen clothing. Decent camping equipment can be obtained from **Condor Explorer**, Dussen 357, T067-670349. **La Casa del Mate**, Errázuriz 268. Everything for the connoisseur of the South American herb. There are large supermarkets at Prat y Lautaro and Lautaro y Cochrane. Good sheep's cheese is often available from a kiosk by the plaza.

Activities and tours

Lago Yelcho and the border *p250*
Fishing
Isla Monita Lodge, near Puerto Cárdenas, offers packages for anglers and non-anglers on a private island on Lago Yelcho, as well as fishing in many nearby locations; contact **Turismo Grant**, PO Box 52311, Santiago, T02-6395524, F6337133.

Kayaking
Patagonian Waters, main road in Puyuhuapi, T067-314300, www.patagonianwaters.com, offers canoeing and sea kayak trips in the fjord, as well as trekking and horse riding. There is also an office in La Junta.

Río Cisnes *p251*
Fishing
There are good opportunities for fishing on Río Futaleufú and Lago Espolón (see page 250; ask for the Valebote family's motorboat on the lake) and in the area around Puerto Cisnes (see page 251). For the latter, contact **German Hipp**, Costanera 51, Puerto Cisnes, T067-346587, or **Cabañas Río Cisnes** (see above). For further information contact **Turismo Lago Las Torres**, 130 km Carretera Austral Norte, T067-234242.

Futaleufú *p250, map p253*
Tour operators in Futaleufú can arrange whitewater rafting. Prices start at US$75 pp. There are several local fishing guides who can be contacted in the village.
Earth River, www.earthriver.com. Excellent choice for river rafting and kayaking trips, book in advance.
Expediciones Chile, Mistral 296, Futaleufú, T065- 721386, www.exchile.com. Offers the best multi-day trips. Book in advance. Day trips can be booked on site.
Futaleufú Expediciones, O'Higgins 397, Futaleufú, T/F065-258634. Organizes rafting, canyoning, trekking and horse riding expeditions around Futaleufú.
Futaleufú Explore, O'Higgins 772, Futaleufú T065-721411, www.futaleufuexplore.com. Another respected rafting company.

Puyuhuapi and around *p251*
Patagonia Connection, Fidel Oteíza 1921, oficina 1006, Providencia, Santiago, T02-2256489. Operates a 3-night catamaran tour to Laguna San Rafael via **Puyuhuapi Lodge and Spa** (see page 254) on board the *Patagonia Express*. Also offers special fly-fishing programmes and other excursions.

Coyhaique *p252, map p255*
A full list of specialist tours and fishing guides is available from **Sernatur**, see page 252. Excursions and good trekking information is available from **Albergue Las Salamandras**

Angling for a catch

The rivers around Coyhaique provide the greatest fishing in Chile; each year the international fishing fraternity converge on the town for the season, which runs from 15 November to 15 April. Rivers range from the typically English slow chalk stream to fast-flowing Andean snowmelt torrents, requiring diverse angling techniques.

On the outskirts of Coyhaique, the spectacular **Río Simpson** teems with rainbow and brown trout. It is renowned for its evening hatches (sedge and mayfly), which take place throughout the season. Catches in excess of five pounds are frequent and rainbow trout weighing over 12 pounds have been landed.

Near the Argentine border, a scenic one-hour drive from Coyhaique, **Río Nirehuao** is a fly-fisher's dream as brown trout feed voraciously on grasshoppers and dragonfly. The easy wading and moderate casting distances make this river a favourite.

South of Coyhaique, the **Río Baker** offers a unique fishing experience in its turquoise blue water. The Baker is huge and intimidating, as are its fish: rainbows up to 12 pounds lurk here and anglers regularly take fish of seven pound. The **Río Cochrane,** a gin-clear tributary of the Baker, also holds large rainbows. The Cochrane is mainly a 'sight-fishing' river, which requires skill, patience and an experienced guide.

(see Sleeping, page 253). There is also an association of independent local guides who offer (as a rule) good-value and well-informed excursions within the region. See www.escueladeguias.cl for more detailed information.

Fishing

There are excellent opportunities for fishing in the Coyhaique area, especially southwest at Lagos Atrevesado (20 km) and Elizalde (also yachting and camping), and southeast at lagos Frío, Castor and Pollux. In addition to those listed below, most of the general tour operators offer specialist fishing trips.

Alex Prior, T067-234732. Recommended for fly-fishing.

General tours

Aike Bikers, T067-258307, juan.orellanam@123mail.cl. Mountain bike tours of the city and surrounding countryside.

Andes Patagónicos, Horn 48 y 40, local 11, T067-216711, www.ap.cl. Trips to local lakes as well as Tortel, historically based tours and bespoke trips all year round. Good, but not cheap. Provides general tourist information.

Aysen Tour, Gral Parra 97, T067-237070, www.aysentour.cl. Typical range of tours along the Carretera Austral.

Camello Patagón, Simpson 169, T067-244327, www.camellopatagon.cl. Trips to Capilla de Marmol in Río Tranquilo.

Condor Explorer, Dussen 357, T067-670349, www.condorexplorer.com. Good small-scale agency who specialize in trekking but also do general Carretera tours. English spoken. Recommended.

El Puesto Expeditions, Moraleda 299, T067-233785, elpuesto@entelchile.net. Hiking, fishing, climbing.

Expediciones Coyhaique, Portales 195, T067-232300, juliomeier@entelchile.net. Tours of local lakes and other sights, Laguna San Rafael trips, fishing and birdwatching trips and excursions down the Río Baker.

Geo Turismo, Lillo 315, T067-237456, www.geoturismopatagonia.cl. Offers wide range of tours throughout the region, English spoken, professional, recommended.

Patagonia Adventure Expeditions, Riquelme 372, T067-219894, www.adventurepatagonia.com. Agency famed for its rafting tours. Various other multi-day adventure tours also offered. English spoken. Recommended.

Turismo Prado de la Patagonia, 21 de Mayo 417, T067-231271, www.turismopradopatagonia.cl. Tours of local lakes and other sights, Laguna San Rafael trips and historical tours. Also offers general tourist information.

Horse riding

Baltazar Araneda, T067-231047 or book through **Hospedaje Natti** (see Sleeping, page 253). Horse riding trips to lagos Palomo, Azul and Desierto, US$300 per person for 4 days, US$375 for 5 days.
Cabot, Lautaro 339, T067-230101, www.cabot.cl. Horse riding excursions to Cerro Castillo and other tours.

Scenic flights

Patagonia Explorer, T099-8172172, stonepiloto@hotmail.com. Pilot Willy Stone offers charter flights to the Laguna San Rafael, US$250 per person, recommended.

Skiing

El Fraile, office in Coyhaique at Dussen y Plaza de Armas 376, T067-231690. Near Lago Frío, 29 km southeast of Coyhaique, this ski resort has 5 pistes, 2 lifts, a basic café and equipment hire (season Jun-Sep).

Puerto Aisén *p252*

Turismo Rucaray, on the plaza, rucaray@entelchile.net. Recommended for local tours. Internet access.

Transport

Lago Yelcho and the border *p250*

Transporte Patagonia Norte, T065-741257, runs a weekly bus from Palena to **Puerto** Montt via Argentina, Mon 0630, 13 hrs, US$28.

Futaleufú *p250, map p253*

Bus

To **Chaitén**, daily, 5 hrs; to **Puerto Montt**, Tue and Fri, US$33; to the **Argentine border** Mon and Fri 0900 and 1800 from Balmaceda 419, 30 mins, US$4; on the Argentine side there are connecting services to **Trevelin** and **Esquel**.

La Junta and around *p251*

There is no bus terminal in La Junta. All minibuses should be booked in advance. To **Puerto Cisnes**, Buses Emanuel, Manuel Montt, esq Esmerelda, T067-314198, Mon and Fri, US$8. To **Coyhaique**, Buses Emanuel, Tue and Sat, US$16; Buses Daniela, T067-231701, 2 weekly, US$16; Buses Norte, 3 weekly. To **Chaitén**, Buses Emanuel, Mon-Sat, US$11; Transportes Lago Verde, Varas s/n, T067-314108, 3 weekly, US$11; Buses Norte, 3 weekly. To **Lago Verde**, Buses Daniela, 2 weekly. Book all in advance.

Puyuhuapi and around *p251*

Daily buses from Puyuhuapi north to **Chaitén** and south to **Coyhaique**, plus 2 weekly to **Lago Verde**.

Río Cisnes *p251*

Transportes Terra Austral, T067-346757, runs services from Puerto Cisnes to **Coyhaique**, Mon-Sat 0600, US$9; Buses Norte, T067-346440 offers the same route once a week, US$8.

Coyhaique *p252, map p255*

Air

Airline offices Sky, Prat 203, T067-240826, local calls 600-6002828; LanChile, Moraleda 402, T067-231188, local calls 600-5262000; Don Carlos, Subteniente Cruz 63, T067-231981; Aerohein, Baquedano 500, T067-232772, www.aerohein.cl; Transportes Aéreos San Rafael, 18 Septiembre 469, T067-233408.

Tte Vidal airport Don Carlos flies to **Chile Chico**, Mon-Sat, US$50; to **Cochrane**, Mon and Thu, 45 mins, US$75, and to **Villa O'Higgins**, Mon and Thu, US$100, recommended only for those who have strong stomachs, or are in a hurry. There are also flights to **Tortel**, Wed, US$35, but these are subsidized for residents of the village.

Balmaceda airport LanChile and Sky to **Santiago**, several daily, US$130-250 return plus tax; to **Puerto Montt**, daily in summer, US$75-150 return plus tax. LanChile also to **Punta Arenas**, Sat, US$75-150 return plus tax. One-way fares are usually more expensive. For transport to/from the airport, see page 250. For flights to Laguna San Rafael, see page 261.

Bus

The main terminal is at Lautaro y Magallanes. In the terminal are: Bus São Paulo, T067-237630; Bus Sur, T067-211460, www.bus-sur.cl; Don Oscar, T067-254335, Giobbi, T067-232607; Interlagos, T067-240840, www.patagoniainterlagos.cl, recommended; Queilen Bus; Transportes Terra Austral, T067-254475. Other companies are Alegría, Errázuriz 145; Bus Bronco, Magallanes 560; Buses Becker, Ibáñez 358, T067-35050; Buses Daniela,

Going further ... Glaciar San Rafael

Situated some 200 km south of Puerto Chacabuco, the San Rafael glacier is one of the highlights for many travellers to Chile. About 45 km in length and towering 30 m above water level, the deep blue glacier groans and cracks as it carves off icebergs, which are carried across the Laguna San Rafael and out to sea via the Río Tempano. Around the shores of the laguna is thick vegetation and above are snowy mountain peaks.

The San Rafael is one of many glaciers flowing from the giant **Campo de Hielo Norte**, which covers much of the 1,740,000- ha **Parque Nacional Laguna San Rafael** (entry fee US$6). In the national park are puma, pudu, foxes, dolphins, occasional sea-lions and sea otters, and many species of bird.

There is a small ranger station on the shore of Laguna San Rafael, which provides information on the national park. Walking trails are limited (about 10 km in all) but a lookout platform has been constructed, with fine views of the glacier. The rangers are willing to row you out to the glacier in calm weather: an awesome three-hour adventure, past icebergs and swells created when huge chunks of ice break off the glacier and crash into the laguna.

The glacier is rapidly disintegrating and is likely to have disappeared entirely by 2011. It is thought that waves created by motorized tourist boats are adding to the problem. Visitors should insist that their boats do not go too close to the glacier creating further damage.

Getting there Aerohein and Don Carlos provide air taxis from Coyhaique, US$200 each for party of five; some pilots in Puerto Aisén will also fly to the glacier for around US$95 per person, but many are unwilling to land on the rough airstrip. Other air-tour options available from Coyhaique, see page 260. **Boats from Puerto Montt** Slow service with Navimag (via Puerto Chacabuco); official cruises by Skorpios; tours with Patagonia Connection; also private yacht charters. See page 235. **Boats from Puerto Chacabuco** Slow service with Navimag; one- or three-day trips with Catamaranes del Sur; luxury catamaran cruises with Iceberg Express. Local fishing boats from Puerto Chacabuco/Puerto Aisén (enquire at the port) take about 18-20 hours each way and charge the same as the tourist boats. Note that they might not have adequate facilities or a licence for the trip. Out of season, trips are difficult to arrange. See page 262.

Baquedano 1122, T067-231701; **Bus Norte**, Parra 337, T067-232167; **Don Carlos**, Subteniente Cruz 63, T067-232981; **Suray**, Prat 265, T067-238387; **Turibus**, Baquedano 1171, T067-231333.

Carretera Austral north Suray, São Paulo, Interlagos and Don Carlos minibuses run to **Puerto Aisén** every 15 mins, 1 hr, US$2. To **Chaitén** via Puyuhuapi and La Junta, **Don Oscar**, 3 weekly, 12 hrs, US$28. Also **Buses Norte**, **Buses Daniela**, **Buses Becker**, several weekly between them. To **Lago Verde** via La Junta, **Buses Daniela**, Tue, Sat, US$18; also **Bus Bronco**, Wed, Fri, Sat. To **Puerto Cisnes**, Transportes Terra Austral and **Alegría**, each Mon-Sat, US$9.

Carretera Austral south To **Cochrane**, **Interlagos**, 0930 Mon, Wed, Thu, Sat, Sun, US$20, recommended, and **Don Carlos**, 0930 Tue, Thu, Sat, US$17. Buses to Cochrane stop at **Cerro Castillo**, US$5, **Bahía Murta**, US$9, **Puerto Río Tranquilo**, US$12, and **Puerto Bertrand** , US$14. *Colectivos* to **Puerto Ibáñez**, 2 hrs, book the day before, US$6, pick up at 0700 from your hotel to connect with **El Pilchero** ferry to Chile Chico: **Dario Figueroa Castro**, T067-233286, **Tour Aisen**, T09-9898 2643, **Colectivos Sr Parra**, T067-251073, Sat and Sun only; **Minibus Don Tito Segovia**, T067-250280; **Sr Yamil**, T067 -250346, and **Humberto Gomez**, T067-423262.

Long distance To **Puerto Montt**, via Bariloche, all year, **Turibus**, Tue and Sat 1700, US$40; **Queilen Bus**, Mon, Thu, US$40, with connections to Osorno, Valdivia, Temuco, Santiago and Castro, often heavily booked. To **Punta Arenas** via Coyhaique Alto and Comodoro Rivadavia, **Bus Sur**, Tue, US$55. To **Comodoro Rivadavia** (Argentina), **Turibus**, Mon, Fri, also **Giobbi**, Tue, Sat, from terminal, 12 hrs, US$35.

Car hire

Hire from: **AGS**, Av Ogana 1298, T067-235354; **Automóvil Club de Chile**, Carrera 333, T067-231649, rents jeeps and other vehicles; **Automundo AVR**, Bilbao 510, T067-231621; **Río Baker**, Balmaceda airport, T067-272163; **Sur Nativo Renta Car**; Baquedano 457, T067-235500; **Traeger- Hertz**, Baquedano 457, T067-231648; **Turismo Prado**, 21 de Mayo 417, T/F067-231271. Mechanic at **Automotores Santiago**, C Los Ñires 811, T067-238330, T099-6406896, speaks English, can obtain spare parts quickly.

Ferry

Shipping offices are at **Catamaranes del Sur**, Carrera 50, T067-351112, www.catamaranes delsur.cl; **Naviera Río Cisnes**, Magallanes 303, T067-432702, www.navierariocisnes.cl; **Navimag**, Ibáñez 347, T067-233306, www. navimag.com; **Skorpios**, Gral Parra 21, T067-213755, www.skorpios.cl.

Taxi

Fares are 50% extra after 2100. *Colectivos* congregate at Prat y Bilbao, fare US$0.70.

Puerto Aisén /Puerto Chacabuco *p252*

Bus

Suray runs buses between the 2 ports every 20 mins, US$0.75. **Interlagos** and **Suray** have frequent services to **Coyhaique**, 1 hr, US$2 (see above).

Ferry

To Puerto Montt Naviera Austral, www.navieraustral.cl, and **Navimag**, Terminal de Transbordadores, T067-351111, www.navimag.com, year-round ferry services via the Canal Moraleda once a week in summer, irregular off-season, 24 hrs, US$40.

To Laguna San Rafael It is best to make reservations for this trip at the ferry's offices in Puerto Montt, Coyhaique or Santiago (or, for **Naviera Austral**, in Chaitén or Ancud). **Catamaranes del Sur**, Carrera 50, T067-351112, www.catamaranesdelsur.cl, 1-3 weekly Sep-Apr, 1-day trips US$299, 3-day trips from $550. **Compañía Naviera Puerto Montt**, Sgto Aldea 679, Puerto Aisén, T067-332908 /3511066. Motorized sailing boats, the *Odisea* and the *Visun*, sail Dec-Mar on 6-day trips to the Laguna San Rafael. **Iceberg Express**, Av Providencia 2331, of 602, Santiago, T02-3350580. 12-hr luxury catamaran cruises. **Navimag**, Terminal de Transbordadores, T067-351111, www.navi mag.com. Official services, all year, reduced service off season, 24 hrs, from US$259.

Directory

Futaleufú *p250, map p253*

Banks Banco del Estado, Futaleufú, but no ATM. Changing foreign currency is difficult, but US dollars and Argentine pesos are accepted in many places.

Coyhaique *p252, map p303*

Bank Several with Redbanc ATMs in centre, for dollars, TCs and Argentine pesos. Both the following *casas de cambio* are recommended: **Casa de Cambio Emperador**, Bilbao 222, and **Lucía Saldivia**, Baquedano 285. **Hospital** C Hospital 068, T067-233172. **Internet** **Ciber Patagonia**, 21 de Mayo 525, best value; **Entel**, Prat 340; **Hechizos**, 21 de Mayo 460, also cheap; several others. **Language schools** Baquedano Language School, Baquedano 20, T067-232520, www.balasch.cl. US$400 per week, including 4 hrs one-to-one tuition daily, lodging and all meals, other activities organized at discount rates, friendly, informative, highly recommended. **Laundry** **Lavaseco Universal**, Gral Parra 55; **QL**, Bilbao 160. **Post office** Cochrane 202, Mon-Fri 0900-1230, 1430-1800, Sat 0830-1200. **Telephone** Several call centres; shop around as prices are relatively expensive.

Puerto Aisén *p252*

Banks BCI, Prat, for Visa; **Banco de Chile**, Plaza de Armas, only changes cash, not TCs. There's a Redbanc ATM machine in Puerto Chacabuco. **Post office** South side of bridge. **Telephone** Plaza de Armas, next to Turismo Rucuray; **ENTEL**, Libertad 408, internet access.

Lago General Carrera and beyond

The section of the Carretera Austral around the north and western sides of Lago General Carrera is reckoned by many to be the most spectacular stretch of all. Straddling the frontier with Argentina, the lake is the largest in South America after Lake Titicaca and is believed to be the deepest on the continent, with a maximum depth of 590 m. The region has 300 days of sunshine a year and rainfall is low. In general, the climate has more in common with Argentine Patagonia than with the rest of the Carretera Austral.

South from Cochrane, the scenery becomes increasingly remote and dramatic. The final stretch of the Carretera Austral leads to the small town of Villa O'Higgins at the end of the road. ▸▸ *For Sleeping, Eating and other listings see pages 267-270.*

Ins and outs → *Colour map 2, B3*

Getting there and around There are direct buses and flights to Cochrane from Coyhaique. Minibuses also run along the Carretera Austral in summer to Puerto Ibañez (five weekly), from where, a ferry connects with Chile Chico. Overland routes between Coyhaique and Chile Chico are much longer, passing either through Argentina via Los Antiguos, or along the Carretera Austral and west around the lake. Public transport is scarce: air taxis link the small towns but there are only two weekly buses from Chile Chico to Cochrane and from Cochrane to Villa O'Higgins. A 4WD makes getting around much easier. ▸▸ *See Transport page 269.*

Deer, oh deer

The Andean **huemul** (pronounced 'way-mool') is a shy mountain deer native to southern Chile and Argentina. It's a medium-sized, stocky creature, adapted to survival in rugged terrain. Males grow antlers and have distinctive black face masks. Although it used to range from just south of Santiago to the Straits of Magellan, human pressures have pushed the huemul to the brink of extinction, with current numbers estimated at just 1000-1500. Your best chance of seeing one is in the Reserva Nacional Río Claro, just outside Coyhaique (see page 252), or the Reserva Nacional Tamango, near Cochrane (see page 266). To visit either of these you will need to be accompanied by a warden.

The Carretera Austral area is also one of the best places for trying to spot the equally rare **pudu**. This miniature creature, around 40 cm tall and weighing only 10 kg, is the smallest member of the deer family in the world. Native to southern Argentina and Chile, the pudu is vulnerable to extinction, largely due to habitat loss, but also because its unique appearance (the males grow two short spiked antlers) has made it a target for poaching for zoos. Reddish-brown in colour, the pudú is ideally adapted to the dense temperate rainforests of Patagonia, scooting along trails through the undergrowth, leaving behind minuscule cloven tracks.

Reserva Nacional Cerro Castillo → *Colour map 2, B3*

Beyond Coyhaique, the Carretera Austral runs southwest through the Reserva Nacional Cerro Castillo, which extends over 179,550 ha. The park is named after the fabulous **Cerro Castillo** (2675 m), which resembles a fairytale castle with rock pinnacles jutting out from a covering of snow. It also includes Cerro Bandera (2040 m) just west of Balmaceda and several other peaks in the northern wall of the valley of the Río Ibañez. The park has a number of excellent day treks; ask at the *guardería* at the northeastern end of the park near Laguna Chinguay. There is a **CONAF campsite** ⓘ *T067-237070, US$8*. At Km 83 the road crosses the Portezuelo Ibañez (1120 m) and drops through the Cuesta del Diablo, a series of bends with fine views over the Río Ibañez.

Puerto Ibáñez and around → *Colour map 2, B3*

At **Bajada Ibáñez**, 97 km south of Coyhaique, a branch road heads southeast for 31 km to **Puerto Ibáñez** (officially Puerto Ingeniero Ibáñez), the principal port on the Chilean section of Lago General Carrera. From here boats depart for Chile Chico on the southern shore; this is a very cold crossing even in summer, so take warm clothing. The Carretera Austral, meanwhile, continues from Bajada Ibañez 8 km to **Villa Cerro Castillo**. Near the village is the **Monumento Nacional Manos de Cerro Castillo**, where traces of ancient rock paintings, estimated to be 10,000 years old, have been found. The road climbs out of the valley, passing the emerald-green **Laguna Verde** and the Portezuelo Cofré, before descending to the boggy Manso valley.

Lago General Carrera » *pp267-270.*

Known as General Carrera in Chile and as Buenos Aires in Argentina, this lake is a beautiful azure blue, surrounded at its Chilean end by predominantly Alpine terrain and at the Argentine end by dry pampa. The eruption of Volcán Hudson in 1991 (south of Chile Chico) polluted parts of Lago General Carrera and many rivers and, although the waters are now clear, the effects can still be seen in some places.

The western shore

Some 5 km from the Carretera Austral, at Km 203, **Bahía Murta** is situated on the northern tip of the central 'arm' of Lago General Carrera. The village dates from the 1930s, when it exported timber to Argentina via Chile Chico. From here, the road follows the lake's western shore to **Río Tranquilo** (228 km from Coyhaique), where buses stop for lunch and fuel. Close to Río Tranquilo is the unusual **Catedral de Mármol**, a peninsula made of marble, with fascinating **caves** ⓘ *boat hire with guide US$35*. The village also has an unusual cemetery. A new branch of the Carretera Austral heads northwest from Río Tranquilo to **Puerto Grosse** on the coast at Bahía Exploradores.

The southern shore

At the southwestern tip of Lago General Carrera, at Km 279, is **El Maitén**, from where a road branches off east along the south shore of the lake towards Chile Chico. Ten kilometres east of El Maitén, **Puerto Guadal** is a picturesque town that is a centre for fishing. It also has shops, accommodation, restaurants, a post office and petrol. Further east, just past the village of **Mallin Grande**, Km 40, the road runs through the **Paso de las Llaves**, a 30-km stretch carved out of the rock-face on the edge of the lake. The road climbs and drops, offering wonderful views across the water and the icefields to the west. At Km 74, a turning runs to **Fachinal**. A further 8 km east, there is an open cast mine, which produces gold and other precious metals.

Chile Chico and around → *Colour map 2, B3*

Chile Chico is a quiet, friendly but dusty town situated on the lake shore 122 km east of El Maitén, close to the Argentine border. The town dates from 1909 when settlers crossed from Argentina and occupied the land, leading to conflict with cattle ranchers who had been given settlement rights by the Chilean government. In the showdown that followed (known as the war of Chile Chico) the ranchers were driven out by the settlers, and it was not until 1931 that the Chilean government recognized the town's existence.

Now the centre of a fruit-growing region, it has an annual festival at the end of January and a small museum open in summer; outside is a boat that carried cargo on the lake before the opening of the new road along the southern shore. There are fine views from the **Cerro de las Banderas** at the western end of town. The **tourist office** ⓘ *Municipalidad, O'Higgins 333*, can help in arranging tours. From Chile Chico a road runs 2 km east to the border and on for 5 km to **Los Antiguos** (see page 148)

The country to the south and west of Chile Chico provides good walking terrain, through weird rock formations and dry brush scrub. The northern and higher peak of **Cerro Pico del Sur** (2168 m) can be climbed by the agile from Los Cipres (beware dogs in the farmyard). You will need a long summer's day and the 1:50,000 map. From the summit you'll enjoy indescribable views of the Lake and the Andes. Twenty kilometres south of Chile Chico towards Lago Jeinimeni is the **Cueva de las Manos**, a cave full of Tehuelche paintings, the most famous of which are the *manos azules* (blue hands). The path is difficult, and partly hidden, so you're recommended to take a guide.

Reserva Nacional Lago Jeinemeni → *Colour map 2, B3*

ⓘ *53 km south of Chile Chico, open all year but access limited between Apr and Oct due to high river levels, US$3, camping US$6.* This park covers 160,000 ha and includes two lakes, **Lago Jeinemeni** and **Lago Verde**, which lie surrounded by forests in the narrow valley of the Río Jeinemeni. Impressive cliffs, waterfalls and small glaciers provide habitat for huemul deer, pumas and condors. Activities include fishing for salmon and rainbow trout, trekking and rowing. Access is via an unpaved road, which branches south off the road to Los Antiguos and crosses five rivers. At Km 42, there is a small lake, **Laguna de los Flamencos**, where large numbers of flamingos can be seen. The park entrance is at Km 53; just beyond is a ranger station, a campsite and fishing area at the eastern end of Lago Jeinemeni. Take all supplies, including a good map.

Towards Cochrane » pp267-270.

South of El Maitén, the Carretera Austral becomes steeper and more winding; in winter this stretch is icy and dangerous. **Puerto Bertrand,** 5 km away, is a good place for fishing. Beyond Puerto Bertrand, the road climbs up to high moorland, passing the confluence of the rivers Neff and Baker, before winding south along the east bank of the Río Baker to Cochrane. The road is rough but not treacherous and the scenery is splendid. Watch out for cattle and hares on the road (and huemuls in winter) and take blind corners slowly.

Cochrane and around → *Colour map 2, B2*

Sitting in a hollow on the northern banks of the Río Cochrane, 343 km south of Coyhaique, Cochrane is a simple place, good for walking and fishing. The **tourist office** ⓘ *Mon-Sat 0900-1300, 1430-2000*, is open in summer only; in winter go to the Municipalidad at Esmeralda 398. Excursions can be made from the town to **Lago Cochrane**, which covers over 17,500 ha, straddling the frontier with Argentina (the Argentine section is called Lago Puerredón). On the northern shore is the **Reserva Nacional Tamango** ⓘ *Dec-Mar 0830-2100, Apr-Nov 0830-1830, US$4, guided visits to see the huemal, Tue, Thu, Sat, US$80 for a group of 6 people*, a lenga-forest reserve that is home to one of the largest colonies of rare huemul as well as guanaco, foxes, woodpeckers and hummingbirds. There are several marked trails affording views over the town, the nearby lakes and even to the Campo de Hielo Norte to the west. Tourist facilities, however, are rudimentary.

Some 17 km north of Cochrane, a road runs east for 78 km through Villa Chacabuco to the border at **Paso Roballos**. On the Argentine side the road continues to **Bajo Caracoles**, an isolated settlement on Ruta 40 (see page 149). There is no public transport along this route and the road is often flooded in spring. » *Border crossing, page 185.*

South of Cochrane » pp267-270.

Travelling by bus on the final 224-km stretch of the Carretera Austral from Cochrane to Villa O'Higgins can be frustrating, as you will want to stop every 15 minutes to marvel at the views. From **Vagabundo**, Km 98, boats sail regularly down the Río Baker to Tortel. This is a beautiful trip through thick forest, with vistas of snow-capped mountains and waterfalls.

Tortel → *Colour map 2, B2*

Built on a hill at the mouth of the river 135 km from Cochrane, Tortel has no streets, only wooden walkways and became famous in October 2000 as the place where British Prince William spent three months working for **Raleigh International**; it is also where Rosie Swale ended her epic horseback journey through Chile, as recorded in *Back to Cape Horn*. A branch of the Carretera Austral, beginning 2 km south of Vagabundo and reaching south to Tortel, was completed in 2003, so the village is now accessible by road, and the repercussions on its character will be enormous. From Tortel, you can hire a boat to visit two spectacular glaciers: **Ventisquero Jorge Montt**, five hours southwest, or **Ventisquero Steffens**, on the edge of the Parque Nacional San Rafael. On the Río Baker nearby is the **Isla de los Muertos**, where some hundred Chilote workers died under mysterious circumstances early in the 20th century.

The Carretera continues southwards to **Puerto Yungay**, a tiny village with a military post and a pretty church. This section of the road is hilly and in places very bad; don't drive along it at night. From Puerto Yungay, there is a regular **ferry** to Río Bravo, from where the road continues through more spectacular scenery – lakes moors, swamps, rivers and waterfalls – before arriving at its final destination.

Villa O'Higgins → *Colour map 2, C2*

Situated at the southernmost end of the Carretera Austral, Villa O'Higgins has the atmosphere of a frontier town. It lies 2 km from a northerly 'arm' of **Lago O'Higgins,** which straddles the Argentine border as Lago San Martín. The lake is dotted with numerous icebergs that have split off the Campo de Hielo Sur to the west; these can be visited by boat from **Bahía Bahamóndez**, 7 km south. **Tourist information** ⓘ *T067-211849, www.villaohiggins.cl*, is available in the plaza in summer or from the Municipalidad, which can also provide guides and information on trekking. Behind the town, a mirador affords spectacular views of nearby mountains, lakes and glaciers.

It is now possible, if arduous, to get from Villa O'Higgins to **El Chaltén** in Argentina on foot or by horse. From **Bahía Bahamóndez**, a boat sets off across Lago O'Higgins ⓘ *T067-670313, www.villaohiggins.cl, 3 times per week Dec-Mar, 3 hrs, US$35*, to **Candelario Mancila** on the southern shore. Here you'll find accommodation, horses and guides for hire (US$22) and **Chilean immigration** ⓘ *open winter 0800-2000, summer 0800-2200. Prior permission to cross must be sought from the international police at Coyhaique (Condell 14)*. From Candelario Mancila, it is 15 km to the Argentine border and a further 5 km to the Argentine immigration post on **Lago del Desierto** (see page 160); allow two days on foot with a guide. You can catch a boat across the lake, 45 Argentine pesos per person, or walk the 15 km to the southern shore, from where there is transport in summer to El Chaltén. With the opening of this route, it is now possible to travel along the whole of the Carretera Austral and on to Torres del Paine without having to double back on yourself.

Sleeping

Puerto Ibañez and around *p264*

C **Cabañas Shehen Aike**, Risopatrón 55, Puerto Ibáñez, T067-423284 www.shehenaike.cl. Children-friendly cabin complex run by a Swiss-Chilean family. Lots of information on the local area as well as horse riding and fishing trips. English, German, French spoken.

C **Hostería Villarrica**, O'Higgins 59, Villa Cerro Castillo. **G** singles. Basic accommodation, good mid-price meals and a grocery store. Cheap meals are also available at **Restaurante La Querencia**, O'Higgins s/n, Villa Cerro Castillo.

E **Residencial Ibáñez**, Bertrán Dixon 31, Puerto Ibáñez, T067-423227. **G** singles. Clean, warm, hot water. Similar next door at No 29.

E **Vientos del Sur**, Bertrán Dixon 282, Puerto Ibáñez, T067-423208. **G** singles. Cheap meals available, good.

Camping

Municipal campsite, Puerto Ibáñez, T067-423234. Open Dec-Mar, US$10 per site.

The western shore *p265*

A **Hostal el Puesto**, Pedro Lagos 258, Río Tranquilo, T02-1964555, www.elpuesto.cl. Without a doubt the most comfortable place in Río Tranquilo. The owners can organize tours.

C **Campo Alacaluf**, Km 44 on the Río Tranquilo-Bahía Exploradores side road, T067-419500. Wonderful guesthouse hidden miles away from civilization and run by a very friendly German family. Recommended.

C-D **Hostal Los Pinos**, 2 Oriente 41, T067-411576, Río Tranquilo. Family run, well maintained, good mid-price meals. Friendly. Recommended.

D **Cabañas Jacricalor**, 1 Sur s/n, Río Tranquilo, T067-419500. **G** singles. Tent-sized *cabañas*.

D **Hostería Carretera Austral**, 1 Sur 223, Río Tranquilo, T067-419500, lopezpinuer@yahoo.es. Serves mid-range/cheap meals.

F **Hostería Lago General Carrera**, Av 5 de Abril 647 y Colombia, Bahía Murta, public phone 067-419600. **G** singles. Cheap meals.

For an explanation of sleeping and eating price codes, and other relevant information, see Essentials pages 25-26.

F Residencial Patagonia, Pasaje España 64, Bahía Murta, public telephone 067-419600. **G** singles. Very basic, without bath.

Free camping is possible by the lake in Bahía Murta, with good views of Cerro Castillo.

Chile Chico and around *p265*

All the following are in Chile Chico:

D pp **Casa Quinta No Me Olvides**, Camino Internacional s/n. Without bath. Clean, cooking facilities. Also camping. Tours arranged to Lago Jeinimeni and Cueva de las Manos.

D Hostería de la Patagonia, Camino Internacional s/n, T067-411337, F411414. **F** singles; full board available. Clean, excellent food, English, French and Italian spoken, trekking, horse riding and whitewater rafting organized, also camping.

D-E Ventura, Carrera 290, T067-411311. Modern suites.

E Plaza, O'Higgins y Balmaceda, T067-411510. Basic, clean. Recommended.

F Residencial Don Luis, Balmaceda 175, T067-411384. **G** singles. Clean, meals available.

Camping

Free campsite at **Bahía Jarra**, 5 km from Chile Chico, then 12 km north. **Camping del Sol** at the eastern end of the town.

Towards Cochrane *p266*

AL Mallín Colorado, 2 km west of El Maitén, T067-2741807, chile@patagonia-pacific.cl. *Cabañas*, adventure activities, horse riding, rafting, fishing, English and German spoken.

B-C Hostería Campo Baker, Puerto Bertrand, T067-411477. *Cabañas*, sleep 5.

D Doña Ester, Puerto Bertrand. Rooms in a pink house. **G** singles. Good.

D Hostería Puerto Bertrand, Sector Costanera, Puerto Bertrand, T067-419900. **F** singles. Also meals, *cabañas*, and tours (see Activities and tours).

Cochrane *p266*

In summer it is best to book rooms in advance. The following are all in Cochrane:

A Ultimo Paraíso, Lago Brown 455, T067-522361. Regarded as the best place to stay. Also arranges fishing trips.

B Cabañas Rogery, Tte Merino 502, T067-522264. Cabins sleep 4, with kitchen facilities. Breakfast included.

B Hotel Wellmann, Las Golondrinas 36, T067-522171. Hot water, comfortable, warm, good meals. Recommended.

C Residencial Rubio, Tte Merino 4, T067-522173. **F** singles, breakfast included, lunch and dinner extra. With bath. Very good.

D Hostal Latitud 47 sur, Lago Brown 564. **F** singles. Clean, hot water, internet, tours.

D Residencial Cero a Cero, Lago Brown 464, T067-522158, ceroacero@ze.cl. **F** singles, with breakfast, cheaper without bath, welcoming, recommended.

D Residencial Sur Austral, Prat 334, T067-522150. **F** singles, with breakfast and hot water.

E Hospedaje Cochrane, Dr Steffens 451, T067-522377. **G** singles. Good meals, camping available. Recommended.

E Hospedaje Paola, Lago Brown 150, T067-522215. **G** singles. Also camping.

E Residencial El Fogón, San Valentín 651, T067-522240. **G** singles. Its pub is one of few eating places open in the low season.

Camping

In the Reserva Nacional Tamango, there are campsites and *cabañas* at **Los Correntadas**, US$14 per site, and **Los Coigües**, US$18 per site. Details and booking through **CONAF**, Av Ogana 1060, T067-212125.

South of Cochrane *p266*

D Doña Berta Muñoz, Tortel. Full board. One guest comments: "Expect fresh mutton meals and if you are squeamish... don't look out of the window when they butcher the 2 lambs a day on the front porch."

D Sergio Barrio, Tortel. Full board available, good food.

E Casa Rural, Tortel. Full board or B&B.

E Hospedaje Costanera, Tortel, T067-234815. Price includes breakfast (also open to non-residents). Clean, warm, with attractive garden, recommended.

E Apocalipsis 1:3, Villa O'Higgins, T067-216927. **G** singles. Shared baths, friendly, serves food.

D Hospedaje Patagonia, Villa O'Higgins, T067- 234813. **F** singles. Basic accommodation.

Eating

Hosterías are your best bet for food (see Sleeping, above).

Chile Chico and around *p265*

Café Holiday, C González. Good coffee, friendly service.

Cafetería Loly y Elizabeth, González 25, on plaza. Serves coffee, ice cream and cakes.

Cochrane *p266*

There are a couple of mid-range options on Tte Merino and San Valentín too.

La Costa, plaza, Cochrane. Friendly.

Tortel *p266*

Café Celes Salom, Tortel. Basic cheap meals and disco on Sat with occasional bands.

Bars and clubs

Chile Chico and around *p265*

Pub El Minero, Carrera 205. Recommended for a drink.

Zebra, O'Higgins 750 Interior. This disco is the place to be seen in Chile Chico.

Festivals and events

Chile Chico and around *p265*

Last week of Jan The town hosts the Festival Internacional de la Voz.

Activities and tours

Lago General Carrera *p265*

El Puesto Expediciones, Lagos 258, Río Tranquilo, T067-233785, www.elpuesto.cl. Fishing trips and other excursions.

Towards Cochrane *p266*

Jonathan Leidich, Puerto Bertrand, T067-411330. Lives on the edge of the lake, and is highly recommended for rafting, horse riding and other activities.

La Red de Turismo Río Baker, Hostería Puerto Bertrand, Puerto Bertrand, T067-419900. Rafting, horse riding and other activities.

Patagonia Baker Lodges, Orillas del Río Baker, Puerto Bertrand, T067-411903. Fishing trips on the lake.

Río Baker Lodges, T067-411499. Fishing trips on the lake.

Cochrane *p266*

Fishing

Lago Cochrane offers excellent fishing all-year round; boats can be hired for US$12 pp; fishing trips are run by **Hotel Ultimo Paraíso** (see Sleeping).

Tour operators

Excursions can be arranged through Guillermo Paso at **Transportes Los Ñadis** (see Transport, below); fishing tours are available from **Hotel Ultimo Paraíso** (see Sleeping, above.

Don Pedro Muñoz, T067-522244. Hires out horses for excursions in the surrounding countryside.

Red de Turismo Río Baker, San Valentín 438, T067-522646, trural@patagoniachile.cl. Offers tours of all kinds within the region.

Samuel Smiol, T067-522487. Offers tours to the icefields and mountains, English spoken.

Siesta Oppi, 3176 Neuenegg, Switzerland, T+41-31-7419192. This Swiss canoe shop organizes canoe trips in Jan and Feb.

Tortel *p266*

Charter boats can be arranged through Viviana Muñoz or Hernán Ovando at the Municipalidad, T067-211876. Prices to **Ventisquero Jorge Montt**, speedboat 2 hrs, US$120 per person; *lancha* 5 hrs, US$150. To **Ventisquero Steffens**, speedboat 1 hr, US$80 per person; *lancha* 2½ hrs, $100.

Villa O'Higgins *p267*

Nelson Henríquez, Lago Cisnes 201. Fishing trips on the lake.

Transport

Puerto Ibañez and around *p264*

Buses and jeeps meet the ferry in Puerto Ibáñez for connections to **Coyhaique**, 2 hrs, US$7. There is also a road from Puerto Ibáñez to **Perito Moreno** in Argentina, but no public transport. **Transportes Amin Ali**, O'Higgins s/n, Villa Cerro Castillo, T067-419200, provides transport from Villa Cerro Castillo to **Coyhaique**, US$6.

Ferry

The car ferry, *El Pilchero*, sails from Puerto Ibáñez to **Chile Chico**, Mon 1800, Wed 1000, Thu 1630, Sat 1100, Sun 1700, return departures Mon 0800, Tue 0800, Wed 1600, Fri 1630, Sun 1330, 2½ hrs, cars US$40, passengers US$4.50, bicycles US$3. The number of passengers is limited to 105; arrive 30 mins before departure. Reserve at least 2 days in advance through **Mar del Sur**, Baquedano 146, Coyhaique, T067-231255. This is a very cold crossing, even in summer; take warm clothing.

Chile Chico and around *p265*

Air

Don Carlos flies to **Coyhaique** (Tte Vidal airport), 5 weekly, US$50, from an airstrip just outside Chile Chico.

Bus

Transportes Ales, T067-411739, runs minibuses along the south side of the lake to **Puerto Guadal**, Wed, Sat, US$11, and **Cochrane**, US$19. Additional services to Puerto Guadal are provided by **Sr Sergio Haro Ramos**, T067-411251, Wed, Sat, US$13, and **Transportes Seguel**, 2 weekly, US$12. Minibuses from Chile Chico to **Los Antiguos** (Argentina), 45 mins including formalities, US$4 (payable in Chilean pesos only), are run by **Arcotrans**, T067-411841, and **Transportes Padilla**, T067-411904. The buses depart when they are full – usually about 5 times daily each. For onward transport, see page 152.

Ferry

For services to **Puerto Ibáñez**, see above. Tickets should be reserved in advance from the terminal in Chile Chico.

Cochrane *p266*

Air

Don Carlos flies to **Coyhaique**, Mon, Thu, US$75, from an airstrip just north of town.

Bus

To **Coyhaique**, Don Carlos, Prat 344, T/F067-522150, 2 weekly, US$18; **Inter Lagos**, 6 weekly, US$20, recommended; **Los Ñadis**, Los Helechos 490, T/F067-522196, 3 weekly, US$11; **Acuario 13**, Río Baker 349, T/F067- 522143, 3 weekly, US$22. To **Vagabundo**, US$8, **Los Ñadis**, 3 weekly; **Acuario 13**, 4 weekly. To **Villa O'Higgins**, Los Ñadis, 1 service Mon, US$12; **Acuario 13**, 1 weekly, US$11. To **Chile Chico**, **Transportes Ale**, Thu and Sun, US$20. To **Tortel**, Acuarcio, 4 weekly, US$9.

Tortel *p266*

Air

Don Carlos to **Coyhaique** (Tte Vidal), Mon and Wed, US$35. This is a subsidized price for residents of the village. Other travellers must buy a standby ticket and should expect to pay much more.

Boat

To **Vagabundo**, Tue, Sun 0900, 5 hrs, US$3 one way; return trip Tue, Sun 1500, 3 hrs. There is also a boat once a fortnight from Tortel to **Puerto Yungay**, or you can arrange a charter for 6-10 people by contacting Viviana Muñoz or Hernán Ovando at the Municipalidad, T067-211876, 8 hrs, US$150 return.

Villa O'Higgins *p267*

Don Carlos air taxi flies to Villa O'Higgins from **Coyhaique**, via Cochrane, Mon, Thu, US$100. There are also 2 buses weekly to **Cochrane**, US$12. Boats across Lago O'Higgins depart from Bahía Bahamóndez.

Directory

Chile Chico and around *p265*

Banks Generally it's best to change money in Coyhaique or Argentina, but dollars and Argentine pesos can be changed in small amounts (at poor rates) at shops and cafés in Chile Chico, including **Cafetería Loly y Elizabeth**. **Hospital** Lautaro s/n, T067-411334.

Cochrane *p266*

Banks **Banco del Estado**, on the plaza, changes dollars. ATM accepts MasterCard and Cirrus but not Visa. **Internet** There are 2 on the plaza, one run by nuns (closed Sun). **Supermarket** Melero, Las Golondrinas 148.

Tortel *p266*

Banks There is no bank in Tortel but a mobile bank comes twice a month. **Medical services** Medical centre staffed by doctors, nurses and dentists visits Tortel monthly. **Post office** Mon-Fri 0830-1330, post leaves Tortel weekly by air.

Far South

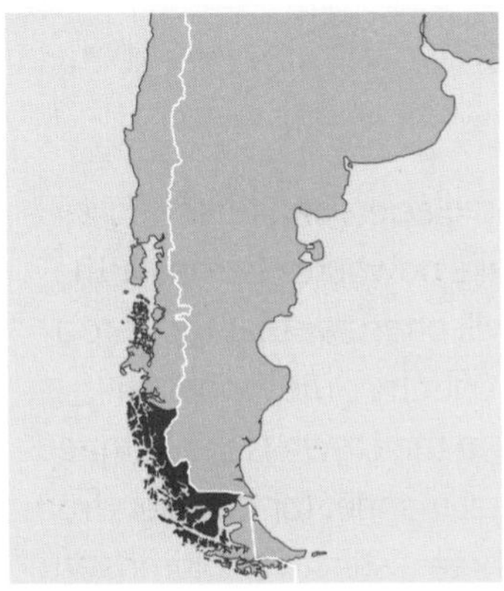

Footprint features

Introduction

A spectacular land of fragmenting glaciers and teetering icy peaks, southern Patagonia feels like nowhere else on earth. Although Chileans posted here will often say that they are a "long way from Chile", this is the country's most popular destination for visitors. The jewel in the crown is the Parque Nacional Torres del Paine, a natural magnet for travellers from all over the world. The 'towers', three distinctive columns after which the park is named, point vertically upwards from the Paine massif like fingers, surrounded by imposing glaciers, turquoise-coloured lakes and thick forests of native trees.

Puerto Natales is the base for exploration of Torres del Paine and for boat trips to the glaciers in the Parque Nacional Bernardo O'Higgins. It also provides access to the Parque Nacional Los Glaciares in Argentina. Further south, Punta Arenas is a European-style city with a lively Chilote community and remnants of earlier English and Croatian influences.

Villa O'Higgins
L Strobel
Lago O'Higgins
Lago San Martín
L Cardiel
Estancia La Maipu
Estancia La Angostura
Puerto Edén
Isla Wellington
Fitz Roy (3405m)
El Chaltén
40
Glaciar Viedma
Lago Viedma
Estancia Helsingfors
Tres Lagos
Estancia La Leona
Cerro Norte
Parque Nacional Los Glaciares
Glaciar Upsala
Golfo Trinidad
Leona
Lago Argentino
Río Santa Cruz
Puerto Bandera
Estancia Arice
Río Bote
Glaciar Perito Moreno
El Calafate
Gendarme Barreto
Parque Nacional Bernardo O'Higgins
Estancia Alta Vista
ARGENTINA
Estancia Nibepo Aike
El Cerrito
Lago Sarmiento
Fuentes del Coyle
Pacific Ocean
Parque Nacional Torres del Paine
La Esperanza
Paso Cancha Carrera
Cerro Castillo
REGION XII
Gobernador Mayer
Río Coig
Seno Última Esperanza
Ferry to Puerto Montt
Balmaceda (2035m)
Paso Dorotea
Río Turbio
Monumento Nacional Cueva Milodón
Paso Casas Viejas
El Turbio
Río Gallegos
Puerto Natales
Bella Vista
Cordillera Sarmiento
El Zurdo
N
Morro Chico
40 km
40 miles
CHILE
9
Villa Tehuelches
Río Verde
Monumento Natural Los Pingüinos
Isla Magdalena
Cordillera Riesco
Parque Nacional Alacalufes
Seno Otway
Isla Isabel
Reserva Forestal Magallanes
Punta Arenas
Reserva Forestal Laguna Parillar
Fuerte Bulnes
Estrecho de Magallanes
Isla Dawson
Parque Nacional Alberto de Agostini
★ Don't miss ...
❶ Penguins at Seno Otway, page 278.
❷ Skiing at Cerro Mirador, page 282.
❸ A cruise to Tierra del Fuego, page 283.
❹ A boat trip to Parque Nacional Bernardo O'Higgins, page 286.
❺ Trekking 'El Circuito', page 293.

Punta Arenas and around

Capital of Región XII, Punta Arenas lies 2140 km due south of Santiago. The city was originally named 'Sandy Point' by the English, but adopted the Hispanic equivalent under Chilean colonization. A centre for the local sheep farming and fishing industries, it is also the home of La Polar, one of the most southerly breweries in the world. Although Punta Arenas has expanded rapidly, it remains a tranquil and pleasant city. The climate and architecture give it a distinctively northern European atmosphere, quite unlike anywhere else in Chile. » *For Sleeping,. Eating and other listings, see pages 279-284.*

Ins and outs → *Colour map 3, B3*

Getting there Punta Arenas is cut off from the rest of Chile. The only road connections are through Argentina: either via Comodoro Rivadavia and Río Gallegos to Coyhaique and the Carretera Austral or via Bariloche to Puerto Montt. It is quicker, and often cheaper, to take one of the many daily flights to/from Puerto Montt or Santiago instead. There are also direct flights to Porvenir, Puerto Williams and Ushuaia. **Carlos Ibáñez del Campo airport** is 20 km north of town; **Buses Transfer** and **Buses Pacheco** are scheduled to meet flights, US$2. A taxi costs US$9. The many buses from Punta Arenas to Puerto Natales, 247 km north, will only stop at the airport if they are scheduled to pick up passengers. For ferry routes to Tierra del Fuego, see page 302. » *See Transport, page 283.*

Tourist information The municipal **tourist office** on the plaza is good, T061-200610, or try **Sernatur** ⓘ *Magallanes 960, T061-225385, www.patagonia-chile.com, 0830-1845, closed weekends in winter*, and **CONAF** ⓘ *Bulnes 0309, opposite the shepherd monument, between the racetrack and cemetery, T061-238544, Mon-Fri.*

Background

After its foundation in 1848, Punta Arenas became a penal colony modelled on Australia. In 1867, it was opened to foreign settlers and given free port status. From the 1880s, it prospered as a refuelling and provisioning centre for steam ships and whaling vessels. It also became a centre for the new sheep *estancias* since it afforded the best harbour facilities. The city's importance was reduced overnight by the opening of the Panama Canal in 1914. Most of those who came to work in the *estancias* were from Chiloé; many people in the city have relatives in Chiloé and feel an affinity with the island (the *barrios* on either side of the upper reaches of Independencia are known as Chilote areas); the Chilotes who returned north took Patagonian customs with them, hence the number of *maté* drinkers on Chiloé.

Sights » *pp279-284.*

Punta Arenas is not a huge city and walking about is a pleasant way of getting to know it. Around the attractive **Plaza Muñoz Gamero** are a number of mansions that once belonged to the great sheep-ranching families of the late 19th century. A good example is the **Palacio Sara Braun** ⓘ *Tue-Sun, US$2*, built between 1894 and 1905 with materials from Europe; the Palacio has several elegantly decorated rooms open to the public and also houses the **Hotel José Nogueira**. In the centre of the plaza is a statue of Magellan with a mermaid and two Fuegian Indians at his feet. According to local wisdom, those who rub or kiss the big toe of one of the Fuegians will return to Punta Arenas.

Just north of the plaza is the **Museo de Historia Regional Braun Menéndez** ⓘ *Magallanes 949, T061-244216, Mon-Sat 1030- 1700, Sun 1030-1400 (summer) or*

1100-1300 (winter), US$2, children half-price, the opulent former mansion of Mauricio Braun, built in 1905. A visit is recommended. Part of the museum is set out as a room-by-room regional history; the rest of the house has been left with its original furniture. Guided tours are in Spanish only but a somewhat confusing information sheet in English is also available. One block further north is the **Teatro Cervantes**, now a cinema with an ornate interior.

Punta Arenas

To 6, Museo del Recuerdo, Zona Franca, Airport, Puerto Natales & Ferry to Porvenir

To 14 & Parque María Behety

To Fuerte Bulnes & Puerto del Hambre

To 16

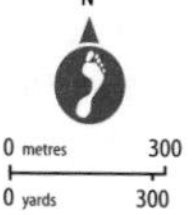

Sleeping
Aikén 1 *D2*
Backpackers Paradise 2 *C3*
Cabo de Hornos 3 *C2*
Cóndor del Plata 20 *C2*
Hospedaje Miramar 28 *D1*
Hospedaje Quo Vadis 16 *D1*
Hostal al Fin del Mundo 25 *C3*
Hostal del Estrecho 18 *C3*
Hostal del Sur 7 *B1*
Hostal Dinka's House 6 *B3*
Hostal Green House 11 *B3*
Hostal Independencia 26 *D1*
Hostal La Estancia 27 *C3*
Hostal O'Higgins 4 *D3*
Hostal Parediso 8 *B3*
Hostal Rubio 5 *B1*
Hostal Sonia Kuscevic 9 *A2*
José Nogueira 10 *C2*
Monte Carlo 26 *C2*
Oro Fueguino 15 *C1*
Pink House 13 *A3*
Plaza 22 *D2*
Ritz 14 *C3*
Savoy 29 *C3*
Tierra del Fuego 17 *C2*

Eating
Calypso 2 *C2*
Carioca 11 *C2*
Centro Español 3 *D2*
Damiana Elena 1 *C3*
Dino's Pizza 16 *B2*
El Estribo 4 *C2*
El Quijote 7 *C2*
Golden Dragon 8 *C1*
La Luna 9 *C3*
La Marmite 5 *C2*
Lomit's 10 *C2*
Parilla Los Ganaderos 6 *A2*
Puerto Viejo 12 *D3*
Remezón 14 *D2*
Sabores de Chiloé 13 *D2*
Santino 18 *C2*
Sotitos 15 *D2*

Buses
Fernández 4 *C2*
Pacheco 2 *C2*
Sur 1 *C2*
Transfer 3 *C2*

Three blocks east, the **Museo Naval y Maritimo** ⓘ *Pedro Montt 981, T061-205479, terzona@armarda.cl, Tue-Sun 0930-1230, 1400-1700, US$1.50*, houses an exhibition of local and national maritime history, with sections on naval instruments, cartography, meteorology and shipwrecks. There is a video in Spanish and information in English.

Three blocks further west is **Museo Militar** ⓘ *Zenteno y Balmaceda, Tue-Sun 0900-1300, 1500-1700, free*, at the Regimiento Pudeto. Lots of knives, guns, flags and other military memorabilia are displayed here plus many items brought from Fuerte Bulnes. Explanatory notes in excruciating English.

North of the centre along Bulnes is the excellent **Museo Regional Salesiano Mayorino Borgatello** ⓘ *Colegio Salesiano, Av Bulnes 374, entrance next to church, Tue-Sun 1000-1800, US$4*, an excellent introduction to Patagonia with a large collection of stuffed birds and animals from the region, exhibits on local history, geology, athropology, aviation and industry. Three blocks further on, the **cemetery** ⓘ *Av Bulnes, daily 0800-1800*, is one of the most interesting places in the city, with cypress avenues, gravestones in many languages, which bear testimony to the cosmopolitan provenance of Patagonian pioneers, and many mausolea and memorials to pioneer families and victims of shipping disasters. Look out for the statue of Indicito, the little Indian, on the northwest side, which is now an object of reverence, bedecked with flowers. Further north still, the Instituto de la Patagonia houses the **Museo del Recuerdo** ⓘ *Av Bulnes 1890, Km 4 north (opposite the zona franca), T061-207056, Mon-Fri 0830-1130, 1430-1815, Sat 0830-1300, US$2, children free*, an open-air museum with artefacts used by the early settlers, pioneer homes and botanical gardens.

On 21 de May, south of Independencia, is Chile's only Hindu temple, while further along the same street, on the southern outskirts of the city, the wooded **Parque María Behety**, features a scale model of Fuerte Bulnes, a campsite and children's playground, popular for Sunday picnics. In winter, there is an ice rink here.

Around Punta Arenas

Reserva Forestal Magallanes → *Colour map 3, B3*

ⓘ *7 km west of town, administration at CONAF, Menéndez 1147, 2nd fl, Punta Arenas, T061-223841, Mon-Fri, US$5*. Known locally as the Parque Japonés, this forest reserve extends over 13,500 ha and rises to 600 m. **Viento Sur** (see Activities and tours, page 283) offers a scheduled transport service to the reserve, but it can also be reached on foot or by bike: follow Independencia up the hill and take a right turning for Río de las Minas, about 3 km from the edge of town; the entrance to the reserve is 2 km beyond. Here you will find a self-guided nature trail through lenga and coigue trees. The road continues through the woods for 14 km passing several picnic sites. From the top end of the road a short path leads to a lookout over the **Garganta del Diablo** (Devil's Throat), a gorge with views over Punta Arenas and Tierra del Fuego. From here a slippery path leads down to the Río de las Minas Valley and then back to Punta Arenas. Also within the reserve, **Cerro Mirador** is one of the few places in the world where you can ski with a sea view (see page 282). There's also a good two-hour hike here in summer; the trail is clearly marked and flora is labelled.

Fuerte Bulnes and south → *Colour map 3, B3*

About 25 km south of Punta Arenas, a fork to the right leads to the very peaceful **Reserva Forestal Laguna Parrillar**, surrounded by snow-capped hills. It has older forest than the Magallanes Reserve and sphagnum bogs, and offers excellent salmon trout fishing. There is a three-hour walk to the tree-line along poorly marked, boggy paths, and fine views from the Mirador. Camping is forbidden but there are sites for cooking on gas stoves. There is no public transport to the reserve; a radio taxi will cost about US$50.

Shackleton and the rescue from Elephant Island

Shackleton's 1914-1916 Antarctic expedition is one of the epics of polar exploration. Shackleton's vessel, *Endurance*, which left England in August 1914 with 28 men aboard, became trapped in pack-ice in January 1915. After drifting northwards with the ice for eight months, the ship was crushed by the floes and sank. With three boats, supplies and the dogs, the group camped on an ice floe which continued to drift north for eight months. In April 1916, after surviving on a diet of seals and penguins, the party took to the boats as the ice broke up. After seven days at sea they reached Elephant Island. From there Shackleton and five other men sailed 1300 km in 17 days to South Georgia, where there were whaling stations. On reaching the south shore of South Georgia, Shackleton and two men crossed the island (the first such crossing) to find help. Shackleton, from whom nothing had been heard by the outside world since leaving the island 18 months before, was not at first recognized.

The British government sent a rescue vessel to Elephant Island, but the delays involved led Shackleton to seek help locally. After ice had prevented three rescue attempts – the first from South Georgia, the second from the Falkland Islands/Islas Malvinas and the third from Punta Arenas – Shackleton persuaded the Chilean authorities to permit a fourth attempt using the tug *Yelcho*. Leaving Punta Arenas on 25 August 1916, the vessel encountered thick fog but, unusually for the time of year, little ice and it quickly reached Elephant Island where the men, who had endured an Antarctic winter under upturned boats, were down to four days of supplies.

Although the expedition failed to cross Antarctica, Shackleton's achievement was outstanding: despite the loss of *Endurance*, the party had survived two Antarctic winters without loss of life. Shackleton himself returned to the region in 1921 to lead another expedition but, in January 1922, aged only 47, he suffered a fatal heart attack in South Georgia.

Some 56 km south of Punta Arenas, **Fuerte Bulnes** is a replica of the wooden fort erected in 1843 by the crew of the Chilean vessel *Ancud*. Built in the 1940s and originally designed to house a museum, nearly all the interesting exhibits and artefacts were moved to museums in Punta Arenas and Santiago in 1986 and now only the empty shells of the various buildings remain.

Nearby is **Puerto Hambre** (see box, page 324), where there are ruins of the church built in 1584 by a group of ill-fated Spanish colonists led by Sarmiento de Gamboa. Disaster struck the fledgling colony when their only remaining ship, with Sarmiento on board, was blown into the Atlantic, leaving many men stranded on land. Sarmiento organized two rescue missions, but was captured by the English and imprisoned. When the English corsair Thomas Cavendish sailed through the Straits in 1587 he found only 18 survivors. Only one of them trusted Cavendish enough to set sail with him; the rest of the men were left to die and Cavendish named the place Port Famine as a reminder of their grisly fate. This is a very beautiful area with views towards the towering ice mountains near Pico Sarmiento; it was of Puerto Hambre that Darwin wrote: "looking due southward... the distant channels between the mountains appeared from their gloominess to lead beyond the confines of this world".

Bypassing Fuerte Bulnes, the road south continues past a memorial to Captain Pringle Stokes, Captain of the *Beagle* before Fitz Roy, who committed suicide here in 1829, before running out 5 km further on at San Juan. Beyond is the southernmost point of the continent of South America at **Cape Froward**.

Going furher: Falkland Islands/Las Malvinas

These remote southern outposts, where there are more penguins than people, are the only part of South America where UK sterling is the currency and the British monarch's head appears on the stamps. Windswept they may be, but the islands are a haven for wildlife and for those who wish to see it: albatross nest in the tussac, sea lions breed on the beaches and orca whales cruise off the coast.

About 640 km east of the South American mainland, the Falkland Islands/Islas Malvinas are made up of two large islands and hundreds of smaller ones. The capital, Stanley, is a small modern town with reminders of its seafaring past in the wrecks of sailing ships in the bay. Its residents live mostly in brightly-painted houses, many of which have corrugated iron roofs. Surrounded by rolling moorland, Stanley resembles parts of the Scottish Hebrides. To visit the Camp, as the land outside Stanley is known, 4WD vehicles make tours, or you can fly to farming outposts for warm hospitality, huge skies and unparalleled nature watching. In the southeast, Sea Lion Island is a delightful place to explore and relax; and it's worth taking the one-hour flight to West Falkland or one of the smaller islands for the stunning scenery.

Ins and outs The best time to visit is October to March. The climate is cool and oceanic and the weather is very unpredictable. Average temperatures are 15°C in January, and 4°C in June.

Stanley has two small hotels, three guesthouses and a growing number of B&Bs. Elsewhere are tourist lodges offering comfortable full-board, cottages to rent, and the opportunity to share in the life and work of a farm.

All visitors must have a full passport. Citizens of Britain, USA, Chile and most Commonwealth or EU countries do not need a visa. Visitors are issued a one-month visitor permit on arrival upon presentation of a return ticket. Visitors should book accommodation in advance and have sufficient funds. There are ATMs on the islands. Visa and Mastercard are widely accepted.

Flights from Santiago, via Puerto Montt and Punta Arenas with **LAN** every Saturday. Return fares: Santiago £530, Punta Arenas £285. Once a month, the flight calls at Río Gallegos, Argentina. Trips can be arranged through **International Tours and Travel**, see page 282. For further information contact the **Falkland Islands Tourist Board**, PO Box 618, Stanley, FIQQ 1ZZ, T+500 22215 /27019, www.visitorfalklands.com.

North of Punta Arenas

Seventy kilometres north of Punta Arenas, **Seno Otway** is the site of a colony of Magellanic penguins, which can be visited ⓘ *Oct-mid Mar, US$5*. There are beautiful views across the sound to the mountains to the north and rheas, skunks and foxes can also be seen. Several agencies offer trips to the colony, (five hours, US$14 peak season); if you wish to visit independently, a taxi from Punta Arenas will cost US$40 return.

A small island, 30 km northeast, **Isla Magdalena** is the location of the **Monumento Natural Los Pingüinos**, a colony of 150,000 penguins, administered by **CONAF**. Deserted apart from during the breeding season from November to early February, Magdalena is one of a group of three islands visited by Drake (the others are Marta and Isabel), whose men killed 3000 penguins for food. Boat trips to the island are run by **Comapa** ⓘ *Tue, Thu, Sat, 1600 (Dec-Feb), 2 hrs each way, with 2 hrs on the island, US$30, subject to cancellation if windy; full refund given.* Tours are also organized by several operators in Punta Arenas.

Beyond, Route 255 heads northeast via Punta Delgada to the Argentine border and then along Route 3 to Río Gallegos. For routes to El Calafate, see page 286.

Sleeping

Punta Arenas *p274, map p275*
Hotel prices are substantially lower during winter months (Apr/May-Sep). Most hotels include breakfast in the room price. Accommodation is also available in many private houses; ask at tourist office. There are no campsites in or near the city.

L-AL Cabo de Hornos, Muñoz Gamero 1039 on the plaza, T061-715000, www.hoteles-australis.com. 4 star, newly refurbished and comfortable. Bright and spacious rooms. Good views from the 4th floor up, either of the Magellan straights or the plaza.

L José Nogueira, Bories 959, in former Palacio Sara Braun, T061-248840, www.hotelnogueira.com. Beautiful *loggia*. Slightly small rooms, but high ceilings. The rooms on the 2nd floor are best. Good suites, lovely dining room, parking. Probably the nicest hotel in town. Recommended.

AL Tierra del Fuego, Colón 716, T061-226200, www.puntaarenas.com. Good breakfast, parking. Decent sized rooms, some rooms with kitchenette. **Café 1900** is downstairs.

A Cóndor del Plata, Colón 556, T061-247987, www.condordeplata.cl. Small hotel often used by polar expeditions. Rooms with cable TV and full bathtubs. Cash discounts.

A Hostería Yaganes, Camino Antiguo Norte Km 7.5, T061-211600, www.pehoe.cl/yaganes.htm. *Cabañas* on the shores of the Straits of Magellan, nice setting.

A Plaza, Nogueira 1116, piso 2, T061-248613, www.hotelplaza.cl. Historic building with high ceilings and old- fashioned charm, redone recently. English spoken. Limited parking. Recommended.

B Hostal Sonia Kuscevic, Pasaje Darwin 175, T061-248543, www.hostalsk.50megs.com. One of the oldest guesthouses in Punta Arenas. Impeccably kept rooms with TV and bath. Very quiet. Good breakfast including omelette. Good value off-season.

B Oro Fueguino, Fagnano 356, T061-249401, www.orofueguino.cl. Recently refurbished, TV and phone. Some rooms with no windows. Good breakfast. Often fills up with groups so book ahead. Cheaper in US$dollars than pesos. Recommended.

B Savoy, Menéndez 1073, T061-247979, www.hotelsavoy.cl. Garish pink carpets and low ceilings. Pleasant rooms but some lack windows, slightly claustrophobic. Better value in US dollars than in pesos.

B-C Monte Carlo, Colón 605, T061-222120, www.montecarlohotel.cl. Old wooden building. Rooms are heated, carpeted and have seen better days. The last refit seems circa 1970. Cheaper without bath.

C Hostal del Estrecho, Menéndez 1048, T061-241011, www.chileanpatagonia.com/estrecho. With large breakfast and bath (cheaper without), central heating, cable TV.

C Hostal del Sur, Mejicana 151, T061-227249. Homely and impeccably kept late 19th-century house. The living room is top of the range 1960s, but the rooms are modern. Excellent breakfast with cereal and cakes. Not central, but in a peaceful neighbourhood. Advance booking advised in summer. Highly recommended.

C Hostal La Estancia, O'Higgins 765, T061-249130, www.hostallaestancia.cl. Simple but comfortable rooms, some with bath. Heating in passageways but not in rooms. Very good kitchen facilities, internet, lots of information, friendly. English spoken. Excellent breakfast with real coffee. A little expensive but still Recommended.

C Hostal O'Higgins, O'Higgins 1205, T061-227999. With bath and breakfast, very clean. **F** pp with shared bath.

C Hostal Rubio, España 640, T061-226458, www.hostalrubio.cl. Small rooms with bath, parking, laundry facilities, helpful. Tours and transport arranged.

C-D Hostal al Fin del Mundo, O'Higgins 1026, T061-710185, www.alfindelmundo.cl. **F** singles. With breakfast. Bright cosy and friendly. Shared baths, central, helpful, laundry service, book exchange, internet, English spoken, helpful, recommended.

C-D Hostal Green House, Angamos 1146, T061-227939, www.hostalgreenhouse.cl. Friendly hostel run by Christina, an anthropologist and Mario, a psychologist. Kitchen facilities, laundry, internet. German and a

For an explanation of sleeping and eating price codes, and other relevant information, see Essentials pages 25-26.

little English spoken. If Mario is in the mood he will get out his bagpipes. Recommended.

C-D **Hostal Paprediso**, Angamos 1073, T061-224212. D-F singles. Decent rooms with cable TV and heating, with or without bath (some cheaper rooms have no window). Good breakfast, parking, use of kitchen. Friendly, basic information given, some English spoken. Recommended.

C-D **The Pink House**, Caupolicán 99, T061- 222436,pinkhous@ctcinternet.cl. F singles. Impeccable rooms with or without bath, breakfast included. Pickup from bus station. English spoken, internet, recommended.

D **Hostal Dinka's House**, Caupolicán 169, T061-226056, www.dinkashouse.cl. With bath, breakfast, use of kitchen, laundry.

D **Ritz**, Pedro Montt 1102, T061-224422. E singles. All rooms with shared bathrooms. Breakfast extra. Old, clean and cosy and with a kind of run-down charm. Recommended. (Bruce Chatwin stayed here: check out his name in the guest book.)

D-E **Aikén**, Errázuriz 612, T061-222629, www.aiken.cl. G pp in dorms. Good beds with duvets. Some rooms with view. Large bathrooms, internet, TV lounge, heating, kitchen facilities, friendly, English spoken.

E **Backpackers Paradise**, Carrera Pinto 1022, T061-240104, backpackersparadise@hotmail.com. G pp in basic dorms. Fun cheap hostel with cooking facilities, limited bathroom facilities, lots of info, good meeting place, luggage store, internet, laundry service, little privacy, book exchange. Expensive bike rental. Recommended.

E **Hospedaje Miramar**, Almte Señoret 1190, T061-215446. G per person in dorms. Slightly exotic location on the edge of the red-light district. Friendly staff, good views over the bay. Breakfast extra.

E **Hospedaje Quo Vadis**, Paraguaya 150, T061-247687. G singles. Motorcycle parking, meals, safe, quiet. Recommended.

F **Hostal Independencia**, Independencia 374, T061-227572, www.chileaustral.com/independencia. G pp in shared rooms. Friendly, small basic rooms. Breakfast extra, kitchen facilities, laundry service, internet, bike rental and cheap camping. Also *cabañas* away from the centre. Good value. Recommended.

Eating

Punta Arenas *p274, map p275*

𝕐𝕐𝕐 **Remezón**, 21 de Mayo 1469, T061-241029, www.patagoniasalvaje.net. Regional specialities such as krill. Very good, and so it should be given the exorbitant prices.

𝕐𝕐𝕐-𝕐𝕐 **Centro Español**, Plaza Muñoz Gamero 771, above Teatro Cervantes. Large helpings, limited selection. Decent lunch menu.

𝕐𝕐𝕐-𝕐𝕐 **El Estribo**, Carrera Pinto 762, T061-244714. Specializes in local and exotic dishes such as guanaco.

𝕐𝕐𝕐-𝕐𝕐 **Sotitos**, O'Higgins 1138. Good service and excellent cuisine. Elegant, expensive. Recommended.

𝕐𝕐 **Damiana Elena**, O'Higgins 694, T061-222818. Popular, stylish restaurant serving Mediterranean food with a Patagonian touch. Advance booking essential at weekends.

𝕐𝕐 **Golden Dragon**, Señoret 908. Slightly upmarket Chinese with views.

𝕐𝕐 **La Luna**, O'Higgins 1017, T061-228555. Fish and shellfish including local specialities, huge *pisco sours*, lively atmosphere.

𝕐𝕐 **La Marmite**, Plaza Sampaio. Intimate restaurant decorated in desert pastel colours. Self-styled 'mestizo' restaurant – regional food with an international touch. Friendly service. Good value for Punta Arenas.

𝕐𝕐 **Parrilla Los Ganaderos**, Bulnes 0977, T061-222818. Best place for spit-roast lamb. It's a long walk past the hippodrome from the town centre. Take a taxi or a *colectivo* going towards the Zona Franca.

𝕐𝕐 **Puerto Viejo**, O'Higgins 1205, T061-225296. By the port. The most traditional of the seafood restaurants. Slightly tacky decor and surprisingly no views considering its location. Over-attentive waiters used to cruise ship clientele speak comedy pigeon English.

𝕐𝕐 **Santino**, Colón 657, T061-220511. Good pizzas, large bar, good service.

𝕐 **Calypso**, Bories 817. Open Sun evening, busy at night, smoky, cheap.

𝕐 **Carioca**, Menéndez 600 y Chiloé. Cheap lunches, snacks and beer, good service.

𝕐 **Cocinerías**, Lautaro Navarro, south of the port entrance. Stalls serving cheap fish meals.

Fishy business

Visitors to Punta Arenas and the surrounding region should be especially wary of eating shellfish. In recent years, the nearby waters have been affected by a marea roja (red tide) of poisonous algae. Infected molluscs can kill humans almost instantly, so never pick up mussels along the shore of Punta Arenas. However, all shellfish sold in restaurants have been inspected and so are theoretically safe. There are seasonal bans on centolla (king crab) fishing to protect dwindling stocks; do not purchase centolla out of season.

Dino's Pizza, Bories 557. Good pizzas, huge sandwiches. For something different, try the rhubarb juice. Recommended.
El Quijote, Lautaro Navarro 1087, T061- 241225. Good burgers, sandwiches and fish dishes. Good value set lunch. Recommended.
La Terraza, 21 de Mayo 1288. Sandwiches, *empanadas* and beer, cheap and good.
Lomit's, Menéndez 722. A Punta Arenas fast food institution serving cheap snacks and drinks, open when the others are closed, always busy, recommended.
Los Años 60 The Mitchel, Chiloé 1231. One of several along this strip serving economic set lunches.
Restaurant de Turismo Punta Arenas, Chiloé 1280. Good, friendly. Recommended. Also serves beer and 26 varieties of sandwiches, open 24 hrs.
Sabores de Chiloé, Chiloé esq Balmaceda. Chilote food as the name implies.

Cafés

Casa del Pastel, Carrera Pinto y O'Higgins. Very good pastries.
Chocolatta, Bories 852. Probably the best coffee in town.
Coffeenet, Waldo Seguel 670. Proper internet café serving espresso.
Entre Fierros, Roca 875, T061-223436. Small diner that by all accounts has remained unchanged since the 1950s. It is famous for its banana milkshakes and tiny *choripan* (spicy sausage-meat sandwiches).
La Espiga, Errázuriz 632. Bread, pastries and snacks.
Pancal, 21 de Mayo 1280. Excellent *empanadas*, bread and pastries.

Bars and clubs

Punta Arenas *p274, map p275*
Be aware that anywhere that calls itself a 'nightclub' is in fact a brothel.
La Taberna del Club de la Unión, Plaza Muñoz Gamero y Seguel. Atmospheric pub in the basement of the **Nogueira** hotel, smoky.
Olijoe, Errázuriz 970. Reasonably plush British-style pub, leather interior, recommended.
Pub 1900, Av Colón esq Bories. Friendly, relaxed atmosphere.

Festivals and events

Punta Arenas *p274, map p275*
Feb Muestra custumbrista de Chiloe, when the Chilote community celebrates its culture.
21 Jun Carnaval de invierno is the winter solstice marked by a carnival on the weekend closest to 21 Jun.

Shopping

Punta Arenas *p274, map p275*
Zona Franca, 3½ km north of the centre, on the right-hand side of the road to the airport, take bus E or A from Plaza Muñoz Gamero or a colectivo. Punta Arenas has certain free-port facilities. Cheap electrical goods are especially worth seeking out, as is camping equipment. The quality of most other goods is low and the prices little better than elsewhere. Open Mon-Sat 1000-1230, 1500-2000.

Handicrafts and local products

Punta Arenas is famous for the quality of its handmade **chocolate**, sold at several shops on Calle Bories.

Artesanía Ramas, Independencia 799. A wide selection of handicrafts.

Casa Diaz, Bories 712/546. Handicrafts.

Chile Típico, Carrera Pinto 1015, T061-225827. Chilean souvenirs

Chocolates Norweisser, Carrera 663. Good chocolate factory.

North Face, Bories 887. Outdoor gear.

Patagonia Gourmet, Mejicana 608. Local marmalades and other specialities.

Pingüi, Bories 404. Crafts and books on Tierra del Fuego, Patagonia and Antarctica.

Sports Nativa, Colón 614. Camping and Skiing equipment.

The Wool House Patagonia, Fagnano 675, by the plaza. Good quality, reasonably priced woollen clothes.

Activities and tours

Punta Arenas *p274, map p275*

Skiing

Cerro Mirador, 9 km west of Punta Arenas in the Reserva Nacional Magallanes, is one of the few places in the world where you can ski with a sea view. Season Jun to Sep, weather permitting. Daily lift-ticket, US$11; equipment rental, US$9 per adult. There's a mid-way lodge with food, drink and equipment. For cross-country skiing facilities, contact the **Club Andino**, T061-241479, www.clubandino.tierra.cl. However, the ski centre is often closed due to lack of snow. There's also a good 2-hr hike here in summer; the trail is clearly marked and flora is labelled. Skiing is also available at **Tres Morros**.

Tour operators

Most organize tours to Torres del Paine, Fuerte Bulnes and *pingüineras* on Otway sound. Several also offer bespoke tours: shop around as prices vary. Specify in advance if you want a tour in English. There are many more tour operators than these listed. For more information ask at the Sernatur office.

Arka Patagonia, Magallanes 345, T061-248167, www.arkapatagonia.com. All types of tours, rafting, fishing, etc.

International Tours & Travel, LAN GSA, PO Box 408, Stanley, F1QQ 1ZZ, Falkland Islands, T+500-22041, www.falklandstravel.com. **LanChile** agents on the Falkland Islands and offers tailor-made and special-interest tours.

Kayak Tour, T061-240028, www.kayak tour.cl. Kayak tours in the Magellan Straights.

Pali Alke, Lautaro Navarro 1125, T061-229388, www.turismopaliaike.com. Wide range of tours including horse riding trips.

Sandy Point, Lautaro Navarro 975, T061-222241, www.sandypoint.cl. Offers transport to Seno Otway and Fuerte Bulnes with or without guide. Also has airport shuttlebuses that will pick you up from your lodgings, US$5.

Turismo Aonikenk, Magallanes 619, T061-221982, www.aonikenk.com. Expensive but very good bespoke excursions. Recommended.

Turismo Aventour, Nogueira 1255, T061-241197, www.aventourpatagonia.com. English spoken, specializes in fishing trips and organizes tours to Tierra del Fuego.

Cruising to Tierra del Fuego

The Chilean company, **Crucero Australis** offers spectacular luxury cruises around the fjords and islets south of Punta Arenas. The *Magellanes* departs Punta Arenas on Saturdays in season (five days, four nights, US$785-1903 per person) stopping to explore remote glaciers and wildlife colonies en route to Puerto Williams and Ushuaia. The cruise from Ushuaia departs on Wednesdays and takes the more southerly route back to Punta Arenas (four days, three nights, US$490- 1649) via the end of the world at Cape Horn.

For further information and advance bookings, contact **Cruceros Australis**, Miraflores 178, piso 12, Santiago, T02-6963211, www.australis.com (Buenos Aires office T011-4325 4000).

Turismo Comapa, Magallanes 990, T061-200200, www.comapa.com. Tours to Torres del Paine, Tierra del Fuego and Isla Magdalena, also agents for trips to the Falklands/Malvinas, Ushuaia and Cape Horn.
Turismo Pehoé, Menéndez 918, T061-241373, www.pehoe.com. Organizes tours and hotels; enquire about catamaran services.
Turismo Renta Club Internacional, Carrera Pinto 1142, T061-223371. Bike hire, US$2 per hr.
Turismo Viento Sur, Fagnano 585, T061-226930, www.vientosur.com. For camping equipment, fishing excursions, sea kayaking, cycle hire, English spoken, good tours.

Transport

Punta Arenas *p274, map p275*
Transport is heavily booked from late Dec to Mar; advance booking is advised.

Air

Airline offices Aerovías DAP, O'Higgins 891, T061-223340, www.dap.cl, 0900-1230, 1430-1930; **LanChile**, Bories 884, T600-5262000, www.lan.com; **Sky Airline**, Roca 933, www.skyairline.cl; **Aerolíneas del Sur**, Fagnano 817, www.aerolineasdelsur.cl.

Local To **Balmaceda** (for Coyhaique), with **LanChile (LanExpress)**, daily in summer, US$80, otherwise 1 a week or daily via Puerto Montt (more expensive). To **Puerto Montt**, with **LanChile (LanExpress)**, **Aerolíneas del Sur** and **Sky Airline**, 10 daily from US$160 return. Cheapest one-way tickets with **Aerolíneas del Sur**. To **Santiago**, **LanChile** (LanExpress), several daily, from US$200 return, via Puerto Montt. To **Porvenir**, **Aerovías DAP**, 2 daily Mon-Sat, US$26 one way, plus other irregular flights, with Twin-Otter and Cessna aircraft. To **Puerto Williams**, **Aerovías DAP**, daily in summer, US$95 one way.

Long-distance To **Ushuaia** (Argentina), **LanChile**, 3 weekly in summer, 1 hr, US$140 one way; reserve in advance from mid-Dec to Feb. To **Falkland Islands/Islas Malvinas**, LanChile, Sat, US$500 return. **International Tours & Travel**, T+500- 22041, www.falklands travel.com, serve as LanChile agents on the Falkland Islands.

Bus

Buses depart from the company offices as follows: **Bus Sur**, Menéndez 565 T061-227145, www.bus-sur.cl; **Buses Sur**, Menédez 552; **Buses Transfer**, Pedro Montt 966, T061-229613; **Cruz del Sur**, **Pingüino** and **Fernández**, Sanhueza 745, T061-242313, www.busesfernandez.com; **Gesell**, Menéndez 556, T061-222896; **Ghisoni**, Lautaro Navarro 971, T061-222078, www.ghisoni.terra.cl; **Los Carlos**, Plaza Muñoz Gamero 1039, T061-241321; **Pacheco**, Colón 900, T061-242174, www.busespacheco.com; **Turbus**, Errázuriz 932, T061-225315.

Services and frequencies change every year, so check on arrival at the helpful Sernatur office. Timetables are also printed daily in El Austral. The services detailed below are for high season only.

Fernández, **Transfer** (cheapest), **Buses Pacheco** and **Buses Sur**, all run several services each day to **Puerto Natales**, 3 hrs, last departure 2000, US$6 one way, US$10.50 return (although this means you have to return with the same company). Buses will pick up at the airport with advance notice.

To **Coyhaique**, 20 hrs, **Buses Sur**, 1 per week via Argentina, US$55, meals not included. **Cruz del Sur**, **Queilen Bus** and **Pacheco** have services through Argentina to **Osorno**, **Puerto Montt** and **Castro**, several weekly, 36 hrs to Castro, US$60.

To Argentina To **Río Gallegos**, Pingüino departs daily 1245, returns 1300; **Ghisoni**, 4 weekly departs 1100; **Pacheco**, 5 weekly, departs 1130. All cost US$14 and take about 5 hrs. For services to **Buenos Aires** it is cheaper to go to Río Gallegos and buy an onward ticket from there. **Pacheco** and **Ghisoni** also have buses most days to **Río Grande** via Punta Delgada, 8 hrs, US$18, heavily booked. To Ushuaia via Punta Deglada 12-14 hrs, US$46, book any return at same time, **Tecni Austral** (from Ghisoni office), Tue, Thu, Sat, Sun 0800; **Pacheco**, Mon, Wed, Fri.

Car

Bargain if you want to hire a car for several days. **Autómovil Club**, O'Higgins 931, T061-243675, and at airport; **Budget**, O'Higgins 964, T061-241696; **Hertz**, O'Higgins 987, T061-229049, English spoken; also at airport T061-210096; **Internacional**, Seguel 443 and at airport, T061-228323, recommended; **Lotus Rentacar**, Mejicana 694, T061-241697; **Lubac**, Magallanes 970, T/F061-242023; **Magallanes Rent a Car**, O'Higgins 949, T/F061-221601; **Paine Rent a Car**, Menéndez 631, T/F061-240852, try bargaining, friendly; **Willemsen**, Lautaro Navarro 1038, T061-247787.

Ferry

For ferry services to **Tierra del Fuego**, see page 302. All tickets on ships must be booked in advance for Jan and Feb.

Visits to the beautiful fjords and glaciers south of Punta Arenas are a highlight. **Comapa** runs a fortnightly 22-hr, 320-km round trip to the 30-km **fjord d'Agostino**, where many glaciers descend to the sea. **Cruceros Australis SA**, runs 5-day luxury cruises from Punta Arenas to **Ushuaia** (see box, page 283).

Most **cruise ships** to **Antarctica** (see page 315) leave from Ushuaia.

Shipping offices **Comapa** (Compañía Marítima de Punta Arenas), Magallanes 990, T061-200200, www.compapa.com; **Navimag**, Magallanes 990, T061-244400, www.navimag.com.

Taxis

Ordinary taxis have yellow roofs. Reliable service is available from **Radio Taxi Austral**, T061-247710/244409. *Colectivos* (all black) run on fixed routes within the city, US$0.60 for anywhere on the route.

Directory

Punta Arenas *p274, map p275*

Banks and currency exchange

Several banks around Plaza Muñoz Gamero, all have ATMs. Argentine pesos can be bought at **Cambio Gasic**, Roca 915, Of 8, T061-242396. **Consulates** Argentina, 21 de Mayo 1878, T061-261912, open weekdays 1000-1530, visas take 24 hrs; **UK**, Catarates de Niaguara 01325, T061-211535, helpful, information on Falkland Islands. For others, ask the tourist office. **Hospitals** **Hospital Regional Lautaro Navarro**, Angamos 180, T061-244040; **Clínica Magallanes**, Bulnes 01448, T061-211527, private clinic; minimum US$45 per visit. A list of English-speaking doctors is available from Sernatur. **Internet** Lots of places offer access, including at Magallanes y Menendez, and below Hostal Calafate on Magallanes, ½ block north of Plaza. Prices are generally US$1 per hour. **Laundry** **Lavasol**, O'Higgins 969, the only self-service laundry, Mon-Sat 0900-2030, Sun 1000-1800, US$6 per machine, wash and dry, good but busy. **Post office** Bories 911 y Menéndez, Mon-Fri 0830-1930, Sat 0900-1400. **Telephone** There are several call centres in the centre (shop around as prices vary).

Puerto Natales and around

From Punta Arenas a good paved road runs 247 km north to Puerto Natales through forests of southern beech and prime pastureland; this is the best sheep-raising area in Chile. Ñandúes and guanacos can be seen en route. Founded in 1911, the town grew as an industrial centre and, until recent years, its prosperity was based upon employment in the coal mines of Río Turbio, Argentina. Today, Puerto Natales is the starting point for trips to the magnificent Bernardo O'Higgins and Torres del Paine national parks and also provides access across the border to the Parque Nacional Los Glaciares. Unsurprisingly, tourism is the mainstay of the town's economy. ➡ *For Sleeping, Eating and other listings, see pages 286-291.*

Ins and outs → *See map page 287. Colour map 3, A2.*

Getting there Puerto Natales is easily reached by daily buses from Punta Arenas and from El Calafate (less frequent in winter) via Río Turbio or Cerro Castillo (both roads part *ripio*). There are also two buses weekly from Río Gallegos. The town is the terminus of the *Magallanes* ship from Puerto Montt (see page 290). If driving between Punta Arenas and Puerto Natales make sure you have enough fuel.

Tourist information There is a kiosk on the waterfront ⓘ *Av Pedro Montt y Phillipi, T061-412125*. Information is also available from the **Municipalidad** ⓘ *Bulnes 285, T061-411263*, and from **CONAF** ⓘ *O'Higgins 584*.

Sights

The **Museo historico municipal** ⓘ *Bulnes 285, T061-411263, museonat@123mail.cl, Mon-Fri 0800-1900, Sat 1000-1300, 1500-1900, closed Sat off season, US$2*, houses a small collection of archaeological and native artefacts as well as exhibits on late 19th-century European colonization. Reasonable descriptions in English.

The colourful old steam train in the main square was once used to take workers to the the meatpacking factory at **Puerto Bories**, 5 km north of town. It is a pleasant hour-long walk along the shore to Bories (US$4 by taxi), with glimpses of the Balmaceda Glacier across the sound. In its heyday the plant was the biggest of its kind in Chile with a capacity for 250,000 sheep. Bankrupted in the early 1990s, much of the plant was dismantled in 1993. Belatedly the plant was given National Monument status and is slowly being restored. Fascinating tours of the remaining buildings and machine rooms are given in English. **Museo Frigorífico Puerto Bories** ⓘ *T061-414328, Mon-Sun 1000-1900 in summer, US$5 or US$7 with guided tour.*

The slab-like **Cerro Dorotea** dominates the town, with superb views of the whole Seno Ultima Esperanza. It can be reached on foot or by any Río Turbio bus or taxi (recommended, as the hill is farther off than it seems). The trail entrance is marked by a sign marked 'Mirador Cerro Dorotea'. Expect to be charged US$5-8 in one of the local houses, where you will be given a broomstick handle which makes a surprisingly good walking stick. It is a 1½-trek up to the 600 m lookout along a well-marked trail.

Monumento Nacional Cueva Milodón → *Colour map 3, A2*

ⓘ *25 km north of Puerto Natales, US$6. Buses JB US$5, taxi US$24 return.*

The cave, a massive 70 m wide, 220 m deep and 30 m high, contains a plastic model of the prehistoric ground-sloth whose remains were found there in 1895. The remains are now in London, although there is talk of returning them to the site. Evidence has also been found of occupation by Patagonians some 11,000 years ago. Nearby, there is a visitor centre, with summaries in English. Most tours to Torres del Paine stop at the cave.

Parque Nacional Bernardo O'Higgins → *Colour map 3, A2*

Often referred to as the **Parque Nacional Monte Balmaceda**, this park covers much of the Campo de Hielo Sur, plus the fjords and offshore islands further west. A three-hour boat trip from Puerto Natales up the Seno de Ultima Esperanza takes you to the southernmost section, passing the **Glaciar Balmaceda**, which drops from the eastern slopes of Monte Balmaceda (2035 m). The glacier is retreating; in 1986 its foot was at sea level. The boat docks one hour further north at **Puerto Toro**, from where it is a 1-km walk to the base of the **Glaciar Serrano** on the north slope of Monte Balmaceda. On the trip, dolphins, sea-lions (in season), black-necked swans, flightless steamer ducks and cormorants can be seen. Take warm clothes, including a hat and gloves.

There is a route from Puerto Toro along the Río Serrano for 35 km to the Torres del Paine administration centre (see page 292); guided tours are available. It is also possible to travel to the Paine administration centre by boat or zodiac ⓘ *5 hrs, US$90*; details from tour agencies in Puerto Natales.

Towards Argentina

From Puerto Natales, the Argentine frontier can be crossed at three points: Paso Casas Viejas, Paso Dorotea and Paso Cancha Carrera (see page 159). They all eventually meet Route 40, which runs north to El Calafate and east to Río Gallegos. All buses use the Río Turbio crossing, but if you're driving to El Calafate, the Cerro Castillo crossing is a shorter route. » *For onward routes from the border to El Calafate, see page 167.*

Sleeping

Puerto Natales *p285, map p287*
Most prices include breakfast. Hotels in the countryside are open only in the summer months; specific dates vary. In season, cheaper accommodation fills up quickly after the arrival of the **Navimag** ferry from Puerto Montt. Most of the more expensive hotels are much of a muchness give or take the view. Occasionally one of these will have a special offer. Call round for quotes.

L Indigo Patagonia, Ladrilleros 105, T061-413609, www.indigopatagonia.com. Old 3-storey house on the waterfront with fantastic views, recently expanded and converted into a boutique hotel, together with restaurant (open to the public) and roof-top spa.

AL-A Juan Ladrilleros, Pedro Montt 161, T061- 411652, afv@entelchile.net. Small basic rooms with great views. With bath, but no TV. Often willing to give discounts.

A Aquaterra, Bulnes 299, T061-412239, www.aquaterrapatagonia.cl Understated design. No frills but thought and effort have gone into it. Not cheap, but unlike many other places in the same price bracket you get the feeling that the staff are there to help and are able to answer any question you might have. Living room upstairs and a resto-bar downstairs. Alternative therapies also offered.

A Glaciares, Eberhard 104, T061-411452, www.hotelglaciares.co.cl. A standard 3-star. Some rooms have a partial view. Good day tours to Torres del Paine.

A Martín Gusinde, Bories 278, T061-412770, www.austrohoteles.cl. Comfy 3-star, although the carpets could do with a change. Good value rates off season.

A Weskar Ecolodge, Km 1, road to Bories, T061-414168, www.weskar.cl. Quiet lodge overlooking the bay, understated wooden interior. Most rooms with extensive views. There is a restaurant for guests and bike rental. A good out-of-town place to relax.

B Hostal Sir Francis Drake, Phillipi 383, T061-411553, www.chileaustral.com/francisdrake. Simple, smallish but comfortable rooms with bath and cable TV. There is a pleasant living room on the upper floor with views. Recommended.

B Hostel Natales, Ladrilleros 209, T061-411081, www.hostelnatales.cl. **E** pp in dorms. All rooms with bath. Recently converted into a luxury hostel. Fully refurbished and very comfortable, if a little overpriced.

C Residencial Oasis, Señoret 332, resoasis@hotmail. com. Comfortable rooms, with or without bath, cable TV. Breakfast included. Some rooms have no window.

C-D Casa Cecilia, Tomás Rogers 60, T061-411797, www.casaceciliahostal.com.
F singles. With good breakfast, some rooms with bath, clean, cooking facilities, English, French and German spoken, heating, luggage store, camping equipment rental, tours, bus tickets sold, credit cards accepted. Better value in US dollars. Warmly recommended.

C-D Hostal Bulnes, Bulnes 407, T061-411307, www.hostalbulnes.com. With breakfast, some rooms with bath, laundry facilities, luggage store.

D Blanquita, Carrera Pinto 409, T061-411674.
F singles. Basic quiet hotel that looks like a giant portacabin. With bath, heating and breakfast, friendly. Recommended.

D Natalino, Eberhard 371, T061-411968. Clean and very friendly. Rooms with bath and breakfast, parking.

D Patagonia Adventure, Tomás Rogers 179, T061-411028, www.apatagonia.com.
G pp in dorms. Friendly, clean, English spoken, camping equipment for hire, luggage store, book exchange. Good bike and kayak tours offered. Also a general agent selling trips to Torres del Paine. Breakfast is served in the café annex. Recommended.

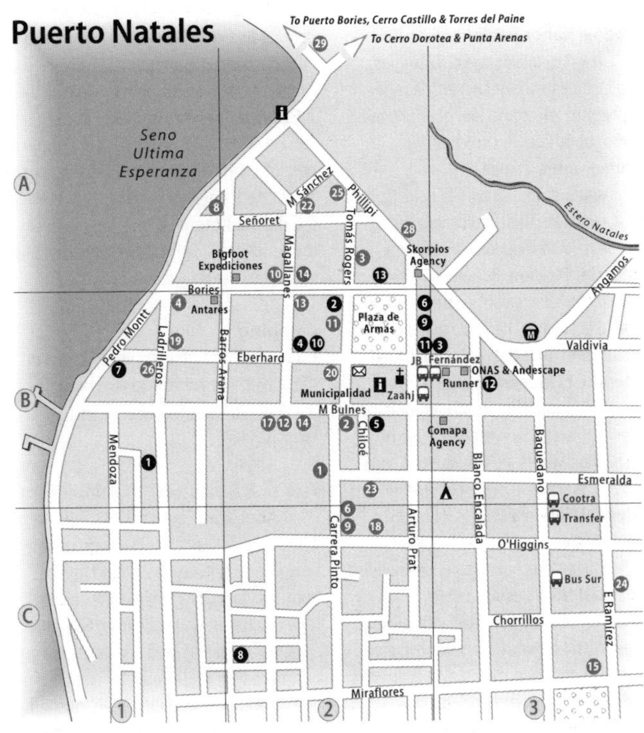

Sleeping
Aquaterra 17 *B2*
Blanquita 1 *B2*
Casa Cecilia 3 *A2*
Casa Teresa 23 *B2*
El Refugio 18 *C2*
Glaciares 19 *B1*
Hospedaje Chila 6 *C2*
Hospedaje Nancy 24 *C3*
Hostal Bulnes 2 *B2*
Hostal Sir Francis Drake 25 *A2*
Hostel Natales 26 *B1*
Indigo Patagonia 4 *B1*
Juan Ladrilleros 8 *A1*
Los Inmigrantes 9 *C2*
Martín Gusinde 10 *A2*
Natalino 20 *B2*
Patagonia Adventure 11 *B2*
Residencial Dickson 12 *B2*
Residencial El Mundial 13 *B2*
Residencial Gabriela 14 *B2*
Residencial Niko's 15 *C3*
Residencial Niko's II 28 *A2*
Residencial Oasis 22 *A2*
Weskar Ecolodge 29 *A2*

Eating
Andrés 1 *B1*
Angelicas 3 *B3*
Club Deportivo Natales 4 *B2*
Cristal 5 *B2*
El Asador Patagónico 9 *B2*
El Living 6 *B2*
El Marítimo 7 *B1*
El Rincón de Don Chicho 8 *C2*
La Casa de Pepe 2 *B2*
La Mesita Grande 11 *B2*
La Oveja Negra 2 *B2*
La Repizza 12 *B3*
La Ultima Esperanza 10 *B2*
Masay 5 *B2*
Parrilla Don Jorge 13 *A2*

Bars & clubs
Casino 14 *A2*

D-E Residencial Niko's II, Phillipi 528, T061-411500, residencialnicosii@hotmail.com. With good breakfast. Some rooms with bath and cable TV, English spoken, tours, tent hire, book exchange.
E Casa Teresa, Esmeralda 463, T061-410472, freepatagonia@hotmail.com. **G** singles. Good value, warm, cheap meals, quiet, friendly. Tours to Torres del Paine. Recommended.
E El Refugio, O'Higgins 456, T061-414881. **G** singles. Youthful and lively place to stay. Offers tours. Internet access.
E Hospedaje Chila, Carrera Pinto 442, T061-412328. **G** singles. Use of kitchen, welcoming, laundry facilities, luggage store, bakes bread. Recommended.
E Hospedaje Nancy, E Ramírez 540, T061-4510022, www.nataleslodge.cl. **G** singles. Cooking facilities, internet access, laundry service, helpful, tours and lots of information. Good budget option. Recommended.
E Los Inmigrantes, Carrera Pinto 480, T061-413482, losinmigrantes@hotmail.com. Good breakfast, clean, kitchen, equipment rental, luggage store. **G** singles. Recommended.
E Residencial Dickson, Bulnes 307, T061-411871, lodging@chilaustral.com. **G** singles. Good breakfast, clean, helpful, cooking and laundry facilities, internet. Recommended.
E Residencial El Mundial, Bories 315, T061-412476, omar@fortalezapatagonia.cl. **G** singles. Some rooms with bath. Use of kitchen (if the owners are not using it), good value meals, luggage stored. Recommended.
E Residencial Gabriela, Bulnes 317, T061-411061. **G** singles. Clean, good breakfast, helpful, luggage store, heating. Recommended.
E Residencial Niko's, Ramírez 669, T061-412810, nikoresidencial@hotmail.com. **G** singles. With breakfast, basic rooms, some rooms with bath, good meals, also dormitory accommodation, recommended.
E Tierra del Fuego, Bulnes 23, T061-412138. **G** singles. Clean, parking, will store luggage, good.

Parque Nacional Bernardo O'Higgins *p286*

AL Hostería Monte Balmaceda, T061-220174. Although the park is uninhabited, guest accommodation is available here.

Road from Punta Arenas

AL Hostal Río Penitente, Km 138, T061-331694. In an old *estancia*. Recommended.
A Hostería Río Verde, Km 90, east off the highway on Seno Skyring, T061-311122. Private bath, heating. Recommended.
B Hostería Llanuras de Diana, Km 215 (30 km south of Puerto Natales), T061-410661. Hidden from road, beautifully situated. Recommended.
C Hotel Rubens, Km 183, T061-226916. Popular for fishing.

North of town

AL-A Cisne de Cuello Negro, 6 km from town, Km 275 near Puerto Bories, for bookings contact Av Colón 782, Punta Arenas, T061-244506, pehoe1@ctcinternet.cl. Clean, excellent cooking. Recommended.
A Estancia Tres Pasos, 40 km north, T061-221930, www.trespasos.cl. Simple and beautiful lodge between Puerto Natales and Torres del Paine. Horse riding trips offered.
B Cabañas Kotenk Aike, 2 km north of town, T061-412581. Sleeps 4, modern, very comfortable, great location.

Camping

There is a campsite in town on Esmeralda y Prat with hot water and tent hire.

Eating

Puerto Natales *p285, map p287*

ΨΨΨ-ΨΨ Angelicas, Eberhard 532, T061-410365, angelicas@rest.cl. A sign of how Puerto Natales has turned into a boutique town. Elegant Mediterranean-style restaurant originally from Santiago. Quality ingredients well prepared. Pricy but more than reasonable for Natales, and customers invariably leave satisfied. Staff can be a little flustered when the restaurant is full. Recommended.
ΨΨΨ-ΨΨ El Asador Patagónico, Prat 158 on the plaza. Specializes in spit-roast lamb. Recommended.
ΨΨΨ-ΨΨ Parrilla Don Jorge, Bories 430 on plaza, T061-410999. Another restaurant specializing in Cordero al Palo, but also serving fish, etc. The open plan leaves

For an explanation of sleeping and eating price codes, and other relevant information, see Essentials pages 25-26.

you feeling a little exposed when the restaurant is not full. Decent service.

¶¶ **El Marítimo**, Pedro Montt 214. Seafood and salmon, good views, popular.

¶¶ **El Rincón de Don Chicho**, Luiz Cruz Martínez 206, T061-414339. All-you-can-eat *parrillada*. Vegetarian options on request. 15 mins' walk from town centre. Recommended.

¶¶ **La Casa de Pepe**, Tomás Rogers 131 on the plaza. For those who want to sample the traditional food of central Chile – *pernil, pastel de choclo* etc. Uncomfortable seats.

¶¶ **La Mesita Grande**, Prat 196 on the plaza, T061-411571, www.mesitagrande.cl. Fresh pizzas made in a wood-burning clay oven. Also pasta and good desserts. Not much atmosphere, but there's a fantastic antique till.

¶¶-¶ **La Caleta Economica**, Eberhard 261, T061-413969. Excellent seafood, also meat and chicken dishes, large portions, good value for money.

¶¶-¶ **La Oveja Negra**, Tomás Rogers 169, on the plaza. Typical Chilean dishes, book swap. Ownership of this restaurant seems to change every year.

¶¶ **La Ultima Esperanza**, Eberhard 354. Recommended for salmon, seafood, huge portions, not cheap but worth it.

¶ **Andrés**, Ladrilleros 381. Excellent, good fish dishes, good service.

¶ **Club Deportivo Natales**, Eberhard 332. Very cheap, decent meals

¶ **Cristal**, Bulnes 439. Tasty sandwiches and salmon, good value.

¶ **La Repizza**, Blanco Encalada 294, T061-410361. Good-value sarnies and light meals.

¶ **Masay**, Bulnes 429. Cheap sandwiches.

Cafés

Aquaterra, Bulnes 299. Cosy, good, also a shiatsu and reiki centre.

Café & Books, Blanco Encalada 224. Cosy café with an extensive 2 for 1 book exchange.

El Living, on the plaza. Cosy, British run, with English newspapers and magazines. Wide variety of cakes, good tea and coffee, wine and vegetarian food. Book exchange.

Emporio de la Pampa, Eberhard 226C, T061-510520. Small café/delicatessen selling wine and local gourmet products.

Patagonia Adventure, Tomás Rogers 179 on the plaza. Opens at 0630 for early risers.

Patagonia Dulce, Barros Arana 233, T061-415285, www.patagoniadulce.cl. For the best hot chocolate in town.

Bars and clubs

Puerto Natales *p285, map p287*

There are a couple of discos on Blanco Encalada.

Casino, Bories 314, T061-411834, daily 1300-0400. Modest, tables open from 2100.

El Bar de Ruperto, Bulnes 371. Good, English-run pub with a lively mix of locals and tourists. For a kick, try the chile vodka.

Kaweshkar, Eberhard 161. European style lounge bar.

Iguana, Magallanes y Eberhard. There is invariably a bar here, but it seems to change name and ownership each year.

Shopping

Puerto Natales *p285, map p287*

Camping equipment

Camping gas is available in hardware stores, eg at Baquedano y O'Higgins. Wares tend to be more expensive than the Zona Franca in Punta Arenas.

Alfgal, Barros Arana 299, T061-413622.

Balfer, Esmeralda y Baquedano.

La Maddera, Prat 297, T061-41331. Outdoor clothing.

Patagonia Adventure and **Casa Cecilia** hire out good-quality gear (see Sleeping, above). Check all equipment and prices carefully. Average charges, per day: tent US$8, sleeping bag US$4-6, mat US$2, raincoat US$1, also cooking gear US$2. Deposits sometimes required: tent US$200, sleeping bag US$100. Note that it is often difficult to hire walking boots.

Food

Food prices are variable so shop around, although everything tends to be more expensive than in Punta Arenas. There's a 24-hr supermarket on the Bulnes 300 block, and at Bulnes 1085. The town markets are also good.

Handicrafts

Ñandu, Eberhard 586. Popular craft store. Another branch at Baquedano y Chorrillos.

Activities and tours

Puerto Natales *p285, map p287*
Reports of the reliability of agencies, especially for their trips to Parque Nacional Torres del Paine, are very mixed. It is better to book tours direct with operators in Puerto Natales than through agents in Punta Arenas or Santiago, where huge commissions may be charged.

Some agencies offer 1-day tours to the Perito Moreno glacier in Argentina (see page 148), 14-hr trip, 2 hrs at the glacier, US$60 excluding food and park entry fee; take US$ cash or Argentine pesos as Chilean pesos are not accepted. However, if you have more time it is better to break the trip by staying in Calafate, and organizing a tour from there.

Antares, Barros Arana 111, T061-414611, www.antarespatagonia.com. Kayaking and trekking.

Bigfoot Expediciones, Bories 206, T061-413247, www.bigfootpatagonia.com. Sea kayaking, trekking, mountaineering and ice-hiking trips on the Grey glacier. Unforgettable if expensive. Recommended.

Chile Nativo, Eberhard 230, casilla 42, T061-411835, www.chilenativo.com. Specializes in multi-day and bespoke tours of Torres del Paine and surroundings.

Comapa, Bulnes 533, T061-411300, www.comapa.cl. Large regional operator offering decent day tours to the park.

Erratic Rock, Baquedano 719, T061-410355, www.erraticrock.com. New agency offering interesting and alternative trekking routes from half a day to 2 weeks.

Estancia Travel, Casa 13B, Puerto Bories (5 km north of Puerto Natales), T061-412221, www.estanciatravel.com. English/Chilean operator offering a different way of experiencing Patagonia – on horseback. Bilingual guides and well-kept horses. Good half-day trips to the cueva del Milodón. Prices start from US$35 for 2 hrs. Multi-day trips only for the well off. Book direct or through agencies in Natales.

Fishing Patagonia, Magallanes 180, T061-410349, www.fishing-patagonia.com. Expensive fly-fishing trips.

Onas, Eberhard 595, T061-414349, www.onaspatagonia.com. Tours of Torres del Paine and kayak trips. Also trips to and from the park down the Río Serrano in zodiac boats to the Serrano glacier in the Parque National Bernardo O'Higgins, and from there on the tour boats to Puerto Natales, US$90 each all inclusive. Book in advance.

Skorpios, Prat 62, T061-412409, www.skorpios.cl. Catamaran trips up to the Fjordo de las montañas. Truly spectacular close up vistas of glaciers and waterfalls given good weather. 2 sailings weekly, US$130.

Sendero Aventura, **Hostal Patagonia Adventure**, Tomás Rogers 179, T061-415636, sendero_aventura@terra.cl. Trekking in Torres del Paine, cycle and kayak trips to the park, boats to Parque Nacional Bernado O'Higgins, camping equipment and bike hire. Recommended.

Turismo 21 de Mayo, Eberhard 554, T061-411476, www.turismo21demayo.cl. Runs boat trips to Parque Nacional Bernardo O'Higgins and on to Torres del Paine in motor zodiac. This can be combined in a very long day with a trip to the park returning by bus. US$150 including park entry and food.

Turismo Runner, Eberhard 555, T061-414141, www.turismorunner.cl. Specializes in day trips to Torres del Paine combined with a boat trip to the face of the Grey Glacier, US$150 per person including park entrance and a decent lunch at the **Hostería Grey**.

Turismo Zaahj, Prat 236, T061-412260. Day trips to Torres del Paine cost around US$35, excluding park entry.

Transport

Puerto Natales *p285, map p287*

Bus

There are buses to **Punta Arenas** by **Bus Fernández**, Eberhard 555, T061-411111; **Bus Sur**, Baquedano 534, T061-411325; and **Bus Transfer**, Baquedano 414, T061-421616; several daily, 3 hrs, US$4, book in advance. **Bus Sur** runs to **Coyhaique**, Mon, US$55. For details of buses to **Torres del Paine**, see page 298.

To Argentina Bus Sur has 3 weekly direct services to **Río Gallegos**, US$18. **Lagoper** (Baquedano y Valdivia), **Turisur**,

Bus Sur and Cootra run hourly services to **Río Turbio** (change bus at border), 2 hrs (depending on customs), US$5. To **El Calafate**, Bus Sur and Zaahj Bus, 4½ hrs, US$19, daily; Cootra also runs a service via Río Turbio, 7 hrs, reserve at least 1 day ahead.

Boat

The Navimag ferry *Magallanes* sails every Fri in summer to **Puerto Montt**, less often off season (see page 232); confirmation of reservations is advised.

Shipping offices Navimag, Pedro Montt 262, Loc B, Terminal Marítimo, T061-411421, www.navimag.com.

Car hire

Avis, Bulnes 632, T061-410775; Motor Cars, Blanco 330, T061-415593, www.motorcars.cl; Ultima Esperanza, Blanco Encalada 206, T061-410461. Hire agents can arrange permission to drive into Argentina, but this is expensive and takes 24 hrs to arrange.

Parque Nacional Bernardo O'Higgins *p286*

The cutter 21 de Mayo and the sailing boat Nueva Galicia sail every morning from Puerto Natales to **Parque Nacional Bernardo O'Higgins** in summer and on Sun only in the winter, US$60 per person, minimum 10 passengers. Book through Casa Cecilia (see Sleeping), or Turismo 21 de Mayo (see Activities and tours). Lunch extra, so take own food; snacks and drinks available on board. The trip can be combined with a visit to Torres del Paine. Pay the full return fare on the boat.

Directory

Puerto Natales *p285, map p287*

Banks and casas de cambio Some *casas* offer very poor rates (much better to change money in Punta Arenas). Banco Santiago, Bulnes y Blanco Encalada, Mastercard and Visa, ATM; Enio America, Blanco Encalada 266, Argentine pesos can be changed here. Others on Bulnes and Prat. **Internet** Several places in the centre. **Laundry** Lavandería Catch, Bories 218, friendly service. **Post office** Eberhard 417, open Mon-Fri 0830-1230, 1430-1745, Sat 0900-1230. **Telephone** CTC, Blanco Encalada 23 y Bulnes; Entel, Baquedano y Bulnes, phone and fax; Telefonica, Blanco Encalada y Phillipi.

Parque Nacional Torres del Paine

Covering 242,242 ha, 145 km northwest of Puerto Natales, this Chilean national park is a UNESCO Biosphere Reserve and a must-visit thanks to its diverse wildlife and spectacular surroundings. Taking its name from the Tehuelche word Paine, meaning 'blue', the park encompasses some truly stunning scenery, with constantly changing panoramas of peaks, glaciers and icebergs, vividly coloured lakes of turquoise, ultramarine and grey, and quiet green valleys filled with wild flowers. In the centre of the park is one of the most impressive mountain areas on earth, a granite massif from which rise oddly shaped peaks of over 2600 m, known as the Torres (towers) and Cuernos (horns) of Paine.

In total, there are 15 peaks above 2000 m, of which the highest is Cerro Paine Grande (3050 m); few places can compare to its steep forested talus slopes topped by 1000-m vertical shafts of basalt with conical caps. These are the remains of frozen magma in ancient volcanic throats, everything else having been eroded. On the western edge of the park is the enormous Campo de Hielo Sur icefield; four main glaciers – Grey, Dickson, Zapata and Tyndall – branch off it, their meltwater forming a complex of lakes and streams, which lead into Pacific fjords. Two other glaciers, Francés and Los Perros, descend on the western side of the central massif. » *For Sleeping, Eating and other listings, see pages 296-298.*

Tourists del Paine

→ The park has become increasingly popular, receiving over 100,000 a year. Despite efforts to manage the ever-growing numbers, the impact of such a large influx is starting to show.
→ Litter has become a problem, especially around *refugios* and camping areas; please take all your rubbish out of the park, including all toilet paper; human waste should be buried.
→ Bring all necessary equipment and your own food from Puerto Natales; don't rely on the shops within the park, which are expensive and have a limited selection.
→ The wind tends to increase in the evening so, if you're camping, it is a good idea to pitch tents by 1600.
→ Rats and mice can be a problem around campsites and *refugios*, so do not leave food in your pack (which may be chewed through), instead, hang food in a bag on a wire.
→ Forest fires are a serious hazard; you are not allowed to build fires in the park. Bring a stove if camping.

Ins and outs → *Colour map 3, A2*

Getting there The most practical way to get to Torres del Paine is with one of the many bus or tour companies that leave Puerto Natales daily. If you want to drive, hiring a pickup from Punta Arenas or Puerto Natales is an economical proposition for a group (up to nine people), US$400 for four days. The road from Puerto Natales is being improved; it takes about three hours from Puerto Natales to the administration. Petrol is available at Río Serrano, but fill up in case. There is a new road being built to the south side of the park which should cut the journey time to around two hours. ▸▸ *See Transport, page 298.*

Getting around Allow a week or 10 days to see the park properly. Most visitors will find that they get around on foot, however, there are minibuses between the CONAF administration and Guardería Laguna Amarga, as well as boats across Lago Pehoé. Roads inside the park are narrow and bendy with blind corners. Rangers keep a check on the whereabouts of all visitors: you are required to register and show your passport when entering the park or setting off on any hike.

Tourist information Entrances at Laguna Amarga, Lago Sarmiento and Laguna Azul, entry fee foreigners US$19 (proceeds are shared between all Chilean national parks). **CONAF** ⓘ *administration centre at the northern end of Lago del Toro, T061-691931, daily 0830-2000 in summer, 0830-1230, 1400-1830 off season*. It provides a good slide show at 2000 on Saturday and Sunday and there are also excellent exhibitions on the flora and fauna of the park in Spanish and English. There are six ranger stations (*guarderías*) in the park staffed by *guardaparques*, who give advice and also store luggage (not at Laguna Amarga). A basic map is provided with your park entrance ticket; other maps (US$4) are obtainable at **CONAF** offices in Punta Arenas or Puerto Natales but most are unreliable. The maps produced by **Cartographia Digital** and **Patagonia Interactiva** have been recommended as more accurate.

Best time to visit The weather in the park can change in a few minutes. The warmest months are December to March, although it can be wet and windy at this time of year. Most visitors come to the park during January and February, which, if possible, should be avoided due to overcrowding and the unpredictability of the weather. Many parts of the park are now open all year round, although after mid-March, there is less public transport and trucks are irregular. October and November are recommended for wild flowers, and visiting in winter is increasingly popular as there is little wind. Snow may prevent access but well-equipped hikers can do some good walking, when conditions are stable. Rain and snowfall are heavier the further west you go and bad weather sweeps off the Campo de Hielo Sur without warning. For information in Spanish on weather conditions, phone the administration centre.

Wildlife

The park enjoys a micro-climate especially favourable to plants and wildlife. Over 200 species of plants have been identified and, although few trees reach great size, several valleys are thickly forested and little light penetrates. There are 105 species of birds in the park, including 18 species of waterfowl and 11 birds of prey. Particularly noteworthy are condors, blacknecked swans, rheas, kelp geese, ibis, flamingos and austral parakeets. The park is also one of the best places for viewing rheas and guanacos. Other mammals include hares, foxes, skunks, huemules (see box, page 264) and pumas (the last two only very rarely).

Trekking

There are about 250 km of well-marked trails. Visitors must keep to the trails: cross country trekking is not permitted. It is vital not to underestimate the unpredictability of the weather, nor the arduousness of some stretches on the long hikes. Some paths are confusingly marked and it is all too easy to end up on precipices with glaciers or churning rivers awaiting below; be particularly careful to follow the path at the Paso John Gardner on 'El Circuito' (see below). The only means of rescue are on horseback or by boat; the nearest helicopter is in Punta Arenas and high winds usually prevent its operation in the park. It is essential to be properly equipped against cold, wind and rain. A strong, streamlined, waterproof tent is essential if doing El Circuito (although you can hire camping equipment for a single night at most *refugios*). Also essential are protective clothing, strong waterproof footwear, compass, good sleeping bag and sleeping mat. In summer also take shorts and sunscreen.

El Circuito

The most popular trek is a circuit round the Torres and Cuernos del Paine. It is usually done anticlockwise starting from the *guardería* at **Laguna Amarga** and, although some people complete the route in less time, it normally takes five to six days. The circuit is often closed in winter because of snow; major rivers are crossed by footbridges, but these are occasionally washed away. From Laguna Amarga the route is north along the western side of the Río Paine to **Lago Paine**, before turning west to follow the lush pastures of the valley of the Río Paine to the southern end of **Lago Dickson** (it is possible to add a journey to the *campamento* by the Torres on day one of this route); the *refugio* at Lago Dickson lies in a breathtaking position in front of the icy white lake with mountains beyond. From Lago Dickson the path runs along the wooded valley of the **Río de los Perros**, past the Glaciar de los Perros, before climbing through bogs and up scree to **Paso John Gadner** (1241 m, the highest point on the route), then dropping steeply through forest to follow Glaciar Grey southeast to **Lago Grey**, continuing to **Lago Pehoé** and the administration centre. There are superb views en route, particularly from the top of Paso John Gadner.

The longest stretch is between Refugio Laguna Amarga and Refugio Dickson (30 km, 10 hours in good weather; two campsites on the way at Serón and Cairon), but the most difficult section is the very steep, slippery slope from Paso John Gadner down to the Campamento Paso; the path is not well signed at the top of the pass, and some people have got dangerously lost and ended up on Glaciar Grey itself. Camping gear must be carried, as some *campamentos* (including Campamento Paso and Campamento Torres) do not have *refugios*.

The W

A popular alternative to El Circuito, this four- to five-day route can be completed without camping equipment as there is accommodation in *refugios* en route. It combines several of the hikes described separately below. From Refugio Laguna Amarga the first stage runs west via **Hostería Las Torres** and up the valley of the **Río Ascensio** via Refugio Chileno to the base of the **Torres del Paine** (see below). From

Parque Nacional Torres del Paine

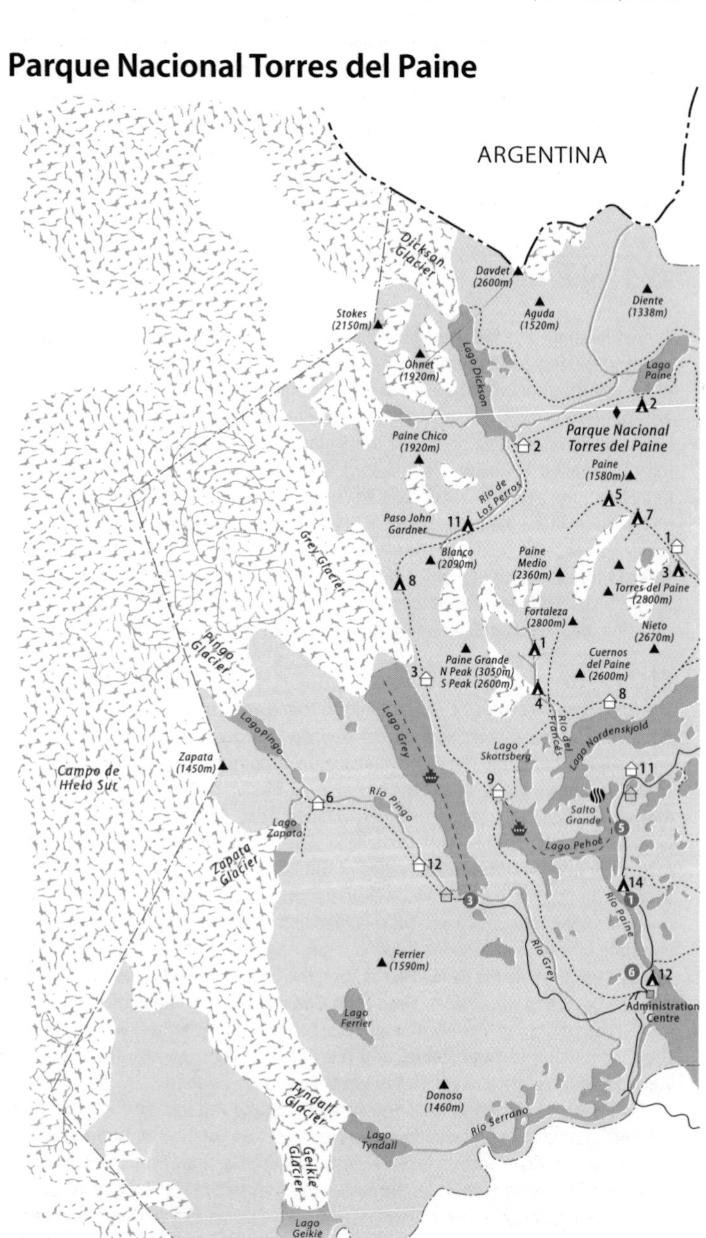

here return to the Hostería Las Torres and then walk along the northern shore of **Lago Nordenskjold** via Refugio Los Cuernos to Campamento Italiano. From here climb the Valley of the **Río del Francés** (see below) before continuing to Lodge Paine Grande. From here you can complete the third part of the 'W' by walking west along the northern shore of **Lago Grey** to Refugio Grey and the Grey Glacier before returning to Lodge Paine Grande and the boat back across the lake to the Refugio Pudeto.

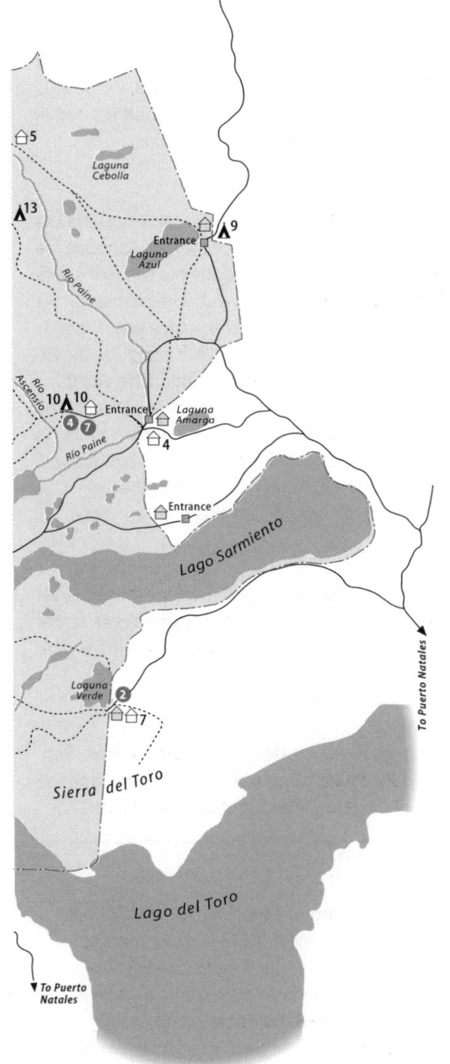

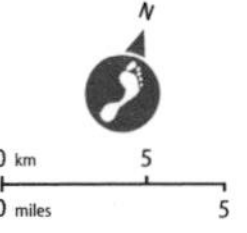

Sleeping
Explora **1**
Hostería Lago Grey **3**
Hostería Las Torres **4**
Hostería Mirador del Payne **2**
Hostería Pehoé **5**
Patagonia Ecocamp **7**
Posada Río Serrano **6**

Refugios
Chileno (Fantástico Sur) **1**
Grey (Andescape) **3**
Lago Dickson (Andescape) **2**
Lago Paine **5**
Laguna Amarga **4**
Laguna Verde **7**
Las Torres (Fantástico Sur) **10**
Lodge Paine Grande (Vertice) **9**
Los Cuernos (Fantástico Sur) **8**
Pingo **12**
Pudeto **11**
Zapata **6**

Camping
Campamento Británico **1**
Campamento Cairon **2**
Campamento Chileno **3**
Campamento Italiano **4**
Campamento Japonés **5**
Campamento Las Torres **7**
Campamento Paso **8**
Lago Pehoé **14**
Laguna Azul **9**
Las Torres **10**
Los Perros **11**
Serón **13**
Serrano **12**

Ranger stations (*guarderías*)

Valley of the Río del Francés

From Lodge Paine Grande this route leads north across undulating country along the western edge of **Lago Skottberg** to Campamento Italiano and then follows the valley of the Río del Francés, which climbs between Cerro Paine Grande and the Ventisquero del Francés (to the west) and the Cuernos del Paine (to the east) to Campamento Británico; the views from the mirador an hour's walk above Campamento Británico are superb. Allow two and a half hours from Lodge Paine Grande to Campamento Italiano, two and a half hours further to Campamento Británico.

Treks from Guardería Grey

Guardería Grey, 18 km west by road from the administration centre, is the starting point for a five-hour trek to Lago Pingo. From the *guardería* follow the **Río Pingo**, via Refugio Pingo and Refugio Zapata (four hours), with views south over Ventisquero Zapata (look out for plenty of wildlife and for icebergs in the lake) to reach the lake. **Ventisquero Pingo** can be seen 3 km away over the lake. Two short signposted walks from Guardería Grey have also been suggested: one is a steep climb up the hill behind the ranger post to **Mirador Ferrier**, from where there are fine views; the other is via a suspension bridge across the Río Pingo to the peninsula at the southern end of **Lago Grey**, from where there are good views of the icebergs on the lakes.

To the base of the Torres del Paine

From Refugio Laguna Amarga, this six-hour route follows the road west to **Hostería Las Torres** (1½ hours), before climbing along the western side of the **Río Ascensio** via Refugio Chileno (two hours) and Campamento Chileno to Campamento Las Torres (two hours), close to the base of the **Torres del Paine** (be careful when crossing the suspension bridge over the Río Ascensio near Hostería Las Torres, as the path is poorly marked and you can end up on the wrong side of the ravine). The path alongside the Río Ascensio is well marked, and the Campamento Las Torres is in an attractive wood (no *refugio*). A further 30 minutes up the morraine takes you to a lake at the base of the towers themselves; they seem so close that you almost feel you could touch them. To see the Torres lit by sunrise (spectacular but you must have good weather), it's well worth carrying your camping gear up to Campamento Torres and spending the night. One hour beyond Campamento Torres is Campamento Japonés, another good campsite.

To Laguna Verde

From the administration centre follow the road north 2 km, before taking the path east over the **Sierra del Toro** and then along the southern side of **Laguna Verde** to the Guardería Laguna Verde. Allow four hours. This is one of the easiest walks in the park and may be a good first hike.

To Laguna Azul and Lago Paine

This route runs north from Laguna Amarga to the western tip of **Laguna Azul**, from where it continues across the sheltered **Río Paine** valley past Laguna Cebolla to the Refugio Lago Paine at the western end of the lake. Allow eight and a half hours.

Sleeping

Parque Nacional Torres del Paine

p291, map p294

LL Explora, Salto Chico on edge of Lago Pehoé, T061-411247, www.explora.com. Ugly building but the most luxurious hotel in the park, offering spectacular views, pool, gym, tours and transfer from Punta Arenas.

LL Hostería Lago Grey, T061-410172, reservations T061-229512, www.turismolagogrey.com.cl. Small rooms on edge of Lago Grey with views of the glacier, restaurant.

LL Hostería Las Torres, head office Magallanes 960, Punta Arenas, T061-710050, www.lastorres.com. Probably the best of the *hosterías* in the park. Nice rooms, decent restaurant, disabled access, horse riding, transport from Laguna Amarga ranger station.

LL-L Hostería Lago Tyndall, T061-413139 www.hoteltyndall.cl. Expensive, cafeteria-style restaurant, electricity during the day only. Only come here if other places are full.

LL-L Patagonia Ecocamp, toll free T0800-051 7095 (UK) and T1-800-901 6987, www.eco camp.travel. Luxury all-inclusive tented camp with geodesic design and powered by renewable energy. See also **Cascada Expediciones**, Activities and tours.

L-A Hostería Pehoé, 5 km south of Pehoé ranger station, 11 km north of park administration, T061-411390, www.pehoe.com. On an island with spectacular view across the lake, but it doesn't make the most of its stunning location, run-down, overpriced.

A Hostería Mirador del Payne (Estancia Lazo), eastern edge of the park, reservations Fagnano 585, Punta Arenas, T061-226930, www.miradordelpayne.com. Beautifully situated on Laguna Verde with spectacular views with a restaurant and good fishing. Recommended but an inconvenient base for visiting the park; own transport essential, or you can trek to it from within the park.

A Posada Río Serrano, book ahead through Baqueano Zamora, Baquedano 534B, Puerto Natales, T061-412911, www.baqueano zamora.com. An old *estancia*, some rooms with bath, breakfast extra, near park administration, good restaurant and shop.

Private refugios

3 companies between them run half of the *refugios* in the park, providing dormitory space only (bring your own sleeping bag or hire one for US$6). Prices are around US$30 pp, with full board about US$30 extra. Take US$ cash and your passport as you will save 19% tax. *Refugios* have kitchens, hot showers and space for camping. Most will hire out tents for around US$12 per night. In high season accommodation and meals in the non-CONAF *refugios* should be booked in advance in Puerto Natales, or by asking staff in one *refugio* to radio another. In winter most of the *refugios* close, although 1 or 2 stay open depending on the weather. Note that the administration rights for many *refugios* are up for tender in 2007 so the following details may change.

Andescape refugios, book through agencies in Puerto Natales or direct at Andescape, Eberhard 599, Puerto Natales, T061-412877, www.andescape.cl. It owns: **Refugio Grey**, on the eastern shore of Lago Grey. **Refugio** Lago Dickson, on the northern part of the circuit.

Fantástico Sur refugios, book in agencies in Puerto Natales or direct on T061-710050, www.wcircuit.com. It owns: **Refugio Las Torres**, next to the Hostería Las Torres. Refugio Los Cuernos, on the northern shore of Lago Nordenskjold. **Refugio Chileno**, valley of the Río Ascensio at the foot of the Torres.

Vertice refugios, book through agencies in Puerto Natales or via www.verticepata gonia.cl. It owns: **Lodge Paine Grande**, new and large on the northwestern edge of Lago Pehoe. In theory the most comfortable of all, but in practice has had teething troubles and several complaints regarding customer service.

In addition, there are 6 free *refugios*: Zapata, Pingo, Laguna Verde, Laguna Amarga, Lago Paine and Pudeto. Most have cooking areas (wood stove or fireplace) but Laguna Verde and Pingo are in very poor condition.

Campsites

The wind tends to increase in the evening so it is a good idea to pitch tents by 1600. Free camping is permitted in 7 locations in the park; these sites are known as *campamentos*. Fires are not allowed as forest fires are a serious hazard. Use camping stoves. Campers are also required to have a trowel to bury their waste. Equipment can be hired in Puerto Natales (see Shopping above).

In addition to sites at the private *refugios*, there are the following sites: **Lago Pehoé**, run by Turismo Río Serrano (see Sleeping, above), US$20 per site, max 6 persons, hot showers, beware of mice. **Laguna Azul**, hot showers. **Las Torres**, run by Estancia Cerro Paine, US$4, hot showers. **Los Perros**, run by Andescape, with shop and hot showers. **Serón**, run by Estancia Cerro Paine, US$4, hot showers. **Serrano**, run by Turismo Río Serrano (see Sleeping, above), US$15 per site, maximum 6, cold showers, basic.

Activities and tours

Parque Nacional Torres del Paine

p291, map p294

Before booking a tour check all the details carefully and get a copy in writing, as there have been increasingly mixed reports of the quality of some tours. Many companies who claim to visit the Grey Glacier, for example, only visit Lago Grey (you see the glacier in the distance). After mid-Mar there is less public transport and trucks are irregular.

Agencies in Puerto Natales offer 1-day minibus tours, US$35 plus park entry; these give a good impression of the lower parts of the park, but you spend most of the day in the vehicle. Ideally you need to stay several days, or at least overnight, to appreciate it fully. Cheaper tours are also available, but both guide and vehicle may not be as good. There are many more operators based in Puerto Natales offering trekking, kayaking, ice-hiking, boat trips (see page 290).

Cascada Expediciones, T02-232 9878, www.cascada-travel. Based in Santiago and Puerto Natales. 5- to 7-day all-inclusive treks to Torres del Paine, Los Glaciares and Cerro Fitz Roy. Also 4-day wildlife-watching trips.

Chile Nativo, Eberhard 230, Casilla 42, Puerto Natales, T061-411835, www.chile nativo.com. Specialists in tailor-made trips.

Experience Chile, T07977-223326, www.experiencechile.org. UK company that arranges itineraries and accommodation.

Hostería Grey, see Sleeping, above, provides excursions by boat to the face of the Grey Glacier at 0900 and 1500 daily, 3½ hrs, US$60 per person. Book direct or through **Turismo Runner** in Puerto Natales.

Transport

Parque Nacional Torres del Paine

p291, map p294

Bus

From early Nov to mid-Apr daily bus services run from Puerto Natales to the park, leaving between 0630 and 0800, and around 1430, 2½ hrs to Laguna Amarga, 3 hrs to the administration centre; return departures are around 1300 and 1800. Generally, buses will drop you at Laguna Amarga and pick you up at the administration centre for the return. The buses wait at Refugio Pudeto until the 1200 boat from Refugio Lago Pehoé arrives. Travel between 2 points within the park (eg Pudeto–Laguna Amarga) is US$4. Services are run by **Bus Sur**, Baquedano 534, T061-411325; **JB**, Prat 258, T061-412824; and **Fortaleza**, Prat 258, T061-410595. In season there are also minibuses from Laguna Amarga to **Hostería Los Torres**, US$4, and from the administration centre to **Hostería Lago Grey**.

At other times, services by travel agencies are subject to demand; arrange your return date with the driver and try to coincide with other groups to keep costs down; **Luis Díaz** has been recommended, about US$17, minimum 3 persons.

In season, there is a direct bus service from Torres del Paine to **El Calafate** (Argentina), with **Chaltén Travel**, US$50. At other times you must either return to Puerto Natales and catch a bus, or get a ride from the park to Villa Cerro Castillo and try to link with the Natales–El Calafate bus schedule.

Boat

A boat service runs across Lago Pehoé from Refugio Lago Pehoé to Refugio Pudeto, daily, 30 mins, US$19 one-way with one piece of baggage free, tickets available on board. Departures from Pehoé 1000, 1230, 1830; from Pudeto 0930, 1200, 1800. Reduced service off season, no service May-Sep.

Tierra del Fuego

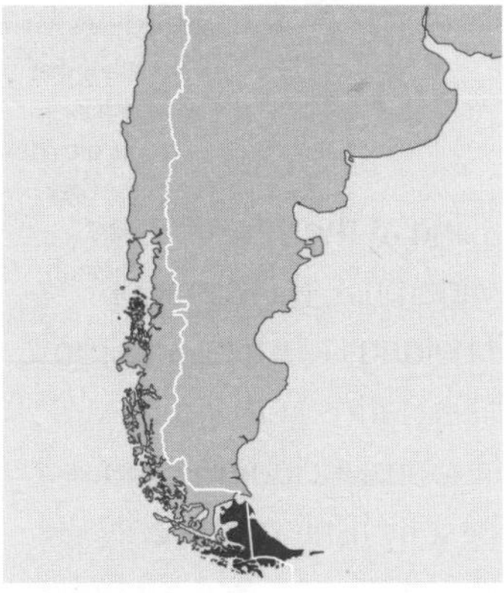

Footprint features

Introduction

At the southern end of Patagonia and at the very end of the world lies its last remaining wilderness, the island of Tierra del Fuego. The eastern half belongs to Chile, an almost untamed expanse of immense sheep farms and virgin mountains, dotted with remote lagoons, including Lago Blanco, which offers the world's best fly fishing. The only settlement is the tiny town of Porvenir.

Argentine Tierra del Fuego boasts a welcoming city with a splendid setting: Ushuaia nestles below the mighty Darwin Range at the very tail of the Andes and looks out over the Beagle Channel to the jagged peaks of Isla Navarino beyond. Visit in autumn, and you'll think the island's name, 'Land of Fire', derives from the blaze of scarlet and orange beech forest covering the mountains but, in winter, the slopes of Cerro Castor offer good powder snow and spectacular views. Head to Parque Nacional Tierra del Fuego for excellent hikes for every ability or be inspired by original pioneer Thomas Bridges to sail forth along the Beagle Canal, past islands covered with basking fur seals, to Estancia Harberton. And if this isn't remote enough, take a boat from Ushuaia to Cape Horn or even Antarctica.

★ Don't miss ...

1. **Fishing at Lago Blanco**, page 305.
2. **Hiking to the Dientes de Navarino**, page 305, or **Bahía Lapataia**, page 313.
3. **The view from Cerro Martial**, page 311.
4. **A boat trip to Estancia Harberton**, page 311.
5. **Staying on a pioneer estancia**, page 314 and page 317.

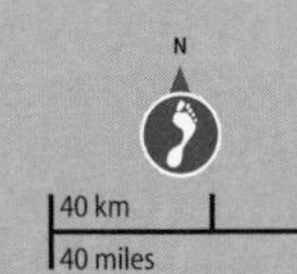

Ins and outs

→ Ins and outs, p303 and p308; Transport, p307 and p319.

There are frequent flights into Porvenir, Río Grand and Ushuaia, but all land access to Tierra del Fuego is via the Chilean side of the island. Transport to the island is heavily booked in summer, especially in January, and even the buses fill quickly, so this part of your journey requires some careful forward planning.

Getting there

Air There are flights to **Río Grande** and **Ushuaia** in Argentine Tierra del Fuego, from Buenos Aires and El Calafate, and flights from many other towns in Patagonia with the army airline **LADE**. There are also daily flights from Punta Arenas to **Porvenir** in Chilean Tierra del Fuego and, less frequently, to **Puerto Williams** on Isla Navarino. Ushuaia is the best entry point for most visitors, with hiking, boat trips and winter sports all nearby; Río Grande provides access to some fantastic estancias, while Porvenir is better for exploration of the remote Chilean plains and isolated lakes.

Ferry There are two ferry crossings to Tierra del Fuego: from **Tres Puentes**, just north of Punta Arenas, to **Porvenir**; and from **Punta Delgada** across the Primera Angostura (First Narrows) to the tiny port of **Punta Espora**. All buses from mainland Argentina and most services from Punta Arenas use the quicker and more frequent Punta Delgada crossing, which is 59 km south of the Argentine border at **Monte Aymond** and 170 km northeast of Punta Arenas, via Route 255. There's a cosy tea room on the northern side, with hot snacks and toilets.

Getting around

The only legal crossing between the Chilean and Argentine parts of Tierra del Fuego is 142 km east of Porvenir. There are two settlements called **San Sebastián**, one on each side of the border, but they are 14 km apart and taxis are not allowed to cross the frontier, which means you must travel on one of the scheduled buses or with your own transport. **Chilean immigration and customs** ⓘ *San Sebastián (Chile), 0800-2200.* **Argentine immigration and customs** ⓘ *San Sebastián (Arg), 24 hrs daily.* From Argentine San Sebastián Route 3 heads east to Río Grande and then south to Ushuaia. This is the main route through the Argentine half of the island and is surfaced apart from a 50 km section between Ushuaia and Tolhuin. Other roads on Tierra del Fuego are narrow and gravelled. Fuel is available in Porvenir, Cerro Sombrero and Cullen (Chile) and Río Grande, Ushuaia and San Sebastián (Argentina). There are scheduled buses linking Punta Arenas with Río Grande and Ushuaia in summer; a few travel via Porvenir. However, there is no guaranteed public transport along the *ripio* roads either south of Porvenir or east of Ushuaia to Harberton and Estancia Moat on the south coast.

Tourist information

Information on Chilean Tierra del Fuego is best sought from tour operators in Punta Arenas (see page 282) or from **Sernatur** (www.sernatur.com). The excellent tourist office in Ushuaia (see page 310) is a good source for information on the Argentine side of the island. See also www.tierradelfuego.org.ar.

Best time to visit

Summer is best for trekking, when daytime temperatures hover around 15°C. Try to avoid Ushuaia in January, however, when it is swamped with tourists. There are very stiff winds at this time of year, particularly further north, around Río Grande, where they can gust up to 200 kph. Ushuaia is at its most beautiful in autumn, when the dense forests turn rich red and yellow, and there are many bright clear days. The ski season is from mid-June to October, when temperatures hover around zero, but the wind drops.

Making the most of Tierra del Fuego

→ Avoid visiting in January. Beds and buses are full, and Tierra del Fuego is not at its most tranquil. March and April are blissful.
→ To save time and avoid disappointment, arrange hiking trips before you arrive, with a reputable adventure tourism company, like **Compania de Guias de Patagonia** or **Canal Fun**. See page 319.
→ Tolhuin has a fabulous bakery that's open 24 hours. It's worth a detour to see the tranquil lakeside, too. See page 309.
→ Agency tours will only allow you two hours at Estancia Harberton. For a fuller experience of pioneer life and the chance to walk around the beautiful coastline, hire a car and drive. See page 311.
→ Boat trips from Ushuaia along the Beagle Channel are much more pleasant on board the charming old *Barracuda* than on the modern catamarans, and the commentary is better too. See page 319.
→ Parque Nacional Tierra del Fuego is best in the late afternoon when the tour buses have gone, particularly Lago Roca and Bahía Lapataia. But make sure you allow enough daylight to get back! See page 313.

Chilean Tierra del Fuego

Chilean Tierra del Fuego forms part of Región XII (Magallanes), of which the capital is Punta Arenas. It is a wild spot, less populated than the Argentine side of the island, and is characterized by a mixture of thick forests, wide rolling pampas and imposing glaciers. There are peaks of well over 2000 m and numerous lakes and rivers, rich in trout and salmon. To the south of Tierra del Fuego, across the Beagle Channel, Isla Navarino is even more remote and inaccessible. ▸▸ *For Sleeping, Eating and other listings, see pages 306-308.*

Ins and outs

Visitors to Chilean Tierra del Fuego arrive either by air to Porvenir or by ferry to Porvenir or Punta Espora. The ferry is recommended for occasional sightings of porpoises following the ships, though arriving by air gives a memorable view of the island. From the Porvenir ferry, buses (US$1.50) and taxis (US$5) run to the town's bus terminal, where local buses depart for Cameron and the Argentine side of the island. There is no local bus service to or from Punta Espora. The only reliable way of reaching Isla Navarino is by air from Punta Arenas.

Porvenir → *Colour map 3, A4*

Chilean Tierra del Fuego has a population of 7000, most of whom live in Porvenir. Founded in 1894 as a port serving the sheep *estancias* of the island, this is the only town on the Chilean side of the island. It is quiet and pleasant, with painted zinc houses and tall trees lining the main avenue. Many inhabitants are descended from Croatian goldminers who came to seek their fortune during the gold boom of the 1890s; the signpost at the port marks the distance to Croatia. There is a small museum, **Museo Fernando Cordero Rusque** ⓘ *Samuel Valdivieso 402, T061-580098*, with archaeological and photographic displays on the Ona people, sections on natural history and gold mining, and a small **tourist annexe**.

Although it's small and not geared up for tourism, Porvenir is the base for exploring the wonderful virgin territory of western Tierra del Fuego and for fly fishing for brown trout, sea run brook trout and steelheads in the island's richly stocked lakes and rivers.

The people of Tierra del Fuego

Human habitation on Tierra del Fuego dates back some 10,000 years; four indigenous groups inhabited the island until the early 20th century. The most numerous, the **Onas** (also known as the Selk'nam), were hunter-gatherers in the north, living mainly on guanaco and several species of rodents. The southeastern corner of the island was inhabited by hunter-gatherers known as the Haus or **Hausch**, while the Yaganes or **Yámanas** lived along the Beagle Channel and on the islands further south. A seafaring people who survived mainly on seafood, fish and seabirds, they developed strong upper bodies for rowing long distances. The fourth group, the **Alacalufe**, lived in the west of Tierra del Fuego as well as on the Chonos Archipelago, surviving by fishing and hunting seals.

The first Europeans to visit the island came with the Portuguese navigator **Fernão Magalhães** (Magellan), who, in 1520, sailed through the channel that bears his name. He saw fires lit on shore and so named the island 'Tierra del Fuego' ('the land of fire'). However, numerous maritime disasters meant that the indigenous population were left undisturbed for three centuries.

Robert Fitzroy and Charles Darwin visited in 1832 and 1833 and several disastrous attempts to convert the indigenous groups followed but it wasn't until 1869 that the first successful mission was finally established. In 1884, the **Reverend Thomas Bridges** (see page 312) founded a mission at Ushuaia and soon many Yámana had settled nearby. Bridges learnt the Yámana language and compiled a Yámana-English dictionary to ease the conversion process. Charles Darwin had written that the Yámana language "barely deserves to be called articulate" but, in fact, it turned out to have an extraordinarily rich vocabulary: the dictionary had 32,000 words and was not complete at the time of Bridges' death in 1898.

The work of the missionaries was disturbed by the discovery of gold in 1887 and the growth of sheep farming. The gold rush began when Julio Popper, a German settler, founded the successful El Paramó mine at San Sebastián. He was followed by treasure seekers from north America and Europe, including many Croatians, whose descendents still live on the island. Sheep farms were created as the Argentine and Chilean governments attempted to populate the island following a border settlement in 1883. The Ona hunted the 'white guanacos' and the colonists responded by offering two sheep for each Ona that was killed (proof was provided by a pair of Ona ears). The indigenous groups were further ravaged by epidemics of European diseases. Despite the efforts of Salesian missionaries in the early 20th century, the Ona went into terminal decline; the last Ona died in 1999. The Hausch have also died out. One old Yámana lady survives near Puerto Williams and there is a handful of Alacalufe at Puerto Edén in the Chonos Archipelago.

Beyond Porvenir

About 90 km east of Porvenir, roads head north to San Sebastián and south to **Cameron**. This large farm settlement is the only other community of any size on the Chilean part of the island and lies 149 km southeast of Porvenir on the opposite shore of windswept Bahía Inútil. Nearing Cameron, the southern mountains loom ahead and the road passes secluded canyons and bays, interspersed with a few farms.

From Cameron a road runs southeast for a further 40 km before splitting north to San Sebastián and south to **Sección Río Grande** (7 km from the junction) – there is very little traffic here. The road south climbs into the hills, through woods where guanacos hoot and run off into glades and the banks are covered with red and purple moss. The north shores of **Lago Blanco** can be reached by cutting through the woods from Sección Río Grande, with superb views of the mountains surrounding the lake and the snows in the south. In the centre of the lake is Isla Victoria, which has accommodation (see Sleeping below). The lake area can be very cold, even in mid-summer, when biting winds sweep in from the south, so wrap up warmly.

Isla Navarino and Cape Horn » *p306-308.*

Situated on the southern shore of the Beagle Channel, Isla Navarino is unspoilt and beautiful, and encompasses great geographical diversity: the **Dientes de Navarino** range has peaks over 1000 m, covered with southern beech forest up to 500 m, while, to the south, stretch great plains covered with peat bogs and lagoons abundant in flora. Wildlife is prolific: guanacos and condors can be seen inland, as well as large numbers of beavers, which were introduced to the island and have done a lot of damage. The island was the centre of the indigenous Yámana culture, and has 500 archaeological sites, dating back 3000 years. The flight from Punta Arenas – the only reliable way of reaching the island – is beautiful, with superb views of Tierra del Fuego, the Cordillera Darwin and the islands stretching south to Cape Horn.

Puerto Williams → *Colour map 3, C4*

The only settlement of any size on the island is Puerto Williams, a Chilean naval base situated about 50 km east of Ushuaia (Argentina). Puerto Williams is the southernmost permanently inhabited town in the world; Puerto Toro, 50 km east-south-east, is the world's southernmost permanently inhabited settlement. Due to the long-running border dispute with Argentina here, Puerto Williams is controlled by the Chilean Navy. Outside the Naval headquarters, you can see the bow section of the *Yelcho*, the tug chartered by Shackleton to rescue men stranded on Elephant Island (see box, page 277).

Museo Martín Gusinde ⓘ *Mon-Thu 1000-1300, 1500-1800, 1500-1800 Sat and Sun, US$1*, known as the Museo del Fin del Mundo ('End of the World Museum') is full of information about vanished indigenous tribes, local wildlife and famous voyages by Charles Darwin and Fitzroy of the *Beagle*. A visit is highly recommended. There is a **tourist office** ⓘ *Municipalidad de Cabos de Hornos, Pres Ibañez 130, T061-621011, closed in winter*, near the museum, which can provide maps and information on hiking. A kilometre west of the town is the yacht club (one of Puerto Williams' two nightspots), whose wharf is made from a sunken 1930s Chilean warship. The last of the Yámana people live at **Villa Ukika**, 2 km east, where there are beaver dams and waterfalls.

Exploring the island

For superb views, climb **Cerro Bandera**, which is reached by a path from the dam 4 km west of the town (a steep three- to four-hour round trip). A challenging 53-km circuit of the **Dientes de Navarino** begins here. This is the southernmost trail in the world and passes through impressive mountain landscapes, frozen lagoons and snowy peaks. It takes four to five days and is possible only between December and March; ask at the Puerto Williams tourist office for further information. At the southernmost point of the walk, there are views of Cape Horn in clear weather, but conditions change quickly and it can snow on the hills, even in high summer, so take warm clothes.

Beyond Cerro Bandera, a road leads 56 km west of Puerto Williams towards Puerto Navarino. There is little or no traffic on this route and it is very beautiful, with forests of *lengas* stretching right down to the water's edge. At **Mejillones**, 32 km from

Puerto Williams, is a graveyard and memorial to the Yámana people. At **Puerto Navarino** there are a handful of marines and an abandoned police post, where you may be allowed to sleep. There are beautiful views across to Ushuaia and west to icebound Hoste Island and the Darwin Massif. A path continues to a cliff above the Murray Narrows: blue, tranquil and utterly calm.

Cape Horn → *Colour map 3, C5*

It is possible to catch a boat south from Isla Navarino to Cape Horn (the most southerly piece of land on earth apart from Antarctica). There is one pebbly beach on the north side of the island; boats anchor in the bay and passengers are taken ashore by motorized dinghy. A rotting stairway climbs the cliff above the beach, up to the building where three marines run the naval post. A path leads from here to the impressive monument of an albatross overlooking the wild, churning waters of the Drake Passage below. » *See Transport, page 308.*

Sleeping

Porvenir *p303*

B **Hostería Los Flamencos**, Tte Merino 018, T061-580049, www.hosterialosflamencos.com. One of the town's best places to stay with wonderful views of the bay, good food, and a pleasant place for a drink. Recommended. Also organizes tours.

D **Hostería y Turismo Yendegaia**, Croacia 702, T061-581665, www.turismoyendegaia.com. A charming, bright yellow house just 2 blocks from the plaza, built by a Croatian pioneer in 1926, this has 7 comfortable and light rooms, all with bath and TV, a good restaurant, and plenty of tourist information from the travel company which is also housed here. Recommended.

D **Rozas**, Phillippi 296, T061-580088. With bath, hot water, heating, restaurant and bar, internet, laundry facilities. Recommended.

E **Hostel Kawi**, Pedro Silva 144, T061-581638, www.tierradelfuegoandtrouts.com. A comfortable hostel, with rooms for 3, all with bath, and offering fly-fishing trips on the island.

E **Restaurant y Hostal El Chispa**, Señoret 202, T061-580 054. Simple rooms, some with shared bath, and a good restaurant, serving seafood and other Chilean dishes.

F pp **España**, Croacia 698, T061-580160. Some rooms with bath, breakfast extra. Good restaurant with fixed-price lunch.

Beyond Porvenir *p304*

If you get stuck in the wilds, it is usually possible to camp in a barn at an estancia.

C-F **Hostería de la Frontera**, San Sebastián, T061-696004, escabini@tie.cl. Rooms with bath and a decent restaurant. Avoid the more basic accommodation in an annexe.

C-F **Hostería Tunkelen**, Cerro Sombrero, 46 km south of Primera Angostura, T061-345001, hosteria_tunkelen@hotmail.com. Private rooms and dorms. Recommended.

F **Posada Las Flores**, Km 127 on the Porvenir-San Sebastián road. Reservations via **Hostal de la Patagonia** in Punta Arenas.

G **Pensión del Señor Alarcón**, Cerro Sombrero, 46 km south of Primera Angostura. Good, friendly.

G **Refugio Lago Blanco**, Lago Blanco, T061-241197. The only accommodation on the lake.

Puerto Williams *p305*

B-C **Hostería Wala**, on the edge of Lauta bay, 2 km out of town, T061-621114. Splendid walks in the area. Very hospitable.

D pp **Pensíon Temuco**, Piloto Pardo 244, T061-621113. Price for full board. Good food and hot showers. Slightly overpriced, but comfortable and recommended.

E pp **Hostería Camblor**, T061-621033, hosteriacamblor@terra.cl. Price for full board. Gets very booked up. Good value.

F pp **Hostal Yagan**, Piloto Pardo 260, T061-621334, hostalyagan@hotmail.com. Single and double rooms. Good meals available. Clean and comfortable, friendly, tours offered.

F **Jeanette Talavera**, Maragaño 168, T061-621150, www.simltd.com. Small dorms, shared bathrooms, kitchen and laundry. Organizes sailing trips, treks and other activities.

F pp **Residencial Onashaga**, Uspashun 15, T061-621564, run by Señor Ortiz – everyone knows him. Accommodation is basic, but the welcomes is warm. Good meals, helpful, full board available.

Eating

Porvenir *p303*

Fishermen will prepare lobster on the spot.
Hostería Los Flamencos, Tte Merino 018. Very good food.
Hostería y Turismo Yendegaia, Croacia 702. Great range of seafood.
Club Croata, Señoret y Phillippi. On the waterfront, good food, lively.
Restaurante Puerto Montt, Croacia 1169. Recommended for seafood.

Puerto Williams *p305*

There are several grocery stores; prices are high because of the remoteness.

Activities and tours

Porvenir *p303*

For adventure tourism and trekking, tour operators in Punta Arenas are the best bet: **Turismo Aonikenk**, Magallanes 619, T061-221982, www.aonikenk.com. Excellent hiking and adventures on Isla Navarino and south of Porvenir. Superb trip around Dientes de Navarino, fly-fishing and horse riding. **Turismo Cordillera de Darwin**, Croacia 675, T061-580206, www.explorepatagonia.cl. For tours of the island from a day to a week. **Hostería y Turismo Yendegaia**, Croacia 702, T061-581665, www.turismoyendegaia.com. Lots of conventional tours, and fishing.

Puerto Williams *p305*

There is no outdoors equipment available on Isla Navarino, so stock up in Punta Arenas.

Sailing

Captain Ben Garrett offers recommended sailing trips in his schooner *Victory* Dec-Jan, including special trips to Ushuaia, cruises in the canals and voyages to Cape Horn, the glaciers, Puerto Montt and Antarctica. Write to **Victory Cruises**, Annex No 1 Puerto Williams; or call collect to Punta Arenas and leave a message with the Puerto Williams operator.

Transport

Porvenir *p303*

Air

Aerovías DAP, Señoret s/n, Porvenir, T061-580089, www.aeroviasdap.cl, flies from **Punta Arenas** (weather and bookings permitting), twice daily Mon-Sat, US$50 one way. Heavily booked so make sure you have your return reservation confirmed.

Bus

Buses from Punta Arenas to Ushuaia don't take on passengers here. **Transportes Gessell**, Duble Almeyda 257, T061-580488 (also in Punta Arenas at José Menéndez 556, T061-222896) runs buses to **Río Grande** (Argentina), Tue and Sat 1400, 5 hrs, US$20; return service Wed and Sun 0800. Local buses run to **Cameron** from Manuel Señor, in theory Mon and Fri 1700, US$13.

Ferry

The *Melinka* sails from **Tres Puentes** (5 km north of Punta Arenas; catch bus A or E from Av Magallanes, US$1; taxi US$3) to **Bahía Chilota**, 5 km west of Porvenir, Tue-Sun 0900 with an extra afternoon sailing Tue-Thu in season, 2½ hrs, pedestrians US$8, cars US$50. The boat returns from Porvenir in the afternoon Tue-Sun.

Timetable dependent on tides and subject to change: check in advance. The crossing can be rough and cold; watch for dolphins. Reservations are essential especially in summer (at least 24 hrs in advance for cars); obtainable from **Transbordadora Austral Broom**, Bulnes 05075, Punta Arenas, T061-218100 (T061-580089 in Porvenir), www.tabsa.cl.

The ferry service from **Punta Delgada** on the mainland to **Punta Espora**, 80 km north of Porvenir, departs usually every 40 mins 0830-2300 (schedules vary with the tides) and takes just 15 mins, pedestrians US$4, cars US$25. This is the main route for buses and trucks between Ushuaia and mainland Argentina. Before 1000 most space is taken by trucks.

Puerto Williams *p305*

Air

Aerovías DAP, Centro Comercial s/n, T061-621051, www.aeroviasdap.cl, flies 20-seater Cessna aircraft from Punta Arenas Mon-Sat, departure time varies, 1¼ hrs, US$64 one way. Book well in advance; there are long waiting lists. Luggage allowance 10 kg (US$2 per kg extra). **Aeropetrel** will charter a plane from Puerto Williams to Cape Horn (US$2600 for 8-10 people).

Ferry
Despite its proximity, there are no regular sailings to Isla Navarino from Ushuaia (Argentina). The following all depart from **Punta Arenas**: **Austral Broom** ferry *Cruz Australis*, www.tabsa.cl, once a week, 36 hrs, US$130 for a reclining seat, US$170 for a bunk, meals included; *Navarino* (contact Carlos Aguilera, 21 de Mayo 1460, Punta Arenas, T061-228066), 3rd week of every month, US$180 one way, 12 passengers; *Beaulieu* cargo boat, once a month, US$350 return, 6 days. Some cruises to **Ushuaia** also stop at Puerto Williams.

Cape Horn *p306*
Crucero Australis cruises from **Ushuaia** stop at Cape Horn (see box page 283). In addition, the naval vessel *PSG Micalvi*, which sails once every 3 months from Punta Arenas via Puerto Williams, may take passengers to Cape Horn for US$250 (letters of recommendation will help). Navy and port authorities in Puerto Williams may deny any knowledge, but everyone else knows when a boat is due; ask at the *Armada* in Punta Arenas (see page 284). Otherwise ask at the yacht club about hitching a ride to Cape Horn.

Directory

Porvenir *p303*
Currency exchange Available at Estrella del Sur, *Santos Mardones*.

Puerto Williams *p305*
Post office Closes 1900. **Telephone** CTC, Mon-Sat 0930-2230, Sun 1000-1300, 1600-2200.

Argentine Tierra del Fuego

Argentine Tierra del Fuego belongs to the province of Tierra del Fuego, Antártida y Las Islas del Atlántico Sur, the capital of which is the welcoming tourist centre Ushuaia. The population of the Argentine sector is around 85,000, most of whom live in the two towns of Río Grande and Ushuaia. Both bigger and more developed than the Chilean side of the island, it provides good territory for guided explorations of the wilderness.
» *For Sleeping, Eating and other listings, see pages 314-320.*

Ins and outs

Getting there The main point of entry is **Aeropuerto Internacional Malvinas Argentinas** ⓘ *4 km from Ushuaia, on a peninsula in the Beagle channel, T02901-423970*, which receives daily **flights** from Buenos Aires (four hours), frequent flights from El Calafate and Punta Arenas, as well as weekly flights with army airline **LADE** from many towns in Patagonia. This is by far the easiest way to get to the Argentine side of the island and the view from the plane as you land over jagged mountains onto the quiet channel below is magical. From the airport, a taxi to the centre of town costs US$2. There is another airport at Río Grande with flights to/from Buenos Aires and Ushuaia. **Buses** from mainland Argentina and from Punta Arenas in Chile travel to Río Grande and Ushuaia via Punta Delgada and San Sebastián. There are also buses from Porvenir to Río Grande.

Getting around If you fly in and out of Ushuaia, you can probably get around fine by bus and boat for the national park and visits along the Beagle Channel, including Harberton. However, if you want to visit Lago Fagnano or more remote estancias or hike in places not visited by the many adventure tourism companies, you could consider hiring a car. Buses from Río Grande and Ushuaia are frequent, but are heavily booked in summer. There are abundant tours from Ushuaia to suit most needs, and some great hiking adventures on offer, too. » *Transport, page 319.*

Río Grande → *Colour map 3, B5*

Río Grande is a sprawling modern coastal town, the centre for a rural sheep-farming community, which grew rapidly in the oil boom of the 1970s and suffered when tax benefits were withdrawn in recent years, leading to increasing unemployment and emigration and leaving a rather sad, windy town today. The people are friendly but there's little culture, and you're most likely to visit in order to change buses. There are a couple of good places to stay, however, and two small museums: the **Museo de Ciencias Naturales y Historias** ⓘ *El Cano 225, Tue-Fri 0900-1700, Sat and Sun 1500-2000*, and the **Museo de la Ciudad** ⓘ *Alberdi 555, T02964-430414, Tue-Fri 1000-1700*, which recounts the city's history through sheep, missions, pioneers and oil. In the blue-roofed hut on the plaza is the small but helpful **tourist office** ⓘ *Rosales 350, T02964-431324, www.tierradelfuego.org.ar, Mon-Fri 0900-2100, Sat 1000-1700*.

The Salesian mission **La Candelaria** ⓘ *11 km north on Route 3, T02964-421642, Mon-Sat 1000-1230, 1500-1900, Sun 1500-1900, US$1.50, afternoon tea US$3*, was founded in 1893 by José Fagnano to try to protect the Ona people from gold prospectors and sheep farmers. It now houses displays of natural history and indigenous artefacts, with strawberry plantations, piglets and an aviary.

South of Río Grande

A fan of roads spreads out south and west from Río Grande to numerous *estancias*; these are unpaved and best attempted in a 4WD vehicle. **Estancia Viamonte**, on the coast 40 km south, is a working sheep farm with a fascinating history. Here, Lucas Bridges, son of Tierra del Fuego's first settler, built a home to protect the large tribe of indigenous Onas, who were fast dying out. The *estancia* is still inhabited by his descendants, who can take you riding and to see the life of the farm. Accommodation is also available. It's highly recommended for an insight into Fuegian life and a cosy place to read '*Uttermost part of the Earth*, see box, page 312.

The paved road south, Route 3, continues across wonderfully open land, more forested than the expanses of Patagonian steppe further north, and increasingly hilly as you near Ushuaia. After around 160 km, you could turn left along a track to the coast, to find **Estancia Cabo San Pablo**, 120 km from Río Grande. This simple working estancia is in a beautiful position, surrounded by native woodland for walking and riding, birdwatching and fishing. It's open all year, but reserve in advance.

Route 3 then climbs high above **Lago Fagnano**, a large expanse of water at the heart of Tierra del Fuego, which straddles the border with Chile. In the small settlement of **Tolhuin** there's a YPF service station just off the main road and a tiny, friendly **tourist office**. Drive into the village to visit the famous bakery **La Union**, where you can buy all kinds of bread, great *empanadas* and delicious fresh *facturas* (pastries), before heading down to the tranquil lake shore, where there's a quiet, unexploited stretch of beach and a couple of good places to stay.

Further along Route 3, about 50 km from Ushuaia, a road to the right swoops down to **Lago Escondido**, a long, fjord-like lake with steep green mountains descending into the water on all sides. There are *cabañas* and a couple of *hosterias*, one with a good restaurant for lunch.

Ushuaia » *pp314-320.*

→ *Colour map 3, C4*

Ushuaia's setting is spectacular. Its brightly coloured houses look like toys against the dramatic backdrop of snow-covered Cerro Martial to the north. Opposite are the forbidding peaks of Isla Navarino, and between flows the green Beagle Channel. Sailing these waters, it is easy to imagine what it was like when Darwin arrived here in 1832 and when the Bridges family first settled here in 1871. Although the town has expanded in recent years, sprawling untidily along the coast, Ushuaia still retains the feel of a pioneer town, isolated and expectant. There are lots of places to stay, which fill up entirely in January, a fine museum, and some great fish restaurants. There is dramatic landscape to be explored in all directions, with good treks in the Parque Nacional Tierra del Fuego just to the west of the city and more adventurous expeditions into the wild heart of the island, trekking, climbing or riding. There's splendid cross-country skiing nearby in winter, as well as downhill skiing at **Cerro Castor** (see page 319). And to the east, along a beautiful stretch of coastline is the historic *estancia* of Harberton, which you can reach by a boat trip along the Beagle Channel.

Tourist information ⓘ *San Martín 674, corner with Fadul, T/F02901-432000, www.tierradelfuego.org.ar, Mon-Fri 0800-2200, Sat, Sun and holidays 0900-2000.* Quite the best tourist office in Argentina. The friendly and helpful staff speak several languages and will find you somewhere to stay, even in the busiest period. They also have a great series of leaflets in English, French, German and Dutch about all the things to see and do, including bus and boat times. There's also an office at the airport, T02901-423970. **Tierra del Fuego National Park Office** ⓘ *San Martín 1395, T02901-421315*, has a useful little map of the park.

Background

Missionary Thomas Bridges first established a mission here in 1884 and the fledgling settlement soon attracted pioneers in search of gold. A penal colony, on nearby Staten Island, moved to the town in 1902 and Croatian and Spanish immigrants, together with shipwreck survivors, began to settle here. However, the town remained isolated until planes arrived in 1935. When the prison closed it was replaced by a naval base and, in the 1970s, a wave of new inhabitants arrived, many of them from Buenos Aires, attracted by reduced income taxes and cheap car prices. Now the city is capital of Argentina's most southerly province and, although fishing still plays a key role in the local economy, Ushuaia has become an important tourist centre as the departure point for voyages to Antarctica.

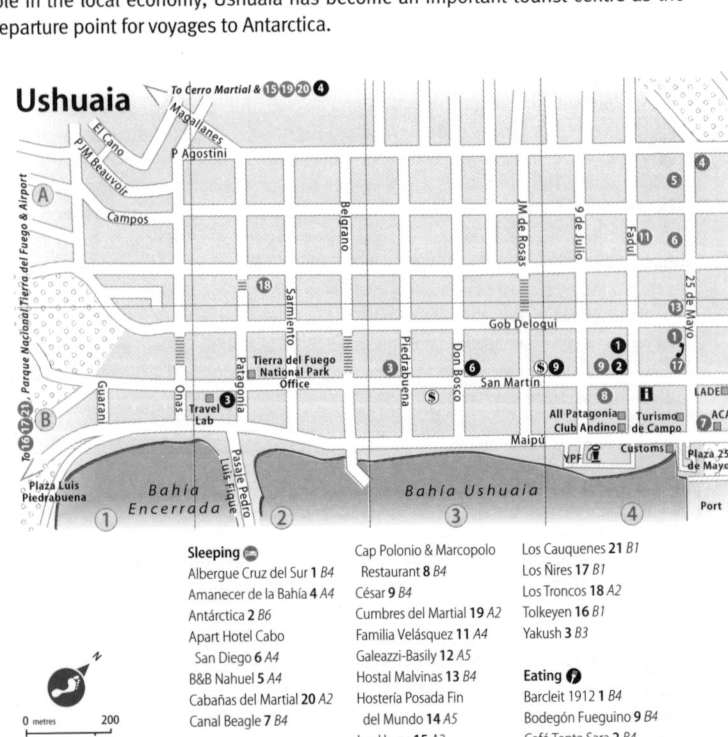

Sights

It's easy to walk around the town in a morning, since all its sights are close together. You'll find banks, restaurants, hotels and shops along Calle San Martín, which runs parallel to the shore, a block north of the coast road, Maipú. Boat trips leave from the **Muelle Turistico** (tourist pier) by a small plaza, 25 de Mayo, on the seafront. There are several museums worth looking at, if bad weather forces you indoors. The most fascinating is **Museo del Fin del Mundo** ⓘ *on the seafront at Maipú y Rivadavia, T02901-421863, www.tierradelfuego.org.ar/museo, Nov-Apr daily 0900-1900, May-Oct Mon-Sat 1200-1900, US$3.50*, in the 1912 bank building, which tells the history of the town through a small collection of carefully chosen exhibits on the indigenous groups, missionaries, pioneers and shipwrecks. There's also a stuffed collection of Tierra del Fuego's birdlife and an extensive reference library. Further east, the old prison, Presidio, at the Naval Base, houses the **Museo Marítimo** ⓘ *Yaganes y Gob Paz, www.museomaritimo.com, daily 1000-2000, US$8.50*, which has models and artefacts from seafaring days, and, in the cells, the **Museo Penitenciario**, which details the history of the prison. **Museo Yámana** ⓘ *Rivadavia 56, T02901-422874, www.tierradelfuego.org.ar/mundoyamana, daily 1000-2000 (winter 1200-1900), US$1.70*, has interesting scale models of everyday indigenous life.

For exhilarating views along the Beagle Channel and to Isla Navarinho beyond, don't miss a trip on the chair lift up to **Cerro Martial** ⓘ *daily 1000-1800 (winter 1030-1630), US$3.50*, about 7 km behind the town. From the top of the lift, you can walk for 90 minutes through *lenga* forest to Glaciar Martial, where there's limited skiing in winter. There's also a splendid tea shop, *refugio* and *cabañas* at the Cerro. Several companies, including **Lautaro** and **Kaupen**, run minibuses from the corner of Maipu and Roca to the bottom of the chairlift, hourly in summer, US$3-4 return, last buses return at 1900 and 2100. Otherwise it's a 1½ hour walk from town via Magallanes.

The **Tren del Fin del Mundo** ⓘ *Fin del Mundo station, 8 km west of Ushuaia (bus US$2 from Maipu and Roca, taxi US$3), T02901-431600, www.trendelfindelmundo.com.ar, 50 mins, 2 departures daily in summer, 1 in winter, US$20 return, plus US$7 park entrance, sit on the left for best views*, is the world's southernmost steam train, running new locomotives and carriages on track first laid by prisoners to carry wood to Ushuaia. It travels from the Fin del Mundo station into the Tierra del Fuego National Park (see page 313) and is an unashamedly touristy experience with relentless commentary in English and Spanish. However, it might be fun for children and is one way of getting into the national park to start a walk. Sit on the left on the outbound journey for the best views. Tickets are available at the station or from travel agencies in town.

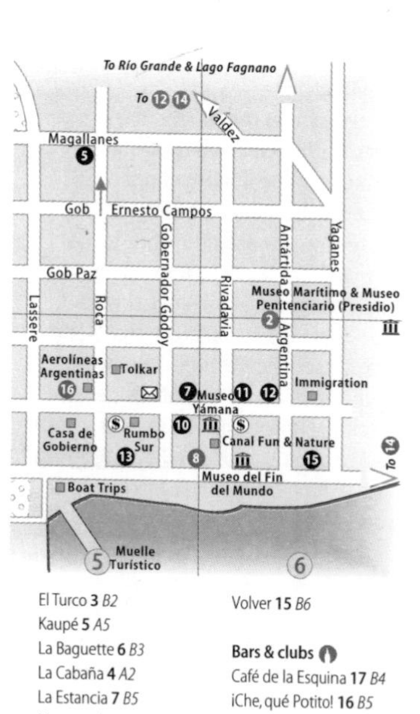

El Turco **3** *B2*
Kaupé **5** *A5*
La Baguette **6** *B3*
La Cabaña **4** *A2*
La Estancia **7** *B5*
Moustacchio **10** *B5*
Parrilla La Rueda **11** *B6*
Tante Sara Pizzas & Pastas **12** *B6*
Tía Elvira **13** *B5*
Volver **15** *B6*

Bars & clubs
Café de la Esquina **17** *B4*
¡Che, qué Potito! **16** *B5*
Küar **14** *B6*
Lennon Pub **8** *B5*

Estancia Harberton

ⓘ *85 km east of Ushuaia (2 hrs' drive), T02901-422742, www.acatushun.org, 15 Oct-15 Apr daily except holidays. Tour of the estancia US$5, museum entrance US$2.*

Building bridges

The story of the first successful missionary to Tierra del Fuego, **Thomas Bridges**, is one of the most stirring in the whole history of pioneers in Argentina. An orphan from Bristol, Thomas Bridges was so called because he was found as a child under a bridge with a letter 'T' on his clothing. He was adopted by a reverand and, as a young man, was taken to start a Christian mission in wild, uncharted Tierra del Fuego where no white man had survived.

Until his death in 1898, Bridges lived with his young wife and child near the Beagle Channel, first creating the settlement of Ushuaia and then Harberton. He devoted his life to working with the Yámanas (Yaghanes) and gave up converting them in favour of compiling a dictionary of their language, and protecting them from persecution.

Thomas's son **Lucas** (1874-1949), one of six children, spent his early life among the Yámanas and Onas, living and hunting as one of them, learning their language, and even, almost fatally, becoming involved in their blood feuds and magic rituals. Lucas became both defender and protector of the indigenous people whose culture he loved, creating a haven for them at Harberton and Estancia Viamonte (see page 314), at a time when most sheep farmers were more interested in shooting them. His compelling memoirs, *Uttermost Part of the Earth* (1947) trace the tragic fate of the native population with whom he grew up; it is now out of print, but available from www.abebooks.co.uk.

In a land of extremes and superlatives, Harberton still stands out as special. The oldest estancia in Tierra del Fuego was built in 1886 on a narrow peninsula overlooking the Beagle Channel by the missionary Thomas Bridges (see above). He was granted the land by President Roca for his work with the indigenous peoples and for rescuing victims of shipwrecks in the channels. Harberton is named after the Devonshire village where Thomas's wife Mary was born; the farmhouse was pre-fabricated by her father in England and assembled on a spot chosen by the Yámana. The English connection is evident in the neat garden of lawns, shrubs and trees between the jetty and the farmhouse; behind the buildings is a large vegetable garden, a real rarity on the island.

Still operating as a working farm, Harberton is run by Thomas Goodall, great-grandson of the founder. Visitors receive an excellent guided walk (bilingual guides) through protected forest around the estancia, where there are reconstructions of the Yámana dwellings, plus a tour of the impressive **Museo Acatushun**, founded by Thomas' wife, Natalie Goodall. The museum is the result of 23 years' scientific investigation into the area's rich marine life and contains the complete skeletons of dolphins, whales and seals. Tea or lunch (if you reserve ahead) are served in the room overlooking the bay. You can camp free, with permission from the owners, or rent one of the two simple cottages on the shore. There are wonderful walks along the coast, and noticeably more wildlife here than in the Tierra del Fuego National Park, probably owing to the estancia's remoteness. » *See Transport, page 320.*

Beagle Channel → *Colour map 3, C4*

A sea trip along the Beagle Channel can be rough but is highly recommended. Excursions can be booked through most agencies and leave from the Muelle Turistico in Ushuaia. Destinations include the sea lion colony at **Isla de los Lobos, Isla de los Pájaros, Les Eclaireurs lighthouse** and the penguin colony at **Isla Martillo**. You can visit Estancia Harberton by boat but always check that your tour actually includes the estancia and not just Harberton bay. » *See Activities and tours, page 318.*

Parque Nacional Tierra del Fuego » pp314-320.

ⓘ *Park administration: San Martín 1395, Ushuaia, T02901-421315, www.parques nacionales.gov.ar, US$7. Park entrance 11 km west of Ushuaia. Note there are no legal crossing points to Chile from the national park.* Covering 63,000 ha of mountains, lakes, rivers and deep valleys, this small but beautiful park stretches west to the Chilean border and north from Bahía Lapataia on the Beagle Channel to beyond Lago Fagnano. Large areas are closed to tourists to protect the environment, but there are marvellous walks for every level fitness. Lower parts of the park are forested with lenga, ñirre and coihue and are rich in birdlife, including geese, the beautiful torrent duck, Magellanic woodpeckers and austral parakeets. Even if you have just a couple of hours to spare, take a bus or taxi to Lago Roca or Bahía Lapataia

Walking in the park

You'll be given a basic map with marked walks at the entrance. More detailed topographical maps are sold in Ushuaia at **Oficina Antárctica**, Maipú and Laserre, or consult the Ushuaia tourist office. All walks are best attempted in the early morning or afternoon to avoid the tour buses. Wear warm, waterproof clothing: in winter the temperature drops to as low as -12°C and in summer, although it can reach 25°C, evenings can be chilly. For a longer hike and a really rich experience of the park, go with guides who know the territory well and can tell you about wildlife. » *See Activities and tours, page 318.*

Senda Costera (6.5 km, three hours each way) This lovely easy walk along the shore of the Beagle Channel gives you the essence of the park: its rocky coastline, edged with a rich forest of beech trees and glorious views of the low islands and steep mountains. Start at **Bahía Ensenada** (where the bus can drop you off and where boats leave for trips to Bahía Lapataia, daily 1000-1700, two hours, US$15, reservation essential). Walk along a well-marked path along the shoreline and then rejoin the road briefly to cross Río Lapataia (ignoring signs to Lago Roca to your right). After crossing the broad green river and a second stretch of water (where there's a small camping spot and the *gendarmería*), it's a pleasant stroll inland to the beautifully tranquil **Bahía Lapataia**, an idyllic spot, with views across the sound.

Lago Roca or Sendo Hito XXIV (4 km, 1½ hours one way). Another easy walk, this time alongside peaceful Lago Roca, where there's a very helpful *guardaparque*, plus camping and a *confiteria*. It takes in lovely pebble beaches and dense forest, with lots of bird life and is especially recommended in the evening, when most visitors have left. Get off the bus at the junction for Lago Roca, turn right along the road to the car park (passing the *guardaparque*'s house) and follow the lake side.

Cerro Guanaco (4 km, four hours one way). Starting at the car park for Lago Roca, this is a challenging, steep hike up through forest to a mirador with splendid views over Lago Roca, the Beagle Channel and far-off mountains. The ground is slippery after rain: take care and don't rush. Allow plenty of time to return in daylight, especially in winter.

Sleeping

Río Grande *p308*

Book ahead, as there are few decent choices.
B Posada de los Sauces, Elcano 839, T02964-432895, info@posadadelossauces.com.ar. By far the best choice. Breakfast included, beautifully decorated and comfortable rooms, good restaurant and cosy bar. Recommended.
C Apart Hotel Keyuk'n, Colón 630, T02964-424435. A good apart hotel, with simple well-equipped flats for 2-4.
C Hotel Atlántida, Belgrano 582, T02964-431915, atlantida@netcombbs.com.ar. A modern, rather uninspiring place, with plain comfortable rooms all with bath and cable TV, but good value with breakfast included.
D Hotel Isla del Mar, Güemes 963, T02964-422883, www.hotelguia.com/hotelisladelmar. Right on the sea shore, looks very bleak in bad weather and is frankly run-down, but cheap, with bathrooms and breakfast included, and the staff are welcoming.
F pp **Hotel Argentina**, San Martín 64, T02964- 422546, hotelargentino@yahoo.com. Quite the best cheap place to stay and much more than a youth hostel. Set in a beautifully renovated 1920s building close to the sea with kitchen facilities, a bright sunny dining room and welcoming owner, Graciela, who knows all about the local area. Highly recommended.

Estancias around Río Grande

LL Estancia María Behety, 15 km from Río Grande. Established in 1897 on a 40-km stretch of river that has become legendary for brown trout fishing. 18 comfortable rooms and good food. At US$5350 per week, this is one of the country's priciest fishing lodges, apparently deservedly so. Reservations through **Fly shop**, www.flyfishingtravel.com.
L Estancia Rivadvia, 100 km from Río Grande, on the route H, www.estanciarivadavia.com, T02901-492186. A 10,000-ha sheep farm, owned by descendants of the original Croatian pioneer who built the place. Luxurious accommodation in a splendid house near the mountains and lakes at the heart of Tierra del Fuego, where you can enjoy a trip around the *estancia* to see wild horses and guanacos, good food, and trekking to the trout lake of Chepelmut and Yehuin.
L Estancia Viamonte, some 40 km southeast on the coast, T02964-430861, www.estanciaviamonte.com. For a really authentic experience of Tierra del Fuego, stay as a guest here. Built in 1902 by pioneer Lucas Bridges, see box, page , this working *estancia* is run by his descendants. You'll be warmly welcomed as their guest, in traditional, beautifully furnished rooms, with comfortable bathrooms, and delicious meals (extra cost). Also a spacious cottage to let, US$315 for 7. Join in the farm activities, read the famous book by blazing fires, ride horses over the estate and completely relax. Warmly recommended. Reserve a week ahead.

Camping

Club Náutico Ioshlelk-Oten, Montilla 1047, 2 km from town on river. Clean, cooking facilities, camping in heated building in cold weather. YPF petrol station has hot showers.

South of Río Grande *p309*

A Hostería Petrel, RN 3, Km 3186, Lago Escondido, T02901-433569, hpetrel@infovia.com.ar. The only place to stay in this idyllic spot. In a secluded forest position on a tranquil beach of the lake, with decent rooms with bath, and a good restaurant overlooking

Going further ... Antarctica

Ushuaia is the starting point for a number of excellent expeditions to Antarctica. These usually run from mid-November to mid-March and last between eight and 11 days, taking in the Antarctic peninsula and the Wedell sea. Some offer extra activities, such as camping and kayaking. Its not exactly a luxury cruise: trips are usually made in non-tourist boats used for scientific exploration, so the accommodation is informal and simple and the food is reasonable but not excessive. The expedition leader organizes lectures during the three-day journey to reach the Antarctic, with at least two disembarkations a day in a zodiac to see icebergs and penguins. When selecting your trip, bear in mind that there's most ice in November and December, more baby penguins in January and February, and whales in March. The landscape, however, is always impressive.

A longer trip of 18 to 19 days, combines the Antarctic with the Malvinas/Falklands and South Georgia islands. There are weekly departures in season. It's worth turning up in Ushuaia and asking the major tour operators for availability; there's a 30% discount if you book last minute in Ushuaia, when the price is around US$2500pp.

For further information and bookings contact **Rumbo Sur, Turismo de Campo** and **All Patagonia**, see Activities and tours, page 318. Seats can also sometimes be purchased on Chilean Naval supply vessels heading for Antarctica, though this requires patience and a long period of waiting in Punta Arenas, see Transport, page 284, for further details.

the lake which serves delicious lamb, open to non-residents. Also has tiny *cabañas* right on the water, US$40 for 2-4 people.

D **Cabañas Khami** , T02964-15611243, www.cabaniaskhami.com.ar. Isolated in a lovely open spot at the head of the lake on low-lying and very comfortable and well-equipped *cabañas*, nicely decorated and with great views of the lake. Good value at US$40 per day for 6. Recommended.

D **Terrazas del Lago**, RN 3, Km 2938, T02964-1560 4851, terrazas@uol.com.ar. A little way from the shore, smart wooden *cabañas*, well decorated, and also a *confitería* and *parrilla*.

D **Parador Kawi Shiken**, off the main road on the way to Ushuaia, 4 km south of Tolhuin on RN 3, Km 2940, T02964-1561 1505, www.hotelguia.com/hoteles/kawi-shiken. Rustic, with 3 rooms, shared bathrooms, *casa de té* and restaurant. Phone ahead to arrange a *cordero al asador* (barbecued lamb). Horse riding.

F pp **Refugio Solar del Bosque**, 18 km from Ushuaia, RN 3, Km 3020, Lago Escondido, T02964-453276, solardelbosque@tierradelfuego.org.ar. Further along the road is this basic hostel for walkers, with shared bathrooms in dorms for 4, breakfast included.

Camping

Camping Hain del Lago, T02964-425951, 156-03606, robertoberbel@hotmail.com. Lovely views, fireplaces, hot showers, and a *quincho* for when it rains.

Camping La Correntina, T156-05020, 17 km from Tolhuin. In woodland, with bathrooms, and horses for hire.

Ushuaia *p309, map p310*

The tourist office has lists of all accommodation, and can help find you somewhere to stay, but in Jan you must reserve ahead.

LL **Las Hayas**, Camino Glaciar Martial, Km 3, T02901-430710, www.lashayas.com.ar. A 5-star hotel, in a spectacular setting, high up on the mountainside with outstanding views over the Beagle Channel. Light, tasteful, impeccable rooms. Breakfast included and use of pool, sauna, gym, squash court, 9-hole golf course, shuttle from town in high season, and transfer from airport. A lovely calm atmosphere, friendly staff, recommended.

L **Cumbres del Martial**, Luis F Martial 3560, T02901-424779, www.cumbresdelmartial.com.ar. This charming cottage by a mountain stream in the forested slopes of

Martial range has very comfortable rooms with balconies looking out to the Beagle Channel. A homely, relaxed feel in a secluded location, 7 km from town. There are also 4 *cabañas* with fireplace and big windows opening onto the woods. Superb fondues are served in the restaurant and tea room.

L Los Cauquenes, 7 km west of Ushuaia, C Reinamora, Barrio Bahía Cauquen, T02901-441300, www.loscauquenesushuaia.com.ar. A 5-star by the sea. An exclusive retreat wonderfully set on the shores of the Beagle Channel. Wood and stone are predominant in its architecture, while a relaxing minimalist decor prevails inside. Suites have their own private balconies. There is a restaurant, spa and frequent transfers to the town centre.

AL Canal Beagle, Maipú y 25 de Mayo, T02901-432303, www.hotelcanalbeagle.com.ar. Good ACA hotel (discounts for members) with a small pool, gym and sauna, with clear views over the channel from some of its comfortable and tastefully decorated rooms, and a good, reasonably priced restaurant.

A Cabañas del Martial, L F Martial 2109, T02901-430475, www.delmartial.com.ar. Wonderful views from these comfortable and well-equipped *cabañas*, set on wooded slopes. Price quoted for 5 people.

A Los Ñires, Av de los Ñires 3040, T02901-443781, www.nires.com.ar. The setting is the feature here, with lovely views, comfortable rooms in simple rustic style, and a good restaurant. Transfers and breakfast included.

A Tolkeyen, Del Tolkeyen 2145, 4 km from town towards national park, T02901-445315, www.tolkeyenhotel.com. A lovely traditional rustic place in a superb setting, with open views from its rooms, which vary between plain and flouncy, but are all spacious and comfortable. Lots of land to walk in, and close to the national park, with free buses into town. The excellent restaurant serves king crab and Fuegian lamb. Very relaxing. Recommended.

B Apart Hotel Cabo San Diego, 25 de Mayo 368, T02901-435600, www.cabosandiego.com.ar. Really comfortable and spacious apartments, spick and span, well equipped for cooking, good bathrooms and comfortable beds. Great for couples or families. Excellent value.

B Cap Polonio, San Martín 746, T02901-422140, www.hotelcappolonio.com.ar. A smart central modern city hotel with very comfortable minimalist rooms, all with bath, phone, TV, internet; some have views of the canal. There's a chic restaurant downstairs.

B César, San Martín 753, T02901-421460, www.hotelcesarhostal.com.ar. Very central, this big tourist place is often booked by groups, but is reasonable value. Simple rooms with bath, breakfast included.

B Hostal Malvinas, Gobernador Deloqui 615, T/F02901-422626, www.hostalmalvinas.net. Neat, comfortable if rather small rooms with excellent bathrooms, and good views, in this central and well-run town house hotel. Breakfast is included, and all day tea and coffee. Recommended.

B Hostería Posada Fin del Mundo, Gobernador Valdez 281, T02901-437345, www.posadafindelmundo.com.ar. A relaxed family atmosphere in a quiet residential area close to centre, homely rooms, and friendly staff. Good value.

D B&B Nahuel, 25 de Mayo 440, T02901-423068. byb_nahuel@yahoo.com.ar. A family house with views over channel, with brightly painted and tastefully decorated rooms, and a lovely welcome from the charming and talkative owner. Great value. Recommended.

E-F pp **Amanecer de la Bahía**, Magallanes 594, T02901-424405, www.ushuaiahostel.com.ar. A light, spacious, impeccably kept *hostal*, with shared rooms for 4 and cramped for 6, also a good double and triples with shared bath. Internet, living rooms, breakfast included.

F pp **Albergue Cruz del Sur**, Deloqui 636, T02901-434099, www.xdelsur.com.ar.There's a very friendly atmosphere in this relaxed small Italian-owned *hostal*, with cosy dorms, use of kitchen, and a lovely quiet library room for reading. Recommended.

F pp **Antárctica**, Antártida Argentina 270, T02901-435774, www.antarcticahostel.com. Welcoming and central hostel with a spacious chill-out room and an excellent bar open till late. Dorms are rather basic and cramped, with **C** larger private doubles. Cooking facilities, breakfast and the use of internet are included. Bikes for hire.

F pp **Yakush**, Piedrabuena y San Martín, T02901-435807, www.hostelyakush.com.ar. A very well-run hostel with spacious rooms to share and a few private ones, a light kitchen and dining room, and a steep tiny garden with views.

Private homes

D Familia Velásquez, Juana Fadul 361, T02901-421719. Basic rooms with breakfast in cosy cheerful pioneer family home, where the kind owners look after you.

D Galeazzi-Basily, Gobernador Valdez 323, T02901-423213, www.avesdelsur.com.ar. The best option by far. A cosy and stylish family home, with welcoming owners who speak excellent English, in a pleasant residential area 5 blocks from the centre. Delicious breakfast included. There are also excellent-value *cabañas* in the garden. Highly recommended.

D Los Troncos, Gobernador Paz 1344, T02901-421895, lostroncos@speedy.com.ar. A welcoming house run by charming Mrs Clarisa Ulloa, with simple rooms, breakfast, TV and free internet.

Estancias

LL Harberton, T02901-422742, estancia harberton@tierradelfuego.org.ar. 2 impeccably restored historical buildings on the tranquil lakeside, giving space and privacy from the main house. Simple accommodation, but wonderful views, and beautiful walks on the *estancia*'s coastline. 90 km east of Ushuaia, along RN 3 and 33, a spectacular drive. Price for 6 people. Open mid-Oct to mid-Apr.

L Estancia Rolito, Route 21 (ex 'A'), Km 14, T02901-492007, rolitotdf@hotmail.com. A magical place on the wooded heart of the island, with cosy accommodation in traditionally built houses, and friendly hosts Annie and Pepe, booked through **Turismo de Campo** (see page 319). Also day visits with recommended walks or horse rides in mature southern beech forest.

Camping

Camping del Solar del Bosque, RN 3, Km 19, heading to Río Grande, T02901-421228. US$2.50 per person. At a small ski resort that in summer offers plenty of activities. Hot showers, and also a large dorm with good facilities.

Camping Haruwen, Haruwen Winter Sports complex (Km 36), en route to Río Grande, T02901-431099. US$3 per tent, electricity, shop, bar, restaurant in a winter sports centre, open also in summer for outdoor activities.

Kawi Yoppen, RN 3 Km 3020, heading to Río Grande, T02901-435135, 10 km from Ushuaia, US$2 per person.

La Pista del Andino, Leandro N Alem 2873, T02901-435890, www.lapistadelandino.com.ar. Set in the **Club Andino** ski premises in a woodland area, it has wonderful views over the town and channel. Electricity, hot showers, tea room and grocery store, US$3 per person.

Parque Nacional Tierra del Fuego *p313*

Camping

Camping Lago Roca, T02901-433313 (entry fee US$ 7), 21 km from Ushuaia. By the forested shore of tranquil Lago Roc, this is a beautiful site with good facilities, reached by bus Jan-Feb, expensive small shop, *cafetería*, US$4 per person.

There are also various sites with no facilities: **Bahía Ensenada Camping**, 14 km from Ushuaia; **Río Pipo**, 16 km from Ushuaia, and **Camping Las Bandurrias**, Cauquenes and **Camping Laguna Verde**, 20 km from Ushuaia.

Eating

Río Grande *p308*

La Nueva Colonial, Fagnano 669. Half a block from the plaza, next to **Casino Club**, where the locals go for delicious pasta in a warm family atmosphere.

La Nueva Piamontesa, Belgrano y Mackinlay, T02964-423620, to the side of the charming 24-hr grocery store. Cheap set menus and also delivers food.

La Rueda, Islas Malvinas 954, 1st floor. Excellent *parrilla* in a welcoming place.

Leymi, 25 de Mayo 1335. Cheap fixed menu.

South of Río Grande *p309*

The following are all in Tolhuin.

Pizzería Amistad, on the same block as the famous **La Unión** bakery. Pizzas 24 hrs daily except Mon 2400-Tue 0600.

La Posada de los Ramírez, a cosy restaurant and *rotisería*. 3 courses will cost you US$4, weekends only, lunch and dinner.

Parrilla La Victoria, Koshten 324, T02964-4922970. Open daily, with beef and lamb on the *asado*, and also pizzas, call before for delicious Fuegian lamb.

Ushuaia *p309, map p310*

Bodegón Fueguino, San Martín 859. In a stylishly renovated 1896 house in the main street, this stands out from the crowd by serving *picadas* with delicious and imaginative dips, good roast lamb, and unusual *cazuelas*, *picadas* and dips. A buzzy atmosphere and welcoming staff.

🍴🍴🍴 **Kaupé**, Roca 470 y Magallanes, T02901-437396. The best restaurant in town, with exquisite food. King crab and meat dishes all beautifully served, in a lovely environment – a great treat.

🍴🍴🍴 **La Cabaña**, Luis F Martial 3560, T02901-424779. The cosy restaurant and tea room of **Cumbres del Martial** hotel serves several excellent types of fondue for dinner, that may be preceded at teatime by a rich list of cakes, scones and brownies.

🍴🍴🍴 **Marcopolo**, San Martín 746. A chic modern international-style café restaurant for seafood and everything else. Soothing decor, good service.

🍴🍴🍴 **Tía Elvira**, Maipú 349. Retains its reputation for excellent seafood, with a good choice of fresh fish and views over the channel.

🍴🍴🍴 **Volver**, Maipú 37. In an atmospheric old 1898 house, with ancient newspaper all over the walls (read intriguing fragments while you eat). Cosy stoves and an intimate atmosphere. Delicious salmon and *arroz con mariscos*.

🍴🍴 **Barcleit 1912**, Juana Fadul 148. Serves good Italian food, pizzas and pastas.

🍴🍴 **La Estancia**, San Martín 253. Cheery and good-value *parrilla tenedor libre*. Packed in high season.

🍴🍴 **Moustacchio**, San Martín y Gobernador Godoy. Long-established, good for seafood in a cosy atmosphere. Next door is a cheaper all-you-can-eat sister restaurant.

🍴🍴 **Parrilla La Rueda**, San Martín y Rivadavia. A good *tenedor libre* for beef, lamb and a great range of salads.

🍴🍴 **Tante Sara Pizzas and Pastas**, San Martín 137. A brightly-lit functional place with tasty filling food. Also take-away.

🍴 **El Turco**, San Martín 1410. One of few good and cheap places, popular with locals, serves generous *milanesas*, pastas, steaks and pizzas.

Cafés

Café Tante Sara, Fadul y San Martín. The most appealing of the cafés on San Martín. Smart and modern with an airy feel, serving good coffee and tasty sandwiches.

La Baguette, Don Bosco y San Martín. The best fresh takeaway sandwiches, and also delicious *empanadas* and *facturas* (pastries).

Bars and clubs

Ushuaia *p309, map p310*

Café de la Esquina, 25 de Mayo y San Martín. Light meals and drinks, in a good atmosphere.

¡Che, qué potito!, San Martín 452. A lively place with Mexican and Brazilian food.

Küar, Av Perito Moreno 2232, east of town. Great setting by the sea, restaurant, bar and brewery open from 1800.

Lennon Pub, Maipú 263. A lively friendly atmosphere and live music.

Festivals and events

Río Grande *p308*

Jan The **sheep shearing festival** is definitely worth seeing, if you're in the area.

2nd week of Feb **Rural exhibition** with handicrafts.

1st week of Mar **Shepherd's day**, with impressive sheepdog display.

20-21 Jun **Winter solstice**, the longest night, has fireworks and ice skating contests, though this is a very inhospitable time of year.

Activities and tours

Río Grande *p308*

Tour operators

Fiesta Travel, 9 de Julio 663, T02964-431800, fiestatravel@arnet.com.ar.

Mariani Travel Rosales 259, T02964-426010, mariani@netcombbs.com.ar.

Techni Austral, Moyano 516, T02964-430610. Bus tickets to Ushuaia.

Ushuaia *p309, map p310*

Fishing

The lakes and rivers of Tierra del Fuego offer great fishing, for brown and rainbow trout, and stream trout in Lago Fagnano. Both fly-casting and spinning are allowed, and permits must be bought. The trout season is 1 Nov- Apr (though this varies slightly every year), licences US$10 per day (an extra fee is charged for some rivers and lakes). Contact Asociación de Caza y Pesca at Maipú 822, T02901-423168, cazapescush@infovia.com.ar.

Fly Casting, T02901-423340. Offer a range of fishing excursions, provide equipment.

Yishka, Gobernador Godoy 62, T02901-437606, www.yishkaevt.com.ar. Arranges fishing excursions to Lago Fagnano.

Skiing, hiking, climbing

For information in sking, hiking and climbing contact **Club Andino Ushaia**, Fadul 50, T02901-422335, www.clubandinoushuaia.com.ar. Maps and trekking guidebooks for sale, free guided walks once a month in summer. Winter sports resorts along RN 3 (see below) are an excellent base for summer trekking and many arrange excursions.
Cerro Castor, 27 km from Ushuaia, a small but modern resort, with runs suitable for all levels. Good off-piste skiing.
Nunatak, 19½ km from Ushuaia, nunatak@tierradelfuego.org.ar, is a small centre from where amazing day treks to nearby glaciers and lakes are possible. To get to the remote areas of the island from Ushuaia, it's worth going with an agency. See Tour operators, for some excellent packages and day hikes.

Tour operators

Lots of companies now offer imaginative adventure tourism expeditions. All agencies charge the same fees for excursions; ask tourist office for a complete list: Tierra del Fuego National Park, 4 hrs, from US$ 17 (entry fee US$ 7 extra); Lagos Escondido and Fagnano, 7-8 hrs, US$25 without lunch. With 3 or 4 people it might be worth hiring a taxi.
All Patagonia, Juana Fadul 60, T02901-433622, www.allpatagonia.com/Eng. A wonderful range of tours, sailing, hiking, birdwatching, all making the most of the wild land around Ushuaia. Ask about the birdwatching trip to the centre of the island, and the 6-day trip crossing the Fuegian cordillera. Also Antarctic trips. Well organized and recommended.
Canal Fun & Nature, Rivadavia 82, T02901-437395, www.canalfun.com. Oriented to young people, it offers a huge range of activities, including trekking, canoeing, horse riding, 4WD excursions. And they also run their own bar **Küar**. Recommended.
Comapa, San Martín 245, T02901-430727, www.comapa.com. A complete range of excursions and accommodation arrangements in Chile, including tickets for **Buses Pacheco** (to Punta Arenas), **Cruceros Australis** (to Cabo de Hornos and **Punta Arenas**), and **Navimag** ferries (Puerto Natales-Puerto Montt); also trips to Antarctica.
Compañía de Guías de Patagonia at Posada Nido de Cóndores, Gobernador Campos 795 (y 9 de Julio), T02901-437753, www.companiadeguias.com.ar. The best walking guides. Well-run expeditions for all levels to the national park, and also to more inaccessible places, for the day, or several days, including the beautiful 3-day walk along the Lucas Bridges path, some equipment and food included. Also ice climbing (training and equipment provided) to Cerro Alvear. Professional, friendly and knowledgeable. Highly recommended.
Rumbo Sur, San Martín 350, T02901-421139, www.rumbosur.com.ar. Flights, buses and all the conventional tours, including Harberton, fishing excursions, plus wonderful Antarctic expeditions, mid-Nov to mid-Mar, friendly.
Tolkar Viajes y Turismo, Roca 157, T02901-431412, www.tolkarturismo.com.ar. Flights, bus tickets to Punta Arenas, Río Grande and Río Gallegos, conventional and adventure tourism, including a full-day mountain biking and canoeing trip in Lago Fagnano and Lago Escondido area.
Travel Lab, San Martín 1444, T02901-436555, www.travel-labpatagonia-com.ar. *Tren del fin del Mundo*, unconventional tours, mountain biking, trekking, etc. English and French spoken, very helpful.
Turismo de Campo, Fuegia Basket 414, T02901-437351, www.turismodecampo.com.ar. Adventure tourism in small groups with English/French speaking guides. Boat and trekking combinations in the National Park, and trekking for all levels in other remoter places, visiting Estancia Rolito, birdwatching tours, fishing excursions, horse riding in central Tierra del Fuego woodlands, sailing in the Beagle Channel. Also Antarctica. Highly recommended.

Transport

Book ahead in summer, as flights fill up fast. In winter, poor weather often causes delays. Passport needed to buy tickets.

Río Grande *p308*

Air

The airport is 4 km west of town, T02964-420600. A taxi to the centre costs US$2. To **Buenos Aires**, **Aerolíneas Argentinas**, San Martín 607, T02901-424467, daily, 3½ hrs direct. **LADE** flies to **Ushuaia**, once a week and to other Patagonian towns.

Bus

Buses leave from the terminal Elcano y Güemes, T02964-420997, or from the office of **Tecni Austral**, Moyano 516, T02964-430610. To **Porvenir** (Chile), 5 hrs, **Gesell**, Wed and Sun 0800, US$9, passport and luggage control at San Sebastián. To **Punta Arenas** (Chile), via Punta Delgada, 10 hrs, **Pacheco**, Tue, Thu, Sat 0730, US$15. To **Río Gallegos** for connections to **El Calafate**, **Tecni Austral**, 3 times a week, US$15. To **Ushuaia**, **Tecni Austral**, 3-4 hrs, 2 daily (heavily booked in summer), US$12; also **Tolkeyen**, US$7.

Ushuaia *p309, map p310*

Air

Schedules tend to change from season to season, so call airline offices for times and prices: **Aerolíneas Argentinas**, Roca 116, T02901-422267, www.aerolineas.com.ar; **Aerovias DAP**, 25 de Mayo 64, T02901-431110; **LADE**, San Martín 542, Loc 5, T02901-421123, www.lade.com.ar.

Aerolíneas and LADE fly to **Buenos Aires**, 3½-5 hrs depending on whether service is direct, and **El Calafate**, 1¼ hrs. Also flights to **Río Gallegos**, 1 hr, and **Río Grande**, 1 hr, but check with agents. To **Punta Arenas** (Chile), **Aerovias DAP**, 1 hr.

Bus

Long distance Buses arrive at offices around town: **Tecni Austral/Tolkar**, Roca 157, T02901-431412; **Líder**, Gob Paz 921, T02901-436421; **Tolkeyen**, Maipú 237, T02901- 437073. To **Buenos Aires**, 36 hrs, US$70, **TAC**, **Don Otto**, **El Pinguino** and **Transportadora Patagonica**. To **Río Grande**, 4 hrs, **Tecni Austral** and **Líder**, both US$, 2 daily; **Tolkeyen**, US$10. No through services from Ushuaia to **Río Gallegos**; instead, go to Río Grande, and change (total 8-10 hrs); book a ticket for the journey with **Tolkar** in Ushuaia, US$18.

To **Punta Arenas** (Chile), via Punta Delgada (15-min ferry crossing), 12 hrs, **Tecni Austral**, Mon, Wed, Fri 0600, US$30; **Tolkeyen/Pacheco**, Tue, Thu, Sat, 0630, US$35; also less frequent via **Porvenir**, 12 hrs (2½-hr ferry crossing), US$50.

Local Ebenezer and Bella Vista, daily to **Lago Escondido**, US$10 return, and **Lago Fagnano**, US$12. In summer, various companies, hourly to **Lago Roca**, US$3 return, and **Bahía Lapataia**, US$7, from the tourist pier; last return 2000 /2100. **Ebenezer** and **Gonzalo** to the **Fin del Mundo station** (see page 311) 0800, 0900, 1400; return 1700, US$3. For services to Harberton, see below.

Car hire

Most companies charge US$45 per day including insurance and 150 km per day. **Hertz**, at the airport, T02901-432429. **Localiza**, San Martín 1222, T02901-430739.

Sea

For cruises to Cape Horn and Punta Arenas, see box, page 283. For trips to Antarctica, see box, page 315.

Taxi

Remise Carlitos, T02901-422222; **Tienda Leon**, San Martín 995, T02901-422222.

Estancia Harberton *p311*

Access by car is along a good unpaved road which branches off Route 3, 40 km east of Ushuaia. Marvellous views en route but no petrol beyond Ushuaia. **Boat** trips twice weekly in summer from the Muelle Turistico, US$20 for a day trip. Daily **minibuses**, **Bella Vista** and **Lautaro**, from Maipu and Juana Fadul, US$14 return. **Tours**, US$40 plus entrance.

Directory

Río Grande *p308*

Banks and currency exchange

4 banks with ATMs on San Martín between 100 and 300. **Post office** Piedrabuena y Ameghino. **Telephone** *Centro de llamada* at San Martín 170 and 458.

Ushuaia *p309, map p310*

Banks and currency exchange

ATMs are plentiful along San Martín. Changing TCs is difficult but possible at **Banco de Tierra del Fuego**, San Martín 396. **Consulate** Chile, Malvinas Argentinas y Jainen, Casilla 21, T02901- 421279. **Internet and telephone** Cyber cafes and *centros de llamada* along San Martín. **Post office** San Martín, Mon-Fri 0900-1300, 1700-1900, Sat 0830-1200.

Background

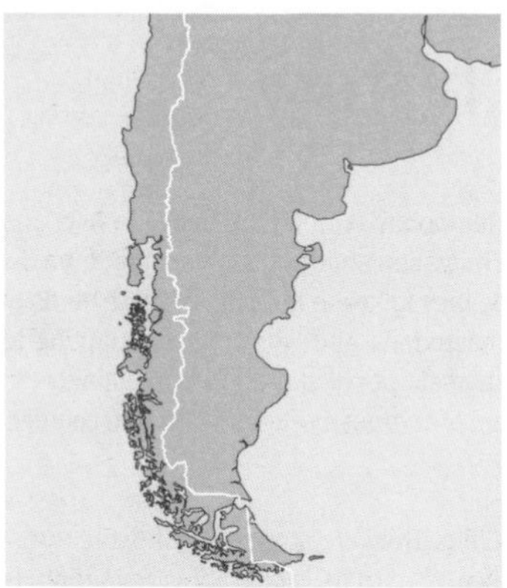

Footprint features

A sprint through history

Early days

50,000 years ago, the first people cross the temporary land bridge between Asia and America at the Bering Straits and begin a long migration southwards, reaching Tierra del Fuego 12,000 years ago. Hunters and foragers, they follow in the path of huge herds of animals such as mammoths, giant sloths, mastodons and wild horses, adapting to fishing along the coasts. The area remains sparsely populated and many Patagonian peoples remain nomadic until the encroachment of European settlers in the 19th century.

15-16th centuries

The Incas expand their empire into central Chile. They are stopped by hostile forest tribes at the Rio Maule, near present-day Talca. Due to its topography, Patagonia is not touched by Inca incursions.

1516

Juan de Solis arrives in the Plata estuary. He and his men are killed by the indigenous Querandí. Other Europeans follow, including Portuguese explorer Ferdinand Magellan who ventures south into the Pacific via the straits north of Tierra del Fuego. The straits become an important trade route until the building of the Panama Canal in 1914.

1541

Following the overthrow of the Incas by a tiny force of Spaniards led by Francisco Pizarro, Pedro de Valdivia is given the task of conquering Chile. He reaches the fertile Mapocho Valley and founds Santiago. The settlements of Concepcion, Valdivia and Villarica follow.

1580s

Buenos Aires is established, but the discovery of precious metals in Peru and Bolivia, focuses colonial attention elsewhere, and it remains a backwater for 200 years. Meanwhile, a group of settlers led by Pedro de Sarmiento seeks to found a colony on the north banks of the Magellan Straits. The colony is a disaster, and only two people survive. This is the end of attempts at European settlement in southern Patagonia for centuries.

1598

A rebellion by the Mapuche tribe in the Chilean Lake District (see box, page 197) drives the Spanish back to the north of the Rio Biobío, leaving isolated groups of settlers in Valdivia and on the island of Chiloe, and ensuring that European influence in Patagonia will remain marginal.

17th century

In 1616, a Dutch navigator names the southernmost tip of Argentina Cape Horn after his hometown, Hoorn. Meanwhile, the indigenous groups and the Spanish authorities are in a state of permanent war. The Spanish want to enslave the natives into a system of *encomiendas* – a feudal regime that has been successful in Peru. The colonizers have more sophisticated weapons, but the indigenous peoples use guerilla warfare and fight using spears, bows and arrows. The Spanish are unable to defeat the Mapuche and there is something of a standoff. During this period a generation of *criollos* (Spaniards born in the colonies) develops and intermarriage takes place resulting in *mestizo* populations. The indigenous people are gradually weakened due to famine, lack of resistence to diseases such as small pox and the production of alcohol. However, It is not until 1881 that the treaty ending Mapuche Independence from Chile is signed.

The original big foots

The dry Patagonian plateau was originally inhabited by one principle indigenous group, the **Tehuelches**, who lived along the eastern side of the Andes, as far north as modern-day Bariloche, and were hunters of rheas and guanaco. In the 18th century, they began to domesticate the local wild horses and sailed down the Patagonian rivers to reach the Atlantic Coast.

The Tehuelches were very large: it is said that when the Spanish first arrived in this area, they discovered Tehuelche footprints in the sand, exclaiming 'qué patagón' ('what a large foot'), hence the name Patagonia.

In the 18th and early 19th centuries, the Tehuelche interacted with European whalers and were patronizingly described as 'semi-civilized'. The granting by the Chilean government of large land concessions in the late 19th century, combined with Argentine president Julio Roca's wars of extermination against Patagonian natives in the 1870s, spelled the end for the Tehuelches. They were persecuted by settlers and only a few survived diseases and the change of lifestyle.

Towards the end of the 20th century, a belated sense of moral guilt arose among the colonizers, but it was too late to preserve the Tehuelche way of life. Today only a few isolated groups remain in Patagonia. For details of other indigenous groups, see page 304.

1776

Buenos Aires is made the capital of the new Viceroyalty of the Rio de la Plata and becomes an important trade route for European goods and contraband. Estancias are formed to farm and export cattle in the area around Buenos Aires.

1808-1816

Napoleon invades Spain and deposes King Ferdinand VII. Argentine independence from Spain is declared on 9 July 1816 by Jose de San Martin, who goes on to lead armies of freedom fighters into Chile with Simon Bolivar. But independence brings neither stability nor unity in Argentina, with fighting by federalist groups.

1827

The royalist citizens of Carmen de Patagones – an outpost at the gateway to Patagonia – are reluctant to accept the *criollo* government and, in 1827, soldiers, gauchos, slaves and pirates are sent to stamp the new government's authority on the region.

1832-1833

General Rosas, dictator of Argentina and military supremo, leads a campaign against the Pampas Indians, destroying their independence and their way of life. This is the beginning of the incursion of European forces into Patagonia. Charles Darwin wrote that he doubted any indigenous Pampas people would be left within a generation.

1843

Alarmed by widespread naval activity in the region, the Chilean navy sends a cutter to the Magellan Strait and erects a fort at Fuerte Bulnes, to claim the straits for Chile – the rest of Patagonia between here and the mainland now falls under Chilean jurisdiction.

1845-80

The Chilean government encourages settlement around Lago Llanquihue, provoking extensive immigration to the area by German colonists. Legacy of this settlement can be seen in the German-looking buildings around Puerto Octay, Frutillar and Puerto Varas.

Port Famine (Puerto Hambre)

In 1582, Felipe II of Spain, alarmed by Drake's passage through the Straits of Magellan, decided to establish a Spanish presence on the Straits. A fleet of 15 ships and 4000 men, commanded by Pedro Sarmiento de Gamboa, was despatched in 1584. However, before they had even left the Bay of Biscay a storm scattered the fleet, sinking seven ships and killing 800 people. Further depleted by disease, the remaining three ships arrived at the Straits with just 300 men on board. This small force founded two cities: Nombre de Jesús on Punta Dungeness at the eastern entrance to the Straits and Rey Don Felipe near Puerto Hambre.

Disaster struck again when their only remaining vessel broke its anchorage; the ship, with Sarmiento on board, was blown into the Atlantic, leaving many of his men stranded on land. After attempts to re-enter the Straits, he set sail for Rio de Janeiro and organized two rescue missions: the first ended in shipwreck, the second in mutiny. Captured by the English, Sarmiento was taken to England and imprisoned. Until his death in 1608, Sarmiento besieged Felipe II with letters urging him to rescue the stranded men.

When the English corsair Thomas Cavendish sailed through the Straits in 1587 he found only 18 survivors. With the English and Spanish at war, only one man – Tomé Hernández – trusted Cavendish. They set sail, leaving the rest of the men to die. He named the place Port Famine as a reminder of their grisly fate.

In 1848, Chile founds Punta Arenas, making Chile's claim of the Strait of Magellan permanent. It becomes a penal colony modelled on Australia, and in 1867 is opened to foreigners and given free port status. The town prospers as a refuelling and provisioning centre for steam ships until the opening of the Panama Canal in 1914.

1853

In 1853 Juan de Rosas, a powerful governor of Buenos Aires, brings order, gaining support by seizing lands from indigenous peoples and handing them to friends in the 'Campaign of the Desert'. This is followed by a new era of growth and prosperity.

1865

Welsh immigrants arrive in Puerto Madryn on the Atlantic Coast and settle inland along the Chubut Valley. Their aim is to free themselves of their English oppressors and to find a haven in which to practise their religion in their own language. They learn from the indigenous Tehuelche people and successfully irrigate the valley for agriculture. In 1889 a railway connects Puerto Madryn with Trelew, enabling the Welsh to export their produce.

1879

Expansion in the south becomes more aggressive with increasing confrontation with indigenous populations. President Julio Roca's 'Conquest of the Wilderness' sends a force against the indigenous peoples of Patagonia, exterminating many of them and herding the rest into settlements. The government pushes the frontier, and the railway, south, paving the way for further European settlement.

Late 19th century

Large swaths of land are divided up and settlers are allocated 40 ha apiece. Argentina is transformed by a stable economy based on cattle farming, foreign investment and European immigration. Thomas Bridges founds a mission in Tierra del Fuego (see page 312).

igrate here because of the Andes, the desert, the ice and the sea, and the country's isolation has contributed to a range of endemic wildlife. Specialist wildlife and birdwatching tours led by experts are available in most areas and are detailed throughout the guide.

Land mammals

Typical of Patagonia, is the **guanaco** – a coffee-coloured, cousin of the llama, with a long neck and small head. Standing at 1.5 m tall and weighing 55 kg, they are very agile and fast runners. Both grazers and browsers, they live in deserts, shrub land, savannah and occasionally on forest fringes. An estimated 20,000 now survive. Two species of deer found in Patagonia are the **huemul** and the **pudú**. The huemul appears on Chile's coat of arms, along with the condor. Both the huemul and the pudú are very rare and difficult to spot, see page 264, Deer, oh deer. A large, reddish-brown species of **puma** can still be found in the mountain valleys, although it's a solitary, nocturnal creature and understandably shy of humans. Other land mammals typical of Patagonia include a small hairless vole called the **tucotuco**, unique to Tierra del Fuego; a type of chinchilla called a **vizcacha**; a rodent called a **mara**; as well as the **otter**, **cougar**, **armadillo**, **skunk** and several species of **fox**.

Marine mammals

Numerous colonies of **seal** (including the elephant seal which can weigh up to three tonnes) and **sea lion** live all along the Patagonian coast and come ashore to mate in December and January. Five species of **dolphin**, including the Fitzroy, Commerson and Peale, can be spotted, frequently off the coast of Chiloé. Types of **whale** include the southern right whale, which comes to breed off the coast of Península Valdés and can be spotted from June to December; and the killer whale, which arrives to feed on the young seal pups from March to April.

Birds

The **choique**, known as 'Darwin's rhea', is a large, flightless, ostrich-like bird, which roams the Patagonian steppes. Once hunted for its feathers, it is now farmed for meat and protected in the wild. Another long-legged bird is the southern **flamingo**, most commonly seen around lake shores, it also inhabits coastal areas on the Península Valdés and the Isla de los Pájaros. From the coast to the mountains, **geese** can be seen flying in pairs; other species to look out for are the black-necked **swan**, the Andean **duck**, the austral **parakeet** and the Magellanic **woodpecker**. Birds of prey include the **condor**, with a wingspan of more than four metres; and various species of **eagle**, **hawk**, and **buzzard**. Two regional birds of prey, the **jote** and the **tiuque**, are also common. Half the world's species of **penguin** can be found along the coast of Chile, including the Humbolt, Magellanic and King species. They live in the sea for most of the year, but colonize Patagonia and Tierra del Fuego by the thousand, as they come onto land from October to March in order to breed. Other coastal birds include the **petrel**, **oystercatcher**, **cormorant**, **heron** and **albatross**.

Books

Argentina

Reference/travel

Bigongiari, Diego (ed) *Pirelli Guide*, including map for cultural, historical and nature information, highly recommended.

Hudson, W H *Far Away and Long Ago* and *Idle Days in Patagonia*, deal with this English writer's early life in the countryside.

Kirbus, Federico B *Guía de Aventuras y Turismo de la Argentina* (with comprehensive English index – 1989); and *La Argentina, país* *de maravillas*, Manrique Zago ediciones (1993), a beautiful book of photographs with text in Spanish and English; *Patagonia* (with **Jorge Schulte**) and *Ruta Cuarenta*, both fine photo- graphic records with text (both Capuz Varela). Also by Kirbus, *Mágica Ruta 40* and *Quebrada de Humahuaca*; see www.magicaruta40.com.ar and www.kirbus.com.ar.

Lucas Bridges, E *Uttermost Part of the Earth*, about the early colonization of Tierra del Fuego.

Literature

Borges, Jorge Luis (1899-1986) Argentina's most famous writer, and at the forefront of avant-garde experimental and urban themes. He is best known for his teasing, revolutionary and poetic short stories, best seen in *Ficciones* (1944) and *El Aleph* (1949).

Cortázar, Julio (1914-1984) The leading Argentine representative of the 1960s 'boom'. His novel *Rayuela* (Hopscotch, 1963) typifies the philosophy and freedom of the period.

Güiraldes, Ricardo (1886-1927) *Don Segundo Sombra*, a second great gaucho work (see Hernández below), further cementing the figure of the gaucho as national hero.

Hernández, José *El gaucho Martín Fierro* (1872), an epic poem about the disruption of local communities by the march of progress; the eponymous hero and dispossessed outlaw came to symbolize Argentine nationhood.

Martínez, Tomás Eloy (1934-) Two highly acclaimed novels on Argentina's enduring 20th-century figures, *Santa Evita* (1995) and *La novela de Perón* (The Perón Novel, 1985).

Puig, Manuel (1932-1990) A writer fascinated by mass culture, gender roles and the banal as art who expressed these ideas in novels such as *El beso de la Mujer Araña* (The Kiss of the Spider Woman, 1976 – made into a renowned film).

Sábato, Ernesto (1911-) Important 1960s writer whose most famous novel is *Sobre héroes y tumbas* (On Heroes and Tombs, 1961) and who also wrote the preface to *Nunca más* (Never again, 1984), the report of the commission into the disappearances in the 1970s 'dirty war'.

Soriano, Osvaldo (1943-1998) Another writer dealing with dictatorship and the 'dirty war' in *No habrá más penas ni olvido* (A Funny, Dirty Little War, 1982).

Chile

Reference/travel

Green, Toby *Saddled with Darwin* (Phoenix, 2000).

Keenan, Brian and **McCarthy, John** *Between Extremes* (Transworld, 1999).

Swale, Rosie *Back to Cape Horn* (Fontana, 1988) desribes her epic horse ride through Chile.

Wheeler, Sara *Travels in a Thin Country* (Little, Brown and Co, 1994).

Poetry

Huidobro, Vicente (1893-1948) Among many books, see *Altazor* (1931).

Mistral, Gabriela (1889-1957; Nobel Prize 1945). *Desolación* (1923). *Tala* (1938), *Lagar* (1954).

Neruda, Pablo (1904-1973; Nobel Prize 1971) Of Neruda's many collections, see *Veinte poemas de amor y una canción deseperada* (1924), *Tercer residencia* (1947), *Canto general* (1950) and his memoirs *Confieso que he vivido* (1974). See also **Feinstein, Adam**, *Pablo Neruda, a passion for life* (Bloomsbury, 2004).

Nicanor Parra (1914-) Brother of the famous singer and artist Violeta Parra *Poemas y antipoemas*, (1954).

20th-century prose

Allende, Isabel (born 1942) Novels such as *The House of the Spirits*, *Of Love and Shadows* and *Eva Luna* are world-famous.

Bolaño, Roberto *By Night in Chile* (Harvill, 2002).

Bombal, María Luisa (1910-80) *La última niebla* (1935).

Brunet, Marta (1901-1967) *Montaña adentro* 1923, *María Nadie* (1957).

Donoso, José (1924-1996) *El obsceno pájaro de la noche*.

Dorfman, Ariel (born 1942) *La muerte y la doncella* (Death and the Maiden), *La última canción de Manuel Sendero* (The Last Song of Manuel Sendero).

Eltit, Damiela (born 1949) *Vaca sagrada* (1991), *El cuarto mundo* (1988).

Skármeta, Antonio (born 1940) Best known for *Ardiente paciencia*, retitled *El cartero de Neruda* and filmed as *Il Postino* (The Postman).**Valenzuela, Luisa** (1938-) *Cola de lagartija* (The Lizard's Tail, 1983).

Jan 2002

Eduardo Duhalde becomes Argentina's fifth president in two weeks. He is forced to devalue the peso in order to borrow money from the International Monetary Fund. The middle class is devastated, many losing their life savings. Widespread poverty becomes a reality, with child malnutrition, and unemployment over 20%.

2003

Argentine elections threaten to return Menem to power, even though he bankrupted the nation by selling off national industries. Kirchner wins by a narrow lead, promising to reduce corruption and reduce the burden of government employees. The country recovers some stability. Tourism flourishes – both from foreigners enjoying low prices, and Argentines realising that their own country is more magnificent than Miami holidays which became the aspirant norm under Menem.

Today

Patagonia remains very much an extremity of both Argentina and Chile. Historically absent from the national boundaries until the 19th century, it still feels very different to the rest of the countries. Some long for the utopia of a united Patagonia, free of the internal wranglings of the power bases of Buenos Aires and Santiago.

Arts and crafts

Indigenous crafts

Present-day handicrafts represent either the transformation of utilitarian objects into works of art, or the continued manufacture of pieces that retain symbolic value. A number of factors threaten these traditions: the loss of types of wood and plant fibres through the destruction of forests; the mechanisation of farm labour; and migration from the countryside to the city. However, city dwellers and tourists have created a demand for 'traditional' crafts so their future is to some degree assured.

Knitwear and textiles

Chiloé is famous for its woollen goods, hand-knitted and coloured with natural dyes. Sweaters, knitted caps, *mantas*, socks are very popular. Rugs, blankets and patch dolls are all sold locally and in Puerto Montt. The Mapuche are also weavers of sheep's wool, making ponchos, *mantas*, sashes (*fajas*), reversible rugs (*lamas*) with geometric designs and bedspreads (*pontros*). The colours come from natural dyes.

Silverware

Although silverware is one of the traditional crafts of the Mapuche, its production is in decline owing to the cost of the metal. Traditional women's jewellery includes earrings, headbands, necklaces, brooches and *tupus* (pins for fastening the *manta* or shawl). Nowadays, the most common items are *chawai* (earrings), but these are smaller than those traditionally worn by Mapuche women. It is not known whether Mapuche silversmiths had perfected their skills before the arrival of the Spaniards; certainly the circulation of silver coins in the 18th century gave great impetus to this form of metalwork.

Specialist crafts

The Mapuche make musical instruments: the *trutruca*, a horn 1½ to 4 m long; *pifilka* (or *pifüllka*), a wooden whistle; the *kultrún* drum; *cascahuilla*, a string of bells; and *trompe*, similar to a Jew's harp. The village of Rari, near the Termas de Panimávida, some 25 km northeast of Linares (Región VII), specialises in beautiful, delicate items made from dyed horsehair: bangles and brooches in the shape of butterflies, little hats, flowers, etc.

Early 20th century

Rural poverty in both countries leads to urbanization and high unemployment, wealth is concentrated in the hands of the very few. The wool boom encourages the creation of large farms for sheep-raising in Patagonia. Many migrants come from the island of Chiloé to work at farms in Argentine Patagonia and on Chilean Tierra del Fuego.

1940s-50s

Following a military coup in 1943, Juan Peron wins the presidency in 1946 and 1952. An authoritarian and charismatic leader, he institutes stringent reforms against the economic elite and in favour of the workers. In 1955 he is ousted and exiled to Spain, but remains popular with the people, making a brief return to power in 1973.

1960s-1970s

Chile's politics become increasingly polarized. The Marxist coalition led by Salvador Allende, introduces sweeping reforms, such as redistribution of income and the takeover of many private enterprises. The country is plunged into economic chaos.

11 Sep 1973

General Pinochet seizes power in a bloody coup. Allende allegedly commits suicide and thousands of his supporters are murdered. During the dictatorship which follows, an estimated 80,000 are tortured, murdered or exiled; one of the early detention centres is on Isla Dawson in the Magellan Straits.

1976-1983

In Chile, the building of the Carretera Austral begins. The new military government in Argentina institutes a reign of terror known as the 'Dirty War'. Any vaguely left-wing thinking, opposition or criticism of the military is met with violent torture and elimination by death squads. Up to 30,000 people 'disappear'. Internal conflict ends with the war against Britain over the disputed Malvinas (Falkland Islands). Democracy of a kind returns, when Alfonsín becomes president in 1983.

1978

Argentina and Chile nearly go to war over a territorial dispute over three islands – Lennox, Nueva and Picton – in the Beagle Channel. The Pope has to intervene, and the islands are awarded to Chile.

1973-1990

Pinochet dissolves Congress in Chile, bans leftist parties and suspends all opposition. His economic policies bring relative prosperity, but a referendum in 1988 sees him rejected by a majority of 12%. Democracy returns and Christian democrat, Patricio Aylwin is elected President in 1990.

1990s

In Argentina, Peronist president Carlos Menem institutes major economic reforms, selling off nationalized industries, and opening the economy to foreign investment. The country falls heavily into debt. In 1999 President Fernando de la Rua of the UCR centre-left Alliance, promises a crackdown on corruption and tough measures to balance Argentina's budget.

2001

In December, nationwide demonstrations erupt when access to bank accounts is restricted in the 'corralito'. Argentina is plunged into serious economic and political crisis. Rioting, looting and widespread civil chaos result in the death of 27 people.

Footnotes

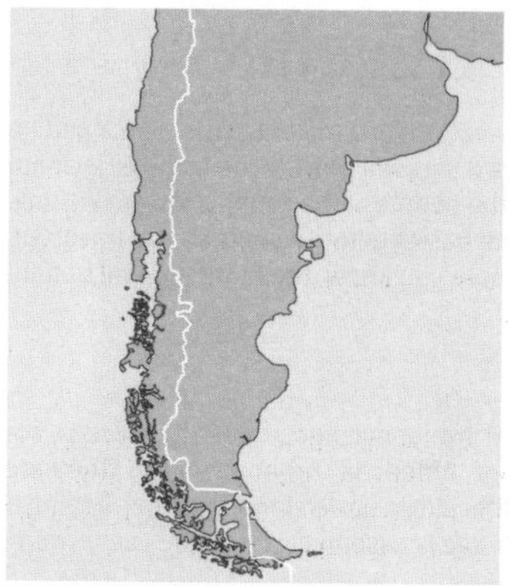

Basic Spanish for travellers

Learning Spanish is a useful part of the preparation for a trip to Latin America and no volumes of dictionaries, phrase books or word lists will provide the same enjoyment as being able to communicate directly with the people of the country you are visiting. It is a good idea to make an effort to grasp the basics before you go. As you travel you will pick up more of the language and the more you know, the more you will benefit from your stay.

General pronunciation

Whether you have been taught the 'Castilian' pronounciation (*z* and *c* followed by *i* or *e* are pronounced as the *th* in think) or the 'American' pronounciation (they are pronounced as *s*), you will encounter little difficulty in understanding either. Regional accents and usages vary, but the basic language is essentially the same everywhere.

Vowels

a	as in English *cat*
e	as in English *best*
i	as the *ee* in English *feet*
o	as in English *shop*
u	as the *oo* in English *food*
ai	as the *i* in English *ride*
ei	as *ey* in English *they*
oi	as *oy* in English *toy*

Consonants

Most consonants can be pronounced more or less as they are in English. The exceptions are:

	before *e* or *i* is the same as *j*
h	is always silent (except in *ch* as in *chair*)
j	as the *ch* in Scottish *loch*
ll	as the *y* in *yellow*
ñ	as the *ni* in English *onion*
rr	trilled much more than in English
x	depending on its location, pronounced *x*, *s*, *sh* or *j*

Spanish words and phrases

Greetings, courtesies

hello	*hola*
good morning	*buenos días*
good afternoon/evening/night	*buenas tardes/noches*
goodbye	*adiós/chao*
pleased to meet you	*mucho gusto*
see you later	*hasta luego*
how are you?	*¿cómo está?¿cómo estás?*
I'm fine, thanks	*estoy muy bien, gracias*
I'm called...	*me llamo...*
what is your name?	*¿cómo se llama? ¿cómo te llamas?*
yes/no	*sí/no*
please	*por favor*
thank you (very much)	*(muchas) gracias*
I speak Spanish	*hablo español*
I don't speak Spanish	*no hablo español*
do you speak English?	*¿habla inglés?*
I don't understand	*no entiendo/no comprendo*
please speak slowly	*hable despacio por favor*
I am very sorry	*lo siento mucho/disculpe*
what do you want?	*¿qué quiere? ¿qué quieres?*
I want	*quiero*
I don't want it	*no lo quiero*
leave me alone	*déjeme en paz/no me moleste*
good/bad	*bueno/malo*

Basic questions and requests

have you got a room for two people?	*¿tiene una habitación para dos personas?*
how do I get to_?	*¿cómo llego a_?*
how much does it cost?	*¿cuánto cuesta? ¿cuánto es?*
I'd like to make a long-distance phone call	*quisiera hacer una llamada de larga distancia*
is service included?	*¿está incluido el servicio?*
is tax included?	*¿están incluidos los impuestos?*
when does the bus leave (arrive)?	*¿a qué hora sale (llega) el autobús?*
when?	*¿cuándo?*
where is_?	*¿dónde está_?*
where can I buy tickets?	*¿dónde puedo comprar boletos?*
where is the nearest petrol station?	*¿dónde está la gasolinera más cercana?*
why?	*¿por qué?*

Basic words and phrases

bank	*el banco*
bathroom/toilet	*el baño*
to be	*ser, estar*
bill	*la factura/la cuenta*
cash	*el efectivo*
cheap	*barato/a*
credit card	*la tarjeta de crédito*
exchange house	*la casa de cambio*
exchange rate	*el tipo de cambio*
expensive	*caro/a*
to go	*ir*
to have	*tener, haber*
market	*el mercado*
note/coin	*el billete/la moneda*
police (policeman)	*la policía (el policía)*
post office	*el correo*
public telephone	*el teléfono público*
shop	*la tienda*
supermarket	*el supermercado*
there is/are	*hay*
there isn't/aren't	*no hay*
ticket office	*la taquilla*
travellers' cheques	*los cheques de viajero/los travelers*

Getting around

aeroplane	*el avión*
airport	*el aeropuerto*
arrival/departure	*la llegada/salida*
avenue	*la avenida*
block	*la cuadra*
border	*la frontera*
bus station	*la terminal de autobuses/camiones*
bus	*el bus/el autobús/el camión*
collective/fixed-route taxi	*el colectivo*
corner	*la esquina*
customs	*la aduana*
first/second class	*la primera/segunda clase*
left/right	*izquierda/derecha*
ticket	*el boleto*
empty/full	*vacío/lleno*
highway, main road	*la carretera*
immigration	*la inmigración*
insurance	*el seguro*
insured person	*el asegurado/la asegurada*

to insure yourself against	*asegurarse contra*
luggage	*el equipaje*
motorway, freeway	*el autopista/la carretera*
north, south, west, east	*el norte, el sur, el oeste (occidente), el este (oriente)*
oil	*el aceite*
to park	*estacionarse*
passport	*el pasaporte*
petrol/gasoline	*la gasolina*
puncture	*el pinchazo/la ponchadura*
street	*la calle*
that way	*por allí/por allá*
this way	*por aquí/por acá*
tourist card/visa	*la tarjeta de turista/visa*
tyre	*la llanta*
unleaded	*sin plomo*
waiting room	*la sala de espera*
to walk	*caminar/andar*

Accommodation

air conditioning	*el aire acondicionado*
all-inclusive	*todo incluido*
bathroom, private	*el baño privado*
bed, double/single	*la cama matrimonial/sencilla*
blankets	*las cobijas/mantas*
to clean	*limpiar*
dining room	*el comedor*
guesthouse	*la casa de huéspedes*
hotel	*el hotel*
noisy	*ruidoso*
pillows	*las almohadas*
power cut	*el apagón/corte*
restaurant	*el restaurante*
room/bedroom	*el cuarto/la habitación*
sheets	*las sábanas*
shower	*la ducha/regadera*
soap	*el jabón*
toilet	*el sanitario/excusado*
toilet paper	*el papel higiénico*
towels, clean/dirty	*las toallas limpias/sucias*
water, hot/cold	*el agua caliente/fría*

Health

aspirin	*la aspirina*
blood	*la sangre*
chemist	*la farmacia*
condoms	*los preservativos, los condones*
contact lenses	*los lentes de contacto*
contraceptives	*los anticonceptivos*
contraceptive pill	*la píldora anticonceptiva*
diarrhoea	*la diarrea*
doctor	*el médico*
fever/sweat	*la fiebre/el sudor*
pain	*el dolor*
head	*la cabeza*
period/sanitary towels	*la regla/las toallas femininas*
stomach	*el estómago*
altitude sickness	*el soroche*

Family

family	*la familia*
brother/sister	*el hermano/la hermana*
daughter/son	*la hija/el hijo*
father/mother	*el padre/la madre*
husband/wife	*el esposo (marido)/la esposa*
boyfriend/girlfriend	*el novio/la novia*
friend	*el amigo/la amiga*
married	*casado/a*
single/unmarried	*soltero/a*

Months, days and time

January	*enero*
February	*febrero*
March	*marzo*
April	*abril*
May	*mayo*
June	*junio*
July	*julio*
August	*agosto*
September	*septiembre*
October	*octubre*
November	*noviembre*
December	*diciembre*
Monday	*lunes*
Tuesday	*martes*
Wednesday	*miércoles*
Thursday	*jueves*
Friday	*viernes*
Saturday	*sábado*
Sunday	*domingo*
at one o'clock	*a la una*
at half past two	*a las dos y media*
at a quarter to three	*a cuarto para las tres/a las tres menos quince*
it's one o'clock	*es la una*
it's seven o'clock	*son las siete*
it's six twenty	*son las seis y veinte*
it's five to nine	*son cinco para las nueve/las nueve menos cinco*
in ten minutes	*en diez minutos*
five hours	*cinco horas*
does it take long?	*¿tarda mucho?*

Numbers

one	*uno/una*
two	*dos*
three	*tres*
four	*cuatro*
five	*cinco*
six	*seis*
seven	*siete*
eight	*ocho*
nine	*nueve*
ten	*diez*
eleven	*once*
twelve	*doce*
thirteen	*trece*
fourteen	*catorce*

fifteen	*quince*
sixteen	*dieciséis*
seventeen	*diecisiete*
eighteen	*dieciocho*
nineteen	*diecinueve*
twenty	*veinte*
twenty-one	*veintiuno*
thirty	*treinta*
forty	*cuarenta*
fifty	*cincuenta*
sixty	*sesenta*
seventy	*setenta*
eighty	*ochenta*
ninety	*noventa*
hundred	*cien/ciento*
thousand	*mil*

Food

avocado	*el aguacate*
baked	*al horno*
bakery	*la panadería*
banana	*el plátano*
beans	*los frijoles/las habichuelas*
beef	*la carne de res*
beef steak or pork fillet	*el bistec*
boiled rice	*el arroz blanco*
bread	*el pan*
breakfast	*el desayuno*
butter	*la mantequilla*
cake	*el pastel*
chewing gum	*el chicle*
chicken	*el pollo*
chilli pepper or green pepper	*el ají/el chile/el pimiento*
clear soup, stock	*el caldo*
cooked	*cocido*
dining room	*el comedor*
egg	*el huevo*
fish	*el pescado*
fork	*el tenedor*
fried	*frito*
garlic	*el ajo*
goat	*el chivo*
grapefruit	*la toronja/el pomelo*
grill	*la parrilla*
guava	*la guayaba*
ham	*el jamón*
hamburger	*la hamburguesa*
hot, spicy	*picante*
ice cream	*el helado*
jam	*la mermelada*
knife	*el cuchillo*
lime	*el limón*
lobster	*la langosta*
lunch	*el almuerzo/la comida*
meal	*la comida*
meat	*la carne*
minced meat	*el picadillo*
onion	*la cebolla*
orange	*la naranja*

pepper	*el pimiento*
pasty, turnover	*la empanada/el pastelito*
pork	*el cerdo*
potato	*la papa*
prawns	*los camarones*
raw	*crudo*
restaurant	*el restaurante*
salad	*la ensalada*
salt	*la sal*
sandwich	*el bocadillo*
sauce	*la salsa*
sausage	*la longaniza/el chorizo*
scrambled eggs	*los huevos revueltos*
seafood	*los mariscos*
soup	*la sopa*
spoon	*la cuchara*
squash	*la calabaza*
squid	*los calamares*
supper	*la cena*
sweet	*dulce*
to eat	*comer*
toasted	*tostado*
turkey	*el pavo*
vegetables	*los legumbres/vegetales*
without meat	*sin carne*
yam	*el camote*

Drink

beer	*la cerveza*
boiled	*hervido/a*
bottled	*en botella*
camomile tea	*té de manzanilla*
canned	*en lata*
coffee	*el café*
coffee, white	*el café con leche*
cold	*frío*
cup	*la taza*
drink	*la bebida*
drunk	*borracho/a*
firewater	*el aguardiente*
fruit milkshake	*el batido/licuado*
glass	*el vaso*
hot	*caliente*
ice/without ice	*el hielo/sin hielo*
juice	*el jugo*
lemonade	*la limonada*
milk	*la leche*
mint	*la menta/la hierbabuena*
rum	*el ron*
soft drink	*el refresco*
sugar	*el azúcar*
tea	*el té*
to drink	*beber/tomar*
water	*el agua*
water, carbonated	*el agua mineral con gas*
water, still mineral	*el agua mineral sin gas*
wine, red	*el vino tinto*
wine, white	*el vino blanco*

Index → *Entries in* ***bold*** *refer to maps.*

Advertisers' index

Credits

Footprint credits
Editor: Nicola Gibbs
Map editor: Sarah Sorensen
Picture editor: Robert Lunn

Publisher: Patrick Dawson
Editorial: Sophie Blacksell, Felicity Laughton, Alan Murphy, Jo Williams
Cartography: Kevin Feeney, Robert Lunn, Daniel Manning
Sales and marketing: Andy Riddle
Advertising: Debbie Wylde, Zoë Jackson
Finance and administration: Elizabeth Taylor

Photography credits
Front cover: Superstock
Back cover: Superstock
Inside colour section: Christabelle Dilks, South American Pictures, Alamy, Superstock, James Sturcke

Print
Manufactured in India by Nutech Photolithographers, Delhi
Pulp from sustainable forests

Footprint feedback
We try as hard as we can to make each Footprint guide as up to date as possible but, of course, things always change. If you want to let us know about your experiences – good, bad or ugly – then don't delay, go to **www.footprintbooks.com** and send in your comments.

Hotel and restaurant price codes should only be taken as a guide to the prices and facilities offered by the establishment. It is at the discretion of the owners to vary them from time to time.

Publishing information
Footprint Patagonia
2nd edition

July 2007

ISBN: 978 1 906098 00 1
CIP DATA: A catalogue record for this book is available from the British Library

Published by Footprint
6 Riverside Court
Lower Bristol Road
Bath BA2 3DZ, UK
T +44 (0)1225 469141
F +44 (0)1225 469461
discover@footprintbooks.com
www.footprintbooks.com

Neither the black and white nor colour maps are intended to have any political significance.

Every effort has been made to ensure that the facts in this guidebook are accurate. However, travellers should still obtain advice from consulates, airlines etc about travel and visa requirements before travelling. The authors and publishers cannot accept responsibility for any loss, injury or inconvenience however caused.

Map 1
Altitude in metres
2000
1000
500
200
0
Highway paved
Highway unpaved
Primary road paved
Primary road unpaved
Secondary road paved
Secondary road unpaved
Track
Path
N
0 km 40
0 miles 40
A
B
C
1
2
3
Pacific Ocean
REGION IX
REGION X
Lanalhue
Lago Lanalhue
Los Sauces
Contulmo
Purén
Collipulli
Ralco
Caviahue
Lago Lleulleu
Cap Pastene
Victoria
Traiguén
Púa
Parque Nacional Tolhuaco
Termas de Tolhuaco
Lonquimay (2865m)
Reserva Nacional Malalcahuello
Tirúa
Galvarino
Curacautín
Malacahuello
Sierra Nevada
Lonquimay
Lautaro
Chol Chol
Vilcún
Lago Conguillo
Llaima
Parque Nacional Conguillio
Nehuentué
Carahue
Nueva Imperial
Temuco
Cherquenco
Vol Llaima (3050m)
Icalma
Puerto Saavedra
Barros Arana
Lago Budi
Freire
Los Laureles
Cunco
Melipeuco
Paso de Icalma
Teodoro Schmidt
Río Toltén
Radal
Río Colico
Lago Colico
Playa Negra
Lago Alumine
Moquehue
Lago Huilipilún
Lago Caburga
Caburga
Parque Nacional Huerquehue
Toltén
Villarrica
Lago Villarrica
Pucón
Termas de Palquin
Aluminé
Lonchoche
Villarrica (2840m)
Quetrupillán (2009m)
Quillén
Mehuín
Lanco
Lican-Ray
San José de la Mariquina
Río Cruces
Lago Calafquén
Parque Nacional Villarrica
Puesco
Paso Mamuil Malal
Panguipulli
Coñaripe
Lanín (3768m)
Río Calle Calle
Lago Panguipulli
Liquiñe
Riñihue
Lago Riñihue
Lago Neltume
Paso Carririñe
Niebla
Corral
Valdivia
Antilhue
Los Lagos
Choshuenco
Puerto Fuy
Lago Huechulafquen
Lago Pirehueico
Parque Nacional Lanín
Monumento Natural Alerce Costero
Paillaco
Futrono
Paso Hua Hum
Junín de los Andes
Puerto Nuevo
Llifén
Lago Lacar
Río Bueno
La Unión
Lago Ranco
San Martín de los Andes
Trumao
Lago Maihue
Río Bueno
Lago Ranco
Lago Huishue
Osorno
Salto Pilmaiquén
Lago Gris
Lago Constancia
Río Golgol
Lago Puyehue
215
Entre Lagos
Termas de Puyehue
Portezuelo de Paso Puyehue
Río Negro
Rupanco
Villa La Angostura
Lago Rupanco
Parque Nacional Puyehue
Parque Nacional Los Arrayanes
Parque Nacional Nahuel Huapi
Puerto Octay
Islote
Lago Nahuel Huapi
Punteagudo (2490m)
Osorno (2652m)
La Picada
Bariloche
Frutillar
Río Negro
Lago Llanquihue
Petrohué
Peulla
Paso Pérez Rosales
Ensenada
Lago Todos los Santos
Tronador (3460m)
Catedral
La Poza
Calbuco
Parque Nacional Vicente Pérez Rosales
Lago Mascardi
Cayutué
Puerto Varas
Ralún
Villa Mascardi
Lago Chapo
Puerto Montt
Pelluco
Cochamó
Río Maullín
Parque Nacional Alerce Andino
Isla Tenglo
Lenca
258
Maullín
La Arena
Puelo
Carelmapu
Pargua
Calbuco
Isla Huar
Faro Corona
Caulín
Puelche
El Bolsón
Chacao
Contao
Norquinco
Ancud
Río Negro/Hornopirén
Pumillahue
Linao
Golfo de Ancud
Los Repollos
Vilcún
Belbén
Parque Nacional Hornopirén
Chepu
Isla Caucahue
Isla Llancahué
El Maitén
Degán
Quemchi
Isla Butachauques
Peninsula Huequi
Parque Pumalín
Parque Nacional Lago Puelo
Chiloé
Isla Mechuque
Epuyén
Dalcahue
Tenaún
Ayacara
Castro
Isla Quinchao
Fiordo Reñihue
Fiordo Largo
Leptepu
Cholila
Parque Nacional Chiloé
Nercón
Achao
Leleque
Vilopulli
Puqueldón
Isla Apiao
Isla Chulín
Parque Pumalín
Cucao
Chonchi
Teupa
Caleta Gonzalo
Huillinco
Isla Lemuy
Isla Cahulinec
Caleta Santa Bárbara
Lago Menéndez
La Bolsa
Chiloé
Isla Talcán
Parque Nacional Los Alerces
Queilén
Chaitén
Lago Futulaufquen
Esquel
Isla Tranquil
Río Yelcho
Amarillo
Quellón
Trevelin
40
Trincao
Puerto Cárdenas
Lago Espolón
Corcovado (2290m)
Futaleufú
Paso Futaleufú
Lago Yelcho
Golfo de Corcovado
Villa Santa Lucía
Puerto Piedra
Paso Palena
Corcovado
Carretera Austral
7
Nevada (2042m)
Puerto Ramírez
Palena
Melinka
Lago Palena
Lago General Vinttner
Lago Vinttner
Río Palena
La Junta
Map 2
Alto Río Pico
Lago Rosselot
Río Figueroa
Paso Las Pampas-Lago Verde
Río Pico

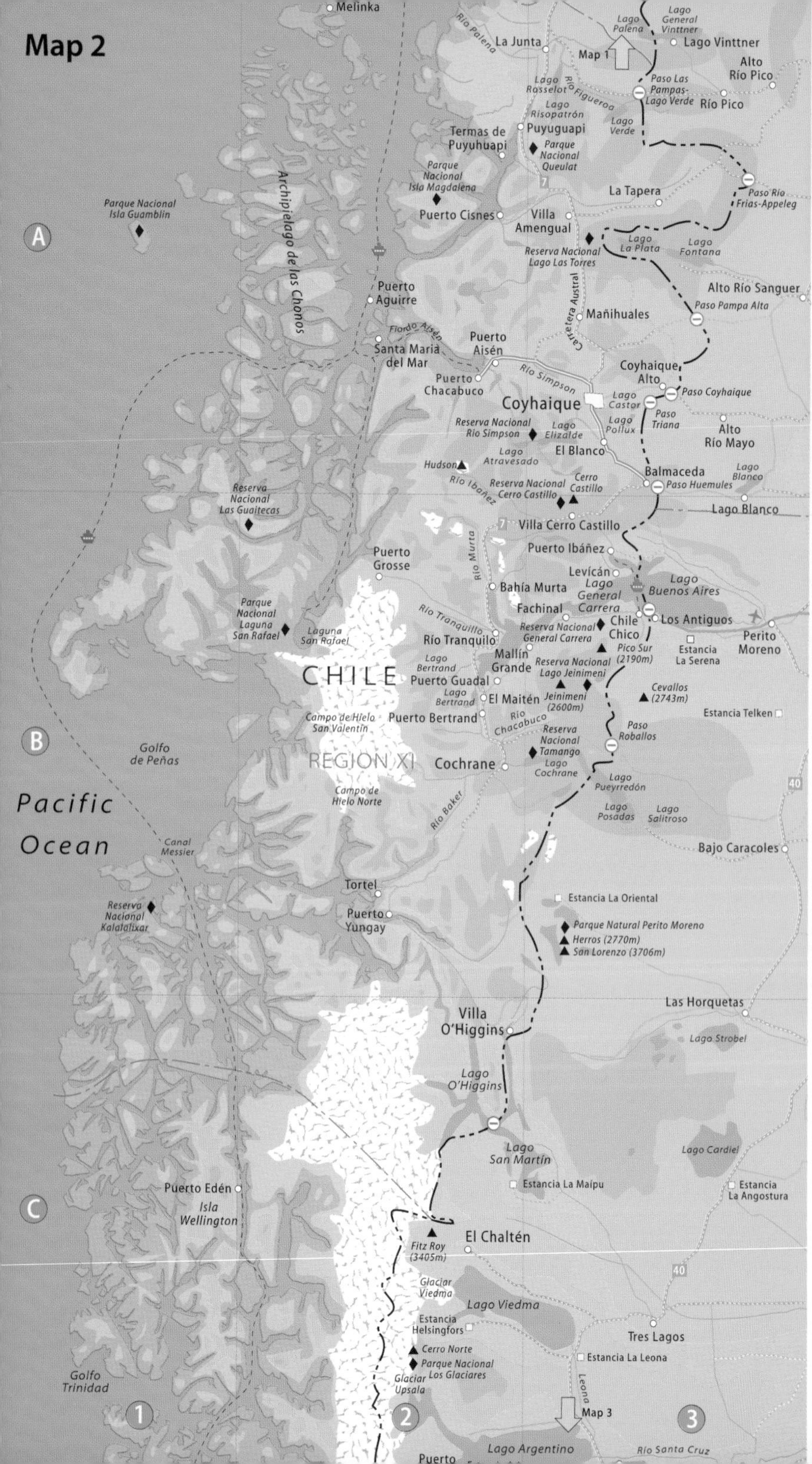
Map 2
Melinka
Río Palena
La Junta
Lago Palena
Lago General Vinttner
Lago Vinttner
Map 1
Alto Río Pico
Lago Rosselot
Río Figueroa
Paso Las Pampas-Lago Verde
Río Pico
Lago Risopatrón
Lago Verde
Termas de Puyuhuapi
Puyuguapi
Parque Nacional Queulat
7
Parque Nacional Isla Magdalena
La Tapera
Paso Río Frias-Appeleg
Parque Nacional Isla Guamblin
Puerto Cisnes
Villa Amengual
A
Archipiélago de las Chonos
Lago La Plata
Lago Fontana
Reserva Nacional Lago Las Torres
Puerto Aguirre
Alto Río Sanguer
Carretera Austral
Paso Pampa Alta
Mañihuales
Fiordo Aisén
Puerto Aisén
Santa Maria del Mar
Coyhaique Alto
Puerto Chacabuco
Río Simpson
Paso Coyhaique
Coyhaique
Lago Castor
Paso Triana
Reserva Nacional Río Simpson
Lago Elizalde
Lago Pollux
Alto Río Mayo
El Blanco
Lago Atravesado
Hudson
Balmaceda
Lago Blanco
Río Ibañez
Reserva Nacional Cerro Castillo
Cerro Castillo
Paso Huemules
Reserva Nacional Las Guaitecas
Lago Blanco
Villa Cerro Castillo
Puerto Ibáñez
Puerto Grosse
Río Murta
Levicán
Lago General Carrera
Lago Buenos Aires
Bahía Murta
Parque Nacional Laguna San Rafael
Fachinal
Chile Chico
Los Antiguos
Perito Moreno
Río Tranquilo
Reserva Nacional General Carrera
Laguna San Rafael
Río Tranquilo
Pico Sur (2190m)
Estancia La Serena
Mallín Grande
Lago Bertrand
Reserva Nacional Lago Jeinimeni
CHILE
Puerto Guadal
Cevallos (2743m)
Lago Bertrand
El Maitén
Jeinimeni (2600m)
Campo de Hielo San Valentín
Puerto Bertrand
Río Chacabuco
Estancia Telken
Paso Roballos
B
Golfo de Peñas
Reserva Nacional Tamango
REGION XI
Cochrane
Lago Cochrane
Lago Pueyrredón
40
Pacific Ocean
Campo de Hielo Norte
Río Baker
Lago Posadas
Lago Salitroso
Canal Messier
Bajo Caracoles
Tortel
Estancia La Oriental
Reserva Nacional Kalalalixar
Puerto Yungay
Parque Natural Perito Moreno
Herros (2770m)
San Lorenzo (3706m)
Las Horquetas
Villa O'Higgins
Lago Strobel
Lago O'Higgins
Lago San Martín
Lago Cardiel
Estancia La Maipu
Estancia La Angostura
Puerto Edén
C
Isla Wellington
Fitz Roy (3405m)
El Chaltén
40
Glaciar Viedma
Lago Viedma
Estancia Helsingfors
Tres Lagos
Estancia La Leona
Cerro Norte
Parque Nacional Los Glaciares
Glaciar Upsala
Golfo Trinidad
Leona
Map 3
1
2
3
Lago Argentino
Río Santa Cruz
Puerto

El Pajarito
Pampa de Agria
Paso de Indios
Los Altaires
25
Las Plumas
Dique F Ameghino
Florentino Ameghino (Merayo)
Embalse Florentino Ameghino
José de San Martín
Gobernador Costa
Uzcudún
3
Map 4
A
Garyalde
Río Chico
Los Tamariscos
Buen Pasto
40
Facundo
Pico Salamanca
Lago Musters
Lago Colhué Huapi
20
Sarmiento
Río Mayo
Colhué Huapí
26
Astra
General Mosconi
Río Guenguel
Comodoro Rivadavia
SANTA CRUZ
Golfo San Jorge
Cañadón Seco
Caleta Olivia
520
Las Heras
Río Deseado
Koluel Kayke
Río Pinturas
ARGENTINA
Pico Truncado
B
Fitz Roy
Cueva de los Manos
Jaramillo
Monumento Natural Bosque Petrificados
Antonio de Biedma
Río Deseado
Puerto Deseado
Reserva Natural San Julián
Estancia La Maria
Gobernador Gregores
C
Río Chico
Puerto San Julián
La Julia
N
Laguna Grande
0 km 40
0 miles 40
Piedrabuena
Santa Cruz
4
5
6
Estancia Monte León
Puerto de Punta Quilla
Rincón Grande
Parque Nacional